INCLUDES VERSIONS 1.3 & 1.4

murach's beginning Java 2

Andrea Steelman

2560 West Shaw Lane, Suite 101 • Fresno, CA 93711-2765

Author: Andrea Steelman
Writer/editor: Joel Murach
Contributing editor: Donna Dean, The Chubb Institute
Production editor: Judy Taylor
Cover Design: Zylka Design
Production: Tom Murach

Books in the Murach series

Murach's Beginning Java 2

Murach's Visual Basic 6

Murach's Structured COBOL

Murach's CICS for the COBOL Programmer

Printed in the United States of America

10 9 8 7 6 5 4 3 2 1
ISBN: 1-890774-12-X

Library of Congress Cataloging-in-Publication Data

Steelman, Andrea, 1973-
Murach's beginning Java 2 / Andrea Steelman.
p. cm.
"Includes versions 1.3 & 1.4."
ISBN 1-890774-12-X
1. Java (Computer program language) I. Title: Beginning Java 2. II. Title.

QA76.73.J38 S84 2001
005.2'762—dc21

2001044046

Contents

Expanded contents

Section 1 The essence of Java programming

Chapter 1 How to get started with Java

Chapter 2 Java language essentials (part 1)

Chapter 6 How to design and test object-oriented programs

Section 2 More Java essentials

Chapter 7 How to work with operators and dates

Chapter 8 How to code control statements

Chapter 9 How to work with arrays, strings, and vectors

Chapter 10 How to handle exceptions and debug code

Section 3 Java for graphical user interfaces

Chapter 11 How to code a graphical user interface (part 1)

Chapter 12 How to code a graphical user interface (part 2)

Chapter 15 How to develop applets

Section 4 Java for file input and output

Chapter 16 An introduction to file input and output

Chapter 17 How to work with text files

Introduction

If you're new to Java or object-oriented programming, this book gets you started right. By the end of chapter 2, you'll be writing programs that use Java classes. By chapter 4, you'll be developing your own classes. And by chapter 6, you'll be able to design, code, and test object-oriented programs in Java.

But this isn't just a beginning book. By the time you finish this book, you'll know how to develop graphical user interfaces with Swing components; how to read and write data that's stored in files; how to use JDBC to work with the data in databases; how to develop applets that are run from Internet browsers; and much more. In short, you'll have a set of professional Java skills that you can use for developing real-world business applications.

Can one book do all that? Yes...but it has to be better than the competing books in more ways than one.

5 ways the content is better

- If you're a beginner, you'll learn how to develop object-oriented Java programs in the first four chapters. No other book gets you started that fast.
- In chapter 5, you'll learn how to work with inheritance and interfaces since they are critical to the effective use of the hundreds of classes that are available with Java. Unlike other books that present theory without application, this chapter focuses just on what you need to know to use Java classes effectively.
- In chapter 6, you'll learn how to design and test object-oriented programs. Although you can't do an effective job of developing a Java program without knowing how to design one, no other beginning book has a chapter like this.
- Figuring out how to create a graphical user interface can be a nightmare with other books, but this one has you create your first GUI from start to finish in chapter 11. Then, chapters 12-14 show you how to enhance that interface. And chapter 15

shows you how to use these skills as you develop Java applets that can be run from a web browser.

- Because stored data is critical to most business applications, chapters 16-18 show you how to work with files, and chapter 19 shows you how to work with databases. In particular, chapters 18 and 19 teach you how to use files and databases to provide the data for the business objects of Java applications. And no other book has content like that.

4 ways the instruction is better

- Realistic business applications and examples throughout this book provide the models that you need for building your own object-oriented programs. In contrast, most competing books present "toy" applications that have little resemblance to applications in the real world.
- Since one of the keys to Java programming is understanding how all of the pieces fit together, this book presents 24 complete Java applications. For the largest application, chapter 6 presents its design, chapter 12 presents its GUI classes, chapter 18 presents the class that can be used if the data is stored in a file, and chapter 19 presents the class that can be used if the data is stored in a database. This is ambitious, effective, and no other book even tries to do anything like it.
- The exercises at the end of each chapter use the source code and data on the CD ROM to give you a maximum amount of practice in a minimum amount of time. This leads to dramatic improvements in learning efficiency.
- All of the information in this book is presented in user-friendly "paired pages," with the essential details and examples on the right and the perspective on the left. This lets you learn faster by reading less. And nobody else has anything like it.

Who this book is for

This book is for anyone who wants to learn how to program with Java. It works if you have no programming experience at all. It works if you have programming experience with another language like COBOL or Visual Basic. And it works if you've already read three or four other Java books and still don't know how to develop a real-world business application.

If you're completely new to programming, the prerequisites are minimal. You just need to be familiar with the operation of the platform that you're using. If, for example, you're using Windows on a PC, you should know how to use the Windows interface to perform tasks like opening, saving, printing, and closing files.

What Java versions and platforms this book supports

Since Java 1.0 was first released in 1996, three other versions have been released: 1.1, 1.2, and 1.3. With version 1.2, Java became known as Java 2, and that name is still in use today. As this book goes to press, the current release of Java is version 1.3.1. So that's the version that's on the CD ROM at the back of this book, and that's the version that we used to develop all of the program examples.

Note, however, that version 1.4 is currently in beta test, and it should be released later this year. That's why we tested all of the programs in this book using the 1.4 beta, too. We have also covered the most useful new features of version 1.4 in this book. Whenever you want to upgrade to this version, you can download it from the Sun web site as explained in chapter 1.

As you work with Java, please keep in mind that all versions are upwards-compatible. That means that everything in the previous versions will work with the new versions. In general, a new version just provides some new classes and methods. Some of these provide new capabilities; some improve upon the old ones. As a result, you'll want to use some of the new classes and methods in your new programs. But you can usually leave the old classes and methods in your old programs because they will still work.

Since Java is platform-independent, a Java program can be run on any platform that supports Java. That means that this book teaches you how to write Java programs that will run on computers that use operating systems like Windows, Solaris, or Linux. However, since the platform for most computer users today is Windows, this book uses Windows to illustrate any platform-dependent procedures. If you're working on another platform, you may need to download information from the Sun web site to learn how to do some of those procedures on your system.

What's on the bound-in CD ROM

To start, the CD ROM that comes with this book contains all the source code and data that you need to do the exercises in this book. That way, you don't have to start every exercise from scratch. In addition, the CD ROM contains the source code and data for all of the applications, applets, and examples that are presented in this book.

To make it easier for you to get started, the CD ROM also provides version 1.3.1 of the Java Software Development Kit (SDK), along with the HTML-based documentation for this version of the SDK. Although these products are available for free from the Java web site, they're large files that may take several hours to download. As a result, the files on this CD ROM can save you some time.

This CD ROM also contains an evaluation copy of the TextPad text editor. This text editor is specifically designed to help you develop Java applications on Windows systems. If you like this product and want to use it beyond the evaluation period, please pay the reasonable fee (around $27) to register your copy. It's a small price to pay for an excellent product.

Last, the CD ROM contains an integrated development environment for Java applications known as Forte for Java. It too is available for free from the Java web site, but having it on the CD can save you hours of download time.

In chapter 1 of this book, you'll learn more about all of these items. You'll also learn how to install them on your system. For a quick look at the installation procedures, though, please refer to the last page in this book.

Support materials for trainers and instructors

If you're a trainer or instructor who would like to use this book as the basis for a course, a complete set of instructional materials is available for it. To start, take a look at the exercises for each chapter. Note how they give your students a maximum amount of practice in a controlled, time-effective way.

Then, to complete the instructional package, we are developing student projects and an instructor's guide. The student projects will give your students a chance to develop complete applications on their own. The instructor's guide will include solutions to the exercises, solutions to the student projects, tests, answers, and PowerPoint slides for classroom presentations. Taken together, this book, its CD, and the instructional materials make a powerful teaching package.

To find out more, please go to the "Instructor Info" section of our web site at www.murach.com, call us at 1-800-221-5528, or e-mail us at murachbooks@murach.com. And if you feel that something is missing from our instructional materials, please let us know so we can fix that.

Please let us know how this book works for you

When we started this book, our goals were (1) to teach you Java as quickly and easily as possible, and (2) to teach you the practical Java concepts and skills that you need for developing real-world business applications. Now, we sincerely hope that we've succeeded.

If you have any comments about this book, we'd appreciate hearing from you. In particular, we'd like to know whether this book has lived up to your expectations. To reply, you can e-mail us at murachbooks@murach.com or send your comments to our street address.

Thanks for buying this book. Thanks for reading it. And good luck with your Java programming.

Andrea Steelman, Author
July 6, 2001

Joel Murach, Editor
July 6, 2001

Section 1

The essence of Java programming

The best way to learn Java programming is to start doing it, and that's the approach the chapters in this section take. So in chapter 1, you get started right as you learn how to get Java on your system and how to compile and run Java programs. Then, in chapters 2 and 3, you learn how to use the Java language essentials as you write your first Java applications. At this point, you're using some of the basic Java classes and objects, but you're not writing object-oriented programs.

To develop programs the way the professionals do, however, you need to write object-oriented programs. So that's what you'll learn how to do in the next two chapters. In chapter 4, you learn how to write programs that consist of two or more classes. In chapter 5, you are introduced to all of the object-oriented concepts and skills that you need as you work with Java. These are useful as you create and use your own classes and objects, and they are absolutely essential for making effective use of the hundreds of classes that Java provides.

Before you can write an effective object-oriented program, though, you need to know how to design and test an object-oriented program. So that's what you'll learn to do in the last chapter of this section. When you complete it, you'll have the essential skills that you need for designing, coding, and testing object-oriented Java programs. You'll also have a clear view of what Java programming is and what you have to do to become proficient at it. That's why we call this section "The essence of Java programming."

1

How to get started with Java

Before you can begin learning the Java language, you need to install Java and you need to learn how to use some tools for working with Java. So that's what you'll learn in this chapter. Along the way, you'll be introduced to some of the concepts and terms you need for working with Java.

Introduction to Java

In 1996, Sun Microsystems released a new programming language called Java. This language had some unique features that gave it great promise as a language that could be used on all platforms for all types of applications. In the three figures that follow, you'll learn more about this language, its features, and its applications.

Toolkits and platforms

Figure 1-1 describes all major releases of Java to date starting with version 1.0 and ending with version 1.4. As you can see, Sun referred to versions 1.0 and 1.1 of the Java toolkit as the *Java Development Kit* (*JDK*). With version 1.2, however, Sun began using the term *Software Development Kit* (*SDK*) to describe the Java toolkit. In practice, these two terms are often used interchangeably. In this book, we'll use the term *SDK* since it's the most current term.

All versions of the SDK since version 1.2 are referred to as *Java 2* because they all run under the *Java 2 Platform*. This book will show you how to use the *Java 2 Platform, Standard Edition* (*J2SE*). Once you master the Standard Edition, you will have all the skills you need to begin learning how to use the *Java 2 Platform, Enterprise Edition* (*J2EE*). In fact, many of the same skills apply to both editions.

One reason that Java has become so widely used is that it can create programs that can run on any of the operating systems shown in this figure. In addition, Java programs can also be run under the Macintosh operating system. You'll learn more about the details of how this works later in this chapter.

Java compared to C++

When Sun's developers created Java, they tried to keep the syntax for Java similar to the syntax for Microsoft C++ so it would be easy for C++ programmers to learn Java. That's one of the four features that are used for comparing Java and C++ in this figure.

The second feature is one of the most touted Java features. Specifically, Java is designed so its applications can be run on any computer platform. In contrast, C++ needs to have a specific compiler for each platform that its applications are going to run on. You'll learn more about this in figure 1-3.

The third feature, though, indicates one of the weaknesses of Java. Specifically, the speed (or performance) of its applications is often considerably slower than the speed of traditional applications. In fact, this is an issue that limits the use of Java for some types of applications.

The fourth feature has to do with the use of internal memory. Specifically, Java is easier to use than C++ because it handles many operations involving the creation and destruction of memory automatically. This also makes it easier to write bug-free code.

Java timeline

Year	Month	Event
1996	January	Sun releases Java Development Kit 1.0 (JDK 1.0).
1997	February	Sun releases Java Development Kit 1.1 (JDK 1.1).
1998	December	Sun releases the Java 2 Platform with version 1.2 of the Software Development Kit (SDK 1.2).
1999	August	Sun releases Java 2 Platform, Standard Edition (J2SE).
	December	Sun releases Java 2 Platform, Enterprise Edition (J2EE).
2000	May	Sun releases J2SE with version 1.3 of the SDK.
2001	April	Sun releases J2SE with version 1.3.1 of the SDK.
	May	Sun releases beta version of the J2SE with version 1.4 of the SDK.

Operating systems supported by Sun

- Win-32 (Windows NT, Windows 95, Windows 98, Windows 2000, and Windows XT)
- Solaris (SPARC or Intel platform)
- Linux

Java compared to C++

Feature	Description
Syntax	Since Sun wanted to make Java easy to learn for C++ programmers, they made the syntax similar to the syntax for C++.
Platforms	After a Java program has been compiled, it can be run on any platform that has a Java interpreter (see figure 1-3). In contrast, a C++ program needs to be compiled once for each type of system that it is going to be run on.
Speed	C++ runs faster than Java, partly because it is compiled for a specific platform, but Java is getting faster with each new version.
Memory	Since most memory operations are handled automatically by Java, it's easier to write bug-free code with Java than it is with C++.

Description

- Versions 1.0 and 1.1 of the Java toolkit were called the *Java Development Kit*, or *JDK*.
- Versions 1.2 through 1.4 of the Java toolkit are called the *Software Development Kit*, or *SDK*.
- The *Java 2 Platform, Standard Edition,* or *J2SE*, supports versions 1.2 through 1.4 of the SDK.
- The *Java 2 Platform, Enterprise Edition,* or *J2EE*, can be used to create enterprise-level, server-side applications.

Figure 1-1 Introduction to Java

Applications, applets, and servlets

Figure 1-2 describes the three types of programs that you can create with Java. First, you can use Java to create *applications*. This figure shows an application that uses a *graphical user interface*, or *GUI*, to get user input and perform a calculation. In this book, you'll be introduced to a variety of applications with the emphasis on GUI applications that get data from files and databases.

One of the unique characteristics of Java is that you can use it to create a special type of web-based application known as an *applet*. For instance, this figure shows an applet that works the same way as the application above it. The main difference between an application and an applet is that an applet can be stored in an HTML page and can run inside a Java-enabled browser. As a result, you can distribute applets via the Internet or an intranet. After you master the basics of building GUI applications, chapter 15 shows you how to create applets.

The Enterprise Edition of the Java 2 Platform can be used to create a special type of server-side application known as a *servlet*. Servlets can access enterprise databases and make that data available via the web. Since servlets are an advanced subject, they aren't presented in this book.

An application

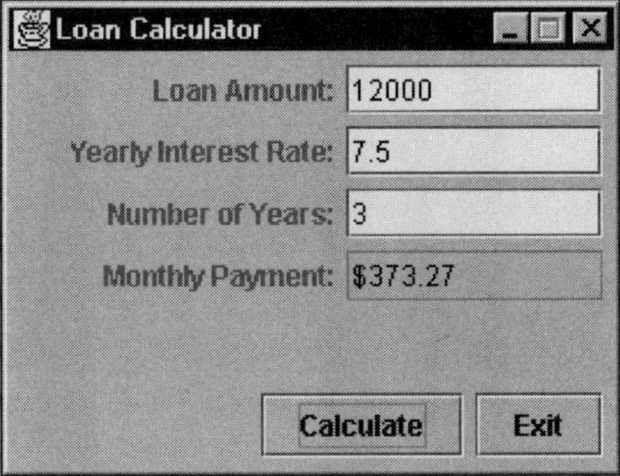

An applet

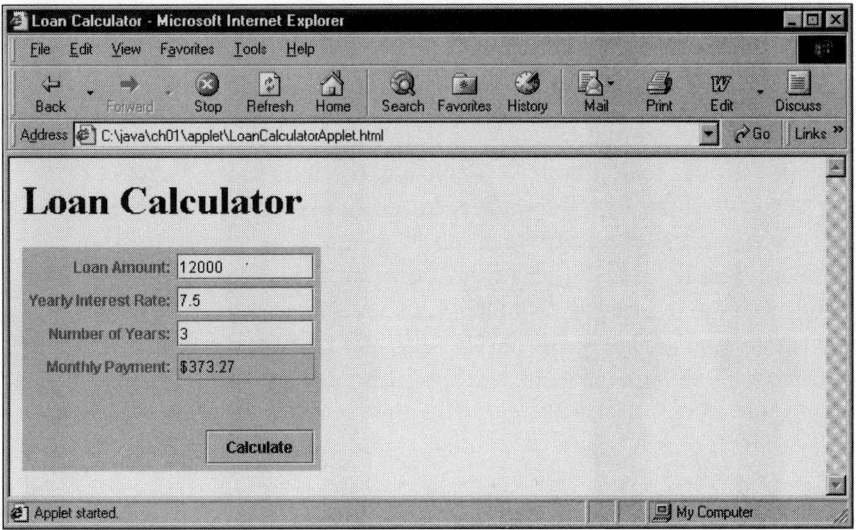

Description

- An *application* is a program that runs in a window. The application shown above uses a *graphical user interface*, or *GUI*, to get input and display output.
- An *applet* is a special type of program that runs within a web browser after it has been retrieved from the Internet or an intranet. You'll learn how to create applets in chapter 15.
- A *servlet* is a special type of program that does server-side processing.

Figure 1-2 Applications, applets, and servlets

How Java compiles and interprets code

Figure 1-3 shows how Java compiles and runs an application. To start, you can use any text editor to enter and edit Java *source code*. Then, you use the *Java compiler* to compile the source code into a format known as Java *bytecodes*. At this point, the bytecodes can be run on any platform that has a *Java interpreter* to interpret (or translate) the Java bytecodes into code that can be understood by the underlying operating system.

Since Java interpreters are available for all major operating systems, you can run Java on most platforms. This is what gives Java applications their *platform independence*. In contrast, C++ requires a specific compiler for each type of platform that its programs are going to run on. When a platform has a Java interpreter installed on it, it can be considered an implementation of a *Java virtual machine*, or *JVM*.

To enhance the platform independence of Java, some web browsers like Netscape and the Internet Explorer are Java-enabled. In other words, these browsers contain Java interpreters. This allows applets, which are bytecodes that are downloaded from the Internet or an intranet, to run within a web browser.

The problem with this is that both Netscape and the Internet Explorer only support older versions of the Java interpreter. In addition, Netscape and the Internet Explorer support slightly different subsets of the Java language. To solve this problem, Sun has developed a tool known as the *Java plug-in*, which lets the user upgrade the interpreter to a later version. This make it possible to develop applets that take advantage of the latest features of Java, but this works better for intranet applications than Internet applications. You'll learn more about this in chapter 15.

How Java compiles and interprets code

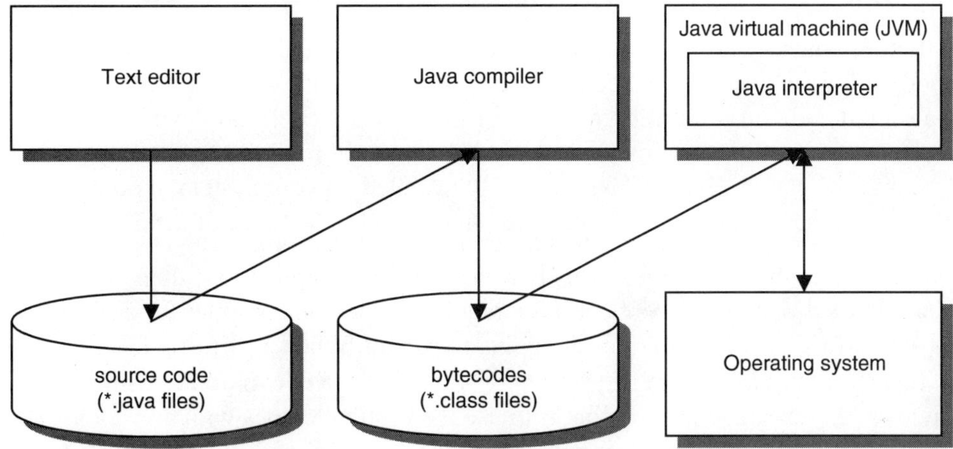

Description

- Any text editor can save and edit the *source code* for a Java application. Source code files use the *java* extension.
- The *Java compiler* translates source code into a *platform-independent* format known as Java *bytecodes*. Files that contain Java bytecodes use the *class* extension.
- The *Java interpreter* executes Java bytecodes. Since Java interpreters exist for all major operating systems, Java bytecodes can be run on most platforms. Any computer with a Java interpreter can be considered an implementation of a *Java virtual machine* (*JVM*).
- Some web browsers like Netscape and the Internet Explorer contain Java interpreters. This lets applets run within these browsers. However, both Netscape and the Internet Explorer only provide older versions of the Java interpreter.
- Sun provides a tool known as the *Java plug-in* that allows the Netscape and Internet Explorer browsers to use the most current version of the Java virtual machine.

Figure 1-3 How Java compiles and interprets code

How to get Java on your system

Before you can start to use Java, the SDK must be installed on your system. In addition, your system may need to be configured to work with the SDK. If Java isn't already installed and your system isn't already configured, you can use the next three figures to make sure it is. Then, you'll be ready to create your first Java application. Even if Java is already installed on your system, though, you should read the summary of files and directories that are part of the SDK.

How to install the SDK

Figure 1-4 shows how to install version 1.3.1 of the SDK. If you're using Windows, the easiest way to do that is to use the CD that comes with this book. Just navigate to the directory that holds the Windows SDK and run the setup file. Then, respond to the resulting dialog boxes. However, if you want to install a different version of Java, you can download that version from the Java web site as described in this figure.

Since Sun is continually updating the Java web site, the procedure shown in this figure may not be up-to-date by the time you read this. As a result, you may have to do some searching to find the current version of the SDK. In general, you can start by looking for products for the Java 2 Platform, Standard Edition. Then, you can find the most current version of the SDK for your operating system.

The Java web site address

```
www.java.sun.com
```

How to download and install the SDK from the Java web site

1. Go to the Java web site.
2. Locate Java products and find the Java 2 Platform, Standard Edition.
3. Go to the download page for the most current SDK version that's available for your platform.
4. After clicking on the download button, follow the instructions. Note the name of the file and the download size.
5. Select one of the FTP download options, unless you're behind a firewall and you need to use the HTTP option.
6. Save the setup file to your hard disk. On a 56K modem, it takes about 2 hours to download this file.
7. Once the entire package has downloaded, check to make sure that you got the executable and that the size is correct. Otherwise, you will get an error when you try to run the executable.
8. Run the exe file, and respond to the resulting dialog boxes. When you're prompted for the SDK directory, use the default directory and install all of the components unless disk space is a problem.

How to install the Windows SDK from the CD that comes with this book

1. Put the CD that comes with this book into your CD drive, and navigate to the WindowsSDK directory. (If you want to use some other platform, you need to download it from the Java web site.)
2. Double-click on the exe file, and respond to the resulting dialog boxes. When you're prompted for the SDK directory, use the default directory. Then, install all of the components unless disk space is a problem.

Figure 1-4 How to install the SDK

A summary of the directories and files of the SDK

Figure 1-5 shows the directories and files that are created when you install the SDK. Here, the SDK is stored in the c:\jdk1.3.1 directory. By default, this directory has six subdirectories: bin, demo, include, include-old, jre, and lib.

The *bin* directory holds all the tools necessary for developing and testing a program including the Java compiler. The *demo* directory contains many sample applications and applets. You can browse through these to learn more about what Java can do, and you can review the source code. The two *include* directories hold header files for the C programming language. These directories allow you to incorporate C code into a Java program.

The *jre* directory contains the Java interpreter, or *Java Runtime Environment* (*JRE*), that's needed to run Java applications once they've been compiled. Although the SDK uses this internal version of the JRE, you can also download a standalone version of the JRE from the Java web site. Once you're done developing a Java application, for example, you can distribute the standalone JRE to other computers so they can run your application. The *lib* directory contains libraries and support files required by the development tools.

The last directory is the *docs* directory, which is used to store the Java documentation. In chapter 3, you'll learn how to download and install this documentation.

In the jdk1.3.1 directory, you can find two *readme* files that contain much of the information that's presented in this figure as well as more technical and detailed information about the SDK. You can view the HTML file with a web browser, and you can open the text file with a text editor.

The jdk1.3.1 directory also contains the src.jar file, which is a type of compressed file known as a *Java Archive file*, or *JAR file*. This file holds the source code for the SDK. Before you can view the source code, though, you must extract the files that contain the source code from this JAR file. You'll learn how to do this in chapter 15.

When you work with Windows, you'll find that it uses the terms *folder* and *subfolder* to refer to DOS directories and subdirectories. For consistency, though, we use the term *directory* throughout this book. In practice, these terms are often used interchangeably.

The file structure of the SDK

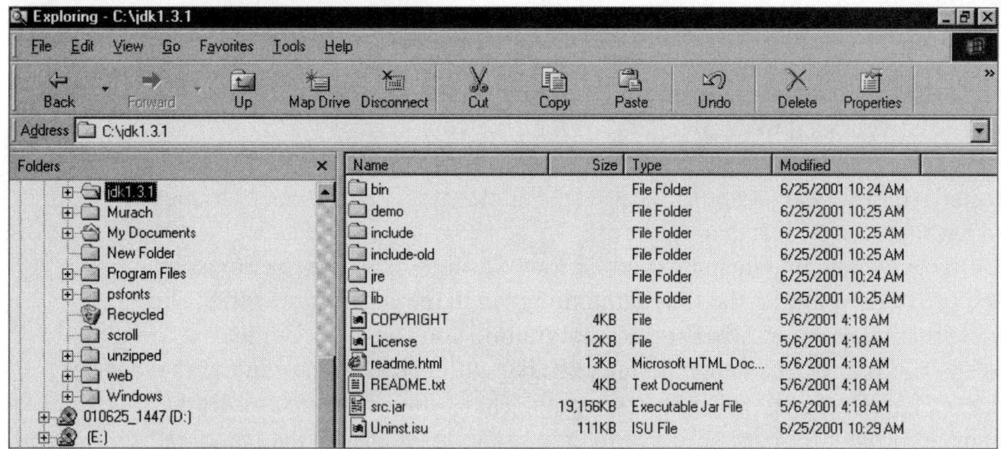

The subdirectories of the SDK

Directory	Description
bin	The Java development tools and commands
demo	Sample applications and applets with source code
include	C header files for combining C code with Java code
include-old	Older C header files for backwards compatibility
jre	The root directory of the Java Runtime Environment (JRE)
lib	Additional libraries of code that are required by the development tools
docs (optional)	The online documentation that you can download (see chapter 3)

The files of the SDK

File	Description
readme.html	An HTML page that provides information on Java 2, including system requirements, features, and documentation links
readme.txt	The text version of the readme.html file
src.jar	A file containing the source code for the SDK

Description

- The *Java Runtime Environment*, or *JRE*, is the Java interpreter that allows you to run compiled programs in Java. The jre directory is an internal copy of the runtime environment that works with the SDK. You can also download a standalone version of the JRE for computers that don't have the SDK installed on them.
- The src.jar file is a compressed file known as a *Java Archive file*, or *JAR file*. If you use the jar tool that comes with the SDK to extract the files from this JAR file, you can view the source code of the Java API.

Figure 1-5   A summary of the directories and files of the SDK

How to configure Windows to work with the SDK

Figure 1-6 shows you how to configure Windows to make it easier to work with the SDK. If you're not using Windows, you can refer to the Java web site to see what you need to do to configure Java for your system.

To configure Windows to work with the SDK, you need to add the bin directory to the *command path*. That way, Windows will know where to look to find the Java commands that you use.

One way to update the path for Windows 95 or 98 is to use the procedure in this figure to edit the Path or Set Path command in the *autoexec.bat* file. This is the file that is automatically executed every time you start your computer. After you edit the file, you can enter c:\autoexec.bat at the DOS prompt to run the autoexec.bat file and establish the new path. Then, you can enter *path* at the command prompt to make sure that the bin directory is now in the command path.

When you edit the autoexec.bat file, be careful! Since this file may affect the operation of other programs on your PC, you don't want to delete or modify any of the commands that this file contains. You only want to add one directory to the command path. If that doesn't work, be sure that you're able to restore the autoexec.bat file to its original condition.

If you're using a later version of Windows, you can use the second procedure in this figure to set the command path. It is easier to use with less chance that you'll do something that will affect the operation of other programs.

If you don't configure Windows in this way, you can still compile and run Java programs, but it's more difficult. In particular, you need to enter the path for each program that you're going to run. For instance, you need to enter

```
\jdk1.3.1\bin\javac
```

to run the javac command that's stored in the c:\jdk1.3.1\bin directory. This is illustrated by the last example in this figure. If you understand DOS, you should understand how this works.

A typical Path statement in the autoexec.bat file

How to set the path for Windows 95/98/2000

1. Go to the Start menu and select the Run option.
2. In the Run dialog box, enter "sysedit" and select OK. This should start the System Configuration Editor.
3. If necessary, use the Window menu to switch to the autoexec.bat file.
4. If the file contains a Path or Set Path command, type a semicolon at the end of the command; then, type "c:\jdk1.3\bin" as shown above. If no such command is there, enter "path=c:\jdk1.3\bin" at the beginning of the file.
5. Save the file and exit the System Configuration Editor.
6. To have the new path take effect, you can restart your computer (which runs the autoexec.bat file) or you can open up an MS-DOS window and enter c:\autoexec.bat at the DOS prompt.

How to set the path for Windows NT

1. Go to the Start menu, point to Settings, and select the Control Panel.
2. Select the Environment option.
3. Add c:\jdk1.3.1\bin to the far right side of the current path in User Variables or System Variables and select OK.

The commands for compiling and running a program if you set the path

```
C:\java\ch01>javac BookOrderApp.java

C:\java\ch01>java BookOrderApp
Title: War and Peace
```

The same commands if you don't set the path

```
C:\java\ch01>\jdk1.3.1\bin\javac BookOrderApp.java

C:\java\ch01>\jdk1.3.1\bin\java BookOrderApp
Title: War and Peace
```

Description

- After you add the Java bin directory to the path, Windows is able to find the commands that you use to compile and run your Java programs. From any DOS prompt, you can display the current path by typing "path".
- To configure other operating systems, you can refer to the Java web site.

Figure 1-6 How to configure Windows to work with the SDK

How to use Windows tools to work with Java

Once the SDK is installed on your computer and configured for your operating system, you're ready to create your first application. Since most Java programmers use Windows, you will now learn how to use the Windows tools for compiling and running Java programs. In particular, you will learn how to use Notepad for entering and editing a program and the DOS prompt for compiling and testing it.

This will give you the general idea of how a Java program is developed on any platform. Then, if you're using another operating system, you can learn similar procedures for developing programs on that system.

Note, however, that this chapter will soon show you how to use a product named TextPad for entering, compiling, and running Java programs on a Windows system. Since this is simpler than using Notepad and DOS commands and since TextPad is included on the CD for this book, we recommend that you use TextPad as you develop the programs for this book. As a result, you should read the procedures that follow primarily for the perspective that they give. Later, if you actually need to use these procedures, you can refer back to them for specific details.

How to use Notepad to save and edit source code

Figure 1-7 shows how to use the Notepad *text editor* to save and edit the source code for an application. After you start Notepad, you can enter and edit the code just as you would with any text editor. However, saving a source code file can be tricky for two reasons.

First, you must use the four-letter *java* extension. Second, since Java is a *case-sensitive* language, you must save the file with the proper capitalization. If the capitalization of the filename doesn't match the capitalization of the class name that's used in the Java code, you'll get an error message when you try to compile the code. In this figure, you can see that "BookOrderApp" is used in both the code and the filename.

To make sure you get the capitalization and the java extension right, you should enclose the filename in quotation marks as shown in this figure. Otherwise, Notepad may truncate the extension to jav or change the capitalization in the filename. Either way, you'll get errors when you try to compile the source code.

In addition, you must save the source code in a standard text-only format such as the *ASCII format* or the *ANSI format*. Since Notepad only supports ASCII, you can't go wrong when you're using Notepad. If, however, you're using a text editor or word processor that supports other formats, you'll need to make sure that you save the file in one of these standard text-only formats.

The Notepad text editor with source code in it

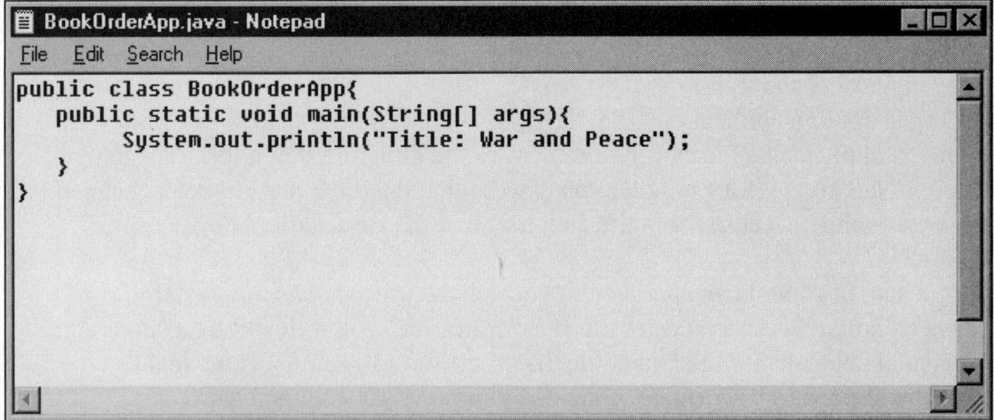

The bottom part of Notepad's Save As dialog box

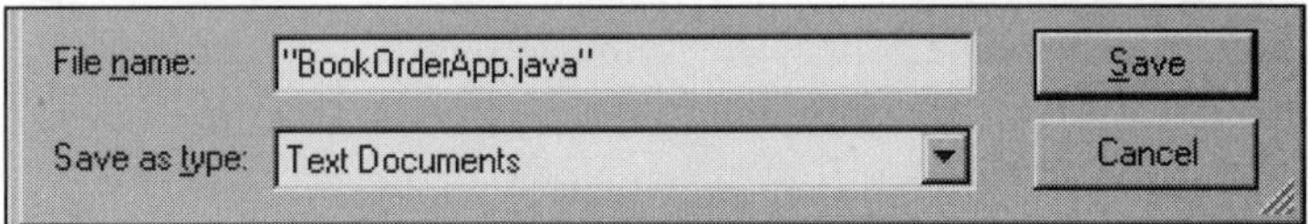

Syntax to save the code in a file

```
"ProgramName.java"
```

Typical capitalization for file names

```
Book.java
BookOrderApp.java
```

Operation

- To start Notepad, click on the Start menu, select Programs, select Accessories, and select Notepad.
- To enter or edit code, use the same techniques that you use with any other text editor or word processor.
- To save the source code, select the Save command from the File menu and enter the filename within quotation marks. That way, the file will be saved with the capitalization that you've used and with the java extension. Otherwise, the capitalization may be changed or the extension may be truncated to jav. (On some versions of Windows, the quotation marks may not be necessary, so you may want to experiment with this.)

Figure 1-7 How to use NotePad to save and edit source code

How to use the DOS prompt to compile source code

Figure 1-8 shows how to use the *DOS prompt*, or *command prompt*, to compile and run applications. To start, you should use the change directory (cd) command to change the current directory to the directory that holds the application. In this figure, for example, you can see that the directory has been changed to c:\java\ch01 because that's the directory that the BookOrderApp.java file is stored in.

Then, to compile an application, you use the *javac command* to start the Java compiler. When you enter the javac command, you follow it by a space and the complete name of the *.java file that you want to compile. Here again, because Java is case-sensitive, you need to use the same capitalization that you used when you saved the *.java file.

If the application doesn't compile successfully, the Java compiler will display one or more error messages. Usually, you can get an idea of what caused each error by reading its message. Then, you can use Notepad to correct and resave the *.java file, and you can compile the program again. Since this means that you'll be switching back and forth between Notepad and the DOS prompt, you'll want to leave both windows open.

When you compile an application successfully, the Java compiler will create a *.class file that has the same filename as the *.java file. For example, a successful compilation of the BookOrderApp.java file will create the BookOrderApp.class file.

How to use the DOS prompt to run an application

To run a program, you use the *java command* to start the Java interpreter. Although you need to use the proper capitalization when you use the java command, you don't need to include an extension for the file. When you enter the java command correctly, the Java interpreter will run the *.class file for the application.

Most of the time, running a Java program will display a graphical user interface like the one shown in figure 1-2. However, you can also print information to the DOS prompt, which in that case is called the *console*. For example, the BookOrderApp file in this figure prints a single line of text to the console.

When an application ends properly, you will be returned to the DOS prompt. Then, you can enter another command. If an application doesn't end properly, though, you can press Ctrl+C to cancel the execution of the program and return to the DOS prompt.

The commands for compiling and running an application

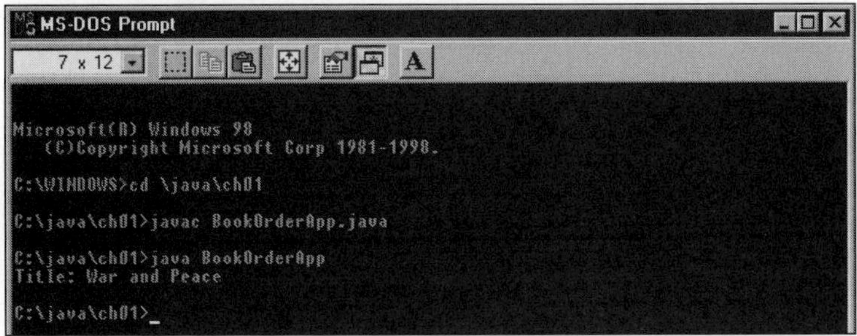

Syntax to compile an application

```
javac ProgramName.java
```

Syntax to run an application

```
java ProgramName
```

Description

- The *DOS prompt*, or *command prompt*, is the prompt that indicates that the operating system is waiting for the next command. When you use DOS, this prompt usually shows the current directory, and it always ends with >. In the example above, the last line is the command prompt, which shows that the current directory is c:\java\ch01.

Operation

- To open the DOS Prompt window with Windows 95, 98 or NT, click on the Start button, select Programs, and select MS-DOS Prompt. With Windows 2000, click on the Start button, select Accessories, and select Command Prompt.
- To change to the directory that contains the file with your source code, use the change directory command (cd) as shown above.
- To compile the source code, enter the Java compile command (javac), followed by the filename (including the java extension).
- If the code compiles successfully, the compiler generates another file with the same name, but with class as the extension. This file contains the bytecodes.
- If the code doesn't compile successfully, the java compiler will generate error messages. Then, you must switch back to your text editor, fix the errors, save your changes, and try compiling the program again.
- To run the compiled version of your source code, enter the Java command (java), followed by the program name without any extension. Since this is a case-sensitive command, make sure to use the same capitalization that you used when naming the file.

Note

- The code shown in the DOS Prompt window above will only work if c:\jdk1.3.1\bin has been added to the command path as in figure 1-6.

Figure 1-8 How to use the DOS prompt to compile and run an application

Common error messages and solutions

Figure 1-9 summarizes some common error messages. The first two errors illustrate *compile-time errors*. These are errors that occur when the Java compiler tries to compile the program. In contrast, the third error illustrates a *run-time error*. That is an error that occurs while the Java interpreter is trying to run the program.

The first error message in this figure involves a syntax error. When the compiler encounters a syntax error, it prints two lines for each error. The first line prints the name of the *.java file, followed by a colon, followed by the line number for the error, followed by a brief description of the error. The second line prints the code that caused the error including a caret character that tries to identify the location where the syntax error occurred. In this example, the syntax error is that a semicolon is missing at the end of the line.

The second error message in this figure involves a problem defining the *public class* for the file. The compiler displays an error message like this when the filename for the *.java file doesn't match the name of the public class defined in the source code. For example, a *.java file that defines a class named BookOrderApp must contain this code

```
public class BookOrderApp{
```

and this file must be saved as BookOrderApp.java. If the name of the file doesn't match the name of the public class (including capitalization), the compiler will give you an error like the one shown in this figure. You'll learn more about the syntax for defining a public class in the next chapter.

The third error message in this figure occurs if you enter the wrong name after the java command. If, for example, you enter "bookorderapp" after the java command, you'll get an error like this. That's because the capitalization for the class isn't correct. If, on the other hand, you enter "BookOrderApp.class" after the java command, you'll get a similar error. That's because you shouldn't include the extension when you use the java command.

Most of the time, the information displayed by an error message will give you an idea of how to fix the problem. Sometimes, though, the compiler doesn't give you accurate error messages. In that case, you'll need to double-check all of your code. You'll learn more about debugging error messages like these as you progress through this book.

A common error message

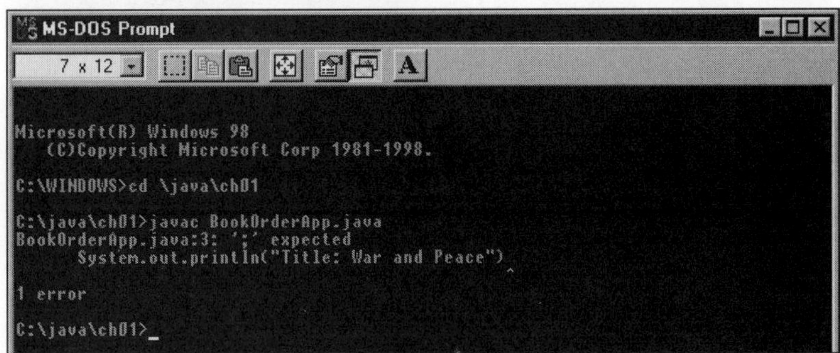

Two common compile-time error messages and solutions

Error:

```
BookOrderApp.java:3: ';' expected
System.out.println("Title: War and Peace")
                                          ^
```

Description: The first line in this error message displays the filename of the *.java file, a number indicating the line where the error occurred, and a brief description of the error. The second line displays the line of code that may have caused the error with a caret symbol (^) below the location where there may be improper syntax.

Solution: Use a text editor to correct the problem and save the file.

Error:

```
BookOrderApp.java:1: class BookOrder is public, should be
declared in a file named BookOrder.java
public class BookOrder{
       ^
```

Description: The *.java filename doesn't match the name of the public class. Remember, you must save the file with the same name as the name that's coded after the words "public class". In addition, you must add the java extension to the filename.

Solution: Enter the correct filename after the javac command. Or, use the text editor to save the java file with the proper spelling and capitalization.

A common run-time error message and solution

Error:

```
Exception in thread "main"
java.lang.NoClassDefFoundError:
bookorderapp (wrong name: BookOrderApp)
```

Description: The name that was entered for the *.class file isn't correct. Remember, you must use the proper capitalization and you must omit the class extension.

Solution: Enter the correct name after the java command. You can use the dir command to check the capitalization for the file as shown in the next figure. If necessary, you may need to use the javac command to recreate the *.class file from the *.java file.

Figure 1-9 Common error messages and solutions

Essential DOS skills for working with Java

Figure 1-10 summarizes some of the most useful commands and keystrokes for working with DOS. In addition, it shows how to install and use a DOS program called DOSKey, which makes entering and editing DOS commands easier. If you're going to use DOS to work with Java, you should review these DOS commands and keystrokes, and you will probably want to turn on the DOSKey program. If you aren't going to use DOS, of course, you can skip this figure.

At the top of this figure, you can see a DOS Prompt window that shows two DOS commands and a directory listing. In this window, the first command changes the current directory to c:\java\ch01. The next command displays a directory listing. If you study this listing, you can see that this directory contains two files with one line of information for each file. At the right side of each line, you can see the complete filenames for these two files (BookOrderApp.java and BookOrderApp.class), and you can see the capitalization for these files as well.

If you master the DOS commands summarized in this figure, you should be able to use DOS to work with Java. To switch to another drive, type the letter of the drive followed by a colon. To change the current directory to another directory, use the cd command. To display a directory listing for the current directory, use the dir command. To return to the DOS prompt when an application hasn't ended properly, press Ctrl+C. Although DOS provides many more commands that let you create directories, move files, copy files, and rename files, you can also use the Windows Explorer to perform those types of tasks.

Although you don't need to use the DOSKey program, it can save you a lot of typing and frustration. If, for example, you compile a program and you encounter a syntax error, you will need to use a text editor to fix the error in the source code. Then, you will need to compile the program again. If you're using DOSKey, you can do that by pressing the up-arrow key to display the command and by pressing the Enter key to execute the command. And if you make a mistake when entering a command, you can use the left- and right-arrow keys to edit the command instead of having to enter the entire command again.

A directory listing

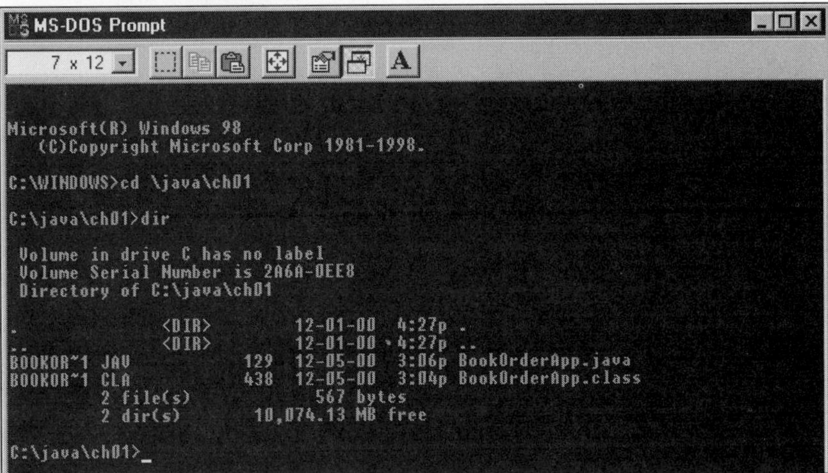

A review of DOS commands and keystrokes

Command	Description
`dir`	Displays a directory listing.
`dir /p`	Displays a directory listing that pauses if the listing is too long to fit on one screen.
`cd \`	Changes the current directory to the root directory for the current drive.
`cd ..`	Changes the current directory to the parent directory.
`cd` *`directory name`*	Changes the current directory to the subdirectory with the specified name.
`letter``:`	Changes the current drive to the drive specified by the letter. For example, entering d: changes the current drive to the d drive.

Keystroke	Description
Ctrl+C	Interrupts the execution of the program and cancels it.
Ctrl+S	Stops the scrolling of the display screen.
F3	Types the last command that was run.

How to start the DOSKey program

- To start the DOSKey program, enter "doskey /insert" at the command prompt.
- To automatically start the DOSKey program for all future sessions, enter the "doskey /insert" statement after the "path" statement in the autoexec.bat file. For help on editing the autoexec.bat file, see figure 1-6.

How to use the DOSKey program

Key	Description
Up or down arrow	Cycles through previous DOS commands in the current session.
Left or right arrow	Moves cursor to allow normal editing of the text at the DOS prompt.

Figure 1-10 Essential DOS skills for working with Java

How to use TextPad to work with Java

Now that you've learned how to use Notepad and the DOS prompt for working with Java, you're ready to learn how to use TextPad. Since this text editor is designed for working with Java, it's a big improvement over Notepad. As a result, we recommend that you use the trial version that's included on the CD that comes with this book.

Unfortunately, TextPad only runs under Windows. So if you're not using Windows, you can use the text editor that comes with your operating system or you can search the web to find a better text editor.

How to use TextPad to save and edit source code

Figure 1-11 shows how to use TextPad to save and edit source code. In short, you can use the standard Windows shortcut keystrokes and menus to enter, edit, and save your code. You can use the File menu to open and close files. You can use the Edit menu to cut, copy, and paste text. And you can use the Search menu to find and replace text. In addition, TextPad color codes the source files so it's easier to recognize the Java syntax, and TextPad makes it easier to save *.java files with the proper capitalization and extension.

Unlike Notepad, TextPad doesn't come as a part of Windows. As a result, you must install it before you can use it. To do that, run the setup file that's on the CD that comes with this book. Then, respond to the resulting dialog boxes. Since this version of TextPad is a trial version, you should pay for TextPad if you decide to use it beyond the initial trial period. Fortunately, this program is relatively inexpensive (about $27), especially when you consider how much time and effort it can save you.

The TextPad text editor with source code in it

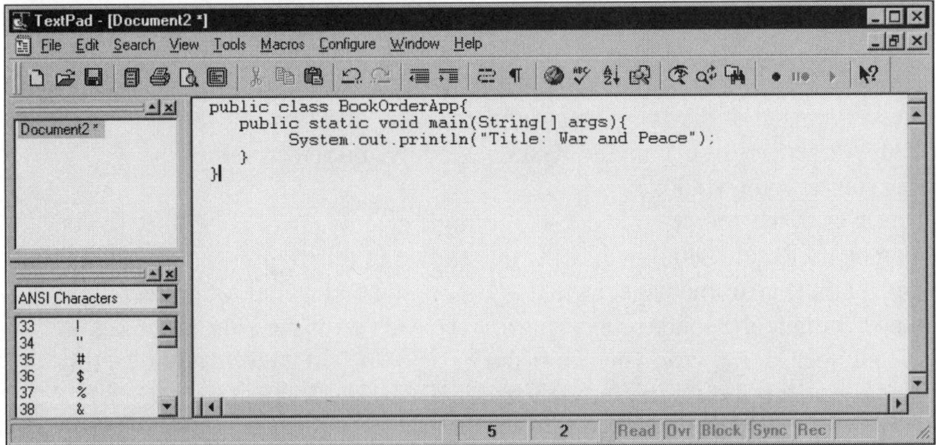

TextPad's Save As dialog box

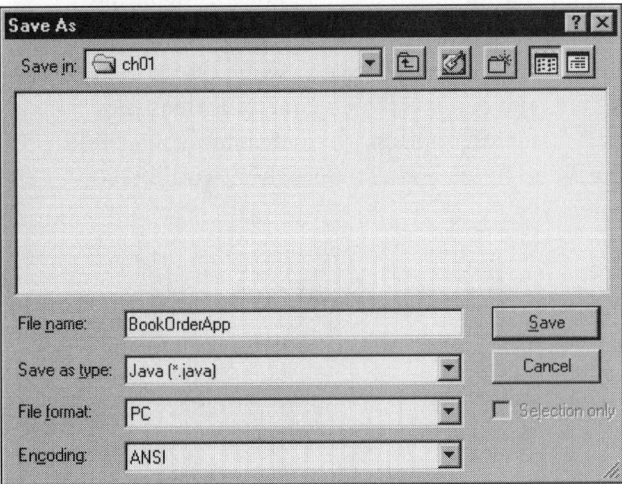

How to install TextPad on your PC

- Navigate to the TextPadSetup directory on the CD that comes with this book. Then, double-click on the exe file and respond to the resulting dialog boxes.

How to enter, edit, and save source code

- To enter and edit source code, you can use the same techniques that you use for working with any other Windows text editor.
- To save the source code, select the Save command from the File menu (Ctrl+S). Then, enter the filename so it's exactly the same as the class name, and select the Java option from the Save As Type list so TextPad adds the four-letter java extension to the filename. (On earlier versions of Windows, you may need to enter the four-letter extension with the filename as in BookOrderApp.java. Otherwise, the extension will be truncated to jav.)

Figure 1-11 How to use TextPad to save and edit source code

How to use TextPad to compile source code

Figure 1-12 shows how to use TextPad to compile the source code for a Java application. The quickest way to do that is to press Ctrl+1 to execute the Compile Java command of the Tools menu. If the source code compiles cleanly, TextPad will generate a Command Results window and return you to the original source code window.

However, if the source code doesn't compile cleanly, TextPad will leave you at a Command Results window like the one shown in this figure. In this case, you can read the error message, switch to the source code window, correct the error, and compile the source code again. Since each error message identifies the line number of the error, you can make it easier to find the error by selecting the Line Number option from the View menu. That way, TextPad will display line numbers as shown in this figure.

When you have several Java files open at once, you can use the Document Selector pane to switch between files. In this figure, only two documents are open (BookOrderApp and Command Results), but you can open as many Java files as you like. You can also use the Window menu and standard Windows keystrokes (Ctrl+F6 and Ctrl+Shift+F6) to switch between windows.

To edit as efficiently as possible, you can use the Document Properties command in the View menu to set formatting options. In particular, you should set the tab settings so you can easily align the code in a program. You'll learn more about that in the next chapter.

How to use TextPad to run an application

Once you've compiled the source code for an application, you can run that application by pressing Ctrl+2. If the application that you run prints text to the console, TextPad will start a DOS Prompt window like the one shown in this figure. Then, you can press any key to end the application. If necessary, you can also click on the Close button or press Alt+F4 to close the DOS Prompt window.

The Tools menu

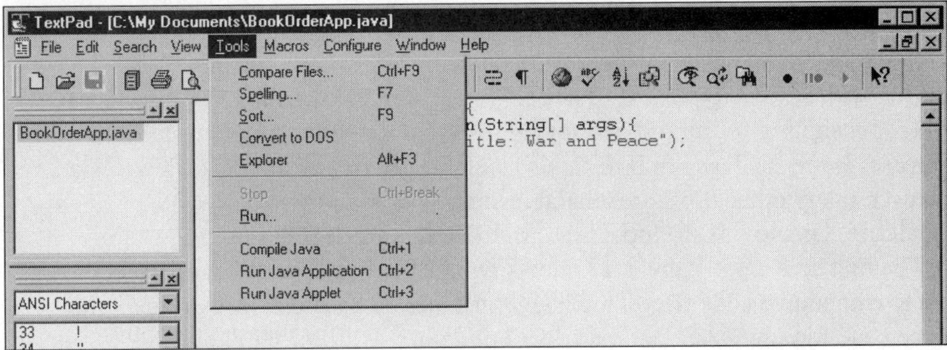

A compile-time error

Text printed to the console

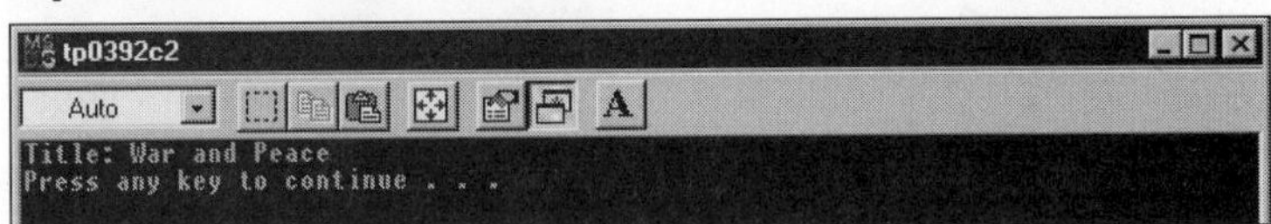

How to compile and run an application

- To compile the current source code, press Ctrl+1 or select the Compile Java command from the Tools menu.
- To run the current application, press Ctrl+2 or select the Run Java Application command.
- If you encounter compile-time errors, TextPad will print them to a window named Command Results. To switch between this window and the window that holds the source code, you can press Ctrl+F6 or use the Document Selector pane that's on the left side of the TextPad window.
- When you print to the console, a DOS window like the one above is displayed, and you need to press any key to end the application. If necessary, you can press Alt+F4 or click on the Close button to close the window.

How to display line numbers and set options

- To display the line numbers for the source code, check Line Numbers in the View menu.
- To set formatting options like tab settings, choose Document Properties in the View menu.

Figure 1-12 How to use TextPad to compile and run an application

Introduction to Java IDEs

Many *Integrated Development Environments* (*IDEs*) are available for working with Java. A typical IDE not only provides a text editor, but also visual tools for designing forms and debugging code. To illustrate a typical IDE, this topic uses Forte for Java, an IDE that's available for free from the Java web site. However, many other IDEs are available such as Borland's JBuilder, WebGain's VisualCafé, Oracle's JDeveloper, and Metrowerk's CodeWarrior.

The first screen in figure 1-13 shows two of the Forte windows that can be used to edit source code. Here, the Explorer window has been used to open the source code for a program named ClockFrame in the Editor window.

The second screen in this figure shows the windows that can be used to visually create the forms of a graphical user interface. Here, you can place visual components such as labels, text boxes, and buttons on a form. Then, you can use the Component Inspector window to view and modify the properties of these components. When you're done, you can use Forte to generate the appropriate code for the form.

In addition, Forte provides many advanced debugging features that aren't available from a simple tool like TextPad. For example, Forte provides a Debugger window and a Debug menu that allows you to set breakpoints and step through code line by line.

Why we don't recommend using an IDE when you're learning Java

We don't recommend using an IDE when you're learning Java for two reasons. First, an IDE will often generate code for you. Although this can save time and effort once you've learned Java, this won't help you learn. While you're learning, you need to have complete control over the code. Second, an IDE is a complex tool with operational details that are themselves difficult to learn. And that can distract you from your learning goals.

Why we recommend using an IDE once you've mastered Java

Once you've got a solid grasp on the use of Java, an IDE is a sophisticated tool that can make working with Java easier. In particular, an IDE can make it easier to develop graphical user interfaces and to debug your code. So when you're through reading this book, you'll be ready to start using one of these tools. That's why we've included Forte for Java on the CD that comes with this book.

Forte's Editing workspace

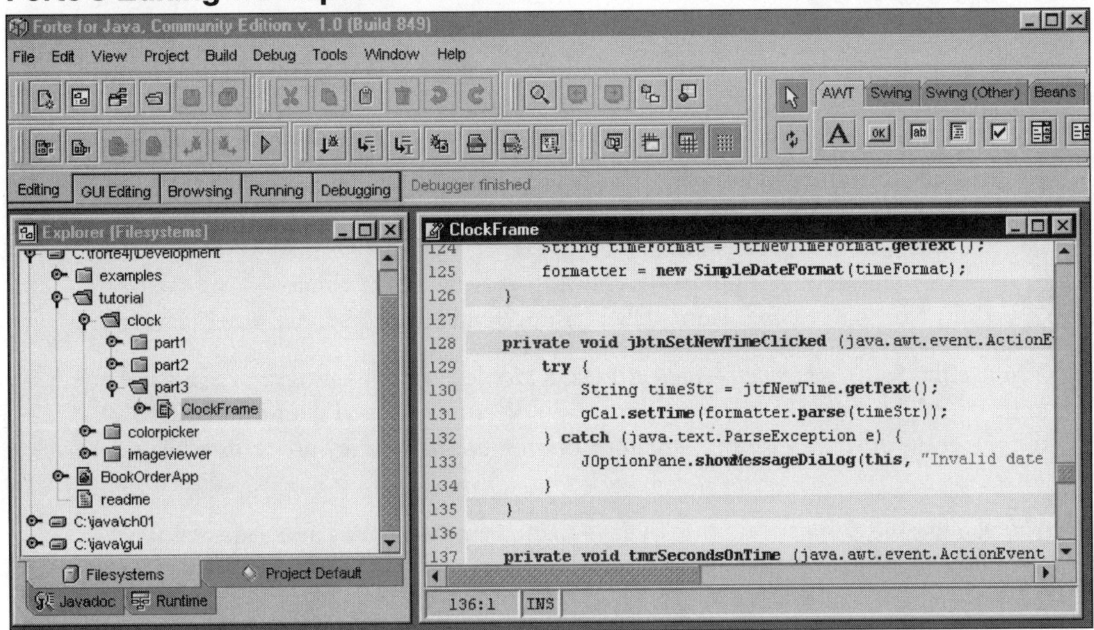

Forte's GUI Editing workspace

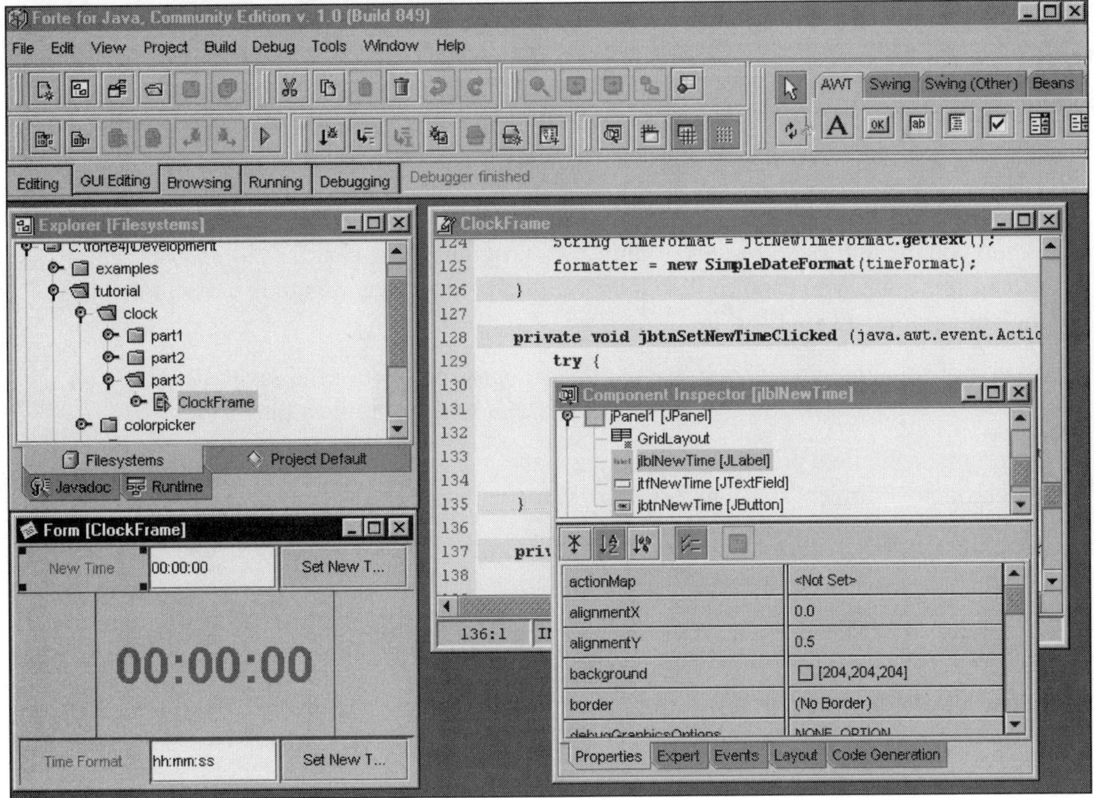

Figure 1-13 The Integrated Development Environment for Forte

Perspective

In this chapter, you learned how to install and configure the SDK for developing Java programs. You also learned how to use either the Windows tools or TextPad to enter, edit, compile, and run a program. With that as background, you're ready to start writing your own Java programs. And that's what you'll learn to do in the next chapter.

Summary

- You use the *Software Development Kit* (*SDK*) to develop Java programs. This used to be called the *Java Development Kit* (*JDK*). Versions 1.2 and later of the SDK run under the *Java 2 Platform, Standard Edition* (*J2SE*) so they are referred to as *Java 2*.
- You can use the Standard Edition of Java to create *applications* and a special type of Internet-based application known as an *applet*. In addition, you can use the *Java 2 Platform, Enterprise Edition* (*J2EE*) to create server-side applications known as *servlets*.
- The *Java compiler* translates *source code* into a *platform-independent* format known as Java *bytecodes*. Then, the *Java interpreter*, or *Java Runtime Environment* (*JRE*), translates the bytecodes into instructions that can be run by a specific operating system. Any machine that has a Java interpreter installed on it can be considered an implementation of a *Java virtual machine* (*JVM*).
- When you use the SDK with Windows, you should add the bin directory to the *command path*.
- When you use Windows for developing Java programs, you can use Notepad as the *text editor*. Then, you can use the *DOS prompt* to enter the commands for compiling and running an application.
- To compile an application, you use the *javac command* to start the Java compiler. To run an application, you use the *java command* to start the Java interpreter.
- When you compile a program, you may get *compile-time errors*. When you run a program, you may get *run-time errors*.
- A text editor like TextPad provides features that make it easier to enter, edit, compile, and test Java programs.
- Once you've mastered the basics of Java, an *Integrated Development Environment* (*IDE*) can make working with Java easier. While you're learning, though, it's better to use a text editor like TextPad.

Terms

Java Development Kit (JDK)
Software Development Kit (SDK)
Java 2
Java 2 Platform, Standard Edition (J2SE)
Java 2 Platform, Enterprise Edition (J2EE)
application
graphical user interface (GUI)
applet
servlet
source code
Java compiler
bytecodes
Java interpreter
platform independence
Java virtual machine (JVM)
Java plug-in
Java Runtime Environment (JRE)
Java Archive file (JAR file)
folder
subfolder
directory
subdirectory
command path
autoexec.bat file
text editor
case-sensitive
ASCII format
ANSI format
DOS prompt
command prompt
javac command
java command
console
compile-time error
run-time error
Integrated Development Environment (IDE)

Objectives

- Describe how Java compares with C++ based on these features: syntax, platform independence, and speed.
- Name and describe the three types of programs that you can create with Java.
- Explain how the use of bytecodes helps Java achieve platform independence.
- Install version 1.3.1 of the SDK for the Java 2 Platform, Standard Edition. If necessary, configure your system to work with the SDK.
- Given the source code for a Java application, use Notepad and the DOS prompt to enter, edit, compile, and run a program.
- Given the source code for a Java application, use TextPad to enter, edit, compile, and run the program.

Before you do the exercises for this chapter

Before you begin the exercises that follow, you should run the install program for the CD that comes with this book to install its directories and files. Then, you should copy the Java directory that's in the c:\Murach\Java2\ExerciseStarts directory to your c drive. You should use the procedure in figure 1-4 to install the SDK. You should use the procedure in figure 1-6 to set the command path for your system. And you should use the procedure in figure 1-11 to install TextPad.

Exercise 1-1 Use TextPad to develop an application

This exercise will guide you through the process of using TextPad to enter, save, compile, and run a simple application.

Enter and save the source code

1. Start TextPad. You should be able to do that by clicking on the Start button, pointing to Programs, pointing to TextPad, and clicking on TextPad.
2. Enter this code (type carefully and use the same capitalization):

```
public class TextPadTest{
   public static void main(String[] args){
      System.out.println("TextPad test");
   }
}
```

3. Use the Save command in the File menu to display the Save As dialog box. Next, navigate to the c:\java\ch01 directory and enter TextPadTest in the File name box. If necessary, select the Java option from the Save as Type combo box. Then, click on the Save button to save the file. (If this saves the file with jav as the extension, use the Save As command to save the file again. This time, type TextPadTest.java as the filename.)

Compile the source code and run the application

4. Press Ctrl+1 to compile the source code.
5. If you get an error message, read the error message, edit the text file, save your changes, and compile the application again. Repeat this process until you compile the application cleanly.
6. Press Ctrl+2 to run the application.
7. This application should start a DOS prompt that displays a line that reads "TextPad test" followed by a line that reads "Press any key to continue…" so press any key. Then, press Alt+F4 to close the DOS Prompt window if it's still open. You should be returned to the TextPad window.

Introduce and correct a compile-time error

8. In the TextPad window, delete the semicolon at the end of the System.out.println statement. Then, press Ctrl+1 to compile the source code. TextPad should display an error message in the Command Result window that indicates that the semicolon is missing.
9. In the Document Selector pane, click on the TextPadTest.java file to switch back to the source code. Then, press Ctrl+F6 twice to toggle back and forth between the Command Result window and the source code.
10. Correct the error and compile the file again (this automatically saves your changes). This time the file should compile cleanly. Then, close the file and exit TextPad.

Exercise 1-2 Use Windows tools to develop an application

If you want to see how the Windows tools work for developing an application, this exercise will guide you through the process of using Notepad and the DOS prompt to save, compile, and run a simple application. This will also give you a good idea of how you can use a text editor and the command prompt on any operating system.

Use Notepad to enter and save the source code

1. Start Notepad. On most systems, you can do that by clicking on the Start button, pointing to Programs, pointing to Accessories, and clicking on Notepad.
2. Enter this code (type carefully and use the same capitalization):

```
public class NotepadTest{
   public static void main(String[] args){
      System.out.println("Notepad test");
   }
}
```

3. Select the Save command from the File menu to display the Save As dialog box. Next, navigate to the c:\java\ch01 directory. Then, enter "NotepadTest.java" in the File Name text box (with the quotation marks), and click on the Save button to save the file. (If you want to see whether the quotation marks are needed, use the Save As command again without the quotation marks to see if the file already exists. If it does, you don't need the quotation marks the next time you save a new file.)

Use the DOS prompt to compile and run the application

4. Open a DOS Prompt window. On most systems, you can do that by clicking on the Start button, pointing to Programs, and clicking on MS-DOS Prompt.
5. Use the cd command to change the current directory to the c:\java\ch01 directory.
6. Use the dir command to view the files that are stored in this directory. If you are in the correct directory, you should see the NotepadTest.java file. Notice how the right side of the directory listing shows the long filename.
7. Use the javac command to compile the NotepadTest.java file. If you get an error message, read the error message, edit the text file, save your changes, and compile the application again. Repeat this process until you compile the application cleanly.
8. Use the dir command to view the files again. Notice that the file named NotepadTest.class has been created.
9. Use the java command to run the NotepadTest application (make sure to use the proper capitalization). This should display the words "Notepad test" after the DOS prompt. Then, close the Notepad and DOS Prompt windows.

Exercise 1-3 Use the DOS prompt to run an existing application

This exercise shows how to run any Java application from the DOS prompt.

1. Open the DOS Prompt window (see step 4 of exercise 1-2). Then, use the cd command to change the current directory to c:\java\ch01.
2. Use the java command to run the InvoiceApp application. When the first dialog box is displayed, enter 1000 as the order total. Then, note the results that are displayed in the second dialog box, and press the Enter key to try this again. When you're done experimenting, enter "x" to end the application. Then, close the DOS Prompt window.

This is the application that you'll learn how to develop in the next chapter. And this shows how the Java virtual machine can be used to run any Java application, whether or not it has been compiled on that machine.

Exercise 1-4 Use any tools to develop an application

If you aren't going to use Windows tools or TextPad to develop your Java programs, you can try whatever tools you are going to use with this generic exercise.

Use any text editor to enter and save the source code

1. Start the text editor and enter this code (type carefully and use the same capitalization):

```
public class Test{
   public static void main(String[] args){
      System.out.println("Test");
   }
}
```

2. Save this code in the c:\java\ch01 directory in a file named "Test.java".

Compile the source code and run the application

3. Compile the source code. If you're using a text editor that has a compile command, use this command. Otherwise, use your command prompt to compile the source code. To do that, start your command prompt and navigate to the c:\java\ch01 directory. Then, enter the javac command like this (make sure to use the same capitalization):

```
javac Test.java
```

4. Run the application. If you're using a text editor that has a run or execute command, use this command. Otherwise, use your command prompt to run the application. To do that, enter the java command like this (make sure to use the same capitalization):

```
java Test
```

5. When you enter this command, the application should print "Test" to the console (the console's appearance will depend on the tool that you're using).

2

Java language essentials (part 1)

Once you've got Java on your system, the quickest and best way to *learn* Java programming is to *do* Java programming. That's why this chapter shows you how to write a complete Java program that uses dialog boxes for input and output. When you finish this chapter, you should be able to write comparable programs of your own.

Basic coding skills

To start, this chapter introduces you to some basic coding skills. First, you'll learn how to code comments and Java statements. Next, you'll learn how create the identifiers that you'll use in your programs. Then, you'll learn how declare the class and main method for a Java application.

How to code comments

Comments can be used to document what a program does, what specific blocks of code do, and what specific lines of code do. Since the Java compiler ignores comments, you can include them anywhere in a program without affecting how your code works. Figure 2-1 shows you how to code two types of comments.

The first example shows a *block comment* at the start of a program. This type of comment can be used to document information that applies to the entire program. That can include the author's name, program completion date, the purpose of the program, the files used by the program, and so on. Block comments can also be used in the body of a program to describe and explain the code that follows.

To document the purpose of a single line of code, you can use *end-of-line comments*. Once the compiler reads the slashes (//) that start this type of comment, it ignores all characters until the end of the current line. In the second example in this figure, end-of-line comments indicate the beginnings and endings of each block of code in a class. Since this can make it easier to keep track of the pairs of braces that are used within a Java application, this can be useful, especially for beginning Java programmers.

In practice, a block comment is commonly used at the start of the program to give general information about the program. In addition, comments should be used to document the portions of the program that are difficult to understand. The trick is to provide comments for the portions of code that need explanation without cluttering the program with unnecessary comments.

How to code statements

The *statements* in a Java program direct the operation of the program. When you code a statement, you can start it anywhere in a coding line, you can continue it from one line to another, and you can code one or more spaces anywhere a single space is valid. To end most statements, you code a semicolon. But when a statement requires a set of braces {}, it ends with the right brace.

To make a program easier to read, you should use indentation and spacing to align statements and parts of statements. This is illustrated by the program in this figure and by all of the programs and examples in this book.

Incidentally, you'll know how to code every statement in this program by the time you complete this chapter. As you read, you may want to refer back to this figure to see how what you've just learned is used in this program.

A block comment at the start of a program

```
/*
 * Date:    4/3/01
 * Author:  A. Steelman
 * Purpose: Uses one dialog box to get the order total from the user.
 *          Then, it calculates the discount amount and invoice total
 *          and displays all three values in a second dialog box.
 */
```

An application that uses end-of-line comments

```
import javax.swing.JOptionPane; // needed to display dialog boxes

public class InvoiceApp{ // begin class
   public static void main(String[] args){ // begin main method
      String choice = "";
      while (!(choice.equalsIgnoreCase("x"))){ // begin while loop
         String inputString = JOptionPane.showInputDialog(
            "Enter order total: ");
         double orderTotal = Double.parseDouble(inputString);
         double discountAmount = 0;
         if (orderTotal >= 100)
            discountAmount = orderTotal * .2;
         else
            discountAmount = orderTotal * .1;
         double invoiceTotal = orderTotal - discountAmount;
         String message = "Order total: " + orderTotal + "\n"
                        + "Discount amount: " + discountAmount + "\n"
                        + "Invoice total: " + invoiceTotal + "\n\n"
                        + "To continue, press Enter.\n"
                        + "To exit, enter 'x': ";
         choice = JOptionPane.showInputDialog(message);
      } // end while loop
      System.exit(0);
   } // end main method
} // end class
```

Description

- *Comments* are used to help document what a program does and what the code within it does, while Java *statements* direct what the program does.

How to code comments

- To code a *block comment*, type /* at the start of the block and */ at the end. You can also code asterisks to identify the lines in the block, but that isn't necessary.
- To code an *end-of-line comment*, type // followed by the comment.

How to code statements

- You can start a statement at any point in a line and continue the statement from one line to the next. To make a program easier to read, you can use indentation and extra spaces to align statements and parts of statements.
- Although most statements end with a semicolon, some statements like the while statement end with the right brace (}) of a pair of braces ({}).

Figure 2-1 How to code comments and statements

How to create identifiers

As you code a Java program, you need to create and use *identifiers*. These are the names in the program that you define. In each program, for example, you need to create an identifier for the name of the program and for the variables that are used by the program.

Figure 2-2 shows you how to create identifiers. In brief, you must start each identifier with a letter, underscore, or dollar sign. After that first character, you can use any combination of letters, underscores, dollar signs, or digits.

Since Java is case-sensitive, you need to pay attention to capitalization when you create and use identifiers. If, for example, you define an identifier as CustomerAddress, you can't refer to it later as Customeraddress. That's a common compile-time error.

When you create an identifier, you should always try to make the name both meaningful and easy to remember. To make a name meaningful, you should use as many characters as you need, so it's easy for other programmers to read and understand your code. For instance, netPrice is more meaningful than nPrice, and nPrice is more meaningful than np. To make a name easy to remember, you should avoid abbreviations. If, for example, you use nwCst as an identifier, you may have difficulty remembering whether it was nCust, nwCust, or nwCst later on. If you code the name as newCustomer, though, you won't have any trouble remembering what it was. Yes, you type more characters when you create identifiers that are meaningful and easy to remember, but that will be justified by the time you'll save when you test, debug, and maintain the program.

Notice that you can't create an identifier that is the same as one of the Java *keywords*. These are the words that are reserved by the Java language, and you'll learn how to use many of them in this chapter. Note, however, that the entire language consists of just 50 keywords.

Valid identifiers

`InvoiceApp`	`choice`	`TITLE`
`Book`	`inputString`	`MONTHS_PER_YEAR`
`BookOrder`	`orderTotal`	`$orderTotal`
`BookOrderApp`	`getOrderTotal`	`_orderTotal`
`BookOrderApp2`	`x`	`input_string`
`BookGUI`	`book1`	`_get_total`
`BookPanel`	`book2`	`$_64_Valid`

The rules for naming an identifier

- Start each identifier with a letter, underscore, or dollar sign. Use letters, dollar signs, underscores, or digits for subsequent characters.
- Use up to 255 characters.
- Don't use Java keywords.

Keywords

`boolean`	`if`	`interface`	`class`	`true`
`char`	`else`	`package`	`volatile`	`false`
`byte`	`final`	`switch`	`while`	`throws`
`float`	`private`	`case`	`return`	`native`
`void`	`protected`	`break`	`throw`	`implements`
`short`	`public`	`default`	`try`	`import`
`double`	`static`	`for`	`catch`	`synchronized`
`int`	`new`	`continue`	`finally`	`const`
`long`	`this`	`do`	`transient`	`goto`
`abstract`	`super`	`extends`	`instanceof`	`null`

Description

- An *identifier* is any name that you create in a Java program. These can be the names of classes, methods, variables, and so on.
- A *keyword* is a word that's reserved by the Java language. As a result, you can't use keywords as identifiers.
- When you refer to an identifier, be sure to use the correct uppercase and lowercase letters because Java is a case-sensitive language.

Figure 2-2 How to create identifiers

How to declare a class

When you develop a Java application, you develop one or more *classes* that do the processing for the program. As you learned in chapter 1, the code for each class is stored in a *.java file, and the compiled code is stored in a *.class file. Within each class that you develop, you code one *class declaration* as shown in figure 2-3.

In the syntax for declaring a class, the boldfaced words are Java keywords, and the words that aren't boldfaced represent code that the programmer supplies. The bar (|) in this syntax means that you have a choice between the two items that the bar separates. In this case, the bar means that you can start the declaration with either the word *public* or the word *private*.

The words *public* and *private* are *access modifiers* that control the *scope* of a class. Usually, a class is declared public, which means that other classes can access it. In fact, you must declare one (and only one) public class for every *.java file. Later in this book, though, you'll learn when and how to use private classes.

After the keywords *public* and *class*, you code the name of the class using the basic rules for creating an identifier. In addition, though, it's a common Java coding convention to start a class name with a capital letter and to use letters and digits only. Beyond that, I recommend that you use a noun or a noun that's preceded by one or more adjectives for each class, and I recommend that you start every word within the name with a capital letter. In this figure, all four class names adhere to these rules and guidelines.

After the class name, the syntax summary shows a left brace, the statements that make up the class, and a right brace. It's a good coding practice, though, to type your ending brace right after you type the starting brace, and then type your code between the two braces. That prevents missing braces, which is a common compile-time error.

This figure also shows a complete class named InvoiceApp with the class declaration shaded. The portion of the code that's between the braces for this class is called the *class definition*. In this simple example, the class definition contains three lines of code, and you'll learn more about them in the next figure.

When you save your class on disk, you save it with a name that consists of the public class name and the *java* extension. As a result, you save the class in this figure with the name InvoiceApp.java.

The syntax for declaring a class

```
public|private class ClassName{
   statements
}
```

Typical class declarations

```
public class InvoiceApp{}
public class BookOrderApp{}
public class Book{}
public class BookOrder{}
```

A public class named InvoiceApp

```
public class InvoiceApp{                          // begin class
   public static void main(String[] args){
      System.out.println("Invoice application");
   }
}                                                 // end class
```

The rules for naming a class

- Start the name with a capital letter.
- Use letters and digits only.
- Follow the other rules for naming an identifier.

Naming recommendations

- Start every word within a class name with an initial cap.
- Each class name should be a noun or a noun that's preceded by one or more adjectives.

Description

- When you develop a Java application, you code one or more *classes* for it. Within each class, you code one *class declaration.*
- The words *public* and *private* are *access modifiers* that control what parts of the program can use the class. If a class is public, the class can be used by all parts of the program.
- Most classes are declared public, and each file must contain one and only one public class. The file name for a class is the same as the class name with *java* as the extension.
- The statements between the braces in a class declaration are the *class definition.*

Figure 2-3 How to declare a class

How to declare a main method

Every Java application contains one or more *methods*, which are pieces of code that perform tasks (they're similar to *functions* in some other programming languages). The *main method* is a special kind of method that's automatically executed when the class that holds it is run. All Java applications contain a main method that starts the program.

To start the coding for the main method, you code a *main method declaration* as shown in figure 2-4. For now, you can code every main method declaration using the code exactly as it's shown, even if you don't completely understand what each keyword means. Although this figure gives a partial explanation for each keyword, you can skip that if you like. We included it for those who are already familiar with object-oriented programming. As you go through this book, of course, you'll much more about each term in a method declaration.

The complete class shows how the main method declaration is coded within the class declaration. Here, the main method is indented so that it's easy to match its starting brace with its ending brace. Between the braces, you can see the one statement that this main method performs.

The syntax for declaring a main method

```
public static void main(String[] args){
   statements
}
```

The main method of the InvoiceApp class

```
public class InvoiceApp{
   public static void main(String[] args){  // begin main method
      System.out.println("Invoice application");
   }                                         // end main method
}
```

Description

- A *method* is a block of code that performs a task.
- Every Java application contains one *main method* that's declared just the way it's shown above. This is called the *main method declaration.*
- The statements between the braces in a main method declaration are run when the program is executed.

Partial explanation of the terms in the main method declaration

- The *public* keyword in the declaration means that other classes can access the main method. The *static* keyword means that the method can be called directly from the other classes without first creating an object. And the *void* keyword means that the method won't return any values.
- The *main* identifier is the name of the method. When you code a method, always include parentheses after the name of the method.
- The code in the parentheses lists the arguments that the method uses, and every main method receives an argument named *args*, which is defined as an array of strings. You'll learn more about arguments and strings later in this chapter, and you'll learn more about arrays in chapter 9.

Figure 2-4 How to declare a main method

How to work with the primitive data types

In this topic, you'll learn about the primitive *data types* of the Java language. Then, you'll learn how to use variables to store data that can change during the execution of a program, and you'll learn how to use constants to store data that doesn't change during the execution of a program. In addition, you'll learn how to perform calculations on the numeric data types.

The eight primitive data types

Figure 2-5 shows the eight *primitive data types* provided by Java. You can use the first four data types to store *integers*, which are numbers that don't contain decimal places (whole numbers). When you use one of the integer types, you should select an appropriate size. Most of the time, you can use the *int* type for working with integers. However, you may need to use the *long* type if the value is too big for the int type. Although the use of the *short* and *byte* types is less common, you can use them when you're working with smaller integers and you need to save system resources.

You can use the next two primitive types to store *floating-point numbers*, which are numbers that contain decimal places. Since the *double* type has more *significant digits* than the *float* type, you'll probably want to use the double type for most floating-point numbers.

To express the value of a floating-point number, you can use *scientific notation*. This lets you express very large and very small numbers in a sort of shorthand. To use this notation, you type the letter *e* or *E* followed by a power of 10. For instance, 3.65e+9 is equal to 3.65 times 10^9 (or 3,650,000,000), and 3.65e-9 is equal to 3.65 times 10^{-9} (or .00000000365). If you have a scientific or mathematical background, of course, you're already familiar with this notation. And if you don't, you probably won't need it for business programs.

You can use the *char* type to store one character. Since Java uses the two-byte *Unicode character set*, it can store practically any character from any language. As a result, you can use Java to create programs that read and print Greek or Chinese characters. In practice, though, you'll usually work with the characters that are stored in the older one-byte *ASCII character set*. These characters are the first 256 characters of the Unicode character set.

Last, you can use the *boolean* type to store a true value or a false value. This can also be thought of as a binary digit (*bit*) that has a value of either 1 (on) or 0 (off).

The eight primitive data types

Type	Bytes	Use
byte	1	Very short integers from -128 to 127.
short	2	Short integers from -32,768 to 32,767.
int	4	Integers from -2,147,483,648 to 2,147,483,647.
long	8	Long integers from -9,223,372,036,854,775,808 to 9,223,372,036,854,775,807.
float	4	Single-precision, floating-point numbers from -3.4E38 to 3.4E38 with 6 or 7 significant digits.
double	8	Double-precision, floating-point numbers from –1.7E308 to 1.7E308 with from 14 to 15 significant digits.
char	2	A single Unicode character that's stored in two bytes.
boolean	1	A *true* (1) or *false* (0) value.

Description

- A *bit* is a binary digit that can have a value of one or zero. A *byte* is a group of eight bits. As a result, the number of bits for each data type is the number of bytes multiplied by 8.
- *Integers* are whole numbers, and the first four data types above provide for integers of various sizes.
- *Floating-point numbers* provide for very large and very small numbers that require decimal positions, but with a limited number of *significant digits*. A *single-precision number* provides for numbers with up to 7 significant digits. A *double-precision number* provides for numbers with up to 15 significant digits. The *double* data type is commonly used for business programs because it provides the precision (number of significant digits) that those programs require.
- To express the value of a floating-point number, you can use *scientific notation* like 2.382E+5, which means 2.382 times 10^5 (a value of 238,200), or 3.25E-8, which means 3.25 times 10^{-8} (a value of .0000000325). Java will sometimes use this notation to display the value of a float or double data type.
- The *Unicode character set* provides for over 65,000 characters with two bytes used for each character.
- The older *ASCII character set* that's used by most operating systems provides for 256 characters with one byte used for each character. In the Unicode character set, the first 256 characters correspond to the 256 ASCII characters.
- A *boolean* data type holds a *true* or *false* value. This is often stored internally as a 1 (for true) or a 0 (for false).

Figure 2-5 The eight primitive data types

How to initialize variables

A *variable* is used to store a data type that can change as the program executes. In figure 2-6, you can learn how to *initialize* a variable. To do that, you create a name (identifier) for the variable, *declare* its data type, and *assign* an initial value to it.

As this figure shows, you can initialize a variable in two different ways. The first way uses a *declaration statement* to declare the data type and an *assignment statement* to assign a value to the variable. The second way uses a single *initialization statement.*

The first one-statement example in this figure does the same task as both statements in the two-statement example. Then, the second example shows how you can initialize two variables in one statement. To do this, you just separate the assignments with a comma.

The third one-statement example shows how to initialize a double type. When assigning values to the double and float types, it's a good coding practice to include a decimal point. For example, if you want to assign the number 29 to the variable, you should code the number as 29.0.

The fourth and fifth examples show how to assign values to the float and long types. To do that, you need to add a letter after the value. For a float type, you add an f or F after the value. For a long type, you add an L. You can also use a lowercase l, but it's not a good coding practice since the lowercase L can easily be mistaken for the number 1. If you omit the letter in one of these assignments, you'll get a compile-time error.

The sixth statement shows how you can use scientific notation. The seventh and eighth examples show that you can assign a character to the char type by enclosing a character in single quotes or by supplying the integer that corresponds to the character. And the ninth example shows how to initialize a variable named valid as a boolean type with a false value.

How to initialize constants

A *constant* is used to store a data type that can't be changed as the program executes, and many of the skills for initializing variables also apply to initializing constants. However, you begin the initialization statement for a constant with the *final* keyword. As a result, constants are sometimes called *final variables*. In addition, it's a common coding convention to use all uppercase letters for the name of a constant and to separate the words in a constant name with underscores.

How to initialize a variable in two statements

Syntax

```
type variableName;
variableName = value;
```

Example

```
int counter;                    // declaration statement
counter = 1;                    // assignment statement
```

How to initialize a variable in one statement

Syntax

```
type variableName = value;
```

Examples

```
int counter = 1;                // initialization statement
int x = 0, y = 0;               // initialize 2 variables with 1 statement
double price = 14.95;
float interestRate = 8.125F;    // F indicates a float type
long numberOfBytes = 20000L;    // L indicates a long type
double distance = 3.65e+9;      // scientific notation
char letter = 'A';              // stored as a two-byte Unicode character
char letter = 65;               // integer value for a Unicode character
boolean valid = false;          // where false is a keyword
```

How to initialize a constant

Syntax

```
final type CONSTANT_NAME = value;
```

Examples

```
final int DAYS_IN_NOVEMBER = 30;
final double SALES_TAX = .075;
```

Description

- A *variable* stores a value that can change as a program executes, while a *constant* stores a value that can't be changed.
- To *initialize* a variable or constant, you *declare* a type and *assign* an initial value. As default values, it's common to initialize integer types to 0, floating-point types to 0.0, and boolean types to false.
- To initialize more than one variable for a single data type in a single statement, use commas to separate the assignments.
- To identify float values, you must type an f or F after the number. To identify long values, you must type an l or L after the number.

Naming guidelines

- Start variable names with a lowercase letter and capitalize the first letter in all words after the first word.
- Capitalize all of the letters in constants and separate the words with underscores.
- Try to use meaningful names that are easy to remember as you code.

Figure 2-6 How to initialize variables and constants

How to code assignment statements

After you initialize a variable, you can change its value. To do that, you code an *assignment statement* as summarized in figure 2-7. In a simple assignment statement, you just code the variable name, an equals sign, and an expression. The expression can be as simple as a *numeric literal* (or just *literal*) like 1 or 22.5. It can be the name of another variable. Or, it can be an *arithmetic expression.*

To create an arithmetic expression, you use the *arithmetic operators* to indicate what operations are to be performed on the *operands* in the expression. An operand can be a literal or a variable. For business programs, most arithmetic expressions are relatively simple, so you shouldn't have any trouble coding them. But you can learn more about coding them in the next figure.

If you study the operators in this figure, you can see that the first five operators work on two operands. As a result, they're referred to as *binary operators*. For example, when you use the subtraction operator (-), you subtract one operand from another. In contrast, the last four operators work on one operand. As a result, they're referred to as *unary operators*. For example, you can code the negative sign operator (-) in front of an operand to reverse the value of the operand. And you can code the positive sign operator in front of a byte, short, or char operand to change its value to the integer type.

Please note in the examples of typical assignment statements that you can code the same variable name on both sides of the equals sign, as shown by the second and last examples. In the second example, if month has a value of 7 when the statement starts, it has a value of 8 after the statement has been executed. In other words, the current value of the variable is used in the arithmetic expression, and then the result of the expression is stored in the variable. This works the same in the last example. If index has a starting value of 5, it has a value of 6 after the statement has been executed.

Besides the equals sign, Java provides for the other *assignment operators* shown in this figure. Here again, if you study the examples, you shouldn't have any trouble using them. Although these operators don't provide any new functionality, you can use them to write shorter code. This can be useful when you're working with variables that have long names.

The syntax for a simple assignment statement

```
variableName = expression;
```

Typical assignment statements

```
month = 1;
month = month + 1;
discountAmount = orderTotal * .2;
invoiceTotal = orderTotal - discountAmount;
salesChange = thisYearSales - lastYearSales;
changePercent = salesChange / lastYearSales * 100;
changePercent = (thisYearSales - lastYearSales) / lastYearSales * 100;
index = index++;
```

Arithmetic operators

Operator	Name	Description
+	Addition	Adds two operands.
-	Subtraction	Subtracts the right operand from the left operand.
*	Multiplication	Multiplies the right operand and the left operand.
/	Division	Divides the right operand into the left operand. If both operands are integers, then the result is an integer.
%	Modulus	Returns the value that is left over after dividing the right operand into the left operand.
++	Increment	Adds 1 to the operand (x = x + 1).
--	Decrement	Subtracts 1 from the operand (x = x - 1).
+	Positive sign	Promotes byte, short, or char types to the int type.
-	Negative sign	Changes a positive value to negative, and vice versa.

Other assignment operators (assume int c = 13)

Operator	Example	Description	Result
+=	c += 5;	c = c + 5;	c = 18
-=	c -= 8;	c = c - 8;	c = 5
*=	c *= 2;	c = c * 2;	c = 26
/=	c /= 2;	c = c / 2;	c = 6
%=	c %= 9;	c = c % 9;	c = 4

Description

- A simple *assignment statement* consists of a variable, an equals sign, and an expression. When the assignment statement is executed, the value of the expression is determined and the result is stored in the variable.
- An *arithmetic expression* consists of one or more *operands* and *arithmetic operators*. The first five operators above are called *binary operators* because they operate on two operands. The next four are called *unary operators* because they operate on just one operand. In the next figure, you can learn more about the way arithmetic expressions are evaluated.
- Besides the equals sign, Java provides for the five other *assignment operators* shown above. These operators provide a shorthand for coding common operations.

Figure 2-7 How to code assignment statements

How to code arithmetic expressions

Figure 2-8 gives the *order of precedence* of the arithmetic operations. This means that all of the increment and decrement operations in an expression are done first, followed by all of the positive and negative operations, and so on. If there is more than one operation at each order of precedence, the operations are done from left to right.

Because this sequence of operations doesn't always work the way you want it to, you may need to override the sequence by using parentheses. Then, the expressions in the innermost sets of parentheses are done first, followed by the next sets of parentheses, and so on. Within the parentheses, though, the operations are done left to right by order of precedence. Since you use the parentheses just as in high school algebra, you shouldn't have any trouble coding them.

If you study the examples in this figure, you can see how the arithmetic operators work. Since the addition (+), subtraction (-), and multiplication (*) operators are easy to understand, the first four examples focus on the division (/) and modulus (%) operators. The first and second examples show how to use these operators with integers. The third and fourth examples show how to use them with double values.

Since each char type is a Unicode character that has a numeric code that maps to an integer, you can perform some integer operations on char types. For instance, the seventh and eighth examples show how you can use the increment operator to change the numeric value for a char variable from 67 to 68 which changes the character from 'C' to 'D'. (Note that you use single quotation marks to assign character values to the char data type).

After these examples, this figure shows how to *cast* one numeric type to another numeric type. To start, it shows how *implicit casts* work. In particular, it shows how Java automatically converts less precise types to more precise types. This will work even when Java evaluates operands connected by arithmetic operators such as multiplication or addition. First, Java will check if any of the operands in an expression use the double type (the most precise type). If so, Java will evaluate the entire expression as a double. If not, Java continues looking for the next most precise type and makes any necessary conversions. Most of the time, that's what you want.

However, if you ever need to override an implicit cast, you can use parentheses to perform an *explicit cast* as shown in the second part of this figure. In this case, you just code the desired data type in parentheses before the data type that you want to convert. When you do this, of course, you may lose some precision as illustrated by the example which converts a value of 93.25 to 93. Note, however, that if you don't code an explicit cast in this example, you'll get a compile-time error because Java doesn't automatically cast a more precise data type to a less precise type.

Although you typically cast between numeric data types, you can also cast between the int and char type. That's because every char type corresponds to an int value that identifies it in the Unicode character set.

The order of precedence for arithmetic operations

1. Increment and decrement
2. Positive and negative
3. Multiplication, division, and modulus
4. Addition and subtraction

The use of parentheses

- Unless parentheses are used, the operations in an expression take place from left to right in the *order of precedence*.
- To clarify or override the sequence of operations, you can use parentheses. Then, the operations in the innermost sets of parentheses are done first, followed by the operations in the next sets, and so on.

Examples of arithmetic expressions

```
int x = 14, y = 8;          // assume this for all examples
double a = 8.5, b = 3.4;    // assume this for all examples

int result = x / y;         // result = 1
int result = x % y;         // result = 6
double result = a / b;      // result = 2.5
double result = a % b;      // result = 1.7   or 8.5-(3.4*2)
int result = y++;           // result = 9     or 8+1
int result = y--;           // result = 7     or 8-1
char letter = 'C';          // letter = 'C'   Unicode integer is 67
letter++;                   // letter = 'D'   Unicode integer is 68
int result = -y;            // result = -8
int result = -y + x;        // result = 6
```

How implicit casting affects the results of an arithmetic expression

Description

Java automatically converts less precise data types to more precise data types.

Casting from less precise to more precise data types

byte → short → int → long → float → double

char → int

Example

```
double a = 95.0;                 // a is a double
int b = 86, c = 91;              // b and c are ints
double average = (a+b+c)/3;      // average is 90.666666...
```

How you can code an explicit cast

Syntax

```
(type) operand
```

Example

```
double average = 93.25;
int gradeInCourse = (int) average;   // gradeInCourse is 93
```

Figure 2-8 How to code arithmetic expressions

Four classes for working with data

Although the Java language consists of just 50 keywords, Java provides hundreds of *classes* that you can use in your programs. These classes provide functions that the language itself doesn't provide. To get you started with your use of classes, this chapter now presents four that you'll use all the time. These are the first of many Java classes that you'll learn how to use in this book.

How to use the String class to create a String object

A *string* can contain any characters in the character set. Although Java doesn't provide a primitive data type for strings, it does provide a String class. Then, you use the String class to create a String *object* that contains a string, and you use that object as a variable. In other words, an object is just a container for data.

When you create an object from a class, it can be referred as creating a new *instance* of the class. This is standard terminology for object-oriented programming. This process can be referred to as *instantiation*.

Figure 2-9 shows two ways to create an object from the String class. First, it shows how to use the *new* keyword to create a new instance of the String class with the starting value of the object in parentheses. This is the standard syntax for creating objects when you use other classes.

When you use the String class, though, it's more common to use the shortcut syntax in this figure to create String objects. This syntax is similar to the syntax for initializing a primitive type. However, the String class begins with an uppercase letter, while a primitive data type begins with a lowercase letter. In addition, you must enclose any *string literal* in double quotation marks.

If you look at the examples, you can see that the first statement creates a String object named title that contains the title of Herman Melville's classic book, *Moby Dick*. The second statement creates a String object named book and sets it equal to the String object created in the previous statement. The third statement creates a String object and uses an empty set of quotation marks to set the string equal to an *empty string*. This means that the variable refers to a String object, but that object doesn't contain any characters. And the fourth statement creates a String object that uses the *null* keyword to set the object equal to a *null value*. This means that a variable for working with a String object has been declared, but it doesn't refer to any object yet.

When you assign values to String objects, you can use the *escape sequences* shown in this figure as part of a string. This lets you put backslashes, quotation marks, and control characters such as new lines, tabs, and returns in a string. Here, the first example shows how to include a new line character in a string. The second example shows how to include tab and return characters in a string. The third example shows how to include a backslash. And the fourth example shows how to include quotation marks.

Two ways to create a String object

Using the *new* keyword

```
String title = new String("War and Peace");
```

Using a shortcut

```
String title = "War and Peace";
```

Examples

```
String title = "Moby Dick";
String book = title;
String code = "";
String inputValue = null;
```

Escape sequences

Key	Description	Key	Description
`\n`	New line	`\f`	Form feed
`\t`	Tab	`\\`	Backslash
`\r`	Return	`\"`	Quotation mark

Escape sequence examples

Code	Resulting string
`"Code: warp\nPrice: $14.95"`	`Code: warp` `Price: $14.95`
`"Joe\tSmith\rKate\tLewis\r"`	`Joe    Smith` `Kate   Lewis`
`"Directory - c:\\java\\test"`	`Directory - c:\java\test`
`"Type \"x\" to exit"`	`Type "x" to exit`

Description

- A *string* is a variable that can consist of any characters in the character set including letters, numbers, and special characters like *, &, and #.
- To work with a string in Java, you create a String *object* from the String *class*. Then, the String object contains the string, and you can use the object as a variable.
- To create a String object, you can use the *new* keyword. This is the standard way to create a new *instance* of an object from a class. However, it's more common to create String objects by using the shortcut coding style.
- To specify the value of a string, you can enclose any text in double quotation marks. This is known as a *string literal* (or *literal string*). Within the literal, you can use *escape sequences* for special purposes.
- To assign a *null value* to a String object, you can use the *null* keyword. This means that the value of the string is unknown.
- To assign an *empty string* to a String object, you can code a set of quotation marks with nothing between them. This usually indicates that the value of the string is known, but the string doesn't contain any characters.

Figure 2-9 How to use the String class to create a String object

How to use two methods of the String class

Once you create an object of a class, you can use the *methods* of the class to perform operations on the object. To *call* a method, you use the syntax shown at the top of figure 2-10. This means that you code the object name, the *dot operator* (or just *dot*), and the method name with the *arguments* for the method in parentheses after the method name. This is the syntax that you use for calling the methods of any object.

To compare two strings, for example, you must call one of the *methods* shown in this figure. The difference in these methods is that the equals method is *case-sensitive* while the equalsIgnoreCase method is not. For both of these methods, only one argument is required, and that argument must provide the String object that you want to compare with the current object.

The two examples show how to use these two methods. The first example compares a variable that refers to a String object with a string literal. In this example, the first statement initializes the choice variable to the string "X". Then, since the first if statement uses the equals method to compare the string literal "x" with this variable, it will return a false value. However, since the second if statement uses the equalsIgnoreCase method, it will return a true value. This shows that the equals method is case-sensitive.

The second example is similar to the first example except that it uses two variables in the comparison. For now, it's OK if you don't completely understand the incomplete if statements that are used in these examples, because you'll learn how to code them later in this chapter.

How to join two or more strings

This figure also shows how to *join*, or *concatenate*, two or more strings because you'll often need to do that when working with String objects. As you can see, you use the plus sign to join them. Here, the first example joins two variables that refer to String objects with a string literal that contains a single space. The second example joins a string with a variable that refers to a price. And the third example joins several strings that use the new line character. To improve the readability of the code, this example splits the message string onto two lines and uses indentation to align the two lines of the string. Note in the second and third examples that when a numeric data type is joined in a string, the data type is converted to a string.

The syntax for calling a method of an object

```
object.method(arguments)
```

Two methods of the String class that can be used to compare strings

Method	Description
`equals(String)`	Compares the current String object with the String object specified as the argument and returns a true value if they are equal. This method makes a case-sensitive comparison.
`equalsIgnoreCase(String)`	Works like the equals method but is not case-sensitive.

Examples

```
String choice = "X";
if (choice.equals("x"))                 // returns a false value
if (choice.equalsIgnoreCase("x"))       // returns a true value

String code = "Warp";
String bookCode = "warp";
if (code.equalsIgnoreCase(bookCode)) // returns a true value
```

How to join strings

How to join three strings

```
String firstName = "Ted";
String lastName = "Steelman";
String name = firstName + " " + lastName;    // name = "Ted Steelman"
```

How to join a string and a number

```
double price = 14.95;
String priceString = "Price: " + price;      // priceString = "Price: 14.95"
```

How to join a string that uses escape sequences

```
String title = "War and Peace";
double price = 14.95;
String message = "Title: " + title + "\n"
               + "Price: " + price + "\n";
```

Description

- To *call a method* of an object, code the object name, followed by a *dot operator* (period), followed by the name of the method, followed by a set of parentheses. Within the parentheses, you code the *arguments* that are required by the method. If a method requires more than one argument, you separate the arguments with commas.
- To use the two String methods shown above, you code an argument that represents the field that the object should be compared to. That argument can be a literal string value or the name of a string variable (another String object).
- To *join* (or *concatenate*) a string with another string or a data type, use a plus sign. If necessary, Java will automatically convert primitive data types so they can be used as part of the string.

Figure 2-10 How to use two methods of the String class and how to join strings

How to use the Integer and Double classes

Figure 2-11 shows how to use the Integer and Double classes to convert String objects to the int and double types. In addition, it shows how to convert int and double types to String objects. Since the Integer and Double classes wrap around the primitive types, they are sometimes referred to as *wrapper classes*. Wrapper classes also exist for the other six primitive data types.

To convert primitive types to String objects and vice versa, you need to use the *static methods* of the Integer and Double classes. Unlike a regular method, which is called from an object, a static method is called from a class. As a result, static methods are sometimes called *class methods*.

To call a static method, you use the syntax at the top of this figure. That is, you type the name of the class, followed by a dot, the name of the method, and a set of parentheses. Within the parentheses, you code any arguments required by the method. If the method requires more than one argument, you separate them with commas.

The first two examples show how to convert a String object to a primitive type. In the first example, the parseInt method of the Integer class converts a String to an integer. Once this statement is executed, you can use the quantity variable in arithmetic expressions. The second example works the same, but it uses the Double class and its parseDouble method to convert a String object to a double type.

But what happens if the string contains a non-numeric value like "ten" that can't be parsed to an int or double type? In that case, the parseInt or parseDouble method will cause a run-time error. Using Java terminology, you can say that the method *throws an exception*. In the next chapter, you'll learn how to *catch* the exception that is thrown by one of these methods.

The third and fourth examples in this figure show how to convert a primitive type to a String object. In the third example, the toString method of the Integer class converts the int variable named counter to a string and returns the value to a String object named counterString. In the fourth example, the toString method of the Double class converts the double variable named price to a string and returns that string to the String object named priceString.

The syntax for using a static method of a class

```
class.method(arguments)
```

Two static methods of the Integer class

Method	Description
`parseInt(String)`	Attempts to convert the String object that's supplied as an argument to an int type. If successful, it returns the int value. If unsuccessful, it throws an exception.
`toString(int)`	Converts the int value that's supplied as an argument to a String object and returns that String object.

Two static methods of the Double class

Method	Description
`parseDouble(String)`	Attempts to convert the String object that's supplied as an argument to a double type. If successful, it returns the double value. If unsuccessful, it throws an exception.
`toString(double)`	Converts the double value that's supplied as an argument to a String object and returns that String object.

How to convert a String object to a primitive type

For an int

```
int quantity = Integer.parseInt(quantityString);
```

For a double

```
double price = Double.parseDouble(priceString);
```

How to convert a primitive type to a String object

For an int

```
String counterString = Integer.toString(counter);
```

For a double

```
String priceString = Double.toString(price);
```

Description

- While regular methods are called from objects, *static methods* are called directly from a class. To call a static method, code the class name, followed by a dot operator, followed by the method name, followed by a set of parentheses. Within the parentheses, you code any arguments that are required by the method.
- If the parseInt and parseDouble methods can't successfully parse the string, they will return an error. In Java terminology, this is known as *throwing an exception*. You'll learn how to handle or *catch* exceptions in the next chapter.
- The Integer and Double classes are known as *wrapper classes* since they wrap around a primitive type. Every primitive type has a wrapper class that works like the two wrapper classes shown here.

Figure 2-11 How to use the Integer and Double classes

How to use two methods of the System.out object to print data to the console

In figure 2-12, you can learn how to use the println and print methods of the System.out object. As you can see, these methods print data to the *console*. Although these are actually methods of the PrintStream class, you won't understand how that works until you read chapter 17. So for now, you can just code them as shown and not worry about what's happening behind the scene.

If you look at the examples in this figure, you can see that you code System.out.println and System.out.print to start one of these methods. Then, you code the string that you want printed as the argument for the method. Although you don't actually create objects when you use these methods, Java refers to System.out as an object of the System class so the println and print methods can be thought of as methods of the System.out object.

If you study the examples, you shouldn't have any trouble using these methods. For instance, the first statement for the println method prints the words "Invoice application" to the console. The second statement prints the string "Order total: " followed by the value of the orderTotal variable (which is converted to a string by this join). The third statement prints the value of the variable named x to the console. And the fourth statement prints the variables named x and y to the console. If x and y are numbers, these numbers will be added together. If they are strings, the two strings will be joined.

The print method of the System.out object works like the println method except that it doesn't automatically start a new line. As a result, you can use this method to print several data arguments on the same line. For instance, the three statements in this example use the print method to print "Price: ", followed by a double variable that holds the price value, followed by a new line character. Of course, you can achieve the same result with a single line of code like this:

```
System.out.print("Price: " + price + "\n");
```

or like this:

```
System.out.println("Price: " + price);
```

This figure also shows an application that uses the println method to print four lines to the console. In the main method of this application, the first three statements set the values for three variables. Then, the next four statements print the title of the application followed by the values for the three variables.

Two methods of the System.out object

Method	Description
`println(data)`	Prints the data argument followed by a new line character to the console.
`print(data)`	Prints the data to the console without starting a new line.

How to use the println method

```
System.out.println("Invoice application");
System.out.println("Order total: " + orderTotal);
System.out.println(x);
System.out.println(x + y);
```

How to use the print method

```
System.out.print("Price: ");
System.out.print(price);
System.out.print("\n");
```

An application that prints data to the console

```
public class InvoiceApp{
   public static void main(String[] args){
      double orderTotal = 100.0;
      double discountAmount = orderTotal * .2;
      double invoiceTotal = orderTotal - discountAmount;
      System.out.println("Invoice application");
      System.out.println("Order total: " + orderTotal);
      System.out.println("Discount amount: " + discountAmount);
      System.out.println("Invoice total: " + invoiceTotal);
   }
}
```

The output of the application shown above

Description

- Although the appearance of a *console* may differ from one system to another, you can always use the print and println methods to print data to the console.

Figure 2-12 How to use two methods of the System class to print data to the console

Exercise 2-1 Practice what you've learned

If you're new to programming, you may feel a bit overwhelmed at this point. If so, we recommend that you do this practice exercise. To edit, compile, and run the program for this exercise and the other exercises in this chapter and book, you can use whatever tools you want. If you are using Windows, though, we recommend that you use TextPad for Windows as shown in chapter 1.

Create the Practice application

1. Start your text editor and enter the PracticeApp class shown here:

```
public class PracticeApp{
   public static void main(String[] args){
      System.out.println("Practice Application");
   }
}
```

2. Save the file as "PracticeApp.java" in the c:\java\ch02 directory. Then, compile, fix any compile-time errors, run the program, and fix any bugs. When the program runs, it should print the words "Practice Application" to the console. Then, you need to press any key to continue, and you may need to close the console by clicking on the exit button in the upper right corner or by pressing Alt+F4.

Initialize and print variables

3. Enter the code that follows at the end of the main method. Before you compile and run the program, though, try to determine what results the program will produce. Then, compile and run the program.

```
int quantity = 3;
double price = 24.95;
float floatNumber = 24.95e+15F;
char character = 75;
boolean valid = true;
System.out.println("Quantity =  " + quantity);
System.out.println("Price =     " + price);
System.out.println("FP Number = " + floatNumber);
System.out.println("Char =      " + character);
System.out.println("Valid =     " + valid);
```

4. If you want to experiment with any of the data types shown in figure 2-5, do that now. If, for example, you delete the F in the scientific notation for the floating-point variable above, you'll see that the statement won't compile.

Work with arithmetic expressions

5. Enter the code that follows at the end of the main method. Then, try to determine what results the program will produce before you compile and run it. (Note that this arithmetic expression as well as some of the ones in later steps use some variables that were entered in earlier steps.)

```
double doubleResult = 0.0;
doubleResult = quantity * price;
System.out.println("Double result =  " + doubleResult);
```

6. The statements that follow illustrate the need for explicit casting. Enter them at the end of the main method, then compile and test. If you doubt the need for the cast, remove it to see what happens when you compile.

```
int integerResult = 0;
integerResult = (int) doubleResult; // casts a double to an integer
System.out.println("Integer result = " + integerResult);
```

7. The statements that follow show how data types can be incremented by 1. Enter these statements at the end of the main method, then compile and test.

```
doubleResult = doubleResult + 1;
integerResult++;
character++;
System.out.println("Double result =  " + doubleResult);
System.out.println("Integer result = " + integerResult);
System.out.println("Character =      " + character);
```

8. The statements that follow illustrate the use of a constant in an arithmetic expression. That expression is supposed to calculate the sales tax for an order (sales tax percent times the order total) before adding it to the order total, and thus deriving the invoice total. If you think parentheses are necessary in this expression, add them as you enter the statements that follow at the end of the main method. Then, compile and test.

```
double orderTotal = 1000.0;
double invoiceTotal = 0.0;
final double SALES_TAX_PERCENT = .0785;
invoiceTotal = orderTotal + orderTotal * SALES_TAX_PERCENT;
System.out.println("\n\n"
                + "Order total =   " + orderTotal + "\n"
                + "Invoice total = " + invoiceTotal + "\n");
```

9. If you want to experiment with more complex arithmetic expressions, you can use figures 2-7 and 2-8 as a guide. Just initialize the variables you need, change the values of existing variables, code the expressions in assignment statements, and print the results.

Create a String object and use a Double method

10. The statements that follow show how a String object can be converted to a double variable. Enter, compile, test, and experiment to see how this works:

```
String stringNumber = "3.146";
double parsedDouble = Double.parseDouble(stringNumber);
String message = "\n\n"
              + "String number =   " + stringNumber + "\n"
              + "Parsed number =   " + parsedDouble + "\n";
System.out.println(message);
```

Exit from the program

11. Close the program. Then, keep this program in mind so you can use it whenever you want to experiment with some code that you don't quite understand.

How to use the JOptionPane class for input and output

To make it easier for you to write programs, Java provides libraries of classes that contain prewritten code. These libraries make up the Java *Application Programming Interface*, or *API*. After you learn how the Java API is organized and how to import classes into your programs, this topic shows you how to use the JOptionPane class to display dialog boxes that get input from a user and display output.

How to import classes

In the Java language, all code is stored in classes. In the Java API, groups of related classes are organized into *packages*. In figure 2-13, you can see a list of some of the commonly used packages. This figure also shows how to import the classes that are stored within each package.

Since the java.lang package contains the classes that are used in almost every Java program (such as the String, Integer, Double, and System classes), this package is automatically available to all programs. To use other packages, though, you usually need to include an *import statement* at the beginning of the program. With this statement, you can import a single class by specifying the class name, or you can import all of the classes in the package by typing an asterisk (*).

If you look at the examples, you can see how to code an import statement. Here, the first three statements import just one class each, while the fourth statement imports all of the Swing classes with a single statement.

As the figure shows, Java provides two different technologies for building a *graphical user interface* (*GUI*) that contains text boxes, command buttons, option buttons, and so on. The older technology known as the *Abstract Windows Toolkit* (*AWT*) was used with versions 1.0 and 1.1 of Java. Its classes are stored in the java.awt package. Since version 1.2 of Java, though, a new technology known as *Swing* has been available. The Swing classes are stored in the javax.swing package. In a moment, you'll learn how to use the JOptionPane class of the javax.swing package to display dialog boxes.

In addition to the packages provided by the Java API, you can get packages from third party sources, either as shareware or by purchasing them. To review some of these packages, check the Java web site. You can also create packages that contain classes that you've written. You'll learn how to do that in chapter 4.

Commonly used packages

Package name	Description
`java.lang`	Provides classes fundamental to Java, including classes that work with primitive data types, strings, and math functions.
`java.text`	Provides classes to handle text, dates, and numbers.
`java.util`	Provides classes to work with collections, including vectors and linked lists.
`java.io`	Provides classes to read data from files and to write data to files.
`java.sql`	Provides classes to read data from databases and to write data to databases.
`java.applet`	An older package that provides classes to create an applet.
`java.awt`	An older package called the *Abstract Windows Toolkit* (*AWT*) that provides classes to create graphical user interfaces.
`java.awt.event`	A package that provides classes necessary to handle events.
`javax.swing`	A newer package called *Swing* that provides classes to create graphical user interfaces and applets.

The syntax of the import statement

```
import packagename.ClassName;
   or
import packagename.*;
```

Examples

```
import java.text.NumberFormat;
import javax.swing.JOptionPane;
import javax.swing.JFrame;
import javax.swing.*;
import java.awt.*;
import java.awt.event.*;
```

Description

- The Java 2, Standard Edition, v1.3.1 *Application Programming Interface*, or *API*, provides all the classes that are included as part of the SDK. These classes are organized into *packages*.
- All classes stored in the java.lang package are automatically available to all Java programs.
- To use classes that aren't in the java.lang package, use the *import statement* as shown above. To import one class from a package, specify the package name followed by the class name. To import all classes in a package, specify the package name followed by an asterisk (*).
- Java provides two technologies for building *graphical user interfaces* (*GUIs*). The older technology is called the *Abstract Windows Toolkit* (*AWT*), and the newer technology is called *Swing*.

Figure 2-13 How to import classes

How to use the JOptionPane class to get input

Figure 2-14 shows how to use the static showInputDialog method of the JOptionPane class to display a dialog box that gets input from a user. To start, this figure describes this method and the exit method of the System class that's used with the showInputDialog method. Then, this figure shows the code for a sample application that displays the two dialog boxes shown in this figure.

The only argument that's required by this method is a string that contains the text that's displayed on the dialog box. To supply this argument, you can type text in quotes or you can type the name of a variable that refers to a String object.

The code for the sample application shows how to use the two methods described in this figure. To start, this code uses an import statement to import the JOptionPane class of the javax.swing package. Then, in the main method of this application, the first statement assigns the String object that's returned by the showInputDialog method to a String object named inputString. When this statement is executed, the first dialog box in this figure is displayed. After the user enters a value in the text box and clicks on the OK button, that value is stored in the String object. If, on the other hand, the user clicks on the Cancel button, a null value is stored in the object. In that case, any method that uses the object may throw an exception if it can't accept a null value. You'll learn how to handle this exception in the next chapter.

The second statement creates a String object named message that contains the string that was entered by the user plus some additional information. Then, the third statement uses the showInputDialog method to display this String object. When this statement is executed, the second dialog box in this figure is displayed. The last statement in the main method is the exit method of the System object, and you can learn more about that next.

How to use the System.exit method to end a JOptionPane thread

When you use a JOptionPane method to display a dialog box, a *thread* is started. Then, you need to terminate that thread before the main method ends. Otherwise, the thread will continue after the program ends, and you will have to press Ctrl+C to cancel that thread.

To terminate all threads, you can code the System.exit method as shown in the application in this figure. Here, a zero value is coded as the argument for the method, which means that the application exited normally.

For now, all you need to know about threads is that some graphical user interface components such as JOptionPane dialog boxes create threads. In that case, to properly exit the application, you must terminate the thread. You'll learn more about threads in chapter 20.

A static method of the JOptionPane class

Method	Description
`showInputDialog(messageString)`	Displays an input dialog box that displays the message specified by the String argument and returns a String object that contains the data that's entered into the dialog box by the user.

A static method of the System class

Method	Description
`exit(intStatus)`	Terminates all threads, passing the int value as a status code where 0 means that the application exited normally.

A sample application

```
import javax.swing.JOptionPane;

public class NameApp{
   public static void main(String[] args){
      String inputString = JOptionPane.showInputDialog(
         "Enter your first name: ");
      String message = "First name: " + inputString + "\n\n"
                     + "Press the Enter key to exit.";
      JOptionPane.showInputDialog(message);
      System.exit(0);
   }
}
```

The first input dialog box displayed by the code above

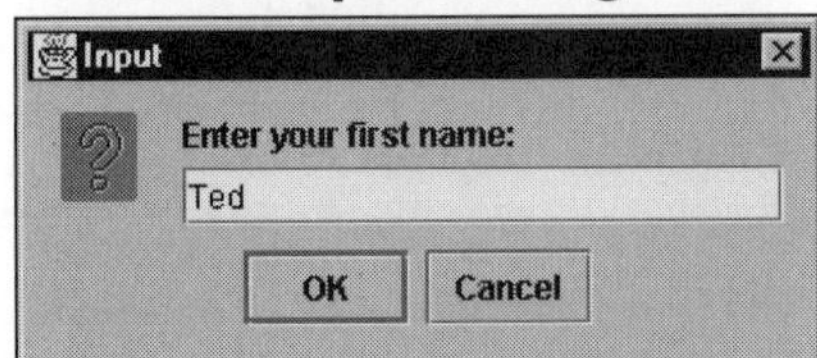

The second input dialog box displayed by the code above

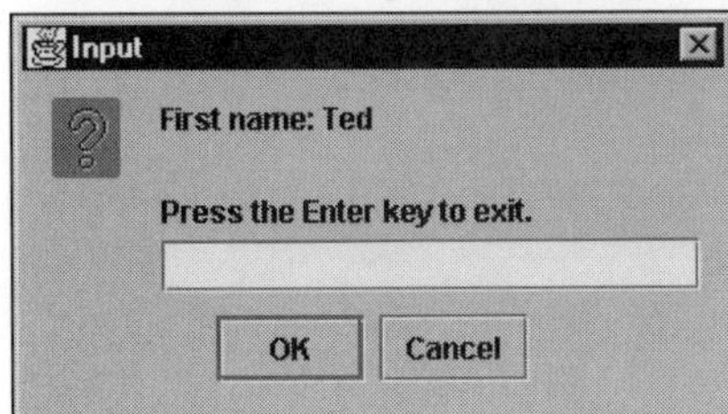

Description

- When you use the showInputDialog method of the JOptionPane class to get input data from a user, a *thread* is started. To terminate this thread before the program ends, you should use the exit method of the System class.
- In chapter 20, you'll learn more about what threads are and how you use them.

Figure 2-14 How to use the JOptionPane class to get input

How to use two more methods of the JOptionPane class

Figure 2-15 shows two more methods of the JOptionPane class that can be used to display enhanced JOptionPane dialog boxes. Both of these methods accept four arguments. The first method displays an input dialog box like the one shown in the previous figure while the second method displays a message dialog box like the one shown at the bottom of this figure. When you use one of these methods, you can set the title and icon for the dialog box.

Although the first method has the same name as the showInputDialog method shown in the previous figure, this method accepts four arguments. In Java terminology, this is another *signature* of the same method name, and it's known as *overloading* a method. If you supply one String object argument for the showInputDialog method, this method will display a dialog box like the one shown in the last figure. But if you supply all four arguments as shown in this figure, you can control the title and icon of the dialog box.

For the first argument, you can use the null keyword so the dialog box is centered on the screen. For the second and third arguments, you can specify a string that sets the message and title of the dialog box. And for the fourth argument, which determines the icon that's used for the box, you can use one of the five JOptionPane fields that are summarized in this figure. To use one, you type JOptionPane, followed by a dot, followed by the name of the field.

When you use Java, the term *field* can be used to refer to any data item that is stored in a class. This includes instance variables as well as static fields, which you'll learn about in chapter 4. In this case, the fields are static fields that can be used as arguments in the JOptionPane methods.

You can see how these arguments are used in the example in this figure, which displays the dialog box shown below it. Here, the first statement defines a String object, and the second statement uses the showMessageDialog method to display the message dialog box. The third and fourth arguments of this method set the title of the dialog box to "Invoice" and its icon to PLAIN_MESSAGE, which means that the dialog box doesn't have an icon.

Two more static methods of the JOptionPane class

Another method for displaying an input dialog box

```
showInputDialog(parentComponent, messageString, titleString,
    messageTypeInt);
```

A method for displaying a message dialog box

```
showMessageDialog(parentComponent, messageString, titleString,
    messageTypeInt);
```

The four arguments of the methods shown above

Argument	Description
`parentComponent`	An object representing the component that's the parent of the dialog box. For now, use null so that the application uses a default component that causes the dialog box to appear in the center of the screen.
`messageString`	A string representing the message to be displayed in the dialog box.
`titleString`	A string representing the title of the dialog box.
`messageTypeInt`	An int that indicates the type of icon that will be used for the dialog box. You can use the fields of the JOptionPane class for this argument.

JOptionPane fields that can be used for the messageTypeInt argument

Message type	Description
`ERROR_MESSAGE`	Display an error icon.
`INFORMATION_MESSAGE`	Display an information icon.
`WARNING_MESSAGE`	Display an exclamation point as a warning icon.
`QUESTION_MESSAGE`	Display a question mark as a question icon.
`PLAIN_MESSAGE`	Doesn't display an icon.

Code that displays a message dialog box with no icon

```
String message = "Order total: $100.00\n"
               + "Discount amount: $20.00\n"
               + "Invoice total: $80.00";
JOptionPane.showMessageDialog(null, message,
               "Invoice", JOptionPane.PLAIN_MESSAGE);
```

The message dialog box that's displayed by the code shown above

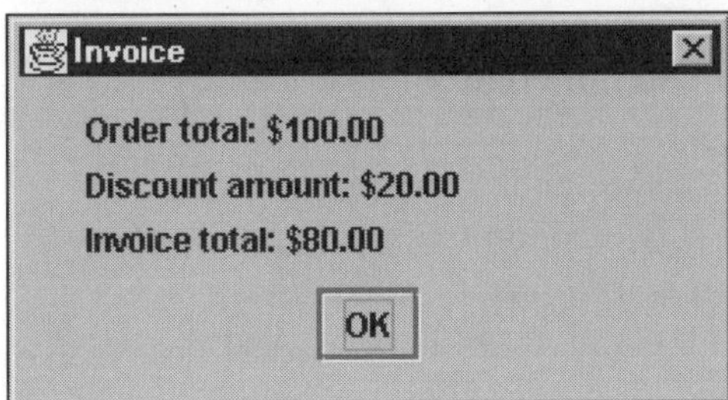

Figure 2-15 How to use two more methods of the JOptionPane class

How to code control statements

As you write programs, you need to determine when certain operations should occur. For instance, you'll often want to execute one or more statements if a certain condition is true and to execute other statements if the condition is false. To get you started, this topic will show you how to code conditional expressions and how to use the two most popular *control statements*. Then, in chapter 8, you can learn how to use the other control statements.

How to code conditional expressions

Before you can code control statements, you need to learn how to code *conditional expressions* like the ones shown in figure 2-16. A conditional expression evaluates to either true or false and can be used in control statements like the if and while statements shown in the next two figures. When you code conditional expressions, you can use the six *relational operators* and the three *logical operators* shown in this figure. However, most expressions require just one relational operator so they're quite easy to code.

When you compare primitive data types, for example, you use one of the relational operators as shown in the first group of examples. Here, the first expression tests to see whether two variables are equal. The second tests to see whether the first variable is less than or equal to the second one. The third tests to see whether a variable is less than or equal to the literal value 0. And the fourth tests to see whether a boolean data type is set to true.

The only trick to coding expressions like these is making sure to use the equals operator (==) for an equals condition, because the equals sign (=) is only used in an assignment statement. Also, remember that you can't use these operators for comparing objects. To compare String objects, for example, you need to use the String methods as shown by the second group of examples. In the first condition in this group, the not operator (!) is used so the condition is true only if the value of the choice variable is not equal to "x".

Occasionally, though, you need to code more complex expressions like those in the third group of examples. Then, Java evaluates the expressions from left to right based on this order of precedence: arithmetic operations first, followed by relational operations, followed by logical operations. Here again, though, you can use parentheses if you want to clarify or control this evaluation sequence.

With that as background, you should be able to decipher the expressions in the third group of examples. For instance, the first two conditions are true if either the first *or* the second relational expression is true. The third condition is true only if both the first *and* the second relational expressions are true. And the last condition shows how you can use the And and Or operators in the same conditional expression. In this case, the statement is true if the first *and* second expressions are true *or* if the third expression is true.

Relational operators

Operator	Name	Returns a true value ...
`==`	Equal to	if both operands are equal.
`!=`	Not equal to	if the left and right operands are not equal.
`>`	Greater than	if the left operand is greater than the right operand.
`<`	Less than	if the left operand is less than the right operand.
`>=`	Greater than or equal to	if the left operand is greater than or equal to the right operand.
`<=`	Less than or equal to	if the left operand is less than or equal to the right operand.

Logical operators

Operator	Name	Description
`&&`	And	Returns a true value if both expressions are true.
`||`	Or	Returns a true value if either expression is true.
`!`	Not	Reverses the value of the expression.

Simple conditional expressions with primitive data types

```
userMonth == systemMonth
onHandQuantity <= reorderPoint
quantity <= 0
switchValue == true
```

Simple conditional expressions with strings

```
!(choice.equals("x"))
code.equalsIgnoreCase(bookCode)
```

More complex expressions

```
(timeInService <= 4) || (timeInService >= 12)
(age != 16) || (height < 60)
(percentTaxed >= 0) && (income >= 35000)
((date > startDate) && (date < expirationDate)) || (valid == true)
```

Description

- To test two primitive types for equality, make sure to use the equals operator (==), not the single equals sign (=). The single equals sign is used for assignment statements.
- To test two strings for equality, use the equals method of the String object, not the equals operator (==). If you use the equals operator, Java will check to see if the two String objects are stored in the same location, which doesn't indicate whether the strings are equal.
- If you compare two numeric operands that are not of the same type, Java will convert the less precise operand to the type of the more precise operand. For example, if you compare an int to a double, Java converts the int to a double before performing the comparison.

Figure 2-16 How to code conditional expressions

How to code if/else statements

Figure 2-17 shows how to use the *if/else statement* (or just *if statement*) to control the logic of your programs. Here, the brackets in the syntax summary indicate that a clause is optional, and the ellipsis (...) indicates that the preceding element can be repeated as many times as needed. In other words, this syntax shows that you can code an *if clause* with or without *else if clauses* or an *else clause*. It also shows that you can code as many else if clauses as you need.

When an if statement is executed, the condition in the if clause is tested first. If it's true, the statements after the condition are executed. Otherwise, the first else if clause (if there is one) is executed. Then, if its condition is true, the statements after the condition are executed. Otherwise, the next else if clause is executed. This continues with any remaining else if clauses. Finally, if none of the conditions in the if clause or else if clauses were true, the statements in the else clause are executed (if there is one).

If you study the examples in this figure, you'll see the many ways that if statements can be coded. One point to note is that you need to code braces when two or more statements are supposed to be executed when a condition is true. But you don't need to code the braces when just one statement is executed.

This is illustrated by the first group of examples. Here, the first if statement executes just one statement if the condition is true so that statement ends with a semicolon. However, the second if statement executes two statements if the condition is true so those statements need to be coded within a set of braces. In either if statement, if the condition isn't true, Java skips to the statement after the if statement so nothing is done by this statement.

When you code statements within braces, you are coding a *block* of statements. In this case, any variables that you declare within the block are only available to the other statements in that block. In other words, the variables have *block scope*. That's one of the reasons why this example declares and initializes the discountAmount and status variables outside of the if block. That way, they will be available outside the if block.

The next example shows an if statement with an else clause. Here, if the orderTotal variable is greater than or equal to 100, the discount amount is calculated by taking 20% of the orderTotal. If the condition isn't true, the else clause is executed and its single statement calculates the discount amount by taking 10% of the orderTotal.

The example after that shows an if statement with else if clauses and an else clause. Here, if the condition in an if or else if clause is true, the statement for that condition is executed. But if none of those conditions are true, the statement in the else clause is executed.

The last example shows how to code *nested if statements*. In this example, if the choice variable equals "x", Java ignores all of the statements in the nested if statement and executes the last else clause, which exits from the program. If, on the other hand, the choice string doesn't equal "x", Java evaluates the nested if statement. When you code nested if statements, it's a good practice to indent the statements and their clauses to show the nesting structure.

The syntax of the if/else statement

```
if (conditionalExpression) {statements}
[else if (conditionalExpression) {statements}] ...
[else {statements}]
```

If statements without else if or else clauses

With a single statement

```
if (orderTotal >= 100)
   discountAmount = orderTotal * .2;
```

With a block of statements

```
if (orderTotal >= 100){
   discountAmount = orderTotal * .2;
   status = "Bulk rate";
}
```

An if statement with an else clause

```
if (orderTotal >= 100)
   discountAmount = orderTotal * .2;
else
   discountAmount = orderTotal * .1;
```

An if statement with else if and else clauses

```
if (orderTotal >= 100 && orderTotal <= 199)
   discountAmount = orderTotal * .2;
else if (orderTotal >= 200 && orderTotal <= 299)
   discountAmount = orderTotal * .3;
else if (orderTotal >= 300)
   discountAmount = orderTotal * .4;
else
   discountAmount = orderTotal * .1;
```

Nested if statements

```
if (!(choice.equals("x"))){
   if (orderTotal >= 100)                  // begin nested if
      discountAmount = orderTotal * .2;
   else
      discountAmount = orderTotal * .1;    // end nested if
}
else
   System.exit(0);
```

Description

- An *if/else statement*, or just *if statement*, always contains an *if clause*. In addition, it can contain one or more *else if clauses* and a final *else clause*.
- If a clause requires just one statement, you don't have to enclose the statement in braces. You can just end the clause with a semicolon.
- If a clause requires more than one statement, you enclose the *block* of statements in braces. Then, any variables or constants that are declared in the block can only be used by statements in the block. In other words, they have *block scope*.

Figure 2-17 How to code if/else statements

How to code while statements

Figure 2-18 shows how to code a *while statement* to perform repetitive processing. By using this statement, you can repeat a series of statements while a conditional expression is true. Once the expression is false, though, even if it's on the first evaluation, the while statement ends.

Because a while statement loops through the statements in its statement block, the code within a while statement is often referred to as a *while loop*. Since you don't know how many times the loop will be executed, while loops are sometimes referred to as *indeterminate loops*. Here again, any variables that are defined in the block of statements within the braces have block scope, which means that they can't be used outside of the block.

The first example in this figure shows how you can use a while loop to calculate the future value of a one-time investment amount that accumulates interest for a specified number of months. In this example, the first statement sets a variable named futureValue to the investment amount, and the second statement initializes an int variable named i to a value of 1. Then, the while statement says that the while loop should continue to execute while i is less than or equal to the number of months.

Within the while loop, the first statement calculates the interest for one month and adds it to the futureValue variable. Then, the second statement uses the increment operator (++) to increment the i variable. As a result, the loop will continue to execute until it has run once for each month. Then, the condition at the beginning of the while loop will no longer be true and the program will exit the loop.

The second example shows how you can use a while loop to repeat all of the statements in an application until the user enters "x" or "X". In this example, the beginning of the while loop is shaded and the ending brace of the while loop is shaded. Before you enter the loop, this application initializes a String object named choice and sets it equal to an empty string. As a result, the condition at the beginning of the loop is true (the choice variable does not equal "x" or "X"), and the application enters the loop and executes all of its statements. Then, the last statement in the loop resets the value of the choice object by getting input from the user. That way, the conditional expression at the beginning of the loop can be evaluated again with a new value. When the user enters "x" or "X", the application will exit the loop, which in this case also exits the application.

Of course, if the condition at the start of a while statement never becomes false, the loop will never end. This can be referred to as an *infinite loop*. This can happen when the condition at the start of the loop hasn't been carefully coded. Then, to end the program, you need to press Ctrl+C. Since this is the type of problem that you want to avoid, it's worth taking some extra time to make sure your conditions are coded properly.

The syntax of the while loop

```
while (conditionalExpression){
    statements
}
```

A while loop that calculates the future value of an investment

```
futureValue = investmentAmount;
int i = 1;
while (i <= months) {
    futureValue = futureValue + (futureValue * monthlyInterestRate);
    i++;
}
```

A while loop that ends when a String object equals "x" or "X"

```
public class InvoiceApp{
    public static void main(String[] args){
        String choice = "";
        while (!(choice.equalsIgnoreCase("x"))){ // begin while loop
            ...
            code that gets input and performs the calculation
            ...
            String message = "To continue, press Enter.\n"
                           + "To exit, enter 'x': ";
            choice = JOptionPane.showInputDialog(message);
        } // end while loop
        System.exit(0);
    }
}
```

Description

- A *while statement* executes the block of statements within its braces as long as its conditional expression is true. When the expression is false, the while statement skips its block of statements.
- Any variables or constants that are declared in the block have block scope so they can only be used by statements in the block.
- If the condition at the start of a while statement never becomes false, the statement never ends. Then, the program goes into an *infinite loop* that you need to cancel.

How to cancel the execution of an infinite loop

- Press Ctrl+C.

Figure 2-18 How to code while statements

The Invoice application

Figure 2-19 shows the dialog boxes and code for an Invoice application. Although this application is simple, it gets input from a user, it performs calculations that use this input, and it displays the results of the calculations. It also uses almost all of the statements and methods presented in this chapter.

The dialog boxes for the application

Both of the dialog boxes shown in this figure use the default title of "Input" and the default icon for input dialog boxes: the question mark icon. Here, the first dialog box allows the user to enter a total for the order. Then, the second dialog box displays the order total that the user entered plus a discount amount and an invoice total that are calculated by the application.

The code for the application

By now, you should understand all of the code in this program. If you have any trouble with any of the statements, please refer back to the related pages for any clarification that you need. Once you do understand what every line of code in this program does, you've learned a lot about Java. Then, you can practice and reinforce what you've learned by doing the exercises at the end of this chapter.

You should realize, though, that this program has a few shortcomings. First, if you don't enter a number in the first dialog box, the parseDouble method of the Double class won't work and the program will end prematurely with a runtime error. Second, the numbers that are displayed in the second dialog aren't formatted properly. In the next chapter, though, you'll learn how to fix both of these problems.

The first dialog box for the Invoice application

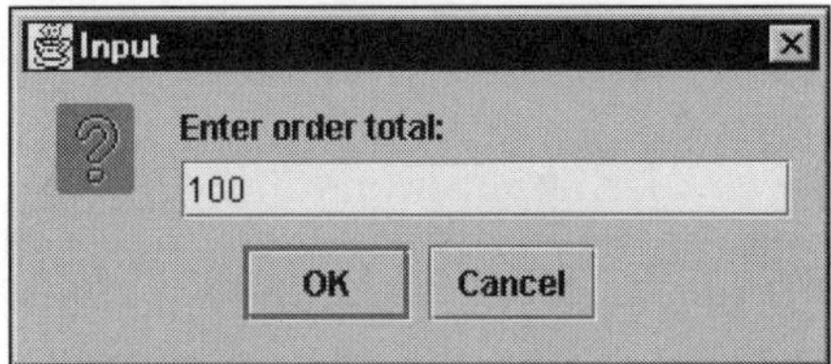

The second dialog box for the Invoice application

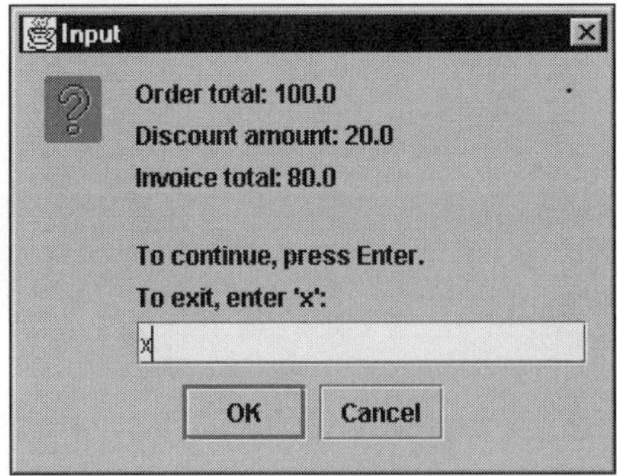

The code for the Invoice application

```
import javax.swing.*;

public class InvoiceApp{
   public static void main(String[] args){
      String choice = "";
      while (!(choice.equalsIgnoreCase("x"))){    // begin while loop
         String inputString = JOptionPane.showInputDialog(
            "Enter order total: ");
         double orderTotal = Double.parseDouble(inputString);
         double discountAmount = 0;
         if (orderTotal >= 100)
            discountAmount = orderTotal * .2;
         else
            discountAmount = orderTotal * .1;
         double invoiceTotal = orderTotal - discountAmount;
         String message = "Order total: " + orderTotal + "\n"
                        + "Discount amount: " + discountAmount + "\n"
                        + "Invoice total: " + invoiceTotal + "\n\n"
                        + "To continue, press Enter.\n"
                        + "To exit, enter 'x': ";
         choice = JOptionPane.showInputDialog(message);
      } // end while loop
      System.exit(0);
   }
}
```

Figure 2-19 The Invoice application

Perspective

The goal of this chapter has been to get you started with Java programming... and get you started fast. Now, if you understand how the Invoice application in figure 2-19 works, you've learned a lot. You should also be able to write comparable programs of your own.

In the next chapter, you will add to what you've learned by learning more of the Java language essentials. You will also see how the Java statements are used in two more complete applications.

Summary

- You can use *comments* to document information about a program.
- You must code at least one public *class* for every Java program that you write. The *main method* of the class is executed when the class is run.
- Java provides eight *primitive data types* to store *integer*, *floating-point*, *character*, and *boolean* values.
- *Variables* store data that changes as a program runs. *Constants* store data that doesn't change as a program runs. You use *assignment statements* to assign values to variables.
- You can use *arithmetic operators* to form *arithmetic expressions*, and you can use *assignment operators* as a shorthand for arithmetic expressions. If necessary, you can *cast* a more precise data type to a less precise type.
- You can create a String *object* from the String class. Then, you can use two methods to compare the object with another string. You can also use the methods of the Double and Integer classes to parse numbers from strings.
- You can call a *method* from an object, and you can call a *static method* from a class. If a method requires *arguments*, you must enter the arguments between the parentheses of the method call.
- You can use two methods of the System class to print data to the *console*.
- The Java *Application Programming Interface*, or *API*, is a library of all the available classes that come as a part of the SDK. This API groups similar classes into *packages*.
- You can use the static methods of the JOptionPane class of the javax.swing package to display dialog boxes that get input and display output.
- You can code *if statements* to control the logic of your program based on the true and false values of *conditional expressions*. You can also code *while statements* to create *while loops* that repeat a series of statements until a conditional expression is true.

Terms

comment
statement
block comment
end-of-line comment
identifier
keyword
class
class declaration
access modifier
scope
class definition
main method
main method declaration
primitive data type
data type
bit
byte
integer
floating-point number
significant digit
single precision
double precision
scientific notation
Unicode character set
ASCII character set
boolean data type
variable
constant
initialization statement
final variable
assignment statement
literal
numeric literal
arithmetic expression
arithmetic operator
operand
binary operator
unary operator
assignment operator
order of precedence
casting
implicit cast
explicit cast
string
instance
instantiation
object
string literal
escape sequence
null value
empty string
method
call a method
dot operator
argument
case-sensitive
join
concatenate
wrapper class
static method
class method
throw an exception
console
Application Programming Interface (API)
package
import statement
graphical user interface (GUI)
Abstract Windows Toolkit (AWT)
Swing
thread
signature of a method
overloading a method
field
control statement
conditional expression
relational operator
logical operator
if/else statement
if statement
if clause
else if clause
else clause
block of statements
block scope
nested if statements
while statement
while loop
indeterminate loop
infinite loop

Objectives

- Given the Java code for a program that uses any of the language elements presented in this chapter, explain what each statement in the program does.
- Given the specifications for a program that requires only the language elements presented in this chapter, write the program.
- List the rules for creating an identifier and the recommended differences in creating class, variable, and constant names.
- Describe any one of the eight primitive data types. Then, distinguish between an integer, a floating-point number, and a boolean value.
- Identify these terms: class, object, instance, method, and static method.
- Explain what “importing a package” means.

Exercise 2-2 Test the Invoice application

In this exercise, you'll compile and test the Invoice application that's presented in figure 2-19.

1. Start your text editor and open the file named "InvoiceApp.java" that you should find in the c:\java\ch02 directory. Then, compile the application, which should compile without errors.
2. Run the program and test it with simple entries like 100, 200, and 1000 so it's easy to see whether or not the calculations are correct. They should be.
3. Enter 233.33 in the first dialog box. This time, the second dialog box will display the discount amount and invoice total with more than 10 decimal places each. In the next chapter, you'll learn how to format numbers so only two decimal places are displayed.
4. Enter "10k" in the dialog box. This time, the application should crash and display an error message on the console. Then, you need to press Ctrl+C or close the console window to terminate the program. Can you tell why this happened? In the next chapter, you'll learn how to fix this bug.

Exercise 2-3 Modify the Invoice application

In this exercise, you'll modify the Invoice application. This will give you a chance to write some code of your own.

1. Save the InvoiceApp program as ModifiedInvoiceApp.java in the c:\java\ch02 directory. Then, change the class name to ModifiedInvoiceApp.
2. Modify the code so the second dialog box displays the information icon, has "Invoice Application" as its title, and prompts the user to enter Y or N to end the program as shown here:

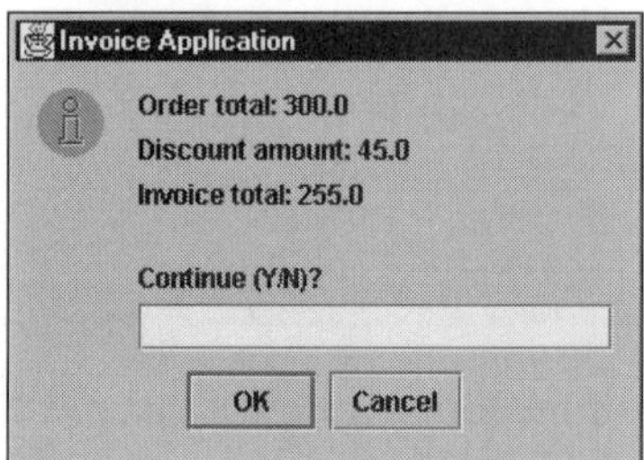

   Next modify the program so it continues if the user enters "Y" or "y", but ends if the user enters "n" or "N". Then, compile and test your changes.
3. Modify the discount calculation so the discount is 20% if the order total is greater than or equal to $500; 15% if the order total is greater than or equal to $250 but less than $500; 10% if the order total is greater than or equal to $100 but less than $250; and zero if the order total is less than $100. Then, compile and test your changes.

3

Java language essentials (part 2)

In the last chapter, you learned how to code an application that got input from a user, performed some calculations, and displayed output to the user. In this chapter, you'll learn how to enhance a program like that by formatting the data that's displayed and by validating the user's entries. Along the way, you'll learn how to use two new classes, how to code two more applications, and how to look up information about any method in any class of the Java API.

Two more classes for working with numbers

In the last chapter, you learned how to work with the eight primitive data types, how to code arithmetic expressions, and how to use the methods of the Integer and Double classes. Now, you're ready to learn about two more classes for working with numbers.

How to use the Math class

Figure 3-1 shows how to use eight of the static methods of the Math class to perform numeric operations. To use one of these methods, you supply zero, one, or two arguments. Then, the method performs its operation on the arguments.

The first example shows how to use the *round* method to round a double or float data type to an integer or long data type. Otherwise, the decimal positions are truncated. In the next figure, though, you'll see that numbers can also be rounded by using the NumberFormat class to format them.

The second example shows how to use the *pow* method to raise the first argument to the power of the second argument. This method returns a double value and accepts two double arguments. However, since Java automatically converts any arguments of a less precise numeric type to a double, the pow method accepts all of the numeric types. In this example, the first statement is equal to 2^2, the second statement is equal to 2^3, and the third and fourth statements are equal to 5^2.

In general, the methods of the Math class work the way you would expect. Sometimes, though, you may need to cast numeric types to get the methods to work the way you want them to. For example, the pow method returns a double type. So if you want to return an int type, you need to cast the double type to an int type as shown in the fourth pow example.

The third example shows how to use the *random* method to generate random numbers. Since this method returns a random double value greater than or equal to 0.0 and less than 1.0, you can return any range of values by multiplying the random number by another number. In this example, the first statement returns a random double value greater than or equal to 0.0 and less than 100.0. Then, the second statement casts this double value to a long data type.

If you have the right mathematical background, you shouldn't have any trouble using these or any of the other Math methods. And if you don't have that background, you probably won't ever need to use them.

The Math class

```
java.lang.Math
```

Some of its static methods

Method	Description
`round(a)`	Returns the closest long or int value to the double or float argument.
`pow(a, b)`	Returns a double value of a double argument, a, raised to another double argument, b.
`random()`	Returns a double value greater than or equal to 0.0 and less than 1.0.
`max(a, b)`	Returns the greater of two float, double, int, or long arguments.
`min(a, b)`	Returns the lesser of two float, double, int, or long arguments.
`abs(a)`	Returns the absolute value of a float, double, or int argument.
`exp(a)`	Returns the exponential number (e) as a double raised to the power of a double argument.
`log(a)`	Returns the natural logarithm as a double of a double argument.

Examples

Example 1: The round method

```
long result = Math.round(1.667);        // result is 2
int result = Math.round(1.49F);         // result is 1
```

Example 2: The pow method

```
double result = Math.pow(2, 2);         // result is 4.0 (2*2)
double result = Math.pow(2, 3);         // result is 8.0 (2*2*2)
double result = Math.pow(5, 2);         // result is 25.0 (5 squared)
int result = (int) Math.pow(5, 2);      // result is 25 (5 squared)
```

Example 3: The random method

```
double x = Math.random() * 100;     // result is a value >= 0.0 and < 100.0
long result = (long) x;             // converts the result from double to long
```

Example 4: The max and min methods

```
int x = 67;
int y = 23;
int max = Math.max(x, y);               // max is 67
int min = Math.min(x, y);               // min is 23
```

Example 5: The abs method

```
double result = Math.abs(-10);          // result is 10.0
```

Description

- When you use one of the static methods of the Math class, you supply the arguments that you want the method performed upon.
- In some cases, you need to cast the result to the data type that you want. This is illustrated by the fourth pow example, which casts a double result to an integer data type.

Figure 3-1 How to use the Math class

How to use the NumberFormat class

When you use numeric values in a program, you'll often need to format them. For example, you may want to apply a standard currency format to a double value. To do that, you need to add a dollar sign and display just two decimal places. Similarly, you may want to display a double value in a standard percentage format. To do that, you need to add a percent sign and move the decimal point two digits to the right.

To do this type of formatting, Java provides the NumberFormat class, which is summarized in figure 3-2. Since this class is part of the java.text package, you must include an import statement for this class before you can use its methods. Once you import the class, you can create a NumberFormat object by using a static method of the NumberFormat class. Then, you can use the format method of the NumberFormat object to return a String object with the appropriate formatting.

To illustrate, the first example shows how to format numbers with the *currency* format. Here, the second statement creates a NumberFormat object named currency and assigns it the result of the static getCurrencyInstance method. Then, the third statement uses the format method of the currency object to return a string that consists of a dollar sign plus the price variable with two decimal places. Because the methods of a NumberFormat object automatically provide rounding, this method returns 45.968 as $45.97 and 1234.572 as $1,234.57. In this format, negative numbers are enclosed in parentheses.

The second example shows how to format numbers with the *percent* format. The main difference between the first and second examples is that you use the getPercentInstance method instead of the getCurrencyInstance method. Then, you can use the format method of the percent object to return a string with a proper percent value followed by a percent sign. For instance, this method returns 0.624 as 62% and 0.626 as 63%. In this format, negative numbers have a leading minus sign.

The third example shows how to format numbers with the *number* format, and how to set the number of decimal places that are returned by any NumberFormat object. Here, the format is changed from the default of three decimal places to just one decimal place. In this format, negative numbers also have a leading minus sign.

The fourth example shows how you can use a NumberFormat object more than once after it has been created. Here, the first statement creates a NumberFormat object. Then, the second statement uses the format method of the NumberFormat object to format three numbers.

The fifth example shows how you can use one statement to create a NumberFormat object and use its format method. Although this example accomplishes the same task as the second example, it doesn't create a NumberFormat object that you can use later in the program. As a result, you should only use code like this when you need to format just one number.

The NumberFormat class

```
java.text.NumberFormat
```

Three static methods of the NumberFormat class

Method	Returns a NumberFormat object that ...
`getCurrencyInstance()`	has the default currency format ($99,999.99).
`getPercentInstance()`	has the default percent format (99%).
`getNumberInstance()`	has the default number format (99,999.999).

Three methods of a NumberFormat object

Method	Description
`format(anyNumberType)`	Returns a String object that has the format specified by the NumberFormat object.
`setMinimumFractionDigits(int)`	Sets the minimum number of decimal places.
`setMaximumFractionDigits(int)`	Sets the maximum number of decimal places.

Examples

Example 1: The currency format

```
double price = 11.575;
NumberFormat currency = NumberFormat.getCurrencyInstance();
String priceString = currency.format(price);        // returns $11.58
```

Example 2: The percent format

```
double majority = .512;
NumberFormat percent = NumberFormat.getPercentInstance();
String majorityString = percent.format(majority);   // returns 51%
```

Example 3: The number format with three decimal places

```
double miles = 15341.256;
NumberFormat number = NumberFormat.getNumberInstance();
number.setMaximumFractionDigits(1);
String milesString = number.format(miles);          // returns 15,341.3
```

Example 4: Using the same NumberFormat object three times

```
NumberFormat currency = NumberFormat.getCurrencyInstance();
String message = "Order total: " + currency.format(orderTotal) + "\n"
   + "Discount amount: " + currency.format(discountAmount) + "\n"
   + "Invoice total: " + currency.format(invoiceTotal);
```

Example 5: Combining two statements on one line

```
String majorityString = NumberFormat.getPercentInstance().format(majority);
```

Description

- Use one of the three static methods to create a NumberFormat object. Then, use the methods of that object to format a number with automatic rounding if that's necessary.
- To change the number of decimal places in the formatted number, use the methods for setting the minimum and maximum number of digits.
- Since the NumberFormat class is in the java.text package, you need to include an import statement when you want to use this class.

Figure 3-2 How to use the NumberFormat class

How to use try/catch statements

You use try/catch statements to test for errors that will otherwise cause your program to fail. Since you usually don't want your program to "crash" in that way, try/catch statements play an important role in most programs.

How to code try/catch statements

An *exception* is an error that can cause a program to fail. For instance, the parseInt or parseDouble method that you learned to use in the last chapter *throws* an exception if the argument can't be converted to an integer or double data type. An exception can also occur when Java can't perform an operation like dividing a value by zero.

To prevent your program from failing when an exception occurs, you can code *try/catch statements* as summarized in figure 3-3. As you can see, you first code a *try block* around the statements that may cause an exception. Then, you code one *catch block* for each type of exception that may occur in the try block. These blocks are coded immediately after the try block.

In the first example in this figure, you can see how try/catch statements are used to catch a NumberFormatException. This type of exception occurs when the parseInt or parseDouble method can't convert the string argument to a valid integer or double value. In this example, the catch block displays an error message and gives the user a chance to enter a valid number.

In the second example, you can see how try/catch statements are used to catch a NullPointerException. This type of exception occurs when a method attempts to use null where an object is expected. For instance, if the user presses the Cancel button in the dialog box, the choice object is set to null. When the equalsIgnoreCase method attempts to compare this object to a string, a NullPointerException is thrown. In this example, the catch statement simply exits the application.

Another way to handle this second type of exception is to test the return value of the showInputDialog method to make sure it isn't null. Then, you don't have to code a try/catch statement for this purpose. However, if you're coding several showInputDialog methods, it may be easier to handle all exceptions in one try/catch statement. In some cases, you have to use a try/catch statement to prevent program failure. For instance, there's no easy way to prevent a NumberFormatException so you have to use a try/catch statement.

For now, this is all you need to know about handling exceptions with try/catch statements. As you go through this book, though, you'll learn about other types of exceptions. And chapter 10 provides a thorough treatment of this subject.

The syntax for the try/catch statement

```
try{statements that may throw an exception}
catch(ExceptionType exceptionName){statements}
```

Two methods that throw an exception

Class	Method	Throws
Integer	parseInt(String)	NumberFormatException
Double	parseDouble(String)	NumberFormatException

Other types of run-time exceptions

```
ArrayIndexOutOfBoundsException
StringIndexOutOfBoundsException
NullPointerException
```

A try/catch statement that catches a NumberFormatException

```
String inputString = JOptionPane.showInputDialog("Enter order total: ");
double orderTotal = 0;
try{
   orderTotal = Double.parseDouble(inputString);
}
catch(NumberFormatException e){
   inputString = JOptionPane.showInputDialog(
      "Invalid order total. \n"
    + "Please enter a number: ");
   orderTotal = Double.parseDouble(inputString);
}
```

A try/catch statement that catches a NullPointerException

```
String choice = "";
try{
   while(!(choice.equalsIgnoreCase("X"))){
      choice = JOptionPane.showInputDialog(
              "Press Enter to continue or enter 'x' to exit.");
   }
}
catch(NullPointerException e){
   System.exit(0);
}
```

Description

- An *exception* is an error that can cause a program to fail. However, you can code try/catch statements to *catch* an exception and to supply code that handles the exception.
- When an error occurs at run time, the method *throws* an exception.
- You can code a *try block* around any statements that may throw an exception. Then, you can code one *catch block* for each type of exception that may occur in the try block. Catch blocks are only executed when an exception is thrown in the try block.
- Any variables or objects that are used in both the try and catch blocks must be created before the try and catch blocks so both the try and catch blocks can access them.

Figure 3-3 How to code try/catch statements

How to use nested while loops to validate input data

Whenever a user enters data, a program should check it to make sure that it is valid. This is referred to as *data validation*. As part of data validation, the user should be given a chance to correct each entry so the program can continue.

One way to give the user more than one chance to make each entry is to use nested while loops as shown in figure 3-4. Here, the main loop repeats all of the statements in the main method until the user exits the application. It starts by displaying a dialog box that asks the user to enter the order total. Then, an outer nested loop is repeated until the user enters a valid number, and an inner nested loop is repeated until the user enters a valid number that's greater than zero. Once that's done, the main loop continues by calculating and displaying the discount amount and invoice total.

If you study this code, you should be able to understand how it works. Note that the condition for the outer nested loop is just

```
tryAgain
```

This is shorthand for

```
tryAgain == true
```

Note also that the tryAgain variable is set to true before this loop is entered, and it's set to false only if the user's entry parses to a valid number that isn't less than or equal to zero. If the entry isn't numeric, the catch block in the outer nested loop asks the user to enter another number. If the entry is numeric but isn't greater than zero, the inner nested loop asks the user to enter a positive number.

In this example, the program has to validate just one user entry. So you can imagine what's involved if the program gets several user entries each time through the main loop. Another way to handle this, though, is to use static methods for data validation, and you'll learn how to create and use them next.

Nested while loops that are used to validate input data

```
public static void main(String[] args){
   String choice = "";
   while (!(choice.equalsIgnoreCase("x"))){ // start outer while loop
      String inputString = JOptionPane.showInputDialog(
         "Enter order total: ");
      double orderTotal = 0;
      boolean tryAgain = true;
      while(tryAgain){ // start outer nested loop
         try{
            orderTotal = Double.parseDouble(inputString);
            while (orderTotal <= 0){ // start inner nested loop
               inputString = JOptionPane.showInputDialog(
                   "Invalid order total. \n"
                 + "Please enter a positive number: ");
               orderTotal = Double.parseDouble(inputString);
            } // end inner nested loop
            tryAgain = false;
         }
         catch(NumberFormatException e){
            inputString = JOptionPane.showInputDialog(
               "Invalid order total. \n"
             + "Please enter a number: ");
         }
      } // end outer nested loop

      // code that calculates and displays the discount amount and invoice
      // total and gives the user a chance to end the program by entering 'x'

   } // end outer while loop
   System.exit(0);
}
```

Description

- Whenever a user enters data, it usually needs to be checked to make sure that it is valid. This is referred to as *data validation.*
- When you use the Integer and Double classes to convert string entries to int or double data types, you need to use try/catch statements to make sure that the entries are numeric. Often, though, you also need to check to make sure that the data is within logical bounds. For example, an order total should be greater than zero.
- When an entry is invalid, the program needs to display an error message and give the user another chance to enter valid data. This needs to be repeated until the entry is valid. One way to code this type of validation routine is to use nested while loops.

Figure 3-4 How to use nested while loops to validate input data

How to create and use static methods

One way to make your programs more manageable is to create your own static methods. Then, you can call them just as you call the static methods that are available through Java classes.

How to create a static method

Figure 3-5 shows how to create a *static method*. To start, you code the *private* and *static* keywords. The static keyword means that you can call this method without having to create an object from this class, while the private keyword means that you can only call this method from within the current class. For now, that's what you want.

After the private and static keywords, you must code a *return type* for the method. Here, you can use any primitive type and most classes. If, for example, you want the method to return a String object, you can code "String" as the return type. And if you want the method to return a double value, you can code "double" as the return type. But if you don't want the method to return any data, you can use the *void* keyword for the return type.

After the return type, you code the method name and any *parameters* required by the method. Since a method performs an action, it's a common coding practice to start the name of a method with a verb. After the name, you code a set of parentheses followed by a set of braces. Within the parentheses, you code the data types and names of the parameters, if any are required. Within the braces, you code the statements that you want the method to perform.

The last statement in the body of the method is the *return statement*. It specifies the name of the variable that is returned by the method. If, however, the method doesn't return a value, you omit this statement.

If you study the examples in this figure, you can see how the statement that *calls* the calculateFutureValue method relates to the complete method. Here, the calling statement supplies three arguments: monthlyPayment, months, and monthlyInterestRate. Then, these arguments are received by the method, which uses a while loop to calculate the future value. The last statement in the method is the return statement, which returns the future value.

In this case, the names of the arguments that are sent to the method are the same as the parameter names used by the method. However, that isn't necessary. As long as the arguments are sent in the right sequence with the right data types, the method will work properly. You'll see this illustrated in a moment.

Did you notice the careful use of the words *argument* and *parameter* in the last few paragraphs? To be precise, a call statement sends arguments to a method, and a method is defined with parameters. The difference is that parameters are the values received by the method, while arguments are the values passed by the caller. You'll see this use of these words throughout this book. In practice, though, these words are often used interchangeably because they are so similar.

The syntax for declaring a private static method with one parameter

```
private static returnType methodName(paramType paramName){
   body of method
   return returnTypeVariable;
}
```

Typical static method declarations

Example 1: A method that doesn't accept any parameters or return any data

```
private static void displayErrorMessage1(){}
```

Example 2: A method that accepts three parameters and returns a double type

```
private static double calculateFutureValue(double monthlyPayment,
   int months, double monthlyInterestRate){}
```

A statement that calls the calculateFutureValue method

```
double futureValue = calculateFutureValue(monthlyPayment,
                     months, monthlyInterestRate);
```

The complete calculateFutureValue method

```
private static double calculateFutureValue(double monthlyPayment,
              int months, double monthlyInterestRate){
   int i = 1;
   double futureValue = 0;
   while (i <= months) {
      futureValue = (futureValue + monthlyPayment) *
      (1 + monthlyInterestRate);
      i++;
   }
   return futureValue;
}
```

Description

- To help organize the code within a program, you can create *static methods*. Then, you can *call* these methods from other parts of the program.
- The *private* keyword at the start of a method means that the method can only be used within the current class. The *static* keyword means that you can call this method without first creating an object from the class.
- After the private and static keywords, you code a *return type* for the method. This is the data type of the result that will be returned by the method. If no result will be returned, you code *void* as the return type.
- After the return type, you code the name of the method followed by a set of parentheses. Within these parentheses, you code a data type and identifier for each of the *parameters* that are going to be sent to the method when the method is called. If the method requires more than one parameter, you separate them with commas.
- Within the set of braces that follows the parameters, you code the statements that do the processing of the method. The last statement is a *return statement* that gives the name of the variable that contains the result that should be returned. But if a method doesn't return a value, you don't need to code the return statement.

Figure 3-5 How to create a static method

How to use a static method to validate input data

Figure 3-6 shows how to use a static method to validate input data. Here, a method named parseTotal receives a String variable and returns a valid double variable. In this case, the calling statement sends a variable named inputString to the method, but the method refers to that variable as totalString. Nevertheless, the method works correctly.

If you study the code in this method, you can see that it does the same validation processing that the nested while loops in figure 3-4 do. However, the static method clearly separates the validation code from the other code. This makes the code easier to read and understand. For a more complicated program, you can code general-purpose validation methods that can be used to validate more than one input entry.

A static method that's used to validate a numeric entry

```
public class EnhancedInvoiceApp{

   public static void main(String[] args){ // the main method
      String choice = "";
      while (!(choice.equalsIgnoreCase("x"))){
         String inputString = JOptionPane.showInputDialog(
            "Enter order total: ");
         double orderTotal = parseTotal(inputString);

      // code that calculates and displays the discount and new total

      } // end while loop
      System.exit(0);
   }

   private static double parseTotal(String totalString){ // a static method
      double orderTotal = 0;
      boolean tryAgain = true;
      while(tryAgain){
         try{
            orderTotal = Double.parseDouble(totalString);
            while (orderTotal <= 0){
               totalString = JOptionPane.showInputDialog(
                    "Invalid order total. \n"
                  + "Please enter a positive number: ");
               orderTotal = Double.parseDouble(totalString);
            }
            tryAgain = false;
         }
         catch(NumberFormatException e){
            totalString = JOptionPane.showInputDialog(
                 "Invalid order total. \n"
               + "Please enter a number: ");
         }
      }
      return orderTotal;
   }

}
```

Description

- The parseTotal method does the same validation processing that's done by the nested while loops in figure 3-4.

Figure 3-6 How to use a static method to validate input data

Two more applications

In the last chapter, you learned how to create an Invoice application that calculates a discount and invoice total. In this topic, you'll learn how to code two more applications. First, you'll learn how to code an application that calculates the future value of a series of monthly payments. Then, you'll learn how to code an application that calculates the total for a book order. By studying these applications, you'll see how what you've learned so far can be applied to a variety of programming requirements.

The Future Value application

Figure 3-7 shows the dialog boxes for the Future Value application. Here, the first dialog box lets you enter an amount for a monthly payment. The second dialog box lets you enter the yearly interest rate. The third dialog box lets you enter the number of years that these monthly payments will be made. And the fourth dialog box displays the future value of the payments when interest is accumulated each month. As you can see in the next figure, the code for this application uses a static method to calculate the future value.

The dialog box for entering the monthly payment

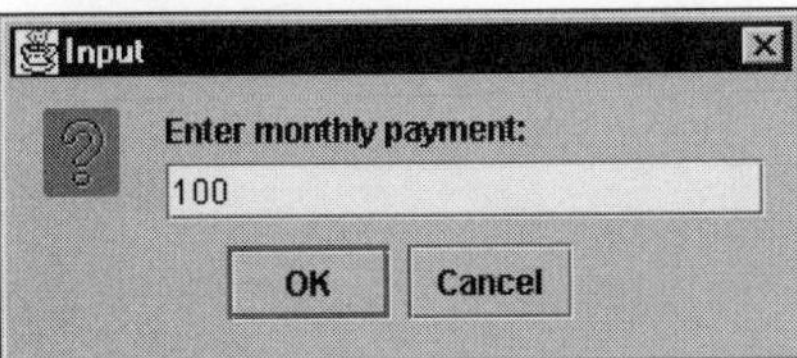

The dialog box for entering the yearly interest rate

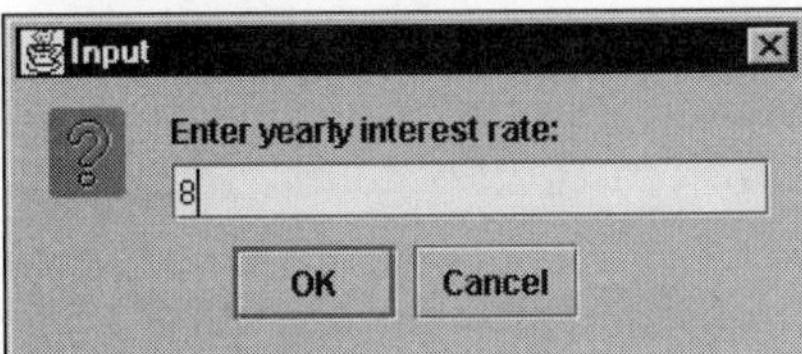

The dialog box for entering the number of years

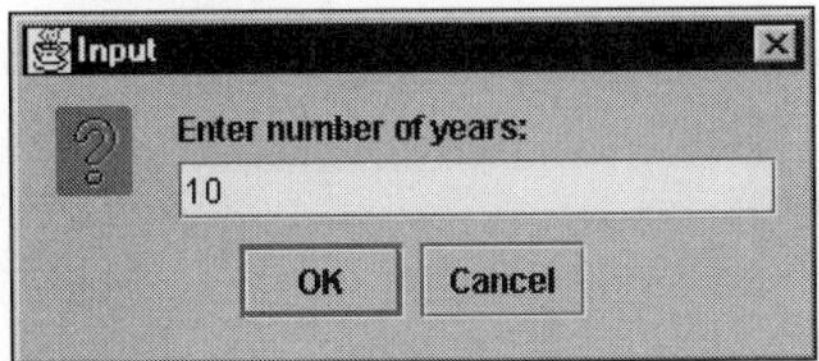

The dialog box that displays the future value

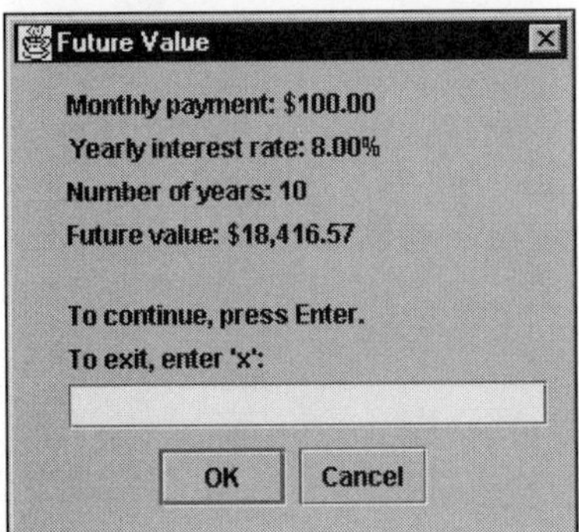

Description

- This program uses the first three dialog boxes to get user entries for monthly payment, yearly interest rate, and number of years.
- This program calculates the future value of the monthly payments with interest accumulated monthly for the specified number of years. Then, it displays the future value in the fourth dialog box.

Figure 3-7 The dialog boxes for the Future Value application

Figure 3-8 shows the code for the Future Value application. Within the main method, a while loop displays the first three dialog boxes and converts the user's entries to numeric values. Then, if necessary, the program converts each entry to monthly units. Specifically, it divides the yearly interest rate by 12 and then by 100 so it becomes the monthly interest rate. And it multiplies the number of years by 12 to get the number of months that the calculation should be based upon.

The program then calls the static method named calculateFutureValue using the variables that hold the monthly payment, number of months, and monthly interest rate as the parameters. Then, the static method uses a while loop to calculate the future value for the number of months indicated by the second parameter. When the static method finishes, it uses the return statement to return the future value to the statement that called it.

The program then uses two NumberFormat objects to apply the currency and percent formats to the values that are displayed by the fourth dialog box. If the user enters x or X in this dialog box, the program ends. Otherwise, the while loop continues by getting the next set of user entries.

Although this code works when the user enters valid numeric data, it will crash if the user enters invalid data. To prevent possible crashes like this, you can include validation code like the code that's shown earlier in this chapter. For instance, you could include one static method for converting a string to a positive double value and use that method for converting both the monthly payment and interest entries. You could also include one static method for converting a string to a positive int value and use that method for converting the years entry.

Please note that you normally wouldn't use three dialog boxes to get three input entries and a fourth dialog box to display the results. Instead, you would use a single dialog box to get the user entries and display the results. That, however, is a complicated undertaking that you'll learn how to do in section 3 of this book.

The code for the FutureValueApp class

```
import javax.swing.*;
import java.text.*;

public class FutureValueApp{
   public static void main(String[] args){
      String choice = "";
      while (!(choice.equalsIgnoreCase("x"))){ // begin while loop

         String paymentString = JOptionPane.showInputDialog(
            "Enter monthly payment: ");
         double monthlyPayment = Double.parseDouble(paymentString);

         String rateString = JOptionPane.showInputDialog(
            "Enter yearly interest rate: ");
         double interestRate = Double.parseDouble(rateString);
         double monthlyInterestRate = interestRate/12/100;

         String yearsString = JOptionPane.showInputDialog(
            "Enter number of years: ");
         int years = Integer.parseInt(yearsString);
         int months = years * 12;

         double futureValue = calculateFutureValue(monthlyPayment,
            months, monthlyInterestRate);

         NumberFormat currency = NumberFormat.getCurrencyInstance();
         NumberFormat percent = NumberFormat.getPercentInstance();
         percent.setMinimumFractionDigits(2);
         String message =
              "Monthly payment: " + currency.format(monthlyPayment) + "\n"
            + "Yearly interest rate: " + percent.format(interestRate/100) + "\n"
            + "Number of years: " +  years + "\n"
            + "Future value: " + currency.format(futureValue) + "\n\n"
            + "To continue, press Enter.\n"
            + "To exit, enter 'x': ";
         choice = JOptionPane.showInputDialog(null,
            message, "Future Value", JOptionPane.PLAIN_MESSAGE);
      } // end while loop
      System.exit(0);
   }

   private static double calculateFutureValue(double monthlyPayment,
                int months, double interestRate){
      int i = 1;
      double futureValue = 0;
      while (i <= months) {
         futureValue = (futureValue + monthlyPayment) *
         (1 + interestRate);
         i++;
      }
      return futureValue;
   }

}
```

Figure 3-8 The code for the Future Value application

The Book Order application

Figure 3-9 shows the dialog boxes for the Book Order application. Here, the first dialog box lets you enter a four-character book code that is used to select a book. The second dialog box lets you enter the number of books that have been ordered. And the third dialog box displays the book's code, title, and price along with the quantity ordered and the order total. You can see the code for this application in the next figure.

The dialog box for entering the book code

The dialog box for entering the quantity ordered

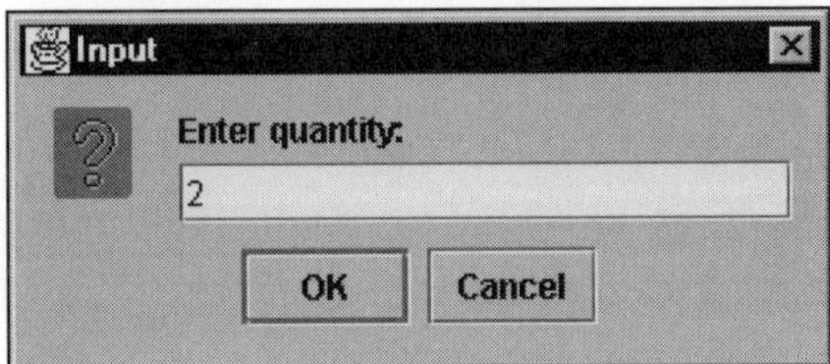

The dialog box for displaying the results

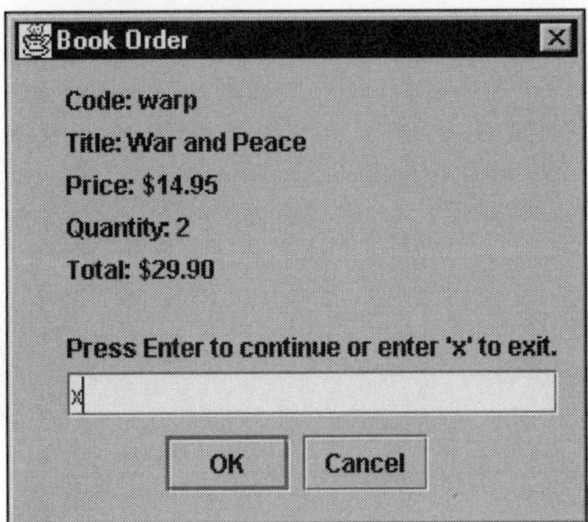

Description

- This program uses the first two dialog boxes to get the code and quantity of the book the user wants to order.
- This program uses the book code to look up the book's title and price. Then, it calculates the total by multiplying quantity by price, and it displays the results in the third dialog box.

Figure 3-9 The dialog boxes for the Book Order application

Figure 3-10 shows the code for the Book Order application, which is similar to the code for the Invoice and Future Value applications. In this case, though, the first dialog box gets an entry that represents a book code. Then, the program uses if/else statements to set the title and price of the book based on the book code that's entered. Although the if/else statements in this example provide book titles and prices for just two books (*War and Peace* and *Moby Dick*), you could easily code more.

In practice, though, you normally get data like this from a file or a database. So in section 4 and chapter 19, you'll learn how to do that. In the meantime, please accept the fact that this application is unrealistic in this respect, and imagine that the application is getting data from a file or database. As you will see in the next chapter, this application is used as the basis for presenting many of the principles of object-oriented programming.

If you study the code in this figure, you shouldn't have any trouble understanding it. Here again, NumberFormat objects are used to format the values that are displayed. And the program doesn't validate the user's entries.

The code for the BookOrderApp class

```
import javax.swing.JOptionPane;
import java.text.NumberFormat;

public class BookOrderApp{
   public static void main(String[] args){
      String choice = "";
      while (!(choice.equalsIgnoreCase("x"))){
         String code = JOptionPane.showInputDialog(
            "Enter book code: ");
         String title = "";
         double price = 0.0;
         if (code.equalsIgnoreCase("WARP")){
            title = "War and Peace";
            price = 14.95;
         }
         else if (code.equalsIgnoreCase("MBDK")){
            title = "Moby Dick";
            price = 12.95;
         }
         else{
            title = "Not Found";
            price = 0.0;
         }
         String inputQuantity = JOptionPane.showInputDialog(
            "Enter quantity: ");
         int quantity = Integer.parseInt(inputQuantity);
         double total = quantity * price;
         NumberFormat currency = NumberFormat.getCurrencyInstance();
         String message = "Code: " + code + "\n"
                        + "Title: " + title + "\n"
                        + "Price: " + currency.format(price) + "\n"
                        + "Quantity: " + quantity + "\n"
                        + "Total: " + currency.format(total) + "\n\n"
                        + "Press Enter to continue or enter 'x' to exit.";
         choice = JOptionPane.showInputDialog(null,
            message, "Book Order", JOptionPane.PLAIN_MESSAGE);
      }
      System.exit(0);
   }
}
```

Description

- Although the code for this program uses if statements to get the title and price for each book code, a program normally gets data like that from a file or database.
- In the next chapter, you'll learn how to write an object-oriented version of this program that uses Book and BookOrder objects. Then, in chapters 18 and 19, you'll learn how to get the data for these objects from a file or a database.

Figure 3-10 The code for the Book Order application

How to use the documentation for the Java API

Now that you've been introduced to some of the classes in the Java API, you're ready to learn how to look up information about these and other Java classes. Since the Java API provides HTML-based documentation, you can browse this documentation with any web browser to get detailed information about every method of every class in the Java API.

How to install the API documentation

Although you can view the documentation for the Java API by browsing the Java web site, you will probably want to install this *API documentation* on your hard drive so you can get the information more quickly. To install it, you can use the procedures shown in figure 3-11. Since the documentation comes in a compressed format called a *zip file*, you need to use an unzip tool like the *Java Archive tool* to extract the HTML pages from the zip file. When you use this tool, it creates a docs directory and its subdirectories beneath the jdk directory.

If you don't want to use the Java Archive tool to unzip files, you can use another tool. For example, WinZip is a popular program for working with zip files. If you use it, you should select the root directory of your hard drive (c:\) as the unzip directory. That way, all of the directories and files for the documentation will be stored under the jdk directory. If you don't already have WinZip installed on your system, you can download a free evaluation copy from www.winzip.com.

How to download the API documentation from the web to your C drive

1. Go to www.java.sun.com.
2. Go to the page for the version of the SDK that you're using.
3. Go to the download page for the version of the SDK that you're using and find the hyperlink for the documentation download.
4. Select the HTML format option and the one bundle option, unless the other options apply to you. Note the filename and size.
5. Select one of the FTP options. If you can't use one of the FTP options, use the HTTP option.
6. Save the file to your hard disk in c:\API_Documentation. Check the filename and size to make sure that the file wasn't corrupted during the download.

How to copy the API documentation from the book's CD to your C drive

1. Find the API_Documentation directory on your CD.
2. Copy the API_Documentation directory from your CD drive to your C drive so it becomes c:\API_Documentation.

How to use the Java Archive tool to install the API documentation from your C drive

1. Use the command prompt to navigate to the c:\API_Documentation directory.
2. Use the Java Archive (JAR) tool to extract the HTML pages from the zip file. To do that, enter this command:

   ```
   jar xvf j2sdk-1_3_1-doc.zip
   ```

3. The Java Archive tool creates the docs directory and its subdirectories subordinate to the c:\API_Documentation directory, and it places the HTML pages for the documentation in these directories.
4. Move the docs directory that you just created to the c:\jdk1.3.1 directory so it becomes c:\jdk1.3.1\docs.

Description

- The CD that comes with this book contains the *API documentation* for version 1.3.1 of the SDK. If you're using another version of the SDK, you can still use this version in most cases. However, you may want to download and install the version that matches your SDK from the Java web site.
- You can use the *Java Archive tool* to extract the HTML pages from the zip file for the API documentation. Or, if you prefer, you can use another tool such as WinZip. To download a free evaluation copy of WinZip, go to www.winzip.com.

Figure 3-11 How to install the API documentation

How to navigate the API documentation

Figure 3-12 shows how to look up any class in the documentation for the Java API. This allows you to get detailed information about a class, such as the arguments that are required by a method. To begin searching this documentation, point your web browser to the index page. Since you'll need to access this page often as you learn about Java, you should use your web browser's bookmark feature to mark this page.

To start, you may want to look up some of the classes that you've already learned about like the String, Double, Integer, JOptionPane, Math, and NumberFormat classes. For example, you can look up all the possible argument combinations for the showInputDialog method of the JOptionPane class.

Conversely, you may want to use the documentation to look up some classes that you aren't familiar with. The more you learn about working with classes, the easier it will be for you to learn about other classes that are similar. For example, if you look up the Long class in the java.lang package, you'll see that it's similar to the Integer class. As a result, once you know how to use the Integer class, you shouldn't have much trouble using the Long class.

In this book, you'll learn about many different classes, and you'll learn much more about how classes work. Along the way, you can always use the documentation for the Java API to help clarify the discussion or further your knowledge.

The index for the documentation

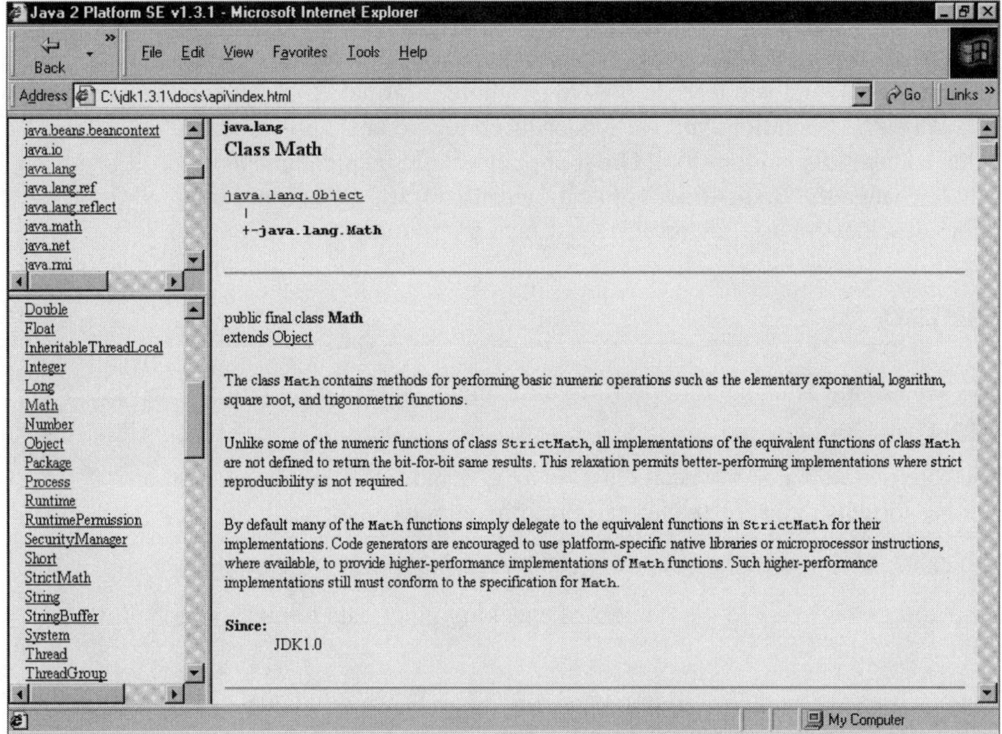

Description

- If you've installed the documentation on your hard drive, you can display an index like the one shown above by using your web browser to go to the index.html file in the \jdk1.3.1\docs\api directory. If you haven't installed the documentation, you can browse through it on the Java web site.
- You can use the upper left frame to select a package. When you do, all classes for that package will be displayed in the lower left frame.
- You can use the lower left frame to select a class. When you do, the documentation for that class will be displayed in the right frame.
- Once you display the documentation for a class, you can scroll through it or click on a hyperlink to get more information.
- The documentation for a class usually provides a wide range of information, including a summary of all of its methods. You'll learn more about what this information means throughout this book. For now, you can focus on the summary of the methods.
- To make it easier to access this documentation, you should bookmark this HTML page. To do that with the Internet Explorer, select the Add To Favorites command from the Favorites menu. Then, you can browse this documentation by selecting the Java 2 Platform SE v1.3.1 command from the Favorites menu.

Figure 3-12 How to navigate the API documentation

Perspective

In this chapter, you learned some essential Java skills for formatting and validating data, and you learned how to get more information about any class in the Java API. In addition, you were introduced to two new applications, the Future Value application and the Book Order application. In the next chapter, you'll learn how to change the Book Order application so that it uses the object-oriented techniques that are used by professional Java programmers.

Summary

- You can use the Math class to perform basic mathematical calculations such as exponentiation.
- You can use the NumberFormat class to apply standard currency, percent, and number formats to any of the numeric primitive types.
- You can code *try/catch statements* to catch *exceptions* that are *thrown* by a class.
- *Data validation* refers to the process of checking input data to make sure that it's valid.
- You can use *static methods* to organize your code. When you code a static method, you can code one *return type* and one or more *parameters*.
- You can get detailed information about any class in the Java API by using a web browser to browse the HTML-based documentation for the Java API.

Terms

exception
throw
try/catch statement
try block
catch block
data validation
static method
call a method
return type
parameter
return statement
API documentation
zip file
Java Archive tool

Objectives

- Use any of the methods of the Math class to perform numeric operations.
- Use the NumberFormat class to format numeric types.
- Write an application that catches exceptions and validates user input.
- Create and use a static method for validating data or performing a calculation.
- Look up information about any method of any class in the API documentation for Java.

Exercise 3-1 Enhance the Invoice application

This exercise guides you through the process of enhancing the Invoice application that you created in the last chapter.

1. Open the InvoiceApp class that you worked with in the last chapter. It should be stored in the c:\java\ch02 directory. Then, save this file as EnhancedInvoiceApp.java in the c:\java\ch03 directory, and change the class name to EnhancedInvoiceApp.
2. Edit the program so it uses the NumberFormat class to apply the currency format to the three numbers displayed in the second dialog box. Then, compile and run the class to make sure it's working properly.
3. Edit the code so it uses one try/catch statement to catch the exceptions that may be thrown if the user presses the Cancel button in the dialog boxes.
4. Edit the code so it uses a nested while loop and a try/catch statement to catch the exception that may be thrown by the parseDouble method of the Double class. When the exception is caught, the program should display another dialog box so the user can correct the entry. After you compile and test the program, you shouldn't be able to crash the application by entering invalid data. However, you should be able to enter a negative number.
5. Edit the code so it prevents the user from entering any number that's less than or equal to zero. Then, compile and run the application to make sure it's working properly.
6. Modify the program so the data validation is done by a static method instead of a nested while loop. Then, test the program to make sure that it still works correctly.

Exercise 3-2 Enhance the Future Value application

This exercise guides you through the process of enhancing the Future Value application that's presented in figures 3-7 and 3-8.

1. Open the FutureValueApp application that's stored in the c:\java\ch03 directory. Then, compile and test the application so you can see how it works. Note that it uses the default input dialog boxes, and it doesn't catch any exceptions or validate any data.
2. Edit the code so the input dialog boxes use "Future Value" as the title and so these dialog boxes don't display icons. Then, compile and test the application to make sure it's working properly.
3. Edit the code so it uses one try/catch statement to catch the exceptions that may be thrown if the user presses the Cancel button in the dialog boxes.
4. Edit the code so it uses static methods to validate the data that's entered for the monthlyPayment, years, and interestRate variables. Then, compile and run the application to make sure it's working properly.

Exercise 3-3 Enhance the Book Order application

This exercise guides you through the process of enhancing the Book Order application that's shown in figures 3-9 and 3-10.

1. Open the BookOrderApp application that's stored in the c:\java\ch03 directory. Then, compile and test the application. Note that it doesn't catch any exceptions or validate any data.
2. Edit the code so it uses one try/catch statement to catch the exceptions that may be thrown if the user presses the Cancel button in the dialog boxes.
3. Edit the program so it uses a static method to validate the data that's entered for the quantity variable. A quick way to do that is to open the Future Value application that you enhanced in the last exercise, copy the method that parses the year entry from that program to this one, and modify the code so it works with the quantity variable. Then, compile and run the class to make sure it's working properly.
4. Edit the program so it uses another static method to set the title of the book depending on the book code. Next, edit the code so it uses a third static method to set the price of the book depending on the book code. Then, compile and run the program to make sure it's working properly.

Exercise 3-4 Browse the Java API documentation

This exercise guides you through the process of using the documentation for the Java API to learn more about classes.

1. Start your web browser and navigate to the index.html page for the API documentation. If you've installed the documentation on your hard drive, it should be in the c:\jdk1.3.1\docs\api directory. Otherwise, go to the Java web site.
2. Bookmark this page with your web browser. For the Internet Explorer, select the Add to Favorites command from the Favorites menu and click OK. When you're done, close your web browser.
3. Start your web browser again. Then, use the bookmark to return to the index.html page.
4. In the upper left frame, select the java.lang package. In the lower left frame, select the Math class. Then, information about the Math class should be displayed in the right frame. Scroll down and skim through the documentation for the Math class. Notice that the documentation shows four signatures for the max method, one method per data type.
5. Browse through the documentation for the classes you've learned about so far: the String class, the Double class, the Integer class, the System class, the JOptionPane class, the Math class, and the NumberFormat class.
6. When you've satisfied your curiosity, close your browser.

4

How to write object-oriented programs

In the last two chapters, you learned how to use Java classes and objects, which is an essential part of object-oriented programming. Now, in this chapter, you'll learn how to create classes for the specific types of objects and methods that your applications require. That too is an essential part of object-oriented programming. When you finish this chapter, you'll begin to see how professional programmers develop Java programs.

An introduction to object-oriented programming

To illustrate some terms and concepts that apply to *object-oriented programming (OOP)*, the next two figures use *Unified Modeling Language* (*UML*) diagrams. This modeling language is the industry standard for working with all object-oriented programming languages including Java.

How encapsulation works

Figure 4-1 shows a *class diagram* for a class named Book. This diagram shows that the class contains three *attributes* and five *operations*. Here, the minus sign (-) identifies attributes and operations that are available only within the current class, while the plus sign (+) identifies attributes and operations that are available to other classes.

In this case, all of the operations are available to other classes, but none of the attributes are. However, some of the operations make the attributes available to other classes. For instance, the getCode operation gets the code attribute, and the getTitle operation gets the title attribute.

This illustrates *encapsulation*, which is a fundamental concept of object-oriented programming. This means that the programmer can hide, or encapsulate, some attributes and operations of a class, while exposing others. Since the attributes (or data) of a class are typically encapsulated within a class, encapsulation is sometimes referred to as *data hiding*. In addition, though, the code that performs the operations of the class is also hidden from the classes that use the operations.

When you use a class, encapsulation lets you think of it as a black box that provides useful attributes and operations. When you use the parseInt method of the Integer class, for example, you don't know how the method converts a string to an integer, and you don't need to know. Similarly, if you use the getPrice operation of the Book class in this figure, you don't know how the operation works, and you don't need to know.

This also means that you can change the internal code for an operation within a class without affecting the classes that use the class. For instance, you can change the code that gets the price of a book for the getPrice operation without changing the classes that use that operation. This makes it easier to upgrade or enhance an application because you only need to change the classes that need upgrading.

A class diagram for the Book class

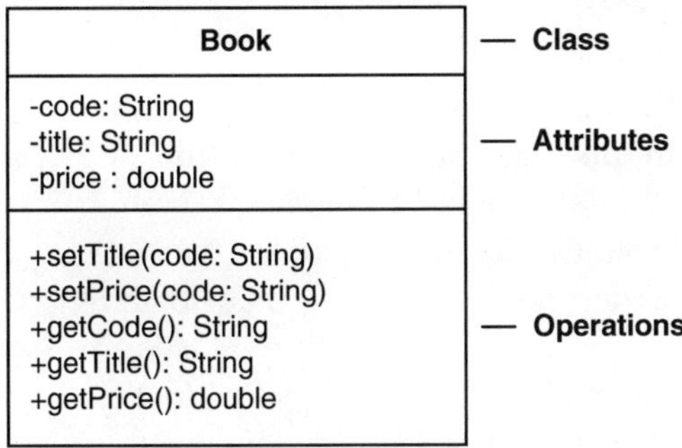

Description

- The *attributes* of a class store the data of a class.
- The *operations* of a class define the tasks that a class can perform. Often, these operations provide a way to work with the attributes of a class.
- *Encapsulation* is one of the fundamental concepts of object-oriented programming. This means that the class controls which of its attributes and operations can be accessed by other classes. As a result, the data in the class can be hidden from other classes (called *data hiding*), and the operations in a class can be modified or improved without changing the way that other classes use them.

Class diagramming notes

- The minus sign (-) in a class diagram marks the attributes and operations that can't be accessed by other classes, while the plus sign (+) marks the attributes and operations that can be accessed by other classes.
- For each attribute, the name is given, followed by a colon, followed by the data type. For each operation, the name is given followed by a set of parentheses. If an operation requires parameters, the name and data type of each parameter is listed in the parentheses. Otherwise, the parentheses are left empty, and the data type of the value that's going to be returned is given after the colon.

Figure 4-1 How encapsulation works

The relationship between a class and its objects

Figure 4-2 uses one class diagram and two *object diagrams* to show how objects are created from a class. Here, the diagrams show only the attributes, not the operations, of the class and its objects. In this case, two objects named book1 and book2 are created from the Book class.

Although an object diagram is similar to a class diagram, there are two differences. First, the name of the object is underlined. Second, each attribute in an object diagram contains a value.

Once an object is created, it has an *identity* and a *state*. An object's identity is its name. An object's state refers to the values that are stored by the object. For example, book1 is the identity of the first Book object, and the state of this object is determined by the three values that it holds. As the program executes, the state of the object may change, but the identity of the object won't.

The relationship between a class and its objects

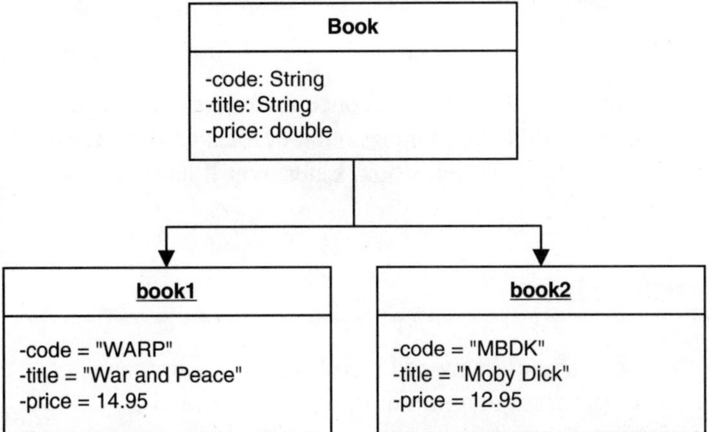

Description

- A *class* can be thought of as a template from which *objects* are made.
- An *object diagram* provides the name of the object and the values of the attributes.
- Once an object is created, it has an *identity* (a unique name) and a *state* (the values that it holds). Although an object's state may change throughout a program, its identity never does.

Figure 4-2 The relationship between a class and its objects

How to code a class that defines an object

Now that you've learned some of the terms and concepts for working with object-oriented programs, you're ready to code a class that defines an object. So to start, you'll learn how to code a class named Book. Later, you'll learn how to create objects from this class.

The code of the Book class

Figure 4-3 presents the code for a class named Book. This code implements the attributes and operations of the class diagram in figure 4-1. Since you learned how to use most of the statements in this class in the last chapter, you should be able to understand most of this code right now. In the next three figures, though, you'll learn how the rest of this code works.

At the top of the class, the three *instance variables* define the data that will be used by the objects created from this class. In UML terms, they define the attributes of the class. Below that, the *constructor* creates the objects of the class by assigning values to the three instance variables of the object. And below that, the five *methods* of the class provide procedures that you can call from an object of the class. In UML terms, these methods define the operations of the class.

The *private* and *public* access modifiers control which instance variables and methods are available to other classes. Since all of the instance variables use the private access modifier, they are only available within the current class. The constructor and the five methods, however, use the public access modifier. As a result, they are available to all classes.

The Book class

```
public class Book{
   private String code;       } Instance variables
   private String title;
   private double price;

   public Book(String bookCode){     } Constructor
      code = bookCode;
      setTitle(bookCode);
      setPrice(bookCode);
   }

   public void setTitle(String bookCode){     } Methods
      if (bookCode.equalsIgnoreCase("WARP"))
         title = "War and Peace";
      else if (bookCode.equalsIgnoreCase("MBDK"))
         title = "Moby Dick";
      else
         title = "Not Found";
   }

   public void setPrice(String bookCode){
      if (bookCode.equalsIgnoreCase("WARP"))
         price = 14.95;
      else if (bookCode.equalsIgnoreCase("MBDK"))
         price = 12.95;
      else
         price = 0.0;
   }

   public String getCode(){
      return code;
   }

   public String getTitle(){
      return title;
   }

   public double getPrice(){
      return price;
   }

}
```

Description

- The *instance variables* of a class hold the attributes, or data, of an object. Each object created from that class has its own copy of these variables with its own values.
- The *constructor* initializes the instance variables and is always called when an object is created from a class.
- The *methods* of a class are the operations that can occur on objects. Methods are the primary way that objects communicate with each other.

Figure 4-3 The code of the Book class

How to code instance variables

Figure 4-4 shows how to code the instance variables that define the types of data that are used by a class. When you declare an instance variable, you should use one of the three access modifiers to control the scope of the variable. For now, you should declare all instance variables as *private* to prevent other classes from directly accessing them. Later in this book, though, you'll learn more about using the public and protected modifiers.

This figure shows four examples of declaring an instance variable. The first example declares a variable of the double type. The second one declares a variable of the int type. The third one declares a variable that's an object of the String class. And the last one declares an object from the Book class...the class that you're learning how to code right now.

Although instance variables work like regular variables, they must be declared within the class body, but not inside methods or constructors. That way, they'll be available throughout the entire class. In this book, all of the examples show the instance variables at the start of the class. When you read through code from other sources, though, you may find the instance variables at the end of the class. In addition, you may find that many programmers place public instance variables at the start of the class and private instance variables at the end of the class.

The syntax for declaring instance variables

```
public|private|protected  primitiveType|ClassName variableName;
```

Examples

```
private double price;
private int quantity;
private String title;
private Book bookObject;
```

Where you can declare instance variables

```
public class Book{

   //common to code instance variables here
   private String code;
   private String title;
   private double price;

   //the constructors and methods of the class
   public Book(String bookCode){}
   public void setTitle(String bookCode){}
   public void setPrice(String bookCode){}
   public String getCode(){ return code; }
   public String getTitle(){ return title; }
   public double getPrice(){ return price; }

   //also common to code instance variables here
   private int test;

}
```

Description

- An instance variable may be a primitive data type, an object created from a Java class such as the String class, or an object created from a programmer-defined class such as the Book class.
- To prevent other classes from accessing instance variables, use the *private* access modifier to declare them as private.

Figure 4-4 How to code instance variables

How to code constructors

Figure 4-5 shows how to code a constructor for a class. When you code one, it's a good coding practice to assign a value to all of the instance variables of the class as shown in the three examples. In addition, you can include any additional statements that you want to execute within the constructor. For instance, the third example ends by calling two methods from the current class.

When you code a constructor, you must use the *public* access modifier and the same name, including capitalization, as the class name. Then, if you don't want to accept arguments, you must code an empty set of parentheses as shown in the first example. On the other hand, if you want to accept arguments, you code the *parameters* for the constructor as shown in the second and third examples. When you code the parameters for a constructor, you must code a data type and a name for each parameter. For the data type, you can code a primitive data type or the class name for any class that defines an object.

The second example shows a constructor with three parameters. Here, the first parameter is a String object named bookCode; the second parameter is a String object named bookTitle; and the third parameter is a double type named bookPrice. Then, the three statements within the constructor use these three parameters to initialize the three instance variables of the class.

The third example shows a constructor with one parameter. Here, the first statement assigns this parameter to the first instance variable of the class. Then, the second and third statements call other methods within the class to initialize the other two instance variables.

When you code a constructor, the class name plus the number of parameters and the data type for each parameter form the *signature* of the constructor. You can code more than one constructor per class as long as each constructor has a unique signature. For example, all three of the constructors shown in this figure have unique signatures so they could be coded within the Book class. This is known as *overloading* a constructor.

If you don't code a constructor, Java will create a default constructor that doesn't accept any parameters and initializes all instance variables to null, zero, or false. To avoid confusion, though, it's a good coding practice to code all of your own constructors. That way, it's easy to see which constructors are available to a class, and it's easy to check the values that each constructor uses to initialize the instance variables.

The syntax for coding constructors

```
public ClassName(parameters){
   statements to initialize instance variables
   other initializing statements (optional)
}
```

The syntax for coding parameters

```
([dataType paramName[, dataType paramName]...])
```

Example 1: A constructor without any parameters

```
public Book(){
   code = "";
   title = "";
   price = 0.0;
}
```

Example 2: A constructor with three parameters

```
public Book(String bookCode, String bookTitle, double bookPrice){
   code = bookCode;
   title = bookTitle;
   price = bookPrice;
}
```

Example 3: A constructor with one parameter

```
public Book(String bookCode){
   code = bookCode;
   setTitle(bookCode);
   setPrice(bookCode);
}
```

Description

- The constructor must use the same name and capitalization as the name of the class, and it must always use the *public* access modifier.
- If you don't code a constructor, Java will create a default constructor that initializes all objects to null, all numeric types to zero, and all boolean types to false.
- To code a constructor that has *parameters*, code a data type and name for each parameter within the parentheses that follow the class name. A data type can be a primitive type or the name of a class. If you code more than one parameter, use commas to separate them.
- The name of the class combined with the parameter list form the *signature* of the constructor. Although you can code more than one constructor per class, each constructor must have a unique signature.

Figure 4-5 How to code constructors

How to code methods

Figure 4-6 shows how to code the methods of a class. To start, this figure shows the syntax for coding a method. Then, this figure shows four methods that could be included in the Book class.

When you code a method, you begin by coding one of the three access modifiers. Most of the time, you'll use the *public* access modifier when declaring a method so the method can be used by other classes. After the access modifier, you code the return type for the method, which refers to the data type that the method returns. After the return type, you code the name of the method followed by any of the parameters for the method. Last, you code the opening and closing braces that contain the statements of the method.

When you code the method name and the parameters of a method, you form the *signature* of a method. If two methods have the same name but accept a different number or type of parameters, they have different signatures. As a result, they can be coded in the same class. This is known as *overloading* a method, which is similar to overloading a constructor.

Since a method name should describe the action that the method performs, it's a common coding practice to start each method name with a verb. Methods that set the value of an instance variable usually begin with *set* and are referred to as *set methods*. Conversely, methods that return the value of an instance variable usually begin with *get* and are referred to as *get methods*.

The first two examples show two ways to code the setTitle method that sets the value of an instance variable named title. In the first example, the method doesn't accept parameters and it doesn't return any values. To do that, it uses the *void* keyword for the return type and it ends with a set of empty parentheses. In the second example, however, the method accepts a String object as a parameter. Then, it uses this parameter to set the instance variable named title.

The third and fourth examples show how to code methods that return data. In the third example, the getTitle method returns the value of the instance variable named title. This method uses a return statement to return the String object that's referred to by the instance variable named title. In the fourth example, the getPrice method returns the value of the instance variable named price, which is a double type.

At this point, you should understand the code for the Book class in figure 4-3. As you can see, the constructor requires one parameter (bookCode) and uses its setTitle and setPrice methods to set the title and price for an object based on that code. The last three methods let other classes get the code, title, and price of a Book object.

The syntax for coding a method

```
public|private|protected returnType methodName(parameters){
    statements
}
```

Example 1: A set method with no parameters

```
public void setTitle(){
    if (code.equalsIgnoreCase("WARP"))
        title = "War and Peace";
    else if (code.equalsIgnoreCase("MBDK"))
        title = "Moby Dick";
    else
        title = "Not Found";
}
```

Example 2: A set method with one parameter

```
public void setTitle(String bookCode){
    if (bookCode.equalsIgnoreCase("WARP"))
        title = "War and Peace";
    else if (bookCode.equalsIgnoreCase("MBDK"))
        title = "Moby Dick";
    else
        title = "Not Found";
}
```

Example 3: A get method that returns a String object

```
public String getTitle(){
    return title;
}
```

Example 4: A get method that returns a double type

```
public double getPrice(){
    return price;
}
```

Description

- To allow other classes to access a method, use the *public* access modifier. To prevent other classes from accessing a method, use the *private* modifier. In the next chapter, you'll learn how to use the *protected* modifier.
- To code a method that doesn't return data, use the *void* keyword for the return type. To code a method that returns data, code a return type in the method declaration and code a return statement in the body of the method as shown in the third and fourth examples.
- When you name a method, you should start each name with a verb. It's a common coding practice to use the verb *set* for methods that set the values of instance variables and to use the verb *get* for methods that return the values of instance variables.
- The name of the method combined with the parameters form the *signature* of the method. Although you can use the same name for more than one method, each method must have a unique signature.

Figure 4-6 How to code methods

How to create an object from a class

Now that you understand the code of the Book class, you're ready to create Book objects from this class and use its methods. First, you'll learn how to code a class named BookApp that creates Book objects from the Book class. Then, you'll learn how to call methods from those objects.

The code of the BookApp class

Figure 4-7 presents the code of the BookApp class. This class contains the main method for the application that creates an object from the Book class. This is often referred to as the *driver class* or *controller class* of an object-oriented application.

To make it easy to tell which class contains the main method that starts an application, it's a common naming convention to add a suffix to this class. In this book, we use "App" as the suffix for the class that's used to start the application.

When coding classes, it's a good coding practice to separate the graphical user interface from the rest of the program. For now, that means that the code that displays dialog boxes should be stored in the BookApp class, not in the Book class. Later in this book, you'll learn how to code classes that define a more complete graphical user interface.

In this figure, the code that uses the Book class is shaded. The first piece of shaded code creates a new Book object named book. Since the Java compiler is case-sensitive, it's OK to use the same name as the class to name the object as long as you use a lowercase letter to start the name of the object. The next two pieces of shaded code call the getTitle and getPrice methods of the Book object. For now, don't worry if you don't understand this code. The next two figures will explain it in more detail.

The BookApp class

```
import javax.swing.JOptionPane;

public class BookApp{
   public static void main(String args[]){
      String choice = "";
      while (!(choice.equalsIgnoreCase("x"))){
         String code = JOptionPane.showInputDialog(
            "Enter a book code:");
         Book book = new Book(code);
         String message = "You have selected:\n"
                        + "   Title: " + book.getTitle() + "\n"
                        + "   Price: " + book.getPrice() + "\n\n"
                        + "Press Enter to continue or enter 'x' to exit:";
         choice = JOptionPane.showInputDialog(null,
            message, "Book", JOptionPane.PLAIN_MESSAGE);
      }//end while
      System.exit(0);
   }
}
```

The dialog boxes that are displayed by the BookApp class

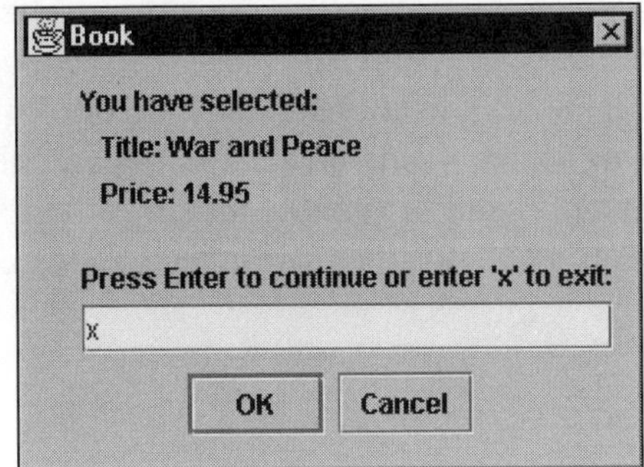

Description

- The class that contains the main method of an application can be called the *driver* or *controller class*. It's a common naming convention to use a suffix such as "App" to identify this class.
- The BookApp class above contains all of the code that provides the user interface of the application. It creates an object from the Book class and calls two methods from that object.
- For now, you should store both the BookApp class and the Book class in the same directory. That way, the Java compiler will let these classes communicate with each other. Later in this chapter, you'll learn how to let user-defined classes communicate with each other even when they're stored in different directories.

Figure 4-7 The code of the BookApp class

How to create an object

Figure 4-8 shows how to create an object with one and with two statements. Most of the time, you'll use the one-line statement to create objects. However, as you'll see later in this book, certain types of coding situations require you to create an object with two statements.

When you use two statements to create an object, the first statement declares the class and the name of the object. However, an *instance* of the object isn't actually created until the second statement is executed. This statement uses the *new* keyword to call the constructor for the object, which initializes the instance variables.

When you send arguments to the constructor of a class, you must make sure that the constructor will be able to accept the arguments. To do that, you must send the right number of arguments, in the right sequence, and with data types that match the data types specified in the parameter list of the constructor. When a class contains more than one constructor, the constructor that matches the arguments that are sent is the constructor that will be executed.

The two-statement example in this figure creates a new Book object without sending any arguments to the Book class. The same task is accomplished by the first one-statement example. Then, the second and third examples show how to send a single argument to the constructor of the Book class. Both of these statements send a String object, but the second example sends a literal while the third example sends a variable that refers to a String object. In contrast, the fourth example sends three arguments to the constructor.

How to create an object in two statements

Syntax

```
ClassName objectName;
objectName = new ClassName(optionalArgumentList);
```

Example 1: No arguments

```
Book book;
book = new Book();
```

How to create an object in one statement

Syntax

```
ClassName objectName = new ClassName(optionalArgumentList);
```

Example 1: No arguments

```
Book book = new Book();
```

Example 2: One literal argument

```
Book book = new Book("WARP");
```

Example 3: One variable argument

```
Book book = new Book(code);
```

Example 4: Three arguments

```
Book book = new Book(code, title, price);
```

Description

- To create an object, you use the *new* keyword to create a new *instance* of a class. Each time the new keyword creates an object, Java calls the constructor for the object, which initializes the instance variables for the object.
- To send arguments to the constructor, code the arguments between the parentheses after the class name. You don't need to specify the types, though, because this has already been done by the parameter list of the constructor.
- When you send arguments to the constructor, the arguments must be in the sequence and with the data types called for by the constructor.

Figure 4-8 How to create an object

How to call the methods of an object

Figure 4-9 shows how to call methods from a Book object. By now, you should be familiar with the basic syntax for calling a method, so this figure should just be review. To start, you type the object name followed by the dot operator and the method name. Then, if the method requires arguments, you can code the argument list between the parentheses, separating multiple arguments with commas. Otherwise, you code an empty set of parentheses.

The first two examples show two ways to call set methods that don't return any data. The first example doesn't send an argument, while the second example sends an argument named bookCode. In this case, the argument is a variable that represents a String object, but the argument could also be a literal value like "WARP". Either way, you need to send the right number of arguments, and you need to match the data types of the arguments with the data types specified in the parameter list of the method.

The third and fourth examples show how to return a value and assign that value to a variable. In the third example, the getPrice method doesn't have any arguments, but it does return a value and assign that value to a double variable named price. In the fourth example, the getPrice method sends a String object as an argument, returns a value, and assigns that value to the double variable named price. Although both methods return a double variable, methods can also return other data types and objects.

The fifth example shows how to call a method from the middle of a statement. Here, the statement calls the getTitle method to return a String object and uses the plus sign to join this String object with string literals that include escape sequences. This shows that a method call doesn't have to come at the end of a statement.

The syntax for calling a method

```
objectName.methodName(optionalArgumentList)
```

Examples of calling a method

Example 1: Sends no arguments and returns no value

```
book.setTitle();
```

Example 2: Sends one argument and returns no value

```
book.setTitle(bookCode);
```

Example 3: Sends no arguments and returns a double value

```
double price = book.getPrice();
```

Example 4: Sends an argument and returns a double value

```
double price = book.getPrice(bookCode);
```

Example 5: A method call within a statement

```
String message = "Title: " + book.getTitle() + "\n\n"
               + "Press Enter to continue or enter 'x' to exit:";
```

Description

- To call a method that doesn't accept arguments, type an empty set of parentheses after the method name.
- To call a method that accepts arguments, enter the arguments between the parentheses that come after the method name. Here, the data type of each argument must match the data type that's specified by the method's parameters.
- To code more than one argument, type a comma between each argument.
- If a method returns a value, you can code an assignment statement to assign the return value to a variable. Here, the data type of the return value must match the data type of the variable that's used in the assignment statement.

Figure 4-9 How to call the methods of an object

The object-oriented code of the Book Order application

In chapter 3, you reviewed the code for a Book Order application that allowed the user to enter a book code and order quantity. Now, you'll see an object-oriented version of that application. It consists of a driver class, the Book class that you've just learned about, and a new class named BookOrder. This class uses a Book object as an instance variable.

The code of the BookOrder class

Figure 4-10 shows the code of the BookOrder class. To start, it defines three instance variables. The first instance variable is an object of the Book class; the second one is an int type that stores the number of books ordered; and the third one is a double type that stores the total for the order.

The constructor of the BookOrder class initializes the three instance variables. The first statement uses the new keyword to pass the bookCode parameter to the constructor for the Book class. This creates an instance of the Book object. Since this code calls the Book constructor from within the BookOrder constructor, creating a BookOrder object also creates a Book object. Then, the second statement assigns the orderQuantity parameter to the quantity instance variable. And the third statement calls the setTotal method, which sets the value of the third instance variable.

As you can see, the setTotal method doesn't have any parameters and it doesn't return any values. However, it calculates the total for the order by multiplying the quantity instance variable by the price that's stored in the Book object. To get the price, it uses the getPrice method of the Book object.

The getBook, getQuantity, and getTotal methods return the values of the instance variables named book, quantity, and total. Since the getBook method returns a Book object, you can get more information on this instance variable by using methods from the Book class. (Incidentally, these methods aren't used by the BookOrderApp class in figure 4-11.)

The toString method returns a String object that presents all of the data for a book order. The first statement in this method creates a NumberFormat object that has the standard currency format, and the second statement creates the String object that presents the data. To do that, it calls methods from the Book object, and it uses the NumberFormat object to format the numbers. For the price variable, the method call that returns the price value is nested within the method call that formats the price value. The last statement in this method uses the return statement to return the String object.

When you write a class like this that uses another class, you don't need to know how the code in the other class works. You just need to know what the name of the class is, what arguments its constructors require, what the names of its methods are, what the methods do, and what arguments they require. Everything else is encapsulated in the other class so you don't need to worry about it.

The BookOrder class

```
import java.text.*;

public class BookOrder{
   private Book book;
   private int quantity;
   private double total;

   public BookOrder(String bookCode, int orderQuantity){
      book = new Book(bookCode);
      quantity = orderQuantity;
      setTotal();
   }

   public void setTotal(){
      total = quantity * book.getPrice();
   }

   public Book getBook(){
      return book;
   }

   public int getQuantity(){
      return quantity;
   }

   public double getTotal(){
      return total;
   }

   public String toString(){
      NumberFormat currency = NumberFormat.getCurrencyInstance();
      String orderString = "Code: " + book.getCode() + "\n"
                         + "Title: " + book.getTitle() + "\n"
                         + "Price: " + currency.format(book.getPrice()) + "\n"
                         + "Quantity: " + quantity + "\n"
                         + "Total: " + currency.format(total) + "\n";
      return orderString;
   }
}
```

Description

- The BookOrder class defines three instance variables. The first one is an instance of the Book class. In other words, the BookOrder class uses the Book class.
- The constructor of the BookOrder class requires two parameters: a book code and an order quantity. This constructor uses these parameters to initialize the three instance variables.
- The BookOrder class provides five methods. The setTotal method sets the order total by multiplying quantity times book price, and it is used by the constructor. The getBook method returns the current Book object, the getQuantity method returns the current quantity, and the getTotal method returns the current total. The toString method returns a string that provides all of the information for the order.

Figure 4-10 The code of the BookOrder class

The code of the BookOrderApp class

Figure 4-11 shows the code for the BookOrderApp class. This is the driver class of the application, and it contains two methods. The first method is the main method that displays the dialog boxes of the application and creates the BookOrder object. The second method parses the quantity that's entered by the user and makes sure that it is valid just like the method in the last chapter.

The main method in this figure is similar to the other ones that you've seen. However, if the user clicks on the Cancel button in one of the dialog boxes, a NullPointerException may be thrown. As a result, the main method includes a try/catch statement to catch this exception if it occurs and exit properly.

After the main method gets the user entries and calls the parseQuantity method, it creates an object from the BookOrder class by passing the book code and order quantity to its constructor. This automatically calculates the total for the BookOrder object. Next, the main method displays a dialog box that shows the book order that the user has entered. To do that, it calls the toString method from the BookOrder object, which returns the String object that describes the book order. Then, it joins this string with some additional text.

Here again, when you write the driver class, you don't need to know how the code in any class that it uses works. You just need to know what the name of the class is, what arguments its constructors require, what the names of its methods are, what the methods do, and what arguments they require. Everything else is encapsulated in the other class so you don't have to worry about it.

The benefits and shortcomings of object-oriented programming

This simple application illustrates some of the benefits of object-oriented programming. First, it lets you divide a large application into smaller classes so the project becomes more manageable. Second, it lets you create classes that can be used by more than one program. Third, it lets you use classes that were created by others. And fourth, it lets you change the way a method works without having to change the classes that use the method.

On the other hand, object-oriented programming also has some shortcomings. First, it requires more code in the form of instance variables, constructors, and the like. Second, it adds to the complexity of an application because you have to document or remember what the constructors require, what the methods require, and so on. You also have to pass variables to the constructors and methods, and use the values and objects that are returned.

The theory, of course, is that the benefits of object-oriented programming far outweigh the shortcomings. To get the full value of the benefits, though, you need to take full advantage of the hundreds of classes that Java provides, and you need to do a good job of designing your own classes. So in chapter 5, you'll learn more about using Java classes, and in chapter 6, you'll learn how to design object-oriented programs of your own.

The BookOrderApp class

```
import javax.swing.JOptionPane;

public class BookOrderApp{
   public static void main(String[] args){
      String choice = "";
      try{
         while (!(choice.equalsIgnoreCase("x"))){
            String code = JOptionPane.showInputDialog(
               "Enter a book code:");
            String inputQuantity = JOptionPane.showInputDialog(
               "Enter a quantity:");
            int quantity = parseQuantity(inputQuantity);
            BookOrder bookOrder = new BookOrder(code, quantity);
            String message = bookOrder.toString() + "\n"
                           + "Press Enter to continue or enter 'x' to exit:";
            choice = JOptionPane.showInputDialog(null,
               message, "Book Order", JOptionPane.PLAIN_MESSAGE);
         }//end while
      catch(NullPointerException e){
         System.exit(0);
      }
      System.exit(0);
   }

   private static int parseQuantity(String quantityString){
      int quantity = 0;
      boolean tryAgain = true;
      while(tryAgain){
         try{
            quantity = Integer.parseInt(quantityString);
            while (quantity <= 0){
               quantityString = JOptionPane.showInputDialog(
                     "Invalid order total. \n"
                  + "Please enter a positive number: ");
                quantity = Integer.parseInt(quantityString);
            }
            tryAgain = false;
         }
         catch(NumberFormatException e){
            quantityString = JOptionPane.showInputDialog(
               "Invalid quantity. \n"
             + "Please enter an integer.");
         }
      }
      return quantity;
   }

}
```

Description

- The BookOrderApp class contains two methods. The main method uses a while loop to display the dialog boxes and control the program. The parseQuantity method is a static method that gets a valid quantity entry from the user.

Figure 4-11 The code of the BookOrderApp class

How to create and use static fields and methods

In chapter 2, you learned how to call static methods from some of the classes in the Java API, and in the last chapter, you learned how to code static methods in the driver class. Now, you'll learn to code static methods and fields in separate classes, and how to call them from other classes.

How to create static fields and methods

Figure 4-12 shows how to code *static fields* and *static methods*. While instance variables and regular methods belong to an object that's created from a class, static fields and static methods belong to the class itself. As a result, they're sometimes called *class fields* and *class methods*.

The top of this figure shows how to code static fields. In short, you use a syntax that's similar to the syntax for a regular variable or constant. However, you use the *static* keyword so the variable or constant belongs to the class, not the object. Then, you supply an initial value for the variable or constant. Typically, the static variables of a class are declared with private access, but the static constants of a class are declared with public access. That way, other classes can access and use these constants.

The first example shows how to code a class that contains static constants. In the next figure, you'll see how you can call these constants from another class. Since this class doesn't contain any instance variables, you don't need to code a constructor for this class.

The second example shows how to code a class that contains a static method that calculates the future value of a series of payments and returns the result as a double value. Here, the method has three parameters that accept the amount of the monthly payment, the number of months, and the monthly interest rate. Then, the method uses a while loop to calculate the future value of the payments. In the last chapter, you saw this method in a driver class, but here it is in a separate class.

The third example shows how you can add a static variable and a static method to the BookOrder class. In this example, the static variable named orderObjectCount counts the number of BookOrder objects that are created from the BookOrder class. First, the variable is declared as private. That way, no other class can manipulate the variable. Then, the constructor increments the variable. Since the constructor is only called when a new instance of an object is created, the class will increment the static variable each time it creates a new object. Then, the static getOrderObjectCount method can be used to return the static orderObjectCount variable.

When you code a class that mixes regular data and methods with static data and methods, you should do your best to keep your data and methods organized. Usually, this means that you group your variables and methods by type (instance or static) and by access modifier (public, protected, or private).

How to declare static fields

```
private static int numberOfObjects = 0;
private static double majorityPercent = .51;
public static final int DAYS_IN_JANUARY = 31;
public static final float EARTH_MASS_IN_KG = 5.972e24F;
```

Example 1: A class that contains static constants

```
public class DateConstants{
   public static final int DAYS_IN_JANUARY = 31;
   public static final int DAYS_IN_FEBRUARY = 28;
   ...
}
```

Example 2: A class that contains a static method that makes a calculation

```
public class FinancialCalculations{
   public static double calculateFutureValue(double monthlyPayment,
   int months, double monthlyInterestRate){
      int i = 1;
      double futureValue = 0;
      while (i <= months) {
         futureValue = (futureValue + monthlyPayment) *
         (1 + monthlyInterestRate);
         i++;
      }
      return futureValue;
   }
}
```

Example 3: A class that contains a static variable and a static method

```
public class BookOrder{
   private Book book;
   private int quantity;
   private double total;
   private static int orderObjectCount = 0;

   public BookOrder(String bookCode, int orderQuantity){
      book = new Book(bookCode);
      quantity = orderQuantity;
      setTotal();
      orderObjectCount++;
   }
   public static int getOrderObjectCount(){
      return orderObjectCount;
   }
   ...
```

Description

- You can use the *static* keyword to code *static variables* and *static methods*. Since static variables and static methods belong to the class, not an object created from the class, they are sometimes called *class variables* and *class methods*.
- When you code a static method, you can only use static variables and variables that are defined in the class. You can't use instance variables in a static method because they belong to an instance of the class, not to the class as a whole.

Figure 4-12 How to create static fields and methods

How to call static fields and methods

Figure 4-13 shows how to call static fields and methods. To start, this figure shows how to call static constants...the most common type of static field. Then, this figure shows how to call static methods. As you would expect, you use the same syntax that you use to call static fields and methods from the Java classes. That is, you code the class name, dot operator, and field or method name.

If you look at the first example of calling a static method from a user-defined class, you can see how this works with the class that's shown in the second example of the previous figure. Here, the class name is FinancialCalculations and the method name is calculateFutureValue. Since the method has three parameters, the call statement sends three arguments. Then, the method returns the future value that's derived from those arguments.

The syntax for calling a static field or method

```
ClassName.fieldName
ClassName.methodName(optionalArgumentList)
```

How to call static fields

From the Java API

```
Math.PI
Math.E
JOptionPane.INFORMATION_MESSAGE
JOptionPane.PLAIN_MESSAGE
```

From a user-defined class

```
DateConstants.DAYS_IN_JANUARY
```

How to call static methods

From Java classes

```
String inputQuantity = JOptionPane.showInputDialog("Enter a quantity:");
int quantity = Integer.parseInt(inputQuantity);
```

From user-defined classes

```
double futureValue =
   FinancialCalculations.calculateFutureValue(
      monthlyPayment, months, monthlyInterestRate);
int orderCount = BookOrder.getOrderObjectCount();
```

Description

- To call a static field or method, type the name of the class, followed by the dot operator, followed by the name of the static field or method. If you call a static method, you need to include the parentheses after the method name and any arguments that the method requires.

Figure 4-13 How to call static fields and methods

How to code a static initialization block

When it takes more than one statement to initialize a static field, you can use a *static initialization block* to initialize the field as shown in figure 4-14. To start, you just code the static keyword followed by braces. Then, you code the statements of the block within the braces. Later, when a method of the class is called for the first time, all of the statements in the static initialization block are executed.

In the example in this figure, the BookDB class contains a static initialization block that executes several statements that initialize the static Connection object, which is used by the other static methods in the class. Since a static initialization block runs as soon as any method of the class is called, this ensures that the Connection object will be available to the rest of the methods in the class.

When to use static fields and methods

Now that you know how to code static fields and methods, you may wonder when to use them and when to use regular fields and methods. In general, when you need to create multiple objects from a class, you should use regular classes and methods. That way, you can create several objects from a class, and each object has its own data in its own instance variables. Then, you can use the methods of each object to process that data.

In contrast, if you just need to perform a single task like a calculation, you can use a static method. Then, you send the method the arguments it needs, and it returns the result that you need without ever creating an object. As you progress through this book, you'll see many examples that will give you a better idea of when static fields and methods are appropriate.

The syntax for coding a static initialization block

```
public class ClassName{
   any field declarations

   static{
      any initialization statements
   }

   the rest of the class
```

A class that uses a static initialization block

```
public class BookDB{
   private static Connection connection;          // static variable

   // the static initialization block
   static{
      try{
         Class.forName("sun.jdbc.odbc.JdbcOdbcDriver");
         String url = "jdbc:odbc:MurachBooks";
         String user = "Admin";
         String password = "";
         connection = DriverManager.getConnection(url, user, password);
      }
      catch (ClassNotFoundException e){
         System.err.println("Driver not found.");
      }
      catch (SQLException e){
         System.err.println("Error connecting to database.");
      }
   }

   // other static methods that use the Connection object
   public static void close(){}
   public static void addRecord(Book book){}
   public static void updateRecord(Book book){}
   public static void deleteRecord(String bookCode){}
   public static Book findOnCode(String bookCode){}
}
```

Description

- To initialize the static variables of a class, you typically code the values in the declarations. If, however, a variable can't be initialized in a single statement, you can code a *static initialization block* that's executed when another class first calls any method of the class.
- When a method of a class is first called by an application, Java initializes all static variables and constants of the class. Then, it executes all static initialization blocks in the order in which they appear.

Figure 4-14 How to code a static initialization block

How to work with packages

In chapter 2, you learned how the Java API uses packages to organize its classes. Now, you'll learn how to use packages to organize your own classes. Then, you'll learn how to make the classes in these packages available to other classes.

How to create and compile packages

Figure 4-15 shows how to create and compile packages. To start, this figure shows a procedure that you can use to create and compile a package. Then, the figure shows some of the details that you need to work with the procedure.

When you name a package, you can use any name you wish, but Sun recommends that you use your Internet domain name in reverse as a prefix. That way, you can be sure that your package will have a unique name. Even if you don't follow this convention, you should avoid using a generic name that might be used by someone else. For example, the name java.text is already used by the Java API.

When you want to include a class as part of a package, you should code a *package statement* as the first statement in the class. To do that, you type the *package* keyword followed by the name of the package as shown in this figure. Although you can code comments before this statement, the package statement must be the first statement in the class.

To keep your packages organized, you should create a subdirectory for each package that corresponds to the package name. Then, you should store all of the *.java and *.class files for each class in the package in that subdirectory. In other words, the pathname of the *.java and *.class files is the same as the name of the package.

When you read step 5 in the procedure for creating and compiling a package, you can see that a single javac command will compile related classes. For instance, compiling BookOrder.java will also compile Book.java because the Book class is used by the BookOrder class. Although this works okay when you're compiling packages, you shouldn't depend on this feature as you're developing the classes. Instead, you should compile each class as you create it to make sure that it doesn't contain syntax errors.

If you're using TextPad, you may have trouble compiling classes that have package statements. To prevent any errors, you can compile classes with a package statement directly in the DOS window, as shown in the figure.

How to create and compile a package

1. Create a subdirectory for the package. If possible, use the naming conventions shown below for the subdirectory path.
2. Move all *.java files that you want to include in the package to this subdirectory.
3. Add a package statement that identifies the name of the package to the beginning of each *.java file. The package name used in this statement must match the subdirectory name that contains the class.
4. Start the command prompt and navigate to the root directory for your application.
5. Use a javac command like the one shown below to compile the classes. Notice how the subdirectory path is included in this command. If the classes depend on each other, this command should compile all of the classes.

Examples of package names

Internet domain	Package name	Subdirectory path
java.sun.com	com.sun.java.text	\com\sun\java\text
murach.com	com.murach.orders	\com\murach\orders

How to code a package statement

```
package com.murach.orders;
```

How to compile the package

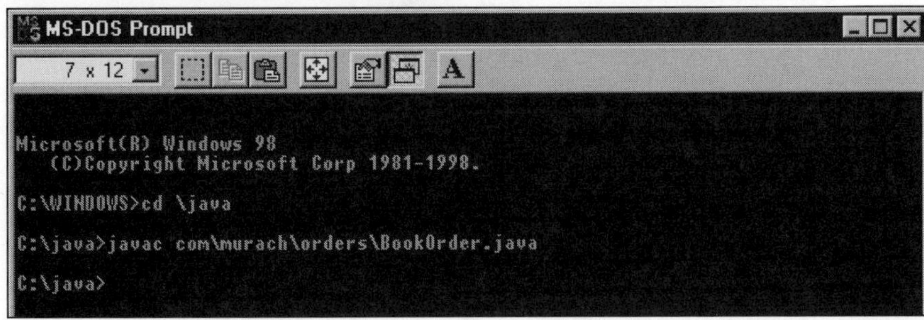

Description

- To ensure that each package name is unique, Sun recommends that all companies preface their package names with a reversed Internet domain name.
- To make the classes in your packages easy to find and manage, you should save all files in the package in a subdirectory with a path that matches the name of the package.
- The *package statement* must be the first statement in the class.

Figure 4-15 How to create and compile packages

How to make packages available to other classes

When you compile a class that contains a package statement, the class becomes a part of a package and classes outside the package can't access it. To make a class within a package available to other classes, though, you can follow the procedure shown in figure 4-16. Then, you can use an import statement to import one or more classes from the package.

To allow other classes to access a class that's stored in a package, you can create a Java Archive (JAR) file that contains the *.class file for the class or classes. When you do this, you must add the *.class files with the subdirectory matching the package name. In other words, you can't just add the *.class files. Then, you must move this JAR file to the \jre\lib\ext directory of your SDK. Alternatively, you can put this file in the \lib\classes directory of your SDK. If this directory doesn't exist, you can create it.

To work with JAR files, you start the command prompt and navigate to the root directory that holds the classes you want to work with. Then, you can use a jar command like the one shown in this figure to create a JAR file for all of the *.class files in that directory. If this command is successful, the command prompt will display some information about the classes that are included in the file as shown in this figure.

How to make a package available to any class in your program

1. Start the command prompt and navigate to the root directory that holds your classes.
2. Use the jar command to create a JAR file for the *.class file or files as shown below.
3. Move the JAR file to the c:\jdk1.3.1\jre\lib\ext directory (where c:\jdk1.3.1 is the directory that stores the SDK).

The syntax for creating a JAR file for a package

```
c:\anydirectory>jar cvf JARFilename.jar classDirectory\*.class
```

Example

```
c:\java>jar cvf orders.jar com\murach\orders\*.class
```

Result

```
C:\java>jar cvf orders.jar com\murach\orders\*.class
added manifest
adding: com/murach/orders/Book.class(in = 716) (out= 459)(deflated 35%)
adding: com/murach/orders/BookOrder.class(in = 1100) (out= 624)(deflated 43%)
```

How to import the package created above

```
import com.murach.orders.*;
```

Description

- When you compile a class that contains a package statement, the class becomes part of a package and classes outside the package can't access it.
- To allow other classes to access a class that's in a package, you must create a Java Archive (JAR) file for it and move the JAR file to the ext directory of the SDK.
- To import any classes that are stored in a jar file in the ext directory, you code an import statement like the one shown above.

Figure 4-16 How to make packages available to other classes

How to use javadoc to document a class

Now that you know how to create your own classes, you're ready to learn how to use the javadoc tool that comes with the SDK to generate the documentation for your classes. This tool allows you to create documentation for your classes that other programmers can use to learn about the fields, constructors, and methods that are available to other classes. This also gives you another way of looking at the classes that you have created.

How to add javadoc comments to a class

Figure 4-17 shows how to add simple *javadoc comments* to a class. In particular, it shows how to code javadoc comments that describe the class and its constructors and methods. For these comments to work, they must be coded directly above the declaration of the class, constructor, or method that they describe.

When you code javadoc comments, it's a common convention to use the *HTML tags* shown in this figure to identify the names of classes. Here, for example, these tags are used to identify the Book and BookOrder classes. In addition to these tags, there are other HTML and javadoc tags that you can use when you need to create more complete documentation for a class. That, however, is beyond the scope of this book. For now, you can use simple javadoc comments like the ones shown in this figure to document your classes.

The Book class with javadoc comments

```
/**********************************************************
 * The <code>Book</code> class represents a book and is used
 * by the <code>BookOrder</code> class.
 **********************************************************/
public class Book{
   private String code;
   private String title;
   private double price;
/***********************************************************
 * Constructs a Book object from a book code.
 ***********************************************************/
   public Book(String bookCode){
      code = bookCode;
      setTitle(bookCode);
      setPrice(bookCode);
   }
/***********************************************************
 * Sets the title of a Book object depending
 * on the book code.
 ***********************************************************/
   public void setTitle(String bookCode){
      if (bookCode.equalsIgnoreCase("WARP"))
         title = "War and Peace";
      else if (bookCode.equalsIgnoreCase("MBDK")){
         title = "Moby Dick";
      else
         title = "Not Found";
   }
/***********************************************************
 * Sets the price of a Book object depending
 * on the book code.
 ***********************************************************/
   public void setPrice(String bookCode){
      if (bookCode.equalsIgnoreCase("WARP"))
         price = 14.95;
      else if (bookCode.equalsIgnoreCase("MBDK")){
         price = 12.95;
      else
         price = 0.0;
   }
```

HTML tags	Description
`<code></code>`	Displays all text between these tags with a special font.

Description

- A *javadoc comment* begins with /** and ends with */, and asterisks within the comment are ignored. You can use javadoc comments to describe the constructors and methods of a class as shown above.
- Within a javadoc comment, you can code *HTML tags* like the one above to identify the names of classes. You can also use other types of tags for more complete documentation.

Figure 4-17 How to add javadoc comments to a class

How to generate the documentation for a class

Figure 4-18 shows how to use the *javadoc tool* to generate the documentation for a class. To start, you can create a directory to store the documentation. Then, you issue a *javadoc command*. When you successfully execute the javadoc command, it generates the HTML pages for the documentation.

When you develop an application that consists of many packages and classes, you can't always use a simple javadoc command like the one shown in this figure. That's why the javadoc command provides more options than the ones shown here. But that too is beyond the scope of this book. For now, you can generate the documentation for all of the classes in a directory as shown in this figure.

How to view the documentation for a class

You can use a web browser to view the documentation for user-defined classes the same way that you view the documentation for the API. The main difference is that the index.html file for user-defined classes will be stored in a different directory. In this figure, for example, it's stored in the c:\java\docs directory.

When you view the documentation for a user-defined class, you can see the constructors and methods that are available for the class. In this figure, for example, the browser shows the constructors and methods for the Book class. This lets you focus on the constructor and method declarations of the class without worrying about the details that are encapsulated within the class.

How to generate the API documentation for a class

Syntax

```
c:\programDirectory>javadoc -d documentationDirectory listOfClassNames
```

Examples

```
c:\java\com\murach\orders>javadoc -d c:\java\docs Book.java
c:\java\com\murach\orders>javadoc -d c:\java\docs Book.java BookOrder.java
c:\java\com\murach\orders>javadoc -d c:\java\docs *.java
```

The documentation that's generated for the Book class

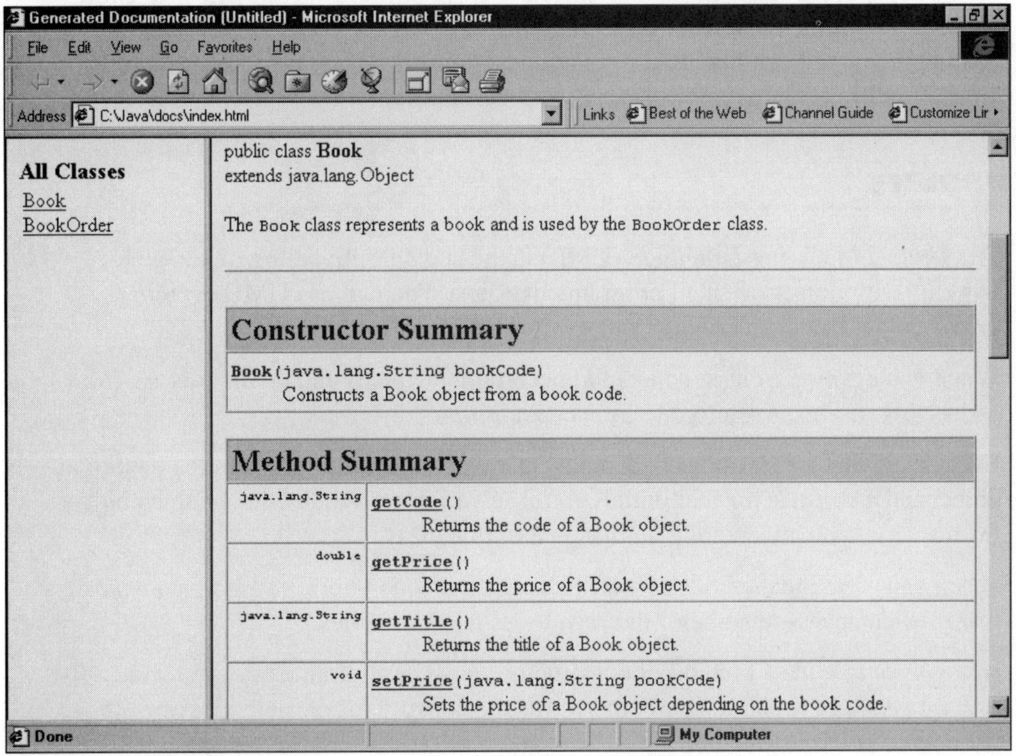

Description

- To use the *javadoc tool* to generate the API documentation for a class, create a directory for the documentation like c:\java\docs. Next, use the command prompt to change the directory to the one that stores the classes that you want to document. Then, enter a *javadoc command* as shown above. This generates the HTML pages for the documentation.
- To view the documentation that's generated by the javadoc tool, start your web browser and point to the index.html file in the directory that stores the documentation.

Figure 4-18 How to generate and view the documentation for a class

Perspective

Now that you've finished this chapter, you should be able to code classes that define objects such as the Book and BookOrder classes. You should be able to use these objects and their methods within an application. You should be able to create and use classes that contain static fields and methods. And you should be able to package and document your classes and methods. These are some of the critical skills of object-oriented programming.

In the next chapter, though, you'll learn some programming skills that expand on the skills that you've learned in this chapter. In particular, chapter 5 will show you how to get the most from the classes that are part of the Java API. Then, in chapter 6, you'll learn how to design and test your own classes, which is another critical skill for effective object-oriented programming.

Summary

- The *Unified Modeling Language* (UML) is the standard modeling language for working with object-oriented programs like Java. You can use UML *class diagrams* to identify the *attributes* and *operations* of a class.
- When you develop a class, you can *hide* certain attributes and coding details from other classes. This is referred to as *encapsulation.*
- Every class that creates objects contains *instance variables* that store the data of an object and a *constructor* that initializes those variables. When you create an object from a class, you are creating an *instance* of that class.
- When you code the methods of a class, you often code public *set* and *get methods* that provide access to some of the private instance variables.
- If you want to code a method or constructor that accepts arguments, you code a list of *parameters* between the parentheses for the constructor or method. For each parameter, you must include a data type and a name.
- The name of a method or constructor combined with the list of parameters is known as the *signature* of the method or constructor. You can *overload* a method or constructor by coding different parameter lists for the same name.
- When you use the *static fields, static methods,* and *static initialization blocks* of a class, you don't create an object from the class. Instead, you call these fields and methods directly from the class.
- You can organize the classes in your application by using a *package statement* to add them to a package. Then, you can use import statements to make the classes in that package available to other classes.
- You can use *javadoc comments* to document a class, its constructors, and its methods. Then, you can use the *javadoc command* to generate HTML-based documentation for your class.

Terms

object-oriented programming (OOP)
Unified Modeling Language (UML)
class diagram
attribute
operation
encapsulation
data hiding
object diagram
identity
state
instance variable
constructor
method
parameter
signature
overloading
set method
get method
driver class
controller class
instance
static field
static method
class field
class method
static initialization block
package statement
javadoc comment
HTML tag
javadoc tool
javadoc command

Objectives

- Describe the concept of encapsulation and explain its importance to object-oriented programming.
- Describe a signature of a constructor or method, and explain what overloading means.
- Code the instance variables, constructors, and methods of a class that defines an object.
- Code a class that creates objects from a user-defined class and then uses the methods of the objects to accomplish the required tasks.
- Code a class that contains static fields and methods, and call these fields and methods from other classes.
- Add two or more classes to a package and make the classes in that package available to other classes.
- Code javadoc comments for a class, and generate the documentation for the class. Then, use your web browser to view that documentation.

Notification of a TextPad bug

If you're using TextPad to do the exercises, you may find that your programs don't end the way they're expected to by returning to the console with the "Press any key to continue" message. Instead, a command prompt is displayed followed by this message: "Batch file missing." In some cases, the program will also restart. Then, you can press Ctrl+C or end the program again to get past this bug.

We've found that this is a TextPad bug that deals with programs that take longer than one minute to run. We just treat this bug as a minor flaw in an otherwise excellent product, and we hope you'll see it that way too.

Exercise 4-1 Test the object-oriented Book Order application

This exercise guides you through the process of testing the object-oriented version of the Book Order application that is presented in this chapter. It consists of three classes: Book, BookOrder, and BookOrderApp.

1. Open the Book, BookOrder, and BookOrderApp classes that you should find in the c:\java\ch04 directory. If you would like to print out and review the code in these classes, print each one.
2. Compile all three classes. Then, run the BookOrderApp class, which is the driver class for this application. When you enter data to test it, this application should work the way it did in the last chapter. But note how much more code the three classes require.
3. Modify the Book class so it provides for one more book. Its code should be "CITR", its title should be "Catcher in the Rye", and its price should be $9.95. Then, compile just this class, and test the BookOrderApp class again with the new book code. This shows that you can make a change to a class without affecting the classes that use it.
4. Add a static field and method to the BookOrder class to keep track of the number of objects that are created from the class (see example 3 in figure 4-12). Then, compile that class. Next, modify the BookOrderApp class so it uses the System.out.println method to display the count of objects when the user enters "X" to end the application. Then, compile and run that class.

Exercise 4-2 Convert the Future Value application to an object-oriented application

This exercise guides you through the process of modifying the Future Value application so it uses a class that provides a static method.

1. Open the FutureValueApp class that's in the c:\java\ch03 directory and save it with the same name in the c:\java\ch04 directory.
2. Start a new class named FinancialCalculations and save this in the c:\java\ch04 directory.
3. Move the static calculateFutureValue method from the FutureValueApp class to the FinancialCalculations class, and edit the access modifier so the method is public. When you're done, this class should look like the class shown in the second example in figure 4-12. Then, compile the class.
4. Modify the FutureValueApp class so it uses the static calculateFutureValue method that's stored in the FinancialCalculations class. Next, compile and run this class to make sure that the application still works properly. Then, close both classes.

Exercise 4-3 Convert the Invoice application to an object-oriented application

This exercise guides you through the process of modifying the Invoice application of chapters 2 and 3 so it uses an Invoice class.

1. Open the InvoiceApp class in c:\java\ch02 or the EnhancedInvoiceApp class in c:\java\ch03, and save it in c:\java\ch04.
2. Start a new class named Invoice and save it in the c:\java\ch04 directory. Then, write the code for this class so it provides all of the data and operations related to an Invoice object. Its constructor should require the order total as its only parameter, and it should initialize instance variables for order total, discount amount, and invoice total. One of its methods should be the toString method, which returns a string that contains all of the data for an invoice. As you work, you may want to move code from the InvoiceApp class to the Invoice class. When you're done, compile the Invoice class.
3. Modify the code in the InvoiceApp class so it creates and uses Invoice objects. Then, compile and test the class to make sure that it works the same way it did before. When you're satisfied that it does, close the classes.

Exercise 4-4 Package the Book and BookOrder classes

This exercise guides you through the process of adding the Book and BookOrder classes to the com.murach.orders package.

1. Create a directory named c:\java\com\murach\orders. Then, move (don't copy) the *.java and *.class files for the Book and BookOrder classes to this directory.
2. Open your text editor and add package statements to the Book and BookOrder classes as shown in figure 4-15.
3. Start the command prompt and change the current directory to c:\java. Then, use the javac command shown in figure 4-15 to compile the BookOrder class. This should compile both the Book and BookOrder classes.
4. From the command prompt, use the jar command to create a JAR file named orders.jar for the Book and BookOrder classes as shown in figure 4-16. Then, move the orders.jar file from the c:\java directory to the \jre\lib\ext directory of your SDK.
5. Open the BookOrderApp class that's stored in the c:\java\ch04 directory, and try to compile this class. You should get several compile-time errors. That's because the BookOrderApp class doesn't know how to access the com.murach.orders package.
6. Add an import statement for the com.murach.orders package as shown in figure 4-16. Then, compile and run the BookOrderApp class to make sure it works correctly.

Exercise 4-5 Document the Book class

This exercise guides you through the process of adding javadoc comments to the Book class and using the javadoc tool to generate the API documentation for the Book class.

1. Start your text editor and open the Book and BookOrder classes that are stored in the c:\java\com\murach\orders directory.
2. Add javadoc comments for the constructor and methods of these classes as shown in figure 4-17. Then, compile the classes.
3. Create a directory named c:\java\docs. Then, start your command prompt and use the javadoc tool to generate the HTML pages for the Book class as shown in figure 4-18. When you're done, these pages should be stored in the c:\java\docs directory.
4. Start your web browser, navigate to the c:\java\docs directory, and open the index.html page. Then, review your documentation.

5

How to work with inheritance and interfaces

Now that you've learned how to code classes that define objects, you're ready to learn how to work with inheritance, interfaces, and other object-oriented features of Java. Although these features are difficult conceptually, they are critical to the effective use of Java. That's why they can't be put off until later in this book.

You don't, however, have to master everything that's presented in this difficult chapter in one reading. Instead, you can focus on the concepts and terms the first time through it. Then, you can refer back to this chapter whenever you need to refresh your memory about concepts, terms, or coding details.

How to work with inheritance

Inheritance is one of the critical concepts of object-oriented programming and Java programming. It lets you create a class that inherits fields and methods from another class. These fields and methods can be referred to as members.

An introduction to inheritance

Figure 5-1 introduces you to inheritance. To use it, you create a *subclass* that inherits the public and *protected* fields and methods from a *superclass*. In addition, it inherits all superclass members that have no access modifier as long as the superclass and subclass are in the same package. Then, the objects that are created from the subclass can use these members of the superclass. In addition, though, the subclass can define its own methods. It can also define methods with the same names and signatures of methods in the superclass. In that case, the methods of the subclass *override* the methods in the superclass.

This is illustrated by the first diagram in this figure, which shows a subclass named DiscountBookOrder that inherits the BookOrder class that you were introduced to in the last chapter. Since the DiscountBookOrder class inherits all of the public methods from the BookOrder class, you can call any of those methods from an object created from the DiscountBookOrder class. In addition, though, the DiscountBookOrder class provides three new methods (setPercentOff, getSubtotal, and getPercentOff). It also provides two methods that will override the ones with the same signatures in the BookOrder class (setTotal and getTotal).

The second diagram shows part of an *inheritance hierarchy* that's taken from the Java API. Although this diagram only shows three levels of inheritance, Java provides for an unlimited number. In addition, this diagram shows that a superclass can have more than one subclass. In this case, the Window superclass has two subclasses, but here again Java provides for an unlimited number. In the Java API, for example, some classes have dozens of subclasses.

As you become more familiar with the classes of the Java API, you'll find that they make widespread use of inheritance. You'll also discover that you have to use inheritance when you create a graphical user interface for an application. In this case, a class that you create inherits the fields and methods from the Java Frame class. You'll see this illustrated in figure 5-3.

If you think you need to use inheritance as you plan the classes for an application, you should make sure that the subclass has an *is-a relationship* with its superclass. This means that the subclass *is a* type of the superclass. For instance, a discount book order *is a* type of book order, and a frame is a type of window.

Incidentally, in this book, we'll primarily use the terms *superclass* and *subclass* to refer to the classes in an inheritance hierarchy. However, a superclass can also be called a *base* or *parent class*, and a subclass can also be called a *derived* or *child class*.

How inheritance works

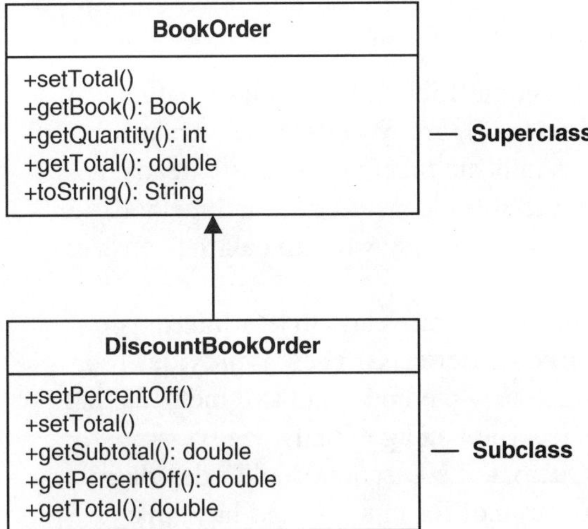

An inheritance hierarchy

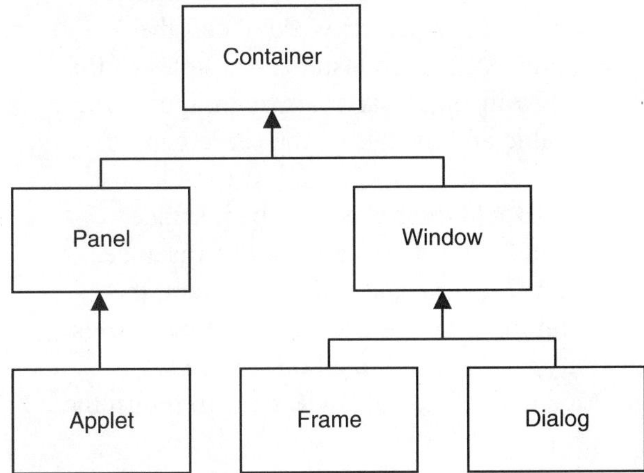

Description

- *Inheritance* lets you define a class that inherits all of the public and *protected* fields and methods of an existing class. Then, the class that inherits the fields and methods is called a *subclass*, *derived class*, or *child class*, while the class that is being inherited is called a *superclass*, *base class*, or *parent class*.
- In a subclass, you can define fields and methods that aren't in the superclass. You can also define methods that have the same names and signatures as those in the superclass. In that case, the method in the subclass *overrides* the method in the superclass.
- Inheritance is used to model an *is-a relationship*. In other words, inheritance is used when a subclass *is a* type of the superclass.
- Inheritance is commonly used in the classes that are in the Java API, so you often need to know what the *inheritance hierarchy* is as you use Java classes.

Figure 5-1 How inheritance works

How to code a class that inherits the BookOrder class

Figure 5-2 shows how to code the DiscountBookOrder subclass that inherits the BookOrder class as shown in the previous figure. Whenever you create a subclass, you use the *extends* keyword to indicate that the subclass extends the superclass. Then, you code the instance variables, constructors, and methods for the subclass. As you do that, you can use the *super* keyword to call the constructors and methods in the superclass.

If you study the code for the DiscountBookOrder class in this figure, you can see that its declaration extends the BookOrder class. Then, it provides four new instance variables, a constructor, three new methods, and two methods that will override methods in the superclass (setTotal and getTotal).

Since a subclass can't inherit constructors, the DiscountBookOrder class must define its own constructor. The constructor for this subclass has three parameters: the book code that indicates the book that's ordered; the quantity of books ordered; and a key code that indicates what (if any) discount should be taken. After the parameter list, the constructor initializes all of the variables in the superclass and the subclass. First, it uses the super keyword to call the constructor for the superclass. This initializes the three instance variables of the superclass. Then, it initializes the three new instance variables by assigning the third parameter to the discountCode variable and by calling the setPercentOff and setTotal methods.

The first two methods in the DiscountBookOrder class set the instance variables of the class. The setPercentOff method sets the percentOff instance variable based on the value of the discountCode instance variable. Then, the setTotal method sets the subtotal and total instance variables. To do that, it uses the super keyword to call the getQuantity and getBook methods of the BookOrder class, and it uses the getPrice method of the Book class to return the price.

The last three methods in the subclass are get methods that return the subtotal, percentOff, and total variables. Because they're so simple, these methods are coded in single lines instead of the expanded format that you're used to seeing.

After the code for this subclass, you can see the code for a driver class named OverrideTest that tests the DiscountBookOrder class. To do that, the driver creates a DiscountBookOrder object and uses its get methods to return the data for the object into a string variable. To return the title and price for the order, the code first calls the getBook method, which returns a Book object, then calls the getTitle and getPrice methods from that object. After all of the data has been returned to the string, the string is displayed in a dialog box.

Now that you've seen how inheritance works, you can ask whether using it makes sense in a case like this. A simple alternative, for example, is to provide for discounts in the BookOrder class itself. To do that, you could add a third parameter to the constructor and adjust the code as needed. Or, you could add a second constructor to that class with a third parameter for the key code. Either way, the coding for the book order application would be simplified.

The syntax for declaring a subclass

```
public class SubclassName extends SuperclassName{}
```

The syntax for calling superclass constructors and methods

```
super(optionalArgumentList)              // calls superclass constructor
super.methodName(optionalArgumentList)   // calls superclass method
```

Code for the DiscountBookOrder subclass

```
public class DiscountBookOrder extends BookOrder{
   private String discountCode;
   private double subtotal, percentOff, total;

   public DiscountBookOrder(String bookCode, int bookQuantity, String keyCode){
      super(bookCode, bookQuantity);
      discountCode = keyCode;
      setPercentOff();
      setTotal();
   }

   public void setPercentOff(){
      if (discountCode.equalsIgnoreCase("a10"))
         percentOff = 0.1;
      else
         percentOff = 0.0;
   }

   public void setTotal(){
      subtotal = super.getQuantity() * super.getBook().getPrice();
      total = subtotal - (subtotal * percentOff);
   }

   public double getSubtotal(){ return subtotal; }
   public double getPercentOff(){ return percentOff; }
   public double getTotal(){ return total; }
}
```

Code that uses the DiscountBookOrder class

```
import javax.swing.JOptionPane;
import java.text.*;

public class OverrideTest{
   public static void main(String[] args){
      NumberFormat currency = NumberFormat.getCurrencyInstance();
      NumberFormat percent = NumberFormat.getPercentInstance();
      DiscountBookOrder order = new DiscountBookOrder("WARP", 2, "a10");
      String test = "Title: " + order.getBook().getTitle() + "\n"
         + "Price: " + order.getBook().getPrice() + "\n"
         + "Quantity: " + order.getQuantity() + "\n"
         + "Subtotal: " + currency.format(order.getSubtotal()) + "\n"
         + "PercentOff: " + percent.format(order.getPercentOff()) + "\n"
         + "Total: " + currency.format(order.getTotal());
      JOptionPane.showMessageDialog(null, test);
      System.exit(0);
   }
}
```

Figure 5-2 How to code a class that inherits the BookOrder class

How to code a class that inherits the JFrame class

Whether or not you use inheritance with your own classes, you will need to create classes that inherit from Java classes. When you use Java to develop a graphical user interface, for example, you need to use inheritance as you define a *frame*. To do that, you typically code a class that inherits the JFrame class of the javax.swing package as shown in figure 5-3.

To use a class from the Java API, you usually need to understand its *inheritance chain*. In this figure, for example, you can see that the JFrame class inherits the Frame class, which inherits the Window class, and so on. As a result, a subclass of the JFrame class can call any of the methods from any of the six classes shown in this figure.

The code in this figure shows the code for a BookOrderFrame class. To start, this class inherits the JFrame class. Then, the constructor calls two methods that set some of the properties of this class. Here, the first method sets the title of the frame while the second method sets the size and position of the frame. Although you call these methods from the BookOrderFrame class, they're actually stored in the Frame and Component classes.

Last, this class contains a main method that creates a BookOrderFrame object and calls the show method to display the object. Since the BookOrderFrame object *is a* JFrame object, you can use a BookOrderFrame object anywhere a JFrame object is expected. For instance, the code in this figure uses a JFrame type to store a reference to a BookOrderFrame object.

The frame that's displayed by this code is shown at the bottom of this figure. As you can see, it has a title and a size, but not much more. In fact, if you click on its close button, it won't even close properly. Later in this chapter, though, you'll learn how to add code that will close the frame.

What you should know about polymorphism

When an object calls an overridden method in an inheritance chain, Java uses *polymorphism* to decide which method it should call. In a Book Order application, for example, you can declare a variable of the BookOrder type. Then, if the user enters a key code, you can create that object as an instance of the DiscountBookOrder class. But if the user doesn't enter a key code, you can create that object as an instance of the BookOrder class. Later, when the setTotal method is called, Java uses polymorphism to determine which method it should use: the one in the DiscountBookOrder class or the one in the BookOrder class.

The key to polymorphism is that this decision is based on the inheritance chain at run time. This can be referred to as *late binding*. At compile time, the compiler simply recognizes that a method with the specified signature exists.

As you develop applications, this has little significance as long as you understand how this works. You just design and code the classes and methods that you need with the skills that you learn in this book. Later, whenever polymorphism is needed, it takes place automatically. I mention this term only because polymorphism is a natural result of inheritance.

The inheritance chain for the JFrame class

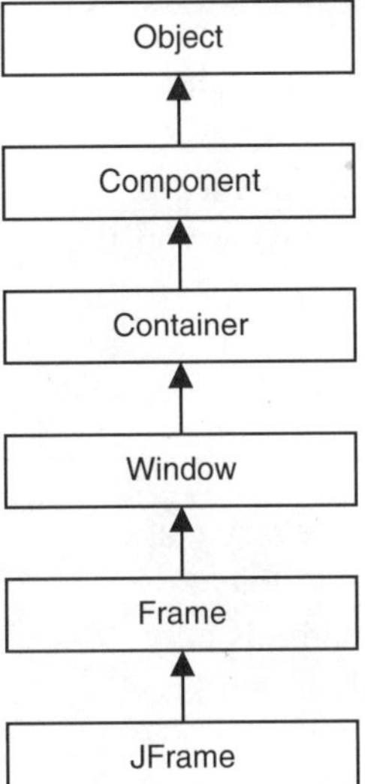

Code for the BookOrderFrame subclass

```
import javax.swing.*;

public class BookOrderFrame extends JFrame{
   public BookOrderFrame(){
      setTitle("Book Order");           // from the Frame class
      setBounds(267, 200, 267, 200);    // from the Component class
   }

   public static void main(String[] args){
      JFrame frame = new BookOrderFrame();
      frame.show();                     // from the Window class
   }
}
```

The BookOrderFrame object that's displayed by the code above

Figure 5-3 How to code a class that inherits the JFrame class

How to work with the Object class

Every class in Java automatically inherits the Object class that was shown in the inheritance chain in figure 5-3. In other words, the Object class is the superclass for all Java classes, including all user-defined classes. This means that you need to know how to work with the Object class. So that's what you'll learn next.

The methods of the Object class

Figure 5-4 summarizes the methods of the Object class. Since every class automatically inherits these methods, they are available from every object. However, since subclasses often override these methods, these methods may work slightly differently from class to class. You'll learn more about working with these methods later in this chapter.

Perhaps the most-used method of the Object class is the toString method. That's because the Java compiler implicitly calls this method when it needs a string representation of an object. For example, when you supply an object as the argument of the println method, this method implicitly calls the toString method of the object.

When you code a class, you typically override the toString method of the Object class to provide more detailed information about the object. Otherwise, the toString method will return the name of the class and the *hash code* of the object, which is a hexadecimal number that indicates the object's location in memory. Similarly, you typically override the equals method of a class.

Unlike C++ and other languages that require you to manage memory, Java uses a mechanism known as the *garbage collector* to automatically manage memory. When the garbage collector determines that the system is running low on memory and that the system is idle, it frees the memory for any objects that don't have any more references to them. Before it does that, though, it calls the *finalize* method for each of those objects.

Although you can code a more specific finalize method for an object, that's generally not a good idea. Since you can't tell when the garbage collector will call this method, you can't be assured that your finalize method will be executed before the program terminates. Therefore, you shouldn't rely on the finalize method to handle any timely tasks.

On the other hand, if you write code for an object that uses non-Java calls to allocate memory, you should code a method for that object that releases those resources. Otherwise, Java won't free this memory, and you will create a "memory leak." If, for example, you code a method named dispose that releases all non-Java resources for an object, you can call that method whenever you need to free those resources.

The Object class

```
java.lang.Object
```

Methods of the Object class

Method	Description
`toString()`	Returns a String object containing the class name, followed by the @ symbol, followed by the hash code for this object. If that's not what you want, you can override this method as shown in figure 5-6.
`equals(Object)`	Returns true (boolean) if this object points to the same space in memory as the specified object. Otherwise, it returns false, even if both objects contain the same data. If that's not what you want, you can override the equals method as shown in figure 5-7.
`getClass()`	Returns a Class object that represents the class of this object. For more information, see figure 5-8.
`clone()`	Returns a copy of this object as an Object object. Before you can use this method, you must implement the Cloneable interface as shown in figure 5-19.
`hashCode()`	Returns the hash code (int) for this object.
`finalize()`	Called by the garbage collector when the garbage collector determines that there are no more references to the object.

Description

- The Object class is the superclass for all classes. As a result, you can call its methods from any object of any class.
- When coding classes, it's a common practice to override the toString and equals methods so they work appropriately for each class.
- The *hash code* for an object is a hexadecimal number that identifies the object's location in memory.
- In general, you don't need to code a finalize method for an object. That's because Java's *garbage collector* automatically reclaims the memory of an object when it needs to. Before it does, it calls the finalize method of the object.

Figure 5-4 The methods of the Object class

How to cast objects

Many methods accept and return objects of the Object class. For example, the equals method accepts an Object object as an argument, and the clone method returns an Object object. To use methods like these, then, you need to *cast* an object of any class to an Object object, and you need to cast an Object object back to an object of the original class. Figure 5-5 shows how.

The diagram at the top of the figure shows the inheritance chain for the BookOrder class. Like all classes, the BookOrder class inherits the Object class. As a result, it can call any of the methods shown in the previous figure.

The first example in this figure shows how to cast a BookOrder object to an Object object and back again. Here, the first statement creates the BookOrder object. Then, the second statement casts the BookOrder object to an Object object. It does this with a simple assignment statement. Since this cast goes up the inheritance chain (from more data to less), this works without any additional code. In contrast, the third statement casts the Object object back to a BookOrder object. Since this cast goes down the inheritance chain (from less data to more), you need to code the class name within parentheses in the assignment statement before you code the name of the object you're casting. When you perform these casts, Java does not lose any of the data that was stored in the original BookOrder object.

The second example shows how casting affects the methods that are available from an object. Here, the first statement creates a BookOrder object and converts it to an Object object. At this point, the object variable can only call methods available to the Object class. As a result, you can't code the statement that's in the comment. The next statement, though, casts the Object object back to the BookOrder class. Then, you can call any of the methods of the BookOrder class. Keep in mind, though, that the object and order variables refer to the same object. As a result, calling the toString method from either variable will execute the toString method that's stored in the BookOrder class.

The third example shows how to code the start of a method that accepts an Object object as a parameter. Then, the method can accept any object created from any class. Here, the first statement uses the *instanceof operator* to see if the object is an instance of the BookOrder class. If so, the Object object is cast to a BookOrder object and the method can continue by processing that type of object. You'll see how this type of code is used to override the equals method in figure 5-7.

The inheritance chain for the BookOrder class

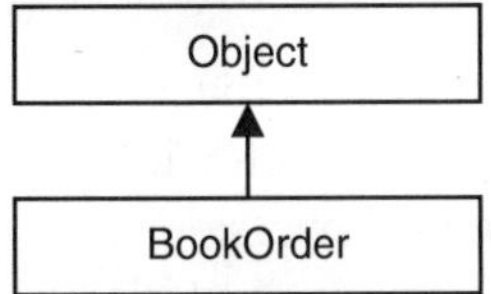

How to cast an object

```
BookOrder order1 = new BookOrder("WARP", 2);
Object object = order1;                    //cast BookOrder to Object
BookOrder order2 = (BookOrder) object;     //cast Object to BookOrder
```

How casting affects methods

```
Object object = new BookOrder("WARP", 2);
String orderString = object.toString();    //OK - method in Object class
// double total = object.getTotal();       //not OK - method in BookOrder class
BookOrder order = (BookOrder) object;      //cast Object to BookOrder
double total = order.getTotal();           //OK
```

The start of a method that accepts an Object object as an argument

```
public boolean equals(Object object){
    if (object instanceof BookOrder){
        BookOrder order2 = (BookOrder) object;
        // the code can continue by processing the BookOrder object
        // as shown in figure 5-7
    }
    return false;
}
```

Description

- To use some of the methods of the Object class, you need to be able to *cast* any type of object to an Object object, and you need to be able to cast an Object object to any other type of object.
- To cast an object up the inheritance chain (from subclass to superclass), you code a simple assignment statement.
- To cast an object down the inheritance chain (from superclass to subclass), you need to code the classname within parentheses to confirm the assignment statement. This type of cast will only work when the object is an instance of the intended class.
- For some methods, you need to code a parameter that accepts an Object object. Then, you can pass any type of object to that method, and the method can use the *instanceof operator* to determine what type of object has been passed to the method.

Figure 5-5 How to cast objects

How to override the toString method

The toString method of the Object class returns a string that includes the class name and the hash code of the object. Since that's not usually the behavior you want when converting objects to strings, many classes in the API override this method. And when you code your own classes, you'll often want to override this method too. Figure 5-6 shows how.

The first example shows the output of the toString method of a Book object if the Book class doesn't override the toString method. Here, the string that's returned begins with the class name, followed by the @ sign, followed by the hash code for the object.

The second example shows how code a toString method in the Book class that overrides the toString method of the Object class. To start, you declare a public toString method that returns a String object and accepts no parameters. Then, you create the string that you want to return and code a return statement for that string. In this figure, the toString method returns a string that includes the three instance variables of the Book object with currency formatting applied to the price variable.

The third example shows two situations where the compiler will automatically call the toString method. First, the compiler will automatically call the toString method when an object is supplied as an argument for the println method of the System.out object. Second, the compiler will automatically call the toString method when you use a plus sign (+) to concatenate an object with a string.

The output for the toString method of the Object class

```
Book@4abc9
```

The toString method of the Book class

```
public String toString(){
   NumberFormat currency = NumberFormat.getCurrencyInstance();
   String orderString = "Code: " + code + "\n"
                      + "Title: " + title + "\n"
                      + "Price: " + currency.format(price) + "\n";
   return orderString;
}
```

Code that implicitly calls the toString method of an object

```
Book book1 = new Book("WARP");
System.out.println(book1);

Book book2 = new Book("MBDK");
String bookString = "Book string: " + book2;
```

Description

- The toString method of the Object class returns a String object that contains the class name, followed by the @ symbol, followed by the hash code for this object.
- To override the toString method of the Object class, code a toString method in the class that you're coding as shown above.
- The Java compiler automatically calls the toString method of an object when you pass any object to the println method of the System.out object or when you use the plus operator (+) to concatenate an object with a string.

Figure 5-6 How to override the toString method of the Object class

How to override the equals method

Figure 5-7 shows how the equals method of the Object class works. In short, this method checks whether two variables refer to the same object, not whether two variables hold the same data. Since that's not usually the behavior you want when comparing objects for equality, many classes in the API, such as the String class, override this method. And when you code your own classes, you'll often want to override this method too.

The first two examples in this figure show how the equals method of the Object class works when the Book class doesn't override the equals method. In the first example, the first two statements create two variables that refer to the same object. Since both variables point to the same space in memory, the expression that uses the equals method to compare these variables evaluates to true. In the second example, the first two statements create two objects that contain the same data. However, since these objects occupy different spaces in memory, the expression that uses the equals method to compare these variables evaluates to false. But that's usually not what you want.

The third example shows how to code an equals method in the Book class that overrides the equals method of the Object class. To start, this method uses the same signature as the equals method of the Object class, which returns a boolean value and accepts a parameter of the Object type. Then, an if statement uses the instanceof operator to make sure that the passed object is an instance of the Book class. If so, it casts the Object object to a Book object. Then, an if statement compares the three instance variables stored in the passed object with the instance variables stored in the current object. If all instance variables are equal, this statement returns true. Otherwise, it returns false. As a result, the first two examples in this figure will return a true value if the Book class contains this method.

The fourth code example shows how to code an equals method in the BookOrder class that overrides the equals method of the Object class. The code for this method works the same as the code for the equals method of the Book class. However, the equals method of the BookOrder class uses the equals method of the Book class. As a result, you must code an equals method for the Book class before this method will work.

How the equals method of the Object class works

Both variables refer to the same object

```
Book book1 = new Book("WARP");
Book book2 = book1;
if (book1.equals(book2))                //expression returns true
```

Both variables refer to different objects that store the same data

```
Book book1 = new Book("WARP");
Book book2 = new Book("WARP");
if (book1.equals(book2))                //expression returns false
```

How to override the equals method of the Object class

The equals method of the Book class

```
public boolean equals(Object object){
   if (object instanceof Book){
      Book book2 = (Book) object;
      if (
          code.equals(book2.getCode()) &&
          title.equals(book2.getTitle()) &&
          price == book2.getPrice()
         )
         return true;
      }
   return false;
}
```

The equals method of the BookOrder class

```
public boolean equals(Object object){
   if (object instanceof BookOrder){
      BookOrder order2 = (BookOrder) object;
      if (
          book.equals(order2.getBook()) &&
          quantity == order2.getQuantity() &&
          total == order2.getTotal()
         )
         return true;
   }
   return false;
}
```

Description

- To test if two objects point to the same space in memory, you can use the equals method of the Object class.
- To test if two objects store the same data, you can override the equals method in the subclass so it tests whether all instance variables in the two objects are equal.

Figure 5-7 How to override the equals method of the Object class

How to use the Class class to get information about an Object object

To show you how complex object-oriented programming with Java can get, this chapter now shows you how to use the Class class to get information about an Object object. *Note, however, that you won't have to do that when you develop Java applications like the ones in this book. So if you want to, you can skip this topic for now and return to it when you need it.* On the other hand, this topic is a good introduction to a skill that you do need when you develop web applications.

When Java runs an application, it uses the Class class to keep track of all of the objects that it loads. This is sometimes referred to as *run-time type identification*, or *RTTI*. To illustrate the use of this information, figure 5-8 shows how to use the getName and getSuperclass methods of the Class class to get the name of an object's class or superclass.

The first two examples show how to get the class name of an object. In the first example, the first statement uses the getClass method of the Object class to return a Class object. Then, the second statement uses the getName method of the Class object to return a String object that holds the name of the class. In the second example, the dot operator connects the getClass and getName methods and returns the String object in a single statement.

The third example shows how to get the name of the superclass for an object. In this example, the first statement returns the Class object for the superclass. Then, the second statement uses the getName method to convert that Class object to a String.

Although the two methods just illustrated are two of the most-commonly used methods of the Class class, you should know that this class contains over 30 methods that let you get a wide range of run-time information about objects. In particular, when combined with the classes in the java.lang.reflect package, the Class class can access detailed information about the fields, constructors, and methods of an object. This lets Java applications work with *JavaBeans*, which are component objects that can be manipulated at run-time. This, however, is well beyond the scope of this book.

The Class class

```
java.lang.Class
```

Common methods of the Class class

Method	Description
`getName()`	Returns a String object that represents the name of this Class object.
`getSuperclass()`	Returns a Class object that represents the superclass of this Class object.

Examples

Code that gets the class name of an object in two statements

```
Class classObject = object.getClass();              //returns Class object
String className = classObject.getName();           //returns String object
```

Code that gets the class name of an object in one statement

```
String className = object.getClass().getName();     //returns String object
```

Code that gets the superclass name of an object

```
Class superclass = object.getClass().getSuperclass();
String className = superclass.getName();
```

Description

- While a program is running, Java uses *run-time type identification* (*RTTI*) to keep track of the classes that each object belongs to and to store detailed information about all loaded classes, arrays, and primitive types. You can use the methods of the Class class to access this information.
- The two methods shown above are only two of the more than 30 methods of the Class class.
- The methods of the Class class can be used with the classes of the java.lang.reflect package to get detailed information about the fields, constructors, and methods of an object. This is the basis for working with *JavaBeans*, which allow your applications to dynamically interact with other classes at run-time.

Figure 5-8 How to use the Class class to get information about an Object object

More skills for coding classes and methods

In this topic, you'll learn other skills for coding classes and methods. To start, you'll learn how to code a method that throws an exception. Next, you'll learn how to work with abstract classes and methods, final classes and methods, and access modifiers. Then, you'll learn an easy way to refer to the object that's defined by the current class. Last, you'll learn more about the difference between coding a method that accepts a primitive type and a method that accepts an object. When you work with Java, you need all of these skills.

How to code a method that throws an exception

In chapter 3, you learned how to catch an exception. Now, figure 5-9 shows how to code a method that *throws* an exception. To do that, you code a *throws clause* at the end of the method declaration. This throws clause specifies the exception or exceptions that the method throws. Then, it's up to the programmer who uses the method to decide whether to catch the exception or to throw the exception to another class.

Although you don't have to catch all types of exceptions, a *checked exception* is checked by the compiler. As a result, you must either catch the exception or throw it. Otherwise, the program won't compile.

The example in this figure shows how to throw an IOException, which is a checked exception that's used by classes that work with file input and output. Since this exception is thrown by the constructor of the FileWriter class and by the close method of the PrintWriter object, the addRecord method in this figure must catch or throw this exception. In this case, the throws clause of the method throws the exception.

As you read through this book, you'll learn more about handling the exceptions that are thrown by Java classes. And chapter 10 provides a more in-depth presentation of exception handling. For now, though, you just need to know how to throw an exception whenever that's required.

The syntax for coding the throws clause of a method

```
method declaration throws ExceptionOne[, ExceptionTwo]...{}
```

A method that throws an exception

```
public static void addRecord(User user) throws IOException{
   PrintWriter out = new PrintWriter(
         new FileWriter("UserEmail.txt", true)); // throws IOException
   out.println(user.getFirstName() + "\t"
             + user.getLastName() + "\t"
             + user.getEmailAddress());
   out.close();                                  // throws IOException
}
```

Description

- When a method includes code that may throw an exception, the method can catch the exception or *throw* it to the class that uses the method. However, not all exceptions need to be caught or thrown.
- A *checked exception* is a type of exception that's checked by the compiler. When you use a method that throws a checked exception, you must supply code that throws or catches that exception or you won't be able to compile your program.
- To throw an exception, you use the *throws* keyword to code a *throws clause* in the method declaration.
- The IOException is a type of checked exception that's thrown by classes that work with file input and output.
- For more information about catching and throwing exceptions, see chapter 10.

Figure 5-9 How to code a method that throws an exception

How to work with abstract classes and methods

Figure 5-10 shows how to work with *abstract classes* and *abstract methods*. To start, it shows a diagram of an inheritance hierarchy that shows how four classes inherit an abstract class. Then, it shows some of the code for the abstract class in this hierarchy. This code shows how to declare an abstract class and how to declare abstract methods.

In general, abstract classes are used in the top levels of an inheritance hierarchy to provide code that can be used by the subclasses and to ensure that certain methods are implemented by the subclasses. In other words, abstract classes are templates for other classes. Although abstract classes are used throughout the Java API, they're rarely used in the classes of a business application.

The diagram in this figure shows five classes in the inheritance hierarchy for the Writer class. As you can see, the Writer class is an abstract class. This means that you can't create an object directly from the Writer class. However, you can create objects from the subclasses of the Writer class.

The code in this figure shows the declaration for the Writer class and the declarations for seven of its methods. Here, the *abstract* keyword is used in the declaration for the class. Then, the first four methods are regular methods that can contain code, while the last three methods are abstract methods. As a result, any subclasses of the Writer class must implement these methods. Otherwise, they won't compile.

The inheritance hierarchy for an abstract class

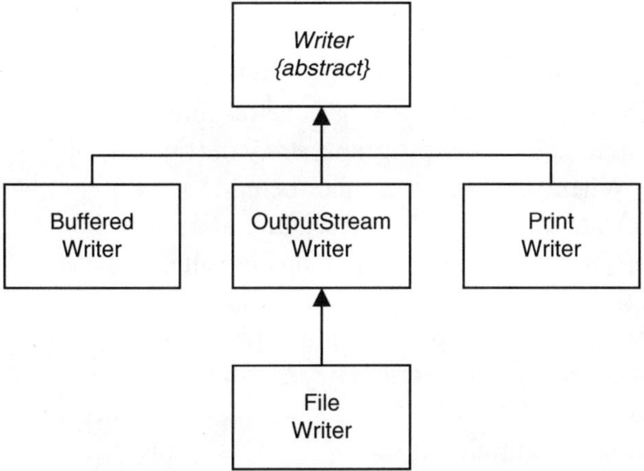

Some of the code for the abstract Writer class

```
public abstract class Writer {

    //regular method declarations
    public void write(int c) throws IOException {}
    public void write(char cbuf[]) throws IOException {}
    public void write(String str) throws IOException {}
    public void write(String str, int off, int len) throws IOException {}

    //abstract method declarations
    public abstract void write(char cbuf[], int off, int len) throws IOException;
    public abstract void flush() throws IOException;
    public abstract void close() throws IOException;
}
```

Description

- An *abstract class* serves as a template that can be inherited by subclasses. However, you can't create an object directly from an abstract class. To declare an abstract class, use the *abstract* keyword in the class declaration.
- When a subclass inherits an abstract class, all *abstract methods* in the abstract class must be overridden in the subclass. To declare an abstract method, use the abstract keyword in the method declaration, don't include braces, and end the statement with a semicolon.
- An abstract class may or may not contain abstract methods. However, any class that contains an abstract method must be declared as abstract.
- All abstract classes and methods must be declared as public.

Figure 5-10 How to work with abstract classes

How to work with final classes and methods

Figure 5-11 shows how to use the *final* keyword to declare *final classes, final methods*, and *final parameters*. You can use this keyword whenever you want to make sure that no one will override or change your classes, methods, or parameters. When you declare a final class, other programmers won't be able to create a subclass from your class. When you declare a final method, other programmers won't be able to override that method. And when you declare a final parameter, other programmers won't be able to assign a new value to the parameter.

Why would want to use final classes, methods, or parameters? First, for design reasons, you may not want other programmers to be able to change the behavior of a method or a class. Second, Java can execute final classes, methods, and parameters faster than regular methods.

When should you use final classes and methods? For the sake of efficiency, you can use a final class or method whenever you're sure that no one else will want to inherit your class or override your methods. Often, though, it's hard to know when that's true. As a result, you should avoid using final classes and methods unless you're certain that no one else will benefit by extending your class or by overriding a method in your class.

The four final class examples in this figure show how to declare final classes. The first two examples are the class declarations for the String and Math classes in the Java API, while the next two are class declarations for user-defined classes. When you declare final classes like these, all methods in the class automatically become final methods.

The two final method examples show how you can declare final methods. Since these methods are in the BookOrder class, which hasn't been declared as final, this class can still be inherited by other classes, such as the DiscountBookOrder class. However, the DiscountBookOrder class won't be able to override either of these methods. Since both of these methods shouldn't do anything but the tasks shown in this figure, though, declaring them as final methods makes sense.

The two final parameter examples show how you can declare final parameters when you're coding a method. Since you would rarely want to assign a new value to the parameter, you can almost always declare parameters as final. However, the performance gain is slight, and the extra keyword clutters the code. As a result, you may or may not want to use final parameters, depending on the type of project that you're working on.

Final classes

```
public final class String{}
public final class Math{}
public final class Book{}
public final class FinancialCalculations{}
```

Final methods

```
public final int getQuantity(){
   return quantity;
}
protected final double getTotal(){
   return total;
}
```

Final parameters

```
public void setQuantity(final int qty){
   quantity = qty;
}
public static void incrementQuantity(final BookOrder order){
   int qty = order.getQuantity();
   order.setQuantity(qty+1);
}
```

Description

- To prevent a class from being inherited, you can create a *final class* by using the *final* keyword in the declaration of the class.
- To prevent subclasses from overriding a method of a superclass, you can create a *final method* by using the final keyword in the declaration of the method. In addition, all methods in a final class are automatically final methods.
- To prevent a method from assigning a new value to a parameter, you can use the final keyword in the method declaration to declare a *final parameter*. Then, if a statement in the method tries to assign a new value to the final parameter, the compiler will report an error.

Figure 5-11 How to work with final classes and methods

How to work with access modifiers

Now that you've learned how to work with packages and subclasses, you're ready for a more complete discussion of how to work with *access modifiers*. That's why figure 5-12 summarizes the four types of access modifiers.

By now, you should be familiar with the private and public access modifiers. To review, you can use the *private* keyword for any fields or methods that you only want to be available within the current class. In contrast, you can use the *public* keyword for any fields or methods that you want to be available to all other classes.

Beyond that, you may occasionally want to use the *protected* keyword for a field or for a method. Then, classes in the same package as well as subclasses will be able to access the field or method. This keyword is typically used to provide access to a method that might be helpful to programmers who are developing classes that inherit your class.

Similarly, there may be times when you don't want to code any access modifier at all for a field or method in a class. Then, the classes in the same package will be able to access the field or method, but subclasses in other packages won't be able to access the field or method.

To encapsulate the data in your classes, you should declare all instance variables with private access. Then, you can use other access modifiers to code methods that provide access to these variables. Although you may be tempted to allow other classes to have direct access to your variables, this defeats the purpose of encapsulation, and it can lead to run-time errors when another class modifies an instance variable in a way that's unexpected.

In general, you should set the *scope* of the fields and methods of your application as small as possible. For instance variables, that almost always means declaring them with private access. However, it's a common coding practice to declare static constants with public access. That way, you can easily access constants that are stored in other classes.

Access modifiers

Keyword	Description
`private`	Available within the current class.
`public`	Available to classes in all packages.
`protected`	Available to classes in the same package and to subclasses.
no keyword coded	Available to classes in the same package.

Description

- To encapsulate the data in your classes, you code private instance variables. Then, you code public set and get methods that set and return the values of the private instance variables.
- You can use the *public* keyword to code static constants. That way, other classes can call those constants from the class.
- You can use the *private* keyword to code methods that are used only within the current class.
- You can use the *protected* keyword to code fields and methods that can be accessed only by other classes in the same package and by any subclasses.
- If you don't code an access modifier, your fields and methods will be available only to other classes in the same package.

Figure 5-12 How to work with access modifiers

How to use the this keyword

When you're coding the methods of a class, you sometimes need to refer to the object that's defined by the current class. To do that, you can use the *this* keyword as shown in figure 5-13. You can use this keyword to refer to instance variables, to call methods, or to pass the current object to another method. In addition, you can use this keyword to call a constructor of the current class, which can be useful when you're overloading constructors.

The first line of the syntax summary shows how to refer to an instance variable of the current object. The second and third lines show how to call a method of the current object or a constructor of the same class. And the fourth and fifth lines show how to use the this keyword to pass the current object to a method.

Since Java implicitly supplies the this keyword for all instance variables and methods, you don't usually need to explicitly code it when referring to instance variables or methods. However, the first example is an exception to this rule. Here, the quantity parameter in the constructor has the same name as the quantity instance variable. As a result, you need to use the this keyword to explicitly identify the instance variable. Of course, another approach would be to change the parameter name so it isn't the same as the instance variable name.

The second example in this figure shows how to use the this keyword to call a method of the current object. As the comments indicate, neither use of this keyword is necessary in this example. However, this does point out that the setTime and getTime methods used in the printTimeToConsole method are actually methods of the current object. They aren't static methods.

The third example shows how to use the this keyword to call another constructor in the same class. Here, two constructors have been added to the BookOrder class. The first constructor doesn't accept any arguments. Instead, it passes two default values to the third BookOrder constructor. Similarly, the second constructor accepts one parameter and passes that parameter and a default value to the third BookOrder constructor. This is an easy way to overload a constructor so it provides default values for missing parameters.

The fourth example shows how to use the this keyword to pass the current object to a method. In this example, the print method sends the current object to the println method of the System.out object. Since this method will automatically invoke the toString method of the object that's passed to it, this method will print a representation of the current object to the console.

The syntax for using the this keyword

```
this.instanceVariable        //refers to an instance variable of current object
this.methodName(arguments)   //calls a method of current object
this(arguments)              //calls another constructor of the same class
object.methodName(this)      //passes the current object to a method
Class.methodName(this)       //passes the current object to a static method
```

Examples

How to refer to an instance variable when a parameter has the same name

```
public BookOrder(String code, int quantity){
   book = new Book(code);
   this.quantity = quantity;
   setTotal();
}
```

How to call a method of the current object

```
public void printTimeToConsole(){
   this.setTime();                    //unnecessary, but clear
   String time = this.getTime();      //unnecessary, but clear
   System.out.println(time);
}
```

How to call another constructor of the same class

```
public BookOrder(){
   this("", 1);
}
public BookOrder(String code){
   this(code, 1);
}
public BookOrder(String code, int quantity){
   // code for initializing instance variables
}
```

How to pass the current object to a method

```
public void print(){
   System.out.println(this);
}
```

Description

- You can use the *this* keyword to refer to an instance variable or method of the current object, to call another constructor of the same class, or to pass the current object to a method.
- Since Java implicitly uses the this keyword for instance variables and methods, you don't need to explicitly code it unless a parameter has the same name as an instance variable.
- If you use the this keyword to call another constructor, the statement must be the first statement in the constructor.

Figure 5-13 How to use the *this* keyword

How primitive types and objects are passed to a method

Figure 5-14 shows that variables with primitive types are passed to a method one way, while objects are passed in another way. Specifically, primitive types are *passed by value*, which means that a copy of the variable's value is passed, not the variable itself. In contrast, objects are *passed by reference*, which means that the method knows where the object's variables are so it can change them directly.

The first example shows how this works when a primitive data type is passed to a method that is supposed to increment the value of the variable by one. In this case, the incrementQuantity method uses a return statement to return the incremented value. Then, the code that calls this method reassigns the return value to the original variable. In other words, the method works with a copy of the value of the variable, but it can't modify the value in the variable itself.

The second example shows how this works when an object is passed to a method. Here, the return type for the incrementQuantity method is void, so no value is returned by the method. Instead, the getQuantity and setQuantity methods of the BookOrder class are used to get and set the quantity variable itself. In other words, the method refers directly to the object and its data so that data is actually changed by the method.

In practice, you usually don't need to know how the values are passed, because your methods work the way you want them to. Occasionally, though, you do need to be aware of the differences in the way that primitive types and objects are passed. When you do, you can refer back to this figure to refresh your memory about it.

Curiously, some programmers disagree about what terminology should be used for these examples. Some agree that Java passes a *reference* to an object instead of the object itself, so this should be referred to as "passing by reference." But others say that Java passes a copy of the reference to the object, so this should be referred to as "passing by value." They argue that the copy of the reference doesn't change. But since it refers directly to the object, you can invoke methods to change the object. No matter what terminology you use, you'll be able to code your methods right if you understand what's happening.

* * *

Because this is a long, difficult chapter, we now recommend that you do the exercises that follow. They will give you a chance to practice and reinforce the most important skills that you've learned so far. This is also a good time to take a break before continuing this chapter.

Example 1: Primitive types are passed by value

A method that changes the value of a primitive type

```
public static int incrementQuantity(int qty){          //returns an int
   return qty+1;
}
```

Code that passes a primitive type to this method

```
int quantity = 2;
quantity = PassTest.incrementQuantity(quantity);   //reassignment statement
   // now the quantity variable is 3
```

Example 2: Objects are passed by reference

A method that changes a value stored in an object

```
public static void incrementQuantity(BookOrder order){  //no return value
   int qty = order.getQuantity();
   order.setQuantity(qty+1);
}
```

Code that passes an object to this method

```
BookOrder order = new BookOrder("WARP", 2);
PassTest.incrementQuantity(order);
   //now the quantity variable in the BookOrder object is 3
```

Description

- When a variable with a primitive type is passed to a method, it is *passed by value*. That means the method can't change the value of the variable itself. Instead, the method must return a new value that gets stored in the variable.
- When an object is passed to a method, it is *passed by reference*. That means that the method can change the data in the object itself so a new value doesn't need to be returned by the method.

Figure 5-14 How primitive types and objects are passed to a method

Exercise 5-1 Use the DiscountBookOrder class

This exercise guides you through the process of using the DiscountBookOrder class that inherits the BookOrder class.

1. Open the DiscountBookOrder class that's in the c:\java\ch05\inherit directory. It contains the code shown in figure 5-2.
2. Add a toString method to this class that returns all of the information about a book order including subtotal, discount percent, discount amount, and total. This should be formatted so it's ready for display in a dialog box. Then, compile the class.
3. Open the Book, BookOrder, and BookOrderApp classes that are in the c:\java\ch05\inherit directory. This is code that you used for the book order application in the last chapter. For now, compile just the Book and BookOrder classes.
4. Modify the BookOrderApp class so (1) it uses another dialog box to get the key code entry from the user; (2) it uses the DiscountBookOrder class instead of the BookOrder class to create order objects and to get the data for a book order; and (3) it displays all of the order data that is returned. Then, compile this class and test the application.

Exercise 5-2 Use alternatives to the DiscountBookOrder class

Just because you can use inheritance doesn't mean that you have to use it. In fact, using inheritance may not be the best way to implement discount book orders. In this exercise, then, you'll get a chance to consider the alternatives.

1. Open the Book, BookOrder, and BookOrderApp classes in the c:\java\ch05\disinherit directory. These are the original classes that you used for the book order application in chapter 4.
2. Modify the BookOrder class so it accepts a third parameter and so its toString method provides for discount orders. To do that, you can (1) create three new instance variables, (2) add a setPercentOff method, and (3) modify the getTotal method. Then, compile this class.
3. Modify the BookOrderApp class so it (1) gets the key code from the user; (2) uses the modified BookOrder class; and (3) displays all of the order data. Then, compile this class and test the application.
4. (Optional) Modify the BookOrder class so it has two constructors: one with two parameters (book code and quantity) for regular orders, and one with three parameters for discount orders. Next, modify the BookOrderApp class so it uses the first constructor for regular orders (no key code) and the second constructor for discount orders. Then, compile these classes and test the application.

Exercise 5-3 Inherit the JFrame class

This exercise guides you through the process of creating the BookOrderFrame class by extending the JFrame class.

1. Create the BookOrderFrame class in figure 5-3. Then, save it in the c:\java\ch05\frame directory.
2. Compile and run this class, which should display a frame. When you click on its close button, the frame should close, but that won't terminate the program. To terminate the program, you're going to have to press Ctrl+C or close the console window. Later in this chapter, though, you'll learn how to fix this problem.

Exercise 5-4 Practice some of the other skills

This exercise guides you through the process of modifying the Book and BookOrder classes so you can practice some of the miscellaneous skills presented in this chapter.

Use final classes and methods

1. Open the Book and BookOrder classes in the c:\java\ch05\order directory. Then, edit the BookOrder class so it's a final class, and compile the class.
2. Try to compile the DiscountBookOrder class. This should give you an error message like: "cannot inherit from final BookOrder."

Use the this keyword to code new constructors

3. Edit the code for the BookOrder class so it uses the this keyword to provide default values for both of the parameters in the original constructor as shown in figure 5-13. Then, compile the code for the BookOrder class.
4. Open the code for the ThisTestApp class in the c:\java\ch05\order directory. Then, compile this code and run the application. It should print three book orders to the console. Notice how the default values are used for the statements that don't pass values to the constructor. Then, close the ThisTestApp class.

Add the equals method (optional)

5. Open the code for the EqualsTestApp1 class in the c:\java\ch05\order directory. Then, compile this code and run the application. Since no equals method exists in the Book class, this should print "false" to the console.
6. Edit the code for the Book class so it includes an equals method like the one shown in figure 5-7. Then, compile the code for the Book class.
7. Run the EqualsTestApp1 class again. This time, this should print "true" to the console. Then, close this class.
8. Repeat steps 5 through 7 with the EqualsTestApp2 class and the BookOrder class.

How to work with interfaces

In Java, a class can only inherit one other class. In some other object-oriented programming languages such as C++, though, a class can inherit more than one class. This is known as *multiple inheritance*.

Although Java doesn't provide for multiple inheritance, it does provide a special type of coding element known as an *interface* that provides many of the advantages of multiple inheritance without some of the problems that are associated with it. So in this topic, you'll learn how to work with interfaces. In particular, you'll learn how to implement two interfaces that are defined in the Java API: the WindowListener interface and the Cloneable interface.

An introduction to interfaces

In some ways, an interface is similar to an abstract class. That's why figure 5-15 compares the two. The main similarity is that both abstract classes and interfaces can contain abstract methods. Similarly, both can contain static constants. However, a class can *implement* more than one interface but it can inherit only one abstract class.

If you use your web browser to view the documentation for the Java API, you'll see that almost every package uses one or more interfaces. In addition, you'll see that the Java documentation italicizes interfaces. That way, it's easy to differentiate between classes and interfaces.

When will you need to use interfaces that are part of the Java API? As you'll see later in this chapter, you need to use interfaces when you want to code a graphical user interface. In particular, you need to use interfaces to handle *events,* such as when a user clicks on a button.

When will you need to code your own interfaces? In general, you won't need to code interfaces for your business applications, but there may be a few occasions when you will want to. For instance, you may want to code an interface to make certain constants available to all classes in a package. Or, you may want to code an interface to force several classes to implement a generic method. As you learn more about how the Java API uses interfaces, you'll begin to understand when coding your own interfaces might be appropriate.

An abstract class compared to an interface

Abstract Class
Variables Constants
Method definitions Static method definitions Abstract methods Abstract static methods

Interface
Static constants
Abstract methods

An interface can contain...

- Static constants
- Abstract methods

A class that implements an interface...

- Can use the constants in the interface.
- Must define all methods in the interface (unless the class is declared as an abstract class).

Advantages of an abstract class

- An abstract class can use instance variables while interfaces can't.
- An abstract class can define regular methods while interfaces can only define abstract methods.
- An abstract class can define static methods while interfaces can't.

Advantages of an interface

- Although a class can only inherit one class, it can *implement* more than one interface. This is how Java provides many of the advantages of *multiple inheritance*.

Figure 5-15 An introduction to interfaces

How to code an interface

Figure 5-16 shows how to code an interface. To start, it shows the inheritance hierarchy for three interfaces that are defined in the Java API. This shows that interfaces can inherit other interfaces. Then, this figure shows the syntax for coding an interface. And finally, this figure shows the code for three interfaces from the Java API. In general, declaring an interface is similar to declaring a class except that you use the *interface* keyword instead of the class keyword.

Although you can't add methods to an existing interface, you can derive new interfaces from existing ones. In the diagram, the WindowListener and ActionListener interfaces only inherit the EventListener interface, but they could inherit other interfaces too. In contrast, some interfaces don't inherit any other interfaces. For example, the SwingConstants interface shown in the third example doesn't inherit any interface.

The first example shows the code for the ActionListener interface. This interface extends the EventListener interface and contains a single abstract method, the actionPerformed method. When you code an abstract method in an interface, you don't have to use the public and abstract keywords. That's because Java automatically supplies these keywords for all methods. Nevertheless, the abstract methods in this figure use the public keyword, which helps document their scope.

The second example shows the code for the WindowListener interface. Like the ActionListener interface, this interface extends the EventListener interface. However, this interface contains seven abstract methods. As with all abstract methods, these methods end with a semicolon instead of braces.

The third example shows how to code an interface that defines constants. When you code constants in an interface, you don't have to code the public, static, and final keywords. That's because Java automatically supplies these keywords for all constants. Here again, though, the three constants in this example use all three of these keywords, which is useful as documentation.

An interface hierarchy

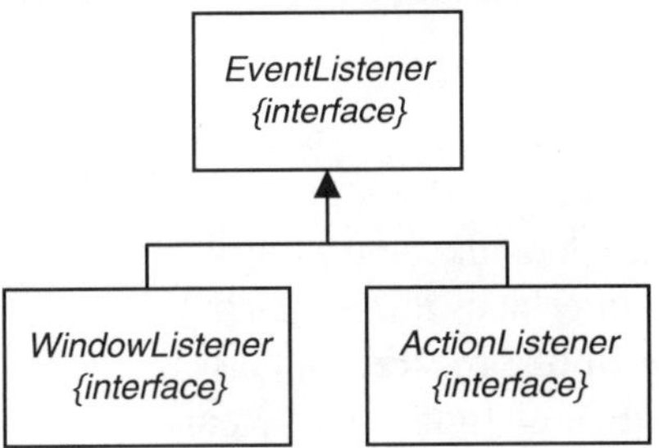

The syntax for declaring an interface

```
public interface InterfaceName{
   dataType CONSTANT_NAME = value;                        //for constants
   returnType MethodName(optionalParameterList);          //for methods
}
```

The syntax for declaring an interface that inherits other interfaces

```
public interface InterfaceName
   [extends SuperInterface1[, SuperInterface2]...]{}
```

Example 1: An interface that defines one abstract method

```
public interface ActionListener extends EventListener {
   public void actionPerformed(ActionEvent e);
}
```

Example 2: An interface that defines seven abstract methods

```
public interface WindowListener extends EventListener {
   public void windowOpened(WindowEvent e);
   public void windowClosing(WindowEvent e);
   public void windowClosed(WindowEvent e);
   public void windowIconified(WindowEvent e);
   public void windowDeiconified(WindowEvent e);
   public void windowActivated(WindowEvent e);
   public void windowDeactivated(WindowEvent e);
}
```

Example 3: An interface that defines constants

```
public interface SwingConstants {
   public static final int CENTER  = 0;
   public static final int TOP     = 1;
   public static final int LEFT    = 2;
   // and so on
}
```

Description

- Declaring an interface is similar to declaring a class except that you use the *interface* keyword instead of the class keyword.
- In an interface, all methods are automatically declared public and abstract, and all constants are automatically declared public, static, and final. Although you can code the public, static, and final keywords, they're optional.

Figure 5-16 How to code an interface

How to implement an interface

Figure 5-17 shows how to code a class that implements an interface. In short, you use the *implements* keyword to implement one or more interfaces, separating interfaces with commas as necessary. Then, the class can use any of the constants contained in any of the interfaces it implements, and it must implement all of the methods defined by all of the interfaces it implements.

The first example in this figure shows how the BookOrderFrame class implements the WindowListener interface in the previous figure. In the constructor, you can see that the this keyword is used as an argument in the addWindowListener method. You'll learn more about this in the next figure.

Because the BookOrderFrame class implements the WindowListener interface, it must define all seven methods contained in the WindowListener interface. Otherwise, the compiler will report an error when it tries to compile this class. So in this first example, all seven methods are defined. Note, however, that the windowClosing method is the only method that contains any code, and this method contains only a single statement that terminates all threads when the frame is closed.

The second example shows the declaration for a class that inherits a class and implements two interfaces. Here, the BookOrderFrame class inherits the JFrame class. Then, it implements the WindowListener interface and the ActionListener interface.

When a class implements an interface that contains constants, the class can use any of the constants in the interface. To refer to these constants, you don't have to type the name of the interface, followed by the dot operator, followed by the name of the constant. Instead, you can just type the name of the constant. In addition, if the interface that you're implementing inherits constants from other interfaces, you can refer to these constants in the same way.

The syntax for implementing an interface

```
public className [extends SuperClass] implements Interface1[, Interface2]...{}
```

A class that extends another class and implements an interface

```
import java.awt.event.*;
import javax.swing.*;

public class BookOrderFrame extends JFrame implements WindowListener{
   public BookOrderFrame(){
      setTitle("Book Order");
      setBounds(267, 200, 267, 200);
      addWindowListener(this);
   }

   public void windowClosing(WindowEvent e){
      System.exit(0);
   }
   public void windowClosed(WindowEvent e){}
   public void windowActivated(WindowEvent e){}
   public void windowDeactivated(WindowEvent e){}
   public void windowDeiconified(WindowEvent e){}
   public void windowIconified(WindowEvent e){}
   public void windowOpened(WindowEvent e){}

   public static void main(String[] args){
      JFrame frame = new BookOrderFrame();
      frame.show();
   }
}
```

The declaration for a class that implements two interfaces

```
public class BookOrderFrame extends JFrame
   implements WindowListener, ActionListener{}
```

Description

- To declare a class that implements an interface, you use the *implements* keyword.
- To refer to a constant declared in an interface, you don't need to specify the interface name as long as the class implements the interface.
- If a class inherits a class that implements interfaces, it also implements those interfaces, so it can access all constants of those interfaces without coding the class name and dot operator.
- A class that implements an interface must also implement all methods that the interface inherits from other interfaces.

Figure 5-17 How to implement an interface

How to use an interface as an argument

Figure 5-18 shows how to use an interface as an argument of a method. That way, the statement that calls the method can pass any object that implements the interface to the method. When this happens, the method ends up calling back one of the interface methods defined in that object's class. This type of code is known as a *callback*, and this creates a flexible design that allows you to plug new classes into various points in your program. In practice, though, you're most likely to use this type of code when you're using classes and methods from the Java API to work with events.

The code in this figure shows how the Java API uses a callback with the WindowListener interface. First, this figure shows the declaration for the addWindowListener method of the Window class. This declaration shows that the addWindowListener method accepts any object that implements the WindowListener interface.

Then, this figure shows the start of the code for the BookOrderFrame class. Here, the third statement in the constructor calls the addWindowListener method and uses the this keyword to supply the current BookOrderFrame object as the argument. Since the BookOrderFrame object implements the WindowListener interface, it's a valid argument for the addWindowListener method.

Once the addWindowListener method is called, an event will cause this method to call a method in this object's class that's defined in the WindowListener interface. For instance, if the user closes the window, the addWindowListener method registers this event and makes sure the windowClosing method in the BookOrderFrame class is called.

Frankly, this is about as difficult as object-oriented programming with Java gets. When you learn how to develop GUIs in section 3 of this book, you will see this in use and it will make more sense. But for now, it may seem bewildering. At a time like that, we say that you just have to click on the "I believe" button and continue.

A method in the Java API that accepts an interface as an argument

```
public void addWindowListener(WindowListener l){}
```

Code that supplies an interface as an argument

```
public class BookOrderFrame extends JFrame implements WindowListener{
   public BookOrderFrame(){
      setTitle("Book Order");
      setBounds(267, 200, 267, 200);
      addWindowListener(this);
   }
   ...
```

Description

- The Window class of the Java API contains the addWindowListener method shown above. Since the JFrame class inherits the Window class, the addWindowListener method is available to the JFrame class.
- A method that accepts an interface as an argument can accept any object that implements the interface. Since the BookOrderFrame class implements the WindowListener interface, the addWindowListener method will accept a BookOrderFrame object as an argument.
- Although it's common to use the this keyword to supply the current object as an argument, you can supply an instance of any object that implements the WindowListener interface.
- To use an interface dynamically, you can use a *callback*. That way, you can use any object that implements the interface as an argument to a method and that method will call the appropriate method in the argument's class.

Figure 5-18 How to use an interface as an argument

How to implement the Cloneable interface

Occasionally, you will have to *clone* an object (make an exact copy of it). Before you can use the clone method of the Object class, though, you must implement the Cloneable interface. You may also have to override the clone method of the Object class. *Note, however, that you usually won't have to clone objects when you develop Java applications like the ones in this book. So if you want to, you can skip this complex topic for now and return to it when you need it.*

Figure 5-19 shows how to clone an object by implementing the Cloneable interface. Since this interface contains no constants or methods, it is known as a *tagging interface*. This interface lets you identify objects that can use the clone method of the Object class. Once you implement this interface for a class, you can call the clone method of the Object class from that class. However, the clone method of the Object class has protected access, and it doesn't work properly when an object contains instance variables that refer to other *mutable objects* (objects that can be changed). So when you code a class, you'll usually want to override the clone method so it has public access and so it works properly when the object contains instance variables that refer to other mutable objects.

The first example in this figure shows how to code a Book class that can be cloned. First, the Book class implements the Cloneable interface so the Book class can use the clone method of the Object class. Then, the Book class defines a public clone method that overrides the clone method of the Object class. That way, the clone method for the Book class will have public access. Last, this method uses the super keyword to call the clone method of the Object class. Since the Book class only contains a primitive type and an *immutable object* (a String object), this clone method will work properly for a Book object.

The second example in this figure shows how to code a BookOrder class that can be cloned. Since this class contains an instance variable of a mutable object (a Book object), you must clone the BookOrder object and the Book object. So the first statement in the clone method clones the BookOrder object. At this point, two BookOrder objects point to the same Book object. Then, the second statement clones the Book object and assigns it to the book instance variable. At this point, each BookOrder object points to its own copy of the Book object. As a result, this clone method will work properly for a BookOrder object.

The third example in this figure shows the code that uses the clone method to clone a BookOrder object. Here, the first statement creates an object from the BookOrder class while the second statement uses the clone method of the Object class to clone the BookOrder object. Then, the third and fourth statements set a new Book object and total for the second book order. And the fifth and sixth statements print both objects to the console so you can verify that the clone method has worked properly.

When you write a method that overrides the clone method of the Object class, your method returns an Object type and throws a checked exception of the

The Cloneable interface defined in the API

```
public interface Cloneable{}
```

Example 1: How the Book class implements the Cloneable interface

```
public class Book implements Cloneable{
   private String code;
   private String title;
   private double price;
   //body of Book class
   public Object clone() throws CloneNotSupportedException{
      return super.clone();
   }
}
```

Example 2: How the BookOrder class implements the Cloneable interface

```
public class BookOrder implements Cloneable{
   private Book book;
   private int quantity;
   private double total;
   //body of BookOrder class
   public Object clone() throws CloneNotSupportedException{
      BookOrder bookOrder = (BookOrder) super.clone();
      book = (Book) book.clone();
      return bookOrder;
   }
}
```

Example 3: Code that uses the clone method

```
public static void main(String[] args) throws CloneNotSupportedException{
   BookOrder order1 = new BookOrder("WARP", 4);
   BookOrder order2 = (BookOrder) order1.clone();
   order2.setBook(new Book("MBDK"));
   order2.setTotal();
   System.out.println(order1);
   System.out.println(order2);
}
```

Description

- To use the clone method of the Object class, you must implement the Cloneable interface. Since the Cloneable interface doesn't require you to implement any methods, it's known as a *tagging interface*.
- The clone method of the Object class has protected access. As a result, it's a common coding practice to override this method with a clone method that has public access.
- The clone method of the Object class doesn't work properly when the class contains an instance variable of a *mutable object* (such as a Book object). As a result, it's a common coding practice to override the clone method of the Object class with a clone method that will clone any instance variables that refer to mutable objects.
- When you override the clone method of the Object class, the method returns an Object type and throws a CloneNotSupportedException. Since this is a checked exception, you either have to throw it or catch it.

Figure 5-19 How to implement the Cloneable interface

CloneNotSupportedException type. As a result, you will often need to cast the object that's returned to another object type. This is illustrated by the second statement in example 3. You will also have to throw the checked exception or catch it. In all three examples, this exception is thrown.

How to code classes that are closely related

So far, all of the applications in this book have declared one class per file. But now, you'll learn when and how to code more than one class per file.

How to code more than one class per file

For most applications, it makes sense to code one class per file. However, there are some coding situations in which two classes are so closely related that it makes sense to store them in the same file. When you work with graphical user interfaces, for example, it often makes sense to code two or more classes within one file.

Figure 5-20 shows how to code more than one class per file. Here, the BookOrder class is declared as the public class so it must be stored in a file named BookOrder.java. However, the Book class can also be stored in this file since it isn't declared as a public class.

The advantage of coding classes in the same file is that you have fewer files to keep track of. In this case, since the Book and BookOrder classes are closely related, it makes sense to store both of them in the same file. When you compile this class, the compiler will generate the class files for both the BookOrder and Book classes.

Two classes declared within the same file

```
public class BookOrder{
   //body of BookOrder class
}
class Book{
   //body of Book class
}
```

The class files that are generated when the code above is compiled

```
BookOrder.class
Book.class
```

Description

- When two classes are closely related, it sometimes makes sense to code them in the same file.
- When you code two or more classes in the same file, you can only have one public class in the file, and that class should be declared first.

Figure 5-20 How to code more than one class per file

An introduction to nested classes

You can code *nested classes* whenever you need to code a class that only makes sense within the context of another class. In practice, though, you may only need to use nested classes when you develop graphical user interfaces.

Figure 5-21 shows the syntax and principles for coding nested classes. After you code the *outer class*, you can code *inner classes* and *static inner classes*. Since these types of classes are members of the outer class, they're sometimes called *member classes*.

The outer class in the first example in this figure works the same as the rest of the classes that you've been working with throughout this book. It must be declared public, and it must be stored in a file that has the same name as the class. Then, it can contain instance variables, static variables, constructors, methods, and static methods.

The first nested class shows the types of data that you can use in an inner class. Since an inner class has direct access to all private variables and methods of the outer class, you may want to use an inner class for some closely related classes. However, an inner class can't contain any static variables or methods.

The second nested class shows the types of data that you can use in a static inner class. Unlike regular inner classes, static inner classes are independent of the outer class. In fact, you can create an object of the static inner class without referring to the outer class. As a result, static inner classes can't access any of the instance variables or methods of the outer class. However, they can access the static variables and methods of the outer class.

The second example in this figure shows how you can nest a class within a method. In this case, the class is known as a *local class* because it can only be called from within the method. In chapter 11, you will see a typical example of a local class.

If you compile the code for the first example in this figure, the compiler will generate the three classes shown. Here, a dollar sign ($) separates the outer class and the inner class. This clearly shows that the inner classes are nested within the outer class.

Example 1: Classes nested within other classes

```
public class OuterClassName{
    //Can contain instance variables and methods
    //Can contain static variables and methods

    class InnerClassName{
        //Can contain instance variables and methods
        //Can't contain static variables or methods
        //Can access all variables and methods of OuterClass
    }
    static class StaticInnerClassName{
        //Can contain instance variables and methods
        //Can contain static variables and methods
        //Can access static data from OuterClass
        //Can't access instance variables or methods from OuterClass
    }
}
```

Example 2: A class nested within a method

```
public class ClassName{
    //body of class
    methodName(){
        class InnerClassName{
            //body of class
        }
    //code of method
    }
}
```

The class files generated when the code for the first example is compiled

```
OuterClassName.class
OuterClassName$InnerClassName.class
OuterClassName$StaticInnerClassName.class
```

Description

- Java has provided support for *nested classes* since version 1.1.
- When you nest classes, the *outer class* must be declared public and must have the same name as the filename of the class.
- Within an outer class, you can nest *inner classes* and *static inner classes*. Since the inner classes are members of the outer class, they are sometimes called *member classes*.
- A class can also be nested inside a method or any other type of block. These types of classes are sometimes called *local classes*.
- Nested classes are often used when developing graphical user interfaces.

Figure 5-21 An introduction to nested classes

Perspective

From a conceptual point of view, at least, this is the most difficult chapter in this book...by far. In practice, though, you actually have to understand these concepts as you work with the Java API. In fact, you'll encounter almost all of these concepts again as you progress through this book.

The good news is that you aren't expected to have a complete understanding of everything in this chapter right now. That will come as you get more experience with Java. For now, if you understand the major concepts of inheritance and interfaces, you're ready to continue. Then, you can refer back to this chapter whenever you need more detailed information.

Summary

- You can use *inheritance* to create a *subclass* (also called a *derived class* or *child class*) that inherits fields and methods from a *superclass* (also called a *base class* or *parent class*).
- If a method in a subclass has the same signature as a method in its superclass, the method in the subclass will *override* the method in the superclass.
- When a subclass object calls an inherited method, Java doesn't decide which method it will call until run time. This is referred to as *polymorphism*.
- The Object class is the superclass for all classes in Java. As a result, the methods in the Object class are always available, though they are often overridden in the subclasses.
- You can *cast* an object up and down its *inheritance chain* without losing any of the data that's stored in the original object.
- When coding method declarations, you can code a *throws clause* to throw an exception. Since the compiler checks for *checked exceptions*, they must be thrown or caught or the code won't compile.
- *Abstract classes* provide code that can be used by subclasses. In addition, they can specify *abstract methods* that must be implemented by subclasses.
- You can use the *final* keyword to declare *final classes*, *final methods*, and *final parameters*. No class can inherit a final class, no method can override a final method, and no statement can assign a new value to a final parameter.
- When coding a class, you can use the *this* keyword to refer to the current object and to call constructors of the current class.
- When Java passes a primitive type to a method, it passes a copy of the value. This is known as *passing by value*. When Java passes an object to a method, it passes a reference to the object. This is known as *passing by reference*.
- An *interface* is a special type of coding element that can contain static constants and abstract methods. Although a class can only inherit one other class, it can *implement* more than one interface.

- If a method accepts an interface as an argument, you can supply any object that implements the interface as an argument.
- Before you can use the clone method of the Object class, you need to implement the Cloneable interface. Then, you can override the clone method so it is public and so it lets you clone *mutable objects*.
- When two or more classes are closely related, it sometimes makes sense to store them all in one file or *nest* them.

Terms

inheritance
member
subclass
superclass
override a method
inheritance hierarchy
is-a relationship
base class
parent class
derived class
child class
frame
inheritance chain
polymorphism
late binding
hash code
garbage collector
cast an object
instanceof operator
run-time type identification (RTTI)
JavaBean
throws clause
checked exception
abstract class
abstract method
final class
final method
final parameter
access modifier
protected
scope
pass by value
pass by reference
multiple inheritance
interface
implement an interface
event
callback
clone
tagging interface
mutable object
immutable object
nested classes
outer class
inner class
static inner class
member class
local class

Objectives

- Describe how inheritance is used in the Java API. When necessary, use inheritance in your own classes.
- Describe how the Object class interacts with other classes in the API. When necessary, override the toString and equals methods in your own classes, or write code that casts an object up or down the inheritance chain.
- Code the following: (1) a method that throws an exception; (2) an abstract class with abstract methods; (3) final classes, methods, and parameters; (4) the this keyword to call constructors and to refer to the current object.
- Explain the difference between passing primitive types to a method and passing objects to a method.
- Describe how interfaces are used in the Java API. When necessary, implement interfaces in your own classes.
- Code more than one class per file. When necessary, use nested classes.

Exercise 5-5 Implement the WindowListener interface

In this exercise, you'll implement the WindowListener interface in the BookOrderFrame class that you created in exercise 5-3.

1. Open the BookOrderFrame class in the c:\java\ch05\frame directory. Then, implement the WindowListener interface as shown in figure 5-17. In the constructor for the class, be sure to add the addWindowListener method.
2. Compile and run the BookOrderFrame class. When you click on the frame's close button, the frame should close and the program should terminate.

Exercise 5-6 Code more than one class per file

1. Open the code for the Book and BookOrder classes that are stored in the c:\java\ch05\classes directory. Next, cut and paste the code for the Book class after the last brace of the BookOrder class. Then, delete the public modifier from the declaration of the Book class, and save the file.
2. View the files in the c:\java\ch05\classes directory. At this point, there shouldn't be any *.class files in this directory. Then, compile the code for the BookOrder class, and view the files in this directory. Now, there should be *.class files for the Book and BookOrder classes.
3. Open the code for the BookOrderApp class in the c:\java\ch05\classes directory. Then, compile the code for this class and run the application. It should work the same as it did earlier in this chapter. This shows that the BookOrderApp uses the *.class files, not the *.java files.

Exercise 5-7 Review the Java API documentation

Now that you know how inheritance and interfaces work, the API documentation will be more meaningful to you. To demonstrate that, do this exercise.

1. Start your web browser and navigate to the index.html page for the API documentation (it should be bookmarked). In the lower left frame, select the JFrame class so you can see its inheritance chain and implemented interfaces in the right frame. Next, scroll through the inner class and field summaries to see the inherited classes and fields. Then scroll through the methods. After that, you can see the methods that this class inherits from other classes.
2. Go to the methods inherited from the Frame class and find the setTitle method. Click on this link to see a description for the method in the Frame class documentation. Then, go back to the inherited methods summary and skim through the methods inherited from the Window and Component classes. Here, you'll see the addWindowListener, show, and setBounds methods.
3. In the lower left frame, select the WindowListener interface. Since it's an interface, its name is italicized. In its documentation, note that just two classes implement this interface, although you will frequently implement it when working with GUIs. Then, scroll through the documentation and review its seven methods.

6

How to design and test object-oriented programs

Now that you know how to code an object-oriented program, you need to know how to design an object-oriented program. That, of course, is what you need to do before you start coding your programs. Although this chapter doesn't presume to show you how to design complete business systems, it will get you started with the design of simple applications. This chapter also shows you how you can test some of the classes in an object-oriented program before all of the other classes are finished.

An introduction to object-oriented design

The Rational Software Corporation has developed or helped to develop many of the standards and tools that have become industry standards for software development. This corporation helped develop the *Unified Modeling Language* (*UML*); it developed an object-oriented design methodology known as the *Rational Unified Process*; and it developed one of the world's leading object-oriented design tools, Rational Rose. To learn more about Rational's development methods and tools, you can visit their web site at www.rational.com.

For a beginning Java programmer, though, the Rational Unified Process can be overwhelming. That's why this topic presents a simplified version of the Rational Unified Process that's appropriate for beginning Java programmers. But first, this topic shows how an object-oriented program is typically divided into three packages, and it shows how to work with class diagrams.

A common architecture for object-oriented programs

Figure 6-1 shows the architecture for a typical object-oriented program. This architecture divides the program into three packages, which helps to organize related classes and minimize unnecessary communication between classes in different packages.

The *user interface package* holds the classes that define the graphical user interface of the application. To create a user interface, for example, you need to code a class that defines a window and you need to add labels, text boxes, buttons, and other controls to that window. In section 3 of this book, you'll learn more about coding user interfaces.

The *business objects package* holds the classes for the *business objects* of the program. The Book and BookOrder classes that you've seen so far are examples of business objects. Since these classes define the logic that's used to solve problems, they can be referred to as the *problem-domain classes* or *logical classes*. They can also be referred to as *business classes*.

The *database package* holds the classes that save business objects to databases or files. If, for example, you want to make Book objects available to your system, you need to store the data for the Book objects in a database or a file. You also need to be able to create Book objects from that stored data, and you need to be able to save new and modified Book objects to that database or file. In other words, the database package makes your business objects *persistent* from one use of an application to another. In section 4, you'll learn how to work with file input and output, and you'll learn how to work with databases in chapter 19.

A common architecture for object-oriented programs

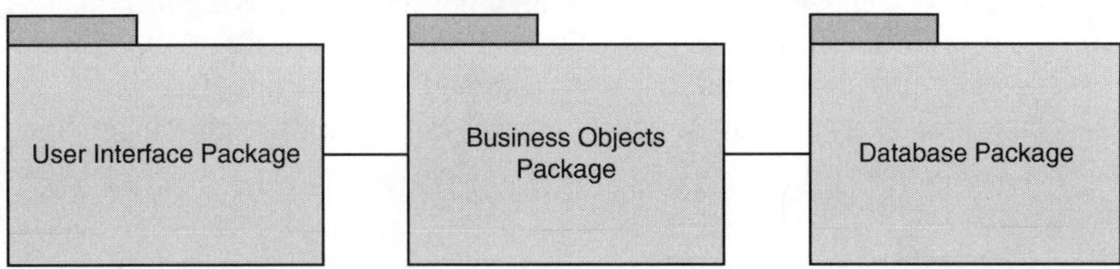

Description

- In 1994, the Rational Software Corporation and the Object Management Group (OMG) helped create a set of standard graphical notations for object-oriented design known as the *Unified Modeling Language* (*UML*).
- The package symbol shown above is a standard UML symbol. Sometimes, the classes within each package are also shown in this type of diagram.
- The *user interface package* holds the classes that define the graphical user interface for the application.
- The *business objects package* holds the classes for the *business objects* of the application. These *business classes* can also be referred to as *problem-domain classes* or *logical classes*.
- The *database package* holds the classes that save and retrieve the data for business objects to or from databases or files. This gives the business objects *persistence.*
- In contrast to the business classes, the user interface and database classes can be referred to as *technical classes.*

Figure 6-1 A common architecture for object-oriented programs

Since the classes in the user interface and database packages implement the technical details of an application, they are sometimes referred to as the *technical classes*. In contrast, the business classes should provide most, if not all, of the business logic of an application. In practice, though, the user interface and database classes are likely to provide some business logic like validating input data in an interface class.

How to work with class diagrams

In chapter 4, you learned how to use a *class diagram* to show the attributes and operations of a single class. Now, figure 6-2 shows how to use a class diagram to show the relationships between the five business classes in an application that allows a customer to enter invoices. Here, all five classes define business objects.

The lines that connect the classes in a class diagram show the relationships between classes, and the numbers on each line show the *cardinality* of each relationship (the numerical relationship). For example, a Customer object in this diagram can relate to more than one Invoice object while an Invoice object must relate to just one Customer object. In addition, a line that ends with a diamond symbol shows that one class can contain one or more objects of another class. This is known as an *aggregate relationship*. For example, an Invoice object can contain one or more LineItem objects, and a LineItem object can contain one or more Item objects.

The class diagram at the top of this figure shows an object-oriented program in the early stages of development. That's why it doesn't show any classes from the user interface or database package. And that's why it doesn't show any of the attributes or operations of the classes.

As your work on the design of a program progresses, though, you add the attributes and operations for each class in the business objects package. You also add the classes in the user interface and database packages to the class diagram. When you're done with that, you convert your class diagrams into Java code that describes the classes, fields, and methods that you've diagrammed. In fact, some of the software tools that you can use to develop class diagrams can also be used to automatically generate Java code from your class diagrams. These tools can also update your class diagrams when you modify the Java code. One such tool is Rational Rose.

If you study the diagram at the top of this figure and if you're familiar with the components of an invoice, you should see how the diagram relates to an invoice. In the heading of an invoice, you find customer data, which includes billing and shipping addresses. So for each Invoice object, there's one Customer object, and there's one or more Address objects. Similarly, in the body of an invoice, you find one line for each item ordered (called a *line item*). So each Invoice object has an aggregate relationship with one or more LineItem objects, which have one-to-one aggregate relationships with Item objects.

A class diagram for five business objects

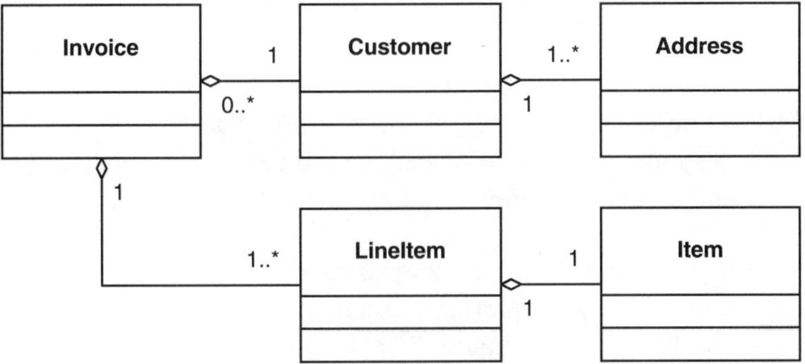

Cardinality

Symbol	Meaning
*	Many
1..*	One to many
0..5	Zero to five

A class diagram that has attributes and operations

LineItem
-lineItemID : long -itemID : long -quantity : int -total : double
+LineItem(lineItemID : long) +getItem() : Item +getQuantity() : int +getTotal() : double

Description

- A *class diagram* is a type of UML diagram that shows the relationships between classes.
- In a class diagram, the lines between the classes indicate the relationships between the classes, and the cardinality symbols indicate the *cardinality* (or numerical relationships). A diamond symbol at the end of a line indicates an *aggregate relationship*, which means that one class can contain one or more instances of the other class.
- In the early phases of analysis and design, you don't need to show the attributes and operations of the class. By the final design phase, though, you should include almost all of the attributes and operations of each class.

Figure 6-2 How to work with class diagrams

A procedure for developing object-oriented programs

Figure 6-3 shows a nine-step procedure that you can use to develop object-oriented programs. When you use this procedure, you will find that the process is *iterative*. In other words, you often have to repeat one or more of the previous steps as you learn more about the requirements and technical details of the program.

In the analysis phase, you gather the requirements, start to identify the business objects, and sketch out the user interface. Often, in fact, it helps to *prototype* the user interface. In this phase, you will be communicating with the people who are going to use the program (the *end users*).

In the design phase, you start by refining the diagrams for the business objects that you identified in step 2. You also add any other business objects that are necessary to the diagram. When you feel that these diagrams are complete, you can begin the diagrams for the classes in the user interface package and the database package.

In the implementation phase, you begin by planning the coding and testing sequence. Then, you can code and test each class. When you use a tool like Rational Rose to design your classes, you can use that tool to generate the starting code for the fields, constructors, and methods of the class. Then, you can code statements within the constructors and methods so they will accomplish the tasks that are specified in the requirements for the program.

In the deployment phase, you begin by documenting the application. To do that, you can use javadoc comments to document your classes. In addition, you may need to prepare the final documentation for the program, which may include class diagrams, and you may need to create a user manual for end users. Then, in step 9, you *deploy* the program, which means to make the program available to the end users.

How to design the classes for a program

As figure 6-3 points out, you identify and design the business classes for an application in steps 2 and 4, and you design the technical classes in step 5. To do those steps, you can follow this general approach.

To identify the business classes, you look for the nouns of the application. For an invoice application, for example, these could be customers, addresses, invoices, line items, items, and the like. For a payroll application, these could be departments, employees, paychecks, W-2 statements, and the like.

Once you've identified the business classes, you try to list the primary attributes and operations (verbs) for each class. The operations can include the set and get methods that let you set and get the attributes of an object, but they should also include the major processing operations (if any). As the design starts to take shape, you can create a class diagram that shows the relationships between the classes as well as the attributes and operations of each class.

A procedure for developing object-oriented programs

Analysis

1. Gather the requirements.
2. Identify the business objects.
3. Diagram or prototype the user interface.

Design

4. Design the classes for the business objects.
5. Design the classes for the user interface and the database packages.

Implementation

6. Plan the coding and testing sequence of the classes.
7. Code and test the classes.

Deployment

8. Document the application.
9. Deploy the application.

Description

- When you use the procedure shown above, you should realize that the process is *iterative*. In other words, you will often have to go back to a previous step as you discover new information in the next step.
- The steps above are an abbreviated version of a process known as the *Rational Unified Process*. For more information about this methodology as well as for information about tools that you can use to analyze and design object-oriented programs, check out the Rational web site at www.rational.com.
- To *prototype* a user interface means to quickly develop a working model that illustrates what the interface is going to look like and how it's going to work, even though most (or all) of the functions aren't actually coded.
- To *deploy* an application means that you make it available to the people who are going to use it. For Java programs, this means that you make the class files available to the *end users*, and you make sure that they have the right version of the Java virtual machine on their systems.

Figure 6-3 A procedure for developing object-oriented programs

Once you have a firm design for the business classes, you can design the technical classes by adding them to the class diagram. Before you can do that, though, you need to know how to code user interfaces and database operations, which you'll learn more about in a moment.

The trouble is that there is no "right" way to design the classes for a business application. For all but the simplest applications, this means that two designers are likely to come up with different designs for the same application, and both approaches will work when you develop the classes in Java. To complicate this problem, the technical classes often conflict with any theory of design so the theory has to be compromised for those classes.

With that as background, this book isn't going to try to present a theory or methodology for the design of object-oriented programs. Instead, it is going to show you examples of how simple object-oriented programs can be designed and coded. Once you understand how these programs work, you'll be able to develop your own techniques for object-oriented design. You'll also have the background you need for learning more about object-oriented design.

How to test an object-oriented program

When you develop an application that consists of several classes, you may want to test some classes before the classes that use them are done. In addition, you may want to use methods before they have been written. That's why this topic presents two skills that you can use for these situations.

How to code a main method that tests a class

Figure 6-4 shows how to code a main method that tests the business class that it's in. That way, you can test the class by running it and checking the information that's printed to the console. Then, when you're satisfied that the class works the way you want it to, you can remove the main method.

In the example in this figure, the assumption is that the BookOrder class is fully developed so it has more than one constructor, get and set methods for all of its instance variables, and a toString method. Then, the main method that's used for testing this class begins by using one of the constructors to create a BookOrder object, after which it prints the data in that object. (Remember that when an object is joined in a string or printed by the System.out.println method, the object's toString method is implicitly called.)

After that, the main method uses the set methods of the BookOrder class to change the values stored in the BookOrder object. This includes using the setBook method to create a new Book object. Last, the main method uses the get methods of the BookOrder object to display new values that are stored in the BookOrder object. By checking the values that the main method prints to the console, you should be able to tell whether or not the BookOrder class works properly.

A class that contains a main method that tests the object

```
public class BookOrder{
   // body of class

   public static void main(String[] args){
      BookOrder bookOrder1 = new BookOrder();
      System.out.println("CONSTRUCTOR 1: \n" + bookOrder1);

      System.out.println("SET METHODS");
      bookOrder1.setBook(new Book("MBDK"));
      System.out.println("setBook method sets book code to MBDK");
      bookOrder1.setQuantity(3);
      System.out.println("setQuantity method sets quantity to 3");
      bookOrder1.setTotal();
      System.out.println("setTotal method calculates total");
      System.out.println();

      System.out.println("GET METHODS");
      System.out.println("getBook method returns: \n"
         + bookOrder1.getBook());
      System.out.println("getQuantity method returns: "
         + bookOrder1.getQuantity());
      System.out.println("getTotal method returns: "
         + bookOrder1.getTotal());
   }
}
```

Output of the main method

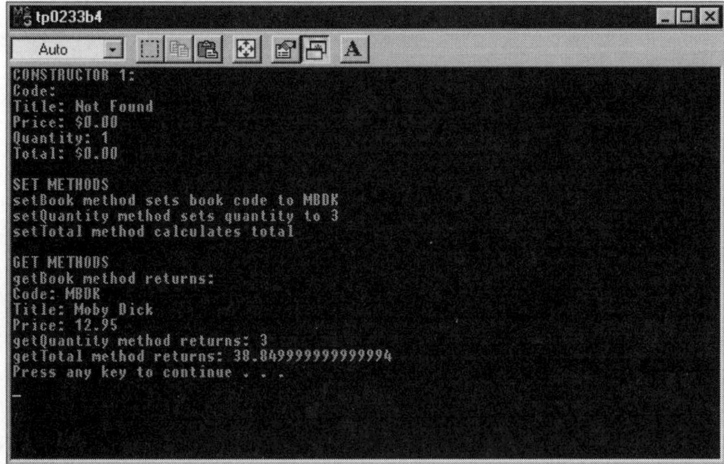

Description

- When you want to test a class before the classes that are going to use it are finished, you can write a main method in the same class. The main method can then test the other methods of the class by sending typical arguments to them and printing the results on the console.
- The main method in the example above works because the BookOrder class has set and get methods for all instance variables and a toString method that overrides the one in the Object class.

Figure 6-4 How to code a main method that tests a class

When and how to code method stubs

When you code a class that calls methods in a class that hasn't been written yet, it sometimes makes sense to code a quick version of that class with *method stubs* instead of the complete methods. Then, your testing can continue. Figure 6-5 shows some examples of how this can work.

If the method stub doesn't have to do anything for a test run, you can code an empty method as shown in the first example. If you just want to check whether a method has been run, you can enter code that prints a message to the console as shown in the second example. And if you need to simulate user input or create an object, you can code a method stub that initializes variables and uses them to create an object as shown in the third example. How you code your methods stubs, of course, is limited only by your ingenuity.

As you create method stubs, though, you must remember that the goal is to get the testing done with a minimum of extra work. In most cases, you can code simple stubs that require little extra work, even for methods that are going to require extensive coding later on. But when a method stub starts getting too elaborate, you're usually better off coding the entire method the way it's supposed to work.

Guidelines for coding stubs

- If a method doesn't have to do anything for the successful completion of a test run, you can code a method stub that doesn't contain any statements.
- If you want to see whether a method gets executed during a test run, you can code a method stub that prints a line to the console.
- If necessary, you can simulate user input by coding test data into a method stub.

Example 1: A method that doesn't contain any statements

```
public void selectCustomer(){}
```

Example 2: A method that displays information

```
public void selectCustomer(){
   System.out.println("The selectCustomer method has been executed.");
}
```

Example 3: A method that simulates user input

```
public void selectCustomer(){
   JOptionPane.showMessageDialog(null,
        "The Select Customer dialog box is under construction. \n"
      + "For testing purposes, 'John Smith' will be the \n"
      + "selected customer.");
   int customerID = 1;
   String customerName = "John Smith";
   customer = new Customer(customerID, customerName);
}
```

Description

- When you're writing a class or method that calls another method that hasn't been coded yet, it sometimes makes sense to quickly write a *method stub* for that method. Then, you can complete the method that you're working on.
- A method stub can be written at any of the levels shown above. But when the stub gets too elaborate, it's often best to write and test the entire method instead of a stub.

Figure 6-5 When and how to code method stubs

The User Email application

To help you understand how to design an object-oriented program, this topic presents the class diagram and code for a simple application. By studying this application, you will see how the classes for a program work together. You'll also see how the Java code relates to the classes in the class diagram. That will give you a much better idea of what you need to do when you design and code your own programs.

The user interface

Figure 6-6 shows the user interface for the User Email application. As you can see, it requires three user entries: first name, last name, and email address. After these entries are made, the user clicks on the Add button to add this data to a record at the end of a file of email records. Otherwise, the user can click on the Exit button at any time to end the application. Although this is about as simple as a real program can be, it illustrates many of the design and coding considerations of much larger programs.

The class diagram

Figure 6-6 also shows the class diagram for this application. Here, the one business class is the User class, which has the three attributes that are entered for each object. This class also has three get methods that make these attributes available to other classes.

In contrast, the UserEmailFrame and UserEmailPanel classes are user interface classes that are used to build the graphical user interface. First, the UserEmailFrame class defines the *frame* or window that the application runs in. It contains a single method that's executed when the window closes. Then, the UserEmailPanel class defines the *panel* that contains the labels, text fields, and buttons of the application. This panel is displayed within the frame of this application, and its lone method contains the code that's executed when the user clicks on any of the buttons in the panel.

Last, the UserIO class contains the methods that provide the input and output (I/O) that lets the application permanently store objects that are created from the User class. For this application, the UserIO class contains a single method that saves the User data in a file or database, but it could also contain methods that retrieve the data for a User object.

From this introduction, you can see that you can't do an adequate job of designing the technical classes for an application until you know how they work. That's why this chapter now introduces the code for all four of the classes in this figure plus the code for the driver class.

The user interface for the User Email application

The class diagram for the User Email application

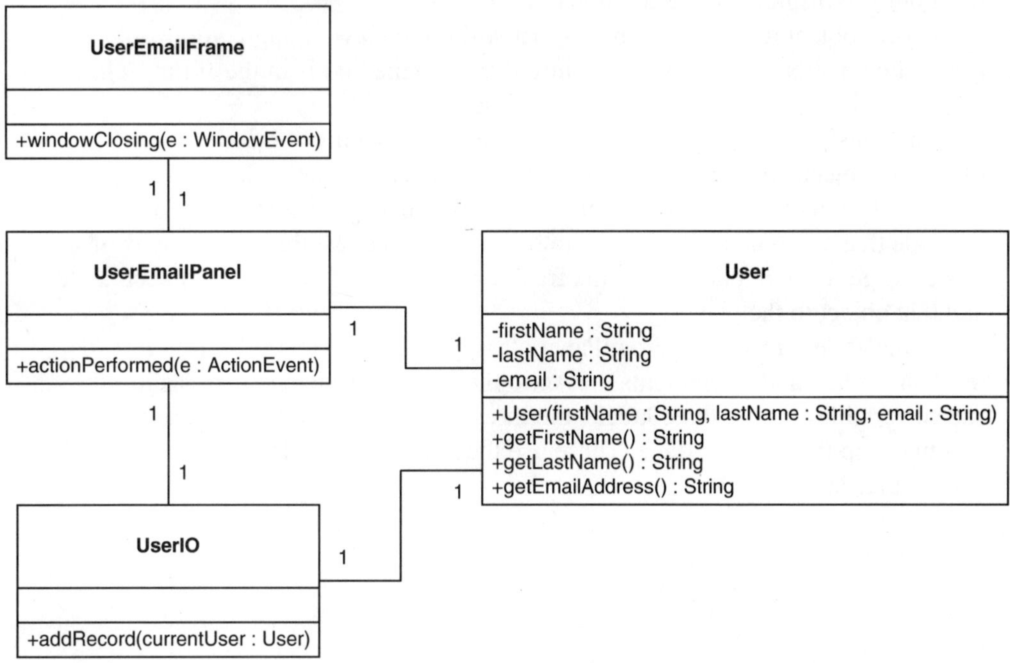

Description

- The UserEmailFrame class defines the JFrame object. This object includes a windowClosing method that's executed whenever the frame is closed.
- The UserEmailPanel class defines the JPanel object that's displayed within the JFrame. This object includes an actionPerformed method that's executed whenever a button on the frame is clicked. If the Add button is clicked, this method creates a new User object from the User class and calls the addRecord method of the UserIO class to add the data in the User object to the end of a file.
- The User class defines the User object.
- The UserIO class contains a static addRecord method that adds the data in a User object to the end of a file.

Figure 6-6 The user interface and class diagram for the User Email application

The code

Figure 6-7 presents the code for all of the classes of the User Email application. As you read through this code, you should begin to get an idea of what it takes to design and code a Java program. Of course, you won't understand most of the code for the user interface and I/O classes, but you should at least understand the shaded code that shows how the classes interact with each other.

This figure starts with the code for the UserEmailApp class, which is the driver class. This class, of course, contains the main method that starts the application. Within the main method, the first statement creates the UserEmailFrame object. Then, the second statement calls the show method of this object to display the frame object.

If you look at the code for the UserEmailFrame class, though, you won't find a show method in it. That's because the show method is in the JFrame class that's inherited by the UserEmailFrame class.

The constructor for the UserEmailFrame class contains the code that defines the frame object. Here, the first seven statements set the title and size of the frame and center the frame on the user's screen. Then, the constructor contains the code that's executed when the frame is closed. The last three statements of this class get the content pane of the frame, create a UserEmailPanel object, and add that object to the pane.

In the code for the UserEmailPanel class, you can see that this class extends the JPanel class and implements the ActionListener interface. It also has instance variables for the three labels, the three text boxes, and the two buttons that make up the user interface. These use the JLabel, JTextField, and JButton classes that Java provides.

The code for the UserEmailApp class

```
import javax.swing.*;

public class UserEmailApp{
   public static void main(String[] args){
      UserEmailFrame frame = new UserEmailFrame();
      frame.show();
   }
}
```

The code for the UserEmailFrame class

```
import java.awt.*;
import java.awt.event.*;
import javax.swing.*;

public class UserEmailFrame extends JFrame{
   public UserEmailFrame(){
      setTitle("User Email");
      Toolkit tk = Toolkit.getDefaultToolkit();
      Dimension d = tk.getScreenSize();
      int width = 300;
      int height = 170;
      setBounds((d.width - width)/2, (d.height-height)/2, width, height);
      setResizable(false);
      addWindowListener(new WindowAdapter(){
         public void windowClosing(WindowEvent e){
            System.exit(0);
         }
      });
      Container contentPane = getContentPane();
      UserEmailPanel panel = new UserEmailPanel();
      contentPane.add(panel);
   }
}
```

The UserEmailPanel class

```
import java.awt.*;
import java.awt.event.*;
import javax.swing.*;
import java.io.*;

public class UserEmailPanel extends JPanel implements ActionListener{
   private JLabel firstNameLabel, lastNameLabel, emailLabel;
   private JTextField firstNameTextField, lastNameTextField, emailTextField;
   private JButton addButton, exitButton;
```

Figure 6-7 The code for the User Email application (part 1 of 3)

The constructor for the UserEmailPanel class creates two panels. The first one, named textFieldPanel, contains the three labels and three text fields. The second one, named buttonPanel, contains the two buttons. Then, the constructor adds these panels to the UserEmailPanel.

Within the constructor for the UserEmailPanel class, you can see that ActionListeners are created for the Add and Exit buttons of the interface. This means that the actionPerformed method will be executed when the user clicks on either button. As a result, the coding for this method determines how the user interface works.

Within the actionPerformed method, you can see that the program exits if the user clicked on the Exit button. However, if the user clicked on the Add button, the code creates a User object from the data that has been entered by the user. Then, it calls the static addRecord method of the UserIO class to add the data in the User object to a file or database. After that, it displays a message dialog box that says that the record has been added. It also sets the text fields in the interface to empty strings.

Note here that you don't need to know how the code in the User or UserIO classes works as you code the actionPerformed method. You just need to know what arguments the User class and addRecord methods require. That's one of the benefits of encapsulation. In fact, when you use a method of the UserIO class, you don't even need to know whether the method uses a file or a database.

The UserEmailPanel class (continued)

```
    public UserEmailPanel(){
        JPanel textFieldPanel = new JPanel();
        textFieldPanel.setLayout(new FlowLayout(FlowLayout.RIGHT));
        firstNameLabel = new JLabel("First name:");
        firstNameTextField = new JTextField(15);
        lastNameLabel = new JLabel("Last name:");
        lastNameTextField = new JTextField(15);
        emailLabel = new JLabel("Email address:");
        emailTextField = new JTextField(15);
        textFieldPanel.add(firstNameLabel);
        textFieldPanel.add(firstNameTextField);
        textFieldPanel.add(lastNameLabel);
        textFieldPanel.add(lastNameTextField);
        textFieldPanel.add(emailLabel);
        textFieldPanel.add(emailTextField);

        JPanel buttonPanel = new JPanel();
        buttonPanel.setLayout(new FlowLayout(FlowLayout.RIGHT));
        addButton = new JButton("Add");
        addButton.addActionListener(this);
        exitButton = new JButton("Exit");
        exitButton.addActionListener(this);
        buttonPanel.add(addButton);
        buttonPanel.add(exitButton);
        setLayout(new BorderLayout());

        add(textFieldPanel, BorderLayout.CENTER);
        add(buttonPanel, BorderLayout.SOUTH);
    }

    public void actionPerformed(ActionEvent e){
        Object source = e.getSource();
        try{
            if (source == exitButton)
                System.exit(0);
            else if (source == addButton){
                User newUser = new User(
                    firstNameTextField.getText(),
                    lastNameTextField.getText(),
                    emailTextField.getText());
                UserIO.addRecord(newUser);
                JOptionPane.showMessageDialog(this,
                    "Your email address has been added to the file.");
                firstNameTextField.setText("");
                lastNameTextField.setText("");
                emailTextField.setText("");
            }
        }
        catch(IOException ioe){
            JOptionPane.showMessageDialog(this, ioe);
        }
    }
}
```

Figure 6-7 The code for the User Email application (part 2 of 3)

When you look at the code for the User and UserIO classes, you can see that they're quite simple. The User class creates a User object with three fields and provides get methods that make that data available to other classes. The UserIO class provides one static method that uses those get methods to add that data to a record at the end of file named UserEmail.txt that's in the current directory.

Remember that the point of going through this code is to give you some idea of how the classes in an application are related. That way, you'll have a better idea of what you have to do when you design a program. So you may want to take a few minutes now to review the relationships.

Keep in mind, though, that you aren't expected to understand the coding details because that's what you'll learn in the rest of this book. In section 3, you'll learn how to develop graphical user interfaces. In section 4, you'll learn how to work with file input and output. And in chapter 19, you'll learn how to work with databases.

The code for the User class

```
public class User{
   private String firstName;
   private String lastName;
   private String emailAddress;

   public User(String first, String last, String email){
      firstName = first;
      lastName = last;
      emailAddress = email;
   }

   public String getFirstName(){ return firstName; }
   public String getLastName(){ return lastName; }
   public String getEmailAddress(){ return emailAddress; }

}
```

The code for the UserIO class

```
import java.io.*;

public class UserIO{
   public static void addRecord(User user) throws IOException{
      PrintWriter out = new PrintWriter(
                        new FileWriter("UserEmail.txt", true));
         out.println(user.getEmailAddress() + " ("
                   + user.getFirstName() + " "
                   + user.getLastName() + ")");
      out.close();
   }
}
```

Figure 6-7 The code for the User Email application (part 3 of 3)

An introduction to the Book Maintenance application

This topic introduces the Book Maintenance application that you'll learn how to code later in this book. It lets a user maintain the records in a file or database that contains the data for Book objects. Although the user interface and database classes for this application are more complex than those for the User Email application, the design and coding concepts are the same.

The user interface

Figure 6-8 shows the graphical user interface for this application. To scroll through the records in the file or database, the user can click on the First, Prev (Previous), Next, and Last buttons. To delete the record that's shown, the user can click on the Delete button. To update a record, the user can change the data, which enables the Update button, and click on that button. And to add a record, the user can click on the Add button, enter the data for a new record, and click on the Update button.

The class diagram

This figure also shows the class diagram for this application. Here again, there's one business class, two user interface classes, and one file or database class. This time, though, a database class is assumed, and it provides methods for all of the operations that may need to be performed.

If you look at the arguments for the methods in the BookDB class, you can see that the first seven don't require any. For instance, the moveNext method moves to the next record in the database. In contrast, the addRecord and updateRecord methods require Book objects as arguments. They use the data in those objects as they add new records or update old records. Finally, the deleteRecord and findOnCode methods require book codes as arguments. Then, they delete or find the records indicated by the book codes.

With this as background, you're ready to learn how to create a user interface by reading section 3. In particular, chapter 12 shows how to create the GUI for this application. As you read, you should keep in mind that you don't need to know how the methods in the file or database class work. You just need to know what their names are, what arguments they require, and what they do.

Then, in chapter 18, you'll learn how to create a class named BookIO that stores the data for this application in a random-access file. And in chapter 19, you'll learn how to create a class named BookDB that uses a database to store the data for this application. In terms of method names, the only difference in these classes is that the BookDB class has a connect method. As a result, it's easy to change this application from a file to a database. Within the methods, though, the coding in these classes is significantly different.

The user interface for the Book Maintenance application

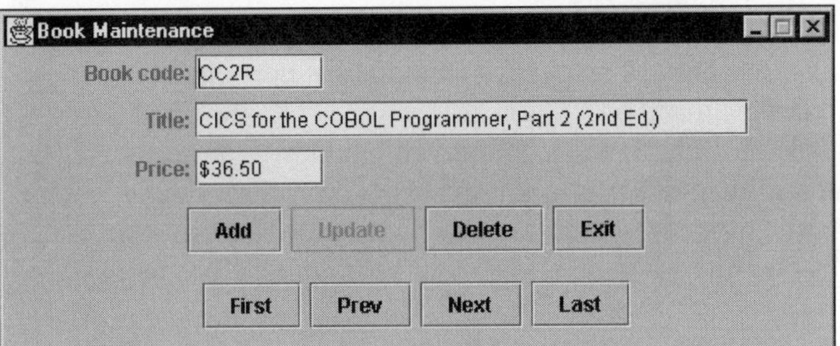

The class diagram for the Book Maintenance application

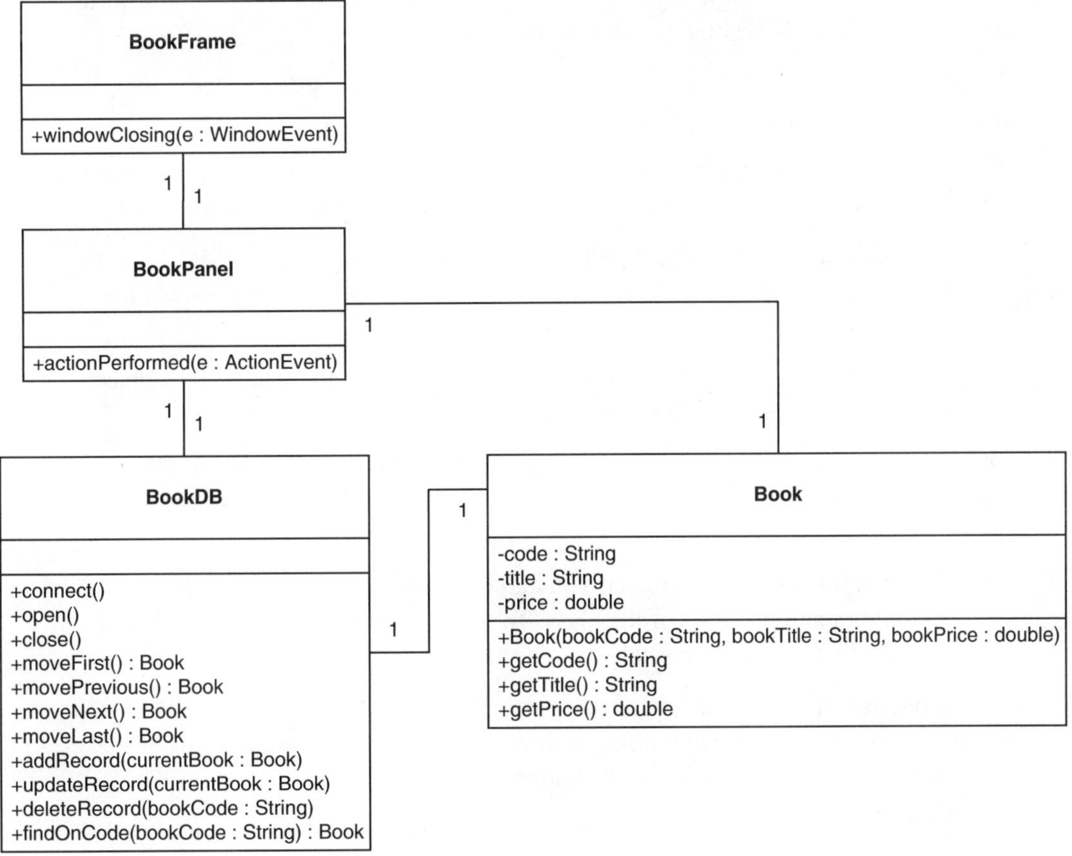

Figure 6-8 The Book Maintenance application

Perspective

The goal of this chapter has been to give you a solid idea of how object-oriented applications are designed and tested. Because you need to see how the code for an object-oriented application works before you're ready to design an object-oriented program, this chapter has also presented the code for a simple application. With that as background, you should now be ready to learn how to code the user interface classes and database classes that your applications require.

Summary

- The *Unified Modeling Language* (UML) is a set of graphical notations for describing software that has become the industry standard.
- The *Rational Unified Process* is an object-oriented software design methodology developed by the Rational Software Corporation.
- The classes in a Java application are typically divided into three packages: a *user interface package*, a *business objects package*, and a *database package*.
- To design the classes of an object-oriented program, you can use a UML diagram known as a *class diagram*. A class diagram shows the relationships between the classes in the application.
- When you design an object-oriented program, you usually go through four phases: analysis, design, implementation, and deployment.
- To design the classes in a program, you start by identifying and designing the business classes. Then, you add the user interface and database classes to the design.
- To test a class that defines an object, you can code a main method that tests all of the constructors and methods of the class. To test related methods, you can code *method stubs* that provide incomplete code that's used for testing purposes only.
- Within the user interface classes of an application, a *frame* displays the window for the application while a *panel* within the frame typically holds the controls of the application such as labels, text fields, buttons, and so on.
- The database classes of an application can store and retrieve data from a file or a database depending on the type of application.

Terms

Unified Modeling Language (UML)
Rational Unified Process
user interface package
business objects package
database package
business object
business class
problem-domain class
logical class
technical class
persistence
class diagram
cardinality
aggregate relationship
line item
iterative
prototype
end user
deploy
method stub
frame
panel

Objectives

- Describe the three packages of a typical object-oriented program.
- Given a class diagram for an application, describe the relationships between the classes that are shown.
- Describe a general procedure for designing the classes of an application.
- Use a main method to test a class, or use a method stub to temporarily implement a method.
- Describe the primary functions of the five classes of the User Email application that was presented in this chapter.
- Given the specifications for an application that requires one business object, a user interface, and database operations that save and retrieve the business object's data, use a class diagram to design its classes.

Exercise 6-1 Test the BookOrder class

This exercise guides you through the process of testing the BookOrder class by itself.

1. Start your text editor and open the BookOrder class that's in the c:\java\ch06\order directory. Note that the Book class is also in this directory.
2. Code a main method within the BookOrder class that tests just the constructor of this class by using code that's similar to the first two lines in the main method in figure 6-4. Note, however, that you will need to pass arguments to the constructor.
3. Add code to the main method that tests the methods in the BookOrder class.
4. When you're done experimenting, close the class.

Exercise 6-2 Test the User Email application

This exercise guides you through the process of running the User Email application so you understand how it works.

1. Start your text editor and open the five classes that are stored in the c:\java\ch06\useremail directory. Then, compile all of them by compiling the UserEmailApp class.
2. Run the UserEmailApp class and enter two or more names and email addresses. Then, use a text editor to view the text file that's created by this application. This file should be named "UserEmail.txt" and it should be stored in the c:\java\ch06\useremail directory. When you open this file, you should see the user email addresses that you entered.
3. If you're going to do exercise 6-3, leave all of the classes open. Otherwise, close all of the open classes.

Exercise 6-3 Write an addRecord method stub

Suppose you want to save the data for the User Email application in a database instead of file. To do that, you want to use a static method named addRecord in a new class named UserDB. Although you haven't even learned how to do database operations yet, you can simulate this change by writing the UserDB class with a method stub for the addRecord method. Then, you can figure out how to write the actual method later on.

1. Start a new class named UserDB that is going to contain one static method named addRecord. The quickest way to do that is to save the UserIO class as UserDB. Then, change UserIO to UserDB in the new class, delete the throws clause, and delete all of the statements in the addRecord method.
2. Write a method stub for the addRecord method and compile the UserDB class. The stub can simply display a line on the console that says the data has been added to the database.
3. Change the code in the UserEmailPanel class so it uses the addRecord method in the UserDB class instead of the UserIO class. Be sure to delete the try/catch statement because the new addRecord method won't throw an IOException. Then, compile this class.
4. Run the UserEmailApp class to see how the method stub works.
5. Enhance the addRecord method stub so it receives the User object and displays the data for it. Then, compile and test again.
6. When you're through experimenting, close all of the open classes.

Section 2

More Java essentials

This section consists of four chapters that show you how to use specific types of Java features. Chapter 7 presents all of the operators that Java provides plus the skills you need for working with dates. Chapter 8 presents all of the control statements that Java provides. Chapter 9 shows you how to work with arrays, strings, and vectors. And chapter 10 gives you more information about handling exceptions and debugging.

Since each chapter in this section is treated as an independent unit, you don't have to read these chapters in sequence. If, for example, you want to learn more about handling exceptions, you can read chapter 10 next. Or, if you want to learn about the other Java control statements, you can read chapter 8 next. We do, however, recommend that you read chapter 8 before you read chapter 9 because chapter 9 uses for loops, which are presented in chapter 8.

Remember, too, that you don't have to read the chapters in this section right after you read the chapters in section 1. If you prefer, you can skip to section 3 to learn how to develop a graphical user interface or to section 4 to learn how to work with file input and output.

7

How to work with operators and dates

In chapter 2, you learned how to use operators in arithmetic and conditional expressions. You also learned how to use the eight primitive data types and strings. Now, in this chapter, you'll learn more about operators. You'll also learn how to work with dates, which are important to most business programs.

Operators, order of precedence, and associativity

This topic begins by reviewing the operators that were presented in chapter 2. Then, it presents the rest of the Java operators and explains how Java evaluates these operators when they're used in expressions.

A review of operators

In chapter 2, you learned how to work with the operators presented in figure 7-1. In particular, you learned how to use *arithmetic operators* to code *arithmetic expressions* that performed calculations on the numeric data types. You learned how to cast one data type to another. You learned how to use *assignment operators* to assign values to variables. And you learned how to use the *relational* and *logical operators* to code *conditional expressions* that were used in if statements and while loops.

Along the way, you learned the difference between binary and unary operators. In short, *binary operators* work on two operands while a *unary operator* works on one operand. For example, since the subtraction operator (-) works on two operands by subtracting one number from another, it's a binary operator. In contrast, since the negative sign operator (-) works on a single operand by reversing the value of the number to its right, it's a unary operator.

Arithmetic operators

Operator	Name	Description
+	Addition	Adds two operands.
-	Subtraction	Subtracts the right operand from the left operand.
*	Multiplication	Multiplies the right operand and the left operand.
/	Division	Divides the right operand into the left operand. If both operands are integers, then the result is an integer.
%	Modulus	Returns the value that is left over after dividing the right operand into the left operand.
++	Increment	Adds 1 to the operand (x = x + 1).
--	Decrement	Subtracts 1 from the operand (x = x - 1).
+	Positive sign	Promotes byte, short, or char types to the int type.
-	Negative sign	Reverses the value of the operand.

The cast operator

Operator	Name	Description
(type)	Cast	Converts the operand to the data type specified in parentheses.

Assignment operators

Operator	Example	Description
=	c = 5;	c = 5;
+=	c += 5;	c = c + 5;
-=	c -= 8;	c = c - 8;
*=	c *= 2;	c = c * 2;
/=	c /= 2;	c = c / 2;
%=	c %= 9;	c = c % 9;

Relational operators

Operator	Name	Returns a true value...
==	Equal to	if the operands are equal.
!=	Not equal to	if the operands aren't equal.
>	Greater than	if the left operand is greater than the right.
<	Less than	if the left operand is less than the right.
>=	Greater than or equal to	if the left operand is greater than or equal to the right.
<=	Less than or equal to	if the left operand is less than or equal to the right.

Logical operators

Operator	Name	Description
&&	And	Returns a true value if both expressions are true.
||	Or	Returns a true value if either expression is true.
!	Not	Reverses the value of the expression.

Figure 7-1 A review of operators

How to work with the increment and decrement operators

Figure 7-2 shows how to work with the increment and decrement operators. In particular, it shows how to use the *prefix* and *postfix* forms of the increment and decrement operators. Although all of the examples in this figure use the increment operator, the same concepts apply to the decrement operator.

When working with the increment and decrement operators, you should realize that the prefix and postfix forms work the same unless they're used in an expression. For instance, in the first example, if the postfix form were used instead of the prefix form, the value displayed would still be 11. However, the next two examples show how you can use the prefix and postfix forms to control when the operand is updated.

The second example shows how to use the prefix form of the increment operator in an expression. In this example, x is initialized to 10. Then, Java increments the operand before it executes the println method. As a result, both println methods display 11.

The third example is the same as the second example, but it uses the postfix form of the increment operator. In this example, Java executes the println method before it increments the operand. As a result, the first println method displays 10 while the second println method displays 11.

Two forms of the increment operator

Form	Syntax	Description
Prefix	++operand	Increments the operand before the statement is executed, using the new value of the operand in the expression.
Postfix	operand++	Increments the operand after the statement is executed, using the current value of the operand in the expression.

Examples

Example 1: The prefix form when it's not in an expression

```
int x = 10;
++x;
System.out.println(x);    // displays 11
```

Example 2: The prefix form used in an expression that prints a number

```
int x = 10;
System.out.println(++x); // displays 11
System.out.println(x);    // displays 11
```

Example 3: The postfix form used in an expression that prints a number

```
int x = 10;
System.out.println(x++); // displays 10
System.out.println(x);    // displays 11
```

Description

- The *prefix* and *postfix* forms of the increment and decrement operators work the same unless they are in an expression. In an expression, though, the prefix form is evaluated before the expression is used; the postfix form is evaluated after the expression is used.

Figure 7-2 How to work with the increment and decrement operators

How to work with the shortcut if/else operator

In chapter 2, you learned how to code if/else statements. Now, figure 7-3 shows you how to use the *shortcut if/else operator* to code a simple if/else statement. When you use this operator, the first operand must be a conditional expression that evaluates to true or false. If it evaluates to true, the second operand is returned. Otherwise, the third operand is returned.

Since the shortcut if/else operator uses three operands, it's often referred to as the *ternary operator*. And since the shortcut if/else operator begins with a conditional expression, it's sometimes called the *conditional ternary operator*.

The examples in this figure show how the shortcut if/else operator can be used to duplicate the logic of a standard if/else statement. Note, however, that the standard if/else statement is easier to read and maintain, even though it requires five lines of code. That's why you should use it for normal if/else logic. In contrast, the shortcut if/else operator is occasionally useful when you need to use if/else logic within an expression as illustrated by the third example.

How to work with the instanceof operator

This figure also shows how to use the *instanceof operator* in a conditional expression. To use this operator, the first operand must be an object, and the second operand must be a class. If the object is an *instance of* the class or any of its subclasses, it returns a true value. Otherwise, it returns a false value.

The example shows how to use the instanceof operator within the equals method of the BookOrder class. Here, the equals method contains a parameter that accepts any object. Then, the first statement uses an if statement to check whether the object that has been passed to the method is an instance of the BookOrder class or any of its subclasses. If so, the expression returns a true value and the statements within the if block are executed. Otherwise, the method returns a false value.

The shortcut if/else operator

Expression

```
operand1 ? operand2 : operand3
```

Description

If operand1 is true, return operand2. Otherwise, return operand3.

Example 1: A regular if statement

```
double discountPercent = 0;
if (orderTotal >= 100)
   discountPercent = .2;
else
   discountPercent = .1;
```

Example 2: The same statement using the shortcut if/else operator

```
double discountPercent = (orderTotal >= 100) ? .2 : .1;
```

Example 3: The shortcut if/else operator within an expression

```
double discountAmount = orderTotal * ((orderTotal >= 100) ? .2 : .1);
```

The instanceof operator

Expression

```
operand1 instanceof operand2
```

Description

If operand1 (an object) is an *instance of* operand2 (a class), return a true value. Otherwise, return a false value. An object is considered an instance of a class if it has been created from a class or any subclass of that class.

Example

```
public boolean equals(Object object){
   if (object instanceof BookOrder){
      // this if block is executed when the object
      // is an instance of the BookOrder class
   }
   return false;
}
```

Figure 7-3 How to work with the shortcut if/else and instanceof operators

How to work with the bitwise and shift operators

For the sake of completeness, figure 7-4 summarizes all of the operators that you can use to work with the *bits* in the *binary numbers* that are stored in Java's four integer data types: byte, short, int, or long. Although you may never need to work with bits, it's worth taking a moment to familiarize yourself with these operators in case you ever do need them.

This figure starts by showing the formula that's used to convert binary values to decimal values. This shows how each bit can hold a one or a zero and how Java calculates the decimal values from the bits. Here, the first four examples use four bits while the fifth example uses eight bits, or one *byte*.

The first four operators in this figure are known as the *bitwise operators*. Of these, the first three operators are binary operators that compare two binary values and return a new binary value. The first is the *and* operator; the second is the *or* operator; and the third is the *xor* operator, which can be referred to as the *exclusive or* operator. The fourth bitwise operator is the *not* operator, which is a unary operator that reverses the values of the bits in a single operand.

The next three operators in this figure are known as the *shift operators*. They shift the bits left or right by the specified number of bits. However, there is a subtle difference between the shift right and shift right unsigned operators. The shift right operator fills in the bits on the left with the sign bit, which is 1 for a negative number or 0 for a positive number. The shift right unsigned operator fills in the bits on the left with zeros. For positive numbers, of course, these operators work the same.

The bitwise assignment operators work similarly to the assignment operators you reviewed earlier in this chapter. Although they don't provide any additional functionality, they do provide a shorter way to code an expression for comparing bit values.

How binary works

Binary value	Formula	Decimal value
0001	0*(2^3) + 0*(2^2) + 0*(2^1) + 1*(2^0)	1
0010	0*(2^3) + 0*(2^2) + 1*(2^1) + 0*(2^0)	2
0100	0*(2^3) + 1*(2^2) + 0*(2^1) + 0*(2^0)	4
1000	1*(2^3) + 0*(2^2) + 0*(2^1) + 0*(2^0)	8
0001 0000	0*(2^7) + 0*(2^6) + 0*(2^5) + 1*(2^4) + 0*(2^3) + 0*(2^2) + 0*(2^1) + 0*(2^0)	16

Bitwise operators and shift operators

Operator	Name	Description
&	Bitwise and	Sets each bit to 1 if both parallel bits are 1.
|	Bitwise or	Sets each bit to 1 if either parallel bit is 1.
^	Bitwise xor	Sets the bit to 1 if the parallel bits are different.
~	Bitwise not	Inverts the value of each bit.
<<	Shift left	Shifts the bits left by the distance specified in the right operand.
>>	Shift right	Shifts the bits right by the distance specified in the right operand, filling the bits on the left with the sign bit (0 for positive, 1 for negative).
>>>	Shift right, unsigned	Shifts the bits right by the distance specified in the right operand, filling the bits on the left with zeros.

Examples

For each example:

```
byte x = 14;     // binary value = 1110
byte y = 6;      // binary value = 0110
```

Expression	Binary result	Decimal result
x & y	0110	6
x | y	1110	14
x ^ y	1000	8
~x	0001	1
x << 1	0001 1100	28
x >> 2	0011	3
x >>> 2	0011	3

Bitwise assignment operators

For each example:

```
byte c = 12;     // binary value: 1100
9 (literal)      // binary value: 1001
```

Operator	Example	Description	Binary result	Decimal result
&=	c &= 9;	c = c & 9;	c = 1000	c = 8
|=	c |= 9;	c = c | 9;	c = 1101	c = 13
^=	c ^= 9;	c = c ^ 9;	c = 0101	c = 5
<<=	c <<= 1;	c = c << 1;	c = 0001 1000	c = 24
>>=	c >>= 2;	c = c >> 2;	c = 0011	c = 3
>>>=	c >>>= 1;	c = c >>> 1;	c = 0110	c = 6

Figure 7-4 How to work with the bitwise and shift operators

How to work with order of precedence and associativity

Figure 7-5 summarizes the *order of precedence* for the operators, and it describes how Java uses the order of precedence when it evaluates expressions that contain the operators summarized in this figure. Most of the time, Java follows rules that you're probably already familiar with. For example, multiplication is performed before addition. However, you can always use parentheses to override the order of precedence. As a result, you don't need to memorize the order of precedence. When in doubt, use parentheses.

This figure lists the operators from the greatest to least precedence. In other words, the first operator to be executed in any expression is the increment or decrement operator; followed by the positive sign, negative sign, the not operator, or the bitwise not operator; followed by the casting operator; and so on. As you would expect, this list shows that multiplication and division are performed before addition and subtraction.

But what if you have both a multiplication and division operator in an expression? Since they both have the same precedence, you need to know which operator will be executed first. To determine this, you use the rules of associativity. *Associativity* tells you the direction to perform the operations. For instance, if you look at the associativity of the multiplication and division operators, you see that its associativity is from left to right. This means that whatever sign Java finds first when reading an equation from left to right will be performed first. Most of the time, the associativity for binary operators is from left to right while the associativity for unary operators is from right to left.

When you use parentheses to control the order of precedence, Java works from the expressions in the innermost sets of parentheses to the expressions in the outer sets of parentheses. When all the expressions in parentheses have been evaluated, the evaluation continues using the order of precedence and associativity rules.

The examples show how to use parentheses to control the *order of evaluation*. The first and second examples show how to use parentheses to override the order of precedence. The third and fourth examples show how to use parentheses to override the rules of associativity. And the fifth and sixth examples show how to use multiple sets of parentheses to clarify an expression. When you apply the rules of associativity to this expression, the division will be evaluated before the multiplication. As a result, both expressions will yield the same value. However, the parentheses in the sixth example make the order of evaluation absolutely clear.

The last example in this figure shows the Java expression for the formula for computing the monthly payment for a loan based on the loan amount, monthly interest rate, and number of months. Here, parentheses are used only when necessary. Otherwise, this expression relies on the order of precedence and the rules of associativity. Note, however, that more sets of parentheses could be used to further clarify the order of evaluation.

Order of precedence

<table>
<tr><th>Operator</th><th>Description</th><th>Associativity</th></tr>
<tr><td>++ --</td><td>Pre-increment, pre-decrement</td><td>Right</td></tr>
<tr><td>++ --</td><td>Post-increment, post-decrement</td><td>Left</td></tr>
<tr><td>+ - ! ~</td><td>Plus, minus, not, bitwise not</td><td>Right</td></tr>
<tr><td>(type)</td><td>Cast</td><td>Right</td></tr>
<tr><td>* / %</td><td>Multiplicative operators</td><td>Left</td></tr>
<tr><td>- +</td><td>Additive operators</td><td>Left</td></tr>
<tr><td><< >> >>></td><td>Bitwise shift</td><td>Left</td></tr>
<tr><td>< <= > >= instanceof</td><td>Relational operators</td><td>Left</td></tr>
<tr><td>== !=</td><td>Equality operators</td><td>Left</td></tr>
<tr><td>&</td><td>Bitwise and</td><td>Left</td></tr>
<tr><td>^</td><td>Bitwise xor</td><td>Left</td></tr>
<tr><td>|</td><td>Bitwise or</td><td>Left</td></tr>
<tr><td>&&</td><td>Conditional and</td><td>Left</td></tr>
<tr><td>||</td><td>Conditional or</td><td>Left</td></tr>
<tr><td>? :</td><td>Shortcut if/else operator</td><td>Right</td></tr>
<tr><td>= += -= *= /= %= <<=
>>= >>>= &= ^= |=</td><td>Assignment operators</td><td>Right</td></tr>
</table>

How to use parentheses to control the order of evaluation

```
10 + 10 * 2         // result is 30
(10 + 10) * 2       // result is 40
10 / 10 * 2         // result is 2
10 / (10 * 2)       // result is 0.5
(salesThisYTD - salesLastYTD) / salesLastYTD * 100;
((salesThisYTD - salesLastYTD) / salesLastYTD) * 100;
```

A formula that computes the monthly payment of a loan

$$\text{monthly payment} = \frac{\text{amount} * \text{monthly interest rate}}{1 - \dfrac{1}{(1 + \text{monthly interest rate})^{\#\text{of months}}}}$$

The arithmetic expression for the formula

```
double monthlyPayment = loanAmount * monthlyInterestRate/
    (1 - 1/Math.pow(1+monthlyInterestRate, months));
```

Description

- You can use parentheses to control the order in which Java performs arithmetic operations. Then, Java works from the inner sets of parentheses outward.
- Java uses the *order of precedence* when evaluating expressions. When two or more operations have equal precedence, Java uses the rules of *associativity* to evaluate the expression from left to right or right to left.

Figure 7-5 How to work with order of precedence and associativity

How to work with dates and times

Although Java doesn't have a primitive data type for working with dates and times, it does have several classes that you can use to work with dates and times. In this topic, you'll learn how to create objects that store dates and times, how to manipulate the values stored in those objects, and how to format those objects.

How to use the GregorianCalendar class to set dates and times

When you create dates and times, you usually use the GregorianCalendar class as shown in figure 7-6. Although you might think that a class named after a calendar would work mainly with dates, this class actually represents a point in time down to the millisecond.

This figure starts by showing four constructors for the GregorianCalendar class. The first constructor creates an object that contains the current date and time. The next three constructors create objects that contain values for a date and time that you specify. For instance, the second constructor creates a date and time using integer values for year, month, and day. In this case, Java sets the hours, minutes, and seconds to 00. However, you can use the third or fourth constructors to set these values.

The first example shows how to get the current date and time. When you call this constructor, it sets the GregorianCalendar object equal to the current date and time. Java gets this date from your computer's internal clock. As a result, the date and time should be set correctly for your time zone.

The five examples in the next group show how to set the values for dates and times. Although setting the year and the day works as you would expect, setting the month isn't as intuitive. To code a month, you enter an integer between 0 to 11 where 0 equals January and 11 equals December. As a result, the first two examples set the date to January, 30, 1998, while the next three examples set the date to December 31, 2005.

When setting times, any values that you don't set will default to 0. In addition, to set the hour, you must enter an integer between 0 and 23 where 0 is equal to midnight and 23 is equal to 11 PM. As a result, the first three examples in the second group set the time to midnight (12:00:00 AM). Here, the first and third examples default to midnight while the second example explicitly sets the time to midnight. The last two examples in this group set the time to 7:30:00 AM and 7:30:30 PM.

In practice, you usually pass variables to the GregorianCalendar constructor when you want to create a new object. This is illustrated by the last example in this figure. Here, year, month, and day variables are passed to the constructor.

The GregorianCalendar class

```
java.util.GregorianCalendar;
```

Constructors for the GregorianCalendar class

```
GregorianCalendar();
GregorianCalendar(intYear, intMonth, intDay);
GregorianCalendar(intYear, intMonth, intDay,
                  intHour, intMinute);
GregorianCalendar(intYear, intMonth, intDay,
                  intHour, intMinute, intSecond);
```

Examples

How to get the current date

```
GregorianCalendar now = new GregorianCalendar();
```

How to set a date with literals

```
GregorianCalendar startDate = new GregorianCalendar(1998,0,30);
GregorianCalendar startDate = new GregorianCalendar(1998,0,30,0,0,0);
GregorianCalendar endDate = new GregorianCalendar(2005,11,31);
GregorianCalendar endDate = new GregorianCalendar(2005,11,31,7,30);
GregorianCalendar endDate = new GregorianCalendar(2005,11,31,19,30,30);
```

How to set a date with variables

```
GregorianCalendar birthDate =
        new GregorianCalendar(birthYear, birthMonth, birthDay);
```

Description

- Year must be a four-digit integer.
- Month must be an integer from 0-11 with 0 being January and 11 being December.
- Day must be an integer from 1-31.
- Hour must be an integer from 0-23, with 0 being 12am (midnight) and 23 being 11pm.
- Minute and second must be integers from 0-59.
- Any time values that aren't set will default to 0.

Figure 7-6 How to use the GregorianCalendar class to set dates and times

How to use the Calendar and GregorianCalendar fields and methods

The GregorianCalendar class is a subclass of the Calendar class. As a result, it inherits all public and protected fields and methods from the Calendar class. Then, the GregorianCalendar class overrides some of the methods of the Calendar class.

Once you create an object from the GregorianCalendar class, you can use the fields and methods shown in figure 7-7 to work with the object. You can also find other fields and methods in the API documentation for these classes.

This figure starts by summarizing the fields and methods that are available for working with GregorianCalendar objects. Then, the examples show how to use these fields and methods. Although these examples show how to work with the date portion of a GregorianCalendar object, you can use the same skills to work with the time portion.

The first set of examples shows how to use the set, add, and roll methods to change the value that's stored in a GregorianCalendar object. The first two examples show how you can use the same arguments for the set method that you used for the constructors of the GregorianCalendar class. In addition, you can use fields from the Calendar class, such as JANUARY and FEBRUARY, to set the month. The rest of the examples show the difference between the add and roll methods. When you use the add method to add 14 months to the date, the year is also increased. But when you use the roll method to roll the current month forward by 14 months, the year isn't affected. As a result, it only changes the month from August to October.

When you manipulate dates and times, you need to make sure to supply values that make sense. For example, since there are only 30 days in November, it doesn't make sense to use 31 as the day argument. If you do that, Java sets the date to December 1.

The second set of examples shows how to use the get method to return various integer values that are stored in the GregorianCalendar object. Here, the year is 2000, the month is 1 (February), the day is 4, the day of the week is 6 (Friday), and the day of the year is 35 (the 31 days of January plus the 4 days of February).

Note that the last method for the Calendar and GregorianCalendar classes is the getTime method, which returns a Date object. You'll learn more about this type of object on the next page.

The Calendar class

```
java.util.Calendar;
```

Fields of the Calendar class

DATE	DAY_OF_MONTH	DAY_OF_WEEK	DAY_OF_YEAR
HOUR	HOUR_OF_DAY	MINUTE	MONTH
SECOND	YEAR	MONDAY...SUNDAY	JANUARY...DECEMBER

Methods of the Calendar and GregorianCalendar classes

Method	Description
`set(intYear, intMonth, etc.)`	Sets the values for year, month, date, hour, minute, and second just as they are set in the constructor for the GregorianCalendar class.
`set(intField, intValue)`	Sets the specified field to the supplied value.
`add(intField, intValue)`	Adds the supplied value to the specified field.
`roll(intField, intValue)`	Adds the supplied value to the specified field, but doesn't affect other fields.
`roll(intField, booleanValue)`	Increments the value of the specified field by 1 for true values and decrements the value of field by 1 for false values.
`get(intField)`	Returns the int value of the specified field.
`getTime()`	Returns a Date object.

Examples

How to change the value of a GregorianCalendar object

```
GregorianCalendar endDate = new
   GregorianCalendar(2000, 0, 1);                    // Jan 1, 2000
endDate.set(2000, 2, 30);                            // Mar 30, 2000
endDate.set(2000, Calendar.MARCH, 30);               // Mar 30, 2000
endDate.set(Calendar.MONTH, Calendar.JANUARY);       // Jan 30, 2000
endDate.add(Calendar.MONTH, 5);                      // June 30, 2000
endDate.add(Calendar.MONTH, 14);                     // Aug 30, 2001
endDate.roll(Calendar.MONTH, 14);                    // Oct 30, 2001
endDate.roll(Calendar.MONTH, true);                  // Nov 30, 2001
endDate.roll(Calendar.DAY_OF_MONTH, false);          // Nov 29, 2001
```

How to return values from a GregorianCalendar object

```
GregorianCalendar birthday = new
   GregorianCalendar(2000, Calendar.FEBRUARY, 4);    // Fri, Feb 4, 2000
int year = birthday.get(Calendar.YEAR);              // year is 2000
int month = birthday.get(Calendar.MONTH);            // month is 1
int day = birthday.get(Calendar.DAY_OF_MONTH);       // day is 4
int dayOfWeek = birthday.get(Calendar.DAY_OF_WEEK); // dayOfWeek is 6
int dayOfYear = birthday.get(Calendar.DAY_OF_YEAR); // dayOfYear is 35
```

Note

- For more information about these and other fields and classes, look up the Calendar and GregorianCalendar classes in the documentation for the Java API.

Figure 7-7 How to use the Calendar and GregorianCalendar fields and methods

How to use the Date class

Figure 7-8 shows how to use the Date class. Unlike the GregorianCalendar class, the Date class doesn't have fields that represent the year, month, day, and so on. Instead, the Date class represents a point in time by the number of milliseconds since January 1, 1970 00:00:00 Greenwich Mean Time (GMT). You need to use Date objects when you want to format a date as shown in the next figure. You may also find Date objects useful when you want to perform arithmetic operations on dates like subtracting one date from another.

Most of the time, you'll create a Date object by invoking the getTime method of a GregorianCalendar object as shown in the first example in this figure. Since the getTime method returns a Date object, you don't need to call either of the Date constructors. However, you can also use either of the constructors in this figure to create a Date object. The first constructor creates a Date object for the current date and time while the second constructor creates a Date object based on the number of milliseconds that are passed to it.

Although you won't need the two methods summarized in this figure very often, they're easy to use if you ever need them. The toString method returns a readable string that displays the day of week, month, date, time, time zone, and year. The getTime method returns a long integer that represents the number of milliseconds since January 1, 1970 00:00:00 GMT.

The last example in this figure shows how Date objects can be useful when you want to calculate the elapsed time between two dates. First, two GregorianCalendar dates are converted to Date objects. Next, the Date objects are converted to milliseconds. Then, the starting date in milliseconds is subtracted from the ending date in milliseconds to get the elapsed milliseconds, and that result is divided by the number of milliseconds in a day to get the elapsed days. This type of routine is useful in many business programs.

The Date class

```
java.util.Date;
```

Constructors

Constructor	Description
`Date()`	Creates a Date object for the current date and time based on your computer's internal clock.
`Date(longMilliseconds)`	Creates a Date object based on the number of milliseconds that is passed to it.

Methods

Method	Description
`getTime()`	Returns a long value that represents the number of milliseconds for the date.
`toString()`	Returns a String object that contains the date and time formatted like this: Wed Aug 02 08:31:25 PDT 2000.

Examples

How to convert a GregorianCalendar object to a Date object

```
Date endDate = gregEndDate.getTime();
```

How to get a Date object for the current date/time

```
Date now = new Date();
```

How to convert Date objects to string and long variables

```
String nowAsString = now.toString();    // converts to a string
long nowInMS = now.getTime();           // converts to milliseconds
```

How to calculate the number of days between two GregorianCalendar dates

```
Date startDate = gregStartDate.getTime();
Date endDate = gregEndDate.getTime();
long startDateMS = startDate.getTime();
long endDateMS = endDate.getTime();
long elapsedMS = endDateMS - startDateMS;
long elapsedDays = elapsedMS / (24 * 60 * 60 * 1000);
```

Description

- A Date object carries a date and time as the number of milliseconds since January 1, 1970 00:00:00 GMT (Greenwich Mean Time).
- You need to convert GregorianCalendar objects to Date objects when you want to use the DateFormat class to format them as shown in the next figure.
- Date objects are also useful when you want to calculate the number of milliseconds (or days) between two dates.

Figure 7-8 How to use the Date class

How to use the DateFormat class to format dates and times

Figure 7-9 shows how to use the DateFormat class to convert a Date object into a string that you can use to display dates and times. In addition, it shows how to control the format of these strings. Since this class works similarly to the NumberFormat class, you shouldn't have much trouble using it.

Before you can format a date, you need to use one of the static methods of the DateFormat class to create a DateFormat object that has a particular format. When you do that, you can choose to return the date only, the time only, or the date and time. If you don't specify a format, the DateFormat object will use the default format. However, you can use one of the four DateFormat fields to override the default date format as shown by the last set of examples. Once you've created a DateFormat object that has the format that you want, you can use its format method to convert a Date object into a string with the specified format.

The first example shows how to format a Date object with the default format. Here, the getDateTimeInstance method is used to return both date and time. Since no arguments are supplied for this method, it will return a string that contains the current date and time with the default format, which should look something like this: Jan 30, 2001 12:10:10 PM.

The second example shows how to format a GregorianCalendar object with the default date format. Here, you can see that you start by using the getTime method to convert the GregorianCalendar object to a Date object. Then, you use the getDateInstance method to return the date only. Since no arguments are supplied for this method, it will return a string that contains this date: Dec 31, 2005.

The final examples show how you can use the fields of the DateFormat class to override the default date format. Here, you can see how to use the SHORT field of the DateFormat class, but the same skills apply to the other three fields. If you use the getDateTimeInstance method, you need to supply the first argument for the date and the second argument for the time. Since both of the arguments are specified as short in this example, they will return a date with a format something like this: 12/31/05 7:30:00 AM.

When you use the LONG and FULL fields, the time portion of the date will end with an abbreviation for the current time zone. In this figure, the examples use the Pacific Standard Time (PST) time zone.

The DateFormat class

```
java.text.DateFormat;
```

Static methods

Method	Description
`getDateInstance()`	Returns a DateFormat object with date, but not time.
`getTimeInstance()`	Returns a DateFormat object with time, but not date.
`getDateTimeInstance()`	Returns a DateFormat object with date and time.
`getDateInstance(intField)`	Same as above, but you can use the fields shown below to override the default date format.
`getTimeInstance(intField)`	Same as above, but you can use the fields shown below to override the default time format.
`getDateTimeInstance(intField, intField)`	Same as above, but you can use the fields shown below to override the default date and time formats.

Fields

Style	Date example	Time example
`SHORT`	12/31/05	12:00 AM.
`MEDIUM`	Dec 31, 2005	7:30:00 PM
`LONG`	December 31, 2005	7:30:00 AM PST
`FULL`	Saturday, December 31, 2005	7:30:00 AM PST

Common method

Method	Description
`format(DateObject)`	Returns a String object of the Date object with the format that's specified by the DateFormat object.

Examples

How to format a Date object with the default date/time format

```
Date now = new Date();
DateFormat defaultDate = DateFormat.getDateTimeInstance();
String nowString = defaultDate.format(now);
```

How to format a GregorianCalendar object with the default date format

```
GregorianCalendar gregEndDate = new GregorianCalendar(2005,11,31,7,30);
Date endDate = gregEndDate.getTime();
DateFormat defaultDate = DateFormat.getDateInstance();
String endDateString = defaultDate.format(endDate);
```

How to change the default formats

```
DateFormat shortDate = DateFormat.getDateInstance(DateFormat.SHORT);
DateFormat shortTime = DateFormat.getTimeInstance(DateFormat.SHORT);
DateFormat shortDateTime =
    DateFormat.getDateTimeInstance(DateFormat.SHORT, DateFormat.SHORT);
```

Figure 7-9 How to use the DateFormat class to format dates and times

Code that adds the current date to the Book Order application

To show how you can use some of these date skills in a program, figure 7-10 shows how to add a date to the BookOrder class. When this code creates a BookOrder object, it sets the date for the object to the current date. Then, you can call the getDate method or the toString method from another class to return a string representation of this date. Although this example uses an instance variable of the String type, it could also use an instance variable of the GregorianCalendar type. Then, the getDate method could return a GregorianCalendar object instead of a String object.

The import statements at the beginning of the file allow the BookOrder class to use the GregorianCalendar, Calendar, Date, and DateFormat classes. Then, the fourth instance variable declares a String object that represents the date, and the constructor calls the setDate method so it sets this instance variable every time it creates a BookOrder object. Last, the getDate method returns a string that represents the date, and the toString method returns a string that begins by displaying the date.

Code that adds the current date to the BookOrder class

```
import java.util.*;
import java.text.*;

public class BookOrder{
   private Book book;
   private int quantity;
   private double total;
   private String date;

   public BookOrder(String bookCode, int orderQuantity){
      book = new Book(bookCode);
      quantity = orderQuantity;
      setTotal();
      setDate();
   }

   public void setTotal(){
      total = quantity * book.getPrice();
   }

   public void setDate(){
      GregorianCalendar gregNow = new GregorianCalendar();
      Date now = gregNow.getTime();
      DateFormat shortDate = DateFormat.getDateInstance(DateFormat.SHORT);
      date = shortDate.format(now); // format the Date object
   }

   public String getDate(){
      return date;
   }

   public Book getBook(){
      return book;
   }

   public int getQuantity(){
      return quantity;
   }

   public double getTotal(){
      return total;
   }

   public String toString(){
      NumberFormat currency = NumberFormat.getCurrencyInstance();
      String orderString = "Date: " + date + "\n\n"
                         + "Code: " + book.getCode() + "\n"
                         + "Title: " + book.getTitle() + "\n"
                         + "Price: " + currency.format(book.getPrice()) + "\n"
                         + "Quantity: " + quantity + "\n"
                         + "Total: " + currency.format(total) + "\n";
      return orderString;
   }

}
```

Figure 7-10 Code that adds the current date to the BookOrder application

Perspective

Now that you've finished this chapter, you should be able to use all of the operators that are provided by Java. You should also be able to work with dates whenever you need to. For most business programs, you can get by with just a small set of operators, but you need a solid set of date-handling skills.

Summary

- You can use the *prefix* and *postfix* forms of the increment and decrement operators to control when a statement increases or decreases the operand.
- You can use the *shortcut if/else operator* to code if/else logic within an expression.
- You can use the *instanceof operator* to check whether an object is created from a class or any of its subclasses.
- You can use *bitwise operators*, *shift operators*, and *bitwise assignment operators* to work with the *bits* of the *binary numbers* that are stored in byte, short, int, or long variables.
- Java uses *order of precedence* and *associativity* to determine the order in which it evaluates arithmetic expressions. To override or clarify this order, you can use parentheses.
- You can use the GregorianCalendar, Calendar, Date, and DateFormat classes to create, manipulate, and format dates and times.

Terms

prefix form
postfix form
shortcut if/else operator
ternary operator
conditional ternary operator
instanceof operator
bit
binary number
byte
bitwise operator
exclusive or
shift operator
order of precedence
associativity
order of evaluation

Objectives

- Use any of the operators provided by Java.
- Explain how the order of precedence and rules of associativity are used for evaluating expressions.
- Explain how you can use parentheses to override the order of evaluation that's used by Java.
- Use the GregorianCalendar, Calendar, Date, and FormatDate classes to get the current date, to set dates, to calculate elapsed days, and to format dates.

Exercise 7-1 Create the Monthly Payment application

This exercise guides you through the process of creating an application that calculates the monthly payment that's due for a loan. It works similarly to the Future Value application that you worked with in chapters 3 and 4.

1. Navigate to the c:\java\ch07\payment directory. It should contain the FutureValueApp and FinancialCalculations classes. Then, rename the FutureValueApp.java file to MonthlyPaymentApp.java.
2. Open the code for the FinancialCalculations class and add a static method named calculateMonthlyPayment. This method should accept three parameters (loanAmount, months, and monthlyInterestRate); it should use the formula shown in figure 7-5 to calculate the monthly payment; and it should return the monthly payment.
3. Open the code for the MonthlyPaymentApp class (formerly, the FutureValueApp class). Then, modify this class so (1) it gets the right entries from the user (loan amount, yearly interest rate, and number of years), (2) it calls the new method to calculate the monthly payment, and (3) it displays the results in a dialog box like this:

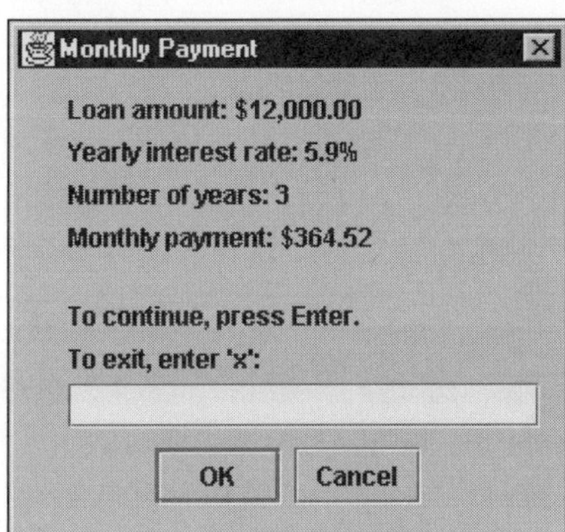

Exercise 7-2 Add a date to the Book Order application

This exercise guides you through the process of adding a date to the Book Order application.

1. Open the Book, BookOrder, and BookOrderApp classes located in the c:\java\ch07\order directory.
2. Add code to the BookOrder class that will add the current date to the toString method of the class as shown in figure 7-10, and compile the class.
3. Run the BookOrderApp class and enter a book order. When you do, the dialog box that displays the book order should also display the current date like this:

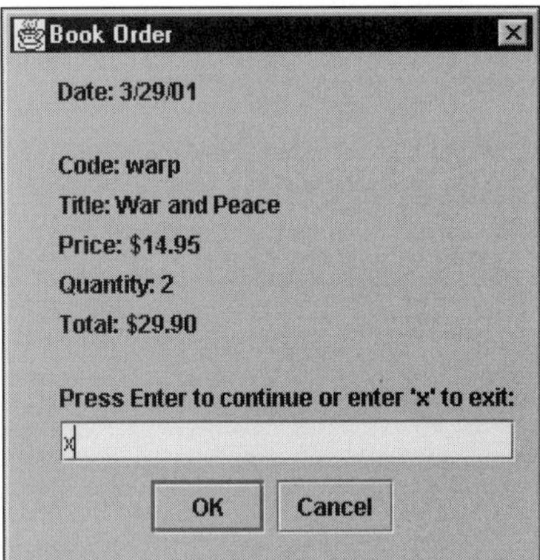

Exercise 7-3 Calculate the elapsed days

Write an application that asks the user to enter the month, day, and year of a date that precedes the current date. Then, display the number of days that have elapsed from the date that is entered to the current date.

How to code control statements

In chapter 2, you learned how to code if/else statements and while loops. Now, in this chapter, you'll learn how to code the rest of the control statements that Java provides. Although you can get by without using most of them, the for loop is commonly used.

How to code if/else and switch statements

In chapter 2, you learned how to code the if/else statement. Now, you'll review that statement, and you'll learn how to code the switch statement, which can be used to provide similar logic in some coding situations.

How to code if/else statements

Figure 8-1 gives the syntax and examples for *if/else statements*. Since this is review, you should understand the examples with no further explanation. Remember, though, that the *else clause* is only executed if none of the conditions in the *if clause* or *else if clauses* are true. Also, only the first if or else if clause with a true condition will be executed.

Remember too that if you include more than one statement after a clause, you need to use braces to create a *block* of statements called an *if block*, an *else if block*, or an *else block*. In that case, any variables that you declare within the block will be available only within that block. In other words, the variables have *block scope*. That's one of the reasons why the title and price variables in the first example are declared outside of the if block. That way, these variables will be available inside and outside of the if block.

The fourth example shows how to use an if/else statement to let a user enter a number to select a book. Here, the first three statements display a dialog box and get a number from the user. Then, the fourth statement declares a variable for a Book object and sets this variable equal to a null value. Last, the if/else statement assigns a Book object to the variable.

The syntax of the if/else statement

```
if (conditionalExpression){statements}
[else if (conditionalExpression){statements}] ...
[else {statements}]
```

Example 1: An if statement

With a block of statements

```
if (bookCode.equalsIgnoreCase("WARP")){
   title = "War and Peace";
   price = 14.95;
}
```

With a single statement

```
if (bookCode.equalsIgnoreCase("WARP"))
   title = "War and Peace";
```

Example 2: An if/else statement with an else clause

```
if (bookCode.equalsIgnoreCase("WARP"))
   title = "War and Peace";
else
   title = "Not Found";
```

Example 3: An if/else statement with else and else if clauses

```
if (bookCode.equalsIgnoreCase("WARP"))
   title = "War and Peace";
else if (bookCode.equalsIgnoreCase("MBDK"))
   title = "Moby Dick";
else if (bookCode.equalsIgnoreCase("CITR"))
   title = "Catcher in the Rye";
else
   title = "Not Found";
```

Example 4: An if/else statement that lets the user select a book by number

```
String message = "1 - War and Peace ($14.95)\n"
               + "2 - Moby Dick ($12.95)\n\n"
               + "To select a book, enter its number: ";
String bookString = JOptionPane.showInputDialog(message);
int bookNumber = Integer.parseInt(bookString);
Book book = null;
if (bookNumber == 1)
   book = new Book("warp");
else if (bookNumber == 2)
   book = new Book("mbdk");
else
   book = new Book("");
```

Figure 8-1 How to code if/else statements

How to code switch statements

Figure 8-2 shows you can use the *switch statement* to work with expressions that evaluate to the char, byte, short, or int types. After the expression in this statement, you can code one or more *case labels* that represent integer values. Then, when the integer value of the expression matches the case label, the statements after the label are executed.

You can code the case labels in any sequence, but you should be sure to follow each label with a colon. Then, after the statements that follow the label, you can code the *break statement* to skip out of the switch statement. Otherwise, the execution of the program *falls through* to the next case label. The default case label is an optional label that identifies the statements that are to be executed if none of the other case labels are matched.

The first example in this figure shows how to code a switch statement that lets the user enter a number to select a book. Although this example provides the same functionality as the fourth example in the previous figure, some programmers feel that the switch statement is easier to code and read than an if/else statement. Here, the first case label creates a new book by sending a book code to the constructor for the Book class. Then, the break statement exits the switch statement. The second case label works the same way. However, the third case label is the default case label, so it is executed whenever the user enters a number that doesn't match one of the other case labels. Since this label is the last case label, it isn't necessary to code a break statement after it.

The second example shows how to code a switch statement that sets the day variable to "weekday" or "weekend" depending on the current day of the week. If you've read the last chapter, you know that the first two statements get the day of the week as an integer with 1 representing Sunday and 7 representing Saturday. Then, the switch statement sets the string variable named day to "weekday" or "weekend" based on the integer for the day of the week. Here, the first break statement is coded after the case labels for 2, 3, 4, 5, and 6. As a result, whenever the dayOfWeek variable equals 2, 3, 4, 5, or 6, program execution falls through these labels and sets the day string to "weekday". Similarly, whenever the dayOfWeek variable equals 1 or 7, program execution falls through these labels and sets the day string to "weekend".

The syntax of the switch statement

```
switch (integerExpression){
   case label1:
      statements
      break;
   case label2:
      statements
      break;
   any other case statements
   default: (optional)
      statements
      break;
}
```

Example 1: A switch statement that lets a user select a book

```
String message = "1 - War and Peace ($14.95)\n"
               + "2 - Moby Dick ($12.95)\n\n"
               + "To select a book, enter its number: ";
String bookString = JOptionPane.showInputDialog(message);
int bookNumber = Integer.parseInt(bookString);
Book book = null;
switch (bookNumber){
   case 1:
      book = new Book("warp");
      break;
   case 2:
      book = new Book("mbdk");
      break;
   default:
      book = new Book("");
}
```

Example 2: A switch statement that checks if the current day is a weekend

```
GregorianCalendar today = new GregorianCalendar();
int dayOfWeek = today.get(Calendar.DAY_OF_WEEK);
String day = "";
switch(dayOfWeek){
   case 2:
   case 3:
   case 4:
   case 5:
   case 6:
      day = "weekday";
      break;
   case 1:
   case 7:
      day = "weekend";
}
```

Description

- The *switch statement* can only be used with expressions that evaluate to one of these integer types: char, byte, short, or int. Then, the *case labels* represent the integer values of that expression, and these labels can be coded in any sequence.
- The *break statement* exits from the switch statement.

Figure 8-2 How to code switch statements

How to code loops

In chapter 2, you learned how to code while loops. Now, you'll learn how to code do-while loops and for loops.

How to code while and do-while loops

Figure 8-3 reviews the code for *while loops* and shows how to use the *do-while statement* to code *do-while loops*. The difference between these types of loops is that the condition is tested first in a while loop and last in a do-while loop. As a result, a do-while loop is always executed at least once.

In the first two examples, you can see how these two types of loops can be used to accomplish the same purpose. In this case, the do-while loop makes sense, because you know that you want to execute the statements in the loop at least once.

In the third example, you can see how you can use a *counter* variable to execute the statements in a loop a certain number of times. In this example, the counter is an int type named i, and this counter is initialized to 1. Then, the last statement in the while loop increments the counter with each repetition of the loop. As a result, the first statement in this loop will be executed until the counter variable becomes greater than or equal to the variable that stores the number of months. Incidentally, it is a common coding practice to name counters with single letters like *i, j,* and *k.*

The fourth example shows how to code a loop that calculates the monthly payments for varying interest rates. Here, the loop executes one time for each of these interest rates: 5.0%, 5.5%, 6.0%, 6.5%, 7.0%, and 7.5%. To make this work, the last statement in the loop increments the counter by .5.

The first two statements within the loop for the fourth example calculate the monthly payment on the loan for the current interest rate. To do that, the second statement calls the calculateMonthlyPayment method from the user-defined FinancialCalculations class. Then, the third statement adds the monthly payment for each interest rate to the end of a message string. When the loop is finished, the message string that has all the interest rates and monthly payments is printed on the console.

Here again, the code within the braces of a while or do-while loop has block scope. As a result, any variables that are declared in the block can't be used outside of the block. That's why the message variable in the fourth example is declared outside of the loop.

When you code loops, you should try to avoid *infinite loops*. If, for example, you forget to code a statement that increments the counter variable, the loop will never end. Then, you have to press Ctrl+C to cancel the program so you can debug your code.

The syntax of the while loop

```
while (conditionalExpression){
   statements
}
```

The syntax of the do-while loop

```
do{
   statements
}
while (conditionalExpression);
```

Example 1: A while loop

```
String choice = "";
while (!(choice.equalsIgnoreCase("x"))){
   // statements within the loop
   choice = JOptionPane.showInputDialog(
            "To continue, press Enter.\n"
         + "To exit, enter 'x': ");
}
```

Example 2: A do-while loop that can be used instead of the while loop

```
String choice = "";
do{
   // statements within the loop
   choice = JOptionPane.showInputDialog(
            "To continue, press Enter.\n"
         + "To exit, enter 'x': ");
}
while (!(choice.equalsIgnoreCase("x")));
```

Example 3: A while loop that makes a calculation

```
int i = 1;
while (i <= months) {
   futureValue = (futureValue + monthlyPayment) *
      (1 + monthlyInterestRate);
   i++;
}
```

Example 4: A while loop that makes a series of calculations

```
String message = "";
double interestRate = 5.0;
while (interestRate < 8.0){
   monthlyInterestRate = interestRate/12/100;
   monthlyPayment = FinancialCalculations.calculateMonthlyPayment(
      loanAmount, months, monthlyInterestRate);
   message += percent.format(interestRate/100) + "     "
         + currency.format(monthlyPayment) + "\n";
   interestRate += .5;
}
System.out.println(message);
```

Description

- In a *while loop*, the condition is tested before the loop is executed. In a *do-while loop*, the condition is tested after the loop is executed.

Figure 8-3 How to code while and do-while loops

How to code for loops

Figure 8-4 shows how to use the *for statement* to code *for loops*. These loops are useful when you need to increment or decrement a counter that determines how many times the loop is going to be executed. In the parentheses of the for statement, you code an *initialization expression* that gives the starting value for the counter, a *termination condition* that determines when the loop will end, and an *increment expression* that determines how much the counter is incremented or decremented each time the loop is executed. To separate these three components, you use semicolons. Then, you code the statements of the loop.

The first example shows how to use the three components at the start of a loop. First, the initialization expression declares the counter that's used to determine the number of loops. In this example, the counter is an int type named i, and this counter is initialized to 0. Next, the termination condition specifies that the loop will be repeated as long as the counter is less than 5. Then, the increment expression increments the counter by 1 at the end of each repetition of the loop. Since the loop uses the println method to print the counter to the console, this code prints the numbers 0 to 4 to the console.

The second example calculates the sum of 8, 6, 4, and 2. In this example, the sum variable is declared before the loop so it will be available outside of the loop because here again any variables declared within braces have block scope. That way, the println method that comes after the loop can use the sum variable. In this case, the initialization expression initializes the counter to 8, and the increment expression uses an assignment operator to subtract 2 from the counter with each repetition of the loop. The loop ends when the counter is no longer greater than zero.

The third example shows how to code a loop that calculates the future value for a series of monthly payments. Here, the loop executes one time for each month. Then, the single statement within the loop adds the monthly payment to the future value and calculates the interest for the month. If you compare this example with the third example in the previous figure, you can see how a for loop improves upon a while loop when a counter is required.

The fourth example shows how to code a loop that calculates the monthly payments for varying interest rates. Like the fourth example in the previous figure, this loop executes one time for each of these interest rates: 5.0%, 5.5%, 6.0%, 6.5%, 7.0%, and 7.5%. But here again, the for loop works better because a counter is required.

The syntax of the for loop

```
for(initializationExpression; terminationCondition; incrementExpression){
   statements
}
```

Example 1: A for loop that prints the numbers 0 through 4

With a single statement

```
for (int i = 0; i < 5; i++)
   System.out.println(i);
```

With a block of statements

```
for (int i = 0; i < 5; i++){
   String counter = "Counter: " + i;
   System.out.println(counter);
}
```

Example 2: A for loop that adds the numbers 8, 6, 4, and 2

```
int sum = 0;
for (int j = 8; j > 0; j-=2){
   sum += j;
}
System.out.println(sum);
```

Example 3: A for loop that makes a calculation

```
for (int i = 1; i <= months; i++) {
   futureValue = (futureValue + monthlyPayment) *
      (1 + monthlyInterestRate);
}
```

Example 4: A for loop that makes a series of calculations

```
String message = "";
for (double interestRate = 5.0; interestRate < 8.0; interestRate += .5){
   double monthlyInterestRate = interestRate/12/100;
   double monthlyPayment = FinancialCalculations.calculateMonthlyPayment(
      loanAmount, months, monthlyInterestRate);
   message += percent.format(interestRate/100) + "     "
           + currency.format(monthlyPayment) + "\n";
}
System.out.println(message);
```

Description

- A *for loop* is useful when you need to increment or decrement a counter that determines how many times the loop is executed.
- Within the parentheses of a *for statement*, you code an *initialization expression* that gives the starting value for the counter, a *termination condition* that determines when the loop ends, and an *increment expression* that increments or decrements the counter.

Figure 8-4 How to code for loops

How to code nested for loops

In chapter 3, you learned how to code nested while loops. Now, figure 8-5 shows how to code nested for loops. As with all *nested loops*, you should use indentation to clearly show the relationships between the loops.

The first example shows two nested for loops that print a table of random numbers. In this example, the inner loop adds three random integers from 0 to 9 to the row string. Then, the outer loop adds the row string to the table string, and it clears the row string so that string can be used in the next loop. Since this code executes each loop three times, these two loops will print a table with three rows and three columns. To get a random number, the inner loop calls the random method of the Math class to return a double type between 0 and 1, multiplies that number by 9, and uses parentheses to cast the result to an int type.

The second example shows nested for loops that print a table of monthly payment calculations. Here, the amount of the loan is set to $12,000, the interest rates vary from 5.0% to 7.5%, and the number of years vary from 2 years to 4 years. To start, the first for loop, which is not nested, adds the headings to the table string. That will be the first line that's displayed by the last statement in this example.

After that, the nested loops add one row for each year to the table string. To do that, the inner loop makes six interest rate calculations per year and adds those calculations to the row string. This works like the fourth example in the previous figure. Then, the outer loop adds the row to the table string and clears the row string so it can be used again in the next loop. This works like the previous example in this figure. Last, when all of the loops have been completed, the println method prints the table string to the console. This shows the lowest monthly payment in the top left corner and the highest monthly payment in the lower right corner. To align these interest rates, this code uses spaces, but you could also use the tab escape sequence (\t) for alignment.

Example 1: Nested for loops that print a table of random numbers

```
String table = "";
String row = "";

for (int i = 1; i < 4; i++){
   for (int j = 1; j < 4; j++){
      int number = (int) (Math.random() * 9);
      row += number + " ";
   }
   table += row + "\n";
   row = "";
}
System.out.println(table);
```

Example 2: Nested for loops that print a table of calculations

```
double loanAmount = 12000;
double monthlyPayment = 0;
String table = "";
String row = "";
NumberFormat currency = NumberFormat.getCurrencyInstance();
NumberFormat percent = NumberFormat.getPercentInstance();
percent.setMinimumFractionDigits(1);

table  = "     ";
for (double interestRate = 5.0; interestRate < 8.0; interestRate += .5){
   table += percent.format(interestRate/100) + "        ";
}
table += "\n";

for (int years = 4; years > 1; years—){
   row = years + "    ";
   for (double interestRate = 5.0; interestRate < 8.0; interestRate += .5){
      int months = years * 12;
      double monthlyInterestRate = interestRate/12/100;
      monthlyPayment = FinancialCalculations.calculateMonthlyPayment(
         loanAmount, months, monthlyInterestRate);
      row += currency.format(monthlyPayment) + "     ";
   }
   table += row + "\n";
   row = "";
}
System.out.println(table);
```

Result of the code shown above

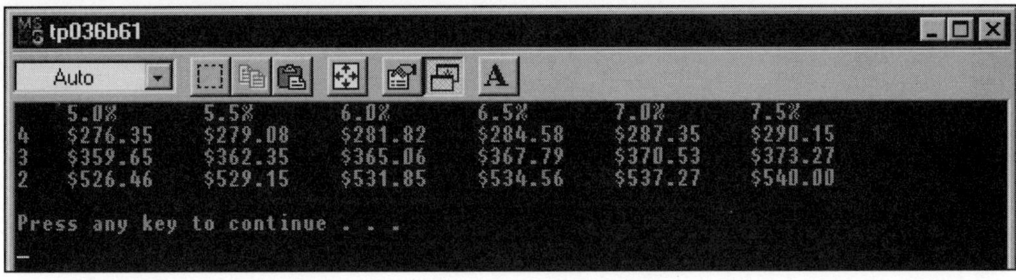

Figure 8-5 How to code nested for loops

How to code break and continue statements

Whenever possible, you should control the logic of your program by using if statements, switch statements, while loops, do-while loops, and for loops. Occasionally, though, you may need to jump out of a loop. In these cases, you can use one of the two statements that are presented next.

How to code break statements

Figure 8-6 shows how to use the *break statement* and the *labeled break statement* to exit loops. If you need to exit the current loop, you can code a break statement. If you need to exit the inner loop and the outer loop, you can use the labeled break statement.

The first example shows how you can use the break statement to exit from an inner loop. Here, a while loop is nested within a for loop. However, the conditional expression for the inner while loop has been set to true. As a result, it will loop until one of the random numbers is greater than 7. Then, it will print some text to the console and the break statement will exit this loop, which will transfer control back to the outer loop. The outer loop will then continue.

If you study the code in this example, you should see that it prints each random number to the console. But after it prints a number that is greater than 7, it also prints a message to that effect and ends the inner loop. This is repeated three times by the outer loop.

The second example shows how you can use the labeled break statement to exit an outer loop from an inner loop. Before you can use a labeled break statement, though, you must code a *label* for the loop that you want to exit. Then, to break out of the outer loop, you just type the break statement followed by the name of the label. This will transfer control to the next statement after the outer loop so the inner loop is only run one time.

The syntax of the break statement

```
break;
```

The syntax of the labeled break statement

```
break labelName;
```

The structure of the labeled break statement

```
labelName:
   loop declaration{
   statements
      another loop declaration{
         statements
         if (conditionalExpression){
            statements
            break labelName;
         }
      }
   }
```

Examples

A break statement that exits the inner loop

```
for (int i = 1; i < 4; i++){
   System.out.println("Outer " + i);
   while (true){
      int number = (int) (Math.random() * 10);
      System.out.println("   Inner " + number);
      if (number > 7){
         System.out.println("   This number is greater than 7");
         break;
      }
   }
}
```

A labeled break statement that exits the outer loop

```
outerLoop:
   for (int i = 1; i < 4; i++){
      System.out.println("Outer " + i);
      while (true){
         int number = (int) (Math.random() * 10);
         System.out.println("   Inner " + number);
         if (number > 7){
            System.out.println("   This number is greater than 7");
            break outerLoop;
         }
      }
   }
```

Description

- To jump to the end of the current loop, you can use the *break statement*.
- To jump to the end of an outer loop from an inner loop, you can label the outer loop and use the *labeled break statement*.
- To code a *label*, type the name of the label and a colon before a loop.

Figure 8-6 How to code break statements

How to code continue statements

Figure 8-7 shows how to use the *continue statement* and *labeled continue statement* to jump to the beginning of a loop. These statements work similarly to the break statements, but they jump to the beginning of a loop instead of the end of a loop. Like the break statements, you can use the unlabeled version of the statement to work with the current loop and you can use the labeled version of the loop to work with nested loops.

The first example shows how to use the continue statement to print 9 random numbers. In this example, the loop generates random numbers from 0 through 10 and prints them to the console. If the random number is less than or equal to 7, though, the continue statement jumps to the beginning of the loop. As a result, the println method that comes after the continue statement is only executed when the random number is greater than 7.

The second example shows how to use the labeled continue statement to print the prime numbers from 1 through 19. In this example, the outer loop loops through the numbers 1 through 19, while the inner loop loops through all numbers from 2 through the outer number minus 1. Then, the remainder variable is set equal to the remainder of the outer loop counter divided by the inner loop counter. If the remainder equals 0, the continue statement causes control of the program to jump to the top of the outer loop. As a result, the outer loop continues with the next number. But if the remainder doesn't equal 0 at any point in the inner loop, which means the number is a prime number, the program finishes the inner loop and the println method prints the number to the console.

The syntax of the continue statement

```
continue;
```

The syntax of the labeled continue statement

```
continue labelName;
```

The structure of the labeled continue statement

```
labelName:
   loop declaration{ ←
      statements
      another loop declaration{
         statements
         if (conditionalExpression){
            statements
            continue labelName;
         }
      }
   }
```

Examples

A continue statement that continues a loop

```
for (int j = 1; j < 10; j++){
   int number = (int) (Math.random() * 10);
   System.out.println(number);
   if (number <= 7)
      continue;
   System.out.println("This number is greater than 7");
}
```

A labeled continue statement that helps print all prime numbers less than 20

```
outerLoop:
   for(int i = 1; i < 20; i++){
      for(int j = 2; j < i-1; j++){
         int remainder = i%j;
         if (remainder == 0)
            continue outerLoop;
      }
      System.out.println(i);
   }
```

Description

- To skip the rest of the statements in the current loop and jump to the top of the current loop, you can use the *continue statement*.
- To skip the rest of the statements in the current loop and jump to the top of a labeled loop, you can add a label to the loop and use the *labeled continue statement*.
- To code a label, type the name of the label and a colon before a while, do-while, or for loop.

Figure 8-7 How to code continue statements

Perspective

Now that you've finished this chapter, you should have a solid understanding of control statements and loops. In the next chapter, you'll see how important loops can be when you work with strings and arrays.

Summary

- You can use *if/else statements* and *switch statements* to control the logic of a program. However, a switch statement can only be used with an expression that evaluates to a char, byte, short, or int type.
- You can use *while*, *do-while*, and *for statements* to repeatedly execute the code within *while*, *do-while*, and *for loops*.
- You can code *nested loops* with do-while and for statements just as you can with while statements.
- You can use the *break statement* to jump to the end of the current loop, and the *labeled break statement* to jump to the end of a labeled loop.
- You can use the *continue statement* to jump to the start of the current loop, and the *labeled continue statement* to jump to the start of a labeled loop.

Terms

if/else statement
if clause
else clause
else if clause
block
if block
else if block
else block
block scope
switch statement
case label
break statement
fall through
while loop
do-while loop
counter
infinite loop
for statement
for loop
initialization expression
termination condition
increment expression
nested loops
labeled break statement
label
continue statement
labeled continue statement

Objectives

- Code if/else statements and switch statements to control the logic of a program.
- Code while, do-while, and for loops to control the repetitive processing that a program requires.
- Code nested loops whenever they are required.
- Use the break, labeled break, continue, and labeled continue statements to jump out of a loop or to jump to the start of a loop.

Exercise 8-1 Enhance the Book application

This exercise guides you through the process of enhancing the Book application so you can select a book by number. This will give you a chance to use a switch statement.

1. Open the BookApp class located in the c:\java\ch08\book directory.
2. Edit the BookApp class using if statements so you can select a book by entering a number for it as in figure 8-1. Then, compile and run the application. When you do, the first dialog box should look like this:

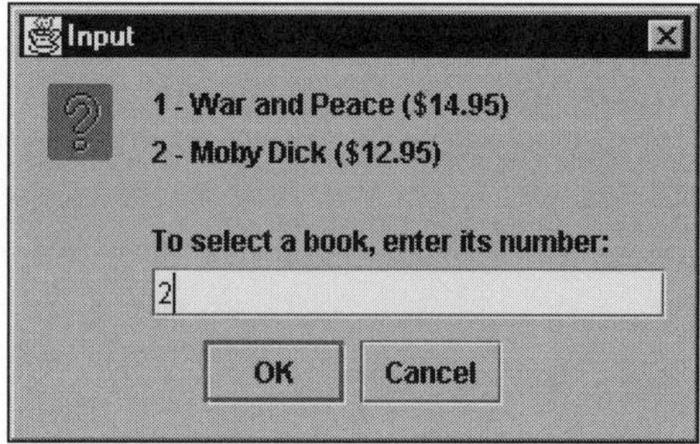

   Then, the second dialog box should display the book that you've selected.
3. Convert the if statements that select a book by number in the BookApp class to a switch statement as shown in figure 8-2. Then, compile and run the application. It should work the same as it did before.
4. Convert the while loop in the BookApp class to a do-while loop as shown in figure 8-3. Then, compile and run the application. It should work the same as it did before.

Exercise 8-2 Enhance the Book Order application

This exercise guides you through the process of enhancing the Book Order application.

1. Open the BookOrderApp class located in the c:\java\ch08\order directory.
2. Edit the code for the BookOrderApp application so it lets the user select a book by entering a number as in exercise 1. To do that, use a switch statement.
3. Compile and run the BookOrderApp class to make sure it works properly.

Exercise 8-3 Enhance the Monthly Payment application

This exercise guides you through the process of enhancing the Monthly Payment application that you created in the last chapter.

1. Open the MonthlyPaymentApp class located in the c:\java\ch08\payment directory.
2. Edit the code for the MonthlyPaymentApp class so it uses a loop like the one shown in figure 8-4 to calculate the monthly payment for these interest rates: 5.0%, 5.5%, 6.0% and 6.5%.
3. Compile the code and run the application. The first dialog box should get the amount of the loan from the user, the second dialog box should get the number of years, and the third dialog box should display the calculations like this:

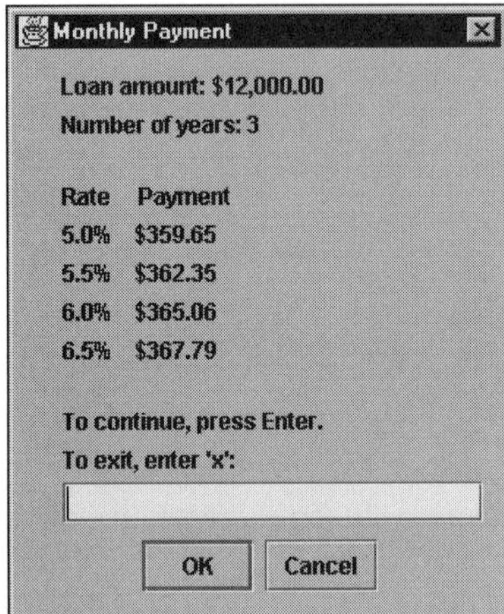

Exercise 8-4 Practice using loops

In this exercise set, you create a Test application so you can practice using loops.

1. Enter the TestApp class shown here and save it in the c:\java\ch08 directory.

```
public class TestApp{
   public static void main(String[] args){
      for (int i=1; i<10; i++){
         System.out.println(i);
      }
   }
}
```

2. Compile and run the application. The application should print the integers 1 through 9.
3. Within the main method, enter any of the code in figures 8-5 through 8-7 that you're not comfortable with. Then, compile and run the application so you can see how the code works.

9

How to work with arrays, strings, and vectors

In this chapter, you'll learn how to work with arrays and vectors, which are important in a variety of Java applications. You'll also learn more about working with strings, which can be thought of as arrays of characters. Before you read this chapter, you should read chapter 8 so you know how to use for loops, because they are commonly used with arrays.

How to work with arrays

In this topic, you'll learn how to use an *array* to work with groups of primitive types or objects. First, you'll learn how to create an array. Next, you'll learn how to assign values to an array. Then, you'll see some examples that show how to work with arrays.

How to create an array

An *array* consists of more than one *element*, and the *length* (or *size*) of an array indicates the number of elements that it contains. The type of an array can be any of the eight primitive types or any class.

In figure 9-1, you can learn how to create an array. Here, the syntax shows how to create an array in one or two statements. When you code the brackets that indicate the number of elements in the array, you can code them after the array type or after the array name. However, it's good coding practice to code them after the array type. This way, you can see that the array is an array of a specific type.

The first three examples show three different ways to create an array of double types that will hold 4 prices. The first example uses two statements, the second example uses one statement, and the third example places the brackets after the array name instead of the array type. When you create an array, each element is given a default value, which is zero for the numeric types, false for boolean types, and null for objects.

The fourth example shows how you can create two arrays of the same type in one statement. This example also shows how to use a constant to specify the array size. Here, both arrays use the same constant to create an array of 100 double values. That way, you can change the value of the constant to change the size of both arrays.

The last two examples show how to create an array of objects from a class. The fifth example creates an array of three String objects, and the sixth example creates an array of five Book objects. These examples show that you can create an array of objects from a class that's in the Java API, such as the String class, or from a user-defined class, such as the Book class.

Once you create an array, you can't change its size. As a result, if you create an array and then need to make it bigger or smaller, you have to create a new array and copy the elements from one array to the other. You'll learn how to do that later in this chapter. But first, you'll learn how to assign values to the elements of an array.

The syntax for creating an array

With two statements

```
type[] arrayName;
arrayName = new type[ARRAY_SIZE];
```

With one statement

```
type[] arrayName = new type[ARRAY_SIZE];
```

How to create an array of double types

With two statements

```
double[] prices;
prices = new double[4];
```

With one statement

```
double[] prices = new double[4];
```

With different bracket location

```
double prices[] = new double[4];
```

Other examples

Two arrays in one statement

```
final int ORDER_COUNT = 100;
double[] prices = new double[ORDER_COUNT],
         totals = new double[ORDER_COUNT];
```

An array of String objects

```
String[] titles = new String[3];
```

An array of Book objects

```
Book[] books = new Book[5];
```

Description

- An *array* can store more than one primitive type or object. An *element* in an array is one of the items in an array. And the *length*, or *size*, of an array is the number of elements in the array.
- When you create an array of primitive types, numeric types are set to zeros and boolean types to false. When you create an array of objects, they are set to null values.

Figure 9-1 How to create an array

How to assign values to the elements of an array

Figure 9-2 shows how to assign values to the elements of an array. As the syntax at the top of the figure shows, you refer to an element in an array by coding the array name followed by an *index* in brackets. Here, the index must be an int value starting at 0 and ending at one less than the size of the array. In other words, an index of 0 refers to the first element in the array, 1 refers to the second element, 2 refers to the third element, and so on.

If you specify an index that's outside of the range of the array, Java will throw an exception at run time of the ArrayIndexOutOfBoundsException type. In chapter 10, you can learn more about working with exceptions like this one.

The first three examples in this figure show how to assign values to the elements in an array by coding one statement per element. The first example creates an array of 4 double values. In this example, the first element holds the value 14.95, the second holds 12.95, the third holds 11.95, and the fourth holds 9.95. The second example creates an array that holds String objects. And the third example creates an array that holds 2 Book objects.

The syntax in the middle of this figure shows how to use the length expression to return the length of an array. Since this expression isn't a method, you don't need to include parentheses after it. You can use this expression to return an int value that represents the length of the array, which is often necessary when you use loops to work with arrays.

The two examples that follow show how to use a loop to assign values to the elements of an array. Both of these examples use the length expression to return the length of the array. That way, these loops will be executed once for each value of the index for the array. In the first example, the statement within the loop uses the counter for the loop to access each element of the array. Since this statement also assigns the value of the counter to each element, the value that's stored within each element is equal to the index for the element. In the second example, the statement within the loop assigns the same book object to all five elements of the array.

The syntax and examples at the bottom of this figure show how to create an array and assign values to the elements of the array in one statement. Here, you start the array definition as before. After the equals sign, though, you use braces to supply the values you want to store in the array. Then, Java creates an array with the number of elements within the braces, and it assigns the values within the braces to each element of the array. For instance, the first statement that follows the syntax does the same task as the five statements in the first example of this figure.

The syntax for referring to an element of an array

```
arrayName[index]
```

Examples that assign values by accessing each element

Code that assigns values to an array of double types

```
double[] prices = new double[4];
prices[0] = 14.95;
prices[1] = 12.95;
prices[2] = 11.95;
prices[3] = 9.95;
```

Code that assigns objects to an array of String objects

```
String[] names = new Strings[3];
names[0] = "Ted Lewis";
names[1] = "Sue Jones";
names[2] = "Ray Thomas";
```

Code that assigns objects to an array of Book objects

```
Book[] books = new Book[2];
books[0] = new Book("warp");
books[1] = new Book("mbdk");
```

The syntax for getting the length of an array

```
arrayName.length
```

Examples that use a for loop to assign values to an array

Code that puts the numbers 0 through 9 in an array

```
int[] values = new int[10];
for (int i = 0; i < values.length; i++){
   values[i] = i;
}
```

Code that puts five Book objects into an array

```
Book[] books = new Book[5];
for (int i = 0; i < books.length; i++){
   books[i] = new Book("warp");
}
```

The syntax for creating an array and assigning values in one statement

```
type[] arrayName = {value1, value2, value3, ...};
```

Examples that create an array and assign values in one statement

```
double[] prices = {14.95, 12.95, 11.95, 9.95};
int[] values = {3, 5, 7, 9};
boolean[] responses = {true, false, true, true, false};
String[] bookCodes = {"warp", "mbdk", "citr"};
Book[] books = {new Book("warp"),
                new Book("mbdk")};
```

Description

- To refer to the elements in an array, you use an *index* that ranges from zero (the first element in the array) to one less than the number of elements in the array.

Figure 9-2 How to assign values to the elements of an array

Code examples that work with arrays

Now that you understand how to store data in arrays, you're ready to see some code examples that show how to work with arrays. As you learned in the last figure, for loops are often used to access each element of an array. That's why most of the examples in figure 9-3 use for loops to work with arrays.

The first example shows how to use individual elements in an expression. Here, the first statement creates an array of 4 doubles. Then, the second statement sets the sum variable equal to the sum of the four elements in the array. And the third statement computes the average by dividing the sum by the number of elements in the array.

The second example performs the same task as the first example, but it uses a loop to access each element. For this task, the first example is shorter and easier to understand than the second example. However, the code in the second example will work for an array of any size while the code in the first example will only work for an array that holds four elements.

The third example shows how to print each element in an array to the console. Here, the loop cycles through each index of the array. Then, the single statement within the loop prints the array to the console. As a result, each statement will be printed on a separate line.

The fourth example shows how you can use a loop to change the value of each element in an array. The first statement in this example creates an array of double values that stores 8 heights in inches. To convert inches to centimeters, the loop multiplies the value for each element by 2.54 and assigns the result to the same element. As a result, after this code runs, 8 new values will replace the eight original values of the array. For example, the first element will store a value of 152.4, the second element will store a value of 157.48, and so on.

The fifth example shows how to print the array created by the fourth example to the console. This code works like the code in the third example except that it uses a NumberFormat object to apply formatting to the numbers, and it adds some text to the end of each number to show that the result is centimeters (cm).

Code that computes the average of an array of prices

```
double[] prices = {14.95, 12.95, 11.95, 9.95};
double sum = prices[0] + prices[1] + prices[2] + prices[3];
double average = sum/prices.length;
```

Code that uses a for loop to compute the average of an array of prices

```
double sum = 0.0;
for (int i = 0; i < prices.length; i++){
   sum += prices[i];
}
double average = sum/prices.length;
```

Code that prints an array of prices to the console

```
for (int i = 0; i < prices.length; i++){
   System.out.println(prices[i]);
}
```

The result of the code shown above

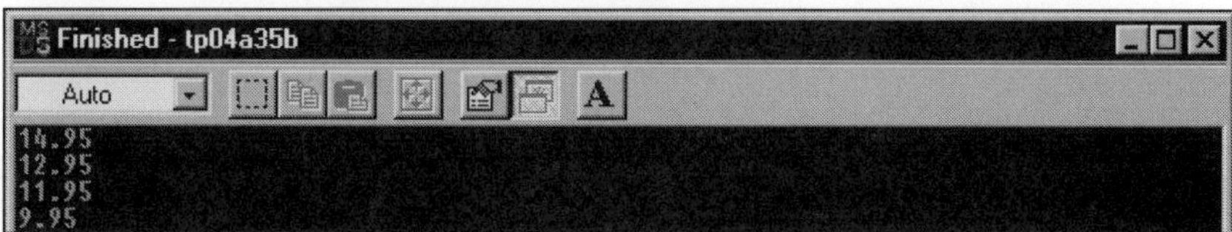

Code that converts an array of heights from inches to centimeters

```
double[] heights = {60, 62, 64, 66, 68, 70, 72, 74};
for (int i = 0; i < heights.length; i++){
   heights[i] *= 2.54;
}
```

Code that prints the converted array of heights to the console

```
NumberFormat number = NumberFormat.getNumberInstance();
for (int i = 0; i < heights.length; i++){
   System.out.println(number.format(heights[i]) + " cm");
}
```

The result of the code shown above

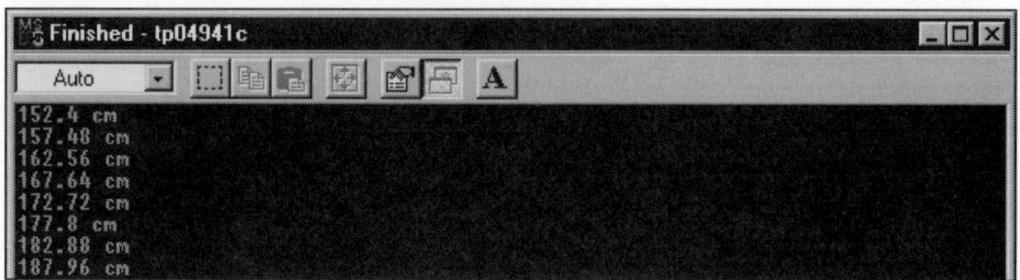

Figure 9-3 Code examples that work with arrays

How to work with two-dimensional arrays

So far, this chapter has shown how to use an array that uses one index to store a single set of elements. You can think of that as a *one-dimensional array*. Now, you'll learn how to work with *two-dimensional arrays* that use two indexes to store data in a table.

How to create a two-dimensional array

Figure 9-4 shows how to create a two-dimensional array and how to assign values to all of its elements. For the most part, two-dimensional arrays work like one-dimensional arrays, except that you use two sets of brackets. Then, you can use the first index to refer to the rows in a table, and you can use the second index to refer to the columns. You can also think of this as an *array of arrays* with the first array representing the number of rows in a table and the other array representing each of the rows.

The figure shows the syntax for two expressions that can be used to determine the length of a two-dimensional array. The first expression is the same expression that's used with one-dimensional arrays. In this context, though, it returns the number of arrays within the array, or the number of rows. To determine the number of elements in any row, you must use the second length expression.

The first example in this figure shows how to create a two-dimensional array. Here, the first statement creates a two-dimensional array of int types with three rows and two columns. As a result, this two-dimensional array can store six integers. Then, the next six statements assign a value to each element in the array.

The second example shows how to create the same array as the first example using a single statement. To do this, you use the same shorthand notation that you used with one-dimensional arrays. However, you code arrays instead of elements. As a result, you must separate each array within the first array with a comma.

The third example shows a two-dimensional array that stores three rows of 4 double values. Here, one line is coded for each row and the column values are aligned so it's easy to see where the values fit into the table.

The fourth example shows that you can create two-dimensional arrays where each row has a different length. In this example, the length of the first row is 3, the length of the second row is 4, and the length of the third row is 2.

When you create a two-dimensional array, you must specify the number of rows that it will use. However, you don't have to specify the length of each row. For instance, the code in the last example creates an array of three rows of unspecified lengths. In the next figure, you'll learn how to work with this type of array.

The syntax for creating a two-dimensional array

```
type[][] arrayName = new type[NUM_OF_ARRAYS][NUM_OF_ELEMENTS_IN_EACH_ARRAY];
```

How to return the number of arrays

```
arrayName.length
```

How to return the number of elements within each array

```
arrayName[index].length
```

How two-dimensional arrays are organized into rows and columns

```
0,0    0,1    0,2    0,3
1,0    1,1    1,2    1,3
2,0    2,1    2,2    2,3
3,0    3,1    3,2    3,3
```

Examples

A two-dimensional array of int types with three rows and two columns

```
int[][] values = new int[3][2];
values[0][0] = 1;
values[0][1] = 2;
values[1][0] = 3;
values[1][1] = 4;
values[2][0] = 5;
values[2][1] = 6;
```

Code that creates the same array shown above with one statement

```
int[][] values = {{1,2}, {3,4}, {5,6}};
```

A two-dimensional array of double types where each row is the same length

```
double[][] grades = {{92.3, 88.0, 95.2, 90.5},
                     {70.2, 79.1, 82.0, 69.8},
                     {88.5, 92.0, 84.4, 97.9}};
```

A two-dimensional array of strings where each row is a different length

```
String[][] titles = {{"War and Peace", "Wuthering Heights", "1984"},
                     {"Casablanca", "Wizard of Oz", "Star Wars", "Birdy"},
                     {"Blue Suede Shoes", "Yellow Submarine"}};
```

A two-dimensional array of int types where the length of each row is unspecified

```
int[][] values = new int[3][];
```

Description

- *Two-dimensional arrays* use two indexes and allow data to be stored in a table that consists of rows and columns. This can also be thought of as an *array of arrays* with each row as a separate array.
- You must specify the number of arrays in a two-dimensional array when it's created. However, you can leave the length of each row array unspecified and set it later.

Figure 9-4 How to create a two-dimensional array

Code examples that work with two-dimensional arrays

Figure 9-5 presents some examples that show how to work with two-dimensional arrays. First, it shows how to use nested loops to assign values to a two-dimensional array, and how to print that array to the console. Then, it shows how to work with a two-dimensional array that contains rows of unspecified lengths.

The first example shows how to use nested for loops to create a two-dimensional array that has three rows and three columns and how to assign values to the elements within that array. Here, each element in the array is an int type that will store a value of 1 or 0 depending on whether its row and column indexes are equal. Since this array is a two-dimensional array, two for loops are needed to cycle through the array. The first for loop cycles through each row, while the second cycles through each column.

The second example shows how to code nested loops to print a two-dimensional array to the console. Here, the first statement declares a String object to store a string representation of the table. Then, the inner loop adds each element to the string followed by a space, while the outer loop adds a new line character to the end of the string.

The third example shows how to define a two-dimensional array without specifying the length of each array. Here, the first statement creates an array that holds 4 arrays of unspecified lengths. To do that, this statement specifies 4 as the first index, but leaves the second index blank. Then, a for loop cycles through each array, and creates a different number of elements for each array. The first time through the loop, the counter will be equal to 0 so the length of the array will be set to 1. The second time through the for loop, i will be equal to 1 so the length of the array will be set to 2. And so on.

The fourth example shows how to code nested loops to print the array created by the third example to the console. This code works like the code shown in the second example. However, it creates a string that includes brackets that show the indexes for each element in the two-dimensional array.

Code that uses nested for loops to create a table

```
int[][] table = new int[3][3];
for (int i = 0; i < table.length; i++){
   for (int j = 0; j < table[i].length; j++){
      if (i == j)
         table[i][j] = 1;
      else
         table[i][j] = 0;
   }
}
```

Code that prints the table created above to the console

```
String tableString = "";
for (int i = 0; i < table.length; i++){
   for (int j = 0; j < table[i].length; j++){
      tableString += table[i][j] + " ";
   }
   tableString += "\n";
}
System.out.println(tableString);
```

The result of the code shown above

Code that creates a two-dimensional array with rows of different lengths

```
int[][] pyramid = new int[4][];
for (int i = 0; i < pyramid.length; i++){
    pyramid[i] = new int[i+1];
}
```

Code that prints the two-dimensional array created above to the console

```
String pyramidString = "";
for (int i = 0; i < pyramid.length; i++){
   for (int j = 0; j < pyramid[i].length; j++){
      pyramidString += "["+ i + "]" + "["+ j + "]" + " ";
   }
   pyramidString += "\n";
}
System.out.println(pyramidString);
```

The result of the code shown above

Figure 9-5 Code examples that work with two-dimensional arrays

More skills for working with arrays

Now that you've learned how to work with one- and two-dimensional arrays, you're ready to learn some new skills for working with arrays. So in this topic, you'll learn how to use the Arrays class, the Comparable interface, and the System class to work with arrays. You'll also learn how to create a second reference to an array.

The methods of the Arrays class

The Arrays class of the java.util package contains several static methods that you can use to compare, sort, and search arrays. In addition, you can use this class to assign a value to one more elements of an array. Figure 9-6 describes these methods.

As you can see, you can use the fill method to assign a value to all or part of an array. You can use the equals method to compare two arrays to check whether they contain the same number of elements with the same values stored within each element. And you can use the sort method to sort all or part of an array. Note, however, that if you want to sort objects that are created from classes that you defined, such as the BookOrder class, you must implement the Comparable interface as shown in figure 9-8.

The last method in this summary is the binarySearch method, which lets you search for an element with a specific value and return its index. Before you can use this method, though, you must use the sort method to sort the array.

In general, the methods in this figure work as you would expect. You can supply an array of primitive types or an array of objects as the array argument for any of the methods, and you can supply any primitive type or object as the value argument. However, you must make sure that the value type matches the array type. In addition, when you supply an index argument, you must make sure that the index falls within the array. Otherwise, the method will throw an exception.

The Arrays class

`java.util.Arrays`

Static methods of the Arrays class

Method	Description
`fill(arrayName, value)`	Fills all elements of the specified array with the specified value.
`fill(arrayName, index1, index2, value)`	Fills elements of the specified array with the specified value from the index1 element to, but not including, the index2 element.
`equals(arrayName1, arrayName2)`	Returns a boolean true value if both arrays are of the same type and all of the elements within the array are equal to each other.
`sort(arrayName)`	Sorts the elements of an array into ascending order.
`sort(arrayName, index1, index2)`	Sorts the elements of an array into ascending order from the index1 element to, but not including, the index2 element.
`binarySearch(arrayName, value)`	Returns an int value for the index of the specified value in the specified array. For this method to work properly, the array must first be sorted by the sort method.

Description

- All of these methods accept arrays of the primitive data types and arrays of objects for the arrayName argument, and they all accept primitive types and objects for the value argument.
- All of the index arguments for these methods must be int types. If an index argument is less than zero or greater than one less than the length of the array, the method will throw an exception of the ArrayIndexOutOfBounds type.
- The sort method will only work on an array of objects created from a user-defined class, such as the Book class, when the class implements the Comparable interface as shown in figure 9-8.

Figure 9-6 The methods of the Arrays class

Code examples that work with the Arrays class

To make sure that you understand how the methods of the Array class work, figure 9-7 presents some examples that show how you can use these methods. Here, the first five examples show how to work with one-dimensional arrays while the last example shows how to work with a two-dimensional array.

The first example shows how to use the fill method to assign a value to all of the elements in an array of int values and an array of Book objects. Here, the first statement creates an array of 5 int values, which automatically initializes all five to 0. Then, the second statement uses the fill method of the Arrays class to set all five values to 1. Similarly, the third statement creates an array of 5 Book objects, which automatically sets all five to a null value. Then, the fourth statement uses the fill method of the Arrays class to set all five Book object references equal to a single Book object. As a result, all five elements of this array will reference the same Book object.

The second example shows how to use the fill method to fill just part of an array. Here, the second and third arguments for the method indicate that elements 0 and 1 should be filled (not including element 2) with a value of 4. This use of indexes works the same way if you want to sort just part of an array.

The third example shows how to use the equals method to compare two arrays. Here, the first two statements create two arrays of String objects. Then, the third statement uses the equals method to compare these arrays. Although these arrays contain the same number of elements, the values stored within each element are different. As a result, the equals method will return a false value.

The fourth example shows how to use the sort method to sort an array of int values. Here, the first statement creates an unsorted array of integers from 0 to 9, and the second statement uses the sort method to sort these values. After the sort, the first element in this array will be 0, the second element will be 1, and so on.

The fifth example shows how to use the binarySearch method. Here, the first statement creates an array of unsorted strings. Then, the second statement uses the sort method to sort this array. For strings, this will result in the array being sorted alphabetically from A to Z. As a result, the binarySearch method used in the third statement will return a value of 2, which means that the string is the third element of the array.

The last example shows how to use the sort method to sort the rows in a two-dimensional array. To do that, this example uses a loop to cycle through each of the rows in the two-dimensional array. Within the loop, it calls the sort method for each row. When the loop finishes, the grades in each row will be sorted from low value to high value.

Code that uses the fill method

```
int[] quantities = new int[5];
Arrays.fill(quantities, 1);
Book[] books = new Book[5];
Arrays.fill(books, new Book("warp"));
```

Code that uses the fill method to fill the first two elements in an array

```
int[] quantities = new int[5];
Arrays.fill(quantities, 0, 2, 4);
```

Code that uses the equals method

```
String[] bookCodes = {"warp", "mbdk"};
String[] newBookCodes = {"warp", "citr"};
boolean bookCodesEqual = Arrays.equals(bookCodes, newBookCodes);
```

Code that uses the sort method

```
int[] numbers = {2,6,4,1,8,5,9,3,7,0};
Arrays.sort(numbers);
```

Code that uses the sort and binarySearch methods

```
String[] bookCodes = {"warp", "mbdk", "citr"};
Arrays.sort(bookCodes);
int index = Arrays.binarySearch(bookCodes, "warp");
```

Code that uses the sort method on a two-dimensional array

```
double[][] grades = {{92.3, 88.0, 95.2, 90.5},
                     {70.2, 79.1, 82.0, 69.8},
                     {88.5, 92.0, 84.4, 97.9}};
for (int i = 0; i < grades.length; i++){
   Arrays.sort(grades[i]);
}
```

Figure 9-7 Code examples that work with the Arrays class

How to implement the Comparable interface

You can only use the sort method of the Arrays class to sort arrays of objects when the classes for those objects implement the Comparable interface. As a result, you need to implement the Comparable interface for any classes that you need to sort. To do that, you must code a compareTo method similar to the one shown in figure 9-8.

If you look up the Comparable interface in the documentation for the Java API, you'll see how it's designed to work. In short, any class that implements the Comparable interface must implement the compareTo method. This method should return -1 if the current object is less than the passed object, 0 if the two objects are equal, and 1 if the current object is greater than the passed object.

This first example in this figure shows one way that the BookOrder class can implement the Comparable interface and its compareTo method. Since the compareTo method accepts an Object type, the first statement casts the object to the BookOrder type. Then, the second and third statements get the total values from the current BookOrder object and the passed BookOrder object. Last, the if statements compare the two values and return the appropriate values.

Because the compareTo method uses the total variable as the basis for comparison, BookOrder objects will be sorted by their total variables when you use the sort method of the Arrays class to sort them. If you wanted to sort them by title or quantity or any other combination of variables, though, you just code the compareTo method that way.

The second example shows how the sort method can be used with BookOrder objects. After the array is created, the sort method of the Arrays class is used to sort the array. Then, a for loop is used to print the objects in sequence. As a result, code like this can be used to test whether the compareTo method (and the sort) is working properly. If it is, the three BookOrder objects will be sorted by their totals.

The Comparable interface defined in the Java API

```
public interface Comparable{
   int compareTo(Object obj);
}
```

A class that implements the Comparable interface

```
public class BookOrder implements Comparable{
   //body of BookOrder class

   public int compareTo(Object o){
      BookOrder bookOrder2 = (BookOrder) o;
      double total1 = this.getTotal();
      double total2 = bookOrder2.getTotal();
      if (total1 < total2)
         return -1;
      if (total1 > total2)
         return 1;
      return 0;
   }
}
```

Code that uses the sort method of the Arrays class (which uses the compareTo method of the BookOrder class)

```
import java.util.*;

public class CompareTestApp{
   public static void main(String args[]){
      BookOrder[] bookOrder = new BookOrder[3];
      bookOrder[0] = new BookOrder("warp", 2);
      bookOrder[1] = new BookOrder("mbdk", 3);
      bookOrder[2] = new BookOrder("warp", 1);
      Arrays.sort(bookOrder);
      for (int i = 0; i < bookOrder.length; i++){
         System.out.println(bookOrder[i]);
      }
   }
}
```

Description

- If you implement the Comparable interface for a class, you have to define the compareTo method. Then, you can use the sort method of the Arrays class to sort an array of objects created from that class. During the sort, the sort method uses the compareTo method of that class.
- When you code the compareTo method in your class, you should return -1 if the current object is less than the passed object, 0 if the objects are equal, and 1 if the current object is greater than the passed object. In this example, the code sorts BookOrder objects by the total field, but you could sort these objects by any field or combination of fields.

Figure 9-8 How to implement the Comparable interface

How to reference an array

The first example in figure 9-9 shows how to create a *reference* to an array by assigning one array variable to a second array variable. Here, the grades variable and the percentages variable both refer to the same array. As a result, any change to the grades variable will be reflected by the percentages variable and vice versa. For instance, the last statement in this example sets the element at index 1 in the percentages array to 70.2, which is also the element that's referred to by index 1 in the grades array.

Since arrays are *immutable*, they can't grow or shrink. However, you can use an existing array variable to reference a larger or smaller array. When you do this, the original elements are erased from memory and the array variable references the new array. For instance, assume you created an array that contains 5 elements. Then, later in the program, you realize that you want that array to have 20 elements. To do this, you just reuse the array variable as shown in the second example and create a new array of 20 elements.

How to copy an array

If you want to create a copy of an array, you can use the arraycopy method of the System class as shown in this figure. Then, each array variable will point to its own copy of the array, and any changes that are made to one array won't affect the other array.

To use the arraycopy method, you specify the five arguments shown in the figure. First, you specify the source array and the starting index. Next, you specify the target array and the starting index. Then, you specify the total number of elements to copy. When you use the arraycopy method, the target array must be large enough to handle the number of elements that you're copying, and both arrays must be of the same type.

The third example in this figure shows how to make a copy of an entire array. Here, both index values are set to 0 and the intLength argument is set to the length of the grades array. As a result, this example copies all of the elements of the grades array into the percentages array.

The fourth example shows how to copy parts of one array into another array. Here, the first statement creates an array of four double values, and the second statement sorts these values from lowest to highest. Next, the third statement creates an array that can hold two double values, and the fourth statement copies the two lowest values into it. Then, the fifth statement creates an array that can hold two double values, and the sixth statement copies the two highest values into it.

The arraycopy method from the System class

```
System.arraycopy(fromArray, intFromIndex, toArray, intToIndex, intLength);
```

Code that creates a reference to an array

```
double[] grades = {92.3, 88.0, 95.2, 90.5};
double[] percentages = grades;
percentages[1] = 70.2;    //grades[1] and percentages[1] are both 70.2
```

Code that reuses an array variable

```
double[] grades = new grades[5];
grades = new grades[20];
```

Code that copies the values of an array

```
double[] grades = {92.3, 88.0, 95.2, 90.5};
double[] percentages = new double[grades.length];
System.arraycopy(grades, 0, percentages, 0, grades.length);
percentages[1] = 70.2;    //grades[1] isn't modified by this statement
```

Code that copies part of one array into another array

```
double[] grades = {92.3, 88.0, 95.2, 90.5};
Arrays.sort(grades);
double[] lowestGrades = new double[2];
System.arraycopy(grades, 0, lowestGrades, 0, 2);
double[] highestGrades = new double[2];
System.arraycopy(grades, 2, highestGrades, 0, 2);
```

Description

- To *reference* an existing array, code an assignment statement like the one shown in the first example. Then, two variables will point to the same array in memory.
- To copy the values of one array into another, use the arraycopy method of the System class as shown in the second and third examples.
- When you copy an array, the target array must be the same type as the sending array and it must be large enough to receive all of the elements that are copied to it.

Figure 9-9 How to reference and copy arrays

How to work with the String class

In chapter 2, you learned how to create a String object and how to use a couple of the methods of the String class that compare two strings. Now, you'll learn some new ways to create String objects, and you'll learn how to use more of the methods of the String class.

Constructors of the String class

Figure 9-10 shows four constructors of the String class. The first constructor provides another way to create an empty string; the second constructor provides another way to create a string from a string; and the third and fourth constructors allow you to create a string from an array of characters or bytes. Although none of these constructors are commonly used, the third and fourth constructors show that you can think of a string as an array of characters.

Code examples that create strings

The first two examples show two ways to create a string. In both of these examples, the first statement uses the shorthand notation you learned how to use in chapter 2. Then, the second statement shows how to do the same task using a constructor of the String class.

The third example creates a string from an array of characters. Here, the second statement converts the entire array of characters to a string named cityString1. Then, the third statement converts the first three characters in the array to a string named cityString2.

The fourth example creates a string from an array of bytes. Here, the first statement creates an array of bytes that represents the same characters as the characters that are used in the third example. That's because every character in the ASCII character set corresponds to a byte value. For example, the byte value of 68 represents the character *D*. Then, the second and third statements in this example work just like they did in the previous example

The String class

```
java.lang.String
```

Some constructors of the String class

Constructor	Description
`String()`	Creates an empty string ("").
`String(String)`	Creates a string from the string value that's supplied to the constructor.
`String(arrayName)`	Creates a string from an array of char types or byte types.
`String(arrayName, intOffset, intLength)`	Creates a string from a subset of an array of char or byte types.

Examples

Two ways to create an empty string

```
String name = "";
String name = new String();
```

Two ways to create a string from another string

```
String title = "Wuthering Heights";
String title = new String("Wuthering Heights");
```

Two ways to create a string from an array of characters

```
char cityArray[] = {'D','a','l','l','a','s'};
String cityString1 = new String(cityArray);
String cityString2 = new String(cityArray, 0, 3);
```

Two ways to create a string from an array of bytes

```
byte cityArray[] = {68, 97, 108, 108, 97, 115};
String cityString1 = new String(cityArray);
String cityString2 = new String(cityArray, 0, 3);
```

Notes

- For the fourth constructor shown above, the characters referenced by the intOffset and intLength arguments must fall within the array. Otherwise, the constructor will throw an exception of the IndexOutOfBounds type.
- Since String objects are *immutable*, they can't grow or shrink. In the next topic, you'll learn how to work with StringBuffer objects that can grow and shrink.

Figure 9-10 How to create strings

Methods of the String class

In chapter 2, you learned how to use the equals and equalsIgnoreCase methods of the String class to compare strings. Now, figure 9-11 reviews these methods and introduces you to 13 more methods that you can use to work with strings. In the next figure, you'll see some examples that use some of these methods. You can also get more information about any of these methods by looking up the String class in the documentation for the Java API.

The first five methods return an int value. Here, the length method returns the total number of characters in the string. In contrast, the indexOf and lastIndexOf methods return a value that represents an index within the string. This index value works as if the string was an array of characters. In other words, the index value for the first character in a string is 0, the index value for the second character is 1, and so on.

The next four methods return a string. Here, the trim method returns the string, but it removes any spaces from the beginning and end of the string. On the other hand, the substring method allows you to return part of a string by specifying index values. When you use this method, you must make sure to specify an index value that's greater than or equal to 0 and less than the length of the string. Otherwise, this method will throw an exception of the StringIndexOutOfBoundsException type.

The last five methods return a boolean value. Here, the equals and equalsIgnoreCase methods compare strings and return a true value if the strings are equal. On the other hand, the startsWith and endsWith methods check whether a string starts or ends with a certain combination of characters and return true values if it does. These methods work similarly to the equals method.

Methods of the String class

Method	Description
`length()`	Returns an int value for the number of characters in this string.
`indexOf(String)`	Returns an int value for the index of the first occurrence of the specified string in this string. If the string isn't found, this method returns -1.
`indexOf(String, startIndex)`	Returns an int value for the index of the first occurrence of the specified string starting at the specified index. If the string isn't found, this method returns -1.
`lastIndexOf(String)`	Returns an int value for the index of the last occurrence of the specified string in this string.
`lastIndexOf(String, startIndex)`	Returns an int value for the index of the last occurrence of the specified string in this string starting at the specified index.
`trim()`	Returns a String object with any spaces removed from beginning and end of this string.
`substring(startIndex)`	Returns a String object that starts at the specified index and goes to the end of the string.
`substring(startIndex, endIndex)`	Returns a String object that starts at the specified start index and goes to, but doesn't include, the end index.
`replace(oldChar, newChar)`	Returns a String object that results from replacing all instances of the specified old char value with the specified new char value.
`charAt(index)`	Returns the char value at the specified index.
`equals(String)`	Returns a boolean true value if the specified string is equal to the current string. This comparison is case-sensitive.
`equalsIgnoreCase(String)`	Returns a boolean true value if the specified string is equal to the current string. This comparison is *not* case-sensitive.
`startsWith(String)`	Returns a boolean true value if this string starts with the specified string.
`startsWith(String, startIndex)`	Returns a boolean true value if this string starts with the specified string starting at the start index.
`endsWith(String)`	Returns a boolean true value if the string ends with the specified string.

Note

- If you supply an index argument that's negative or greater than the length of the string minus one, the method will throw an exception of the StringIndexOutOfBounds type.

Figure 9-11 Methods of the String class

Code examples that work with strings

Figure 9-12 shows some examples of how you can use the methods of the String class. In particular, this figure provides some examples that use the String class to parse strings.

The first example shows how to parse the first name from a string when a user enters a full name. Here, the first statement uses a dialog box that lets a user enter a full name, and the second statement uses the trim method to remove any spaces from the beginning or end of the string that the user may have accidentally typed. Then, the third statement uses the indexOf method to get the index of the first space in the string, which should be between the first name and the middle name or last name. If this method doesn't find a space in the string, it will return -1 and the if/else statement that follows uses the substring method to set the first name variable equal to the entire name string. Otherwise, the if/else statement uses the substring method to set the first name variable equal to the string that begins at the first character of the string and ends at the first space character in the string.

The second example shows how to parse a string that contains an address into the components of the address. In this case, a pipe character (|) separates each component of the address. Here, the second statement uses the trim method to remove any spaces from the beginning and end of the string. Next, an if/else statement sets the value of the streetIndex variable depending on whether the string starts with a pipe character. If it does, the if statement sets the streetIndex to 1 so the pipe character won't be included in the substring. The next three statements use the indexOf and lastIndexOf methods to determine the index values of the first character for each substring. To do that, you find the index of the pipe character and add 1. The last four statements supply these index variables as arguments of the substring method to return the street, city, state, and zip code substrings.

The third example shows how to add dashes to a phone number. To do this, this example creates a second string. Then, it uses the substring method to parse the first string and add the dashes at the appropriate locations in the string. In a moment, you'll learn an easier way to accomplish this task.

The fourth example shows how to remove the dashes from a phone number. To do this, this example creates a second string. Then, it uses a for loop to cycle through each character in the first string. The only statement within this loop uses the charAt method to add all characters in the first string that are not equal to a dash to the second string. As a result, the second string won't contain any dashes. In a moment, you'll learn another way to accomplish this task.

Code that parses a first name from a name string

```
String inputString = JOptionPane.showInputDialog(
   "Enter your full name: ");
String name = inputString.trim();
int indexOfSpace = name.indexOf(" ");
String firstName = null;
if (indexOfSpace == -1)
   firstName = name.substring(0);
else
   firstName = name.substring(0, indexOfSpace);
```

Code that parses a string that contains an address

```
String address = " |805 Main Street|Dallas|TX|12345 ";
address = address.trim();
int streetIndex;
if (address.startsWith("|"))
   streetIndex = 1;
else
   streetIndex = 0;
int cityIndex = 1 + address.indexOf("|", streetIndex+1);
int stateIndex = 1 + address.indexOf("|", cityIndex+1);
int zipIndex = 1 + address.lastIndexOf("|");

String street = address.substring(streetIndex, cityIndex-1);
String city = address.substring(cityIndex, stateIndex-1);
String state = address.substring(stateIndex, zipIndex-1);
String zip = address.substring(zipIndex);
```

Code that adds dashes to a phone number

```
String phoneNumber1 = "9775551212";
String phoneNumber2 = phoneNumber1.substring(0, 3);
phoneNumber2 += "-";
phoneNumber2 += phoneNumber1.substring(3, 6);
phoneNumber2 += "-";
phoneNumber2 += phoneNumber1.substring(6);
```

Code that removes dashes from a phone number

```
String phoneNumber1 = "977-555-1212";
String phoneNumber2 = "";
for(int i = 0; i < phoneNumber1.length(); i++){
   if (phoneNumber1.charAt(i) != '-')
      phoneNumber2 += phoneNumber1.charAt(i);
}
```

Figure 9-12 Code examples that work with strings

How to work with the StringBuffer class

When you use the String class to work with strings, the string is a fixed length, and you can't edit the characters that make up the string. In other words, the String class creates strings that are *immutable*. The only way you can change this type of string is to assign a new string to the String object, which deletes the original string and replaces it with the new string.

If you want more flexibility when working with strings, you can use the StringBuffer class. When you use this class, you create strings that are *mutable*. In other words, you can add, delete, or replace the characters in a StringBuffer object. This makes it easier to write some types of routines, and it can improve the efficiency of your code in some situations.

Constructors and methods of the StringBuffer class

Figure 9-13 shows three constructors and thirteen methods of the StringBuffer class. In the next figure, you'll see some examples that use these constructors and methods. As always, you can find more information on these constructors and methods by looking up the StringBuffer class in the documentation for the Java API.

To create a StringBuffer object, you must use one of the three constructors shown in this figure. The first constructor creates an empty StringBuffer object with a *capacity* of 16 characters. In other words, Java allocates a block of memory, or a *buffer*, that can hold up to 16 characters. Then, if you add characters to this StringBuffer object so the number of characters exceeds 16 characters, Java will automatically increase the capacity.

Whenever possible, you should set the capacity so it's appropriate for your needs. Otherwise, Java will have to allocate memory each time capacity is exceeded, and that can cause your programs to run less efficiently. On the other hand, if you set a large capacity and use a small percentage of it, you waste memory.

The second and third constructors show how to set the capacity for your needs. If you know roughly how many characters you will need, you can use the second constructor to set the capacity. On the other hand, if you need the StringBuffer to be large enough to accommodate the number of characters stored in a particular String object, you can use the third constructor.

Once you create a StringBuffer object, you can use the methods in this figure to work with the object. You can use the first three methods to check the capacity of the object or to check or set the length of the string. You can use the next six methods to add, edit, or delete strings or characters. And you can use the last four methods to return a String object or a character.

The StringBuffer class

`java.lang.StringBuffer`

Constructors of the StringBuffer class

Constructor	Description
`StringBuffer()`	Creates an empty StringBuffer object with an initial capacity of 16 characters.
`StringBuffer(intLength)`	Creates an empty StringBuffer object with initial capacity of the specified number of characters.
`StringBuffer(String)`	Constructs a StringBuffer object that contains the specified string plus an additional capacity of 16 characters.

Methods of the StringBuffer class

Method	Description
`capacity()`	Returns an int value for the capacity of this StringBuffer object.
`length()`	Returns an int value for the number of characters in this StringBuffer object.
`setLength(intNumOfChars)`	Sets the length of this StringBuffer object to the specified number of characters.
`append(value)`	Adds the specified value to the end of the string.
`insert(index, value)`	Inserts the specified value at the specified index pushing the rest of the string back.
`replace(startIndex, endIndex, String)`	Replaces the characters from the start index to, but not including, the end index with the specified string.
`delete(startIndex, endIndex)`	Removes the substring from the start index to, but not including, the end index.
`deleteCharAt(index)`	Removes the character at the specified index.
`setCharAt(index, character)`	Replaces the character at the specified index with the specified character.
`charAt(index)`	Returns a char value for the character at the specified index.
`substring(index)`	Returns a String object that contains the characters starting at the specified index to the end of the string.
`substring(startIndex, endIndex)`	Returns a String object that contains the characters from the start index to, but not including, the end index.
`toString()`	Returns a String object that contains the string that's stored in the StringBuffer object.

Description

- StringBuffer objects are *mutable*, which means you can modify the string in the buffer.
- The *capacity* of a StringBuffer object is the block of memory, or *buffer*, that's allocated to hold the number of characters of the string. If you add characters to a StringBuffer object so it exceeds its capacity, Java automatically increases the capacity by doubling the current capacity and adding two characters (capacity * 2 + 2).
- The append and insert methods accept primitive types, objects, and arrays of characters.

Figure 9-13 Constructors and methods of the StringBuffer class

Code examples that work with the StringBuffer class

Figure 9-14 presents some examples that show how you can use the constructors and methods of the StringBuffer class. In particular, this figure shows how to add characters to the end of a string, how to insert characters into the middle of a string, and how to delete characters from a string.

The first example shows how to use the append method to add characters to the end of a StringBuffer object. Here, the first statement creates an empty StringBuffer object with the default initial capacity of 16 characters. Then, the next three statements use the append method to add 10 characters to the end of the string. As a result, the length of the string is 10 and the capacity of the StringBuffer object is 16.

The second example adds dashes to the string that was created in the first example. Here, the first statement uses the insert method to insert a dash after the first three characters. This pushes the remaining seven numbers back one index. Then, the second statement uses the insert method to insert a dash after the eighth character in the string. This pushes the remaining four numbers in the string back one index.

The third example shows how to remove the dashes from the phone number created by the first two examples. Here, a loop cycles through each character. Within the loop, an if statement uses the charAt method to check if the current character is a dash. If so, the deleteCharAt method is used to delete that character. This causes all characters to the right of the dash to move forward one index.

The fourth example shows how to use the substring method of the StringBuffer class to return a String object. Here, the first statement uses a constructor to create the StringBuffer object from a String object. Then, the next three statements use the substring method to create three String objects from the StringBuffer object. For example, the second statement specifies a substring that goes from the first character up to, but not including, the fourth character. This shows that the substring method works the same for the StringBuffer class as it does for the String class.

The fifth example shows how a StringBuffer object automatically increases its capacity as the length of the string increases. Here, the first statement creates an empty StringBuffer object with a capacity of 8 characters, and the second statement uses the capacity method to check the capacity. Next, the third statement appends a string of 17 characters to the empty string. Since this call exceeds the capacity, Java automatically increases the capacity to twice the initial capacity plus 2 characters. Then, the last two statements check the length and capacity of the modified StringBuffer object.

Code that creates a phone number

```
StringBuffer phoneNumber = new StringBuffer();
phoneNumber.append("977");
phoneNumber.append("555");
phoneNumber.append("1212");
```

Code that adds dashes to a phone number

```
phoneNumber.insert(3, '-');
phoneNumber.insert(7, '-');
```

Code that removes dashes from a phone number

```
for(int i = 0; i < phoneNumber.length(); i++){
   if (phoneNumber.charAt(i) == '-')
      phoneNumber.deleteCharAt(i);
}
```

Code that parses a phone number

```
StringBuffer phoneNumber = new StringBuffer("977-555-1212");
String areaCode = phoneNumber.substring(0,3);
String prefix = phoneNumber.substring(4,7);
String suffix = phoneNumber.substring(8);
```

Code that shows how capacity automatically increases

```
StringBuffer name = new StringBuffer(8);
int capacity1 = name.capacity();     //capacity1 is 8
name.append("Raymond R. Thomas");
int length = name.length();          //length is 17
int capacity2 = name.capacity();     //capacity2 is 18 (2 * capacity1 + 2)
```

Figure 9-14 Code examples that work with the StringBuffer class

How to work with the Vector class

Earlier in this chapter, you learned how to create an array that stores a fixed number of elements. Like an array, a *vector* stores related data items that can be accessed using an integer index. Unlike an array, though, the size of a vector can grow or shrink as elements are added or removed. This makes vectors more flexible and appropriate for certain types of coding situations. Note, however, that vectors can only be used with objects. As a result, you need to use wrapper classes to work with primitive data types as shown in the next figure.

Constructors and methods of the Vector class

Figure 9-15 shows the constructors and methods of the Vector class that you can use to work with a collection of objects. In the next figure, you'll see some examples that show how you can use these constructors and methods. For more information on these and other methods of the Vector class, you can look this class up in the API documentation.

Like a StringBuffer object, each Vector object has a capacity that refers to the block of memory that's allocated for the object. When you code the constructor for a Vector object, you affect how Java manages capacity. If you use the first constructor, the Vector object will start with the default capacity of 10 objects. On the other hand, if you use the second constructor, you can specify a starting capacity. Either way, if the size of a vector exceeds its capacity, Java automatically doubles its capacity.

In contrast, if a vector created from the third constructor exceeds its capacity, Java automatically increases the capacity by the specified increment amount. If the capacity increment amount is 0, though, Java doubles the capacity just as it would with the second constructor. The fourth constructor in this figure lets you create a Vector object by supplying another Vector object as an argument.

Once you create a Vector object, you can use its methods to work with the vector. You can use the first two methods to check the capacity or size of the vector. You can use the third method to get the index of an object in the vector. You can use the next six methods to add, get, set, or remove the objects in a vector. And you can use the last method to convert a vector to an array. Most of these methods work similarly to the methods of the StringBuffer class.

The Vector class

```
java.util.Vector
```

Constructors of the Vector class

Constructor	Description
`Vector()`	Creates an empty vector with an initial capacity of 10 objects.
`Vector(intCapacity)`	Creates an empty vector with the specified capacity.
`Vector(intCapacity, intCapacityIncrement)`	Creates an empty vector with the specified capacity and the specified capacity increment.
`Vector(vectorName)`	Creates a new vector that contains a copy of every object in the specified vector.

Methods of the Vector class

Method	Description
`capacity()`	Returns an int value for the capacity of this vector.
`size()`	Returns an int value for the number of objects in this vector.
`indexOf(object)`	Returns an int value for the index of the first occurrence of the specified object. If the object isn't found, this method returns -1.
`add(object)`	Inserts the specified object at the end of the vector.
`add(index, object)`	Inserts the specified object at the specified index pushing any other objects in the vector back one index.
`get(index)`	Returns an Object type for the object at the specified index.
`set(index, object)`	Replaces the object at the specified index with the specified object.
`remove(index)`	Deletes the object at the specified index from the vector shifting any other objects in the vector to the left.
`remove(object)`	Deletes the first occurrence of the specified object from the vector.
`clear()`	Removes all objects from the vector.
`copyInto(array)`	Copies all objects from the vector into the specified array.

Description

- A *vector* is a data structure similar to an array, but it can change its capacity as objects are added or removed. Although a vector can only hold objects, not primitive types, it can hold wrappers that contain primitive types.
- When you use the first constructor above, Java sets the initial capacity of the vector to 10 objects.
- When you use the first or second constructor above, Java doubles the capacity if the size of the vector becomes larger than its capacity. When you use the third constructor, you can specify an increment amount for the vector that will be used instead of doubling the current capacity.
- If you specify an index that's outside the range of the vector, the vector will throw an exception of the ArrayIndexOutOfBoundsException type.

Figure 9-15 Constructors and methods of the Vector class

Code examples that work with the Vector class

Figure 9-16 presents some examples that show how you can use the constructors and methods in the previous figure to create and work with Vector objects. In particular, it shows how to create vectors, how to add objects to a vector, and how to retrieve objects from a vector.

The first example shows how to create a vector that stores three strings. Here, the first statement creates a Vector object that has the default initial capacity of 10. Then, the second and third statements add strings to the end of this vector while the fourth statement adds a string to the beginning of the vector, which pushes the first two strings back one index. At this point, this vector has a capacity of 10 elements and a size of 3 objects.

The second example shows how to print all of the objects in a vector to the console. Here, a loop cycles through all of the objects in the vector. Within the loop, the first statement uses the get method to retrieve the string. Since the get method returns an object of the Object type, this statement casts the result of the get method to a String type. Then, the second statement prints the string to the console.

The third and fourth examples show how to replace or delete an element in the vector created by the first example. In the third example, the set method is used to replace the third element in the vector with a new string. In the fourth example, both statements delete an object from a vector.

The fifth example shows how to copy all of the elements of a vector into an array. Here, the first statement uses the size method of the vector to create an array that has the same size as the vector. Then, the second statement uses the copyInto method to copy all objects stored in the vector into the array.

The last three examples show how you can use vectors to work with different types of objects. The sixth example uses a wrapper class to store primitive data types in a vector. The seventh example stores GregorianCalendar objects in a vector. And the eighth example stores BookOrder objects in a vector.

Code that creates a vector and adds three objects

```
Vector codesVector = new Vector();
codesVector.add("mbdk");
codesVector.add("citr");
codesVector.add(0, "warp");
```

Code that prints all objects in a vector to the console

```
for (int i = 0; i < codesVector.size(); i++){
    String code = (String) codesVector.get(i);
    System.out.println(code);
}
```

The result of the code shown above

Code that replaces an object with another object

```
codesVector.set(2, "wuth");
```

Two ways to delete an object from a vector

```
codesVector.remove("wuth");
codesVector.remove(2);
```

Code that converts a vector to an array

```
String[] codesArray = new String[codesVector.size()];
codesVector.copyInto(codesArray);
```

A vector that stores integers

```
Vector intVector = new Vector();
intVector.add(new Integer(1));
intVector.add(new Integer(2));
intVector.add(new Integer(3));
```

A vector that stores GregorianCalendar objects

```
Vector datesVector = new Vector();
datesVector.add(new GregorianCalendar(2001, 4, 6));
datesVector.add(new GregorianCalendar(2001, 8, 19));
```

A vector that stores BookOrder objects

```
Vector ordersVector = new Vector();
ordersVector.add(new BookOrder("warp", 2));
ordersVector.add(new BookOrder("mbdk", 1));
```

Figure 9-16 Code examples that work with the Vector class

The Invoice application

To show how vectors can be used in a complete application, this chapter now presents an Invoice application that uses a vector as an instance variable. This is a common use of a vector. As you will see, the Invoice and InvoiceApp classes of this application use the BookOrder and Book classes that have been used throughout this book.

The user interface

Figure 9-17 shows the user interface for the Invoice application. Here, the first dialog box asks the user to enter a number for the invoice. Then, the next three dialog boxes ask the user to enter one or more book orders. When the user enters "x" in the fourth dialog box to stop entering book orders, the fifth dialog box displays the data that's been stored for the invoice. In this figure, two books have been ordered, but the user could have ordered one or more books.

The code

Figure 9-18 shows the code for the Invoice class. This class uses a vector as an instance variable, which allows an Invoice object to contain one or more BookOrder objects. In the constructor of the Invoice class, the reference to the vector of BookOrder objects is set equal to the vector that's passed to the constructor from the InvoiceApp class.

The calculateTotal method of the Invoice class uses a loop to sum the totals for all of the BookOrder objects to get the total for the Invoice object. Within the loop, the first statement retrieves the BookOrder object from the vector. Then, the second statement adds the total for that BookOrder object to the total for the Invoice object.

The toString method of the Invoice class begins by adding the invoice number, date, and total to an invoice string. Then, it uses a loop to add a string representation of all of the BookOrder objects in the Invoice object to the invoice string. To save space, this string includes just the code, price, quantity, and total for each book order. In a more realistic application, though, this loop would also contain a description of the book.

Figure 9-19 shows the code for the InvoiceApp class. This class works much like the BookOrderApp class. However, it uses a vector to store each BookOrder object that's created by the application. Then, when the user enters "x" to exit the loop, the first statement after the loop passes the vector of BookOrder objects to the constructor of the Invoice class. And the second statement displays a string representation of the newly created Invoice object in the final dialog box of the Invoice application.

The first dialog box

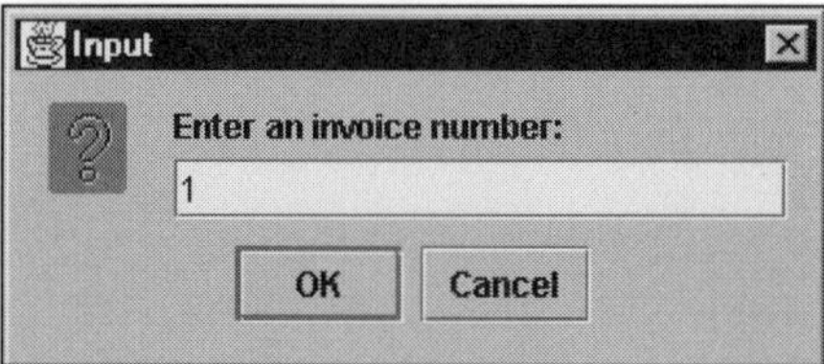

The second dialog box

The third dialog box

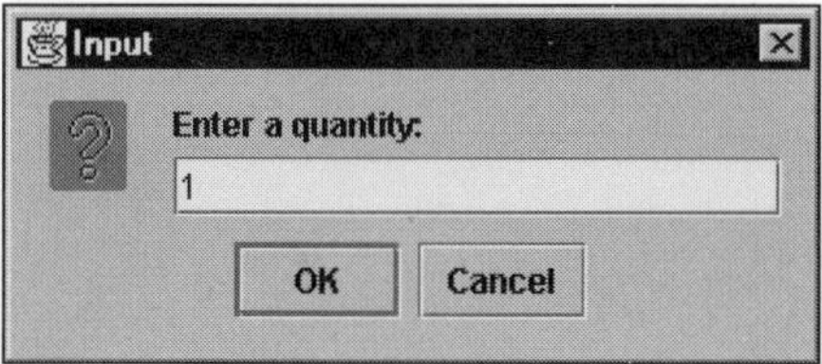

The fourth dialog box

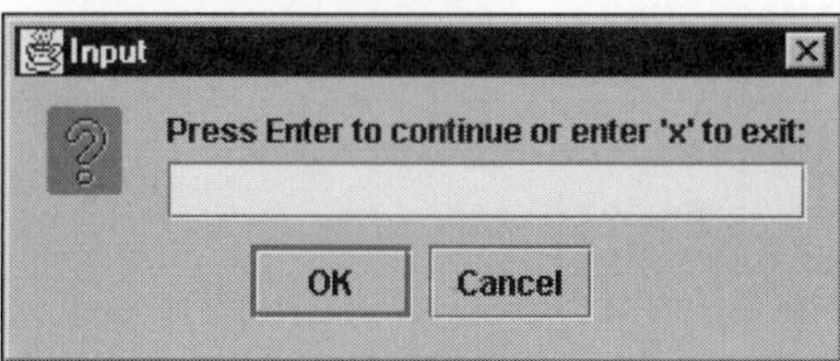

The fifth dialog box

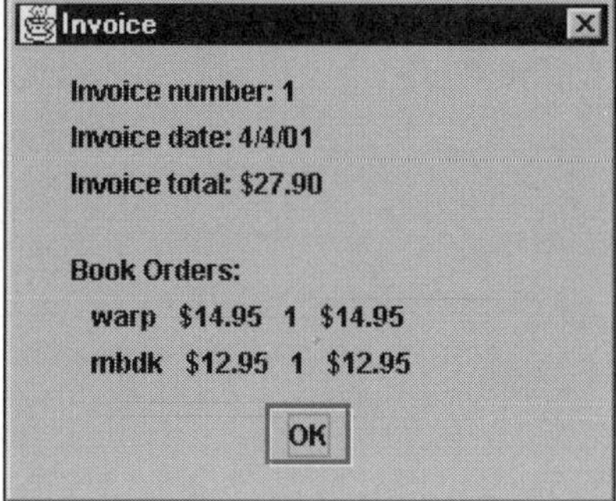

Figure 9-17 The user interface for the Invoice application

The code for the Invoice class

```
import java.text.*;
import java.util.*;

public class Invoice{
   private String number;
   private Date date;
   private Vector bookOrders;
   private double total;

   public Invoice(String invoiceNumber, Vector orders){
      number = invoiceNumber;
      date = new Date();
      bookOrders = new Vector(orders);
      calculateTotal();
   }

   public double calculateTotal(){
      total = 0;
      for(int i = 0; i < bookOrders.size(); i++){
         BookOrder bookOrder = (BookOrder) bookOrders.get(i);
         total += bookOrder.getTotal();
      }
      return total;
   }

   public String toString(){
      DateFormat shortDate = DateFormat.getDateInstance(DateFormat.SHORT);
      NumberFormat currency = NumberFormat.getCurrencyInstance();
      String invoiceString = "Invoice number: " + number + "\n"
         + "Invoice date: " + shortDate.format(date) + "\n"
         + "Invoice total: " + currency.format(total) + "\n\n"
         + "Book Orders: \n";

      for(int i = 0; i < bookOrders.size(); i++){
         BookOrder bookOrder = (BookOrder) bookOrders.get(i);
         invoiceString += "    " + bookOrder.getBook().getCode() + "    "
            + currency.format(bookOrder.getBook().getPrice()) + "    "
            + bookOrder.getQuantity() + "    "
            + currency.format(bookOrder.getTotal()) + "\n";
      }
      return invoiceString;
   }

}
```

Figure 9-18 The code for the Invoice class

The code for the InvoiceApp class

```
import javax.swing.*;
import java.util.*;

public class InvoiceApp{
   public static void main(String args[]){
      String invoiceNumber = JOptionPane.showInputDialog(
         "Enter an invoice number:");
      Vector bookOrders = new Vector();
      String choice = "";
      while (!(choice.equalsIgnoreCase("x"))){
         String code = JOptionPane.showInputDialog(
            "Enter a book code:");
         String inputQuantity = JOptionPane.showInputDialog(
            "Enter a quantity:");
         int quantity = Integer.parseInt(inputQuantity);
         BookOrder bookOrder = new BookOrder(code, quantity);
         bookOrders.add(bookOrder);
         choice = JOptionPane.showInputDialog(
            "Press Enter to continue or enter 'x' to exit:");
      }//end while
      Invoice invoice = new Invoice(invoiceNumber, bookOrders);
      JOptionPane.showMessageDialog(null,
         invoice.toString(), "Invoice", JOptionPane.PLAIN_MESSAGE);
      System.exit(0);
   }

}
```

Figure 9-19 The code for the InvoiceApp class

Perspective

Now that you've finished this chapter, you should know how to work with one-dimensional and two-dimensional arrays. You should also know how to use the String and StringBuffer classes to work with strings, and you should know how to use the Vector class to work with vectors. These are important skills that you'll use in many applications.

Summary

- An *array* is a special type of object that can store more than one primitive data type or object. The *length* (or *size*) of an array is the number of *elements* that are stored in the array. The *index* is the number that is used to identify any element in the array.
- A *one-dimensional array* provides for a single list or column of elements so just one index value is required to identify each element. In contrast, a *two-dimensional array*, or an *array of arrays*, can be used to organize data in a table that has rows and columns. As a result, two index values are required to identify each element.
- You can use the Arrays class to fill, compare, sort, and search arrays. You can use an assignment statement to create a second *reference* to the same array. And you can use the arraycopy method of the System class to make a copy of an array.
- You can use the methods of the String class to find index values for each character in a string, to return parts of the string, and to compare all or part of a string. However, String objects are *immutable* so you can't add, delete, or modify individual characters in a string.
- StringBuffer objects are *mutable* so you can use the StringBuffer methods to add, delete, or change characters in the string that's in the *buffer*. Whenever necessary, Java automatically increases the *capacity* of this buffer.
- You can use the Vector class to create *vectors* that can store other objects. Then, you can use the methods of the Vector class to add, get, remove, and replace the objects that are stored in the vector.

Terms

array
length
size
element
index
one-dimensional array
two-dimensional array
array of arrays
reference
immutable object
mutable object
buffer
capacity
vector

Objectives

- Given a list of values or objects, write code that creates a one-dimensional array that stores those values or objects. Then, write code that uses the values or objects in the array.
- Given a table of values or objects, write code that creates a two-dimensional array that stores those values or objects. Then, write the code that uses the values or objects stored in the array.
- Use the Arrays class, the Comparable interface, the arraycopy method of the System class, and a second reference to work with arrays.
- Use the methods of the String class to parse a string.
- Use the StringBuffer class to create a mutable string, and use the methods of a StringBuffer object to edit the string.
- Given the description of an unspecified number of objects, write code that creates a vector that stores those objects. Then, use the methods of the Vector class to retrieve, modify, add, and remove objects in the vector.

Exercise 9-1 Practice using arrays

In this exercise set, you'll create an Array Test application so you can practice using arrays.

1. Enter the ArrayTestApp class shown here and save it in the c:\java\ch09 directory.

```
public class ArrayTestApp{
   public static void main(String[] args){
      double[] prices = {14.95, 12.95, 11.95, 9.95};
      for (int i = 0; i < prices.length; i++){
         System.out.println(prices[i]);
      }
   }
}
```

2. Compile and run the application. This application should print each price in the array on a separate line.
3. Edit the code so it uses a loop to calculate the average of the prices as in figure 9-3. When you compile and run the code, it should print all of the prices plus the average of the prices to the console.
4. Edit the code so it uses nested for loops to create a table like the first table in figure 9-5. Then, code nested for loops that print the table to the console. When you compile and run the code, it should print a table that has three rows and three columns to the console.
5. Experiment with any of the other array-handling routines that are illustrated in this chapter.

Exercise 9-2 Practice working with strings

In this exercise set, you'll create a String Test application so you can practice working with strings.

1. Enter a class named StringTestApp that contains a main method and save it in the c:\java\ch09 directory.
2. Within the main method, enter code that allows the user to enter a full name in a dialog box. Next, enter code that parses the name so the first name and last name are stored in separate strings. Then, enter code that displays the first and last names in a second dialog box. When you compile and run this code, the first dialog box should look like this:

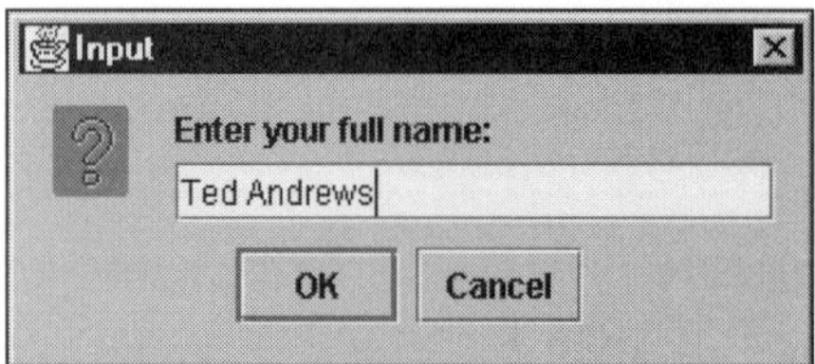

And the second dialog box should look like this:

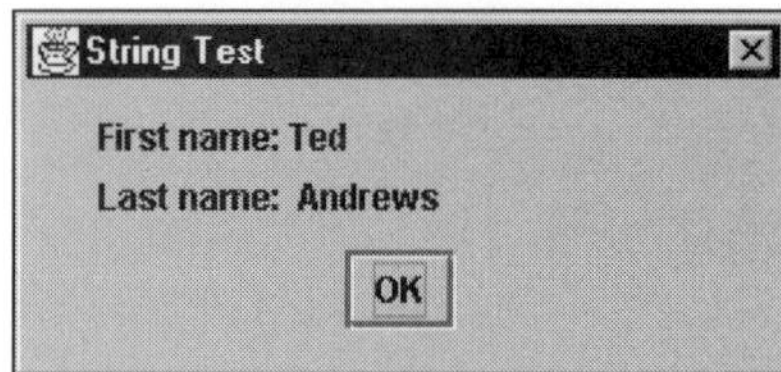

3. If necessary, edit this application so it works even if the user enters a space before or after the name and even if the user enters a middle initial or a middle name.

Exercise 9-3 Create the Invoice application

This exercise guides you through the process of creating and testing the Invoice application that's shown in the last three figures of this chapter.

1. Open the Invoice class that's in the c:\java\ch09\invoice directory. Then, review the code to make sure you know how it works, and compile this class.
2. Open the InvoiceApp class in the same directory, and edit the code so it works the way the code in figure 9-19 works. Then, compile and run the InvoiceApp class. It should display dialog boxes like the ones shown in figure 9-17.
3. Add a loop to the InvoiceApp class so this application lets the user enter more than one invoice. To make that work, you can change the fifth dialog box so it asks whether the user wants to enter more invoices.

10

How to handle exceptions and debug code

In chapter 3, you learned how to catch an exception, and in chapter 5 you learned how to throw an exception. Now, in this chapter, you'll review how to catch and throw exceptions, and you'll learn more about exceptions, including how to throw and define your own exceptions. Then, you'll learn two simple techniques that can help you debug code without using an IDE.

An introduction to exceptions

It's inevitable that your programs will encounter errors. For example, a user may enter data that's not appropriate for the program, or a file that your program needs may get moved or deleted. These types of errors may cause a poorly-coded program to crash and cause the user to lose data. In contrast, when an error occurs in a well-coded program, the program will notify the user, save as much data as possible, clean up resources, and exit the program as smoothly as possible.

To help you handle errors, Java uses a mechanism known as *exception handling*. Before you learn how to handle errors, though, you need to learn about the exception hierarchy and the exception handling mechanism.

The exception hierarchy

In Java, *exceptions* are objects that are created from the Exception class or one of its subclasses. These objects represent errors that have occurred, and they contain information about those errors. All exception classes are derived from the Throwable class as shown by the diagram in figure 10-1.

This diagram shows that the Error and Exception classes are derived from the Throwable class. Since classes in the Error subset describe internal errors and since these errors are rare, you can ignore this subset most of the time. In contrast, you do need to handle most of the exceptions that are derived from the Exception class.

The classes in the Exception subset can be divided into two categories: (1) exceptions derived from the RuntimeException class and (2) all other exceptions. Since the compiler doesn't check the exceptions derived from the RuntimeException class, these exceptions are known as *unchecked exceptions*. On the other hand, the compiler does check the rest of the exceptions derived from the Exception class. As a result, these exceptions are known as *checked exceptions*, and they must be handled or you won't be able to compile your program.

Unchecked exceptions usually occur because of bad code. For example, if a program attempts to access an array with an invalid index, Java will throw an ArrayIndexOutOfBounds exception, which is a type of IndexOutOfBounds exception. If you're careful when you write your code, you can usually prevent these types of exceptions from being thrown.

Checked exceptions, on the other hand, usually occur due to circumstances that are beyond the programmer's control, such as a missing file or a bad network connection. Although you can't avoid these exceptions, you can write code that handles them when they occur.

The Throwable hierarchy

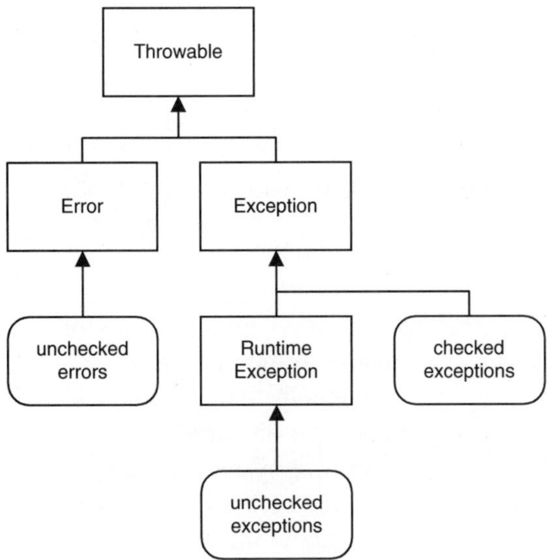

Common exceptions from the Java API

```
Exception
   ClassNotFoundException
   IOException
      EOFException
      FileNotFoundException
   NoSuchMethodException
   RuntimeException
      ArithmeticException
      IllegalArgumentException
         NumberFormatException
      IndexOutOfBoundsException
         ArrayIndexOutOfBoundsException
         StringIndexOutOfBoundsException
      NullPointerException
```

Description

- An *exception* is an object of the Exception class or any of its subclasses. It represents a potential problem that can cause a program to malfunction or crash if it isn't handled properly.
- *Checked exceptions* are checked by the compiler. As a result, you must supply code that handles any checked exceptions or you won't be able to compile your program.
- *Unchecked exceptions* are not checked by the compiler. Although you don't have to handle these exceptions, your program may malfunction or crash if you don't. Since these exceptions result from events like dividing by zero or using an index that's out of the bounds, you can usually avoid them by coding your programs properly.
- Java uses the Error class to identify possible internal errors. Since these types of errors are rare and since there's not much you can do about them, you can usually ignore objects of the Error class.

Figure 10-1 The exception hierarchy

How exceptions are propagated

Figure 10-2 shows how the exception handling mechanism works in Java. To start, when a method encounters a problem that can't be solved within that method, it *throws* an exception. This means that control of the program is transferred, or thrown, to another method.

Most of the time, exceptions are thrown by methods from classes in the Java API. Then, any method that calls a method that throws a checked exception must either throw the exception again or *catch* it and handle it. The code that catches and handles the exception is known as the *exception handler*.

Once a method throws an exception, the run-time system begins looking for the appropriate exception handler. To do this, it searches through the execution *stack trace,* or *call stack*. The stack trace is the list of methods that are called when you call one method. In this diagram, for example, the stack trace is methodA, methodB, methodC, and methodD. If the run-time system doesn't find an appropriate exception handler in the stack trace, the program may crash or become unstable. Then, Java will display information about the exception to the console.

This figure shows how methodD calls methodC, which calls methodB, which calls methodA. Here, methodA may throw an exception. If it does, methodB and methodC choose not to catch the exception. Instead, they throw the exception to methodD, which contains an exception handler.

How Java propagates exceptions

```
MethodD{...
    try{...
        call methodC();
    }
    catch(ExceptionOne e){...
        handle exception
    }
}
```

```
MethodC throws ExceptionOne{...
    call methodB();
}
```

```
MethodB throws ExceptionOne{...
    call methodA();
}
```

```
MethodA throws ExceptionOne{...
    throw new ExceptionOne();
}
```

Two ways to handle checked exceptions

- Throw the exception.
- Catch the exception.

Description

- When a method causes a program to become unstable or crash, that method should *throw* an exception. This warns other programmers who use the method and allows them to handle the exception in a way that's appropriate for their programs. Many methods in the Java API throw exceptions.
- When a method calls another method that throws a checked exception, the method must either throw the exception again or *catch* the exception. Code that catches an exception is known as an *exception handler*.
- When an exception occurs, the run-time system looks for the appropriate exception handler. To do that, it looks through the *stack trace*, or *call stack*, which lists the methods that have been called.

Figure 10-2 How exceptions are propagated

Typical exceptions thrown by the Java API

Figure 10-3 shows some common exceptions that are thrown by the Java API. In addition, this figure shows how you can use the documentation for the Java API to find out what exceptions are thrown by a method.

The two tables at the top of this figure show some of the exceptions that are thrown by the methods of the String, Integer, Double, and RandomAccessFile classes. If, for example, you pass an invalid index to the charAt method of the String class, it will throw an IndexOutOfBoundsException object. Similarly, if the constructor of the RandomAccessFile class can't find the file that's supplied as an argument, it will throw a FileNotFoundException object.

In this figure, all of the exceptions thrown by the methods in the java.lang package are unchecked exceptions. That's why this chapter uses the RandomAccessFile class of the java.io package to illustrate checked exceptions. For now, don't worry if you don't understand the coding details of the RandomAccessFile class. All you need to know about this class is that it allows you to open a file and read data from it. In chapter 18, you'll learn how to use this class.

The screen in this figure shows how you can use the API documentation for a method to see if it throws any exceptions. For instance, if you look up the parseInt method of the Integer class, you'll see the information that's shown. This shows that the parseInt method may throw an exception of the NumberFormatException type, and it briefly explains why this exception may be thrown.

Typical exceptions thrown by the java.lang package

Class	Method	Throws
`String`	`charAt(intIndex)`	`IndexOutOfBoundsException`
	`indexOf(String)`	`NullPointerException`
	`substring(intBeginIndex)`	`IndexOutOfBoundsException`
`Integer`	`parseInt(String)`	`NumberFormatException`
`Double`	`parseDouble(String)`	`NumberFormatException`

Typical exceptions thrown by the java.io package

Class	Constructor / method	Throws
`RandomAccessFile`	`RandomAccessFile(file, mode)`	`FileNotFoundException,` `IOException`
	`length()`	`IOException`
	`close()`	`IOException`

The documentation for the parseInt method of the Integer class

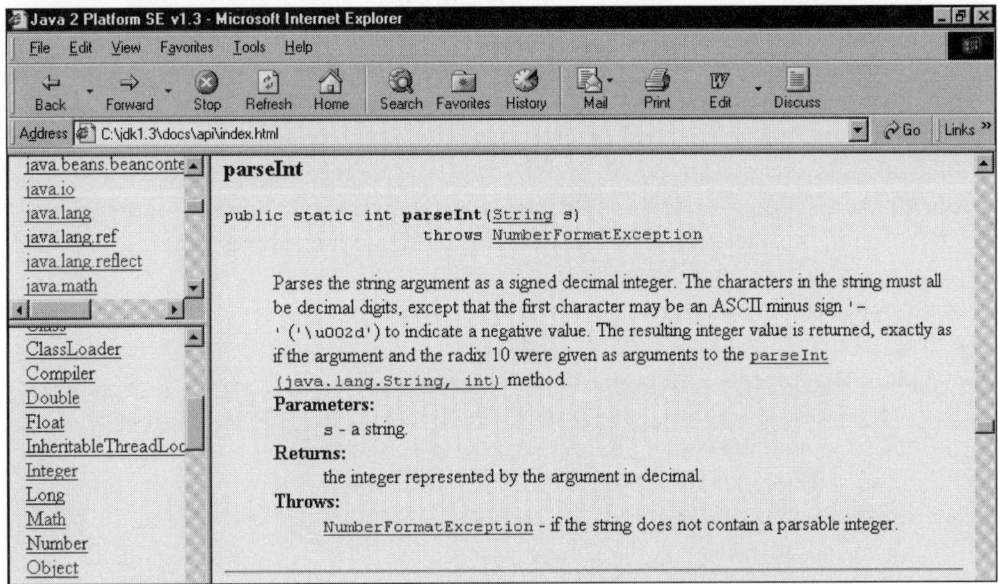

Description

- In the exception lists above, all exceptions thrown by the java.lang package are unchecked exceptions while all exceptions thrown by the java.io package are checked exceptions.
- To find what exceptions are thrown by a method in the Java API, you can look up the method in the API documentation.

Figure 10-3 Typical exceptions thrown by the Java API

How to handle exceptions

Now that you understand how exceptions work, you're ready to write code that handles them. To start, you'll learn how to code a method that throws an exception. Then, you'll learn how to write code that catches and handles an exception. And finally, you'll learn how to write code that prevents exceptions from being thrown in the first place. Since you've already been introduced to throwing and catching exceptions in chapters 2 and 5, most of this material should be review.

How to throw exceptions

When you call a method from the Java API that throws a checked exception, you must either throw the exception or catch it. If you decide that you can't handle the exception properly in the method that you're coding, you code a *throws clause* as shown in figure 10-4. This throws the exception so it can be caught by another method. If a method throws more than one exception, you use commas to separate the exceptions that are in the throws clause.

The first example shows how to code a getFileLength method that throws two types of exceptions. Here, the first statement in this method calls the constructor of the RandomAccessFile class, which may throw an exception of the FileNotFoundException type. Then, the next two statements call methods of the RandomAccessFile class that may throw an exception of the IOException type. As a result, the declaration for the getFileLength method uses a throw statement to identify both of these types of exceptions. Since the FileNotFoundException is a subclass of the IOException class, this method could throw the IOException object only. However, coding both exceptions in the declaration makes the code easier to understand.

The second example shows how to code a getRecordCount method that uses the getFileLength method shown in the first example. Since this method starts by calling the getFileLength method, it must throw or handle the two exceptions that are thrown by that method. In this example, the getRecordCount method uses a throws clause to throw both of these exceptions.

The syntax for coding the throws clause of a method

```
method declaration throws ExceptionOne[, ExceptionTwo] ... {}
```

Example 1: A method that throws two types of exceptions

```
public static long getFileLength() throws FileNotFoundException,
   IOException{
      RandomAccessFile in = new RandomAccessFile("books.dat", "r");
      long length = in.length();
      return length;
}
```

Example 2: A method that calls the getFileLength method shown above

```
public static int getRecordCount() throws FileNotFoundException,
   IOException{
      long length = getFileLength();          // throws two exceptions
      int recordCount = (int) (length / RECORD_SIZE);
      return recordCount;
}
```

Description

- To throw an exception, you code a *throws clause* in the method declaration.
- Any method that calls a method that throws a checked exception must throw the exception as shown above or catch the exception as shown in the next figure. Otherwise, the program won't compile.
- Although you can throw unchecked exceptions, the compiler doesn't force you to handle these exceptions.

Figure 10-4 How to throw exceptions

How to catch exceptions

Figure 10-5 shows how to code *try/catch/finally blocks* to catch exceptions. First, it shows how to code a *try block* and a *catch block* within a loop. Then, it shows how to code a try block with two catch blocks, one for each type of exception. In addition, it shows how to use a *finally block* to release system resources.

The first example shows how to code try/catch blocks within a while loop to catch an exception of the NumberFormatException type. This exception occurs when a user enters a string that can't be converted to an int type by the parseInt method of the Integer class. Here, the try block contains two statements. The first statement calls the parseInt method while the second statement sets the tryAgain variable to false so Java will exit the loop.

If the first statement successfully parses the value that's entered by the user, Java will execute the second statement and exit the loop. However, if the first statement isn't able to parse the entry, it will throw an exception of the NumberFormatException type, thus transferring control to the catch block and skipping the second statement. Here, the catch block contains a single statement that displays a dialog box that informs the user of the exception and asks the user to enter a valid number. Then, Java continues processing at the beginning of the loop. As a result, Java won't exit the loop until the user enters a number that can be parsed by the parseInt method.

The second example shows how to code two catch blocks to handle two types of exceptions. Here, the try block contains two statements. The first statement creates a RandomAccessFile object, which throws an exception of the FileNotFoundException type. The second statement calls the length method from this object, which throws an exception of the IOException type. Since the FileNotFoundException class is a subclass of the IOException class, its catch statement must be coded first. If you coded this catch block second, the catch block for the IOException object would catch all exceptions and the catch block for the FileNotFoundException object would never get executed.

In this example, both catch blocks work similarly. The first statement displays a dialog box that notifies the user of the type of exception, and the second statement exits the program. To indicate that the program exited abnormally, this statement uses a non-zero number as the argument of the exit method.

The second example also shows how to code a finally clause. Since Java executes the code in a finally block whether or not an exception is thrown, finally blocks are often used to release system resources. For instance, it's a common coding practice to use finally blocks to free system resources when working with graphics or input/output operations. In this example, the finally block calls the close method of the RandomAccessFile object, which closes the object and releases any resources used by the object.

Although you usually code one or more catch blocks after a try block, it sometimes makes sense to code just a finally block. If, for example, you want to throw an exception to another method, but you also want to clean up system resources, you can omit the catch block and code a finally block.

The syntax for coding try/catch/finally blocks

```
try{statements}
catch(MostSpecificExceptionType e){statements}
catch(LeastSpecificExceptionType e){statements}
finally{statements}
```

An example that uses a loop to prevent invalid data input

```
String inputQuantity = JOptionPane.showInputDialog(
                       "Enter a quantity:");
int quantity = 0;
boolean tryAgain = true;
while(tryAgain){
   try{
      quantity = Integer.parseInt(inputQuantity);
      tryAgain = false;
   }
   catch(NumberFormatException e){
      inputQuantity = JOptionPane.showInputDialog(
         "Invalid quantity. \n"
       + "Please enter a number.");
   }
}
```

An example that uses two catch blocks and a finally block

```
public static long getFileLength() throws IOException{
   RandomAccessFile in = null;
   long len = 0;
   try{
      in = new RandomAccessFile("books.dat", "r");
      len = in.length();
   }
   catch(FileNotFoundException e){
      JOptionPane.showMessageDialog(null, "books.dat not found.\n"
         + "System will exit.", "Error", JOptionPane.ERROR_MESSAGE);
      System.exit(1);
   }
   catch(IOException e){
      JOptionPane.showMessageDialog(null, "I/O exception.\n"
         + "System will exit.", "Error", JOptionPane.ERROR_MESSAGE);
      System.exit(2);
   }
   finally{
      in.close();
   }
   return len;
}
```

Description

- When you code a *try block* to catch an exception, you must code one or more *catch blocks* or a *finally block* immediately after the try block.
- You should code the catch blocks in sequence from the lowest class in the Throwable hierarchy to the highest.
- A finally block is executed whether or not an exception is thrown.

Figure 10-5 How to catch exceptions

When you code too many try/catch blocks, of course, you clutter the logic of your methods with exception handling code. If possible, then, you should design your methods so they throw exceptions to another method that contains an appropriate exception handler. That way, you can code one exception handler that handles the exceptions from many methods. Another good coding practice is to usually code just one try block within a method. Then, you can code catch blocks for each type of exception that can occur in the method.

When and how to use conventional error trapping

Figure 10-6 shows how to use *conventional error trapping* to avoid throwing an exception. To start, this figure shows some code that may result in an exception. Then, it shows how to handle this exception using a try/catch block. Last, it shows how to avoid this exception by using conventional error trapping. Since conventional error trapping executes faster than using an exception handler, and since conventional error trapping usually requires less code than an exception handler, you should use it whenever possible.

In the first example, if the indexOf method of the String class doesn't find a space character within the string, the substring method will throw an IndexOutOfBoundsException object. That's because the substring method will attempt to access an index that doesn't exist in the string. (If you haven't read chapter 9, you won't understand how the string methods work, but that shouldn't affect your understanding of how you can avoid throwing exceptions.)

Then, to catch the exception that may be thrown by the code in the first example, the code in the second example uses a try/catch statement. Here, the try block is coded around the last three statements in the first example. Then, if the indexOf method doesn't find a space character, the substring method will throw an exception and Java will transfer control to the catch block, which will return the name that was originally passed to the method.

In contrast, the code in the third example uses conventional error trapping to prevent the exception from being thrown in the first place. Since the indexOf method returns a value of -1 when it doesn't find the string that's specified in the argument list, this method can use an if statement to check the int value that's returned. Then, if the value is equal to -1, the method returns the original string. However, if the value isn't equal to -1, the method uses the substring method to parse the first name.

Although you should use conventional error trapping whenever possible, there are times when this is too difficult to be practical. Imagine, for example, how you could use conventional error trapping for the NumberFormatException thrown by the parseInt method shown in the last figure. For an exception like that, it makes more sense to use a try/catch statement.

Code that may throw a StringIndexOutOfBoundsException

```
public static String getFirstName(String inputName){
   String name = inputName.trim();
   int indexOfSpace = name.indexOf(" ");
   String firstName = name.substring(0, indexOfSpace);
   return firstName;
}
```

How to use an exception handler to catch the exception (not the best solution)

```
public static String getFirstName(String inputName){
   String name = inputName.trim();
   try{
      int indexOfSpace = name.indexOf(" ");
      String firstName = name.substring(0, indexOfSpace);
      return firstName;
   }
   catch (StringIndexOutOfBoundsException e){
      return name;
   }
}
```

How to use conventional error trapping so the exception isn't thrown (best solution)

```
public static String getFirstName(String inputName){
   String name = inputName.trim();
   int indexOfSpace = name.indexOf(" ");
   String firstName = null;
   if (indexOfSpace == -1)
      firstName = name;
   else
      firstName = name.substring(0, indexOfSpace);
   return firstName;
}
```

Description

- Whenever possible, you should use *conventional error trapping* to prevent exceptions from being thrown. This is illustrated by the third example.

Figure 10-6 When and how to use conventional error trapping

How to throw and define your own exceptions

Although you usually need to handle only those exceptions that are thrown by the Java API, you may occasionally need to throw your own exceptions. If you do, you should search through the exceptions in the Java API to see if one adequately describes your exception. If you find one, you should throw that exception. On the other hand, if you can't find an appropriate exception in the Java API, you can code a class that defines an exception that is more appropriate.

How to throw your own exceptions

When you're coding a class, you may sometimes need to throw an exception as shown in figure 10-7. However, you should only throw an exception if the current method doesn't have the means to handle the exception, or if you need to throw the exception for testing purposes. Although this figure shows two methods from the Java API that throw exceptions, you can use similar code to throw exceptions when you write your own methods.

To throw an exception, you code a *throw statement* that throws an object of an exception class. To do that, you usually use the new keyword to create an object from the exception class. When you create an object from the exception class, you can use the default constructor, which doesn't accept any arguments, or you can use a constructor that accepts a string that describes the exception in more detail.

The first example in this figure shows the parseInt method from the Integer class in the Java API. This method accepts a string as an argument and attempts to convert this string to an int type. If it can't convert the string, it creates a NumberFormatException object, using the invalid string as the argument for the constructor. Then, it uses the throw statement to throw this object. In the method declaration, the throws clause declares that this method may throw a NumberFormatException object.

The second example shows the readBoolean method from the RandomAccessFile class in the Java API. In the method declaration, the throws clause declares that the method throws an IOException. In the method body, the throw statement throws an EOFException. Since an EOFException object is a type of IOException, this code will work.

The third example shows how to throw an exception for testing purposes. Here, the throw statement throws an IOException object. That way, you can test the exception handler for the IOException object.

The fourth example shows how you can use the throw statement to rethrow an exception after it has been caught. That way, you can catch an exception and do some exception handling. Then, you can throw the exception again so an exception handler in another method can do the rest of the exception handling.

The syntax for throwing an exception

```
throw new ExceptionClass(args);
```

A method from the API that throws an unchecked exception

```
public static int parseInt(String s, int radix)
                           throws NumberFormatException {
   //code for the parseInt method...
   while (i < max) {
      digit = Character.digit(s.charAt(i++),radix);
      if (digit < 0) {
         throw new NumberFormatException(s);
   //more code for the parseInt method
}
```

A method from the API that throws a checked exception

```
public boolean readBoolean() throws IOException {
   int ch = in.read();
   if (ch < 0)
      throw new EOFException();
   return (ch != 0);
}
```

Code that throws an IOException for testing purposes

```
try{
   in = new RandomAccessFile(filename, "r");
   len = in.length();
   throw new IOException();
}
```

Code that rethrows an exception

```
catch(IOException e){
   System.err.println("IOException thrown in getFileLength method");
   throw e;
}
```

When to throw an exception

- When a method encounters a situation where it isn't able to complete its task.
- When you want to generate an exception to test an error handler.
- When you want to catch an exception, perform some exception handling, and then throw the exception again.

Note

- All exception classes in the Java API have two constructors. The default constructor doesn't accept any arguments. The other constructor accepts a string that provides additional information about the exception.

Figure 10-7 How to throw your own exceptions

How to define your own exceptions

Although the Java API contains a wide range of exceptions, you may encounter a situation where none of those exceptions describes your exception accurately. If so, you can code a class that defines an exception as shown in figure 10-8. Then, you can throw your exception just as you would throw any other exception.

Most of the time, you'll want to inherit the Exception class or one of its subclasses to create a checked exception. For example, the diagram in this figure shows the inheritance hierarchy for a programmer-defined exception named BookNotFoundException. However, you can also code a class that defines an unchecked exception by inheriting the RuntimeException class or one of its subclasses.

By convention, all exception classes should have a default constructor that doesn't accept any arguments and another constructor that accepts a string argument. That way, your exception class will behave like the rest of the exception classes in the Java API.

The class shown in this figure provides some skeleton code that you can use to code your own exception classes. To start, this class inherits the Exception class. Then, this class contains two constructors. The first constructor doesn't accept any arguments, while the second constructor accepts a string argument. Here, the second constructor calls the constructor of the superclass. Although this figure presents the minimum amount of code for a programmer-defined exception class, you can add other constructors or instance variables if you need to collect additional information about the exception.

A programmer-defined exception

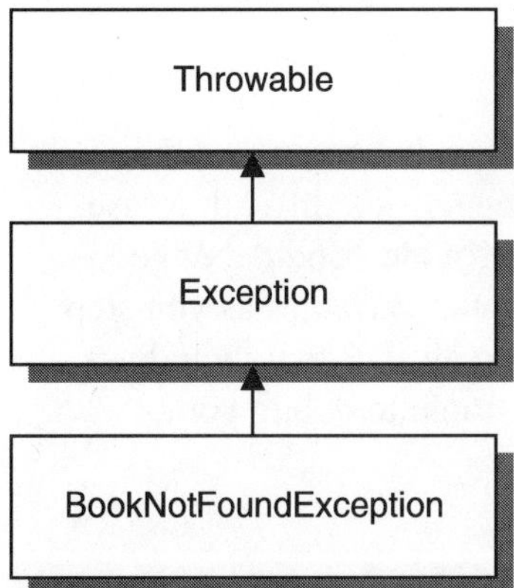

The constructors of the Throwable class

Constructor	Description
`Throwable()`	Creates a Throwable object with null as the message string.
`Throwable(StringMessage)`	Creates a Throwable object with the specified message string.

How to code a programmer-defined exception class

```
public class NewExceptionClass extends Exception{
   public NewExceptionClass(){
   }
   public NewExceptionClass(StringMessage){
      super(message);
   }
}
```

Description

- To define a checked exception, inherit the Exception class or one of its subclasses.
- To define an unchecked exception, inherit the RuntimeException class or any of its subclasses.
- By convention, each exception class should contain a default constructor that doesn't accept any arguments and another constructor that accepts a string argument.

Figure 10-8 How to define your own exceptions

How to debug your classes without an IDE

Locating errors, or *bugs*, in a program and fixing them is known as *debugging*. Although the JDK provides a command line *debugger*, it's difficult to use. One the other hand, most IDEs for working with Java provide good debuggers that can help you locate and fix errors by letting you watch variables as you step through your code. However, if you don't have access to an IDE that includes a good debugger, you can use the skills described in this topic to debug your classes.

How to use print statements to identify bugs

Figure 10-9 shows how to use print statements to identify bugs. To do that, you can use print statements to print the value of a variable to the console. You can also use print statements to determine when a method was entered or exited. Although this isn't as convenient as using a good debugger, it's a rudimentary way to get information about the execution of your program.

The example in this figure shows how to use the println method of the System.out object to help debug a method that computes the average of an array of integers. In this case, the first print statement prints a message that says that execution has entered the method. Within the loop, two print statements print the value of the counter variable and the value of each element of the array. After the loop, the last three print statements print the sum variable, the average variable, and a message that execution has left the method. The comments on these debugging statements make them easy to find and remove after the cause of the bug has been determined.

When you look at the data that's printed to the console, you can tell that the sum isn't being calculated correctly. As a result, the bug must be in the statement that sums the numbers. And if you look at this statement, you'll find that it uses the = operator to assign an int value to the sum variable. To fix this bug, you need to edit this statement so it uses the += operator to add the sum to the current value of the sum variable. Although you could probably find this bug just by studying the code, this illustrates a debugging technique that you can use on more complex problems.

How to use the println method to watch variables

```
System.out.println("variableName: " + variableValue);
```

A method that uses the println method to watch variables

```
public static int getAverage(int[] values){
    System.out.println("enter getAverage method");    //debug code
    int sum = 0;
    for (int i = 0; i < values.length; i++){
        sum = values[i];
        System.out.println("i: " + i);                //debug code
        System.out.println("values[i]: " + values[i]); //debug code
    }
    int average = sum/values.length;
    System.out.println("sum: " + sum);                //debug code
    System.out.println("average: " + average);        //debug code
    System.out.println("leave getAverage method");    //debug code
    return average;
}
```

The output of the code shown above

```
enter getAverage method
i: 0
values[i]: 83
i: 1
values[i]: 95
i: 2
values[i]: 87
i: 3
values[i]: 92
sum: 92
average: 23
leave getAverage method
```

Description

- When a method or routine is producing the wrong result, you can add print statements that display the values of variables as the program progresses. You can also use print statements to indicate when a method or routine is entered and exited.
- To make it easy to remove the debugging statements after you determine the cause of the bug, you can add appropriate comments to the statements.

Figure 10-9 How to use the println method to identify bugs

How to get information about an exception

Since all exception classes ultimately inherit the Throwable class, you can use any of its methods to get information about exception objects. If you look up this class in the Java documentation, you'll see that it contains seven methods. Of these, the three most commonly used methods are shown in figure 10-10.

The first example shows how to use these three methods to display data about an exception. Here, the first statement uses the getMessage method to print the message string of the exception object. If no message is supplied for the exception, this statement will return a null value. Then, the second statement supplies the exception object as the argument of the println method. As a result, Java will automatically call the toString method of the exception, which will print the full name of the exception followed by the message string (if one exists). Last, the third statement prints the full name of the class, followed by the string message, followed by the stack trace. Since this method provides all of the information provided by the first two methods plus some additional information about the stack trace, you can use it instead of using the first two methods.

The first two statements in the first example use the println method of the System.err object, the standard error output stream. Although this works the same as using the System.out object, the standard output stream, it's common to use the System.err object when displaying information about errors and exceptions. This way, even if the standard output stream is redirected to another source (such as a file), the standard error output stream will always come to the attention of the user.

How to print the stack trace to the console

In the first example in this figure, the third statement calls the printStackTrace method of the exception object. This method prints the stack trace to the console, which provides the line numbers of the statements that called the methods in the current stack. In this case, the 17th line in the main method of the BookOrderApp class called the 454th line in the parseInt method of the Integer class, which called the 405th line of the parseInt method of the Integer class where the exception was thrown. By analyzing this information, you can determine that the exception was thrown at the 405th line in the parseInt method of the Integer class. More importantly, though, you can tell that you need to fix the code that's related to the 17th line of the main method of the BookOrderApp class.

The second example shows how to return the stack trace anywhere in your program. To do that, you can create a Throwable object and invoke the printStackTrace method. In this example, you can see that the 10th line of the setPrice method was called by the 7th line of the Book constructor, which was called by the 10th line of the BookOrder constructor, which was called by the 35th line of the main method in BookOrderApp class. Whenever you have a bug in a method, you may want to check the stack trace to see which methods are affected by the bug.

Methods of the Throwable class

Method	Description
`toString()`	Returns a description of this Throwable object.
`getMessage()`	Returns this Throwable object's message string.
`printStackTrace()`	Prints this Throwable object and its stack trace to the console.

Code that uses these three methods

```
catch(NumberFormatException e){
    System.err.println(e.getMessage());
    System.err.println(e);
    e.printStackTrace();
}
```

Output of these three methods

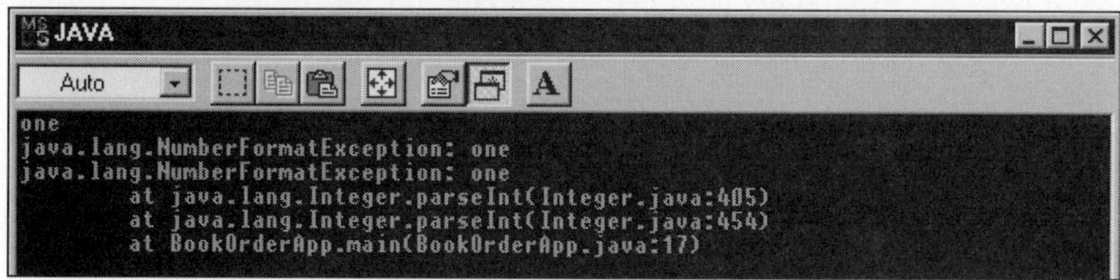

How to use the printStackTrace method anywhere in a program

```
new Throwable().printStackTrace();
```

An example that uses the printStackTrace method in a method

```
public void setPrice(){
    new Throwable().printStackTrace();
    ...
}
```

Output of the printStackTrace method shown above

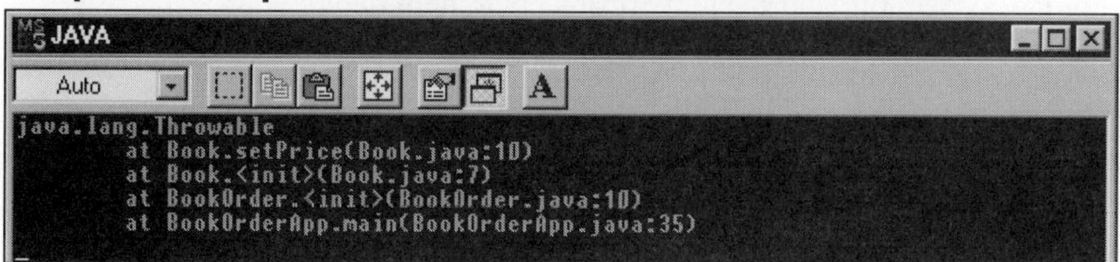

Figure 10-10 How to use the methods of the Throwable class to identify bugs

Perspective

In this chapter, you've learned all the skills that you need to write code that handles exceptions properly. In addition, you've learned some useful debugging techniques. As you develop the applications for the next two sections of this book, you'll see how valuable these skills can be.

Summary

- In Java, an *exception* is an object created from a class that's derived from the Exception class or one of its subclasses. When an exception occurs, a well-coded program notifies its users and minimizes any disruptions or data loss.
- Exceptions derived from the RuntimeException class and its subclasses are *unchecked exceptions* because they aren't checked by the compiler. All other exceptions are *checked exceptions*.
- Any method that calls a method that *throws* a checked exception must either throw the exception by coding a *throws clause* or *catch* it by coding *try/catch/finally blocks*. The code that catches an exception is known as an *exception handler*.
- Whenever practical, you should use *conventional error trapping* to avoid common coding errors. Conventional error trapping runs faster than exception handling and often requires less code.
- When coding your own methods, if you encounter a potential error that can't be handled within that method, you can code a *throw statement* that throws an exception. If you can't find an appropriate exception class in the Java API, you can code your own exception class.
- Most IDEs provide a *debugger* that can help you identify and fix the *bugs* in your programs. If you don't have access to a good debugger, though, you can use the println method of the System.out and System.err objects to help *debug* your programs.
- In Java, the *stack trace*, or *call stack*, is the chain of method calls for any statement that calls a method. You can use the printStackTrace method of an exception object to print the stack trace for any method.

Terms

exception handling
exception
checked exception
unchecked exception
throw an exception
catch an exception
exception handler
stack trace
call stack
throws clause
try block
catch block
finally block
conventional error trapping
bug
debugging
debugger

Objectives

- Describe the difference between checked and unchecked exceptions.
- Given a method that throws an exception, code a method that calls that method and throws that exception.
- Given a method that throws an exception, code a method that calls that method and catches that exception.
- Code a method that throws an exception.
- Code a class that defines a new exception.
- Debug programs by using print statements to watch variables and to mark the entry and exit of methods and routines.
- Debug programs by analyzing the stack trace.

Exercise 10-1 Create the Book IO Test application

In this exercise set, you'll use the Book IO Test application to practice throwing and catching exceptions. Even if you haven't read section 4 yet, you should be able to do this exercise because the focus is on error handling, not file I/O.

1. View the files in the c:\java\ch10\book directory. This directory should contain files named books.dat, BookIO.java, and BookIOTestApp.java.
2. Open the BookIO class, read through it to see what it does, and try to compile it. Java should display an error that indicates that the exceptions in the BookIO class must be caught or thrown. Then, code a throws clause for both methods in the BookIO class as shown in figure 10-4, and compile this class again. It should compile cleanly.
3. Open the BookIOTestApp class and try to compile it. Java should display an error that indicates that the exceptions in the BookIO class must be caught or thrown. Then, code a try/catch statement around the four statements in the BookIOTestApp class that catches the FileNotFoundException and the IOException as shown in figure 10-5. To do that, you'll need to import the java.io package. When you're done, compile and run this class. Java should display the length and number of records in the book.dat file.
4. Edit the BookIO class so it looks for a file named books.txt instead of books.dat. Then, compile this class and run the BookIOTestApp class. When you do, you should get a dialog box that looks like this:

5. Modify the catch clause for the FileNotFoundException so it uses the getMessage method of the Exception object to display the message in the dialog box. Then, compile and run the class. Although this should display a dialog box like the previous one, the message string is from the FileNotFoundException object.

Exercise 10-2 Create the Trap Test application

In this exercise set, you'll use the Trap Test application to practice conventional error trapping.

1. Open the TrapTestApp class that's in the c:\java\ch10\trap directory. Then, read through the code to see what it does, and compile and run the class. In the first dialog box that's displayed, enter a full name like this:

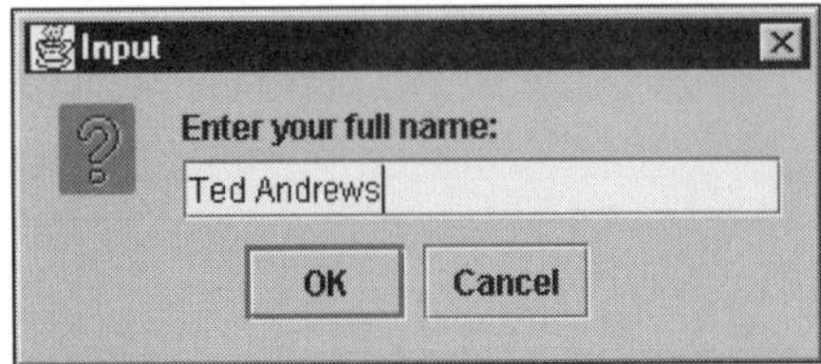

Then, the second dialog box should look like this:

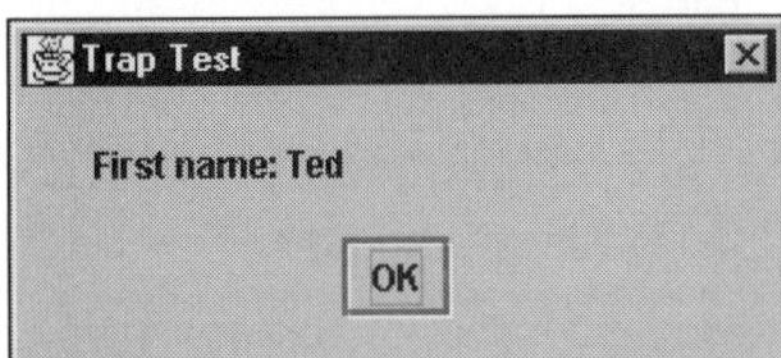

2. Run the TrapTestApp again. This time enter "Test" in the first dialog box. Then, the application should crash and display information about the error to the console like this:

```
JAVA
Exception in thread "main" java.lang.StringIndexOutOfBoundsException: String ind
ex out of range: -1
        at java.lang.String.substring(String.java:1503)
        at TrapTestApp.getFirstName(TrapTestApp.java:15)
        at TrapTestApp.main(TrapTestApp.java:6)
```

To end the application, you'll need to press Ctrl+C.

3. Modify the TrapTestApp so it uses an exception handler to solve this problem as in figure 10-6. Then, test this application to make sure it works properly.
4. Modify the TrapTestApp again so it uses conventional error trapping to solve this problem as in figure 10-6. Then, test this application to make sure it works properly. It should work the same as it did after step 3, but the code should be easier to read and the application should execute faster (through you probably won't be able to notice the difference).

Section 3

Java for graphical user interfaces

In this section, you'll learn how to develop graphical user interfaces for your applications. After chapter 11 shows you the basics of developing a graphical user interface, chapter 12 adds to those skills. When you complete those chapters, you'll be able to develop interfaces at a professional level.

Then, chapter 13 shows you how to add menus to an interface, and chapter 14 shows you how to work with fonts, colors, images, and shapes as you develop your interfaces. Since these are skills that you don't need with every interface, you may want to skip them as you read this section and refer back to them when you need them.

Chapter 15, on the other hand, shows you how to develop a special type of program known as an *applet*. This type of program can be stored in a web page and run within a web browser. To create the user interface for this type of program, you create a regular interface and then convert it to an applet. That's why you should read chapters 11 and 12 before you read chapter 15.

11

How to code a graphical user interface (part 1)

In chapter 2, you learned how to use the JOptionPane class to display dialog boxes. Now, you'll learn how to code a graphical user interface (GUI) that contains labels, text boxes, and buttons. Then, you can learn how to enhance a GUI in the three chapters that follow. When you're done, you'll be able to develop sophisticated GUIs of your own.

An introduction to the Swing classes

In this chapter, you'll learn how to create graphical user interfaces using classes from the javax.swing package. These classes are known as *Swing classes*, or the *Swing set*. This topic presents some general concepts that apply to all Swing classes.

The user interface for the Loan Calculator application

Figure 11-1 presents the graphical user interface for the Loan Calculator application that's presented in this chapter. This shows some of the terminology that Java uses for working with GUIs. For example, Java calls a "decorated" window a *frame*. That is, a frame contains a *title bar* that contains the Java icon, a title, a Minimize button, a Maximize button, and a Close button. In addition, the frame in this figure displays ten *components*: four *labels*, four *text fields*, and two *buttons*. Here, the fourth text field has been modified so it can display output but can't accept input from the user. In this chapter, you'll learn how to write the code that adds these components to the frame.

A user can use this application to calculate the monthly payment of a loan. To start, the user enters the numbers into the first three text fields. Then, the user can select the Calculate button by clicking on it or by pressing the Tab key to move the focus to the Calculate button and then pressing the spacebar to select the button. When this happens, the application displays the amount of the monthly payment in the fourth text field.

By default, Swing components look and act the same on any platform. This is known as the *Metal look and feel*. However, these components look and act slightly different than the components that are native to a particular platform. For example, the user interface shown in this figure looks slightly different than a native Windows user interface. Although the Swing set provides classes that let programmers set the look and feel of a user interface to a particular platform, the Metal look and feel is appropriate for most programs. As a result, that's the look and feel that this book uses in all of its applications.

The user interface for the Loan Calculator application

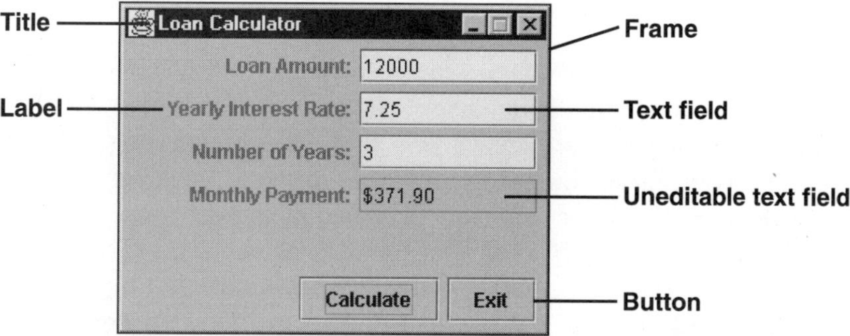

Description

- The window that contains the GUI is called a *frame*.
- The frame in this figure contains four *labels*, four *text fields*, and two *buttons*.
- The last text field in this figure is not editable. As a result, this text field can display output, but the user can't enter data into this field.
- To calculate a monthly payment, the user enters or changes the loan amount, the yearly interest rate, and the number of years. Then, the user selects the Calculate button.
- To exit the program, the user selects the Exit button.
- To select a button, the user can click on the button or use the Tab key to move the focus to the button and then press the spacebar.

Figure 11-1 The user interface for the Loan Calculator application

The inheritance hierarchy

Figure 11-2 presents the inheritance hierarchy for user interface programming. Within this hierarchy, all Swing classes start with the letter J. Although the Java API contains an overwhelming number of classes and methods for GUI programming, the next few chapters will teach you all of the concepts you need to begin using these classes. Once you understand these concepts, you can search through the documentation for the Java API to find the classes and methods that you need.

When Java was first released, it contained only the *Abstract Windowing Toolkit* (*AWT*) for GUI programming. The java.awt package contains most of the classes for the AWT. Since these classes rely on the underlying operating system, they are often called *heavyweight components*. This type of component can make your code perform inconsistently from one system to another and thus difficult to debug. Instead of "write once, run everywhere," Java programming becomes "write once, debug everywhere."

That's why version 1.2 of Java introduced the Swing package for GUI programming. The Swing classes consist of *lightweight components*, which means they are written entirely in Java and don't rely on the underlying operating system as much. However, since Swing classes are derived from classes in the AWT, you need to understand how the AWT works. In fact, you need to use classes and methods from the AWT just to create a simple GUI like the one shown in this chapter.

When creating GUIs, though, you should try to avoid combining AWT components with Swing components. Since AWT components are heavyweight components, they will always be painted over the "lighter" Swing components. This means that the Swing components may not be displayed properly if they are overlapped with AWT components.

Although Swing applets, frames, and dialogs are derived from their AWT counterparts, all other Swing components are derived from the JComponent class. In other words, Swing buttons, labels, and text fields are all derived from the JComponent class.

All GUI components are ultimately derived from the Component class. In addition, most components are derived from the Container class. You can think of a *container* as a component that can hold another component. For instance, a frame can hold buttons, buttons can hold text, and so on. Since all containers are components, a container can hold other containers. The only exception to this is the Window class and its subclasses. If you try to place a window, frame, or dialog box in another container, Java will throw an exception.

The Component hierarchy

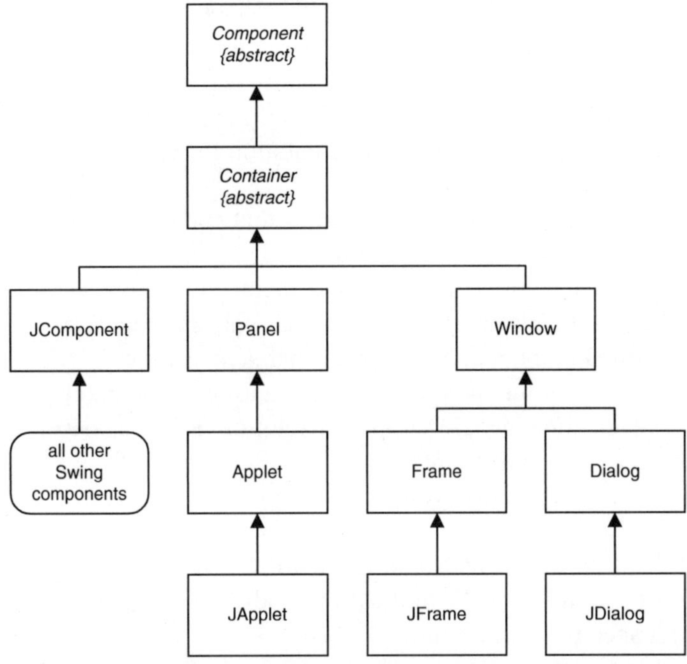

A summary of the classes

Class	Description
Component	An abstract base class that defines any object that can be displayed. For instance, frames, panels, buttons, labels, and text fields are derived from this class.
Container	An abstract class that defines any component that can contain other components.
Window	A class that defines a window without a title or border.
Frame	The AWT class that defines a window with a title and border.
JFrame	The Swing class that defines a window with a title and border.
Dialog	The AWT class that defines a dialog box.
JDialog	The Swing class that defines a dialog box.
JComponent	A base class for Swing components such as JPanel, JButton, JLabel, JTextField, and so on.
Panel	The AWT class that defines a panel.
Applet	The AWT class that defines an applet.
JApplet	The Swing class that defines an applet.

Description

- The *Abstract Windowing Toolkit* (*AWT*) components use an old technology for creating graphical user interfaces that causes them to look and act a little different on each platform. Swing components use a newer technology that allows them to look and act the same on all platforms.
- The AWT classes are stored in the java.awt package, while the Swing classes are stored in the javax.swing package. All Swing classes begin with the letter J.

Figure 11-2 The inheritance hierarchy

Methods of the Component class

Figure 11-3 introduces you to some of the most commonly used methods of the Component class. Since all GUI components are ultimately derived from this class, you can use any of these methods on any component. For more information about these methods, you can use the documentation for the Java API.

The top portion of this figure presents some set methods that can be used to set the properties of a component. Here, the first three methods can be used to size and position a component. When you work with these methods, you use *pixels* as the unit of measurement. Pixels are the tiny dots that your monitor uses to display text and images. Although the number of pixels per screen varies depending on the resolution setting of the monitor, a typical setting is 800 pixels wide by 600 pixels tall. However, some people set their resolution as low as 640 by 480. As a result, if you want your components to fit on the screens of all computer users, you need to size and position your components for the lowest possible resolution.

The middle portion of this figure presents some get methods that you can use to return the properties of a component. With these methods, you can get the size, position, and name of a specific component.

The bottom portion of this figure presents some other methods that you can use to work with components. To start, you can use the first two methods to determine if a component is enabled or visible. Then, you can use one of the last two methods to move the focus to the component. If you're using SDK1.3.1 or earlier SDK versions, you can use the requestFocus method to move the focus to the current component. However, this method is platform dependent and may act differently depending on the system. To overcome this and other focus drawbacks, a new focus model was created in SDK1.4. Part of this model includes the platform independent requestFocusInWindow method. If you're using SDK1.4, then, you should use this method rather than the requestFocus method.

Set methods

Method	Description
`setSize(intWidth, intHeight)`	Resizes this component using two int values.
`setLocation(intX, intY)`	Moves this component to the new location specified by two int values.
`setBounds(intX, intY, intWidth, intHeight)`	Moves and resizes this component.
`setEnabled(booleanValue)`	If the boolean value is true, the component is enabled. If the boolean value is false, the component is disabled.
`setVisible(booleanValue)`	Shows this component if the boolean value is true. Otherwise, hides it.
`setName(StringObject)`	Sets the name of this component to the specified string.

Get methods

Method	Description
`getHeight()`	Returns the height of this component as an int.
`getWidth()`	Returns the width of this component as an int.
`getX()`	Returns the x coordinate of this component as an int.
`getY()`	Returns the y coordinate of this component as an int.
`getName()`	Returns the name of this component as a String object.

Other methods

Method	Description
`isEnabled()`	Returns a true value if the component is enabled.
`isVisible()`	Returns a true value if the component is visible.
`requestFocus()`	Moves the focus to the component. Since this method is platform dependent, it may act differently on different systems.
`requestFocusInWindow()`	A platform independent SDK1.4 method that moves the focus to the component.

Description

- Since all GUI components are ultimately derived from the Component class, you can use its methods on any component.
- When you set the position and size of a component, the unit of measurement is *pixels*, which is the number of dots that your monitor uses to display a screen. The number of pixels per screen varies depending on the resolution setting.

Figure 11-3 Methods of the Component class

How to work with frames

In chapter 5, you were introduced to the JFrame class, you learned how to open a frame, and you learned some concepts for working with frames. In this topic, you'll review some of those skills, and you'll learn more about working with frames.

How to display a frame

Figure 11-4 shows a frame that doesn't contain any components. Then, it shows some code for creating and displaying this frame, and it summarizes some methods that you can use to work with a frame.

The first example shows the code for a class that defines a frame. Since this class uses a Swing component, the first line in the class imports the javax.swing package. Next, the class declaration indicates that the LoanCalculatorFrame class inherits the JFrame class. Then, in the constructor for this class, the first statement uses the setTitle method of the Frame class to set the title of the frame. The second statement uses the setBounds method of the Component class to set the size and position of the frame.

By default, all frames are 0 pixels by 0 pixels and positioned in the top left corner of the screen. In this example, the top left corner of the frame begins 267 pixels to the right of the left edge of the screen and 200 pixels down from the top of the screen. The size of the frame is 267 pixels wide by 200 pixels tall. For a screen running at the 800 x 600 resolution, this setting will center the frame on the screen.

The second example shows a driver class that contains a main method that creates an instance of the LoanCalculatorFrame and displays it. Here, the first statement of the main method creates an object from the LoanCalculatorFrame class. Then, the second statement invokes the show method of that object to display the frame to the screen.

When you use the JFrame class, you can call methods from the Frame, Window, and Component classes. The previous figure showed some of the common methods from the Component class, and this figure shows some of the common methods from the Frame and Window classes. As you work with frames, you can use these methods to control the behavior and appearance of each frame.

A frame that doesn't contain any components

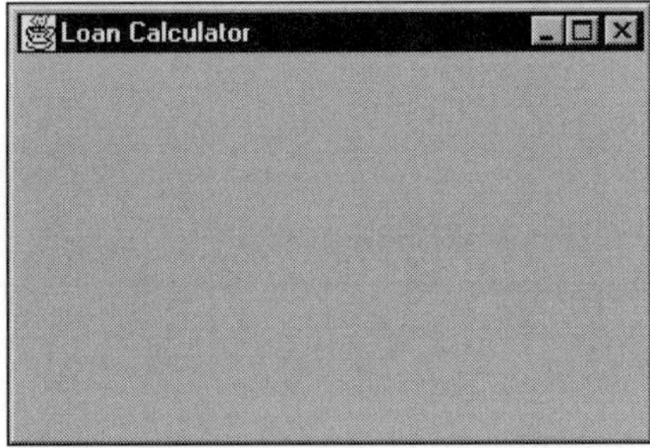

A class that defines a frame

```
import javax.swing.*;

public class LoanCalculatorFrame extends JFrame{

   public LoanCalculatorFrame(){
      setTitle("Loan Calculator");
      setBounds(267, 200, 267, 200);
   }
}
```

A class that displays the frame

```
import javax.swing.*;

public class LoanCalculatorApp{
   public static void main(String[] args){
      JFrame frame = new LoanCalculatorFrame();
      frame.show();
   }
}
```

Methods of the Frame class

Method	Description
setTitle(StringObject)	Sets the title bar to the specified string.
setResizable(booleanValue)	If the boolean value is true, this frame can be resized by the user.
setIconImage(ImageObject)	Sets the icon for this frame.

Methods of the Window class

Method	Description
show()	Makes this window visible.
hide()	Hides this window without closing it.
toBack()	Sends this window to the back.
toFront()	Brings this window to the front.
dispose()	Disposes all system resources used by this window.

Figure 11-4 How to display a frame

How to close a frame

When you create an instance of a frame like the one in the last figure, the frame runs in its own *thread*. As a result, the LoanCalculatorFrame will continue to run even after the main method has ended, and you won't be able to close the frame properly. Instead, you'll be returned to a command prompt window where you can press Ctrl+C to manually terminate this thread. Since this is not an acceptable way to end a program, figure 11-5 provides the code needed to terminate the thread for a frame.

To close a frame or any other window properly, you need to include some code that handles the *event* that's generated when a window closes. In this case, several actions can close the window and generate the event. For example, the user can click on the Close button in the upper right corner of the window, select the Close command from the frame's control menu, or press Alt+F4. No matter how the event is started, though, the code in this figure handles the event by calling the exit method of the System class, which terminates the thread for the frame.

In the next chapter, you'll learn more about how this code works. And in chapter 20, you can learn more about threads. For now, though, all you need to know is that the code shown in this figure is a typical way to terminate the thread for a frame.

The control menu for a frame

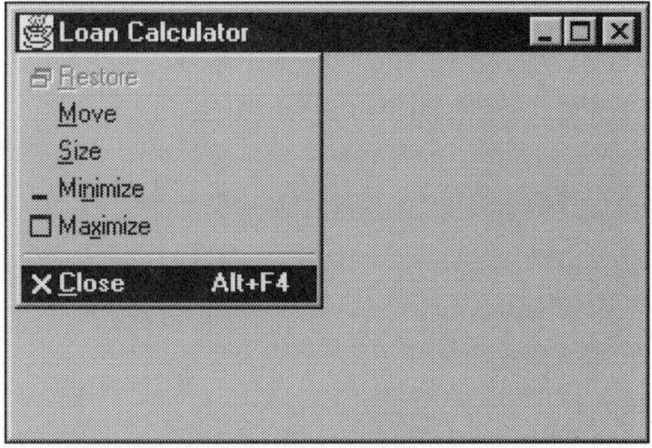

Code that closes a frame

```
public LoanCalculatorFrame(){
    setTitle("Loan Calculator");
    setBounds(267, 200, 267, 200);
    addWindowListener(new WindowAdapter(){
        public void windowClosing(WindowEvent e){
            System.exit(0);
        }
    });
}
```

Description

- To close a frame, the user can click on the Close button in the upper right corner of the frame, press Alt+F4, or pull down the menu for the frame and select the Close command as shown above.
- When you create an instance of a frame in an application, the frame runs in its own *thread*. As a result, the frame continues to run even after the main method has ended.
- To terminate the thread for the frame, you can add the code for a window listener as shown above. This code handles the *event* that occurs when a window closes by executing the exit method of the System class, which terminates the thread for the frame. You'll learn more about handling events later in this chapter and in the next chapter, but this will get you started.
- Before you can use this code to close a frame, you must import the java.awt.event package that contains the WindowAdapter class.

Figure 11-5 How to close a frame

How to center a frame using the Toolkit class

Figure 11-6 shows how to get the height and width of the current user's screen in pixels. To do that, you can use the Toolkit and Dimension classes of the java.awt package. Then, you can use the setBounds method to set the position and size of a frame relative to the height and width of the current user's screen.

To start, you use the getDefaultToolkit method of the Toolkit class to create a Toolkit object, or *toolkit*. Then, you use the getScreenSize method to return the screen resolution of the current system as a Dimension object. Since the Dimension class allows you to access the fields it uses to store height and width, you can use these fields to position and size your frame.

In this figure, for example, the setBounds method centers the frame on the screen. To do that, it gets the x coordinate by subtracting the width of the frame from the width of the screen and dividing the result by two. Then, it gets the y coordinate by performing a similar calculation.

Code that centers a frame on the screen

```
Toolkit tk = Toolkit.getDefaultToolkit();
Dimension d = tk.getScreenSize();
int width = 267;
int height = 200;
setBounds((d.width - width)/2, (d.height - height)/2, width, height);
```

Two methods of the Toolkit class

Method	Description
`getDefaultToolkit()`	Static method that returns the Toolkit object for the current system.
`getScreenSize()`	Returns the screen resolution of the current system as a Dimension object.

Two fields of the Dimension class

Field	Description
`height`	Stores the height of this Dimension object as an int.
`width`	Stores the width of this Dimension object as an int.

Description

- The number of pixels per screen varies depending on the resolution setting of the user's monitor.
- To determine the number of pixels for the current screen, you can use a Toolkit object, or *toolkit*, to return a Dimension object that contains the number of pixels for the current screen.
- The Toolkit and Dimension classes are in the java.awt package.

Figure 11-6 How to center a frame using the Toolkit class

How to work with panels, buttons, and events

Now that you know how to display and close a frame, you're ready to learn how to place other components on it. In this topic, you'll learn how to add two types of components: panels and buttons. Then, you'll learn how to handle the event that's generated when a user clicks on a button.

How to add a panel to a frame

Figure 11-7 shows how to add a *panel*, which is a container component, onto a frame. But before you can add a panel to a frame, you need to understand that a frame contains several *panes*, and you need to learn how to place components on the *content pane*. Although other panes exist, you should place all components on the content pane.

The code in this figure shows how to add a panel to the content pane. Here, the first statement returns a Container object for the content pane by calling the getContentPane method of the JFrame class. The second statement creates a panel by calling the constructor of the JPanel class. And the third statement uses the add method of a Container object to add the panel to the content pane.

Although you can add other components such as buttons directly to the content pane, you typically add components to a panel and then add the panel to the content pane. This helps you organize the components so your code is easier to read and understand.

The JFrame structure

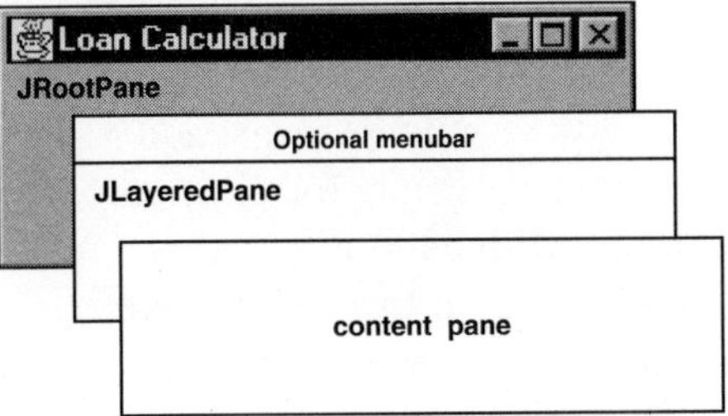

Code that adds a panel to the content pane

```
Container contentPane = getContentPane();
JPanel panel = new JPanel();
contentPane.add(panel);
```

Methods needed to add components to the content pane

Class	Method	Description
JFrame	**getContentPane()**	Returns the content pane as a Container.
Container	**add(**ComponentObject**)**	Adds the component to this Container.

Description

- A JFrame object contains several *panes*. To add components to a frame, you add them to the *content pane* of the frame.
- A *panel* is a component that is also a container. Normally, you add components such as buttons to a panel. Then, you add the panel to the content pane.

Figure 11-7 How to add a panel to a frame

How to add buttons to a panel

Figure 11-8 shows how to add buttons to a panel and how to add the panel to the frame's content pane. To start, this figure shows two examples that add buttons to a panel. Then, this figure summarizes four constructors for the JButton class and three common methods for working with buttons.

The first example shows how to create a button and add it to a panel. Here, the first two statements create the panel and the button. Then, the third statement adds the button to the panel.

The second example shows how to add two buttons to a panel and how to add that panel to the frame. Here, the first three statements create the panel and the two buttons, and the next two statements add the Calculate and Exit buttons to the panel. As a result, the Calculate button appears before the Exit button. Then, the last two statements return the content pane of the frame and add the panel to the content pane.

If you run the code in the second example, you'll see a frame like the one in this figure. Here, the frame displays the buttons in the top center of the frame. Later in this chapter, though, you'll learn how to control the layout that's used by frames and panels so you can display these buttons in the lower right corner of the frame.

The four constructors of the JButton class in this figure let you create buttons that contain text, icons, both, or neither. To place an icon in a button, you must pass it an Icon object. To learn more about working with icons, see chapter 14.

The three methods in this figure let you modify a button after it has been created. To work with the text displayed on a button, you can use the setText and getText methods. To enable or disable a button, you can use the setEnabled method. When you disable a button, the button is grayed out and the button doesn't do anything.

A frame with two buttons

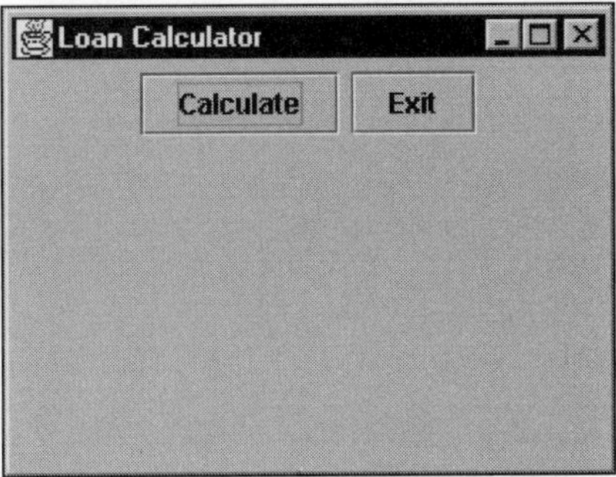

Code that adds a button to a panel

```
JPanel panel = new JPanel();
JButton button = new JButton("OK");
panel.add(button);
```

Code that adds two buttons to a panel

```
JPanel panel = new JPanel();
JButton calculateButton = new JButton("Calculate");
JButton exitButton = new JButton("Exit");
panel.add(calculateButton);
panel.add(exitButton);
Container contentPane = getContentPane();
contentPane.add(panel);
```

Common constructors of the JButton class

Constructor	Description
`JButton()`	Creates a button with no text or icon.
`JButton(StringObject)`	Creates a button with the specified text.
`JButton(IconObject)`	Creates a button with the specified icon.
`JButton(StringObject, IconObject)`	Creates a button with the specified text and icon.

A few methods of the JButton class

Method	Description
`setText(StringObject)`	Sets the text of the button.
`getText()`	Returns a String object of the text of this button.
`setEnabled(booleanValue)`	If boolean value is true, enables this button. Otherwise, disables this button.

Figure 11-8 How to add buttons to a panel

How to handle button events

Figure 11-9 shows how to write the code that's executed when a button is clicked. Although this figure only shows how to handle the event that's generated when a user clicks on a button, the same principles are used to handle other types of events. In the next chapter, you'll learn how to handle other types of events.

The procedure at the top of this figure shows how to handle the event that's generated when a user clicks on an Exit button. In step 1, you declare that the LoanCalculatorFrame class implements the ActionListener interface. This interface is stored in the java.awt.event package, and it contains one method, the actionPerformed method.

In step 2, you add a *listener* to the button. In this case, you use the this keyword to specify that the listener is the current object, which is the LoanCalculatorFrame object. Then, the frame object uses the ActionListener to listen for any events that occur for the Exit button.

In step 3, you implement the ActionListener interface by coding the actionPerformed method. This is the method that handles the ActionEvent object that's passed to it when a button is clicked. The class that contains this method is known as the *event handler class*. Inside the actionPerformed method, the first statement uses the getSource method of the ActionEvent object to return the source of the event as an object of the Object class. Then, the second statement is an if statement that checks if the source of the event is equal to the Exit button. If so, it executes the exit method of the System class, which terminates the thread for the current frame.

The example in this figure shows how the three steps work when you code a class. This class defines a frame that contains two buttons, and it handles the click events for both of those buttons. To start, the declaration for the class states that the LoanCalculatorFrame class implements the ActionListener interface. Then, both buttons are declared as instance variables of this class. That way they're available to the constructor and the actionPerformed method. In the constructor, the code sets up the frame, creates the buttons and the panel, and adds the listener to both buttons.

In the actionPerformed method, the code gets the source object from the ActionEvent object and uses if/else statements to check the source object and execute the appropriate code for each button. If the source is the Exit button, the application exits. If the source is the Calculate button, the application displays a dialog box that says that this button was clicked. Later in this chapter, you'll see how you can code a Calculate button that displays the results of a calculation.

How to handle an action event

1. Specify that a class implements the ActionListener interface.

```
public class LoanCalculatorFrame extends JFrame
   implements ActionListener{}
```

2. Add the ActionListener object to the button by calling the addActionListener method from the button.

```
exitButton.addActionListener(this);
```

3. Implement the ActionListener interface by coding the actionPerformed method.

```
public void actionPerformed(ActionEvent e){
   Object source = e.getSource();
   if (source == exitButton)
      System.exit(0);
}
```

A class that handles two action events

```
import java.awt.*;
import java.awt.event.*;
import javax.swing.*;

public class LoanCalculatorFrame extends JFrame
   implements ActionListener{

   private JButton calculateButton, exitButton;

   public LoanCalculatorFrame(){
      setTitle("Loan Calculator");      // set up the frame
      setBounds(267, 200, 267, 200);
      addWindowListener(new WindowAdapter(){
         public void windowClosing(WindowEvent e){
            System.exit(0);
         }
      });
      JPanel panel = new JPanel();
      calculateButton = new JButton("Calculate");
      calculateButton.addActionListener(this);
      exitButton = new JButton("Exit");
      exitButton.addActionListener(this);
      panel.add(calculateButton);
      panel.add(exitButton);
      Container contentPane = getContentPane();
      contentPane.add(panel);
   }
   public void actionPerformed(ActionEvent e){
      Object source = e.getSource();
      if (source == exitButton)
         System.exit(0);
      else if (source == calculateButton){
         JOptionPane.showMessageDialog(null,
            "You pressed the Calculate button.");
      }
   }
}
```

Figure 11-9 How to handle button events

An introduction to layout managers

This topic shows you how to use two of the most commonly used *layout managers* to position your components within a panel. By combining these layout managers, you can design an effective user interface. In the next chapter, you'll learn more about layout managers.

How to use the Flow layout manager

Figure 11-10 shows how to use the *Flow layout manager*. This layout manager is used by default when you add buttons to a panel. It adds components to the top of the container moving from left to right. When a container runs out of horizontal space, the Flow layout manager creates a new row and begins adding components to the new row. By default, this manager centers components horizontally.

The first frame in this figure shows what happens when five buttons are added to a panel using the Flow layout manager with center alignment. If the frame was wider, the fourth button would appear in the top row, and the fifth button would appear in the center of the next row.

The second frame shows what happens when two buttons are added to a panel using the Flow layout manager with right alignment. Then, the code that follows shows how to create this panel. To do that, the second statement uses the setLayout method of the panel to set Flow layout with right alignment.

To set the layout of a container, you can use the setLayout method that's summarized in this figure. Although this figure shows how to supply a FlowLayout object as an argument, this method accepts any object that implements the LayoutManager interface. In the next figure, you'll see how this method can be used with another type of layout manager.

To create a Flow layout manager with centered alignment, you can use the first FlowLayout constructor that's summarized in this figure. But if you want to change the alignment, you should use the second constructor. Then, you can align components with the left or right side of a container. To specify alignment, you use the fields of the FlowLayout class.

The Flow layout manager with centered alignment

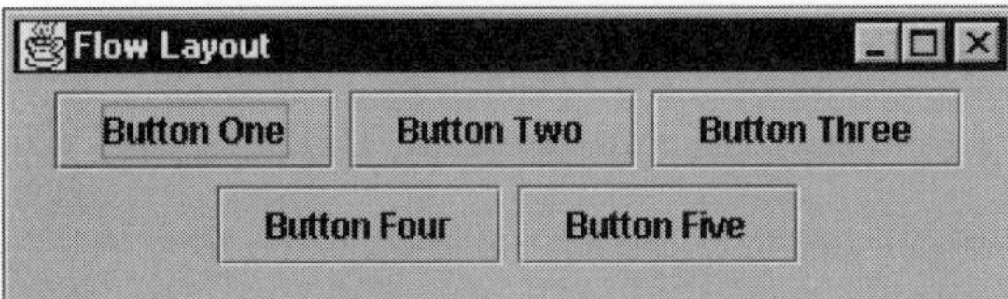

The Flow layout manager with right alignment

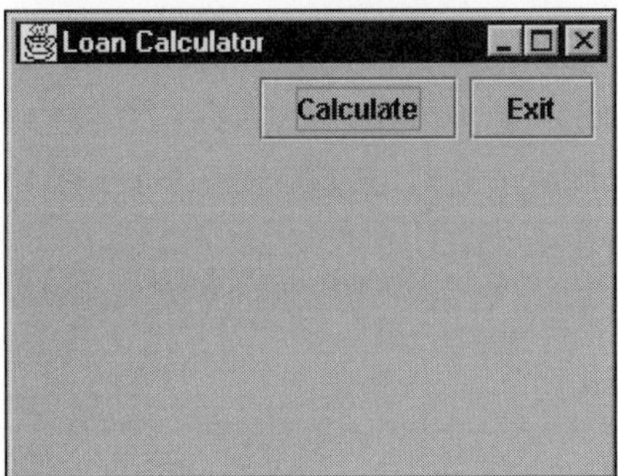

Code that creates a panel that uses right alignment

```
JPanel panel = new JPanel();
panel.setLayout(new FlowLayout(FlowLayout.RIGHT));
calculateButton = new JButton("Calculate");
exitButton = new JButton("Exit");
panel.add(calculateButton);
panel.add(exitButton);
```

Method of the Container class needed to lay out components

Method	Description
setLayout(LayoutManager)	Sets the layout manager for this container.

Common constructors of the FlowLayout class

Constructor	Description
FlowLayout()	Constructs a Flow layout with centered alignment.
FlowLayout(intAlignment)	Constructs a Flow layout with specified alignment.

Alignment fields of the FlowLayout class

CENTER **LEFT** **RIGHT**

Figure 11-10 How to use the Flow layout manager

How to use the Border layout manager

Although the Flow layout manager lets you align buttons with the left or right edge of a container, it doesn't let you place the buttons at the bottom of the container. To do that, you can use the *Border layout manager* as shown in figure 11-11. With this layout manager, you can place components in five different regions of a container: north, south, east, west, and center.

The first frame in this figure shows how the Border layout manager works if you add one button to each of its regions. Here, the Border layout manager stretches the buttons so they are as wide as each region of the container. Although this is okay for some types of user interfaces, you'll usually want to combine the Border layout manager with the Flow layout manager as shown in the second example.

The first code example shows how to set the layout to Border layout and how to add one button to the south region of the container. Here, the first statement uses the setLayout method and the constructor of the BorderLayout class to set the layout for the current container to Border layout. Then, the second statement adds a button to the south region of the container by specifying the component and the region. In this example, if the button is the only button in the south region, the Border layout manager will stretch the button as shown in the first frame.

The second frame in this figure shows what happens when you add two buttons to a panel with Flow layout and right alignment and then add that panel to the south region of a Border layout. In this case, the Border layout manager of the content pane will stretch the panel so it fits the entire south region, but the buttons will not be stretched. This shows how you can combine two or more layout managers to position components.

The second code example shows the code that creates the panel for the second frame. Here, you can see that the layout for the panel is set to Flow layout with right alignment. Then, the buttons are added to that panel, and the panel is added to the south region of the content pane, which has Border layout by default.

To add a panel to a specific region of a Border layout, you supply a second argument that uses one of the five region fields. These fields, of course, correspond to the five regions shown in this figure. Alternatively, you can use these strings for the region fields: "North", "South", "East", "West", and "Center". If you don't specify one of these regions as the second argument, though, the BorderLayout manager uses the default region, which is the center region.

The Border layout manager

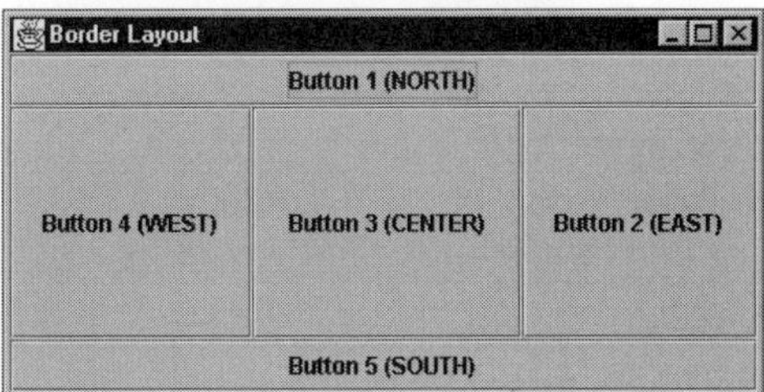

Code that adds a component to the south region of a Border layout

```
setLayout(new BorderLayout());
add(button5, BorderLayout.SOUTH);
```

A panel of buttons in the south region of the content pane

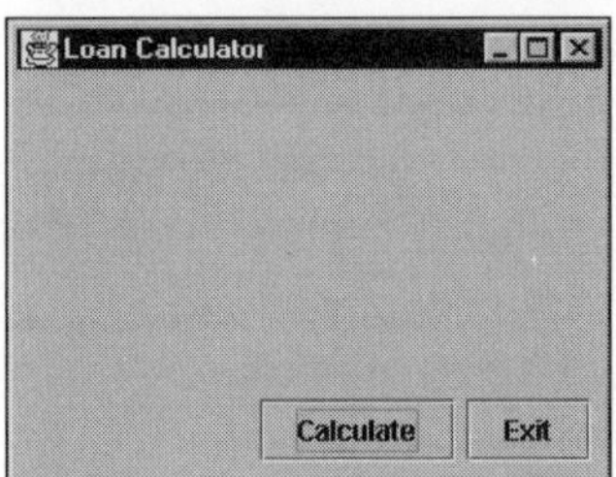

Code that adds a panel of buttons to the south region of the content pane

```
JPanel panel = new JPanel();                    //create the panel
panel.setLayout(new FlowLayout(FlowLayout.RIGHT));
calculateButton = new JButton("Calculate");
exitButton = new JButton("Exit");
panel.add(calculateButton);
panel.add(exitButton);

Container contentPane = getContentPane();        //BorderLayout by default
contentPane.add(panel, BorderLayout.SOUTH);      //add the panel
```

Constructor of the BorderLayout class

Constructor	Description
`BorderLayout()`	Constructs a Border layout.

A method in the Container class used with the Border layout

Method	Description
add(Component, regionField**)**	Adds the component to the region of the container that's specified by the region field of the BorderLayout class.

Region fields of the BorderLayout class

NORTH WEST CENTER EAST SOUTH

Figure 11-11 How to use the Border layout manager

How to structure the layout code

Although you can add multiple components to the content pane of a frame, it's a good coding practice to add all of your components to a single panel and then add that panel to the content pane as shown in figure 11-12. To do that, it helps to divide the code for your user interface into two or more classes. At the least, you should consider storing the code that displays a frame in one class while storing the code that displays the panel in a separate class. This helps you write code that's modular, flexible, and potentially reusable.

The frame in this figure shows a new layout for the Loan Calculator user interface that uses two panels. Here, the first panel is a master panel that uses the Border layout. Then, the second panel is added to the southern region of this master panel. This second panel uses the Flow layout with right alignment.

The code in this figure contains two classes, the LoanCalculatorFrame class and the LoanCalculatorPanel class. The first class contains the code that defines the frame. The second class contains the code that defines the panel that's placed on the frame.

The code for the LoanCalculatorFrame class extends the JFrame class. The first four statements in this class set up the frame and return the content pane. Then, the last statement adds an instance of the LoanCalculatorPanel to the content pane. Since the content pane uses the Border layout by default and since the center region is the default region for Border layout, this adds the LoanCalculatorPanel to the center region of the content pane. In this case, however, because nothing is added to any of the other regions, the center region is stretched to fill the entire content pane.

The code for the LoanCalculatorPanel class extends the JPanel class and implements the ActionListener interface. As a result, this panel class will handle the click events of the buttons. After this class declares both buttons as instance variables, the first eight statements of its constructor create a panel that contains the two buttons. Then, the last two statements set the layout of the current object (which is the LoanCalculatorPanel) to the Border layout and add the button panel to the south region of the current object. Last, the actionPerformed method of this class handles the events that are generated when the user presses the Calculate or Exit buttons.

The layout of a frame

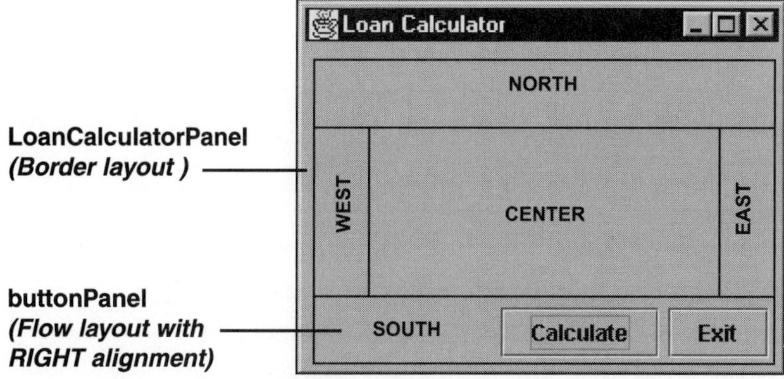

The code that defines this frame

```
import java.awt.*;
import java.awt.event.*;
import javax.swing.*;

public class LoanCalculatorFrame extends JFrame{
   public LoanCalculatorFrame(){
      setTitle("Loan Calculator");
      setBounds(267, 200, 267, 200);
      addWindowListener(new WindowAdapter(){
         public void windowClosing(WindowEvent e){
            System.exit(0);
         }
      });
      Container contentPane = getContentPane();
      contentPane.add(new LoanCalculatorPanel());
   }
}
class LoanCalculatorPanel extends JPanel implements ActionListener{
   private JButton calculateButton, exitButton;

   public LoanCalculatorPanel(){
      JPanel buttonPanel = new JPanel();
      buttonPanel.setLayout(new FlowLayout(FlowLayout.RIGHT));
      calculateButton = new JButton("Calculate");
      calculateButton.addActionListener(this);
      exitButton = new JButton("Exit");
      exitButton.addActionListener(this);
      buttonPanel.add(calculateButton);
      buttonPanel.add(exitButton);
      setLayout(new BorderLayout());
      add(buttonPanel, BorderLayout.SOUTH);
   }
   public void actionPerformed(ActionEvent e){
      Object source = e.getSource();
      if (source == exitButton) System.exit(0);
      else if (source == calculateButton)
         JOptionPane.showMessageDialog(null,
            "You pressed the Calculate button.");
   }
}
```

Figure 11-12 How to structure the layout code

How to work with labels and text fields

This topic shows how to create and work with labels and text fields. First, you'll learn how to use labels to display text. Then, you'll learn how to use text fields to get input from a user and to display output.

How to work with labels

Figure 11-13 shows how to use the JLabel class to add labels to a panel. Labels are typically used to display text that identifies other components. By default, they don't receive the focus when the user presses the Tab key.

For more information about labels, you can look up the JLabel class in the documentation for the Java API. If you do, you'll see that the JLabel class contains many constructors and methods that let you associate a label with a component and to provide keystroke shortcuts for the associated component. For now, though, the skills presented in this figure will get you started with labels.

The first code example in this figure shows how to add a label to a panel. Here, the first statement creates a panel. Then, the second statement creates a label that contains the text "Label One", and the third statement uses the add method of the panel to add the label to the panel. When this panel is displayed in a frame, it will use the default layout manager for a panel, which is the Flow layout with centered alignment.

The second code example shows how to add four labels to a panel. Here, the first statement creates a panel, and the second statement sets the layout for this panel to Flow layout with right alignment. Then, the next four statements create the four labels, and the last four statements add the labels to the panel.

The JLabel constructors in this figure show three ways to create a label. Most of the time, you'll use the constructor that accepts a string argument to create a label that contains text. However, you can create a blank label or one that contains an icon. If you create a blank label, you can use the setText method of the JLabel object to set the text at run time. For more information about working with icons, see chapter 14.

A frame that displays a label

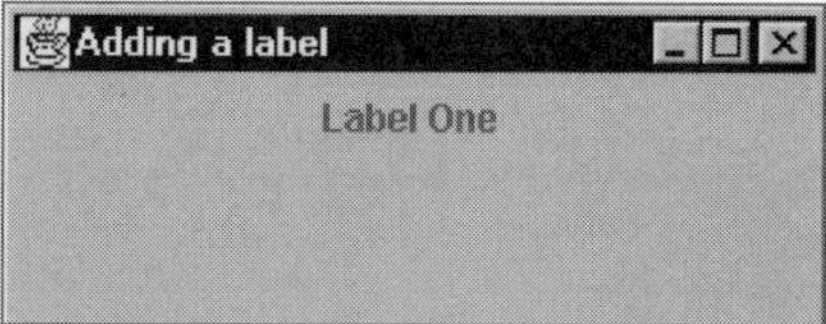

Code that adds a label to a panel

```
JPanel panel = new JPanel();
JLabel label = new JLabel("Label One");
panel.add(label);
```

A frame that displays four labels

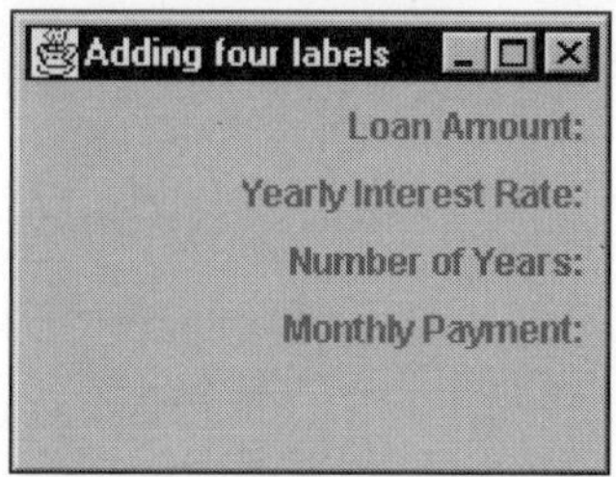

Code that adds four labels to a panel

```
JPanel displayPanel = new JPanel();
displayPanel.setLayout(new FlowLayout(FlowLayout.RIGHT));
JLabel amountLabel = new JLabel("Loan Amount:");
JLabel rateLabel = new JLabel("Yearly Interest Rate:");
JLabel yearsLabel = new JLabel("Number of Years:");
JLabel paymentLabel = new JLabel("Monthly Payment:");
displayPanel.add(amountLabel);
displayPanel.add(rateLabel);
displayPanel.add(yearsLabel);
displayPanel.add(paymentLabel);
```

Common constructors of the JLabel class

Constructors	Description
`JLabel()`	Creates a blank label.
`JLabel(StringObject)`	Creates a label with the specified text.
`JLabel(IconObject)`	Creates a label with the specified icon.

A common method of the JLabel class

Method	Description
`setText()`	Sets the text for the label.

Figure 11-13 How to work with labels

How to work with text fields

Figure 11-14 shows how to use the JTextField class to add *text fields* to a panel. This figure also shows how you can use text fields to get input, and how you can use a disabled text field to display output.

The first code example shows how to create two text fields and add them to a panel. Here, the first statement creates the panel. Then, the second statement uses the first constructor to create a text field that's approximately 20 characters wide and begins with the specified text. The third statement, on the other hand, uses the second constructor to create a field that doesn't contain any text and is approximately 10 characters wide. When you display this panel as shown in the figure, the user can use the Tab key to move between these text fields and the user can enter and edit text in these fields.

The second code example shows how to work with text fields. In particular, it shows how to work with the two text fields that were added in the first code example. Here, the first statement uses the getText method of the first text field to return the text that's stored in that field. The second statement uses the setText method to set the text that's stored in the second text field equal to the text that's stored in the first text field. The third statement uses the setColumns method to set the width of the second text field equal to the width of the first text field. And finally, the fourth statement uses the setEditable method to disable the second text field. This means that the text field will be grayed out and that the user won't be able to enter any text in this field.

This figure also summarizes the two constructors of the JTextField class. The first constructor accepts an argument that specifies the length of the field, and the second constructor accepts arguments that specify a default string and the length of the field. When you specify the length of a field, you specify the maximum number of characters that you want the field to be able to display. However, due to variations in fonts and operating systems, this measurement isn't completely consistent. As a result, it's usually a good coding practice to specify a slightly larger value for the length of the text field. Otherwise, the text field may not be wide enough to display all of its text.

In the application that's shown next, you'll see how to use the setNextFocusableComponent method described in this figure. You can use this method to change the default focus sequence that's used when the user presses the Tab key. For example, you can use this method to skip any disabled text fields. Although this method is commonly called from text fields, it can be called from any class that inherits the JComponent class.

A frame that displays two text fields

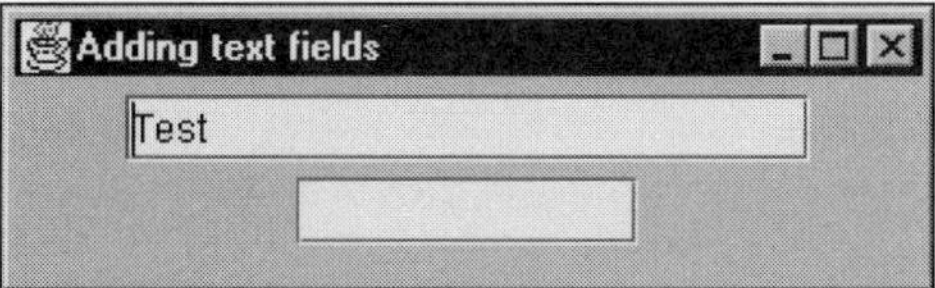

Code that adds two text fields to a panel

```
JPanel panel = new JPanel();
JTextField oneTextField = new JTextField("Test ", 20);
JTextField twoTextField = new JTextField(10);
panel.add(oneTextField);
panel.add(twoTextField);
```

A frame that displays the modified text fields

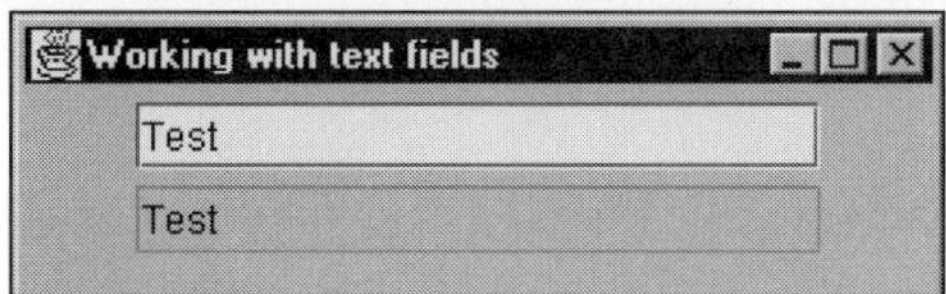

Code that works with text fields

```
String data = oneTextField.getText();
twoTextField.setText(data);
twoTextField.setColumns(20);
twoTextField.setEditable(false);
```

Common constructors of the JTextField class

Constructor	Description
JTextField(intColumns)	Constructs a text field with the specified number of columns.
JTextField(StringObject, intColumns)	Constructs a text field that starts with the specified text and contains the specified number of columns.

A few methods that work with text fields

Method	Description
getText()	Returns the text in this text field as a String object.
setText(StringObject)	Sets the text in this field to the specified string.
setColumns(intValue)	Sets the number of columns to the specified value.
setEditable(booleanValue)	If the boolean value is true, the text in the field is editable. Otherwise, the text isn't editable.
setNextFocusableComponent(Component)	Sets the next component that will receive the focus when the Tab key is pressed to the specified component.

Description

- The JTextField class inherits the JTextComponent class. As a result, it can use the getText, setText, and setEditable methods of the JTextComponent class.

Figure 11-14 How to work with text fields

The Loan Calculator application

In this chapter, you've learned all the skills you need to design a simple graphical user interface. Now, you'll learn how to put all these skills together to create an interface for the Loan Calculator application. Although this interface is simple, it shows how to organize Swing components that create a working graphical user interface.

The user interface

Figure 11-15 begins by showing the user interface for the Loan Calculator application. This user interface uses three panels. The outermost panel is the LoanCalculatorPanel, and it uses a Border layout. Then, the displayPanel is added to the center region of the LoanCalculatorPanel, and the buttonPanel is added to the south region of the LoanCalculatorPanel. Both the displayPanel and the buttonPanel use a Flow layout with right alignment.

The code

The code on this page of this figure shows the LoanCalculatorFrame class that defines the frame of the application. By now, you should understand all the code that's in the constructor for this class. To start, the code defines a frame that's 267 pixels wide by 200 pixels tall and centers this frame on the screen. Then, since you don't want the user to be able to resize this frame, a false value is supplied as the argument for the setResizable method. Next, this constructor contains the code that will terminate the thread for this frame when the frame is closed. Last, the LoanCalculatorPanel object is created and added to the content pane of the frame. You'll see the code for the LoanCalculatorPanel class on the next two pages of this figure.

The main method that's shown on this page displays a frame that's created from the LoanCalculatorFrame class. Within this method, the first statement creates an object from the class. Then, the second statement calls the show method from the frame object to display the frame. Because this main method is coded in this class, you don't need to code a driver class that starts this application. Instead, the LoanCalculatorFrame class will start itself.

The panels of the user interface

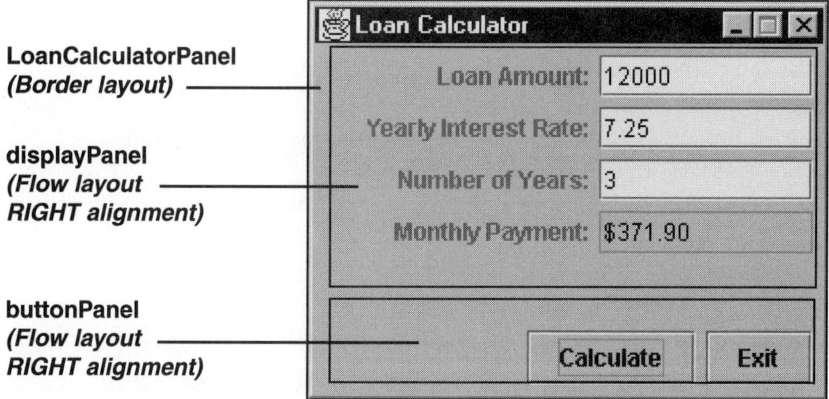

The code for the LoanCalculatorFrame class

```
import java.awt.*;
import java.awt.event.*;
import javax.swing.*;
import java.text.*;

public class LoanCalculatorFrame extends JFrame{
   public LoanCalculatorFrame(){
      setTitle("Loan Calculator");
      Toolkit tk = Toolkit.getDefaultToolkit();
      Dimension d = tk.getScreenSize();
      int height = 200;
      int width = 267;
      setBounds((d.width-width)/2, (d.height-height)/2, width, height);
      setResizable(false);
      addWindowListener(new WindowAdapter(){
         public void windowClosing(WindowEvent e){
            System.exit(0);
         }
      });
      Container contentPane = getContentPane();
      JPanel panel = new LoanCalculatorPanel();
      contentPane.add(panel);
   }
   public static void main(String[] args){
      JFrame frame = new LoanCalculatorFrame();
      frame.show();
   }
}
```

Figure 11-15 The Loan Calculator application (part 1 of 3)

The second page of code is the start of the LoanCalculatorPanel class. The declaration for this class shows that it extends the JPanel class and that it implements the ActionListener interface. Then, the declarations for the instance variables identify the ten components that will be added to this panel: four labels, four text fields, and two buttons.

The constructor for this class begins by creating the display panel that holds the labels and text boxes. Here, the first two statements create the panel and set the layout for the panel to Flow layout with right alignment. Then, the next nine statements create the four labels and four text fields and set the last text field so it isn't editable. The last eight statements add these components to the display panel.

The constructor for this class continues by creating the button panel that holds the two buttons. The first two statements create the buttonPanel and set the layout to Flow layout with right alignment. The next two statements create the buttons. And the last two statements add the components to the button panel.

After creating all of the components for this panel, the constructor adds the listener that's implemented by the current object (the LoanCalculatorPanel object) to the two buttons. In addition, it changes the default focus sequence so the focus will skip from the Years text field to the Calculate button. That way, the disabled Payment text field won't receive the focus when the user presses the Tab key to navigate through the application.

The constructor finishes by setting the layout for the LoanCalculatorPanel object and adding the other two panels to this panel. Here, the first statement sets the layout to Border layout. Then, the second statement adds the displayPanel to the center region of the LoanCalculatorPanel, and the third statement adds the buttonPanel to the south region of the LoanCalculatorPanel.

The code for the LoanCalculatorPanel class

```
class LoanCalculatorPanel extends JPanel implements ActionListener{
   private JTextField amountTextField, rateTextField, yearsTextField,
                      paymentTextField;
   private JLabel amountLabel, rateLabel, yearsLabel, paymentLabel;
   private JButton calculateButton, exitButton;

   public LoanCalculatorPanel(){

      JPanel displayPanel = new JPanel();
      displayPanel.setLayout(new FlowLayout(FlowLayout.RIGHT));
      amountLabel = new JLabel("Loan Amount:");
      rateLabel = new JLabel("Yearly Interest Rate:");
      yearsLabel = new JLabel("Number of Years:");
      paymentLabel = new JLabel("Monthly Payment:");
      amountTextField = new JTextField(10);
      rateTextField = new JTextField(10);
      yearsTextField = new JTextField(10);
      paymentTextField = new JTextField(10);
      paymentTextField.setEditable(false);
      displayPanel.add(amountLabel);
      displayPanel.add(amountTextField);
      displayPanel.add(rateLabel);
      displayPanel.add(rateTextField);
      displayPanel.add(yearsLabel);
      displayPanel.add(yearsTextField);
      displayPanel.add(paymentLabel);
      displayPanel.add(paymentTextField);

      JPanel buttonPanel = new JPanel();
      buttonPanel.setLayout(new FlowLayout(FlowLayout.RIGHT));
      calculateButton = new JButton("Calculate");
      exitButton = new JButton("Exit");
      buttonPanel.add(calculateButton);
      buttonPanel.add(exitButton);

      calculateButton.addActionListener(this);
      exitButton.addActionListener(this);

      yearsTextField.setNextFocusableComponent(calculateButton);

      setLayout(new BorderLayout());
      add(displayPanel, BorderLayout.CENTER);
      add(buttonPanel, BorderLayout.SOUTH);
   }
```

Figure 11-15 The Loan Calculator application (part 2 of 3)

The last page of code shows the actionPerformed method of the LoanCalculatorPanel class. This method contains the code that's executed when the user clicks on the Calculate or Exit buttons. Here, the first statement uses the getSource method of the ActionEvent class to return an object of the Object class. Then, if/else statements are used to compare this Object with the JButton objects. If the Exit button has been clicked, the application terminates the thread for this frame. If the Calculate button has been clicked, the application makes the calculation and displays the result in the fourth text field.

The code that's executed for the Calculate button uses the static calculateMonthlyPayment method of the FinancialCalculations class to perform the calculation. If you've already read chapter 7, you should know how to create that method. But remember that you don't need to know how a method works just to use it. All you need to know is what arguments that method requires.

So before that method is called, the first three statements in the else if block use the getText method to return the arguments that are needed. Since the getText method returns strings, these statements use the static parseDouble and parseInt methods of the Double and Integer classes to convert these strings to the required data types. Then, after the interest rate and year values are adjusted to months, the payment is computed by calling the calculateMonthlyPayment method of the FinancialCalculations class. When the result is returned, it is formatted as currency and set as the text of the Monthly Payment text field.

Since this class will only work properly when valid numbers are entered in the three editable text fields, this method uses a try/catch statement to catch any exceptions of the NumberFormatException type. So if a user doesn't enter valid numbers, Java will throw a NumberFormatException object. Then, the exception handler will display a dialog box that asks the user to check all the entries and try again.

The code for the LoanCalculatorPanel class (continued)

```
    public void actionPerformed(ActionEvent e){
        Object source = e.getSource();
        try{
            if (source == exitButton)
                System.exit(0);
            else if (source == calculateButton){
                double amount = Double.parseDouble(amountTextField.getText());
                double rate = Double.parseDouble(rateTextField.getText());
                int years = Integer.parseInt(yearsTextField.getText());
                double monthlyInterest = rate/12/100;
                int months = years * 12;
                double payment = FinancialCalculations.calculateMonthlyPayment(
                    amount, months, monthlyInterest);
                NumberFormat currency = NumberFormat.getCurrencyInstance();
                paymentTextField.setText(currency.format(payment));
            }
        }
        catch (NumberFormatException nfe){
            JOptionPane.showMessageDialog(this, "Invalid data entered.\n"
                + "Please check all numbers and try again.");
        }
    }
}
```

Figure 11-15 The Loan Calculator application (part 3 of 3)

Perspective

Now that you've finished this chapter, you should be able to create a graphical user interface that can accept user input, display output, and respond appropriately when the user clicks on a button. In particular, you learned how to work with components like frames, panels, labels, text boxes, and buttons. Although that's a good start, there's much more to developing GUIs than that.

In the next chapter, then, you'll expand on this base of knowledge. There, you'll learn how to work with other types of components. You'll learn more about handling events. And you'll learn how to use a more sophisticated layout manager. When you're done with that chapter, you'll be able to develop GUIs at a professional level.

As you learn how to develop GUIs with code, you may remember from chapter 1 that integrated development environments (IDEs) like Forte provide drag-and-drop tools that make it much easier to create a GUI. The trouble is that you still need to understand the code that's generated by the IDE because you often have to modify or enhance it. That's why you need to master the coding skills before you start using an IDE.

Summary

- You can use *Swing* components to create graphical user interfaces that are platform independent and more bug-free than GUIs developed with the older GUI technology known as the *Abstract Windowing Toolkit* (*AWT*).
- All Swing classes inherit the Component and Container classes, are stored in the javax.swing package, and begin with a J. Since all Swing components inherit the Component class, you can call any methods of the Component class from any Swing component.
- You can use Swing components to create a *frame* that contains a title bar and a control menu. Then, you can add *panels*, *labels*, *text fields*, and *buttons* to the *content pane* of that frame.
- You can use the Toolkit class to get the height and width of a user's screen in *pixels*.
- When coding a graphical user interface, you write code that handles *events* that are initiated by the user. To do that, you must write code that defines a *listener* that listens for each event and responds when an event occurs.
- You can use *layout managers* to control how components are displayed within a frame or panel. By default, the content pane of a frame uses the *Border layout manager* while a panel uses the *Flow layout manager*. When using these layout managers, it's common to nest one panel within another panel.

Terms

Swing classes
Swing set
frame
title bar
component
label
text field
button
Metal feel and look
Abstract Windowing Toolkit (AWT)
heavyweight component
lightweight component
container
pixels
thread
event
toolkit
panel
pane
content pane
listener
event handler class
layout manager
Flow layout manager
Border layout manager

Objectives

- Code graphical user interfaces that display labels, text fields, and buttons that respond when a user selects a button.
- Write code that opens a frame, centers it on the screen, and closes it.
- Write code that displays labels and text fields and works with those components.
- Write code that displays a button and handles the event that's generated when a user selects a button.
- Use the Flow layout manager and Border layout manager to control how Java places components on frames and panels.

Exercise 11-1 Create a GUI for the Loan Calculator application

This exercise guides you through the process of creating a GUI for the Loan Calculator application that's described in this chapter.

1. Open the code for the FinancialCalculations class that's saved in the c:\java\ch11\loan directory and read through it to make sure you understand how this class works.
2. Open the code for the LoanCalculatorFrame class that's stored in the c:\java\ch11\loan directory. Notice that this file also contains the code for the LoanCalculatorPanel class. Then, compile and run this class. It should display the user interface, but it won't respond when you click on either of the buttons.
3. Add the code that responds to the buttons as shown in figure 11-15. This code should use one try/catch statement to prevent invalid user entries. Then, compile and run the program. It should display a dialog box like the one in figure 11-15, make an accurate calculation, and respond to any exceptions that are thrown due to invalid input data.

Exercise 11-2 Create a GUI for the Book Order application

This exercise guides you through the process of creating a GUI for the Book Order application.

1. Open the code for the Book and BookOrder classes that are saved in the c:\java\ch11\order directory and read through them to make sure you understand how these classes work.
2. Using the skills and coding style that you learned in this chapter, create the classes that are needed to define a GUI for the Book Order application that looks like the one below. After you start each class, save it in the c:\java\ch11\order directory. When the GUI first appears, all fields should be empty. Then, after the user enters the book code and quantity and clicks on the Calculate button, the program should display the other text fields.

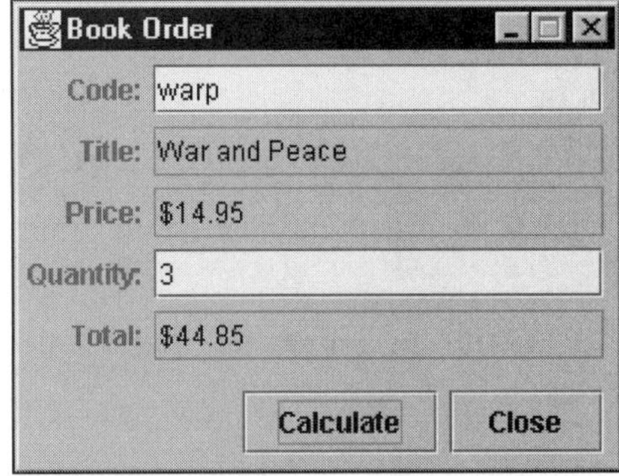

3. Compile the classes and run the application to make sure that it works correctly.
4. Once you're satisfied with the basic operation of the application, enhance the code so it prevents an invalid quantity entry. Then, compile and test this enhancement.

12

How to code a graphical user interface (part 2)

In the last chapter, you learned how to code a graphical user interface by using the most common controls, events, and layout managers. Now, you'll learn how to code a graphical user interface using more sophisticated controls, events, and layout managers. When you complete this chapter, you should be able to develop GUIs at a professional level.

Incidentally, three of the controls that are presented in this chapter require some knowledge of the use of arrays. So if you haven't already read chapter 9, you may want to read the first part of that chapter now. If you don't do that, though, you should still be able to follow what's going on.

How to handle events

In the last chapter, you learned how to handle the event that occurs when you click on a button. In this topic, you'll review how event handling works. Then, you'll learn a general procedure that you can use to code an event handler for any event.

How event handling works

Figure 12-1 shows how event handling works. Here, the first diagram shows how to handle an event that's generated by a button object, while the second diagram shows how to handle any event that's generated from any source. In short, a source generates an *event* object that's handled by an event *listener*.

When a user presses a JButton object, for example, that object generates an ActionEvent object that contains information about the event. Then, any object that implements the ActionListener interface such as a JPanel object can handle the event.

The tables in this figure summarize some common actions along with their events and listeners. These tables divide events into two categories: *semantic events* and *low-level events*. The difference between these two types of events is that semantic events are specific to a component while low-level events are less specific. Since semantic events are easier to handle, you should use them whenever possible. For example, it's easier to handle a mouse click on a button by handling the ActionEvent that's generated by the button than it is to handle a low-level MouseEvent. As a result, low-level events aren't covered until the end of this chapter while the semantic events for a control are covered as each control is presented.

As you can see in these tables, some components generate more than one event. When a user selects an item from a combo box, for example, the combo box generates either an ActionEvent or an ItemEvent object depending on which listener you use. In a case like that, you have to decide which event to handle.

Since the Java event model depends on the Abstract Windows Toolkit (AWT), most of the classes in this figure are stored in the java.awt package and the java.awt.event package. However, some event classes were added with the introduction of Swing and are stored in the javax.swing.event package. For instance, the javax.swing.event package contains the ListSelectionEvent and DocumentListener classes.

What happens when a button is pressed

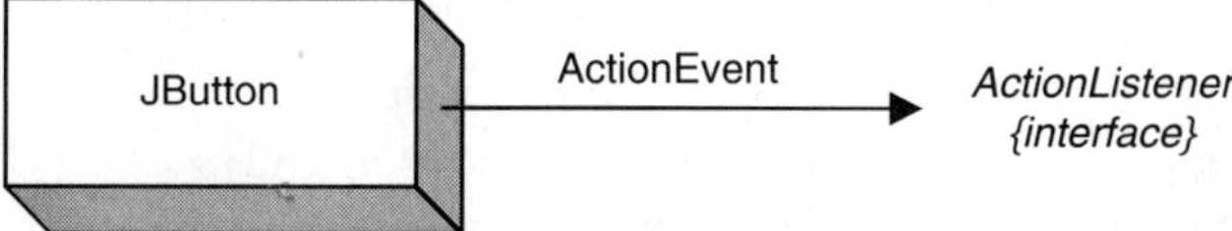

What happens when any event occurs

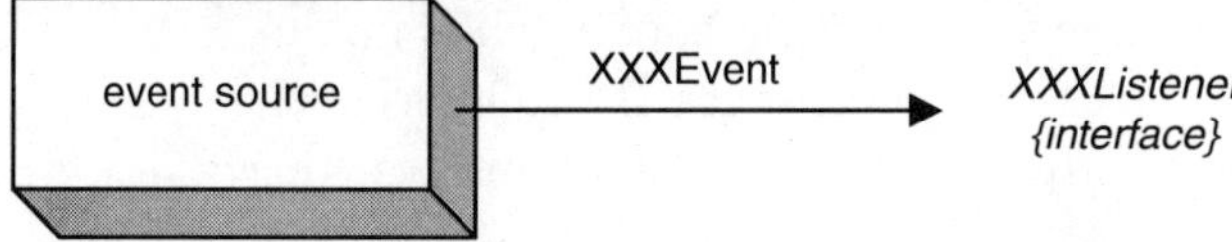

Semantic events

Action	Event object	Listener interface
Button activated	ActionEvent	ActionListener
Combo box item selected	ActionEvent, ItemEvent	ActionListener, ItemListener
List item selected	ListSelectionEvent	ListSelectionListener
Text component changes	DocumentEvent	DocumentListener
Radio button selected	ActionEvent, ItemEvent	ActionListener, ItemListener
Check box selected	ActionEvent, ItemEvent	ActionListener, ItemListener
Scroll bar repositioned	AdjustmentEvent	AdjustmentListener

Low-level events

Action	Event object	Listener interface
Window changes	WindowEvent	WindowListener
Focus changes	FocusEvent	FocusListener
Key pressed	KeyEvent	KeyListener
Mouse clicked	MouseEvent	MouseListener

Description

- An *event* is an object that's created from any class derived from the EventObject class. The event object contains information about the event that occurred.
- An event *listener* is the object that handles the event. The class for an event listener can be called the *event handler class*, and it must implement the appropriate listener interface.
- Two types of events exist in Java: *semantic* events and *low-level* events. A semantic event is related to a specific component such as clicking on a button or selecting an item from a list. Low-level events are less specific like a clicking a mouse button, pressing a key on the keyboard, or closing a window.
- Some components generate more than one event object. This means that you can choose which listener interface to implement.
- Most events and listeners are stored in the java.awt.event package, but some of the newer events and listeners are stored in the javax.swing.event package.

Figure 12-1 How event handling works

A procedure for handling events

Figure 12-2 shows a three-step procedure that you can use to handle any event. Then, it shows the code for a panel that handles three action events. As you learn how to use the controls that are presented in this chapter, you'll also learn how to do these steps for most of the semantic events listed in the previous figure.

In step 1 of the procedure, you declare that the event handler class implements the appropriate listener interface. In the example, the BookOrderPanel class implements the ActionListener interface. However, it could implement more than one listener interface.

In step 2, you add the listener object to any components that generate events that you want to handle. To do that, you call the addXXXListener method from each component. In the example, the three statements in the constructor for the BookOrderPanel call the addActionListener method for three components. Here, the arguments use the this keyword, which says that the current object (the BookOrderPanel) will act as the event handler.

Then, in step 3, you implement the interface by coding the methods required by the interface. To find out what methods you have to code, you can look up the API documentation for the interface. In this book, though, we'll identify the methods that you have to code for each interface.

In this example, the ActionListener interface requires only one method, the actionPerformed method, but some require more. Within the method for the ActionListener interface, the first statement uses the getSource method of the ActionEvent object to return the component that generated the event. Then, an if/else statement executes the right statements for each component. Here, you can see how one method and one event object can be used for two different types of components.

As this figure points out, any class that implements a listener interface can be used as a listener. Often, it makes sense to use the this keyword to indicate that the current object is going to be the listener. But you can code the name of another object instead of the this keyword. Then, that object acts as the event handler, so its class must implement the appropriate listener interface.

Three basic steps to handle any event

1. Declare a class so it implements the appropriate listener interface.
2. Add the listener object to the component by calling the addXXXListener method.
3. Implement the listener interface by coding the methods of the listener interface.

Code for a panel that handles three action events

```
class BookOrderPanel extends JPanel implements ActionListener{
   private JComboBox titleComboBox;
   private JButton calculateButton, closeButton;

   public BookOrderPanel(){
      titleComboBox.addActionListener(this);
      calculateButton.addActionListener(this);
      closeButton.addActionListener(this);
   }

   public void actionPerformed(ActionEvent e){
      Object source = e.getSource();
      if (source == titleComboBox) {
         // code for the Title combo box
      }
      else if (source == calculateButton) {
          // code for the Calculate button
      }
      else if (source == closeButton){
         // code for the Close button
      }
   }
}
```

Description

- Any class that implements a listener interface can act as the listener for events. In the example above, the this keyword indicates that the listener is the current object, which is the current BookOrderPanel object.
- If you don't want the current object to be the listener, you can code the name of another object instead of the this keyword. Then, that object acts as the listener so its class must implement the appropriate listener interface.

Figure 12-2 A procedure for handling events

How to work with controls

In the last chapter, you learned how to work with four *controls*: panels, labels, text fields, and buttons. Now, you'll learn how to work with some other controls.

How to work with combo boxes

Figure 12-3 shows how to work with a *combo box*. After the first part (page) of this figure shows a combo box and some code for using one, the second part (on the next page) summarizes the constructors, methods, and interfaces that you need for working with a combo box. Most of the controls in this chapter are presented in two-part figures like this one because there's too much information for one page. There's also more information than you can remember, so just try to get the concepts as you read about these controls. Then, you can refer back to these figures whenever you need to.

In part 1 of this figure, you can see how a combo box can be used with the Book Order application. With this control, the user can select an item from the drop-down list instead of entering the code for an item. That way, the user always selects a valid item.

The first code example shows how to create a combo box and add it to a panel. Here, the first statement declares the combo box, which is an instance variable of the panel class. Then, the second statement calls the readTitles method of the BookIO class to return an array of Strings. In chapter 18, you'll learn more about this method, but all you need to know right now is that it returns an array with one book title in each element of the array. This array is used as the argument of the constructor in the third statement to populate the list of the new instance of the combo box. The last two statements in this example add a listener to the combo box, and add the combo box to the panel.

The second code example shows how to code the method of the ItemListener interface so it handles the item event that's generated by the Title combo box. In this case, the method is the itemStateChanged method, and the first statement in this method gets the source of the event. Then, the if statement that follows tests to see whether the source is a combo box. If it is, the statements in the if block are executed.

Within the if block, the first statement uses the getSelectedIndex method of a combo box to get the index number of the selected item in the list. Then, the next statement creates a new Book object by using that index plus 1 as the argument for another method of the BookIO class. The last four statements display the price of the book with a currency format, move the focus to the quantity text field, and set the total text field to an empty string.

By default, combo boxes aren't editable so the user can't edit the value that's in the combo box. Although that's usually what you want, you can use the setEditable method to make the combo box editable as shown in the last coding example. Then, the user can type the text of an item into the combo box instead of selecting an item from the list. This, however, means that entry may be invalid.

The Book Order interface with a combo box

Code that adds a combo box to a panel

```
private JComboBox titleComboBox;
String[] titles = BookIO.readTitles();
titleComboBox = new JComboBox(titles);
titleComboBox.addItemListener(this);
displayPanel.add(titleComboBox);
```

The method of the ItemListener class

```
public void itemStateChanged(ItemEvent e){
   Object source = e.getSource();
   if (source == titleComboBox){
      int recordNumber = titleComboBox.getSelectedIndex();
      Book book = BookIO.readRecord(recordNumber+1);
      String priceString = currency.format(book.getPrice());
      priceTextField.setText(priceString);
      quantityTextField.requestFocus();
      totalTextField.setText("");
   }
}
```

The Book Order interface with an editable combo box

Code that changes a combo box so it's editable

```
titleComboBox.setEditable(true);
```

Description

- When you click on the arrow in a *combo box*, a drop-down list appears. Then, you can click on any item in the list to select it.
- To populate the list in a combo box, you pass an array or a vector to it as the argument in the constructor. The items in the array or vector then appear in the drop-down list.
- To handle the events of a combo box, you can implement either the ActionListener or the ItemListener interface, but the ItemListener interface is more logical since you select an item from the list. When you implement the ItemListener interface, you must implement the itemStateChanged method.
- The getSelectedIndex method of a combo box returns the index of the selected item. This is a number from 0 to one less than the number of items in the list.

Figure 12-3 How to work with combo boxes (part 1 of 2)

Part 2 of figure 12-3 summarizes the common constructors and methods of the JComboBox class. Then, this figure summarizes the interfaces and methods that you need for handling the events of a combo box.

As you can see, the two constructors for a combo box accept either an array or a vector of objects. These are used to populate the items in the drop-down list of the combo box. Usually, you'll use an array or a vector to store objects of the String class, but you can also create combo boxes that store other types of objects. (To learn more about arrays and vectors, you can refer back to chapter 9.)

The nine methods of the JComboBox class are the methods you'll use the most with combo boxes. For instance, you can use the getSelectedItem method to return the selected item as an object, and you can use the getSelectedIndex method to return the index of the selected item. In addition, you can use the setEditable method to control whether the combo box can be edited.

The last two methods of the JComboBox class add listeners to the component. The addActionListener method adds an action listener while the addItemListener method adds an item listener. Although an item listener is slightly more flexible than an action listener, both of these listeners are adequate for most coding situations. As a result, you can usually use the listener that's the most convenient for your coding situation. Then, you must code the methods that are required by the class that implements the listener interface.

Since the EventObject class contains the getSource method, every event object can use this method to determine the source of an event. As a result, both ActionEvent and ItemEvent objects can call this method. In addition, the ItemEvent class contains a getItem method that returns the object that was selected and a getStateChanged method that can be used to determine whether an item was selected or deselected.

Common constructors of the JComboBox class

Constructor	Description
JComboBox(Object[])	Creates a combo box that contains the objects stored in the specified array of objects.
JComboBox(Vector)	Creates a combo box that contains the objects stored in the specified Vector object.

Common methods of the JComboBox class

Method	Description
getSelectedItem()	Returns an Object type for the selected item.
getSelectedIndex()	Returns an int value for the index of the selected item.
setEditable(booleanValue)	If the boolean value is true, the combo box can be edited.
getItemCount()	Returns the number of items stored in the combo box.
addItem(Object)	Adds an item to the combo box.
removeItemAt(intValue)	Removes the item at the specified index from the combo box.
removeItem(Object)	Removes the specified item from the combo box.
addActionListener(ActionListener)	Adds an action listener to the combo box.
addItemListener(ItemListener)	Adds an item listener to the combo box.

The event-handler method of the ActionListener interface

Method	Description
void actionPerformed(ActionEvent e)	Invoked when an item is selected.

The event-handler method of the ItemListener interface

Method	Description
void itemStateChanged(ItemEvent e)	Invoked when an item is selected or deselected.

A common method of event objects

Method	Description
getSource()	Returns an Object object for the source of the event.

Two more methods of ItemEvent objects

Method	Description
getItem()	Returns an Object type for the selected item.
getStateChanged()	Returns an int value that indicates whether an item was selected or deselected. The field names for these values are SELECTED and DESELECTED.

Figure 12-3 How to work with combo boxes (part 2 of 2)

How to work with list boxes

Figure 12-4 shows how to work with a *list box*. Part 1 shows two list boxes and the code that relates to them. Then, part 2 shows the constructors, methods, interfaces, and fields that you need for working with them.

In part 1, you can see how a list box can be used with the Book Order application. Here, the user selects a book title from the list box. Then, that selection is used to create a Book object and display the price for the book title.

The first code example shows how to add a list box to a panel. Here, the first statement declares the list box, the second statement uses the readTitles method of the BookIO class to return an array of titles, and the third statement creates the list box and populates it with the items in that array. Then, the fourth statement uses the setSelectionMode method to set the selection mode so the user can select just one item in the list. The last two statements add a listener to the list and add the list to the panel.

The second code example shows how to code the method of the ListSelectionListener interface that's located in the javax.swing.event package so it can handle the event that's generated when the user selects an item from the list. Here, the first statement uses the getSource method to return the source of the event. Then, an if statement checks to see if the source is the title list. If it is, the if block executes six statements that create a Book object based on the list selection, display the price in the panel, set the total field to an empty string, and move the focus to the quantity field. Then, the user can enter the quantity and click on the Calculate button.

The last example in this figure shows a list box that lets a user select more than one item. This is followed by a code example that uses the getSelectedValues and getSelectedIndices methods to return arrays of either the selected values or the indexes of the selected values. Then, the code that handles the events can process these values or the values represented by the indexes.

The Book Order interface with a list box

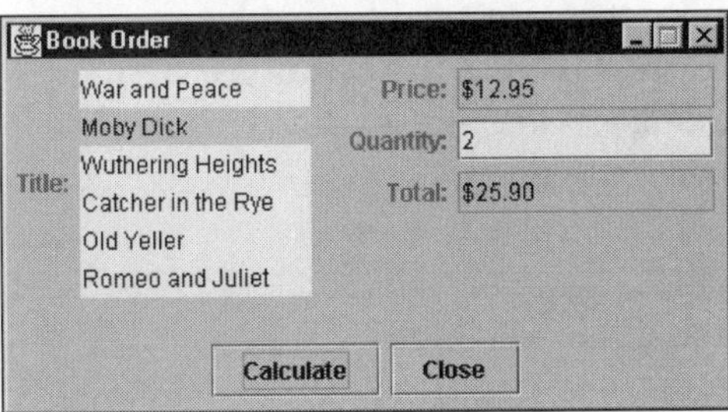

Code that adds a list box to a panel

```
private JList titleList;
String[] titles = BookIO.readTitles();
titleList = new JList(titles);
titleList.setSelectionMode(ListSelectionModel.SINGLE_SELECTION);
titleList.addListSelectionListener(this);
titlePanel.add(titleList);
```

The method of the ListSelectionListener interface

```
public void valueChanged(ListSelectionEvent e){
   Object source = e.getSource();
   if (source == titleList){
      int recordNumber = titleList.getSelectedIndex();
      Book book = BookIO.readRecord(recordNumber+1);
      String priceString = currency.format(book.getPrice());
      priceTextField.setText(priceString);
      totalTextField.setText("");
      quantityTextField.requestFocus();
   }
}
```

A list box that allows multiple selections

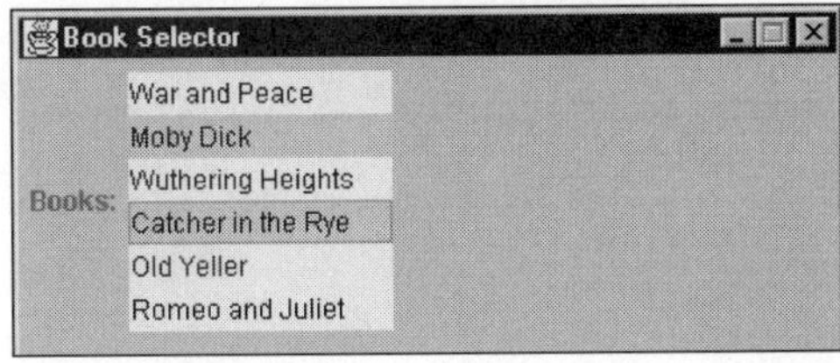

Code that returns an array of selected items or their indexes

```
Object[] title = titleList.getSelectedValues();
int[] recordNumber = titleList.getSelectedIndices();
```

Description

- A *list box* lists an array of items. Then, the user can select an item by clicking on it or deselect an item by clicking on it again.
- To handle the events of a list box, you must implement the ListSelectionListener and its valueChanged method.

Figure 12-4 How to work with list boxes (part 1 of 2)

Part 2 of figure 12-4 summarizes the common constructors and methods for the JList class as well as the interface and fields that you need for working with a list. As you can see, the constructors and methods of the JList class are similar to the constructors and methods of the JComboBox class. In short, you can create a JList from an array of objects or a vector. Then, you can use methods to retrieve the selected item.

Since list boxes can let you select more than one item from a list, the JList class also contains methods that provide for multiple selections. First, you can use the setSelectionMode method and the fields of the ListSelectionModel class to set the mode for the list. Then, if you set the mode to single-interval or multiple-interval selection, you can use the getSelectedValues or getSelectedIndices methods to get the selected items or their indexes.

The JList class also contains a method that lets you control the number of items in the list box. But when you use that method, you should also use a scroll pane as shown in the next figure.

To handle the event that's generated when a user selects an item from a list box, you must implement the ListSelectionListener interface. To do that, you also need to implement the valueChanged method as the event handler.

Common constructors of the JList class

Constructor	Description
`JList(Object[])`	Creates a list that contains the objects stored in the specified array of objects.
`JList(Vector)`	Creates a list that contains the objects stored in the specified Vector object.

Common methods of the JList class

Method	Description
`getSelectedValue()`	Returns the object for the selected item as an Object type.
`getSelectedIndex()`	Returns an int value for the index of the selected item.
`getSelectedValues()`	Returns an array of objects for the selected items.
`getSelectedIndices()`	Returns an array of int values for the indexes of the selected items.
`isSelectedIndex(intVal)`	Returns true if the specified int value matches the index of a selected item in the list.
`setFixedCellWidth(intPixels)`	Sets the cell width to the specified pixel length. Otherwise, the width of the list is slightly wider than the widest item in the array or vector that populates the list.
`setVisibleRowCount(intVal)`	Sets the visible row count to the specified int value. This only works when the list is displayed within a scroll pane as shown in the next figure.
`setSelectionMode(intVal)`	Sets the selection mode to single or multiple selections using fields from the ListSelectionModel class shown below.
`addListSelectionListener( ListSelectionListener)`	Adds a list selection listener to this list.

The ListSelectionListener interface

Method	Description
`void valueChanged( ListSelectionEvent e)`	Invoked when an item selection changes.

Fields of the ListSelectionModel class

Constant	Description
`SINGLE_SELECTION`	Lets the user select one item.
`SINGLE_INTERVAL_SELECTION`	Lets the user select one item or a continuous group of items.
`MULTIPLE_INTERVAL_SELECTION`	Lets the user select any combination of items. This is the default mode.

Figure 12-4 How to work with list boxes (part 2 of 2)

How to work with scroll panes

Figure 12-5 shows how to use the JScrollPane class to add a component like a list box to a *scroll pane*. Here, you can see a version of the Book Order interface with a list box that uses a scroll pane. In this case, the list is too long to fit in the list box so a scroll bar appears that lets the user scroll through the items in the list. Note, however, that the scroll bar isn't displayed if the list fits within its allotted rows.

The code shows how to add a list box to a scroll pane. Here, the first statement uses the setVisibleRowCount method of the JList object to set the number of visible rows for the list. Then, the second statement creates the scroll pane by adding the list to the scroll pane, and the third statement adds the scroll pane to the panel.

The constructor for the JScrollPane class shows that you can add any component to a scroll pane. However, scroll panes are generally used with components that contain rows.

The Book Order interface with a list in a scroll pane

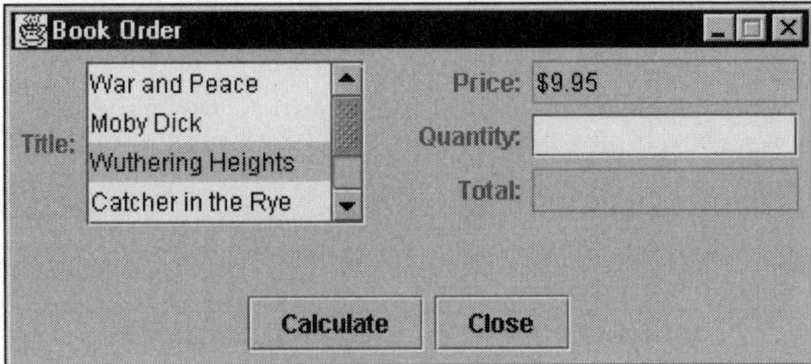

Code that adds a scroll pane to a list on a panel

```
titleList.setVisibleRowCount(4);
JScrollPane titleScroll = new JScrollPane(titleList);
titlePanel.add(titleScroll);
```

Constructor of the JScrollPane class

Constructor	Description
`JScrollPane(Component)`	Creates a scroll pane that displays the contents of the component when its view extends beyond its bounds.

Description

- A *scroll pane* can be used when all of the items in a list won't fit into the component. Then, the user can click on the arrows in the scroll bar or on the scroll bar itself to scroll through the items.
- When you add a list to a scroll pane, you should use the setVisibleRowCount method of the list to set the visible row count.
- If the list doesn't extend beyond the view of the component that has been added to a scroll pane, the scroll bar isn't displayed.

Figure 12-5 How to work with scroll panes

How to work with borders

Figure 12-6 shows how to add a *border* to a component. Although adding borders is an esthetic consideration that doesn't affect functionality, borders also let you add a title to a component. For example, the three text boxes in the BookOrder interface in this figure have etched borders (that you can barely see), but the scroll pane that contains the list box component has a border that adds the word *Title* at the top of the pane.

The first code example shows how to add an etched border to the three text fields. Here, the first statement uses the createEtchedBorder method of the BorderFactory class to create a Border object for an etched border. Then, the next three statements use the setBorder method to apply this border to the three text fields.

The second code example shows how to add an etched border and a title to the scroll pane. Here, the first statement creates the Border object that defines an etched border. Then, the second statement uses this Border object in the createTitledBorder method to create a second Border object that also contains a title. And the third statement uses the setBorder method to apply this Border object to the scroll pane.

The rest of this figure summarizes the methods of the BorderFactory class that are used to create Border objects as well as the method of the JComponent class that you use to set the border for any component. It also lists the packages that store the BorderFactory class and the Border interface, which is the interface that's used by the BorderFactory class. Since the Border interface is located in the javax.swing.border package, you must import this package when you work with borders.

The Book Order interface with etched borders

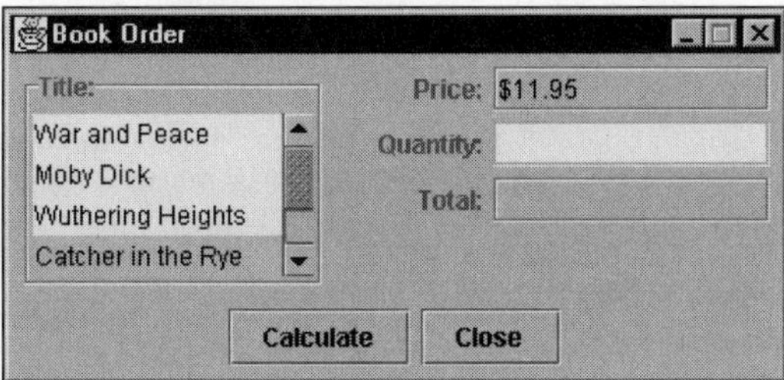

Code that adds an etched border to the three text fields

```
Border etchedBorder = BorderFactory.createEtchedBorder();
priceTextField.setBorder(etchedBorder);
quantityTextField.setBorder(etchedBorder);
totalTextField.setBorder(etchedBorder);
```

Code that adds an etched title border to a scroll pane

```
Border etchedBorder = BorderFactory.createEtchedBorder();
Border titleBorder = BorderFactory.createTitledBorder(
   etchedBorder, "Title:");
titleScroll.setBorder(titleBorder);
```

The Border interface

```
javax.swing.border.Border
```

The BorderFactory class

```
javax.swing.BorderFactory
```

Static methods of the BorderFactory class

Method	Description
createLineBorder()	Returns a Border object with a line border.
createEtchedBorder()	Returns a Border object with an etched border.
createLoweredBevelBorder()	Returns a Border object with a lowered bevel border.
createRaisedBevelBorder()	Returns a Border object with a raised bevel border.
createTitledBorder(Border, String**)**	Returns a Border object that uses the border style specified by the Border object and the title specified by the string.
createTitledBorder(String**)**	Returns a Border object that uses the line border style and a title specified by the string.

Method of the JComponent class used to set borders

Method	Description
setBorder(Border**)**	Sets the border style for a component.

Note

- To set borders as shown above, you must import the javax.swing.border package.

Figure 12-6 How to work with borders

How to work with text fields and text areas

In the last chapter, you learned how to use a *text field* to get one line of input from a user. Now, figure 12-7 shows you how to create a *text area* to get more than one line of input from a user. It also shows how to provide a listener for either a text field or a text area. As before, part 1 of this figure illustrates the use of text fields and areas and the code that makes them work. Then, part 2 summarizes the constructors and methods that you need for working with text fields and areas.

The first code example shows how to add a text area to a scroll pane and how to add that scroll pane to a panel. Here, the first statement declares the text area as an instance of the JTextArea class, and the second statement specifies that the text area should have approximately 4 rows with 20 columns per row. Next, the third statement specifies that each line should wrap to the next line, and the fourth statement specifies that the wrapped lines should be split between words. Then, the fifth statement adds the text area to a scroll pane, and the sixth statement adds the scroll pane to the panel.

The second example shows how to return the text that's stored in a text area as a string. To do that, you use the same method that's used with text fields. That's because this method is actually an inherited method of the JTextComponent class.

The third example shows how to add a document listener to a text field or area. Since text fields and areas are both derived from the JTextComponent class, this works the same for both of these components. Here, the first statement calls the getDocument method from the quantity text field to return a Document object. Then, this statement calls the addDocumentListener method from the Document object to add the listener to the text field. The next statement works the same way for a comment text area.

The fourth example shows how to code the three methods of the DocumentListener interface. Here, the first method contains an if statement that tests to see whether the insert event has occurred for the Document object for the quantity text field. If that's true, the calculateButton is enabled so the user can finish the order. Remember that this type of coding works the same for a text area.

The other two methods in this fourth example are there to remind you that you have to declare them when you implement the DocumentListener interface, although you don't have to code any statements for these methods. To determine whether a user has added or removed a portion of the document, you should use the insertUpdate or removeUpdate methods.

The Book Order interface with a text area

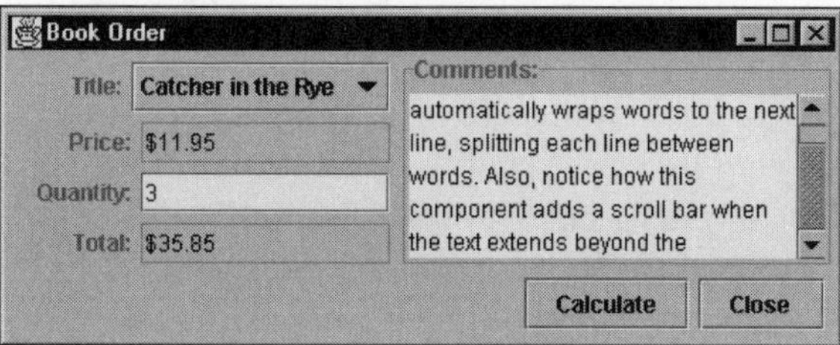

Code that adds a text area

```
private JTextArea commentTextArea;
commentTextArea = new JTextArea(4, 20);
commentTextArea.setLineWrap(true);
commentTextArea.setWrapStyleWord(true);
JScrollPane commentScroll = new JScrollPane(commentTextArea);
displayPanel.add(commentScroll);
```

Code that gets the text stored in a text area

```
String comments = commentTextArea.getText();
```

Code that adds a document listener to a text field and a text area

```
quantityTextField.getDocument().addDocumentListener(this);
commentTextArea.getDocument().addDocumentListener(this);
```

The three methods of the DocumentListener interface

```
public void insertUpdate(DocumentEvent e){
   if (e.getDocument() == quantityTextField.getDocument())
      calculateButton.setEnabled(true);
}
public void removeUpdate(DocumentEvent e){}
public void changedUpdate(DocumentEvent e){}
```

Description

- In contrast to a text field, a *text area* can be used to enter and display more than one line of text.
- When you use the constructor to create a text area, you specify the number of rows and columns for the area. If the text area is going to receive more text than can be viewed, you should add the text area to a scroll pane.
- You can use the setLineWrap and setWrapStyleWord methods to provide for wrapping the lines in the text area when necessary and breaking these lines between words.
- The getText method is actually an inherited method of the JTextComponent class so it works the same for text fields and text areas.
- To add a document listener to a text field or area, you first need to use the getDocument method to get the Document object for the field or area. Then, you use the addDocumentListener method to add the listener to that Document object.
- The three methods for the DocumentListener interface can be used to determine whether a text field or area has had text inserted into it, removed from it, or changed.

Figure 12-7 How to work with text fields and text areas (part 1 of 2)

Part 2 of this figure summarizes the constructors and methods that you need for working with text areas. Note, however, that many of the methods also work with text fields.

To create a text area, you use a constructor of the JTextArea class. The first one creates a blank text area by specifying the number of rows and columns that should be visible. The second one does the same but also specifies an initial string for the text area. When you use one of these constructors, you specify the desired number of rows and columns, but the actual number of rows and columns that are displayed may be slightly different. That depends on a number of variables including the font size and style and the type of layout manager that's being used.

By default, text areas don't wrap text to the next line so a user must press the Enter key to start a new line of text. So if you want the text to wrap, you need to call the setLineWrap method and supply a true value as the argument. By default, though, wrapped lines are split wherever the line reaches the end of the text area, even if that's in the middle of a word. So if you want to make sure that the text is wrapped between words, you can call the setWrapStyleWord method and supply a true value as the argument.

To add a document listener to a text area or field, you should use the addDocumentListener method of the Document class. Before you can do that, though, you must use the getDocument method of the text area or field to get the Document object for the area or field. This means that you add the listener with code like this:

```
commentTextArea.getDocument().addDocumentListener(this);
quantityTextField.getDocument().addDocumentListener(this);
```

Once you've done that, you can implement the three methods for the DocumentListener interface.

Common constructors of the JTextArea class

Constructor	Description
`JTextArea(intRows, intCols)`	Creates an empty text area with the specified number of rows and columns.
`JTextArea(String, intRows, intCols)`	Creates a text area with the specified number of rows and columns starting with the specified text.

Methods that work with text areas

Method	Description
`setLineWrap(boolean)`	If the boolean value is true, then the lines will wrap if they don't fit in the text area.
`setWrapStyleWord(boolean)`	If the boolean value is true and line wrapping is turned on, then wrapped lines will be separated between words.
`append(String)`	Appends the specified text.
`getText()`	Returns the text in this text area as a String object.
`setText(String)`	Sets the text in this text area to the specified string.
`getDocument()`	Returns a Document object that represents a text component, such as a text field or text area.

Method of the Document class

Method	Description
`addDocumentListener(DocumentListener)`	Adds the listener for document changes.

Methods of the DocumentListener interface

Method	Description
`void changedUpdate(DocumentEvent e)`	Called when an attribute of the document has been modified.
`void insertUpdate(DocumentEvent e)`	Called when an insert is made into a document.
`void removeUpdate(DocumentEvent e)`	Called when part of a document is deleted.

Method of the DocumentEvent class

Method	Description
`getDocument()`	Returns the Document object for the component that generated the event.

Description

- The DocumentListener interface is stored in the javax.swing.event package.
- Both the JTextField and JTextArea classes inherit the JTextComponent class. As a result, these classes can call the getText, setText, and setEditable methods that you learned about in the last chapter. Both of these components can also call the getDocument method to return a Document object from the text field or text area.
- To provide a listener for a text area or field, you must implement the DocumentListener interface and its three methods.

Figure 12-7 How to work with text fields and text areas (part 2 of 2)

How to work with radio buttons

Figure 12-8, which is in two parts, shows how to use *radio buttons*. When you work with these buttons, you must put them in a *button group*. Then, the user can select only one button from the group. In the frame in this figure, you can see that the user can select either a Monthly Payment button or a Loan Amount button. This selection then determines what type of calculation the application does.

The first example shows how to add these radio buttons to a button group and how to add the button group to a panel. Here, the first statement declares the two radio buttons from the JRadioButton class, and the next five statements create a panel for the buttons, create the two buttons, and add an action listener to each button. Then, the next three statements create a button group from the ButtonGroup class and add both buttons to the button group. The last four statements add the radio buttons to the panel and create a titled border for the panel.

The second example shows how to code the method of the ActionListener interface for the two radio buttons. If the user selects the Loan Amount radio button, the code clears and disables the Loan Amount text field, enables the Monthly Payment text field, and moves the focus to that field. But if the user selects the Monthly Payment radio button, the code clears and disables the Monthly Payment text field, clears the Loan Amount text field, and moves the focus to that field.

The Loan Calculator interface with radio buttons

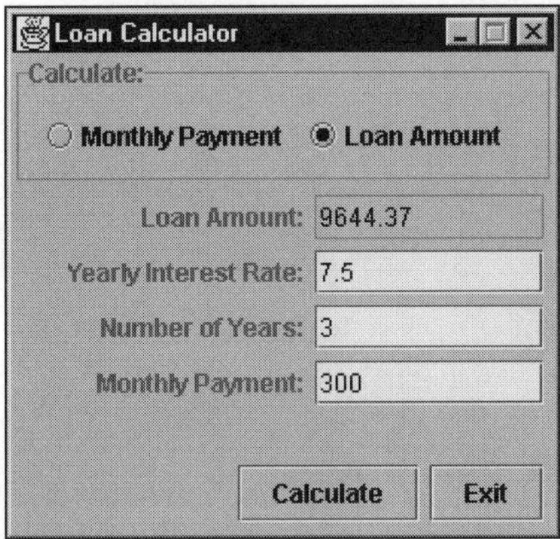

Code that adds the radio buttons to the user interface

```
private JRadioButton paymentRadioButton, amountRadioButton;

JPanel radioPanel = new JPanel();
paymentRadioButton = new JRadioButton("Monthly Payment");
amountRadioButton = new JRadioButton("Loan Amount", true);
paymentRadioButton.addActionListener(this);
amountRadioButton.addActionListener(this);

ButtonGroup radioGroup = new ButtonGroup();
radioGroup.add(paymentRadioButton);
radioGroup.add(amountRadioButton);

radioPanel.add(paymentRadioButton);
radioPanel.add(amountRadioButton);
Border titledRadioBorder =
   BorderFactory.createTitledBorder("Calculate:");
radioPanel.setBorder(titledRadioBorder);
```

Code that implements the ActionListener for the radio buttons

```
public void actionPerformed(ActionEvent e){
   Object source = e.getSource();
   if (source == amountRadioButton){
      amountTextField.setText("");
      amountTextField.setEditable(false);
      paymentTextField.setEditable(true);
      paymentTextField.requestFocus();
   }
   else if (source == paymentRadioButton){
      paymentTextField.setText("");
      paymentTextField.setEditable(false);
      amountTextField.setEditable(true);
      amountTextField.requestFocus();
   }
}
```

Figure 12-8 How to work with radio buttons (part 1 of 2)

Part 2 of this figure shows some of the constructors and methods that you can use when you work with radio buttons. By default, radio buttons are not selected. But if you want to create a radio button that's selected, you can use the second constructor for the JRadioButton class.

If you add more than one radio button to a container, you need to create a button group. To do that, you use the constructor of the ButtonGroup class. Then, you use the add method of this class to add each radio button to the group.

The JRadioButton and JButton classes both inherit the AbstractButton class. As a result, you may find that working with radio buttons is not that different from working with regular buttons. This also allows the add method of the ButtonGroup class to accept a JRadioButton object as an argument.

Constructors of the JRadioButton class

Constructor	Description
`JRadioButton(String)`	Creates an unselected radio button with specified text.
`JRadioButton(String, booleanSelected)`	Creates a radio button with specified text. If the boolean value is true, then the radio button is selected.

Some methods that work with radio buttons

Method	Description
`isSelected()`	Returns true if this radio button is selected.
`addActionListener(ActionListener)`	Adds an action listener to this radio button.
`addItemListener(ItemListener)`	Adds an item listener to this radio button.

Constructor of the ButtonGroup class

Constructor	Description
`ButtonGroup()`	Creates a button group used to hold a group of buttons where only one button can be selected at a time.

Method of the ButtonGroup class

Method	Description
`add(AbstractButton)`	Adds the specified button to the group.

Description

- If you add more than one *radio button* to a container, you must add them to a *button group*. To do that, you add JRadioButton objects to a ButtonGroup object.
- The JRadioButton class inherits the JToggleButton class, which inherits the AbstractButton class. As a result, you can use a JRadioButton object anywhere an AbstractButton object is accepted.

Figure 12-8 How to work with radio buttons (part 2 of 2)

How to work with check boxes

Figure 12-9 shows how to use a *check box* with the Book Order application. Here, if the box is checked, sales tax is added to the order total. Otherwise, the sales tax isn't added to the total.

The first code example shows how to use the JCheckBox class to add a check box to a panel. Here, the first statement declares the check box, the second statement creates the check box, and the third statement adds the check box to a panel.

The second code example shows how you can use the isSelected method to test whether the box is checked. In this case, if the box is checked, 8.75% sales tax is added to the order total.

This figure also summarizes the constructors and methods of the JCheckBox class. Since check boxes are unselected by default, you need to use the second constructor to create a box that is checked. Otherwise, you can use the setSelected method to check or uncheck a box after it has been created. Like the JRadioButton class, the JCheckBox class inherits the AbstractButton class. As a result, these components can call many of the same methods.

Although you can code a listener for a check box, you usually don't need to know *when* a box is checked or unchecked. Instead, you just need to know *if* it is checked. However, if you do need to know when a box is changed, you can implement either an ActionListener or an ItemListener. If, for example, you want to change the values that are displayed when a box is checked, you can implement one of these interfaces.

The Book Order interface with a check box

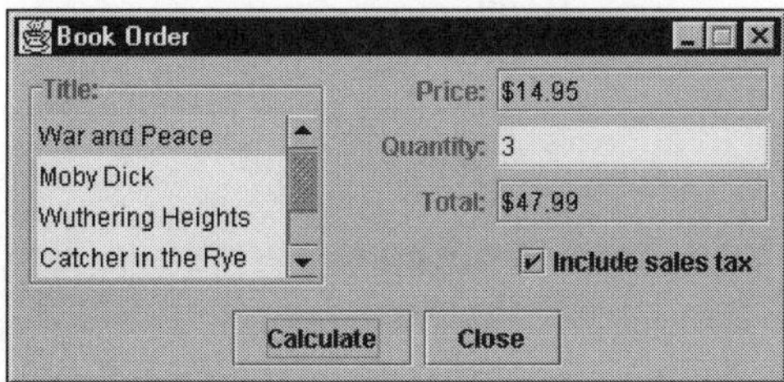

Code that adds a check box to a panel

```
private JCheckBox taxCheckBox;
taxCheckBox = new JCheckBox("Include sales tax", true);
inputPanel.add(taxCheckBox);
```

Code that tests to see whether a check box is checked

```
if (taxCheckBox.isSelected())
    total += total * .0875;
```

Common constructors of the JCheckBox class

Constructor	Description
JCheckBox(String)	Creates an unselected check box with a label that contains the specified string.
JCheckBox(String, booleanSelected)	Creates a check box with a label that contains the specified string. If the boolean value is true, then the check box is selected.

Some methods that work with check boxes

Method	Description
isSelected()	Returns a true value if the checkbox is selected.
setSelected(booleanValue)	Sets the check box to the specified boolean value.
addActionListener(ActionListener)	Adds an action listener to this check box.
addItemListener(ItemListener)	Adds an item listener to this checkbox.

Description

- The user can click on a *check box* to check or uncheck a box. Then, the code for the listener can change the processing that's done based on the setting for the check box.
- In many cases, you don't need to use a listener for a check box because you can use the isSelected method to see whether it's checked.
- If you do need to use a listener, you can use either the ActionListener or the ItemListener.
- Like the JRadioButton class, the JCheckBox class inherits the JToggleButton class, which inherits the AbstractButton class.

Figure 12-9 How to work with check boxes

A summary of other Swing components

In this chapter and the previous chapter, you've learned how to work with the most commonly used Swing components. In addition, figure 12-10 summarizes eight more Swing components that you may find useful and two more event listeners. By now, you should be able to use the API documentation to figure out how to use these components and their event listeners whenever you need them.

The figure presents two Swing components introduced in SDK1.4. First, the JFormattedTextField was added to format numbers, strings, dates, and other arbitrary objects. With this component, you can specify what legal values can be displayed from and entered into a text component. For instance, you can format dates to be displayed in MM/DD/YY notation. Or, you can format strings to include only uppercase letters. You can also format strings to edit telephone numbers, social security numbers, or zip codes.

The second component introduced with SDK1.4 is the JSpinner. A spinner is a single line input field that lets the user select a value from an ordered sequence by using tiny up and down arrow buttons. For instance, spinners are often used to select dates and numbers. If you're interested, you can learn more about these components in the SDK1.4 API documentation.

Other Swing components

Control	Description
JPasswordField	Defines a text field that lets the user enter a password.
JScrollBar	Defines a scroll bar. To process events generated by a scroll bar, you use the AdjustmentListener interface.
JSlider	Defines a slider that lets the user select a value in an interval by sliding a knob. To process events generated by a slider, you use the ChangeListener interface.
JSplitPane	Graphically divides two components. Usually, you add the components to a scroll pane and then add two scroll panes to a split pane.
JTable	Defines a component that displays a table.
JTabbedPane	Defines a component that lets the user select the view of one group of components over another by clicking on a tab. To process events generated by a tabbed pane, you use the ChangeListener interface.

Other Swing components introduced in SDK1.4

Control	Description
JFormattedTextField	Defines a text field that allows formatting of dates, numbers, strings, and other objects. This way, you can specify what values can be displayed and input to a text component. You can learn more about this class in the SDK1.4 API documentation.
JSpinner	Defines a single line input field that allows a user to select a value from an ordered sequence. To process events generated by a JSpinner, you use the ChangeListener interface. You can learn more about this class in the SDK1.4 API documentation.

Other semantic event listeners

Interface	Method
AdjustmentListener	`void adjustmentValueChanged(AdjustmentEvent e)`
ChangeListener	`void stateChanged(ChangeEvent e)`

Figure 12-10 A summary of other Swing components

How to work with layout managers

In the last chapter, you were introduced to the Flow and Border layout managers. Now, you'll be introduced to the rest of the layout managers of the Java API, and you'll learn how to use one of the most sophisticated layout managers, the Grid Bag layout manager.

A summary of layout managers

Figure 12-11 presents a summary of the layout managers provided by the Java API. After the Flow and Border layout managers that you learned about in the last chapter, you can see the Card layout manager, the Box layout manager, the Grid layout manager, and Grid Bag layout manager.

The first user interface in this figure illustrates the Box layout, which can lay components out vertically or horizontally. To set the direction of the layout, you use the constructor of the BoxLayout class. If you want to use the Box layout manager, you can create an object of the Box class. This class acts as a container similar to the JPanel class. The biggest difference is that a Box object uses the Box layout as the default layout manager, while a JPanel object uses the Flow layout.

In SDK 1.3.1 and earlier versions, the Box class isn't a Swing class. That means that the Box objects don't conform to Swing behavior. In SDK1.4, though, the Box class descends from the JComponent class, which means that you can treat Box objects as normal Swing components. In addition, the Box layout supports right to left and bottom to top orientation layouts in SDK1.4.

The second user interface illustrates the Grid layout, which uses a rectangular grid to lay out components. With this layout, each rectangle in the grid is of equal size. To set the grid up, you specify the number of rows and columns in the constructor of the GridLayout class. Then, you add the components to the container. In some situations, though, this layout manager may ignore the number of columns that you specify. If, for example, you create a grid of 4 rows and 3 columns with 8 components, the layout manager will use 4 rows and 2 columns as shown in this figure.

Although the Card, Box, and Grid layouts aren't used much, they're easy to use if you ever need them. To learn more about these layout managers, you can look them up in the documentation of the Java API (they're stored in the java.awt package).

In contrast, the Grid Bag layout manager is the most flexible and sophisticated layout manager, and it's commonly used. That's why it's presented in the next three figures.

Examples of the Box and Grid layouts

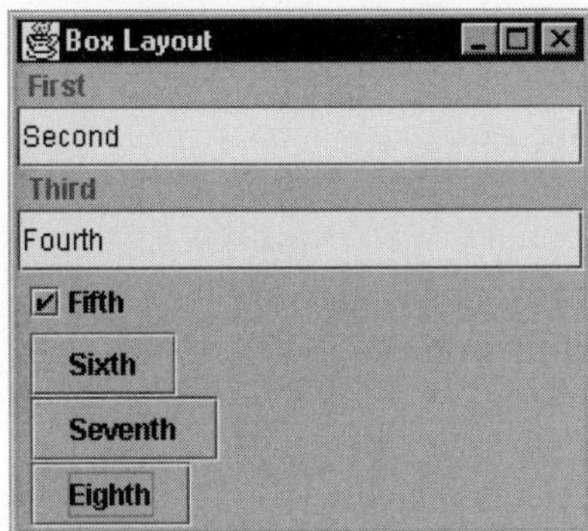

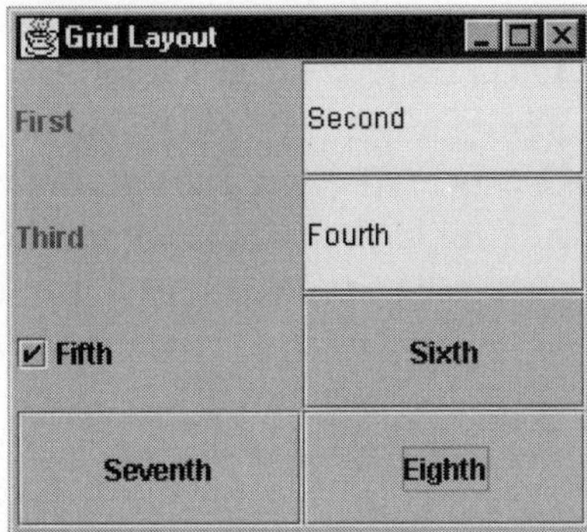

Description of layout managers

Class	Description
FlowLayout	Lays out components from left to right as shown in chapter 11.
BorderLayout	Lays out components in five regions as shown in chapter 11.
CardLayout	Lays out components on a card where only one card is visible at a time. Rather than using this class, you can use the JTabbedPane class.
BoxLayout	Lays out components either horizontally or vertically as shown above. In SDK1.4, this becomes a Swing class, and it supports right to left and bottom to top orientations (as well as left to right and top to bottom orientations).
GridLayout	Lays out components in a rectangular grid where each rectangle is the same size as shown above.
GridBagLayout	Lays out components horizontally and vertically in a rectangular grid as shown in the next three figures.

Note

- Although this figure lists all of the layout managers available from the Java API, it's possible to define other layout managers. As a result, if you use an IDE, it may use another layout manager.

Figure 12-11 A summary of layout managers

How to work with the Grid Bag layout manager

Figure 12-12 shows how to work with the *Grid Bag layout manager*. Here, you can see a user interface with this layout along with the grid that's used to align the components in this user interface. When you use this layout manager, components can differ in size and be aligned both horizontally and vertically. Like the Grid layout, the Grid Bag layout uses a rectangular grid to lay out the components. But unlike the Grid layout, the Grid Bag layout allows components to be displayed in more than one cell.

To use the Grid Bag layout, you specify the location and size of each component within the grid. To do that, you can use the five-step procedure shown in this figure.

In step 1, you can sketch the GUI and divide it into rows and columns. From this, you can see how many rows and columns each component will occupy. For instance, the sketch in this figure shows that the list box in the scroll pane will start at x = 1 and y = 1 and use 2 columns and 3 rows. Similarly, the first text field will start at x = 4 and y = 1 and use 1 row and 2 columns. As you work, you should understand that the size of the overall grid isn't predetermined. Instead, the size is set automatically after you specify the number of rows and columns for each component.

In step 2, as with all layout managers, you need to set the container's layout manager by calling the constructor of the GridBagLayout class. However, this class doesn't hold the size and positioning constraints. So in step 3, you must create an object of the GridBagConstraints class, which will hold these constraints.

In step 4, you supply the constraints for each component, and in step 5, you use the add method of the Container class with the component and its constraints as arguments. You'll learn how to do those steps in the next two figures. Then, as step 6 shows, you repeat steps 4 and 5 for each component of the layout.

A user interface that uses the Grid Bag layout

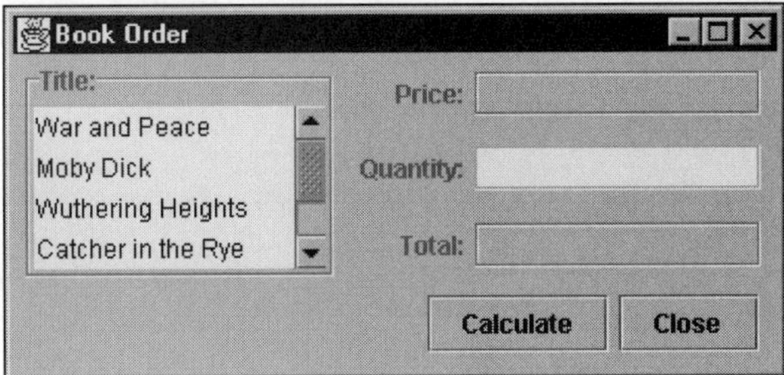

The layout of the user interface shown above

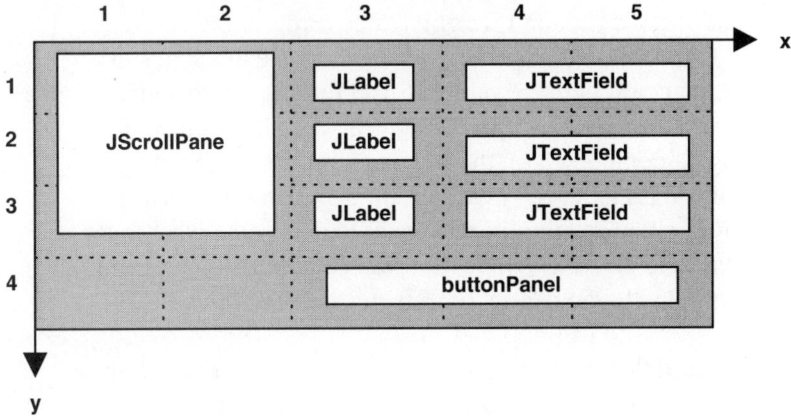

How to work with the Grid Bag layout

1. Diagram or sketch the user interface and divide it into rows and columns.
2. Set the layout to an object of the GridBagLayout class.

```
setLayout(new GridBagLayout());
```

3. Create a GridBagConstraints object to hold positioning data for a component.

```
GridBagConstraints c = new GridBagConstraints();
```

4. Set the constraints in the GridBagConstraints object as shown in the next figure.

```
c.gridx = 1;
c.gridy = 1;
c.gridwidth = 2;
c.gridheight = 3;
```

5. Use the add method of the Container class that specifies the component and its constraints.

```
add(Component, GridBagConstraints)
```

6. Repeat steps 4 and 5 until all components have been added.

Figure 12-12 How to work with the Grid Bag layout manager

How to set the constraints for a Grid Bag layout

Figure 12-13 shows how to set the positioning and size constraints for each component in a Grid Bag layout. To do that, you need to use the fields of the GridBagConstraints class.

The first eight fields in this figure let you set the size and position of each component. You can use the gridx and gridy fields to set the starting position for the component in cells. You can use the gridheight and gridwidth fields to state the overall height and width of the component in cells. You can use the ipadx and ipady fields to specify the amount of padding that's used between cells in pixels. And you can use the weightx and weighty fields to specify how to distribute the extra space when the overall layout doesn't take up the whole container area. By default, the weightx and weighty values are set to 0 so the cells are spaced as close together as possible. If you want some extra space to appear between the cells, you can set these values to 100 for all components.

You can use the anchor constraint to align components within a cell. If, for example, you want to align a component on the left edge of a cell, you can set the anchor constraint to the WEST field. By default, though, components use the CENTER field. Similarly, you use the fill constraint to determine what to do with any extra space in the cell. If, for example, you want a component to grow vertically so it fills the entire cell, you can set the fill constraint to the VERTICAL field.

You can use the last two fields instead of using the gridx, gridy, gridheight, and gridwidth constraints. For example, you can use the RELATIVE field for the gridx constraint to place a component to the right of the previous component. And you can use the REMAINDER field for the gridwidth field to specify when a component is the last in a row. That way, the layout manager knows to move on to the next row.

Fields of the GridBagConstraints class

Field	Description
`gridx`	An int value that specifies the leftmost cell that the component occupies.
`gridy`	An int value that specifies the topmost cell that the component occupies.
`gridheight`	An int value that specifies the number of vertical cells that a component occupies.
`gridwidth`	An int value that specifies the number of horizontal cells that a component occupies.
`ipadx`	An int value that specifies the amount of internal horizontal padding.
`ipady`	An int value that specifies the amount of internal vertical padding.
`weightx`	A double value that specifies how extra horizontal space is distributed if the resulting layout is horizontally smaller than the area allotted. The default value is 0, which means no extra space is allotted between cells if a component doesn't fill the column.
`weighty`	A double value that specifies how extra vertical space is distributed if the resulting layout is vertically smaller that the area allotted. The default value is 0, which means no extra space is allotted between cells if a component doesn't fill the row.
`anchor`	An int value that specifies the alignment of a component within a cell. You can use the fields below to set this constraint.
`fill`	An int value that specifies what to do with extra space in a cell. You can use the fields below to set this constraint.

Fields of the GridBagConstraints class that set the anchor field

CENTER	NORTHEAST	WEST	SOUTHEAST
NORTH	EAST	SOUTH	

Fields of the GridBagConstraints class that set the fill constraint

NONE	HORIZONTAL	VERTICAL	BOTH

Other fields of the GridBagConstraints class

Field	Description
RELATIVE	For the gridx and gridy fields, this field specifies that the component will be placed next to the last added component. For the gridwidth and gridheight fields, this field specifies that the component will be the next-to-last component in a row or column.
REMAINDER	For the gridwidth and gridheight fields, this field specifies that a component is the last component in a row or column.

Description

- For most purposes, the value of 100 will work fine for both the weightx and weighty constraints.
- The ipadx and ipady fields use pixels as the unit of measure where the number of pixels is equal to double the amount of the int value that's stored in the field. For example:

```
int numberOfPixels = ipadx * 2
```

Figure 12-13 How to set the constraints for a Grid Bag layout

An example that uses the Grid Bag layout manager

Figure 12-14 presents the code that uses the Grid Bag layout manager to lay out the components in the Book Order interface shown in figure 12-12. To start, this figure shows how to code the grid values to lay out components. Then, it shows how to get similar results by using the RELATIVE and REMAINDER fields of the GridBagConstraints class.

The first group of statements in the first example sets the current container's layout manager to the Grid Bag layout. Next, it creates an object from the GridBagConstraints class named c, and it sets the weight constraints to 100. Then, it sets the ipadx constraint to 5 so all components will have a minimum of 10 pixels of horizontal padding.

The second group of statements first sets the constraints for the scroll pane that contains the title list box. Here, the component will be located in the top left corner of the grid with a width of 2 cells and a height of 3 cells. This code also uses the NORTHWEST field of the anchor constraint to align the component with the upper left corner of the grid. Then, the last statement in this group adds the title scroll pane to the grid using the constraints that have been set in the GridBagConstraints object (c).

The third group of statements adds the three labels to the container. To start, it sets the size and position of the Price label and adds that label. Then, it sets a new value for the gridy constraint and adds the Quantity label. This works because the rest of the constraints are the same as the constraints for the Price label. Last, it sets a new value for the gridy constraint and adds the Total label.

The fourth group of statements adds the three text fields to the container. This code works like the code for the three labels. And the fifth group of statements adds a panel that contains the two buttons of the user interface.

The second example in this figure shows how you can use the RELATIVE and REMAINDER fields to position and size the text fields that are added to this grid. Here, to set the size of the text fields so they take up the rest of the grid horizontally, the fourth statement uses the REMAINDER field to set the gridwidth constraint. Then, to place the second and third text fields immediately below the previous text field, the sixth and eighth statements use the RELATIVE field to set the gridy constraint. This block of code gets the same result as the fourth block in the first example.

At this point, you should realize that using the Grid Bay layout manager can be tedious, but it's not that difficult. After you set the layout for the container to GridBagLayout and create the GridBagConstraints object, you just set the constraints for each component and add it to the container. This is an efficient way to design and code a layout for most applications.

Code that lays out the Book Order interface in figure 12-12

```
setLayout(new GridBagLayout());
GridBagConstraints c = new GridBagConstraints();
c.weightx = 100;
c.weighty = 100;
c.ipadx = 5;

c.gridx = 1;
c.gridy = 1;
c.gridwidth = 2;
c.gridheight = 3;
c.anchor = GridBagConstraints.NORTHWEST;
add(titleScroll, c);

c.gridx = 3;
c.gridy = 1;
c.gridwidth = 1;
c.gridheight = 1;
c.anchor = GridBagConstraints.EAST;
add(priceLabel, c);
c.gridy = 2;
add(quantityLabel, c);
c.gridy = 3;
add(totalLabel, c);

c.gridx = 4;
c.gridy = 1;
c.gridwidth = 2;
c.anchor = GridBagConstraints.WEST;
add(priceTextField, c);
c.gridy = 2;
add(quantityTextField, c);
c.gridy = 3;
add(totalTextField, c);

c.gridx = 3;
c.gridy = 4;
c.gridwidth = 3;
c.anchor = GridBagConstraints.EAST;
add(buttonPanel, c);
```

Code that uses relative positioning

```
c.gridx = 4;
c.gridy = 1;
c.anchor = GridBagConstraints.WEST;
c.gridwidth = GridBagConstraints.REMAINDER;
add(priceTextField, c);
c.gridy = GridBagConstraints.RELATIVE;
add(quantityTextField, c);
c.gridy = GridBagConstraints.RELATIVE;
add(totalTextField, c);
```

Figure 12-14 An example that uses the Grid Bag layout

How to code low-level events

So far, you've learned how to handle the semantic events that are generated by controls. In the last chapter, you also learned how to handle the low-level event that occurs when you close a window. Now, you'll learn how to work with other low-level events, such as a mouse being moved, and you'll learn why the code that closes a window works the way it does.

A summary of low-level events

Figure 12-15 presents a summary of low-level events. To handle these events, you need to implement the appropriate listener interfaces that are shown. Then, you need to add the listener to a component. However, unlike the listeners for semantic events that often require you to code a single method, the listeners for low-level events require you to code several methods.

The first five events in this figure can occur on any component. In other words, the Component class contains methods that allow you to add these event listeners to any component. The next event can occur on any container, which means that the Container class has an addContainerListener method. The last event can be used with any window because the Window class has an addWindowListener method. To add a listener to a component, you can use the methods presented in this figure.

In the next two figures, you'll learn how to work with the FocusListener and KeyListener interfaces. Then, if you want to learn more about the rest of the low-level events, you can look up the interfaces for these events in the documentation for the Java API. All of these interfaces are stored in the java.awt.event package.

Common low-level events and listeners

Event	Interface	Methods
Moving the focus	FocusListener	`void focusGained(FocusEvent e)` `void focusLost(FocusEvent e)`

Pressing or releasing a key	KeyListener	`void keyPressed(KeyEvent e)`
		`void keyReleased(KeyEvent e)`
		`void keyTyped(KeyEvent e)`

Dragging the mouse	MouseMotionListener	`void mouseDragged(MouseEvent e)` `void mouseMoved(MouseEvent e)`

Clicking the mouse	MouseListener	`void mouseClicked(MouseEvent e)`
		`void mouseEntered(MouseEvent e)`
		`void mouseExited(MouseEvent e)`
		`void mousePressed(MouseEvent e)`
		`void mouseReleased(MouseEvent e)`

Moving or sizing a component	ComponentListener	`void componentHidden(ComponentEvent e)`
		`void componentMoved(ComponentEvent e)`
		`void componentResized(ComponentEvent e)`
		`void componentShown(ComponentEvent e)`

Adding or removing a component	ContainerListener	`void componentAdded(ContainerEvent e)` `void componentRemoved(ContainerEvent e)`

Working with the window	WindowListener	`void windowActivated(WindowEvent e)`
		`void windowClosed(WindowEvent e)`
		`void windowClosing(WindowEvent e)`
		`void windowDeactivated(WindowEvent e)`
		`void windowDeiconified(WindowEvent e)`
		`void windowIconified(WindowEvent e)`
		`void windowOpened(WindowEvent e)`

How to declare a listener for any class

```
class MyClass extends AnotherClass implements XXXListener{
```

Methods that add low-level listeners

Class	Method
Component	`addFocusListener(FocusListener)`
Component	`addKeyListener(KeyListener)`
Component	`addMouseMotionListener(MouseMotionListener)`
Component	`addMouseListener(MouseListener)`
Component	`addComponentListener(ComponentListener)`
Container	`addContainerListener(ContainerListener)`
Window	`addWindowListener(WindowListener)`

Figure 12-15 A summary of low-level events

How to work with focus events

Figure 12-16 shows how to work with *focus events*. To start, this figure describes the two methods that you must code to implement the FocusListener interface. Then, it describes three methods that you can use to get information about the FocusEvent class. Last, it shows some code that implements the two methods of the FocusListener interface for the Book Order application.

In SDK1.4, the getOppositeComponent method is added to the FocusEvent class. This method returns the "opposite" component involved in the focus change. If, for example, a text field loses focus, the "opposite" component is the one that gains the focus. Similarly, if a button gains the focus, the "opposite" component is the one that lost the focus.

In the example, the focusLost method validates the entry in the quantity text field. This means that a focus listener has been added to this text field. Once focus is permanently lost from this field, the code checks to see if a valid integer has been entered. If not, this method displays a dialog box with an error message and moves the focus back to the quantity text field. As a result, the user won't be able to continue until a valid integer has been entered. Although the focusLost method contains all of this code, the focus listener class must also include the focusGained method, even if this method doesn't contain any statements.

Methods of the FocusListener interface

Method	Description
`void focusGained(FocusEvent e)`	Invoked when a component that implements a focus listener gains the focus.
`void focusLost(FocusEvent e)`	Invoked when a component that implements a focus listener loses the focus.

Common methods of the FocusEvent class

Method	Description
`getComponent()`	Returns the Component where event occurred.
`isTemporary()`	Returns true if the focus is a temporary change.
`getOppositeComponent()`	An SDK1.4 method that returns the other component involved in the focus change.

Code that implements the methods of the FocusListener interface

```
public void focusLost(FocusEvent e){
   if (e.getComponent() == quantityTextField && !e.isTemporary()){
      try{
         int quantity = Integer.parseInt(quantityTextField.getText());
      }
      catch(NumberFormatException nfe){
         JOptionPane.showMessageDialog(null, "Invalid quantity.\n"
            + "Please enter a positive number.",
            "Error", JOptionPane.ERROR_MESSAGE);
         quantityTextField.requestFocus();
      }
   }
}
public void focusGained(FocusEvent e){
}
```

Description

- A *focus event* occurs when the focus moves to or from a component.
- To implement the FocusListener, you must implement both of the methods for this interface. However, both methods don't have to include code that processes the event.

Figure 12-16 How to work with focus events

How to work with keyboard events

Figure 12-17 shows how to work with *keyboard events* that result from keys being pressed. To start, it describes the three methods that must be coded to implement the KeyListener interface. Then, it describes some of the methods and fields of the KeyEvent class. For a complete list of the fields in this class, you can use the documentation of the Java API.

The example in this figure shows how to implement the KeyListener interface for the Book Order application. This example assumes that a key listener has been added to the quantity text field. That way, a user can press Alt+C to perform the calculation once the data has been entered.

In this example, all three methods of the KeyListener interface are coded, even though the keyPressed method is the only method that contains any statements. Within this method, the first statement calls the getKeyCode method to return the combination of keys that the user pressed. Then, if the user pressed Alt+C while the focus was on the quantity text field, the application moves the focus to the Calculate button and uses the doClick method to click this button. This has the same effect as if the user clicked the mouse on the Calculate button.

Methods of the KeyListener interface

Method	Description
`void keyPressed(KeyEvent e)`	Invoked when a key is pressed.
`void keyReleased(KeyEvent e)`	Invoked when a key is released.
`void keyTyped(KeyEvent e)`	Invoked when a key is pressed and released.

Common methods of the KeyEvent class

Method	Description
`getKeyCode()`	Returns an int code that represents the key pressed.
`isControlDown()`	Returns a boolean true if the Ctrl key is down.
`isAltDown()`	Returns a boolean true if the Alt key is down.
`isShiftDown()`	Returns a boolean true if the Shift key is down.

Some fields of the KeyEvent class

Field	Description
`VK_A`	An int value representing the A key.
`VK_B`	An int value representing the B key.
`VK_1`	An int value representing the 1 key.
`VK_TAB`	An int value representing the Tab key.

Code that implements the methods of the KeyListener interface

```
public void keyPressed(KeyEvent e){
    int keyCode = e.getKeyCode();
    if ((keyCode == KeyEvent.VK_C) && (e.isAltDown())){
        calculateButton.requestFocus();
        calculateButton.doClick();
    }
}
public void keyReleased(KeyEvent e){
}
public void keyTyped(KeyEvent e){
}
```

Description

- A *keyboard event* occurs when a user presses, releases, or presses and releases a key.
- The key listener only works when the focus is on a component that has the listener added to it. To implement a key listener for an entire user interface, you must add the key listener to every component that can receive the focus.
- The doClick method that's used in the code above is a method in the AbstractButton class.

Figure 12-17 How to work with keyboard events

How to work with adapter classes

Since it can be tedious to code all the methods in a listener interface just to use one of them, the Java API provides *adapter classes*. An adapter class is a class that implements all the methods of a listener interface but doesn't code any statements within these methods. Then, your listener class can inherit the adapter class and override any methods you want to code.

Figure 12-18 shows how to work with adapter classes. To start, it summarizes five adapter classes that correspond with five of the listener interfaces. Then, it shows how an adapter class makes it easier to code a class that implements an interface.

The first two examples illustrate how using an adapter class shortens the amount of code needed to implement a listener interface. Here, the first code example is 11 lines long because it includes all seven methods of the WindowListener interface. However, the second code example takes only 5 lines because it inherits the WindowAdapter class.

The third example shows how to add a listener class to a component. In particular, it shows how to add the WindowWorker class that's created in either of the first two examples to the current component. Here, the first statement creates a WindowWorker object. Then, the second statement adds this object to the current component.

The fourth example combines the code that's used in the second and third code examples to create an *anonymous class*. This example begins by calling the addWindowListener method. Then, to supply the argument for this method, this code creates a WindowAdapter object that includes the code that overrides the windowClosed method. In other words, the entire class is coded as the argument for the addWindowListener method without ever giving this class a name (that's why it's anonymous).

You may recognize this fourth example as the technique that you've been using to handle the window closed event at the end of a program. You should now have a better idea of what this code is doing. If it's still difficult to follow, though, that's because it uses some unusual coding techniques. Just remember that this example is equivalent to the second and third examples combined

Common adapter classes

Class	Interface
WindowAdapter	WindowListener
FocusAdapter	FocusListener
KeyAdapter	KeyListener
MouseAdapter	MouseListener
MouseMotionAdapter	MouseMotionListener

How to implement the WindowListener interface

Without an adapter class

```
class WindowWorker implements WindowListener{
   public void windowActivated(WindowEvent e){}
   public void windowClosed(WindowEvent e){
      System.exit(0);
   }
   public void windowClosing(WindowEvent e){}
   public void windowDeactivated(WindowEvent e){}
   public void windowDeiconified(WindowEvent e){}
   public void windowIconified(WindowEvent e){}
   public void windowOpened(WindowEvent e){}
}
```

With an adapter class

```
class WindowWorker extends WindowAdapter{
   public void windowClosed(WindowEvent e){
      System.exit(0);
   }
}
```

How to add a window listener to a frame

With a named class

```
WindowWorker win = new WindowWorker();
addWindowListener(win);
```

With an anonymous class

```
addWindowListener(new WindowAdapter(){
   public void windowClosed(WindowEvent e){
      System.exit(0);
   }
});
```

Description

- An *adapter class* is a class that implements all the methods of a listener interface as empty methods. This way, your event handler class can inherit the Adapter class and override only the methods that you need in your program.
- Although your event handler class can't inherit an adapter class if it already inherits another class, you can use an adapter class as an *anonymous class*. The fourth example shows how you can add a window listener to a frame by using the WindowAdapter class as an anonymous class.

Figure 12-18 How to work with adapter classes

The Book Maintenance application

In chapter 6, you learned about the design of a program called the Book Maintenance application. This application lets you add, update, or delete the book data that's stored in a file or database. Now, you'll learn how to code the user interface for that application.

As you will see, this application calls methods from the BookIO class to handle input and output operations that add, update, and delete the data for a Book object. In chapter 18, you'll learn how the methods in this class work. For now, though, you just need to use those methods, which is illustrated by the code for this application.

The user interface

Figure 12-19 shows the user interface for the Book Maintenance application. This interface lets the user change the data for any record in the file or database that contains the book records. It also lets the user add records to and delete records from the file or database. In case you aren't familiar with this kind of interface, this figure describes its operation in detail.

Note in the description that the buttons in this interface are enabled or disabled depending on what the user starts to do. When the data for a book is first displayed, for example, only the Update button is disabled. But if the user changes the data in the title or price text fields for a book, all of the buttons are disabled except for the Update and Exit buttons. Then, the user can click on the Update button to save the changes to the record in the file or database.

Note too that clicking on the Add button doesn't add a record to the file or database. Instead, that clears the text fields so the user can enter the data for a new record. That also disables all of the buttons except the Update and Exit buttons. Then, the user can enter the data for a new record and click on the Update button to add the record to the file or database. To cancel an add or update operation, the user can simply press the Escape key when the focus is in the code, title, or price text field.

To navigate through the records in this interface, the user can click on one of the buttons in the bottom row. Although this is acceptable for a file or database that consists of a small number of records, most interfaces provide an easier way to display the data for any record. For instance, some interfaces let you enter the code for the record that you want displayed and then click on a Find button to display that record. Other interfaces provide a combo or list box that lets you select the record that you want displayed. If you understand the code for this interface, though, you should be able to add an enhancement like that.

The user interface

How the interface works

- When the GUI is first displayed, the data for the first book in the file or database is displayed and the Update button is disabled as shown.
- To navigate through the book records, the user can click on the one of the buttons in the bottom row: the First button displays the first record in the file or database; the Prev button displays the previous record; the Next button displays the next record; and the Last button displays the last record. Whenever a new record is displayed, the Update button is disabled.
- To modify the data for a book, the user makes a change to the title or price fields. At that point, the Update button is enabled and the Add, Delete, and navigation buttons are disabled. Then, to save the changes to the file or database, the user clicks on the Update button.
- To add a record to the file or database, the user clicks on the Add button. This clears the text fields, enables the Update button, and disables the Add, Delete, and navigation buttons. Then, the user can enter the code, title, and price (with or without dollar sign) for a new book and click on the Update button to save the new record to the file or database. This record will be added at the end of the file or database.
- To delete a record, the user navigates to that record and clicks on the Delete button. After it deletes the record from the file or database, the program displays the data for the next record (or the new last record if the deleted record was the last record).
- To cancel any add or update operation, the user can press the Esc key when the focus is in one of the text fields. To exit from the program at any time, the user can click on the Exit button. This will cancel any change, addition, or deletion that's in progress.

Two ways this interface has been simplified

- Only three fields are displayed for each book record, although a typical master record like this contains many fields that can be maintained.
- The interface doesn't provide a way to go directly to the data for a specific book like entering the book code and clicking on a Find button.

Figure 12-19 The user interface for the Book Maintenance application

The Grid Bag layout and the code

Figure 12-20 (in five parts) starts with a diagram of the grid that's used by this application's Grid Bag layout manager. This diagram lays out eight components in a 4x5 grid: three labels, three text fields, and two panels with four buttons in each. You can use this as a guide to the code for the interface for this application.

Part 1 of this figure also presents the first page of code, which includes the code for the BookFrame class. To start, the code imports the six packages that the user interface needs. Then, the constructor for the BookFrame class sets up the frame and adds a BookPanel object to the content pane of the frame. Since this code is the same as in the last chapter, you shouldn't have any trouble following it, although you may have new respect for the code that adds the window listener and ends the program when the window is closed.

Note, however, that the windowClosing method now includes a statement that calls the close method of the BookIO class. This method closes the file that is opened in the BookPanel class, as you will see in a moment. This is typical of any program that works with files. Each file is usually opened at the start of the application and closed at the end of it.

After the constructor, the main method for the BookFrame class creates an instance of the BookFrame and displays it on the screen. That way, you can run the BookFrame class by itself, and it will display the user interface for the Book Maintenance application. You won't need to create a separate driver class.

Before you continue, I want you to know that the code for this interface has a few simplifications for illustrative purposes. First, the code lets the user add a new record to the file or database with the same book code as an existing record, which shouldn't be allowed. Second, the code deletes a record when the user clicks on the Delete button without displaying a warning message. If you understand the code that follows, though, you should be able to make these enhancements on your own.

The grid for the Grid Bag layout of the user interface

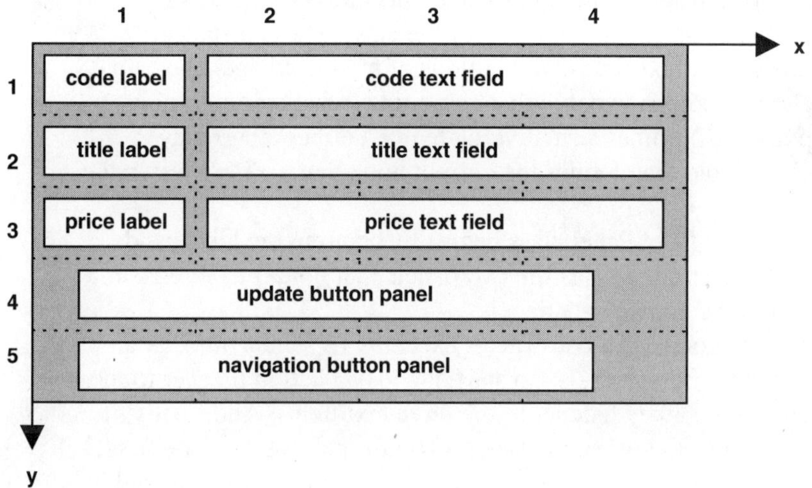

The code

```
import java.awt.*;
import java.awt.event.*;
import javax.swing.*;
import javax.swing.event.*;
import java.text.*;
import java.io.*;

public class BookFrame extends JFrame{
   public BookFrame(){
      setTitle("Book Maintenance");
      Toolkit tk = Toolkit.getDefaultToolkit();
      Dimension d = tk.getScreenSize();
      int width = 400, height = 200;
      setBounds((d.width - width)/2, (d.height - height)/2, width, height);
      setResizable(false);
      addWindowListener(new WindowAdapter(){
         public void windowClosing(WindowEvent e){
            BookIO.close;
            System.exit(0);
         }
      });
      Container contentPane = getContentPane();
      BookPanel panel = new BookPanel();
      contentPane.add(panel);
   }
   public static void main(String[] args){
      JFrame frame = new BookFrame();
      frame.show();
   }
}
```

Figure 12-20 The Book Maintenance application (part 1 of 5)

Part 2 of this figure shows the start of the BookPanel class. It begins by implementing three event listener interfaces and by declaring the instance variables that will be used throughout the rest of the class. These instance variables declare the labels, text fields, and buttons of the BookPanel class. In addition, they declare a boolean variable that determines whether a record is being added or updated, a NumberFormat variable that defines a currency format, and a Book variable that defines the current book that is displayed in the user interface.

The constructor of the BookPanel class begins by creating the labels and text fields of the panel. Then, it creates the two panels that hold the buttons, and it adds those buttons to the appropriate panels.

In the fourth block of code, the constructor executes 13 statements that add the appropriate listeners to the controls. To start, it adds an action listener to the eight buttons. Then, it adds a key listener to the three text fields. And finally, it adds a document listener to the title and price text fields, but not the code field, which shouldn't be changed. You'll see how the document events are handled in part 5 of this figure.

The code for the Book Maintenance application (continued)

```
class BookPanel extends JPanel implements ActionListener,
   DocumentListener, KeyListener{

   private JButton addButton, updateButton, deleteButton, exitButton,
                   firstButton, prevButton, nextButton, lastButton;
   private JLabel codeLabel, titleLabel, priceLabel;
   private JTextField codeField, titleField, priceField;
   private boolean addFlag = false;
   private NumberFormat currency = NumberFormat.getCurrencyInstance();
   private Book currentBook = null;

   public BookPanel(){

      codeLabel = new JLabel("Code: ");
      codeField = new JTextField("", 7);
      titleLabel = new JLabel("Title: ");
      titleField = new JTextField("", 26);
      priceLabel = new JLabel("Price: ");
      priceField = new JTextField("", 7);

      JPanel updatePanel = new JPanel();
      addButton = new JButton("Add");
      updateButton = new JButton("Update");
      deleteButton = new JButton("Delete");
      exitButton = new JButton("Exit");
      updatePanel.add(addButton);
      updatePanel.add(updateButton);
      updatePanel.add(deleteButton);
      updatePanel.add(exitButton);

      JPanel navigationPanel = new JPanel();
      firstButton = new JButton("First");
      prevButton = new JButton("Prev");
      nextButton = new JButton("Next");
      lastButton = new JButton("Last");
      navigationPanel.add(firstButton);
      navigationPanel.add(prevButton);
      navigationPanel.add(nextButton);
      navigationPanel.add(lastButton);

      addButton.addActionListener(this);
      updateButton.addActionListener(this);
      deleteButton.addActionListener(this);
      exitButton.addActionListener(this);
      firstButton.addActionListener(this);
      prevButton.addActionListener(this);
      nextButton.addActionListener(this);
      lastButton.addActionListener(this);
      codeField.addKeyListener(this);
      titleField.addKeyListener(this);
      priceField.addKeyListener(this);
      titleField.getDocument().addDocumentListener(this);
      priceField.getDocument().addDocumentListener(this);
```

Figure 12-20 The Book Maintenance application (part 2 of 5)

Part 3 of this figure shows the code in the BookPanel class that controls the layout for the panel. Here, the first statement sets the layout for the BookPanel class to a Grid Bag layout, and the second statement creates a GridBagConstraints object. Then, the third and fourth statements set the weigthx and weighty constraints to control how extra space is distributed, and the fifth statement sets the ipadx constraint so there will be a minimum of 10 pixels of horizontal space between components.

The next three groups of code add all the components to the layout. To do that, this code uses a helper method called getConstraints that's coded near the bottom of this page right after the BookPanel constructor. This method sets the gridx, gridy, gridwidth, and gridheight fields in a single line of code so it's easier to set these constraints.

After the components are added to the BookPanel class, the open method of the BookIO class is called. This method opens the file that contains the book data. Then, the moveFirst method of the BookIO class is called. This method sets the currentBook instance variable equal to the first book in the file. Since these BookIO methods may throw a FileNotFoundException and an IOException, the constructor uses a try/catch statement to catch these exceptions. Then, the last two statements of the constructor call helper methods named performBookDisplay and enableButtons that are shown in part 4 of this figure. These methods display the data for the current book in the text fields and enable or disable the appropriate buttons.

The code for the Book Maintenance application (continued)

```
        setLayout(new GridBagLayout());
        GridBagConstraints c = new GridBagConstraints();
        c.weightx = 100;
        c.weighty = 100;
        c.ipadx = 5;

        c.anchor = GridBagConstraints.EAST;
        c = getConstraints(c, 1, 1, 1, 1);
        add(codeLabel, c);
        c = getConstraints(c, 1, 2, 1, 1);
        add(titleLabel, c);
        c = getConstraints(c, 1, 3, 1, 1);
        add(priceLabel, c);

        c.anchor = GridBagConstraints.WEST;
        c = getConstraints(c, 2, 1, 3, 1);
        add(codeField, c);
        c = getConstraints(c, 2, 2, 3, 1);
        add(titleField, c);
        c = getConstraints(c, 2, 3, 3, 1);
        add(priceField, c);

        c.anchor = GridBagConstraints.CENTER;
        c = getConstraints(c, 1, 4, 4, 1);
        add(updatePanel, c);
        c = getConstraints(c, 1, 5, 4, 1);
        add(navigationPanel, c);

        try{
           BookIO.open();
           currentBook = BookIO.moveFirst();
        }
        catch (FileNotFoundException e){
           JOptionPane.showMessageDialog(null, "FileNotFoundException");
           System.exit(1);
        }
        catch (IOException e){
           JOptionPane.showMessageDialog(null, "IOException");
        }
        performBookDisplay();
        enableButtons(true);
    }

    private GridBagConstraints getConstraints(GridBagConstraints c,
        int x, int y, int width, int height){
        c.gridx = x;
        c.gridy = y;
        c.gridwidth = width;
        c.gridheight = height;
        return c;
    }
```

Part 4 of this figure starts with the two helper methods that are called by the last two statements of the constructor in part 3. Here, the performBookDisplay method sets the three text fields so they contain the data for the current book. Because the third field is formatted by the currency object, it will include a dollar sign when it is displayed.

Then, the enableButtons method enables or disables the buttons of the user interface depending on the value that's passed to the method. If a true value is passed to the method, all of the buttons except the Update button are enabled. But if a false value is passed to the method, the Update button is the only button that's enabled (except for the Exit button, which is always enabled). That prevents a user from clicking on another button such as the Next button when the user has begun updating the data for a book.

After the two helper methods, you can see the start of the code that implements the actionPerformed method of the ActionListener interface. This is the method that handles all the events that are caused by clicking on one of the buttons. Since the statements within this method call methods that throw exceptions, a try/catch statement has been coded around all of the statements in this method. That way, you only have to code a single try clause with three catch clauses to catch all of the possible exceptions that may be thrown when a user clicks on a button.

Within the actionPerformed method, the first statement returns the source of the event. Then, if/else statements execute the appropriate code for each button. For instance, the first if block calls the close method of the BookIO class and exits the user interface if the user clicks the Exit button. This call to the close method is necessary, even though this method is also called from the windowClosing method of the BookFrame class, because calling the System.exit method doesn't generate a windowClosing event.

Then, the next four else if blocks display the data for the appropriate book when the user clicks the First, Prev, Next, or Last buttons. To do that, each block calls a method from the BookIO class to return a Book object. Then, it sets the currentBook instance variable equal to this Book object, and it calls the performBookDisplay and enableButtons methods to display the book and enable all buttons except the Update button.

The last else if block in this part is the code that's executed when the user clicks on the Add button. Within this block, the first statement moves the focus to the code text field, and the second statement enables the Update button and disables all the other buttons except the Exit button. Then, the next three statements clear the three text fields, and the last statement sets the addFlag instance variable to true. Although this code doesn't actually add a book, it does prepare the user interface to add a record. Later, after the user enters a code, title, and price for the book and clicks on the Update button, the code for the Update button adds the book.

The code for the Book Maintenance application (continued)

```
private void performBookDisplay(){
   codeField.setText(currentBook.getCode());
   titleField.setText(currentBook.getTitle());
   priceField.setText(currency.format(currentBook.getPrice()));
}

private void enableButtons(boolean flag1){
   boolean flag2 = false;
   if (flag1 == false) flag2 = true;
   updateButton.setEnabled(flag2);
   addButton.setEnabled(flag1);
   deleteButton.setEnabled(flag1);
   firstButton.setEnabled(flag1);
   nextButton.setEnabled(flag1);
   prevButton.setEnabled(flag1);
   lastButton.setEnabled(flag1);
}

public void actionPerformed(ActionEvent e){
   try{
      Object source = e.getSource();
      if (source == exitButton){
         BookIO.close();
         System.exit(0);
      }
      else if (source == firstButton){
         currentBook = BookIO.moveFirst();
         performBookDisplay();
         enableButtons(true);
      }
      else if (source == prevButton){
         currentBook = BookIO.movePrevious();
         performBookDisplay();
         enableButtons(true);
      }
      else if (source == nextButton){
         currentBook = BookIO.moveNext();
         performBookDisplay();
         enableButtons(true);
      }
      else if (source == lastButton){
         currentBook = BookIO.moveLast();
         performBookDisplay();
         enableButtons(true);
      }
      else if (source == addButton){
         codeField.requestFocus();
         enableButtons(false);
         codeField.setText("");
         titleField.setText("");
         priceField.setText("");
         addFlag = true;
      }
```

Figure 12-20 The Book Maintenance application (part 4 of 5)

Part 5 of this figure starts with the else if block that's executed when the user clicks on the Update button. Here, the first three statements remove the dollar sign from the price text field and convert it to a double value (see chapter 9 if you don't understand the use of the priceString methods). Then, the fourth statement uses this double value and the values that are stored in the code and title fields to create a Book object. After that, two if statements check the addFlag variable to determine whether to add or update the book. If the addFlag variable is false, the updateRecord method of the BookIO class is called to update the data for the current book. But if the addFlag variable is true, the addRecord method is used to add the current book to the file or database and the addFlag variable is set to false. Finally, this else if block sets the currentBook equal to the book that has just been added or updated, and the helper methods are called to display the data for that book and to enable all of the buttons except the Update button.

The last else if block shows the code that's executed when the user presses the Delete button. Within this block, the first statement calls the deleteRecord method from the BookIO class. This method deletes the current record from the file or database. Then, the next two statements move the focus to the Next button and perform the doClick method for this button, which causes the event handler for this button to set the current record to the next record and display its data.

After the actionPerformed method, the next three methods implement the KeyListener interface, although the keyPressed method is the only method that contains any statements. Here, the first statement returns the key code that indicates the key that was pressed by the user. Then, this method uses an if statement to see if the user pressed the Escape key. If so, the focus is moved to the code text field, the current record is displayed, and all buttons except the Update button are enabled. This has the effect of returning the values in the three text fields to what they were before they were modified. In part 2 of this figure, you can see that the key listener has only been added to the three text fields, so pressing the Escape key will only work when the focus is on one of those fields.

The last three methods in this figure implement the DocumentListener interface. Here, the code includes three methods, even though the insertUpdate and removeUpdate methods are the only methods that contain any statements. These are the methods that are called when the user edits the text in either the title or price fields. Then, the statements within these methods disable all buttons except the Update and Exit buttons. To enable the other buttons, the user must either finish the update by clicking on the Update button or press the Escape key. Since the document listener has only been added to the title and price fields, this code isn't executed when the user edits the text in the code field.

* * *

Now, you should take some time to reflect on the code for this user interface. Although each book object consists of just three fields, this gives you a good idea of what you need to do when you develop an interface for objects with many fields. At this time, you should also do your best to understand every line of code in this application because that's the best way to master Java. If you need to refer back to earlier portions of this chapter or book, by all means do so.

The code for the Book Maintenance application (continued)

```
            else if (source == updateButton){
                String priceString = priceField.getText();
                if (priceString.charAt(0) == '$')
                    priceString = priceString.substring(1);
                double price = Double.parseDouble(priceString);
                Book book = new Book(codeField.getText(),
                    titleField.getText(), price);
                if (addFlag == false){
                    BookIO.updateRecord(book);
                }
                if (addFlag == true){
                    BookIO.addRecord(book);
                    addFlag = false;
                }
                currentBook = book;
                performBookDisplay();
                enableButtons(true);
            }
            else if(source == deleteButton){
                BookIO.deleteRecord(currentBook.getCode());
                nextButton.requestFocus();
                nextButton.doClick();
            }
        }
        catch (FileNotFoundException fnfe){
            JOptionPane.showMessageDialog(this, "FileNotFoundException");
        }
        catch (NumberFormatException nfe){
            JOptionPane.showMessageDialog(this, "NumberFormatException");
        }
        catch (IOException ioe){
            JOptionPane.showMessageDialog(this, "IOException");
        }
    }

    public void keyPressed(KeyEvent e){
        int keyCode = e.getKeyCode();
        if (keyCode == KeyEvent.VK_ESCAPE){
            codeField.requestFocus();
            performBookDisplay();
            enableButtons(true);
        }
    }
    public void keyReleased(KeyEvent e){}
    public void keyTyped(KeyEvent e){}

    public void insertUpdate(DocumentEvent e){
        enableButtons(false);
    }
    public void removeUpdate(DocumentEvent e){
        enableButtons(false);
    }
    public void changedUpdate(DocumentEvent e){}
}
```

Figure 12-20 The Book Maintenance application (part 5 of 5)

Perspective

In this chapter, you learned how to work with some new controls and the events generated by these controls. In addition, you learned how to use the most sophisticated layout manager available from the Java API, and you learned how to handle low-level events. In short, you've learned all of the essential skills for working with graphical user interfaces. This means that you should now be able to develop significant user interfaces on your own.

Summary

- An *event* is an object that's generated by user actions or by system events. An event *listener* is an object that implements the listener interface.
- A *semantic event* is an event that's related to a specific component like clicking on a button. In contrast, a *low-level event* is a less specific event like clicking the mouse.
- To handle an event, you must implement the appropriate listener interface. Then, you must add an object created from the listener class to the appropriate component by using the addXXXListener method, and you must code the methods of the listener interface.
- A *combo box* lets a user select an item from a drop-down list of items, and a *list box* lets a user select one or more items from a list of items.
- You can add a component like a list box to a *scroll pane*, and you can add a *border* to any component.
- You can create a *text area* that can store one or more lines of text, and you can use many of the same techniques to work with *text fields* and text areas.
- You can create two or more *radio buttons* that you can add to a *button group*. Then, the user can select one of the buttons in the group. You can also create a *check box* that lets a user check or uncheck the box.
- The *Grid Bag layout manager* is the most sophisticated and flexible layout manager. When you use the Grid Bag layout manager, you use the fields of the GridBagConstraints class to align components in a grid.
- To make it easier to code the listener interfaces for low-level events, the Java API includes *adapter classes* that contain empty methods for all of the methods in the listener interface.
- An *anonymous class* that uses the WindowAdapter class is commonly used to handle the window closed event for an interface.

Terms

event
listener
event handler class
semantic event
low-level event
control
combo box
list box
scroll pane
border
text field
text area
radio button
button group
check box
Grid Bag layout manager
focus event
keyboard event
adapter class
anonymous class

Objectives

- Code graphical user interfaces that use combo boxes, list boxes, scroll panes, text areas, radio buttons, and check boxes. Then, write code that responds to the semantic events that are generated when a user interacts with these components.
- Use the Grid Bag layout manager to position components on a frame, panel, or other type of container.
- Write code that handles low-level events like focus events and keyboard events, and use adapter classes whenever they are appropriate.

Exercise 12-1 Code the Book Maintenance user interface

1. Use the Explorer to review the files in the c:\java\ch12\book directory. It should include a data file named books.dat and three class files: Book, BookIO, and BookFrame.
2. Open the code for the BookFrame class that's in the c:\java\ch12\book directory. Then, edit its code so it displays the user interface for the Book Maintenance application that's shown in figure 12-19.
3. Compile and run this code to make sure that it works correctly. This should also compile the Book and BookIO classes. When the application runs, it should display a dialog box like the one in figure 12-19, and it should allow you to add, edit, and delete the books that are stored in the books.dat file.

Exercise 12-2 Enhance the Book Order application

1. Open the code for the Book class that's in the c:\java\ch12\order directory. Then, read through this code to make sure you understand it. It uses the readRecord method of the BookIO class to get the code, title, and price for each book from the books.dat file that's stored in this directory.
2. Open the code for the BookOrderFrame class that's in the c:\java\ch12\order directory. Then, edit this code so it uses a combo box to select the title instead of having the user enter a code as shown in figure 12-3. To return the array of book titles, use the static readTitles method of the BookIO class. Since this method throws an IOException, you should place it in a try/catch block.
3. Compile and run this code to make sure that it works correctly. It should display a dialog box like the one in figure 12-3; it should make an accurate calculation; and it should respond to any exceptions that are thrown due to bad input from the user. In addition, the combo box should display all the books that are stored in the books.dat file.

Exercise 12-3 Enhance the Loan Calculator application

1. Open the code for the FinancialCalculations class that's in the c:\java\ch12\loan directory and read through it to make sure you understand how this class works. Notice that this class now contains another method called calculateLoanAmount.
2. Open the code for the LoanCalculatorFrame class that's saved in the c:\java\ch12\loan directory. Using the skills and coding style that you learned in this chapter, modify this class so it uses two radio buttons as shown in figure 12-8.
3. Compile this code and run the application to make sure that it works correctly. It should let you calculate the monthly payment on a loan or calculate the value of the loan based on a series of monthly payments, and it should catch any exceptions that are thrown when the user enters invalid data.

13

How to work with menus

In the last two chapters, you learned how to code graphical user interfaces at a professional level. Now, in this chapter, you'll learn how to add menus to those interfaces, and you'll learn how to handle the events that are generated when a user selects an item from a menu. Although you won't need to use menus with every interface, they do provide another way for users to find the commands they're looking for.

Essential skills for working with menus

This topic presents the basic skills that you need for working with menus. After it shows you how to add menus and submenus to a frame, it shows how to handle the events that are generated by these components. Then, it shows you two ways to allow the user to select menu items with the keyboard. But first, it shows you the hierarchy of Swing classes that you can use to work with menus.

The hierarchy of classes for working with menus

Figure 13-1 shows the Swing hierarchy that you can use to work with menus. Since all of these classes ultimately inherit the JComponent class, they work much like the components you learned about in the last two chapters. Also, since menus and menu items inherit the AbstractButton class, they work much like the other buttons including buttons created from the JButton, JCheckBox, and JRadioButton classes.

This figure also summarizes three common methods of the AbstractButton class. Although these methods can be used with any class that inherits the AbstractButton class, the isSelected and setSelected methods are commonly used with the JRadioButtonMenuItem and JCheckBoxMenuItem. On the other hand, the doClick method is commonly used with the JButton class.

The hierarchy of classes for working with menus

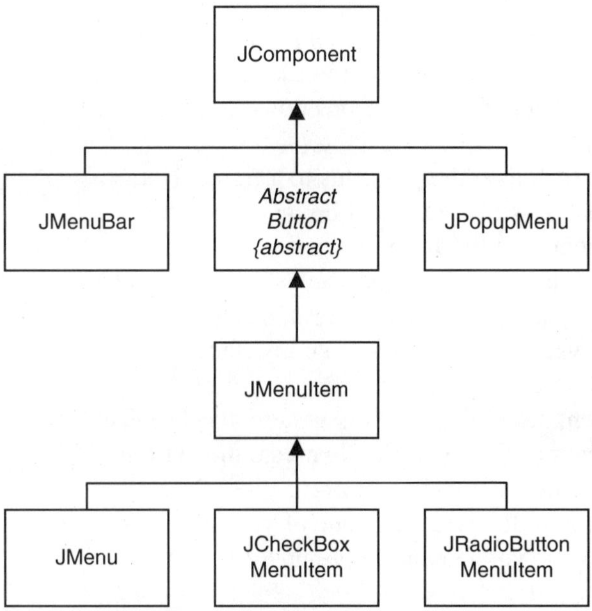

Summary of these classes

Class	Description
JMenuBar	A Swing class that defines a menu bar.
JPopupMenu	A Swing class that defines a menu that's typically displayed when a user right-clicks on a component.
AbstractButton	An abstract class that defines common behavior for Swing button classes, including the JButton, JCheckBox, and JRadioButton classes.
JMenuItem	A Swing class that defines an item on a menu.
JMenu	A Swing class that defines a menu.
JCheckBoxMenuItem	A Swing class that defines a menu item that works similarly to a check box.
JRadioButtonMenuItem	A Swing class that defines a menu item that works similarly to a radio button.

Common methods of the AbstractButton class

Method	Description
`isSelected()`	Returns a true value if the item is selected.
`setSelected(booleanValue)`	Sets the button to the specified boolean value, but doesn't generate the event for the button.
`doClick()`	Generates the event for the button.

Note

- The JButton, JCheckBox, and JRadioButton classes also inherit the AbstractButton class.

Figure 13-1 The hierarchy of classes for working with menus

How to add menus

Figure 13-2 shows how to add a *menu bar* that contains *menus* to a top-level container such as a frame or an applet. To access a menu, the user can click on the name of the menu in the menu bar. Then, the menu drops down from the menu bar.

The example in this figure shows how to add two menus to a frame. Here, the first two statements use the JMenu class to create the File menu and the Records menu. The next three statements use the JMenuBar class to create the menu bar and to add the two menus to the menu bar. And the last statement adds the menu bar to the frame. After this example, you can see a summary of the constructors and methods that can be used to add menus to an interface.

When you use menus, you usually create them in the constructor of the frame class and add them to the content pane. Then, if you want to synchronize the menu items with the buttons in the interface, you should create the buttons in the frame class too. That makes it easier to do the synchronization. When you use menus, then, you probably won't want to divide the code of your interface into a frame class and a panel class as shown in chapters 11 and 12.

An application with a menu bar and two menus

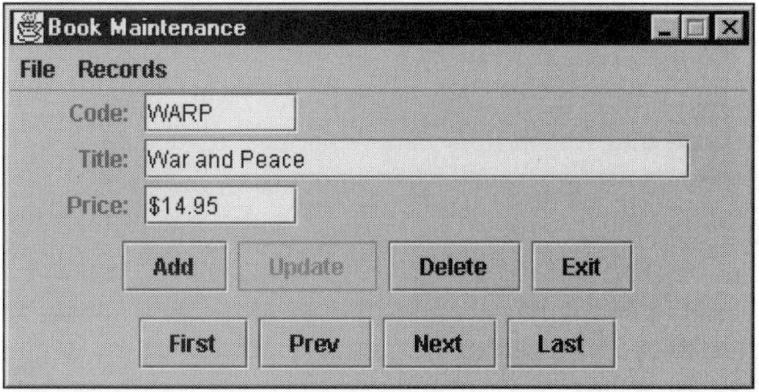

Code that adds two menus to a frame

```
JMenu fileMenu = new JMenu("File");
JMenu recordsMenu = new JMenu("Records");

JMenuBar menuBar = new JMenuBar();
menuBar.add(fileMenu);
menuBar.add(recordsMenu);

setJMenuBar(menuBar);
```

Constructors and methods needed to add a menu to a frame

Class	Constructor/Method	Description
JMenu	**JMenu(**String**)**	Creates a menu with the specified text.
JMenuBar	**JMenuBar()**	Creates a menu bar.
JMenuBar	**add(**JMenu**)**	Adds the specified menu to a menu bar.
JFrame	**setJMenuBar(**JMenuBar**)**	Adds the specified menu bar to a frame.
JApplet	**setJMenuBar(**JMenuBar**)**	Adds the specified menu bar to an applet.

Description

- The *menu bar* in an interface is the bar below the title bar. A *menu* is one of the lists that drops down from a menu bar.
- To select a menu, the user can click on the menu name in the menu bar.
- You usually create the menu bar and the menus in the constructor of the frame class and add these items to its content pane. When you use menus, it also makes sense to develop the rest of the interface in the frame class rather than a separate panel class. This makes it easier to synchronize the menus and the buttons (see figure 13-4).
- You can use the techniques in this chapter to work with normal user interfaces or with applets. To learn more about applets, you can read chapter 15.

Figure 13-2 How to add menus

How to add menu items

Figure 13-3 shows how to add *menu items* to the two menus defined in the last figure. In the user interface that's shown, you can see the four menu items of the Records menu. Here, the third and fourth items are separated by a *separator*, and the second item is disabled. To select an enabled menu item, the user can click on it.

In the code example, you can see how the menu items are added to the two menus. Here, the first statement declares the five menu items that will be added. Since you usually want to be able to access these menu items throughout the entire class, they're usually declared as instance variables of the class. Then, the next three statements create the Exit menu item and add it to the File menu. And the last eleven statements create the four items of the Records menu and add those items to that menu. This code uses the addSeparator method of the JMenu class to add a separator between the Delete and Move items, and it uses the setEnabled method of the JMenuItem class to disable the Update button.

This figure also summarizes the constructors and methods that you can use to work with menu items. To start, you can use either of the constructors of the JMenuItem class to create a menu item. Then, you can call any of the methods of the menu item to enable it, disable it, retrieve its text, or add an action listener to it. Finally, you can use the add method of the JMenu class to add the item to the menu, and you can use the addSeparator method to place a separator between menu items.

An application with a menu that contains four menu items

Code that adds menu items to the two menus

```
private JMenuItem exitMenuItem, addMenuItem, updateMenuItem,
                  deleteMenuItem, moveMenuItem;

JMenu fileMenu = new JMenu("File");
exitMenuItem = new JMenuItem("Exit");
fileMenu.add(exitMenuItem);

JMenu recordsMenu = new JMenu("Records");
addMenuItem = new JMenuItem("Add");
updateMenuItem = new JMenuItem("Update");
deleteMenuItem = new JMenuItem("Delete");
moveMenuItem = new JMenuItem("Move");
recordsMenu.add(addMenuItem);
recordsMenu.add(updateMenuItem);
recordsMenu.add(deleteMenuItem);
recordsMenu.addSeparator();
recordsMenu.add(moveMenuItem);
updateMenuItem.setEnabled(false);
```

Common constructors of the JMenuItem class

Constructor	Description
JMenuItem(String**)**	Creates a menu item with the specified text.
JMenuItem(String, Icon**)**	Creates a menu item with the specified text and icon.

Common methods of the JMenuItem class

Method	Description
setEnabled(booleanValue**)**	If the boolean value is true, the item is enabled.
getText()	Returns the String used as text in the menu item.
addActionListener(ActionEvent**)**	Adds an action listener to this menu item.

Methods from the JMenu class that work with menu items

Method	Description
add(Component**)**	Adds the specified component to a menu.
addSeparator()	Adds a separator to the menu.

Description

- A *menu item* is one of the items in a menu. A *separator* is a line that separates two items.

Figure 13-3 How to add menu items to menus

How to handle menu item events

Figure 13-4 shows how to handle the events that are generated when a user selects a menu item. To start, this figure shows two ways to add an action listener to a menu item. The first way shows how to add an action listener to a menu item when you want the current object from the BookFrame class to listen for the event that's generated when a user selects a menu item. The second way shows how to add an action listener to a menu item when you want an object from the BookPanel class to listen for the event that's generated when a user selects a menu item.

To decide how to structure your code, you need to determine the amount of interaction and synchronization that's necessary between the menu items and the other controls that are displayed on the frame. Then, if you find that you need access to variables that refer to menu items and other controls at the same time, you need to structure your code so all of these controls are available as instance variables of the class that defines the frame. This differs from the structure of the code in the last two chapters, which divided the code for an interface into a frame and a panel class.

The next two examples show two ways to code the event handler for menu events. In the first actionPerformed method, the first statement retrieves the source of the event as an object of the Object class. Next, an if statement checks to see whether the object is an instance of the JMenuItem class. If it is, the next two statements cast the object to the JMenuItem type and use the getText method to return the text that corresponds to the item. Then, a series of if statements executes the doClick methods of the buttons that correspond with the menu selections. This avoids unnecessary duplication of code and insures that the application will execute the same code whether the user selects the menu item or the button.

In the second actionPerformed method, the getActionCommand of the ActionEvent class is used to get the string that's used as text in the menu item that triggered the event. In other words, this one statement replaces the two statements that get the same result in the first event handler. Otherwise, these methods work the same.

The last example in this figure shows the code that synchronizes the buttons that are displayed on the frame with the state of the menu items. To use code like this, though, the menu items and buttons must both be stored in the same class. For example, this code will work if the menu items and buttons are declared as instance variables of the BookFrame class. That way, the enableButtons method will have access to all the buttons and menu items and can enable or disable each button or item depending on the boolean value that's passed to the method.

Two ways to add a listener to a menu item

When the current frame is the listener

```
addMenuItem.addActionListener(this);
```

When a panel defined by another class is the listener

```
BookPanel panel = new BookPanel();
addMenuItem.addActionListener(panel);
```

One way to code the event handler for menu item events

```
public void actionPerformed(ActionEvent e){
   Object source = e.getSource();
   if (source instanceof JMenuItem){
      JMenuItem item = (JMenuItem) source;
      String text = item.getText();
      if (text.equals("Add"))
         addButton.doClick();
      if (text.equals("Update"))
         updateButton.doClick();
      // code for other menu items
   }
   // code for other buttons
}
```

Another way to code the event handler for menu item events

```
public void actionPerformed(ActionEvent e){
   Object source = e.getSource();
   if (source instanceof JMenuItem){
      String item = e.getActionCommand();
      if (item.equals("Add"))
         addButton.doClick();
      if (item.equals("Update"))
         updateButton.doClick();
      // code for other menu items
```

Code that synchronizes buttons and menu items

```
private void enableButtons(boolean flag){
   addButton.setEnabled(flag);
   addMenuItem.setEnabled(flag);
   updateButton.setEnabled(!flag);
   updateMenuItem.setEnabled(!flag);
   deleteButton.setEnabled(flag);
   deleteMenuItem.setEnabled(flag);
   // code for other buttons and menu items
}
```

A useful method of the ActionEvent class

Method	Description
`getActionCommand()`	Returns the string used as text in the item that triggered the event.

Description

- If you want to synchronize the menu items with the buttons, you should create both the items and the buttons in the frame class instead of dividing the code for the interface into a frame and a panel class.

Figure 13-4 How to handle menu item events

How to create submenus

Figure 13-5 shows how to create a *submenu* that drops down from an item in another menu. Here, a submenu drops down from the Move item in the Records menu.

In the code for adding this submenu to the Records menu, you can see that the first statement declares the menu items of the submenu as instance variables of the class. Then, the next nine statements create a Move menu using the JMenu and JMenuItem classes, and the last statement adds the Move menu to the Records menu. Later, when you run the application, an arrow is displayed to the right of the Move menu to indicate that it is a submenu of the Records menu.

Although submenus are easy to create, they force the user to drill down through the menus, which makes the submenu items more difficult to find. That's why you should avoid using submenus if you can. In practice, though, submenus let you pack more choices into less space, which is sometimes what you need to do.

An application with a submenu

Code that adds a submenu to a menu

```
JMenuItem firstMenuItem, prevMenuItem, nextMenuItem, lastMenuItem;

JMenu moveMenu = new JMenu("Move");
firstMenuItem = new JMenuItem("First");
prevMenuItem = new JMenuItem("Prev");
nextMenuItem = new JMenuItem("Next");
lastMenuItem = new JMenuItem("Last");
moveMenu.add(firstMenuItem);
moveMenu.add(prevMenuItem);
moveMenu.add(nextMenuItem);
moveMenu.add(lastMenuItem);

recordsMenu.add(moveMenu);
```

Description

- A *submenu* is a menu that drops down from a menu item in another menu.
- The advantage of using submenus is that it lets you pack more items in less space.
- The disadvantage of using submenus is that the user has to drill down deeper to find the menu items.

Figure 13-5 How to create submenus

How to set keyboard mnemonics

Figure 13-6 shows how to set the *keyboard mnemonics* for menus and menu items so the user can use keystrokes to select menus and menus items. Then, the user can press the Alt key plus a menu's underlined letter to pull down the menu. And the user can press a menu item's underlined letter to select the menu item.

The first example shows how to specify that the keyboard mnemonic for the File menu is the letter *F*. For this to work, the File menu must first be created by the JMenu constructor. Then, the setMnemonic method that the JMenu class ultimately inherits from the AbstractButton class specifies the mnemonic. Since this method isn't case sensitive, the user can use either uppercase or lowercase letters.

The second example shows how to specify that the keyboard mnemonics for the Exit and Add menu items are the letters *x* and *A*. To add these mnemonics, you use the constructor of the JMenuItem class that's shown at the bottom of this figure. When you use this constructor, you can use uppercase or lowercase characters for the second argument and the result isn't case-sensitive. Since the JMenuItem class is also derived from the AbstractButton class, you can use the setMnemonic method to set keyboard mnemonics for menu items too.

If you're using SDK1.4, you can use the setDisplayedMnemonicIndex method to determine which occurrence of a character you want underlined. For instance, if you use the setMnemonic method on a button that contains the text "Save As", the first "a" is automatically underlined. To underline the second "a", you can then call the setDisplayedMnemonicIndex method with an index argument of 5.

An application with keyboard mnemonics

Code that adds keyboard mnemonics to a menu

```
fileMenu.setMnemonic('F');
```

Code that adds keyboard mnemonics to two menu items

```
JMenuItem exitMenuItem = new JMenuItem("Exit", 'x');
JMenuItem addMenuItem = new JMenuItem("Add", 'A');
```

How to add keyboard mnemonics to menus and menu items

Class	Method/Constructor	Description
AbstractButton	**setMnemonic**(charMnemonic)	Adds the specified mnemonic.
AbstractButton	**setDisplayedMnemonicIndex**(intIndex)	An SDK1.4 method that sets the character to be used as the mnemonic when the character occurs more than once.
JMenuItem	**JMenuItem**(String, charMnemonic)	Creates a menu item with the specified text and keyboard mnemonic.

Description

- If you want the user to be able to select menus and menu items with the keyboard, you can provide *keyboard mnemonics* for the menus and menu items.
- To pull down a menu that contains an underlined letter, the user can hold down the Alt key and press the letter. Then, the user can select any item on the menu by pressing its underlined letter.
- To use the setDisplayedMnemonicIndex method included in SDK1.4, you must first call the setMnemonic method. Then, you can use the setDisplayedMnemonicIndex method to specify the index of the character you wish to be underlined.

Figure 13-6 How to set keyboard mnemonics

How to set accelerator keys

Figure 13-7 shows how to set *accelerator keys* for menu items. In the interface that's shown, these keys have been added to the Add, Update, and Delete items of the Records menu. So it's easy for the user to find out what they are, the key combinations are shown to the right of the menu items in the menus. For instance, the accelerator keys for the Update item are Ctrl+U.

The code example shows how to add accelerator keys to the Add and Update menu items. Here, the first statement uses the setAccelerator method to add Ctrl+U as the accelerator for the Update menu item. To do this, this method calls the static getKeystroke method from the KeyStroke class, and it uses fields from the KeyEvent and Event classes.

The second statement in this example works the same way except that it uses a plus sign to add both the Ctrl and Alt keys to the keystroke combination. When working with accelerator keys, you need to make sure that the accelerator keys that you use for menu items don't conflict with the accelerator keys that are already defined for other components of the application. For example, the Ctrl+X, Ctrl+C, and Ctrl+V keys are commonly used by text components to cut, copy, and paste text so you shouldn't use these keys for menu items.

An application with accelerators

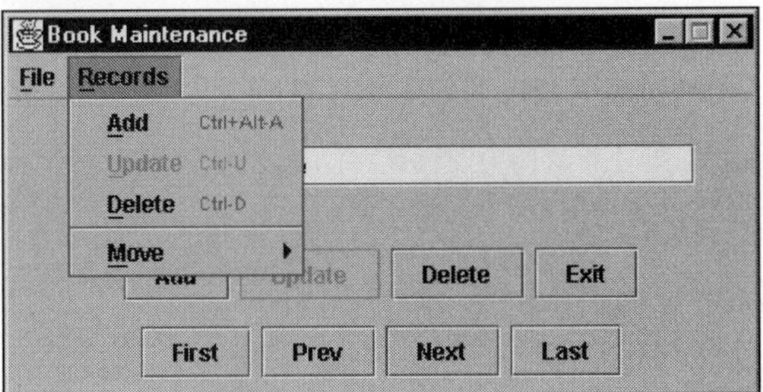

Code that adds accelerators to two menu items

```
updateMenuItem.setAccelerator(KeyStroke.getKeyStroke(KeyEvent.VK_U,
    Event.CTRL_MASK));
addMenuItem.setAccelerator(KeyStroke.getKeyStroke(KeyEvent.VK_A,
    Event.CTRL_MASK + Event.ALT_MASK));
```

A method that sets an accelerator to a JMenuItem object

Method	Description
`setAccelerator(KeyStroke)`	Sets the key combination needed to invoke the action listener of a menu item.

A static method of the KeyStroke class that returns a KeyStroke object

Method	Description
`getKeyStroke(intKeyCode, intModifier)`	Returns a KeyStroke object that contains the key combination of the specified key code and modifier.

Fields for the key codes in the KeyEvent class

`VK_A` `VK_B` `VK_C` ... `VK_Z`

Fields for the modifiers in the Event class

`SHIFT_MASK` `CTRL_MASK` `ALT_MASK`

Description

- If you want the user to be able to select a menu item without pulling down a menu, you can add an *accelerator key* for that item.
- When you plan the accelerator keys for menu items, be sure that they don't conflict with they key combinations that are used for other purposes.
- The Keystroke class is stored in the javax.swing package, the KeyEvent class is stored in the java.awt.event package, and the Event class is stored in the java.awt package.

Figure 13-7 How to set accelerator keys

Advanced skills for working with menus

This topic presents some advanced skills for working with menus and menu items. First, you'll learn how to add special menu items that work like radio buttons and check boxes to menus. Then, you'll learn how to create pop-up menus that appear when you click the right mouse button.

How to work with radio button menu items

Figure 13-8 shows how to add *radio button menu items* to a menu. These items have some characteristics of the radio buttons that you learned about in chapter 12 and some characteristics of the menu items that you learned about earlier in this chapter.

The first code example shows the code that adds two radio button menu items to the Calculate menu. Here, the first statement declares these items as instance variables of the class that defines the frame. That way, these items will be available throughout the entire class. Then, the next four statements create the Calculate menu, a button group, and the two items. After that, the next four statements add the items to the button group and to the menu, and the last two statements add an action listener to the menu items.

The second code example shows how to handle the events that are generated when the user clicks on one of the radio button items. This code is similar to the code that handles the other menu item events. Because JRadioButtonMenuItem is a subclass of JMenuItem, the first if statement can check to see whether the source is a JMenuItem object.

The rest of this figure summarizes two constructors that you can use to create radio button menu items. To create an unselected radio button menu item, you can use the first constructor. To create a selected radio button menu item, you can use the second constructor.

An application with two radio button menu items

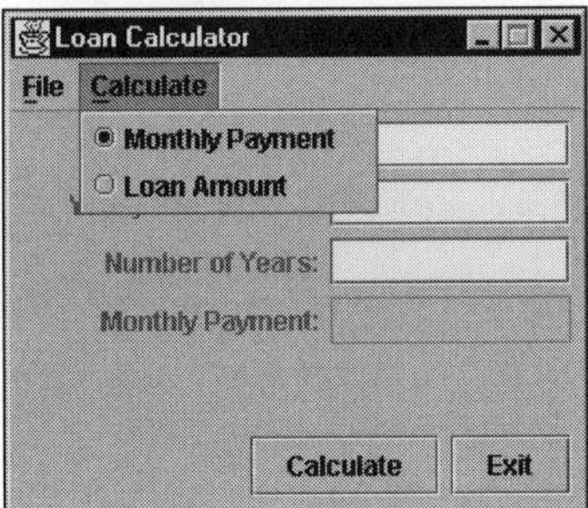

Code that adds two radio button menu items to a menu

```
private JRadioButtonMenuItem paymentItem, amountItem;

JMenu calculateMenu = new JMenu("Calculate");
ButtonGroup group = new ButtonGroup();
paymentItem = new JRadioButtonMenuItem(
    "Monthly Payment", true);
amountItem = new JRadioButtonMenuItem(
    "Loan Amount");

group.add(paymentItem);
group.add(amountItem);
calculateMenu.add(paymentItem);
calculateMenu.add(amountItem);

paymentItem.addActionListener(this);
amountItem.addActionListener(this);
```

The method that handles the radio button menu item events

```
public void actionPerformed(ActionEvent e){
    Object source = e.getSource();
    if (source instanceof JMenuItem){
        String item = e.getActionCommand();
        if (item.equals("Monthly Payment")){
            paymentField.setText("");
            paymentField.setEditable(false);
            amountField.setEditable(true);
            amountField.requestFocus();
        }
        if (item.equals("Loan Amount")){
            // code for the Loan Amount item
        }
    }
}
```

Common constructors of the JRadioButtonMenuItem class

Constructor	Description
`JRadioButtonMenuItem(String)`	Creates an unselected radio button menu item with specified text.
`JRadioButtonMenuItem(String, booleanValue)`	Creates a radio button menu item with specified text. If boolean value is true, then the item is selected.

Figure 13-8 How to work with radio button menu items

How to work with check box menu items

Figure 13-9 shows how to work with *check box menu items*. These components have some characteristics of the check boxes that you learned about in chapter 12 and some characteristics of the menu items that you learned about earlier in this chapter.

The first code example shows how to add a check box menu item to a menu. Here, the first statement declares the check box menu item as an instance variable of the class that defines the frame. That way, the check box menu item is available throughout the entire frame. Then, the next three statements add the check box menu item to the Window menu, and the last statement adds an action listener to the check box menu item.

The second code example shows how to handle the event that's generated when a user clicks on the check box menu item. In short, you just code an actionPerformed method within the ActionListener class like you do for all other menu items. However, this code example also uses the isSelected method to check to see if the button is selected. If it is, the code calls the setResizable method to make the current frame resizable. Since the isSelected method is defined in the AbstractButton class, this method is available to all buttons and menu items.

The rest of this figure summarizes the constructors that you can use to create a check box menu item. To create an unselected check box menu item, you can use the first constructor. To create a selected check box menu item, you can use the second constructor.

An application with a check box menu item

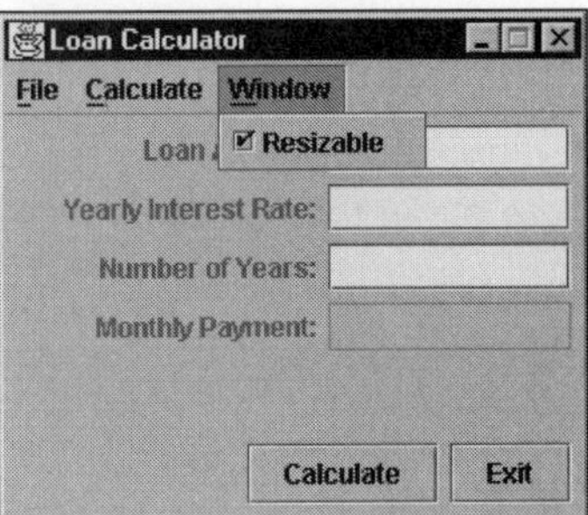

Code that adds a check box menu item to a menu

```
private JCheckBoxMenuItem resizableItem;

JMenu windowMenu = new JMenu("Window");
resizableItem = new JCheckBoxMenuItem("Resizable", true);
windowMenu.add(resizableItem);

resizableItem.addActionListener(this);
```

The method that handles the check box menu item event

```
public void actionPerformed(ActionEvent e){
   Object source = e.getSource();
   if (source instanceof JMenuItem){
      String item = e.getActionCommand();
      if (item.equals("Resizable")){
         if (resizableItem.isSelected())
            setResizable(true);
         else
            setResizable(false);
      }
   }
}
```

Common constructors of the JCheckBoxMenuItem class

Constructor	Description
`JCheckBoxMenuItem(String)`	Creates an unselected check box menu item with specified text.
`JCheckBoxMenuItem(String, booleanValue)`	Creates a check box menu item with specified text. If boolean value is true, then the item is selected.

Figure 13-9 How to work with check box menu items

How to work with pop-up menus

Figure 13-10 shows how to work with *pop-up menus* that appear whenever a user presses the pop-up trigger (which is usually the right mouse button). For instance, the screen at the top of this figure shows a pop-up menu that contains two menu items, the Resizable item and the Exit item. Part 1 of this figure shows the code that adds this pop-up menu to the interface, and part 2 summarizes the constructors and methods that you need for working with these menus.

The code example shows all of the code that you need to create and display a pop-up menu. Here, the first three statements declare the pop-up menu and the two items on the pop-up menu. Usually, these variables are declared as instance variables of the current class. Then, the next eight statements create the items, add them to the pop-up menu, and add action listeners to them.

The last two statements in this example add a mouse listener to the content pane. Here, the first statement returns the content pane. Then, the second statement adds the mouse listener to this pane. In this case, the mouse listener is an anonymous class that's a new instance of the MouseAdapter class. Within this anonymous class, the mouseReleased method contains the code that's executed when a mouse button is released. Within this method, an if statement checks to see if the event should trigger a pop-up menu. Usually, this means that the if statement checks if the right mouse button was clicked. If so, this method uses the show method of the pop-up menu to display the pop-up menu. To do that, it uses three methods of the MouseEvent class to display the pop-up menu at the coordinates where the user released the right mouse button.

An application with a pop-up menu

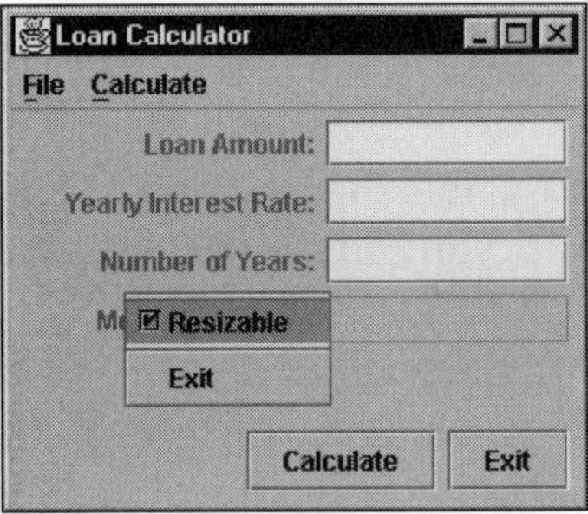

Code that adds a pop-up menu to a content pane

```
private JPopupMenu popupMenu;
private JCheckBoxMenuItem resizablePopupItem;
private JMenuItem exitPopupItem;

popupMenu = new JPopupMenu();
resizablePopupItem = new JCheckBoxMenuItem("Resizable", true);
exitPopupItem = new JMenuItem("Exit");
popupMenu.add(resizablePopupItem);
popupMenu.addSeparator();
popupMenu.add(exitPopupItem);
resizablePopupItem.addActionListener(this);
exitPopupItem.addActionListener(this);

Container contentPane = getContentPane();
contentPane.addMouseListener(new MouseAdapter(){
   public void mouseReleased(MouseEvent e){
      if (e.isPopupTrigger())
         popupMenu.show(e.getComponent(), e.getX(), e.getY());
   }
});
```

Description

- To handle a mouse event, you can use an anonymous class as shown above. As you learned in the last chapter, the MouseAdapter class implements all the methods of the MouseListener interface as empty methods. That way, you only need to override the code for the mouseReleased method.
- If you add the mouse listener to the content pane, then all the mouse events below the menu bar are handled by this listener. In this example, the pop-up menu is displayed when the user clicks the right mouse button anywhere in the content pane.

Figure 13-10 How to work with pop-up menus (part 1 of 2)

Part 2 of this figure summarizes the constructors and methods that you can use to work with pop-up menus. To start, you can use the constructor of the JPopupMenu class to create a pop-up menu. Then, you can use the methods of the JPopupMenu class to work with a pop-up menu.

Below the constructors and methods of the Popup class, this figure shows the five methods of the MouseListener interface. Typically, you can use the MouseAdapter class to implement all five of these methods. Then, you can override the mouseReleased method as shown on the previous page. If necessary, though, you can also code any of the other methods of the MouseListener interface.

To display a pop-up menu, you need to know if the pop-up trigger generated the event. In addition, you may need to know what component was clicked, and you may need to know the x and y coordinates of where the click was released. To get this information, you can use the four methods of the MouseEvent class.

Common constructor of the JPopupMenu class

Constructor	Description
JPopupMenu()	Creates a pop-up menu.

Common methods of the JPopupMenu class

Method	Description
add(JMenuItem**)**	Adds the menu item to the pop-up menu.
addSeparator()	Adds a separator to the pop-up menu.
show(Component, intX, intY**)**	Displays the pop-up menu at the x,y coordinates inside the component.
setLocation(intX, intY**)**	Positions the pop-up menu at the x,y coordinates.

The MouseListener interface

Method	Description
void mouseClicked(MouseEvent e)	Invoked when the mouse is clicked on a component.
void mouseEntered(MouseEvent e)	Invoked when the mouse enters a component.
void mouseExited(MouseEvent e)	Invoked when the mouse exits a component.
void mousePressed(MouseEvent e)	Invoked when the mouse button is pressed in a component.
void mouseReleased(MouseEvent e)	Invoked when the mouse button is released in a component.

Common methods of the MouseEvent class

Method	Description
getComponent()	Returns the Component where the mouse event occurred.
getX()	Returns the horizontal position of the event as an int.
getY()	Returns the vertical position of the event as an int.
isPopupTrigger()	Returns a boolean true value if the pop-up trigger (which is usually the right mouse button) generated the event.

Note

- All x and y coordinates are measured in pixels.

Figure 13-10 How to work with pop-up menus (part 2 of 2)

Perspective

Now that you've finished this chapter, you should be able to add menus to a frame and to handle the events that are generated when a user selects an item from a menu. For many user interfaces, that should be all that you need to know. In the next chapter, though, you can learn how to use fonts, colors, images, and shapes to improve the appearance of your applications.

Summary

- You can add a *menu bar* to a frame or an applet, and you can add *menus* to the menu bar. Then, you can add *menu items* and menu *separators* to the menus.
- If you create the menus in the class that defines the frame, you typically handle all of the menu events within that class.
- If you add a menu to another menu, the menu system will display it as a *submenu*.
- When you set *keystroke mnemonics* for menus and menu items, the users can select menus by holding down Alt and pressing the underlined letter for the menu. Then, the users can select menu items by pressing the underlined letter for the menu item.
- When you set *accelerator keys* for menu items, the users can select items by pressing their key combinations.
- You can add *radio button menu items* and *check box menu items* to menus. These items work much like radio buttons and check boxes.
- You can create a *pop-up menu* that appears when the user right-clicks anywhere on a component.

Terms

menu bar
menu
menu item
separator
submenu
keyboard mnemonic
accelerator key
radio button menu item
check box menu item
pop-up menu

Objectives

- Write code that (1) adds a menu bar and a complete system of menus to an application and (2) handles the events that are generated when the user selects an item from the menu system.
- Write code that (1) displays a pop-up menu when the user right-clicks on a component and (2) handles the events that are generated when the user selects an item from the pop-up menu.
- Identify these terms: menu, menu item, submenu, and pop-up menu.
- Distinguish between these terms: keyboard mnemonics and accelerator keys.

Exercise 13-1 Add menus to the Book Maintenance application

1. Open the code for the BookFrame class that's in the c:\java\ch13\book directory. Notice that this code has been restructured so the BookFrame class contains all the code for the user interface.
2. Edit this class so it displays the File and Record menus that are described in figures 13-3 through 13-7. When you're done, the menu items should do the same actions that are performed by the buttons of the frame. In addition, the menu items should have keyboard mnemonics and accelerator keys.
3. Compile and run this code to make sure that it works correctly. In particular, you should synchronize the menu items with the buttons so the application enables and disables them appropriately.

Exercise 13-2 Add menus to the Loan Calculator application

1. Open the code for the LoanCalculatorFrame class that's in the c:\java\ch13\loan directory. Notice how this code is structured so the LoanCalculatorFrame class contains all the code for the user interface.
2. Edit this class so the frame will display a File menu with an Exit menu item. Then, edit the code so the frame will display a Calculate menu like the one shown in figure 13-8. To do that, you should convert the existing radio buttons to menu items.
3. Compile and run this code to make sure that it works the way it did in the last chapter, but with the radio buttons on the Calculate menu, not on the frame.

(This exercise continues on the next page.)

4. Edit this class so the frame will display a pop-up menu like the one in figure 13-10. To handle the event that's generated when the user selects the Resizable check box menu item, you'll need to add code like the code in figure 13-9.
5. Compile and run this code to make sure that it works correctly. You should be able to use the pop-up menu to exit the application and to allow the frame to be resized.

14

How to work with fonts, colors, images, and shapes

In the last three chapters, you learned how to use components such as labels, text boxes, and menu items to display text in a graphical user interface. Now, you'll learn how to work with fonts, colors, images, and shapes. Although you won't need these features for many of the user interfaces that you develop, you should at least know what's available.

How to work with fonts and colors

This topic shows how to work with fonts and colors. But first, it explains how Java displays components, and it shows how to display text on a component.

How components are painted

Figure 14-1 shows how Java paints Swing and AWT components. Every time Java displays a top-level container such as a frame or applet, it *paints* all the components within the container. Java also repaints these components when a container appears after it has been hidden.

To do that, Java automatically calls the paint method for each component. For AWT components, Java automatically calls the update and paint methods. For Swing components, the AWT paint method also calls the paintComponent method.

If you want to display graphics on an AWT component, you can override the paint method. Similarly, if you want to display graphics on a Swing component, you can override its paintComponent method. If, for example, you want to display an image on a panel, you can create a class that inherits the JPanel class and override the paintComponent method to display the image.

For both AWT and Swing components, you shouldn't call the paint method directly. Instead, when you want to force Java to repaint a component, you should call the component's repaint method. If, for example, you want an image to be displayed after a user clicks on a button, you can invoke the repaint method within the if statement that handles the button event.

Each of the methods presented in this figure has a Graphics object as a parameter. This object represents the component that is going to be painted or repainted. Note, however, that you don't create this type of object by calling a constructor. Instead, Java creates this type of object automatically and passes it to the method that it calls. As you will see, this type of object has many methods that let you set fonts, colors, images, and shapes.

The state of a Graphics object can be referred to as the component's *graphics context*, or its *graphics rendering context*. This context includes its font and color. In the next pages, you'll learn how to change the graphics context for Java components.

How Java paints a Swing component

```
repaint() →
    update(Graphics g) →
        paint(Graphics g) →
            paintComponent(Graphics g) → COMPONENT DRAWN
```

Methods of the Component class used for painting

Method	Description
`repaint()`	Calls the component's update method.
`update(Graphics g)`	Calls the component's paint method.
`paint(Graphics g)`	Automatically called when a component needs to be painted.

Methods of the JComponent class used for painting

Method	Description
`paintComponent(Graphics g)`	Automatically called when a component needs to be painted.

Description

- When a top-level container such as a frame or applet first appears, Java *paints* all the components in the container. If a container is minimized and then restored, Java automatically repaints all the components in the container by calling the paint method for each component.
- When you want to repaint a component within a program, you can call its repaint method.
- To display text, images, or shapes on a Swing component, you can override the component's paintComponent method. To display text, images, or shapes on an AWT component, you can override the component's paint method.
- When Java invokes the update, paint, or paintComponent method, a Graphics object is automatically passed to it. This object represents the component that is going to be painted or repainted.
- The state of a Graphics object can be referred to as the component's *graphics context*, or its *graphics rendering context*. This context includes its font and color.
- In this chapter, you'll learn how to use many of the methods of the Graphics class to work with fonts, colors, images, and shapes.

Figure 14-1 How components are painted

How to display text on a component

For most applications, you use label components to display text. To illustrate how you can work with graphics, though, figure 14-2 shows how to use the Graphics class to display text on a component. This figure starts with an interface that displays text in a panel within a frame.

The first code example defines the panel that displays this text. To start, it declares a class named TextPanel that inherits the JPanel class. Then, the single method in this class overrides the paintComponent method of the JPanel class. Within this method, the first statement calls the paintComponent method of the superclass (the JPanel class). This statement ensures that you don't accidentally interfere with any necessary painting that's done by the superclass.

The last two statements within this paintComponent method create a String object and call the drawString method of the Graphics object, which in this case is the panel. This method displays the text 30 pixels to the right and 40 pixels down from the upper left corner of the panel. Because the font and color haven't been changed, this text will be printed with the font and color of the current graphics context.

The second code example shows some of the code that defines the frame that displays the TextPanel panel. By now, this type of code should be familiar to you. In short, this code defines the frame, creates a TextPanel object, and displays the TextPanel object on the content pane of the frame.

An example that displays text

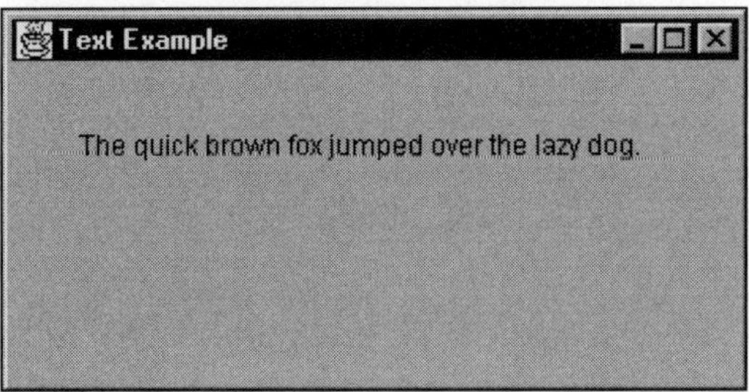

A class that overrides the paintComponent method for a panel

```
class TextPanel extends JPanel{
   public void paintComponent(Graphics g){
      super.paintComponent(g);
      String text = "The quick brown fox jumped over the lazy dog.";
      g.drawString(text, 30, 40);
   }
}
```

A class that displays the panel within a frame

```
public class TextFrame extends JFrame{
   public TextFrame(){
      // code that defines the frame
      TextPanel panel = new TextPanel();
      contentPane.add(panel);
   }
}
```

A method of the Graphics class that renders text

Method	Description
drawString(String, intX, intY)	Draws the specified string at the specified x and y coordinates on the component using the current graphics context.

Description

- Most of the time, you use labels and other text components to display text. However, you can override the paintComponent method of a Swing component or the paint method of a non-Swing component to display a string.
- To display text on a component, create your own class that inherits the component's class. Then, override its paint or paintComponent method with your own method. At the start of this method, you should call the paint or paintComponent method of the superclass so the superclass can run that method.

Figure 14-2 How to display text on a component

How to set fonts

Figure 14-3 shows how to set the font for the graphics context and for individual components. First, this figure shows some examples that set fonts. Then, it summarizes the fields, constructors, and methods that you can use to set fonts.

Since fonts differ from computer to computer, the Java API provides some *logical fonts* that always map to a font available on the local computer. For example, the SansSerif font will map to a sans serif font that's available on the current system, such as Helvetica or Arial. As a result, when you use the logical font names in this figure, you can be sure that they'll be available on all systems.

In case you aren't familiar with font terminology, *serifs* are the top and bottom lines that finish off the main strokes of a letter as in this letter *M*. In contrast, a *sans serif* font doesn't have serifs as in this letter *M*. In this book, the text font has serifs, but the headings don't.

The first example shows how to use the Font class to create a font. Here, the first statement creates a font that has serifs, bold style, and a size of 16 points. To do that, the first argument specifies a logical font, the second argument specifies the style, and the third argument specifies the size. In contrast, the second statement creates a font from the Helvetica font family with a plain style and a size of 12 points. To do that, the first argument specifies a string that indicates the name of the font family name. The third statement in this example shows how you can use the plus sign (+) to combine the bold and italic styles.

The second example shows how to set the font for the graphics context. This shows the paintComponent method that you learned about in the last figure with two new statements that set the font for the graphics context. Here, the second statement creates the font, and the third statement calls the setFont method of the Graphics object to set the font for the graphics context. Then, the text that's displayed by the fifth statement will use the font that's specified in the graphics context.

The third example shows how to set the font for the text that's displayed on a button. To do that, you call the setFont method from the button. Since this method is stored in the Component class, you can call it from any component.

The fourth example shows how to retrieve all the fonts that are available on the current system. Here, the first two statements create a GraphicsEnvironment object. Then, the third statement returns an array of strings that represent the font family names that are available on that system. As a programmer, you can use this array to print or display the font families so you know what you can work with on a specific system.

How to set fonts

Code that creates fonts

```
Font boldSerif16 = new Font("Serif", Font.BOLD, 16);
Font helvetica12 = new Font("Helvetica", Font.PLAIN, 12);
Font font = new Font("Dialog", Font.BOLD + Font.ITALIC, 8);
```

Code that sets the font for a graphics context

```
public void paintComponent(Graphics g){
    super.paintComponent(g);
    Font font = new Font("Dialog", Font.BOLD + Font.ITALIC, 20);
    g.setFont(font);
    String text = "The quick brown fox jumped over the lazy dog.";
    g.drawString(text, 30, 40);
}
```

Code that sets the font of a component

```
Font font = new Font("SansSerif", Font.BOLD, 16);
JButton addButton = new JButton("Add");
addButton.setFont(font);
```

Code that gets a list of the available fonts from the current system

```
GraphicsEnvironment ge = null;
ge = GraphicsEnvironment.getLocalGraphicsEnvironment();
String[] fonts = ge.getAvailableFontFamilyNames();
```

A common constructor of the Font class

Constructor	Description
Font(nameString, intStyle, intSize)	Creates a font with the specified name, style, and size.

Logical font names

Name	Description
SansSerif	Maps to a font that doesn't have serifs such as Helvetica or Arial.
Serif	Maps to a font that has serifs such as Times or Times New Roman.
Monospaced	Maps to a mono-spaced font such as Courier or Courier New.
Dialog, DialogInput	Maps to the system fonts that are used in dialog boxes.

Static fields of the Font class used to set the style

PLAIN **BOLD** **ITALIC**

Classes and methods that set fonts

Class	Method	Description
Graphics	**setFont**(Font)	Sets the font in the graphics context to the specified font.
Component	**setFont**(Font)	Sets the font in this component to the specified font.

Two methods of the GraphicsEnvironment class

Method	Description
getLocalGraphicsEnvironment()	A static method that returns a GraphicsEnvironment object.
getAvailableFontFamilyNames()	Returns an array of Strings of all available fonts for the current system.

Figure 14-3 How to set fonts

How to work with font metrics

The height and width of a displayed string depends on the font family, style and size of the font that's used to display it. As a result, it's often hard to specify the x and y coordinates when you use the drawString method to draw text on a component. That's why figure 14-4 shows how to use the FontMetrics class to find the width and height of a string. Then, you can use this information to position the text on a component. In this figure, for example, you can see how to center a string on a component and how to wrap a string to a second line.

The first example shows how to center a string on a component. Once the first four statements create the font and the string, the fifth statement creates a FontMetrics object. Then, the sixth statement uses the stringWidth method of the FontMetrics object to return the width of the string in pixels, and the seventh statement uses the getHeight method to return the height of the string in pixels. The last three statements get the height and width of the panel in pixels and use those numbers to calculate the x and y coordinates needed by the drawString method to center the string horizontally and vertically. When you use this technique to center a string vertically, the baseline of the leftmost character is positioned on the centerline. This means that the text may not appear centered, but rather positioned above the centerline.

The second example shows how to use the FontMetrics class to wrap a string to the next line. If you've read chapter 9, you should be able to follow this code without too much trouble. This code could be substituted for the last statement of the first example. Then, the two examples combined would both wrap and center the string.

The code in the second example splits the original string into lines that don't exceed the width of the panel minus 20 pixels. This is done by the first for loop, and each of these lines is put into one element of a vector named strings. Then, the second for loop uses the drawString method to draw each string in the vector on a separate line of the panel. Note, however, that this doesn't split the lines between words; it splits the lines whenever the next character will cause the line to exceed the line width.

After the examples, this figure summarizes some of the constructors and methods that you can use to work with font metrics. To create a FontMetrics object, you can use either of the methods of the Graphics object or the constructor of the FontMetrics class. Then, you can use the methods of the FontMetrics class to return the number of pixels for the height and width of a string in the current font.

How to work with font metrics

Code that centers a string

```
public void paintComponent(Graphics g){
   super.paintComponent(g);
   Font f = new Font("SansSerif", Font.BOLD + Font.ITALIC, 16);
   g.setFont(f);
   String text = "The quick brown fox jumped over the lazy dog.";
   FontMetrics fm = g.getFontMetrics();
   int widthString = fm.stringWidth(text);
   int heightString = fm.getHeight();
   int widthPanel = this.getWidth();
   int heightPanel = this.getHeight();
   g.drawString(text, (widthPanel - widthString) / 2,
                      (heightPanel - heightString) / 2);
}
```

Code that wraps a string to the next line

```
int widthLine = widthPanel - 20;
Vector strings = new Vector();
String tempString = "";
int maxLineWidth = 0;
for (int i = 0; i < text.length(); i++){
   tempString += text.charAt(i);
   maxLineWidth += fm.charWidth(text.charAt(i));
   if ((maxLineWidth >= widthLine) || (i==text.length() - 1)){
      strings.add(tempString);
      maxLineWidth = 0;
      tempString = "";
   }
}
int lines = strings.size();
int y = (heightPanel - (heightString * lines)) / 2;
for (int i = 0; i < lines; i++){
   String line = (String) strings.get(i);
   g.drawString(line, 10, y + i * heightString);
}
```

Methods of the Graphics class that return a FontMetrics object

Method	Description
`getFontMetrics()`	Returns a FontMetrics object for the current font.
`getFontMetrics(Font)`	Returns a FontMetrics object for the specified font.

Constructors and methods of the FontMetrics class

Constructor/Method	Description
`FontMetrics(Font)`	Creates a FontMetrics object for the specified font.
`getHeight()`	Returns an int value in pixels for the height of a line of this font.
`stringWidth(String)`	Returns an int value in pixels for the width of the specified string.
`charWidth(char)`	Returns an int value in pixels for the width of the specified character.

Figure 14-4 How to work with font metrics

How to set colors

Figure 14-5 shows how to set the color in a graphics context or for a component. To start, this figure shows some code examples that you can use to set colors. These examples use methods from the Graphics and Component classes that accept objects from the Color class. When you work with colors, you'll often use the fields of the Color or SystemColor class to set colors.

The first example shows how to create a color. Here, the first statement uses a field of the Color class to create a Color object for the color red. Then, the second statement uses a field of the SystemColor class to create a Color object that stores the color that's used by the system for window objects. This color will vary depending on how each system is configured. In contrast to the first two statements that use predefined fields to create colors, the third statement uses a constructor of the Color class to create the color yellow. To create yellow, this statement uses the maximum amount (255) of both red and green and no blue. In practice, though, you won't need to create your own colors unless you need to create colors that aren't already defined by one of the fields of the Color or SystemColor classes.

The second example shows how to set the color for the graphics context. Here, the first statement calls the setColor method from the Graphics object to set the color for the graphics context to red. As a result, the text that's printed by the second statement will be red. This color will stay in effect until it's changed by another statement like the third statement.

The third example shows how to set the foreground and background colors of components. Here, the first statement sets the background color for the Exit button to green so the button will be green. Then, the second statement sets the foreground color to blue so the text will be blue.

In general, the default colors for the components are adequate for most programs so you won't need to change them. If you do want to change them, though, you should consider using colors that are available from the SystemColor class, which has more than 20 color fields. That way, the colors that you use will be consistent with the other colors that are used for the interface.

How to set colors

Code that creates colors

```
Color red = Color.red;
Color windowColor = SystemColor.window;
Color yellow = new Color(255, 255, 0);
```

Code that sets the color in a graphics context

```
g.setColor(Color.red);
g.drawString("This text is red!", 30, 30);
g.setColor(Color.blue);
g.drawString("This text is blue!", 30, 70);
```

Code that sets the color of components

```
exitButton.setBackground(Color.green);
exitButton.setForeground(Color.blue);
```

Fields of the Color class

black	darkGray	lightGray	pink	yellow
blue	gray	magenta	red	
cyan	green	orange	white	

Five fields of the SystemColor class

window	menu	menuText	deskTop	windowBorder

A constructor of the Color class

Constructor	Description
`Color(intRed, intGreen, intBlue)`	Creates a Color object that represents the color specified by the red, green, and blue values. These values are on a scale of 0-255.

A method of the Graphics class that sets colors

Method	Description
`setColor(Color)`	Sets the color of the Graphic object.

Methods of the Component class that set colors

Method	Description
`setBackground(Color)`	Sets the background color of this component.
`setForeground(Color)`	Sets the foreground color of this component.

Figure 14-5 How to set colors

The Fonts and Colors application

To show you how all of this works in the context of a complete application, figure 14-6 presents the Fonts and Colors application. It is a simple application that lets the user change the font family, style, size, and color of the text that's displayed.

The user interface

Part 1 of this figure shows the user interface for this application. As you can see, this interface has three combo boxes that let the user select the font family, font size, and color. It also has two check boxes that let the user select the bold and italic font styles. When the user changes any of these controls, the application changes the appearance of the text that's displayed.

The code

Part 1 of this figure continues with the code that defines the frame for the application. By now, you should be familiar with this type of code. This code defines the FontsFrame class that defines the frame, and it displays a panel of the FontsPanel class within the frame.

Part 2 of this figure presents the code for the start of the FontsPanel class. After it declares that the FontsPanel implements the ItemListener class, it declares the instance variables for the class. These instance variables include the combo boxes and check boxes of the application as well as an instance variable for a Font object and an instance variable for a Color object.

Within the constructor for the class, the first five statements create a combo box that contains all font names available to the current system. The next twelve statements create a combo box that contains seven possible font sizes, a combo box that contains four possible colors, a bold check box, and an italic check box. The rest of the statements add these components to a panel and add the panel to the north region of the current panel. Notice that the constructor sets the combo boxes and the current font so they specify a black, 18 point, sans serif font.

Part 3 of this figure starts with the code for the itemStateChanged method that's executed when the user generates an event by changing an item on the user interface. For each of these events, the statements within this method set the font family, font style, font size, and color based on the user's selections. Then, the last statement calls the repaint method of the current object (the BookPanel object). This method calls a chain of methods that eventually calls the paintComponent method of the current object.

The statements within the paintComponent method set the current font and color of the graphics context based on the user's selections. The statements after that use font metrics to get the width and height of the string. And the last statement draws the string in the center of the panel.

The user interface

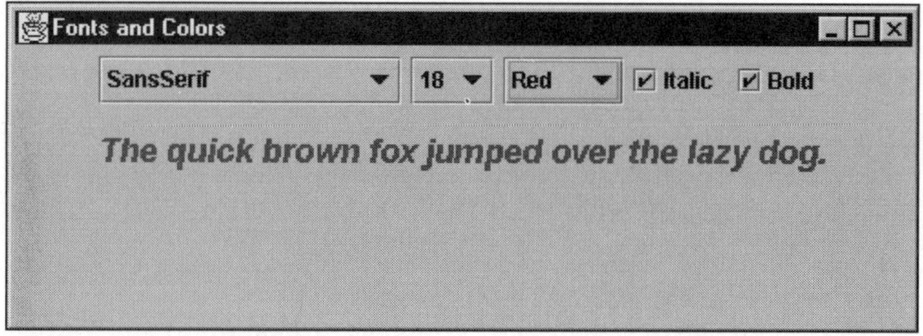

The code

```
import java.awt.*;
import java.awt.event.*;
import javax.swing.*;

public class FontsFrame extends JFrame{
   public FontsFrame(){
      setTitle("Fonts and Colors");
      Toolkit tk = Toolkit.getDefaultToolkit();
      Dimension d = tk.getScreenSize();
      int width = 500;
      int height = 175;
      setBounds((int) (d.width-width)/2,
                (int) (d.height-height)/2, width, height);
      addWindowListener(new WindowAdapter(){
         public void windowClosing(WindowEvent e){
            System.exit(0);
         }
      });
      Container contentPane = getContentPane();
      FontsPanel panel = new FontsPanel();
      contentPane.add(panel);
   }
   public static void main(String[] args){
      FontsFrame frame = new FontsFrame();
      frame.show();
   }
}
```

Figure 14-6 The Fonts and Colors application (part 1 of 3)

The code (continued)

```
class FontsPanel extends JPanel implements ItemListener{
   JComboBox fontComboBox, sizeComboBox, colorComboBox;
   JCheckBox boldCheckBox, italicCheckBox;
   Font font;
   Color color;

   public FontsPanel(){

      GraphicsEnvironment ge;
      ge = GraphicsEnvironment.getLocalGraphicsEnvironment();
      fontComboBox = new JComboBox(ge.getAvailableFontFamilyNames());
      fontComboBox.setSelectedItem("SansSerif");
      fontComboBox.addItemListener(this);

      String[] sizes = {"8", "10", "12", "14", "16", "18", "20"};
      sizeComboBox = new JComboBox(sizes);
      sizeComboBox.setSelectedItem("18");
      sizeComboBox.addItemListener(this);

      String[] colors = {"Black", "Red", "Blue", "Green"};
      colorComboBox = new JComboBox(colors);
      colorComboBox.setSelectedItem("Black");
      colorComboBox.addItemListener(this);

      boldCheckBox = new JCheckBox("Bold");
      boldCheckBox.addItemListener(this);

      italicCheckBox = new JCheckBox("Italic");
      italicCheckBox.addItemListener(this);

      JPanel northPanel = new JPanel();
      northPanel.add(fontComboBox);
      northPanel.add(sizeComboBox);
      northPanel.add(colorComboBox);
      northPanel.add(italicCheckBox);
      northPanel.add(boldCheckBox);

      setLayout(new BorderLayout());
      add(northPanel, BorderLayout.NORTH);
      font = new Font("SansSerif", Font.PLAIN, 18);
   }
```

Figure 14-6 The Fonts and Colors application (part 2 of 3)

The code (continued)

```
    public void itemStateChanged(ItemEvent e){
        String fontFamily = (String) fontComboBox.getSelectedItem();
        int style = Font.PLAIN;
        String sizeInt = (String) sizeComboBox.getSelectedItem();
        int size = Integer.parseInt(sizeInt);
        String colorString = (String) colorComboBox.getSelectedItem();
        if (colorString.equals("Black"))
            color = Color.black;
        else if (colorString.equals("Blue"))
            color = Color.blue;
        else if (colorString.equals("Red"))
            color = Color.red;
        else if (colorString.equals("Green"))
            color = Color.green;
        if ((boldCheckBox.isSelected()) && (italicCheckBox.isSelected()))
            style = Font.BOLD + Font.ITALIC;
        else if (boldCheckBox.isSelected())
            style = Font.BOLD;
        else if (italicCheckBox.isSelected())
            style = Font.ITALIC;
        font = new Font(fontFamily, style, size);
        repaint();
    }

    public void paintComponent(Graphics g){
        super.paintComponent(g);
        g.setFont(font);
        g.setColor(color);
        String text = "The quick brown fox jumped over the lazy dog.";
        FontMetrics fm = g.getFontMetrics();
        int widthPanel= getWidth();
        int heightPanel = getHeight();
        int widthString = fm.stringWidth(text);
        int heightString = fm.getHeight();
        g.drawString(text, (widthPanel - widthString)/2,
            (heightPanel-heightString)/2);
    }
}
```

Figure 14-6 The Fonts and Colors application (part 3 of 3)

How to work with images and icons

In this topic, you'll learn how to work with images and icons. First, you'll learn how to use the Graphics object to display images. Then, you'll learn how to display a special type of image known as an *icon* within certain types of components such as frames and buttons.

How to display images

Figure 14-7 shows how to use the Graphics object to display an image in a component. After it shows some code examples that work with images, this figure summarizes some methods of the Toolkit and Graphics class that you can use to display images.

When you work with images in Java, you need to know that Java only supports images in the GIF or JPG file formats. Before you can work with images in another format, then, you must convert them to GIF or JPG format.

The first example shows how to create an Image object. Here, the first statement creates a Toolkit object. Then, the next four statements use the Toolkit object to retrieve the image for the Murach logo. Each of these statements uses a slightly different string to specify the location of the image. The second statement points to the current directory, the third statement points to the file in the c:\logos directory, the fourth statement points to the file in the logos subdirectory of the current directory, and the fifth statement points to the file one directory up from the current directory.

The second example shows how to draw an image on a component. Typically, this code is located within the paintComponent method for a Graphics object. Here, the first statement displays the image for the Murach logo. This statement specifies the x and y coordinates for the logo and identifies the current object as the ImageObserver. When executed, this code displays a logo like the one shown at the top of the figure. Since no height and width are specified for this image, this code uses the number of pixels that are saved in the file for the height and width. In other words, this statement sizes the image at 100%. In contrast, the second statement sizes the image to the specified width and height so the image is adjusted to that size when it's displayed. To set the width and height of the image to the same dimensions as the component, the getWidth and getHeight methods can be used. These two methods belong to the Component class and can be used to return the current width and height of any component. In this example, these methods return the dimensions of the component with this graphics context.

When Java loads an image, it notifies the ImageObserver object whenever more information about the image becomes available. Since the Component class implements the ImageObserver interface, any component can act as the observer. So for most applications, you can specify the current object as the ImageObserver object.

An example that displays an image

Code that creates Image objects

```
Toolkit tk = Toolkit.getDefaultToolkit();
Image murachLogo1 = tk.getImage("MurachLogo.gif");
Image murachLogo2 = tk.getImage("C:\\logos\\MurachLogo.gif");
Image murachLogo3 = tk.getImage("logos\\MurachLogo.gif");
Image murachLogo4 = tk.getImage("..\\MurachLogo.gif");
```

Code that draws an image in the paintComponent method

```
g.drawImage(murachLogo, 30, 40, this);
g.drawImage(murachLogo, 0, 0, getWidth(), getHeight(), this);
```

Methods of the Toolkit class that work with images

Method	Description
getDefaultToolkit()	A static method that returns a Toolkit object.
getImage(StringFileName**)**	Returns an Image object for the image that corresponds to the specified string.

Methods of the Graphics class that draw images

Method	Description
drawImage(Image, intX, intY, ImageObserver**)**	Draws as much of the image as possible starting at the specified x and y coordinates.
drawImage(Image, intX, intY, intWidth, intHeight, ImageObserver**)**	Draws as much of the image as possible starting at the specified x and y coordinates and scales the image so it fits within the specified width and height.

Description

- Java only supports the GIF and JPEG image formats. So, before you can use images with other formats, you need to convert them to the GIF or JPEG format.
- Besides the two drawImage methods, the Graphics class contains four other drawImage methods that allow other options. For more information about these methods, you can look them up in the documentation for the Java API.
- The ImageObserver object receives information about an image as the image is being loaded. Since the Component class implements the ImageObserver interface, you can use any component as the ImageObserver object. This implementation of the ImageObserver interface lets the component be repainted as more of the image becomes available.

Figure 14-7 How to display images

How to display icons

Figure 14-8 shows how to get images and display them as *icons* in components. In general, icons are small images that are specifically designed to fit on a frame, button, or menu item. To illustrate, this figure starts with a frame that has an icon in its title bar plus two buttons that contain icons. After the code examples show how to create and set icons, this figure summarizes some of the constructors and methods of the ImageIcon class that you can use to work with icons.

The first example shows how to set an icon for a frame. Here, the first two statements use the ImageIcon class to return an Image object for an icon. Alternatively, you could use the Toolkit class to return the Image object as shown in the last figure. However, it's recommended that you use the ImageIcon class to return Image objects when working with Swing components. No matter how the Image object is returned, though, the third statement calls the setIconImage method to set the icon for the current object, which is the frame. This code displays the icon in the upper left corner of the frame and in the taskbar as shown in this figure.

The second example shows how to set an icon for a button. Here, the first statement creates an ImageIcon object. Then, the second statement creates a button, and the third statement uses the setIcon method to set the icon for the button shown in the user interface. Note, however, that you can use similar code to add icons to any class derived from the AbstractButton class, which includes menu items, check boxes, and radio buttons.

You can also display images on Swing components, such as labels, by using a constructor that has an Icon object argument. When you use this constructor, the specified image is displayed full size on the component. If you use this technique, you can prevent interfering with the painting process by overriding the paintComponent method.

An example that displays three icons

A taskbar that shows the icon for a minimized frame

Code that sets the icon of a frame in its constructor

```
ImageIcon murachIconImage = new ImageIcon("MurachIcon.gif");
Image murachIcon = murachIconImage.getImage();
setIconImage(murachIcon);
```

Code that adds an icon to a button

```
ImageIcon buttonIcon = new ImageIcon("MurachIcon.gif");
JButton createOrdersButton = new JButton("Create Book Orders");
createOrdersButton.setIcon(buttonIcon);
```

Some methods that set icons

Class	Method	Description
Frame	`setIconImage(Image)`	Sets the icon for the frame.
AbstractButton	`setIcon(Icon)`	Sets the icon for the button.

Some constructors and methods of the ImageIcon class

Constructor/Method	Description
`ImageIcon(StringFileName)`	Creates an ImageIcon object from the file specified by the string.
`getImage()`	Returns an Image object from the ImageIcon object.

Description

- Since the ImageIcon class implements the Icon interface, you can use an object of the ImageIcon class anywhere an Icon object is accepted.
- If you add a large icon to a component, the component will grow to fit the icon. For instance, if you add a large image as an icon to a button, then the button will appear large enough to fit the image inside it.

Figure 14-8 How to display icons

How to draw and fill shapes with the Graphics class

In this topic, you'll learn how to draw and fill shapes using methods of the Graphics class. This is an older technique for working with shapes that was introduced in version 1.0 of Java. Then, in the next topic, you'll learn how to use a newer technique that was introduced in version 1.2 of Java.

In general, you should use the newer technique whenever possible. But for certain types of programs, such as older applets, you may need to use the Graphics class.

How to draw shapes with the Graphics class

Figure 14-9 shows how to draw shapes with the Graphics class. To start, this figure shows a frame that displays seven types of shapes. Then, this figure shows three examples that draw these shapes, and it summarizes the methods of the Graphics and Polygon classes that you can use to draw shapes. You can use these methods when you override the paint or paintComponent methods.

The first example shows how to draw lines, rectangles, ovals, and arcs. If you compare the statements with the methods below and the shapes above, you should be able to figure out how each statement works. For instance, the second statement draws a rectangle that starts 120 pixels to the right and 30 pixels down from the upper left corner of the panel, and this rectangle has a width of 70 pixels and a height of 40 pixels. Similarly, the fifth statement draws an open arc that starts 30 pixels to the right and 90 pixels down from the upper left corner of the panel, and this arc starts at an angle of 30 degrees and extends for 120 degrees.

The second example shows one way to draw a triangle. Here, the first two statements create the three x and y points for the triangle, and the third statement uses a constructor of the Polygon class to create a triangle from these three points. Then, the last statement uses the drawPolygon method of the Graphics class to draw the triangle.

Similarly, the third example shows one way to create a diamond shape. Here, the first statement creates a Polygon object that doesn't contain any points, and the next four statements use the addPoint method of the Polygon object to add four points. Then, the last statement uses the drawPolygon method of the Graphics class to draw the diamond.

The rest of this figure presents methods of the Graphics class that you can use to draw shapes on a component. Most of these methods are self-explanatory. Before you can use the drawPolygon method, though, you must use the constructors and methods of the Polygon class to create an appropriate Polygon object.

An example that displays shapes

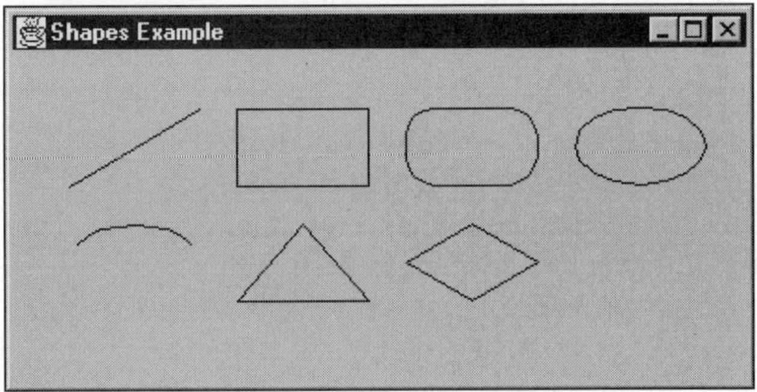

Code that draws lines, rectangles, and ovals

```
g.drawLine(100,30,30,70);
g.drawRect(120,30,70,40);
g.drawRoundRect(210,30,70,40,30,30);
g.drawOval(300,30,70,40);
g.drawArc(30,90,70,40,30,120);
```

Code that draws a triangle

```
int[] xPoints = {120,155,190};
int[] yPoints = {130,90,130};
Polygon triangle = new Polygon(xPoints, yPoints, 3);
g.drawPolygon(triangle);
```

Code that draws a diamond

```
Polygon diamond = new Polygon();
diamond.addPoint(210,110);
diamond.addPoint(245,90);
diamond.addPoint(280,110);
diamond.addPoint(245,130);
g.drawPolygon(diamond);
```

Methods of the Graphics class that draw shapes

```
drawLine(intX1, intY1, intX2, intY2)
drawRect(intX, intY, intWidth, intHeight)
drawRoundRect(intX, intY, intWidth, intHeight, intArcWidth, intArcHeight)
drawOval(intX, intY, intWidth, intHeight)
drawArc(intX, intY, intWidth, intHeight, intStartAngle, intArcAngle)
drawPolygon(Polygon)
```

Constructors and methods of the Polygon class

```
Polygon()
Polygon(xPointsArray, yPointsArray, intNumberOfPoints)
addPoint(intX, intY)
```

Figure 14-9 How to draw shapes with the Graphics class

How to fill shapes with the Graphics class

Figure 14-10 shows how to fill shapes. To start, it shows a frame that shows six figures that have been filled. Then, it shows three code examples that use the fill method to both draw and fill those shapes. These code examples show that the only difference between drawing shapes and filling shapes is that you use the fillXXX method instead of the drawXXX method. As a result, the code shown in this figure and the methods summarized at the bottom of this figure should be review.

When you call one of the fillXXX methods, the color that's used depends on the graphics context. By default, the graphics context uses black, but you can use the setColor method of the Graphics object to change the fill color. For example, you can use a statement like this

```
g.setColor(Color.red);
```

to change the fill color to red. Then, all fillXXX methods that are called after this statement will use red until another statement changes the color again.

An example that displays filled shapes

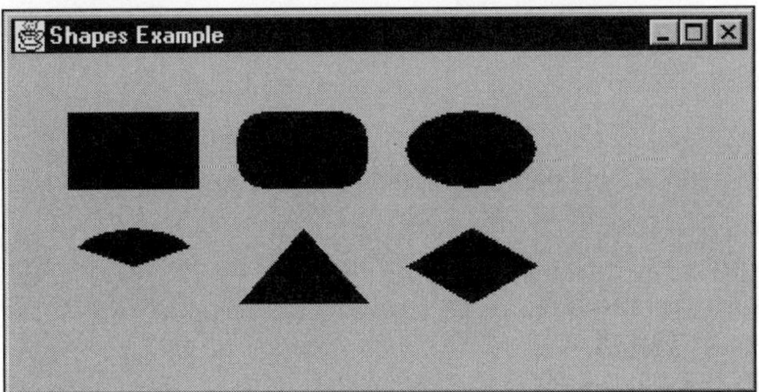

Code that fills lines, rectangles, and ovals

```
g.fillRect(30,30,70,40);
g.fillRoundRect(120,30,70,40,30,30);
g.fillOval(210,30,70,40);
g.fillArc(30,90,70,40,30,120);
```

Code that fills a triangle

```
int[] xPoints = {120,155,190};
int[] yPoints = {130,90,130};
Polygon triangle = new Polygon(xPoints, yPoints, 3);
g.fillPolygon(triangle);
```

Code that fills a diamond

```
Polygon diamond = new Polygon();
diamond.addPoint(210,110);
diamond.addPoint(245,90);
diamond.addPoint(280,110);
diamond.addPoint(245,130);
g.fillPolygon(diamond);
```

Methods of the Graphics class that fill shapes

```
fillRect(intX, intY, intWidth, intHeight)
fill3DRect(intX, intY, intWidth, intHeight, booleanRaised)
fillRoundRect(intX, intY, intWidth, intHeight, intArcWidth, intArcHeight)
fillOval(intX, intY, intWidth, intHeight)
fillArc(intX, intY, intWidth, intHeight, intStartAngle, intArcAngle)
fillPolygon(Polygon)
```

Description

- The fill methods work just like the draw methods except that they both draw and fill the shape.
- The color that's used to fill a shape is the color of the graphics context.

Figure 14-10 How to fill shapes with the Graphics class

How to draw and fill shapes with the Java2D API

Version 1.2 of Java introduced some new classes for working with graphics known as the *Java2D API*. These classes use an architecture that's more consistent with the principles of object-oriented programming. In addition, these classes provide advanced drawing capabilities that go beyond the capabilities that are available from the Graphics class. Although the advanced features of the Java2D API go beyond the scope of this book, this topic shows you how to use the Java2D API to draw the same shapes that you learned how to draw with the Graphics class.

An introduction to the Java2D API

Figure 14-11 introduces you to the Java2D API. To start, it shows that the Graphics2D class inherits the Graphics class. Then, it shows some of the packages that the Java2D API uses, and it summarizes some of the classes that the Java2D API uses to work with shapes.

When you use the Graphics class to draw shapes, you use a method of the Graphics class to draw a shape. When you use the Java2D API to work with shapes, you first create a shape from a class. Then, you call a method of the Graphics2D class to draw the shape. This is an approach that's more consistent with the principles of object-oriented design, and this makes it easier to work with shapes.

The summary in this figure shows some of the classes that you can use to define shapes. All of these classes are located in the java.awt.geom package, and the superclasses are abstract classes. To create an object from these classes, you must use the appropriate subclass, which is an inner class of the superclass. Although these subclasses work similarly, they accept different types of arguments. All of these classes implement the Shape interface.

The graphics hierarchy

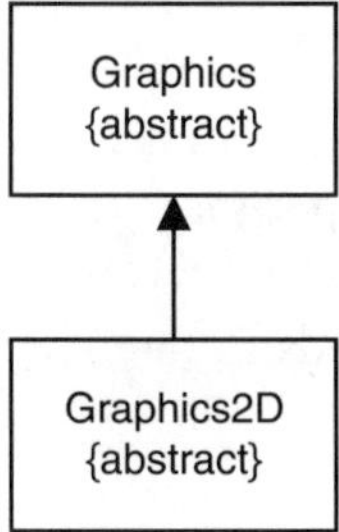

Other packages used by the Java2D API

```
java.awt.font          java.awt.color
java.awt.geom          java.awt.image
java.awt.print         java.awt.image.renderable
```

Some classes of the java.awt.geom package

Class	Subclass	Description
Line2D	Line2D.Double Line2D.Float	Classes that define a straight line.
Ellipse2D	Ellipse2D.Double Ellipse2D.Float	Classes that define a two-dimensional ellipse.
Rectangle2D	Rectangle2D.Double Rectangle2D.Float	Classes that define a rectangle by location and dimension.
RoundRectangle2D	RoundRectangle2D.Double RoundRectangle2D.Float	Classes that define a round rectangle by location, dimension, and the arc dimensions of the corners.
Arc2D	Arc2D.Double Arc2D.Float	Classes that define a two-dimensional arc.

Description

- The Graphics2D class was introduced with JDK1.2 as part of the *Java2D API*. The Java2D API provides graphic capabilities that go beyond the capabilities of the Graphics class. Both of these classes are stored in the java.awt package.
- All of the classes shown in this figure implement the Shape interface. As a result, you can use objects created from these classes anywhere a Shape object is accepted.
- All of the subclasses shown in this figure are inner classes of the abstract superclass. For example, the Line2D.Double and Line2D.Float classes are inner classes of the abstract Line2D class.

Figure 14-11 A summary of the packages and classes in the Java2D API

How to draw and fill shapes with the Java2D API

Part 1 of figure 14-12 shows how to use the Graphics2D class to draw and fill shapes, and part 2 of this figure summarizes the constructors you need to use to create shapes. To start, part 1 shows a frame that displays some shapes that are filled and some that aren't. Then, after this part of the figure shows examples that draw and fill these shapes, it summarizes the two methods of the Graphics2D class that you can use to draw and fill shapes.

The first example shows how to create Shape objects from the Java2D shapes. Here, the first statement creates a line object from the Line2D.Double class. The second statement creates a rectangle object from the Rectangle2D.Double class. And so on. These statements work because all of the Java2D shape objects implement the Shape interface.

The second example shows how to use the Graphics2D object to draw one of these Shape objects. Within the paintComponent method, the first statement casts the Graphics parameter to an object of the Graphics2D type. Then, the second statement creates an ellipse, and the third statement calls the draw method from the Graphics2D object with the Shape object as the argument.

The third example shows a statement that fills an ellipse instead of drawing an ellipse. If you wanted to display a filled ellipse, you could use this statement instead of the third statement in the second example.

The fourth example shows how to draw a triangle. Here, the first three statements use two arrays and the Polygon class to create a triangle. This code is exactly the same as the code presented in the last topic. However, the fourth statement uses the fill method of the Graphics2D object to fill the Polygon.

An example that displays shapes and filled shapes

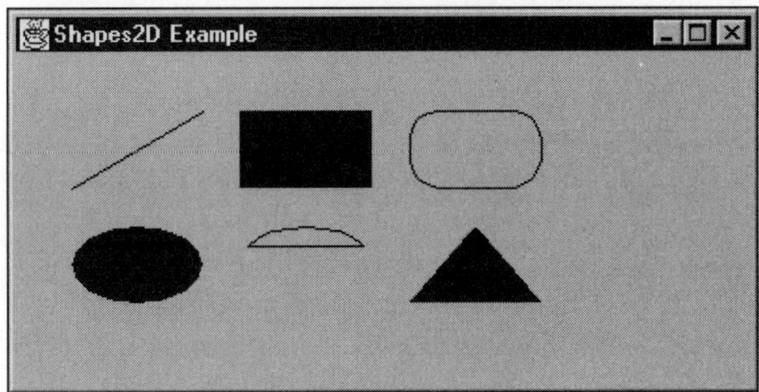

Code that creates Java2D shapes

```
Shape line = new Line2D.Double(100,30,30,70);
Shape rectangle = new Rectangle2D.Double(120,30,70,40);
Shape roundRectangle = new RoundRectangle2D.Double(210,30,70,40,30,30);
Shape ellipse = new Ellipse2D.Double(30,90,70,40);
Shape arc = new Arc2D.Double(120,90,70,40,30,120,Arc2D.CHORD);
```

A method that uses the Graphics2D context to draw a shape

```
public void paintComponent(Graphics g){
    Graphics2D g2D = (Graphics2D) g;
    Shape ellipse = new Ellipse2D.Double(30,90,70,40);
    g2D.draw(ellipse);
}
```

Code that uses the Graphics 2D context to fill a shape

```
g2D.fill(ellipse);
```

Code that creates and fills a triangle

```
int[] xPoints = {210,245,280};
int[] yPoints = {130,90,130};
Polygon triangle = new Polygon(xPoints, yPoints, 3);
g2D.fill(triangle);
```

Methods of the Graphics2D class that draw and fill shapes

Method	Description
draw(Shape)	Draws the outline of the Shape using the current graphics context.
fill(Shape)	Fills the Shape using the current graphics context.

Description

- Since the paintComponent method accepts a Graphics object, you must first cast this object to a Graphics2D object in order to use Java2D API features.
- Since the Polygon class implements the Shape interface, you can supply an object of the Polygon class to the draw or fill method.

Figure 14-12 How to draw and fill shapes using the Java2D API (part 1 of 2)

Part 2 of figure 14-12 summarizes the constructors for the shapes used in part 1. In addition, it summarizes the three fields of the Arc2D class that you can use as the type argument of the Arc2D constructor. Since each of the constructors accepts arguments similar to those for the corresponding draw method in the Graphics class, this figure should be review. For example, the Rectangle2D.Double constructor accepts position and size arguments similar to those for the drawRect method in the Graphics class. And the Ellipse2D.Double constructor accepts arguments similar to those for the drawOval method.

When you use the Arc2D class, you need to supply a type argument. To do that, you can use one of the three fields from the Arc2D class summarized in this figure. If you don't want any lines joining the two end points, you use an open arc. If you want one straight line joining the two end points, you use a chord arc. And if you want one line from each end of the arc to the center of the circle that the arc is a part of, you use a pie arc.

Constructors of the Java2D API classes

```
Line2D.Double(doubleX1, doubleY1, doubleX2, doubleY2)
Line2D.Float(floatX1, floatY1, floatX2, floatY2)
Ellipse2D.Double(doubleX, doubleY, doubleWidth, doubleHeight)
Ellipse2D.Float(floatX, floatY, floatWidth, floatHeight)
Rectangle2D.Double(doubleX, doubleY, doubleWidth, doubleHeight)
Rectangle2D.Float(floatX, floatY, floatWidth, floatHeight)
RoundRectangle2D.Double(doubleX, doubleY, doubleWidth, doubleHeight,
                        doubleArcWidth, doubleArcHeight)
RoundRectangle2D.Float(floatX, floatY, floatWidth, floatHeight,
                       floatArcWidth, floatArcHeight)
Arc2D.Double(doubleX, doubleY, doubleWidth, doubleHeight,
             doubleStartAngle, doubleExtentAngle, intType)
Arc2D.Float(floatX, floatY, floatWidth, floatHeight,
            floatStartAngle, floatExtentAngle, intType)
```

Arc types from the Arc2D class

```
OPEN          CHORD          PIE
```

Description

- The arguments for the constructors of the Java2D API classes are similar to those for the draw methods in the Graphics class.
- When you use a constructor of the Arc2D class, you can use the arc type fields as the last argument to indicate how you want the arc drawn.

Figure 14-12 How to draw and fill shapes using the Java2D API (part 2 of 2)

The Shapes application

To show how all of this code works in the context of a complete application, figure 14-13 presents the Shapes application. Although this application serves no practical purpose, it does illustrate some of the coding issues.

The user interface

The user interface lets the user select a shape from a combo box that lists five shapes. Then, the application displays the selected shape below the combo box.

The code

After the user interface, you can see the code for the ShapesPanel class of this application. This class defines the panel that is displayed within the frame that's defined by the ShapesFrame class. Since the ShapesFrame class works like the FontsFrame class shown earlier in this chapter, it isn't shown in this figure.

The ShapesPanel class begins by declaring that it implements the ItemListener interface. Then, it declares two instance variables. The first instance variable refers to the combo box while the second instance variable refers to the Shape object that's created when the user selects an item from the combo box.

Within the constructor for the class, the first four statements create the combo box and add an item listener to it. Then, the fifth statement sets the initially selected shape to a rectangle, and the sixth statement initializes the instance variable for the Shape object to a Rectangle2D.Double object.

When the user selects an item from the combo box, the itemStateChanged method handles the ItemEvent object that's generated. Within this method, the first statement returns the string for the selected shape, and the second statement sets the x and y coordinates, the width, and height for the shape. Then, a series of if/else statements create an appropriate shape object and assign it to the instance variable for the Shape object. The last statement in this method calls the repaint method, which eventually calls the paintComponent method.

Here again, it is the paintComponent method that actually draws the current Shape object. Since this method is automatically called when the frame is first displayed, it initially draws the rectangle that's defined in the constructor for the panel. Then, whenever a user selects an object, this method draws that object. To do that, the third statement in this method calls the draw method of the Graphics2D object, and it supplies the Shape object instance variable as the argument.

The user interface

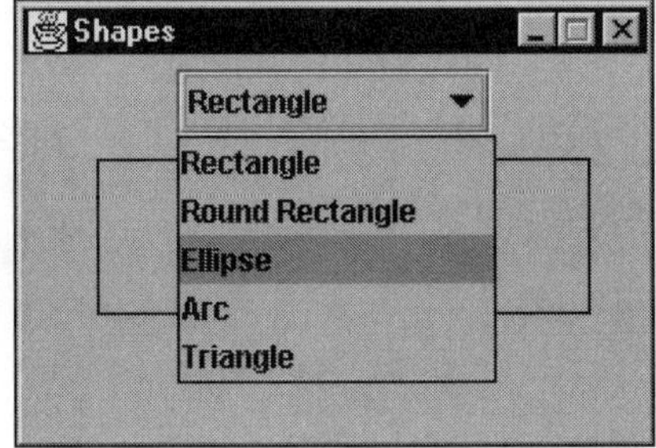

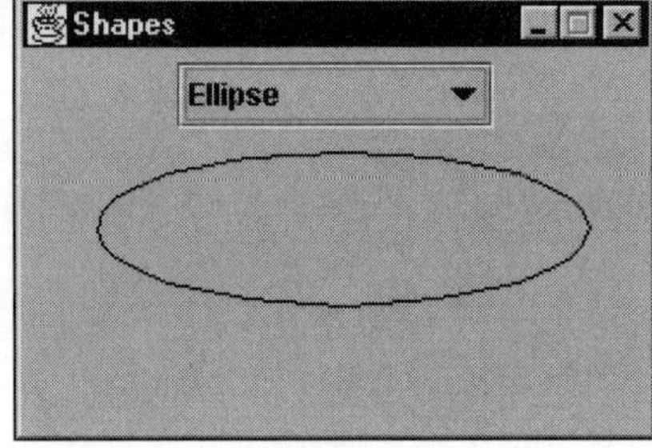

The code for the ShapesPanel class

```
class ShapesPanel extends JPanel implements ItemListener{

   JComboBox shapeComboBox;
   Shape shape;

   public ShapesPanel(){
      String[] shapes = {"Rectangle", "Round Rectangle", "Ellipse",
                         "Arc", "Triangle"};
      shapeComboBox = new JComboBox(shapes);
      shapeComboBox.addItemListener(this);
      add(shapeComboBox);
      shapeComboBox.setSelectedItem("Rectangle");
      shape = new Rectangle2D.Double(30, 40, 200, 60);
   }

   public void itemStateChanged(ItemEvent e){
      String shapeString = (String)shapeComboBox.getSelectedItem();
      int x = 30, y = 40, w = 200, h = 60;
      if (shapeString.equals("Rectangle"))
         shape = new Rectangle2D.Double(x, y, w, h);
      else if (shapeString.equals("Round Rectangle"))
         shape = new RoundRectangle2D.Double(x, y, w, h, 40, 40);
      else if (shapeString.equals("Ellipse"))
         shape = new Ellipse2D.Double(x, y, w, h);
      else if (shapeString.equals("Arc"))
         shape = new Arc2D.Double(x, y, w, h, 30, 210, Arc2D.CHORD);
      else if (shapeString.equals("Triangle")){
         int[] xPoints = {x, (x+w)/2, w};
         int[] yPoints = {y+h, y, y+h};
         shape = new Polygon(xPoints, yPoints, 3);
      }
      repaint();
   }

   public void paintComponent(Graphics g){
      super.paintComponent(g);
      Graphics2D g2D = (Graphics2D) g;
      g2D.draw(shape);
   }
}
```

Figure 14-13 The Shapes application

Perspective

In this chapter, you've learned how to work with fonts, colors, images, and shapes. Skills like these are occasionally useful when you create normal user interfaces. As you will see in the next chapter, though, they can also be used with applets.

Summary

- To access the *graphics context* for a Swing component, you inherit the component and override its paintComponent method. Then, you can use the Graphics object to set fonts and colors, to draw text, to draw shapes, and to fill shapes.
- You can set the font for the graphics context or for a component. To make sure that a font maps to a font that's available on the current system, you can use one of the *logical fonts* provided by the Java API.
- You can use font metrics to determine the height of a specific font or the length of a string with a specific font.
- You can set the color for the graphics context or for the foreground or background of a specific component.
- You can display JPG or GIF images within Java programs, and you can display *icons* within frames and most types of buttons including menu items, radio buttons, and check boxes.
- You can use the methods of the Graphics class to draw and fill shapes such as lines, rectangles, ovals, and triangles. However, the Java API also provides a newer, more sophisticated technology known as the *Java2D API* that can accomplish the same tasks.

Terms

paint
graphics context
graphics rendering context
logical font
icon
Java2D API

Objectives

- Write code that sets fonts and colors.
- Write code that displays images and adds icons to frames and buttons.
- Write code that displays shapes.

Exercise 14-1 Create the Fonts and Colors application

1. Open the code for the FontsFrame class that's in the c:\java\ch14\fonts directory. Then, compile and run this code. When you do, the application should allow you to select a font family, size, style, and color, but it won't display the text with the appropriate selections.
2. Fix this code so it does display the text the right way. Then, compile and run this application to make sure that it works correctly.

Exercise 14-2 Enhance the Shapes application

1. Open the code for the ShapesFrame class that's in the c:\java\ch14\shapes directory. Then, compile and run this code. It should work as shown in figure 14-13.
2. Add a checkbox that lets the user fill the shape. Then, add a color combobox that lets the user select a color for the shape. When you're done, the user interface should look like this:

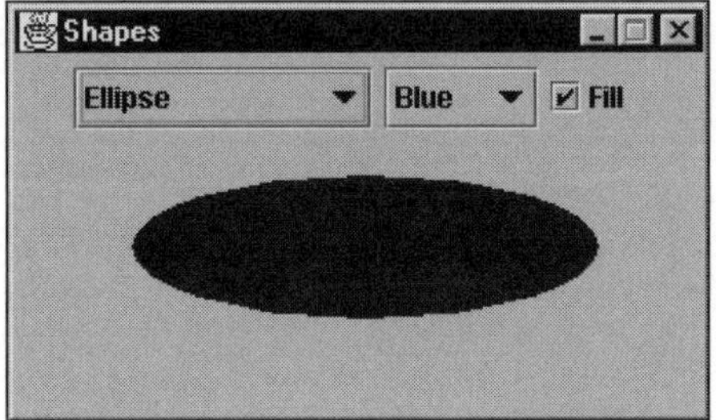

3. Add the event handling code that makes this user interface work correctly.

Exercise 14-3 Add an icon to the Book Order application

1. Open the code for the BookOrderFrame class that's in the c:\java\ch14\book directory. Then, edit this class so the frame displays the icon in the MurachIcon.gif file that's in the c:\java\ch14\book directory. When you're done, the frame should look like this:

2. Compile and test the application to make sure it works correctly.

15

How to develop applets

The last four chapters of this book have shown you how to develop user interfaces for applications that are run in the traditional way. That is, the applications are installed on each user's computer or on a network server so they can be run on each user's computer.

In this chapter, you'll learn how to develop an *applet*, a special type of application that can be stored in a web page and run within a web browser. Applets are unique to the Java language, and they helped fuel the remarkable growth and hype of Java in its early days.

An introduction to applets

This topic gives you the background information you need for working with applets. To start, it shows two types of applets and describes the inheritance chain for working with applets. Then, it summarizes some deployment and security issues, plus the four methods that control the execution of every applet.

Two versions of the Loan Calculator applet

In chapter 11, you learned how to create the Loan Calculator application. In this chapter, you'll learn how to convert that application to an *applet*, and you'll learn how to place the applet within a *web page* that's defined by the *Hypertext Markup Language* (*HTML*). Then, when a web browser views the HTML page, the applet will run within the web browser.

Figure 15-1 shows two versions of the Loan Calculator applet when it's viewed within the Internet Explorer. The first version shows the Loan Calculator applet as a *Swing applet*. This applet uses the Swing components that you learned about in chapter 11. The second version shows the Loan Calculator applet as an *AWT applet*. This applet uses AWT components instead of Swing components. Note that there's little visual difference when the applets are running, although the code is different.

Why would you want to create AWT applets instead of Swing applets? Because both the Internet Explorer and Netscape web browsers contain *Java virtual machines* (*JVMs*) that can run AWT applets. As a result, anyone with one of these web browsers can run AWT applets. In contrast, neither web browser currently supports Swing applets. To get around this problem, Sun has created a plug-in that lets either web browser run Swing applets, but this plug-in needs to be installed on every client system that's going to use the applets. This, of course, limits the use of Swing applets.

The Loan Calculator applet (Swing version)

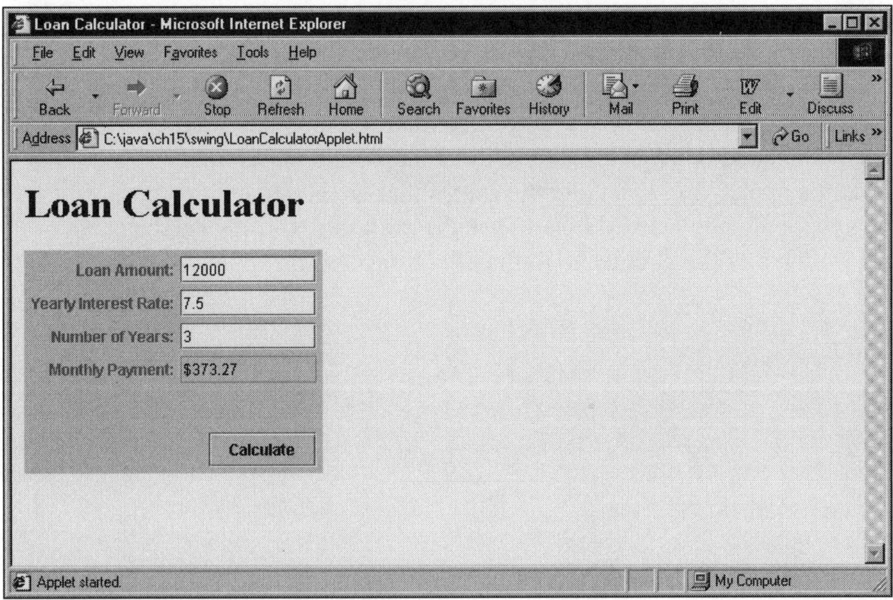

The Loan Calculator applet (AWT version)

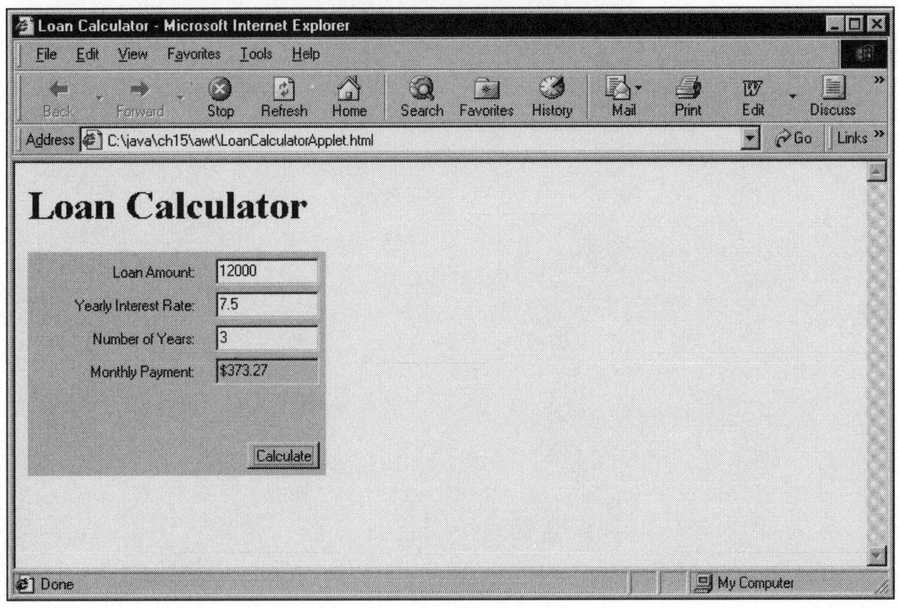

Figure 15-1 An introduction to applets

The inheritance chain for applets

Figure 15-2 presents the inheritance chain for applets. This shows that you can use the Applet class to define an AWT applet, or you can use the JApplet class to define a Swing applet. Either way, you can use the methods from the Component and Container classes to work with the applet, to place other components on the applet, and to handle the events that are generated for the applet. Since you've already learned how to use these classes, this means that you already have most of the skills that you need for developing applets.

The inheritance chain for applets

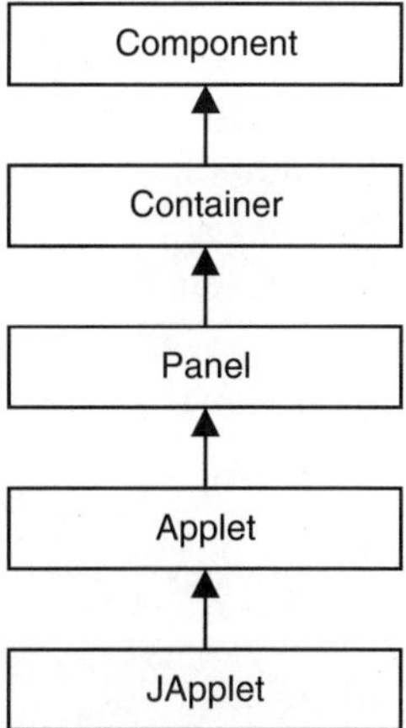

Summary of these classes

Class	Description
Component	An abstract base class that defines any object that can be displayed. For instance, frames, panels, buttons, labels, and text fields are derived from this class.
Container	An abstract class that defines any component that can contain other components.
Panel	The AWT class that defines a panel.
Applet	The AWT class that defines an applet. This class is stored in the java.applet package.
JApplet	The Swing class that defines an applet. This class is stored in the javax.swing package.

Description

- An *applet* is a special type of application that's included as part of an HTML page and runs within a browser.
- To create an applet, you define a class that inherits the Applet or JApplet class.

Figure 15-2 The inheritance chain for applets

Applet deployment issues

After Java 1.0 was released, both the Internet Explorer and Netscape browsers included a Java virtual machine (JVM) that could run Java 1.0. This allowed anyone with one of these web browsers to access applets and run them. Unfortunately, neither browser has kept up with the new versions of Java. As a result, most browsers support Java 1.0 and many browsers support Java 1.1, but few support Java 1.2 and later versions.

To allow the Internet Explorer and Netscape browsers to run Swing applets that use the latest features of Java, Sun created a tool called the *Java Plug-in* that extends the browser's capabilities. If the appropriate Java Plug-in is installed on a system, the browser on that system can run Swing applets that use the most current version of Java. Of course, this creates a deployment issue. That's one of the reasons that web programmers today often use HTML forms, CGI scripts, and animated GIFs instead of applets.

With that as background, figure 15-3 presents two options for deploying applets. On one hand, you can create AWT applets that use only the features from Java 1.0 and perhaps a few features of Java 1.1. This makes the applet easy to deploy, but it prevents you from using the newer features of Java. In addition, since different browsers contain slightly different JVMs, you may need to debug your application for each type of browser.

On the other hand, you can create Swing applets that use the new features of Java. In this case, though, you must make sure that the Java Plug-in is installed on each user's machine. Although you can do that for internal systems that are only used by your own employees, it's often difficult or impractical to do that for external systems that are used by customers or other types of users. That's why Swing applets are used the most for intranets.

Incidentally, when you install SDK versions 1.3 and later, the Java Plug-in is automatically installed on your system. As a result, you don't have to worry about this deployment issue as you develop and test Swing applets.

Two options for deploying applets

1. Write Swing applets and install the Java Plug-in on all of the client machines.
2. Write AWT applets using just the features of Java 1.0 or 1.1.

Swing applets

Pros

- Swing applets can use Swing components.
- Swing applets can use all of the current Java features.

Cons

- The developer needs to run the HTML Converter program on the HTML page before the applet can be viewed with a browser.
- The Java Plug-in must be installed on the client machines before the users can view the applet within a browser.

AWT applets

Pros

- No conversion is necessary for the HTML page.
- The Java plug-in isn't needed to view the applet within a browser.

Cons

- AWT applets can't use Swing components.
- AWT applets can't use any Java features that were introduced after Java 1.1. In most cases, it's best to stick to the Java features of Java 1.0.
- AWT applets are more difficult to debug.

Description

- Most web browsers, including most versions of Microsoft Internet Explorer and Netscape, contain a Java virtual machine that can run applets written in Java 1.0 and 1.1.
- When the Java Plug-in is installed on a client machine, the Internet Explorer and Netscape browsers can run the most current version of Java.
- When you download and install the SDK, the Java Plug-in is automatically installed on your machine so you can run the applets within your browser.
- Swing applets work best when you control the client environment as in an intranet environment. Then, you can make sure the Java Plug-in is installed on each user machine.

Figure 15-3 Applet deployment issues

Applet security issues

Since applets were designed to be downloaded from an Internet server and to be run on client systems, they have more security restrictions than applications. This prevents applets from intentionally or accidentally damaging the client system.

Figure 15-4 lists some of these security restrictions. This shows that an applet can't access any files or databases on the client system, and it can't access much information about the client system. In fact, an applet can only access the information it needs to run, such as the Java version and type of operating system that's used by the client.

Although applets have strong security restrictions by default, you can loosen these security restrictions. To do that, you can create *signed applets* that show that the applets comes from a trusted source. Then, an applet could, for example, read files from the client system's hard drive. Signed applets, though, are an advanced topic that goes beyond the scope of this book.

If you're wondering whether applets can read and write files on Internet, intranet, and network servers, the answer is, Yes. However, applets can't ordinarily do the read and write operations themselves. They can, though, send and receive data from other programs located on the host server. This way, another program can read and write files and transfer the data back and forth to the applet. Of course, this requires some networking techniques that aren't presented in this beginning book. That's why this chapter focuses on applets that don't read and write files or databases on servers.

What an applet can't do

- Read, write, or delete files or databases on the client system.
- Access information about the files or databases on the client system.
- Run programs on the client system.
- Access system properties for the client system except the Java version, the name and version of the operating system, and the characters used to separate directories, paths, and lines.
- Make network connections to other servers available to the client system.

What an applet can do

- Display user interface components and graphics.
- Send keystrokes and mouse clicks back to the applet's server.
- Make network connections to the applet's server.
- Call public methods from other applets on the same web page.

Description

- To prevent applets from damaging a client system or from making it possible to damage a client system, security restrictions limit what an applet can do.
- To overcome these security restrictions, you can create a *signed applet*. This indicates that the applet comes from a trusted source. Then, you can add rights to the signed applet.

Figure 15-4 Applet security issues

Four methods of an applet

Figure 15-5 introduces the four methods of the Applet class that are used to control the execution of any applet. Since the browser automatically calls these methods, you don't need to call them. However, you do need to override them in some cases.

In all but the simplest applets, for example, you'll override the init method to initialize the applet as shown in the next figure. Also, since the start and stop methods are typically used with threads, you'll learn more about them in chapter 20.

Four methods of the Applet class

Method	Description
`public void init()`	Called when the browser first loads the applet.
`public void start()`	Called after the init method and every time the user moves to the web page for the applet.
`public void stop()`	Called before the destroy method and every time the user moves to another web page.
`public void destroy()`	Called when the user exits the browser.

Description

- Since the browser or the Applet Viewer calls these methods when needed, you never need to call them. However, you may need to override them to get your applet to work properly.
- Figure 15-6 shows how to override the init method.
- Chapter 20 shows how to override the start and stop methods.

Figure 15-5 Four methods of an applet

How to develop Swing applets

In this topic, you'll learn how to develop and test a Swing applet by using a procedure like the one at the start of figure 15-6. After you learn how to code a Swing applet, you'll learn how to code the HTML page for the applet, how to test the applet with the Applet Viewer, how to convert the HTML page so it will run on Internet Explorer and Netscape, and how to test the applet within a browser.

How to convert a Swing application to a Swing applet

Instead of showing how to code a Swing applet from scratch, the second procedure in figure 15-6 shows how to convert a Swing application to a Swing applet. This procedure highlights the differences between the code for an applet and the code for an application. Then, this figure shows the code that results when the Loan Calculation application of chapter 11 is converted to an applet.

In step 1 of the conversion procedure, you modify the class so it extends the JApplet class instead of the JFrame class, and you override the init method to initialize the applet. This method then performs some of the same operations that were in the frame's constructor.

In step 2, you remove any code that sets the frame's size, location, or title because the applet's HTML page will accomplish these tasks. You remove any code that's used to exit the frame because an applet runs within a browser, not within a frame. And you remove the main method for the frame if there is one.

The code in this figure shows the Swing version of the Loan Calculation applet. Within the LoanCalculatorApplet class, the init method displays a LoanCalculatorPanel object on the content pane of the applet. Within the LoanCalculationPanel class, most of the code is the same as it was in the Loan Calculator application. The only difference is that all references to the Exit button have been removed. For example, this code doesn't contain an instance variable that refers to the Exit button. As a result, the actionPerformed method for the panel doesn't handle the event that's generated when the user clicks on the Exit button.

A procedure for developing a Swing applet

1. Code and compile the Swing applet.
2. Code the HTML page for the applet.
3. Test the applet with the Applet Viewer.
4. Use the HTML Converter to convert the HTML page for the applet.
5. Test the HTML page with a browser.

How to convert a Swing application to a Swing applet

1. Extend the JApplet class instead of the JFrame class, and convert the constructor of the JFrame class so it becomes the init method of the JApplet class.
2. Remove (1) any code that sets the title, size, and position of the frame; (2) any code that's used to exit the frame; and (3) the main method if one exists.

The code for a Swing applet

```
import java.awt.*;
import java.awt.event.*;
import javax.swing.*;
import java.text.*;

public class LoanCalculatorApplet extends JApplet{
   public void init(){
      Container contentPane = getContentPane();
      JPanel panel = new LoanCalculatorPanel();
      contentPane.add(panel);
   }
}

class LoanCalculatorPanel extends JPanel implements ActionListener{
   private JTextField amountTextField, rateTextField, yearsTextField,
                 paymentTextField;
   private JLabel amountLabel, rateLabel, yearsLabel, paymentLabel;
   private JButton calculateButton;

   public LoanCalculatorPanel(){
      // code that defines the LoanCalculatorPanel without an Exit button
   }

   public void actionPerformed(ActionEvent e){
      Object source = e.getSource();
      if (source == calculateButton){
         double amount = Double.parseDouble(amountTextField.getText());
         double rate = Double.parseDouble(rateTextField.getText())/12/100;
         int months = Integer.parseInt(yearsTextField.getText())*12;
         double payment = FinancialCalculations.calculateMonthlyPayment(
             amount, months, rate);
         NumberFormat currency = NumberFormat.getCurrencyInstance();
         paymentTextField.setText(currency.format(payment));
      }
   }
}
```

Figure 15-6 How to develop a Swing applet

How to code the HTML page for an applet

Figure 15-7 shows how to place the class file for an applet within an HTML page. To start, this figure shows the code for an HTML page that places the class file for the Loan Calculator application within an HTML page. Then, it summarizes seven basic HTML *tags* that you can use to place an applet within an HTML page. Last, it summarizes five *attributes* of the APPLET tag that you can use to provide additional information about the applet.

To code an HTML tag, you start with a tag name (like <HTML>) and end with the tag name preceded by a slash (like </HTML>). As you code, you'll often need to nest one tag within another tag. For instance, the HTML tag marks the start and end of an HTML page so all of the other tags are nested within it. Similarly, the BODY tag is coded around all of the code that makes up the body of the HTML page. This is where you place text, images, applets, and so on. In this figure, for example, the H1 tag displays "Loan Calculator" as a level-1 heading. Then, the APPLET tag tells the browser to display the specified applet with the specified width and height.

Within an APPLET tag, you code the attributes that provide additional information about the applet. In particular, you use the CODE attribute to specify the class file for the applet, and you use the WIDTH and HEIGHT attributes to specify the size of the applet in pixels. After the attributes, you can supply text that will be displayed when the user is unable to load the applet.

To enter and edit an HTML page, you can use any text editor, but you must save the HTML page in a file with HTML as the extension. Of course, you can do this with a general-purpose editor like NotePad or a special-purpose editor like TextPad.

Unfortunately, the APPLET tag that's described in this figure doesn't work for Swing applets. That's because the Java Plug-in doesn't recognize the APPLET tag. Before you can view a Swing applet in a browser, you must convert the APPLET tag to the OBJECT tag that's used by the Internet Explorer or the EMBED tag that's used by Netscape. In addition, when you use these two tags, you need to provide some complex attributes that aren't described in this figure. Fortunately, Sun provides a tool called the HTML Converter that can be used to convert the APPLET tag to the appropriate OBJECT and EMBED tags. In a moment, you'll learn how to use this tool.

How to place an applet in an HTML page

```
<HTML>
<TITLE>Loan Calculator</TITLE>
<BODY>
<H1>Loan Calculator</H1>
<APPLET CODE = "LoanCalculatorApplet.class"
        WIDTH = 240
        HEIGHT = 175>
If you can't see this applet, your web browser may not be Java-enabled.
</APPLET>
</BODY>
</HTML>
```

Some HTML tags

Tag	Description
`<HTML></HTML>`	Marks the beginning and end of an HTML document.
`<TITLE></TITLE>`	Defines the title of the HTML document.
`<BODY></BODY>`	Marks the beginning and end of the body of the HTML document.
`<H1></H1>`	Displays the enclosed text as a level-1 header.
`<APPLET></APPLET>`	Defines an applet within the HTML page. Although this tag has been deprecated (which means you shouldn't use it), most browsers still recognize it.
`<OBJECT></OBJECT>`	Defines an object within a document. Internet Explorer uses this tag to define Swing applets.
`<EMBED></EMBED>`	Embeds an application within the document. Netscape uses this tag to define Swing applets.

Some attributes for working with the APPLET tag

Attribute	Description
CODE	Specifies the class file of the applet to be executed.
WIDTH	Specifies the width of the applet in pixels.
HEIGHT	Specifies the height of the applet in pixels.
ARCHIVE	Specifies the archive file (such as a JAR file) to be downloaded.
CODEBASE	Specifies the location of the code on the server.

File naming convention

```
AppletClassName.html
```

Description

- The *Hypertext Markup Language* (HTML) is the language that's used to create web pages. Each HTML *tag* begins with the tag name and ends with the tag name prefixed by a forward slash. Within a tag, you can set the *attributes* for the tag.
- Although HTML isn't case sensitive, the Java applet filename is.
- Figure 15-9 shows how to use the HTML Converter to convert an APPLET tag to the OBJECT and EMBED tags.

Figure 15-7 How to code the HTML page for an applet

How to view an applet with the Applet Viewer

Although you can't view a Swing applet in a browser until you convert the APPLET tag to the appropriate OBJECT and EMBED tags, figure 15-8 shows how to view a Swing applet with the *Applet Viewer*. This is a tool that's included in the Java SDK, and it can read the APPLET tag.

To run the Applet Viewer from the command prompt, you enter the command shown in this figure. To do that, you start the command prompt and navigate to the directory that holds the class file for the applet and the HTML page for the applet. Then, you enter the appletviewer command followed by the file name of the HTML page.

To run the Applet Viewer from TextPad, you select the Run Java Applet command from the Tools menu. If you're using TextPad, though, you don't even need to create the HTML page before selecting this command. That's because TextPad will automatically create a temporary HTML page for you if one doesn't already exist. But if an HTML page does exist, TextPad will provide a dialog box that lets you select that HTML page.

Note that when you use this viewer, only the applet is displayed. Any other text that's included in the HTML file is ignored. Nevertheless, this is a quick way to test an applet before you do the final testing using a web browser.

An applet in the Applet Viewer

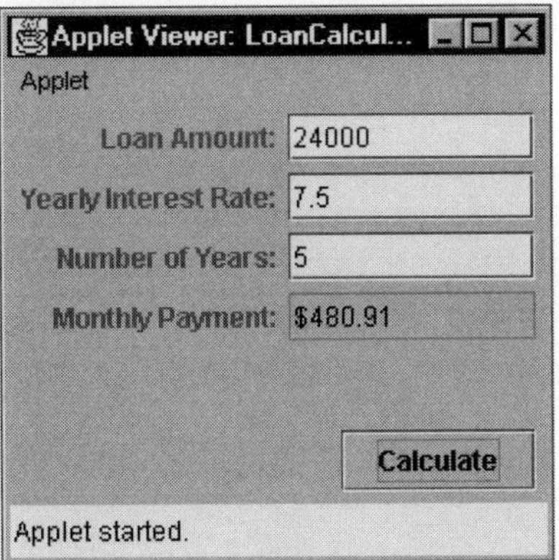

How to run the Applet Viewer from the command prompt

```
c:\java\ch15\swing>appletviewer LoanCalculator.html
```

How to run the Applet Viewer from TextPad

- Select the Run Java Applet command from the Tools menu or press Ctrl+3. If no HTML page exists in the current directory, TextPad will automatically create a temporary one. But if an HTML page exists, TextPad will let the Applet Viewer use it.

Description

- The Applet Viewer that's included in the SDK lets you test an applet before you run it in a browser.
- When you run the Applet Viewer, you will see the applet but you won't see any other elements that are defined by the HTML page.

Figure 15-8 How to view an applet with the Applet Viewer

How to use the Java Plug-in HTML Converter

Before a web browser can use the Java Plug-in to run a Swing applet, you must convert the APPLET tag to the OBJECT and EMBED tags. Since these tags are difficult to code, Sun has created a tool called the *Java Plug-in HTML Converter* that can automatically make this conversion for you as described in figure 15-9. Although this converter is included with SDK versions 1.3.1 and later, you must download the converter for earlier versions from the Java web site. Just make sure to use the converter that corresponds to the version of Java that you're using.

To start the converter, you start the command prompt and navigate to the directory that holds the converter. For versions 1.3.1 and later, a JAR file that contains the converter is located in the lib subdirectory of the jdk. Then, you can execute the command in step 2 of this figure. If you have trouble starting the converter, you can refer to the documentation that's available from the Java web site.

Once the dialog box for the HTML Converter appears, you can specify the file or files that you want to convert. Since the converter replaces your original HTML files with the converted ones, the originals are placed in the backup directory that you specify. Once you specify the files to convert and the backup directory, you can click on the Convert button. Then, a dialog box will appear that tells you how many files were successfully converted.

The Java Plug-in HTML Converter

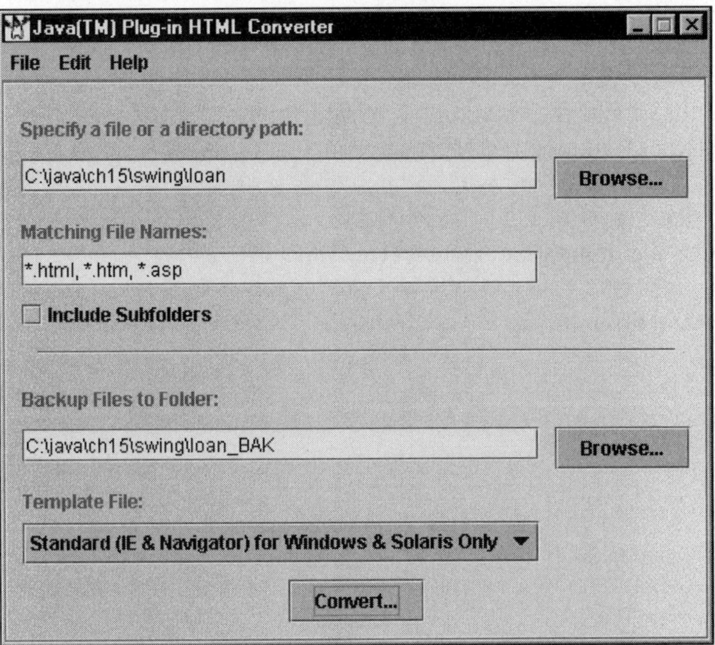

How to use the Plug-in HTML Converter

1. Start the command prompt and navigate to the directory that holds the htmlconverter.jar file. If you're using SDK versions 1.3.1 or later, this file is located in C:\jdkXXX\lib.
2. Start the converter with the following command:
   ```
   java -jar htmlconverter.jar -gui
   ```
3. To convert all HTML files in a directory, click on the Browse button and navigate to the directory. Then, click on the Convert button.

Description

- You should use the Java Plug-in HTML Converter that corresponds to the SDK version that's running on your system.
- Although the Java Plug-in HTML Converter is included with SDK versions 1.3.1 and later, it's not included with SDK versions 1.3 and earlier. If you're using one of these earlier versions, you'll need to download its HTML Converter from the Java web site.

Figure 15-9 How to use the Java Plug-in HTML Converter

The code for the converted HTML page

Figure 15-10 shows the converted HTML code for the HTML file in figure 15-7. This shows that the converter adds the OBJECT tag and the EMBED tag to the HTML page and that it specifies several complex attributes for each tag. As a result, both the Internet Explorer and Netscape can read this HTML page.

Note that the HTML Converter didn't change any code outside of the APPLET tag. Note too that the APPLET tag that was in the original HTML page has been included as a comment in the new HTML page.

Once the HTML is converted, you can still view the applet with the Applet Viewer. However, due to a bug in the Applet Viewer, two Applet Viewer windows may appear.

The HTML file in figure 15-7 after the conversion process

```
<HTML>
<TITLE>Loan Calculator</TITLE>
<BODY>
<h1>Loan Calculator</h1>
<!--"CONVERTED_APPLET"-->
<!-- CONVERTER VERSION 1.3 -->
<OBJECT classid="clsid:8AD9C840-044E-11D1-B3E9-00805F499D93"
WIDTH = 240 HEIGHT = 175
codebase="http://java.sun.com/products/plugin/1.3/jinstall-13-
win32.cab#Version=1,3,0,0">
<PARAM NAME = CODE VALUE = "LoanCalculatorApplet.class" >
<PARAM NAME="type" VALUE="application/x-java-applet;version=1.3">
<PARAM NAME="scriptable" VALUE="false">
<COMMENT>
<EMBED type="application/x-java-applet;version=1.3"  CODE =
"LoanCalculatorApplet.class" WIDTH = 240 HEIGHT = 175  scriptable=false
pluginspage="http://java.sun.com/products/plugin/1.3/plugin-
install.html"><NOEMBED></COMMENT>
If you can't see this applet, your web browser may not be Java-enabled.
</NOEMBED></EMBED>
</OBJECT>
<!--
<APPLET CODE = "LoanCalculatorApplet.class" WIDTH = 240 HEIGHT = 175>
If you can't see this applet, your web browser may not be Java-enabled.
</APPLET>
-->
<!--"END_CONVERTED_APPLET"-->

</BODY>
</HTML>
```

Description

- The HTML conversion results in an HTML page that uses scripting to allow both Internet Explorer and Netscape to read the page…even though these browsers use different tags for working with applets.
- The conversion only affects the code within the APPLET tag.
- The converted page has the original APPLET tag within an HTML comment. An HTML comment starts with <!-- and ends with -->.
- If you attempt to view your applet in the Applet Viewer after this conversion process, the applet may appear twice since the Applet Viewer doesn't recognize the comments and doesn't ignore the original APPLET tag.

Figure 15-10 The code for the converted HTML page

How to test a Swing applet

Since the Java Plug-in is automatically installed on your system, you can view a Swing applet in your browser as shown in figure 15-11. Then, you can test the Swing applet to make sure it runs properly within a browser. As you do that, you can use the *Java Console* to view debugging information.

If you're using version 1.3.1 and you run a Swing applet within a browser, the Java Console icon is displayed in the taskbar. Then, you can display the Java Console by double-clicking on this icon. Note, however, that you can also display the Java Console each time you run a Swing application by changing a system setting. And you should be able to display the Java Console by using one of the menus of your web browser.

If you're using version 1.3 or earlier, the Java Console icon won't be displayed in the taskbar. Then, you can use one of the other methods to display this console.

Once you've displayed the Java Console, you can use it to view any debugging information that the applet has printed to the console using println statements as well as any exceptions that have been thrown by the applet at run time. For example, the Java Console shown in this figure begins by displaying some general information about the current system and a list of commands that you can use to work with the Java Console. Then, it displays three lines that were printed to the console by println statements in the applet, followed by the description of an exception that was thrown by the applet at run time.

If you can't view the Java Console after trying the techniques described in the figure, your browser may have disabled the Java Console. To enable it, you can check the "Enable Java Console" checkbox located in your browser's advanced options.

A Swing applet with the Java Console displayed

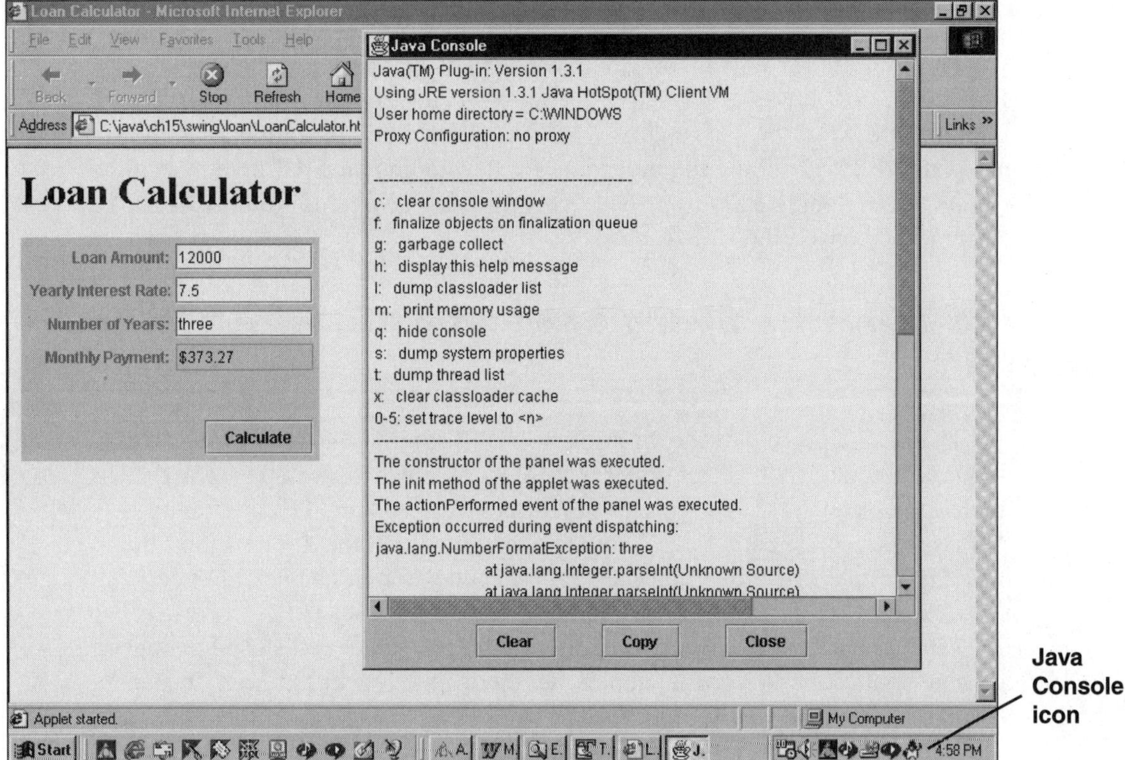

How to test a Swing applet

1. Start your web browser and test the applet to make sure it's working correctly.
2. If necessary, display the Java Console to view the output from println statements or information about any exceptions that have been thrown.

How to display the Java Console

- If you're using SDK version 1.3.1 or later, double-click on the Java Console icon in the task bar.
- To automatically display the Java Console each time you run an applet in a web browser, go to the Control Panel, double-click on the Java Plug-in icon, and select the Show Java Console check box.
- You should also be able to display the Java Console by selecting the Java Console command from one of your web browser's menus. For the Internet Explorer, select this command from the View menu. For Netscape, select this command from the Tools submenu of the Communicator menu.

How work with the Java Console

- You can press any of the letters shown in the Java Console to execute the related command. Although most of these letters execute advanced functions that go beyond the scope of this book, you can press *c* to clear all messages from the Java Console window, and you can press *q* to close the Java Console window.

Figure 15-11 How to test a Swing applet

How to develop AWT applets

This topic shows how to develop AWT applets that only use the features of Java 1.0, or possibly Java 1.1. All of the most recent versions of the Internet Explorer and Netscape can run this type of applet without using the Java Plug-in. As figure 15-12 shows, the procedure for developing an AWT applet is similar to developing a Swing applet, but you don't have to use the HTML converter to convert the HTML code.

How to convert a Swing application to an AWT applet

The second procedure shown in figure 15-12 shows how to convert a Swing application to an AWT applet rather than showing how to develop an AWT applet from scratch. This highlights the differences between the code for an AWT applet and the code for a Swing application. Then, this figure shows the code that results when the Loan Calculation application of chapter 11 is converted to an AWT applet.

The procedure in this figure is similar to the procedure that's used to convert a Swing application to a Swing applet, but there are a few differences. In step 1, you must import the java.applet package so you can access the Applet class, and you extend the Applet class instead of the JApplet class. In step 3, you must replace all Swing components with their corresponding AWT components. To do that, you can usually delete the J at the start of a component name, so a component like JLabel becomes the Label component. In addition, you can remove the import Swing package statement. In step 4, you need to make sure that you aren't using any classes or methods that were introduced after Java 1.1. In fact, depending on the web browsers that you need to support, you may need to limit your code to the classes and methods of Java 1.0 only.

With that in mind, the code in this figure uses Java 1.0 only. Within the init method, the three statements add a LoanCalculatorPanel object to the center region of the Border layout. Within the LoanCalculatorPanel class, the instance variables use AWT components instead of Swing components. And within the actionPerformed method, the first two statements don't use the parseDouble method from the Double class because that method was added in version 1.2 of Java. To fix this problem, the code uses the doubleValue method to return a double value from a new Double object that's created from a text field.

A procedure for developing an AWT applet

1. Code and compile the AWT applet.
2. Code the HTML page for the applet.
3. Test the applet using the Applet Viewer or a browser.

How to convert a Swing application to an AWT applet

1. Import the java.applet package; extend the Applet class instead of the JFrame class; and convert the constructor of the JFrame class so it becomes the init method of the Applet class.
2. Remove (1) any code that sets the title, size, and position of the frame; (2) any code that's used to exit the frame; and (3) the main method if one exists.
3. Replace all Swing components with the corresponding AWT elements.
4. Remove any Java code that uses classes or methods that were introduced after Java 1.0.

A Java 1.1 version of the LoanCalculation applet

```
import java.awt.*;
import java.awt.event.*;
import java.applet.*;
import java.text.*;

public class LoanCalculatorApplet extends Applet{
   public void init(){
      Panel panel = new LoanCalculatorPanel();
      setLayout(new BorderLayout());
      add(panel, BorderLayout.CENTER);
   }
}

class LoanCalculatorPanel extends Panel implements ActionListener{
   private TextField amountTextField, rateTextField, yearsTextField,
                     paymentTextField;
   private Label amountLabel, rateLabel, yearsLabel, paymentLabel;
   private Button calculateButton;

   public LoanCalculatorPanel(){
      // code that defines the LoanCalculatorPanel without an Exit button
      // using AWT components instead of Swing components
   }

   public void actionPerformed(ActionEvent e){
      double amount = new Double(amountTextField.getText()).doubleValue();
      double rate = new Double(rateTextField.getText()).doubleValue()/12/100;
      int months = Integer.parseInt(yearsTextField.getText())*12;
      double payment = FinancialCalculations.calculateMonthlyPayment(
            amount, months, rate);
      NumberFormat currency = NumberFormat.getCurrencyInstance();
      paymentTextField.setText(currency.format(payment));
   }
}
```

Figure 15-12 How to develop an AWT applet

How to test an AWT applet

Figure 15-13 shows how to test an AWT applet by running it in a browser. If you're using version 1.3.1 or later this works essentially the same as if you're testing a Swing applet. If you're using version 1.3 or earlier, though, you need to disable the Java Plug-in before you test your AWT applets. Otherwise, your browser will use the Java Plug-in so it will support all of the current features of Java, which will prevent you from testing the AWT applet properly.

In this example, the debugging information in the Java Console starts with two lines of text that the applet printed to the console using println statements. Then, it shows an exception that was thrown by the applet when the Calculate button was clicked. This exception was thrown because the applet attempted to use the parseDouble method of the Double class to parse the Loan Amount and Yearly Interest Rate text fields, but this version of the Java virtual machine doesn't include this method (which was introduced in version 1.2). As a result, the message says that the method doesn't exist.

An AWT applet with the Java Console displayed

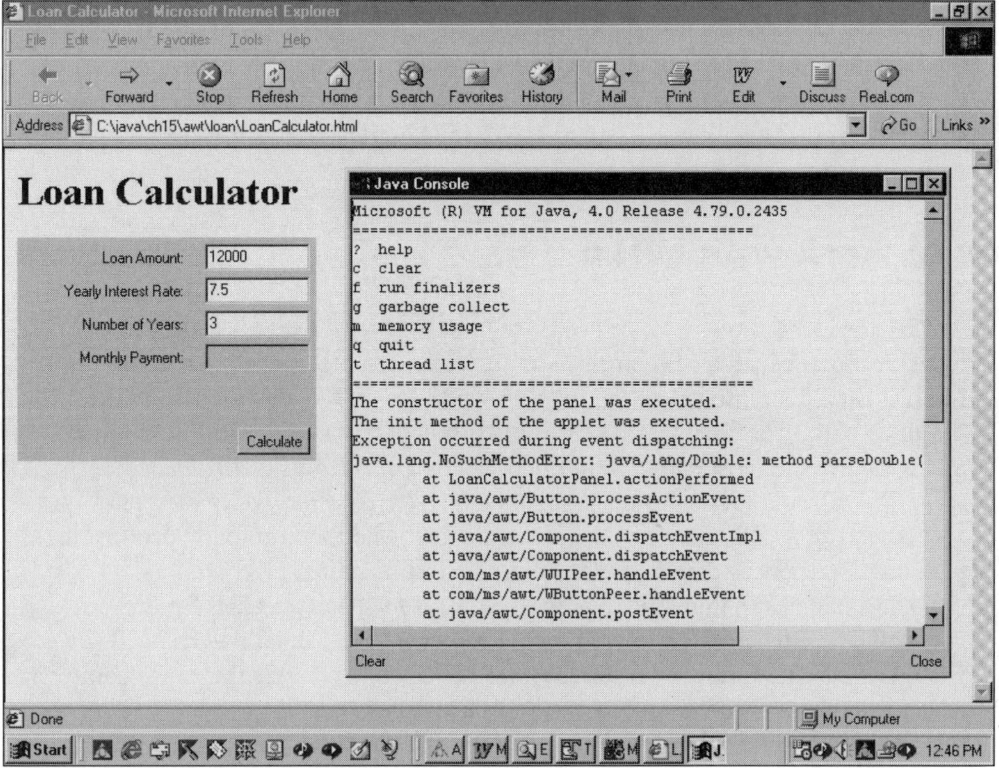

How to test an AWT applet using SDK 1.3.1 or later

1. Start your web browser and test the applet to make sure it's working correctly.
2. If necessary, display the Java Console to view the output from println statements or information about any exceptions that are thrown,

How to test an AWT applet using SDK 1.3 or earlier

1. Disable the Java Plug-in if it's installed on your system. To do that, go to the Control Panel, double-click on the Java Plug-in icon, and deselect the Enable Java Plug-in check box.
2. Start your web browser and test the applet. If necessary, display the Java Console to view any debugging information.

Figure 15-13 How to test an AWT applet

More skills for working with applets

This topic describes some skills that are often used to work with applets. First, you'll learn how to locate resources such as images that are stored on remote servers. Then, you'll learn how to use JAR files to improve the download time of your applets.

How to work with URLs

Figure 15-14 shows how to use a *Uniform Resource Locator* (*URL*) to locate resources such as directories and files on a remote server such as an Internet server, an intranet server, or a network server. As you can see, a URL has three parts. The first part specifies the protocol that's used. For the Internet and intranets, the most common protocol is *Hypertext Transfer Protocol* (*HTTP*), but another common protocol is *File Transfer Protocol* (*FTP*). The second part of a URL specifies the host machine. And the third part specifies the path that represents a directory or file on the host machine.

The examples in this figure show three ways to specify a URL for the MurachLogo GIF file that's stored on the server for the Murach web site. The first example shows how to use an *absolute URL* that specifies the entire name of the resource, while the second and third examples show how to use a *relative URL* to specify the name of a resource relative to another URL. For instance, the first statement in the second example creates an absolute URL that refers to the root directory on the host machine. Then, the second statement uses a relative URL to specify the location of the graphic file relative to the first URL. Similarly, the statement in the third example uses the getCodeBase method of the Applet class to return the URL of the directory that holds the applet class, which becomes part of a relative URL.

After the examples, this figure summarizes the constructors and methods of the URL and Applet classes that you can use to create URLs. To create a URL object, you can use either of the constructors for the URL class. Since this class is located in the java.net package, you should import this package when you're working with URLs. And since both of these constructors throw a checked exception of the MalformedURLException type, you must either throw or catch this exception when you code a constructor for a URL.

To return a URL object from the class that defines an applet, you can use either of the two methods of the Applet class. The first method returns the *code base*, the directory that stores the class file for the applet. The second method returns the *document base*, the directory that stores the HTML file for the applet. Unless the CODEBASE attribute of the APPLET tag specifies another directory, the code base and the document base will be the same directory. Since these two method belong to the Applet class, they are usually called in the init method.

The components of a URL

```
http://www.murach.com/books/index.htm
```

protocol: http | host: www.murach.com | path: /books/index.htm

Code examples that use the URL constructors

Example 1: An absolute URL

```
URL logoURL = new URL("http://www.murach.com/images/MurachLogo.gif");
```

Example 2: A relative URL

```
URL murachURL = new URL("http://www.murach.com");
URL logoURL = new URL(murachURL, "images/MurachLogo.gif");
```

Example 3: Another relative URL

```
URL logoURL = new URL(getCodeBase(), "images/MurachLogo.gif");
```

The URL class

```
java.net.URL
```

Common constructors of the URL class

Constructor	Description
`URL(String)`	Creates an absolute URL object from the string that specifies an absolute URL.
`URL(URL, String)`	Creates a URL object where the string specifies a URL that's relative to the location specified by the URL object.

Two methods of the Applet class that work with URLs

Method	Description
`getCodeBase()`	Returns a URL object that represents the URL of the directory that holds the applet class.
`getDocumentBase()`	Returns a URL object that represents the URL of the directory that holds the HTML page.

Description

- A *Uniform Resource Locator* (*URL*) locates resources on a remove server such as an Internet server, an intranet server, or even a network server.
- An *absolute URL* specifies the entire name of the resource. A *relative URL* specifies the name of a resource relative to another URL.
- The *code base* is the directory that stores the class files for an applet. The *document base* is the directory that stores the HTML file for the applet. Unless the CODEBASE attribute of the APPLET tag specifies a code base, the code base and the document base refer to the same directory.
- Both of the constructors of the URL class shown in this figure throw a checked exception of the MalformedURLException type. As a result, you must throw or catch this exception when you work with URLs.

Figure 15-14 How to work with URLs

How to display images in applets

Figure 15-15 shows how to display an image within an applet. To start, this figure shows two code examples. Then, this figure summarizes the constructors and methods that you can use to display images in applets.

The first example shows a class that displays an image in a Swing applet. Within the init method for this applet, the first statement creates an object of the URL class that locates the image file. To do so, this statement uses the getCodeBase method described in the last figure. Since the constructor for the URL class throws a MalformedURLException, this example uses a try/catch statement to catch this exception. Then, the next four statements create an ImageIcon object from the URL object, place the ImageIcon in a label component, and display the label on the content pane of the applet.

The second example shows a class that displays an image in an AWT applet. To do so, this class overrides the paint method of the Applet class. Within the paint method, the first statement uses the getImage method of the Applet class to create an Image object. Then, the second statement uses the drawImage method of the Graphics class to display the image on the applet.

The rest of this figure summarizes the constructors and methods that you can use to display images in applets. For Swing applets, you can use the constructor of the ImageIcon class to create an ImageIcon object from a URL object. For AWT applets, you can use the getImage method of the Applet class to return an Image object. Either way, you can use the getCodeBase method described in the last figure to return a URL object for the directory that stores the class file for the applet.

A code example that adds an image to a Swing applet

```
public class ImageApplet extends JApplet{
   public void init(){
      try{
         URL imageURL = new URL(getCodeBase(), "images/MurachLogo.gif");
         ImageIcon labelIcon = new ImageIcon(imageURL);
         JLabel label = new JLabel(labelIcon);
         Container contentPane = getContentPane();
         contentPane.add(label);
      }
      catch(MalformedURLException e){
         System.out.println("Can't find image URL.");
      }
   }
}
```

A code example that adds an image to an AWT applet

```
public class ImageApplet extends Applet{
   public void paint(Graphics g){
      Image image = getImage(getCodeBase(), "images/MurachLogo.gif");
      g.drawImage(image, 30, 40, this);
   }
}
```

A constructor of the ImageIcon class

Constructor	Description
`ImageIcon(URL)`	Returns an ImageIcon object for the image file at the specified URL.

Two methods of the Applet class that load images

Method	Description
`getImage(URL)`	Returns an Image object that represents the image file at the specified absolute URL.
`getImage(URL, String)`	Returns an Image object that represents the location of an image file relative to the base URL.

Description

- To work with images in Swing applets, you can use the ImageIcon class to create an ImageIcon object. Then, you can add the ImageIcon object to a component to display it.
- To work with AWT applets, you can use the getImage method of the Applet class to return an Image object. Then, you can override the paint method in the Applet class, to display the image.

Figure 15-15 How to display images in applets

How to work with JAR files

Figure 15-16 shows how to work with *Java Archive files*, or *JAR files*. As you may remember, a JAR file contains one or more files and it stores these files in a compressed format. When you work with applets that need to access more than one file, using a JAR file can dramatically improve the download time of the applet. If, for example, an applet consists of several class files and an image file, you can store all of these files in a single JAR file. Then, the browser only needs to make one HTTP request to get the JAR file from the server. Besides that, the compressed files won't take as long to download.

Since the JAR tool is automatically installed as part of the SDK, you can use the JAR command to create and update a JAR file, to list the contents of a JAR file, and to extract files from a JAR file. To use this command, you start with the command name. Then, you enter one or more of the six options that are summarized in this figure. For example, to create a JAR file with verbose output, you specify the c to create the file, f to specify the name of the file, and v to specify verbose output. After that, you must specify the name of the JAR file followed by any files you want to include in the JAR file. To do this, you can use the wildcard character (*) to specify all files of a particular type. For example, you can use *.class to add all of the class files in a directory to the JAR file.

The examples in this figure show how to work with the JAR command. Here, the first example shows how to create a JAR file named LoanApplet.jar that contains all of the class files in the current directory and all of the GIF files in the images subdirectory. The second example shows how to add the MurachLogo.GIF file to that JAR file, assuming that this file is stored in the images subdirectory. The third example shows how to extract these files from that JAR file. And the fourth example shows how to list the contents of that JAR file. Since you usually want to get feedback about each JAR command, you typically use the verbose output option, especially when working with the create, update, and extract options.

The two screens in this figure show the results of some typical JAR commands. In the first screen, the verbose output of the JAR command shows that the command added three class files to the JAR file, and it shows how much the JAR tool was able to compress these files. In the second screen, the JAR command lists the contents of a JAR file without verbose output.

The syntax for using the JAR tool at the command line

```
jar [options] JARFileName File1 File2 File3 ...
```

Common options of the JAR tool

Option	Description
c	Creates a new JAR file and adds the specified files to it.
f	Specifies the second argument as the JAR file name.
u	Updates an existing JAR file by adding or replacing files.
x	Extracts the files from the specified JAR file.
t	Lists the contents of the JAR file.
v	Creates verbose output that includes compression information about the files that are added to the JAR file.

An example that creates a JAR file

```
C:\java\ch15\swing\loan>jar cfv LoanApplet.jar *.class images/*.gif
```

An example that updates a JAR file

```
C:\java\ch15\swing\loan>jar ufv LoanApplet.jar images/MurachLogo.gif
```

An example that extracts files from a JAR file

```
C:\java\ch15\swing\loan>jar xfv LoanApplet.jar
```

An example that lists the contents of a JAR file

```
C:\java\ch15\swing\loan>jar tf LoanApplet.jar
```

The result when you create a JAR file with verbose output

```
C:\java\ch15\swing\loan>jar cfv LoanApplet.jar *.class
added manifest
adding: FinancialCalculations.class(in = 456) (out= 344)(deflated 24%)
adding: LoanCalculatorApplet.class(in = 461) (out= 300)(deflated 34%)
adding: LoanCalculatorPanel.class(in = 2670) (out= 1444)(deflated 45%)
```

The result when you list the contents of the JAR file

```
C:\java\ch15\swing\loan>jar tf LoanApplet.jar
META-INF/
META-INF/MANIFEST.MF
FinancialCalculations.class
LoanCalculatorApplet.class
LoanCalculatorPanel.class
```

Description

- To specify all files with a certain extension, you can use the * wildcard.
- To use the JAR tool, start the command prompt and navigate to the directory that stores the files you want to archive. Then, you can issue the JAR command. If necessary, you can also use a relative path name to identify files.

Figure 15-16 How to work with JAR files

How to include JAR files in an HTML page

Once you create a JAR file that contains all of the files needed by an applet, you can specify the JAR file in the HTML page that contains the applet as shown in figure 15-17. Before you include a JAR file, though, you should make sure that the users of your applet have browsers that can use JAR files. Although most modern browsers can read JAR files, older browsers that only support Java 1.0 can't use JAR files.

The code in this figure shows how to use the ARCHIVE attribute of the APPLET tag to specify a JAR file that contains the files for the applet. Notice that you still need to use the CODE attribute to specify the class file that defines the applet so the browser knows what file to execute to start the applet. Then, every time it needs another file, it looks for that file in the JAR file. If it can't find it there, it will look for the file on the server. However, since connecting to the server for additional files significantly increases the download time for your applets, you should try to include all the files that the applet needs within the JAR file.

How to include a JAR file in an HTML page

```
<HTML>
<TITLE>Loan Calculator</TITLE>
<BODY>
<APPLET ARCHIVE = "LoanApplet.jar"
        CODE = "LoanCalculatorApplet.class"
        WIDTH = 240
        HEIGHT = 175>
</APPLET>
</BODY>
</HTML>
```

Description

- To improve the download time for your applets, you can place all the files needed by the applet in one JAR file. Then, you can include the JAR file within the applet by specifying the file name in the ARCHIVE attribute. Otherwise, the applet gets the files from the server, which is much slower.
- Browsers that can only run Java 1.0 applets can't use JAR files.

Figure 15-17 How to include JAR files in an HTML page

Perspective

In this chapter, you learned how to develop both Swing and AWT applets that can be run within a web browser. You also learned about some of the limitations of applets that have led web programmers to use other methods for developing web applications. One of the most important of these trends is toward the use of Java Server Pages and servlets for web applications...and that's going to be the subject of the next book in this series.

In chapter 20, you can learn how to develop an applet that works with threads. There, you will see that you can use threads to create applets that display animations and other types of multimedia effects. But there again, it's usually more practical to use other methods to get the same effects.

Summary

- An *applet* is a special type of application that's stored in a *web page* on a remote server and runs within a web browser on a client machine.
- You can use the *Hypertext Markup Language* (*HTML*) to create a web page. Within the HTML file, you use *tags* to define the elements of the page. And within some tags, you define *attributes* that provide additional information.
- If you use the JApplet class to create a *Swing applet*, you can use Swing components and all of the current features of Java. To distribute this type of applet, you must run the *HTML Converter* on the HTML page that contains the applet, and you must install the *Java Plug-in* on all systems that will use the applet.
- Most web browsers contain a *Java virtual machine* (*JVM*) that can run *AWT applets* that use only the features of Java 1.0. Many web browsers, though, also support some of the features of Java 1.1.
- Since applets are downloaded from remote servers and run on client machines, they have stricter security restrictions than applications. To get around these restrictions, it's possible to create a *signed applet*.
- To test an applet but not its HTML page, you can use the *Applet Viewer*. To test an applet and its HTML page, you run the HTML page from a web browser. Then, you can use the *Java Console* to get debugging information.
- To specify a remote resource, you can use a *Uniform Resource Locator* (URL). An *absolute URL* specifies the complete path of a directory or file while a *relative URL* specifies a path that's relative to another URL.
- The *code base* for an applet is the directory that stores the class file for the applet. The *document base* for an applet is the directory that stores the HTML file for the applet.
- You can use a *Java Archive file* (*JAR file*) to store one or more files in a compressed format. To download an applet as efficiently as possible, you should store all files needed by the applet in a JAR file.

Terms

applet
web page
Hypertext Markup Language (HTML)
Swing applet
AWT applet
Java virtual machine (JVM)
Java Plug-in
signed applet
tag
attribute
Applet Viewer
Java Console
Java Plug-in HTML converter
Uniform Resource Locator (URL)
Hypertext Transfer Protocol (HTTP)
File Transfer Protocol (FTP)
absolute URL
relative URL
code base
document base
Java Archive file (JAR file)

Objectives

- Develop a Swing or AWT applet from scratch, or convert a Swing application to a Swing or AWT applet.
- Code an HTML page that uses the APPLET tag to specify the filename, width, and height of an applet.
- Use the Applet Viewer to test an applet.
- For a Swing applet, use the HTML Converter to convert the APPLET tag to the OBJECT and EMBED tags that are used by the Internet Explorer and by Netscape.
- Test a Swing or AWT applet by running it in a web browser. If necessary, use the Java Console to get debugging information.
- Use a URL to specify a directory or file that's located on a remote server.
- Display an image in an applet.
- Use JAR files to compress and store all files that are needed by an applet. Then, specify the JAR file in the HTML page that contains the applet.
- Describe the deployment issues for Swing and AWT applets.
- Describe the security restrictions of applets.

Exercise 15-1 Develop the Swing Loan Calculator applet

1. Convert the code for the Loan Calculator application that's stored in the c:\java\ch15\swing\loan directory to a Swing applet as in figure 15-6. Then, compile the application.
2. Code an HTML page that displays the applet as in figure 15-7. Then, save this file as "LoanCalculator.html" in the c:\java\ch15\swing\loan directory.
3. Use the Applet Viewer to view the applet as in figure 15-8.
4. Run the HTML Converter as in figure 15-9 to convert the HTML page.
5. Use your web browser to test the HTML page and the applet as in figure 15-11. Since the Java Plug-in is automatically installed when you install the SDK, the browser should work properly. While you're testing, you should display the Java Console.

Exercise 15-2 Develop the AWT Loan Calculator applet

1. Convert the code for the Loan Calculator application that's in the c:\java\ch15\awt\loan directory to an AWT applet as in figure 15-12. Then, compile the application.
2. Code an HTML page that displays the applet as in figure 15-7. Then, save this file as "LoanCalculator.html" in the c:\java\ch15\awt\loan directory.
3. Use the Applet Viewer to view the applet as in figure 15-8.
4. Use your web browser to test the HTML page and the applet as shown in 15-13. While you're testing, you should display the Java Console.

Exercise 15-3 Enhance the Swing applet

1. Open the Swing version of the Loan Calculator applet that's in the c:\java\ch15\swing\loanApplet directory. Then, add the icon that's stored in the images subdirectory to the Calculate button as in figure 15-15.
2. Use the JAR tool to create a JAR file that contains all class files needed by the Loan Calculator applet and all image files needed by the applet as in figure 15-16. Then, modify the HTML page so it uses this JAR file as described in figure 15-17. To do this, you may want to code a simple HTML page, then run it through the Java HTML converter. This way, you can run the Swing applet within a browser.

Section 4

Java for file input and output

In a typical business application, the data for business objects is saved in disk files or databases so it can be retrieved whenever it is needed. In this section, then, you'll learn how to use Java for writing data to disk files and reading data from disk files.

In chapter 16, you'll be introduced to file input and output and the two types of files that the Java API provides for: text files and binary files. Then, in chapter 17, you can learn how to work with text files. And in chapter 18, you can learn how to work with binary files and random-access versions of binary files.

Note, however, that you don't have to read all three of these chapters in sequence. After you read chapter 16, you can read either chapter 17 or chapter 18.

16

An introduction to file input and output

In the last section, you learned how to create user interfaces that get input from the user. Unless you save that data to a file or database, though, the data is lost when the user exits the program. That's why Java provides a variety of classes that let you write data to a file and read data from a file.

In this chapter, you'll be introduced to the concepts and terms that you need for working with files as well as the two types of files that Java provides for. You'll also learn how to use the File class with either type of file. Then, in the next two chapters, you'll learn how to write the code that reads data from and writes data to either type of file.

An introduction to file input and output

This topic introduces you to file input and output in Java. It shows how streams and files work, how to layer streams, and how to handle the three types of exceptions that are commonly thrown when working with file input and output.

How files and streams work

Figure 16-1 presents the two types of files and the two types of streams that you use when you do *I/O operations* (or *file I/O*) in Java. In a *text file*, all of the data is stored as text characters with one character per byte on disk. Often, the fields and records in this type of file are separated by delimiters like tabs, bars, or end of line characters. In the text file in this figure, the fields are separated by bars and the records by end of line characters.

In contrast, the data in a *binary file* can include seven primitive types of data plus object data. In the example in this figure, you can see that two bytes are used for each character in the code and title fields of a Book object. However, the third field is a numeric data type so it doesn't display properly in a text editor. Also, since the records in a binary file don't end with end of line characters, one record isn't displayed on each line when a binary file is opened by a text editor.

To handle I/O operations, Java uses *streams*. You can think of a stream as the flow of data from one location to another. For instance, an *output stream* can flow from the internal memory of an application to a disk file, and an *input stream* can flow from a disk file to internal memory. When you work with a text file, you use a *character stream*. When you work with a binary file, you use a *binary stream*.

Although this chapter shows you how to use streams with disk files, Java also uses streams with other types of devices. For instance, you can use an output stream to send data to a PC monitor or a network connection. In fact, the System.out and System.err objects are the standard output streams that are used for printing data to the console. Similarly, you can use an input stream to read data from a source like a keyboard or a network connection. In fact, the System.in object is a standard input stream that is used for reading data from the keyboard.

Since the primary numeric data types can be stored in a binary file, this type of file is more efficient for applications that work with numeric data. In contrast, the numeric data in a text file has to be parsed to the primitive types before it can be used in arithmetic operations. That's one reason why binary files are used for most business applications. When an application works primarily with text data, though, text files can also be efficient.

When you save a text or binary file, you can use any extension for the file name. In this book, though, *txt* is used as the extension for all text files and *dat* for all binary files. For instance, the text file in this figure is named books.txt, and the binary file is named books.dat.

A text file that's opened by a text editor

A binary file that's opened by a text editor

Two types of files

File	Description
Text	A file that contains text characters. The fields and records in this type of file are often delimited by special characters like tab, bar, and end of line characters.
Binary	A file that can contain seven of the primitive data types plus object data.

Two types of streams

Stream	Description
Character	Used to transfer text data to or from an I/O device.
Binary	Used to transfer binary data to or from an I/O device.

Description

- An *input file* is a file that is read by a program; an *output file* is a file that is written by a program. Input and output operations are often referred to as *I/O operations* or *file I/O*.
- A *stream* is the flow of data from one location to another. To write data to a file or a screen from internal storage, you use an *output stream*. To read data from a file or the keyboard into internal storage, you use an *input stream*.
- To read and write *text files*, you use *character streams*. To read and write *binary files*, you use *binary streams*.
- Streams are not only used with disk devices, but also with input devices like keyboards and network connections and output devices like PC monitors and network connections.

Figure 16-1 How files and streams work

How to layer streams

To create one stream that has all the functionality that you need for an application, it's common to *layer* two or more streams into a *filtered stream.* This is illustrated by the diagram in figure 16-2. Here, the PrintWriter class is layered with the FileWriter class to create an output stream for a text file. In this case, the PrintWriter class is used to write strings and numbers to a character stream, but this stream doesn't know where to write the data. That's why it's layered with the FileWriter class, which converts the characters in the character stream to bytes and writes those bytes to the specified text file.

In the code examples, you can see how you layer streams in Java. Quite simply, you use an object of one class as the argument for the constructor of another. For instance, a FileWriter object is used as the argument of the PrintWriter constructor in the first example.

In the second and third examples, a block of internal memory known as a *buffer* is layered with two other streams. This can be referred to as a *buffered stream.* When you use this type of stream for output, the data is stored in the buffer before it is written to the output device. Then, when the buffer is full, all of the data in the buffer is *flushed* to the disk file in a single I/O operation. Similarly, when you use a buffer for input, a full buffer of data is read in a single I/O operation.

The benefit if buffering is that it reduces the number of I/O operations that are done by a disk device. If, for example, a buffer can hold 4000 bytes of data, only one write or read operation is required to flush or fill the buffer. In contrast, if the data is written or read one field at a time, 4000 bytes might require hundreds of I/O operations. For each I/O operation, though, the disk has to rotate to the starting disk location. Since this rotation is extremely slow relative to internal operations, buffering dramatically improves the performance of I/O operations. That's why you should use buffers for all but the most trivial disk operations.

How to layer two or more streams

stream A + stream B + … = filtered stream

How to layer the PrintWriter and FileWriter streams

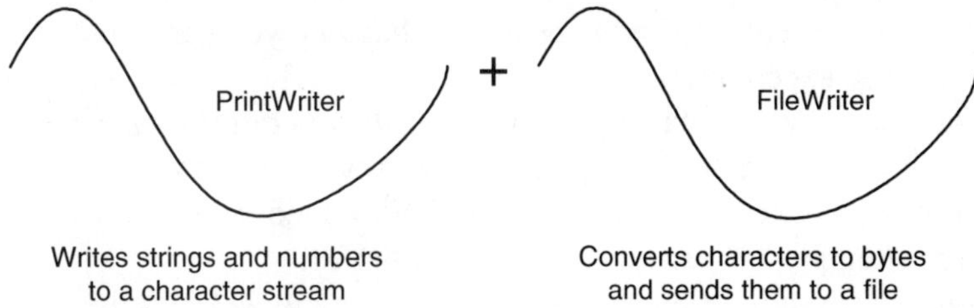

Code that layers two streams for a text file

```
PrintWriter out = new PrintWriter(
                  new FileWriter("books.txt"));
```

Code that layers two streams with a buffer for a text file

```
PrintWriter out = new PrintWriter(
                  new BufferedWriter(
                  new FileWriter("books.txt")));
```

Code that layers two streams with a buffer for a binary file

```
DataOutputStream out = new DataOutputStream(
                       new BufferedOutputStream(
                       new FileOutputStream("books.dat")));
```

Description

- The java.io package contains classes that can be used to create different types of streams that have different types of functionality. In SDK1.4, the java.nio package contains classes and other packages that provide fast buffered I/O, character set conversions, new I/O exception classes, and overall improved I/O performance.
- To get the functionality you need for a stream, you often need to combine, or *layer*, two or more streams. When you layer two or more streams, you create a *filtered stream.*
- To make disk processing more efficient, you can use a *buffered stream* by adding a block of internal memory called a *buffer* to the stream. Then, output data is stored in the buffer before it is written to a file, and input data is read into the buffer before it is processed by a program.
- When an output buffer is full, the program *flushes* the buffer, which means that it sends the data in the buffer to the I/O device. When an input buffer is full, the program stops reading data from the I/O device into the buffer.
- Buffers significantly improve the performance of disk operations because they reduce the number of device operations.

Figure 16-2 How to layer streams

How to work with I/O exceptions

If you've read chapter 10, you know the basic skills for handling exceptions. Now, figure 16-3 summarizes the three types of checked exceptions that must be handled when you're working with certain I/O operations, and it shows a typical way to handle these types of exceptions. In the next two chapters, you can use code like this to handle these exceptions.

All exceptions that are thrown by classes that perform I/O operations inherit the IOException class. In particular, an EOFException is thrown when a program attempts to read beyond the end of a file, and a FileNotFoundException is thrown when a program attempts to open a file that doesn't exist.

The example in this figure shows how to handle these exceptions. Here, the code attempts to read data from a file. As a result, the constructors and methods in the code throw all three types of I/O exceptions. To catch these exceptions, this example uses a single try/catch statement to catch the IOException. This works because both the FileNotFoundException and the EOFException are a type of IOException.

Note, however, that this example doesn't have separate catch blocks for FileNotFoundException and EOFException. Instead, it uses code that prevents these types of exceptions from being thrown. After a File object is created that identifies a file, an if statement checks whether the file exists and proceeds accordingly if it doesn't. This prevents the FileNotFoundException. Then, if the file does exist, a loop reads the records in the file as long as the string that's returned by the readLine method isn't a null value, which means that the end of the file hasn't been reached. If it has, the loop ends, which prevents the EOFException.

Common I/O exception classes

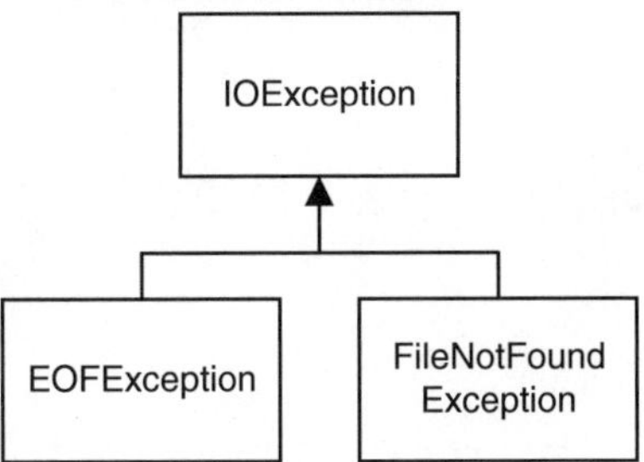

The common I/O exceptions

Exception	Description
`IOException`	Thrown when an error occurs in I/O processing.
`EOFException`	Thrown when a program attempts to read beyond the end of a file.
`FileNotFoundException`	Thrown when a program attempts to open a file that doesn't exist.

Code that handles I/O exceptions

```
try{
    File data = new File("grades.txt");
    if (data.exists()){
        BufferedReader in = new BufferedReader(
                            new FileReader(data));
        String line = in.readLine();
        while(line != null){
            System.out.println(line);
            line = in.readLine();
        }
        in.close();
    }
    else
        System.out.println("The grades.txt file doesn't exist");
}
catch(IOException e){
    System.out.println("An IOException has occurred.");
}
```

Description

- All exceptions that are thrown by classes that perform I/O operations inherit the IOException class.
- For efficiency, it's best to prevent some exceptions from ever occurring instead of catching them with catch blocks. That's why the code above prevents the EOF and FileNotFound exceptions from occurring.

Figure 16-3 How to work with I/O exceptions

How to work with the File class

In this topic, you'll learn how to use the File class to work with directories and files. This is useful whether you're working with text files or binary files. Then, in the next two chapters, you'll learn how to use File objects with those types of files.

How to create a File object

Figure 16-4 shows how to create File objects. After it shows some examples that create File objects, it summarizes three constructors and one field of the File class.

In the first group of examples, all of the statements create File objects for Windows systems. In that case, the backslash is use to separate the parts of a path. To code one backslash in Java, though, you need to use the \\ escape sequence.

The first four statements in this group of examples show how to use the first File constructor. Here, the first statement creates a File object that refers to a file in the current directory. The second statement uses an *absolute pathname* to specify the entire path and filename for the file. And the third statement uses a *relative pathname* to specify the path and filename for the file relative to the current directory. In this case, the File object refers to a file located in the files subdirectory of the current directory.

The fourth statement in this group shows how to use the *Universal Naming Convention* (*UNC*) to specify a file on a remote computer. To do that, you code two backslashes (\\\\), followed by the host name and the share name. In this case, the File object refers to a file located on a computer named server on the C share drive in the editorial directory.

The fifth statement in this group shows how to use the second File constructor. Here, the first argument refers to the parent pathname, while the second one refers to the child pathname. In this case, the first argument refers to the directory and the second argument refers to the file.

The last two statements in this group show how to use the third File constructor. Here, the first statement creates a File object that refers to a directory. Then, the second statement creates a File object that refers to a file located in that directory.

Although Windows uses a backslash (\) to separate files, Unix uses a forward slash (/). How then do you create File objects that will work on either type of system? By using the separator field of the File class. This is illustrated by the last example in this figure. Then, the Java virtual machines will interpret the code the right way for each type of system.

The File class

```
java.io.File
```

Examples that create File objects for Windows systems

```
File file = new File("books.txt");
File file = new File("C:\\java\\ch16\\files\\books.txt");
File file = new File("files\\books.txt");
File file = new File("\\\\server\\c\\editorial\\books.txt");
File file = new File("..\\files", "books.txt");
File dir = new File("C:\\java\\ch16\\files");
File file = new File(dir, "books.txt");
```

An example that uses the separator field

```
File file = new File("files" + File.separator + "books.txt");
```

Common constructors of the File class

Constructor	Description
`File(StringPath)`	Creates a File object that refers to the specified pathname.
`File(StringPath, StringSubPath)`	Creates a File object that refers to the pathname created by combining the specified path with the specified subpath.
`File(File, StringSubPath)`	Creates a File object that refers to the pathname created by combining the pathname in the specified File object with the specified subpath.

A field of the File class

Field	Description
`separator`	Returns the system separator character as a string.

Description

- To identify the name and location of a file, you can use an *absolute pathname* to specify the entire path for a file, or you can use a *relative pathname* to specify the path of the file relative to another directory.
- To code a backslash as a String literal, you must use the escape sequence (\\).
- To create a File object that represents a file on a remote computer, you can use the *Universal Naming Convention* (*UNC*). To do that, code two backslashes (\\\\) followed by the hostname and the share name.
- Windows uses a backslash to separate directories, while Unix uses a forward slash. To write code that will run on either system, you can use the separator field of the File class as the separator.

Figure 16-4 How to create a File object

Methods of the File class

Figure 16-5 summarizes some of the methods of the File class that you can use for working with files and directories. For more information about these methods, you can use the documentation of the Java API.

The first group in this figure presents some common methods that you can use to test a file or directory. You can use the first three methods to check whether a file exists and whether you can read or write the file. You can use the next two methods to test whether the pathname refers to a file or a directory.

The second group presents some methods that you can use to get information about a file or directory. To return the name of the file or directory, for example, you can use the getName method. To return the pathname of the file or directory, you can use the next three methods. To return the length of the file in bytes or the time that the file was last modified, you can use the length and lastModified methods. And to return arrays that describe the available drives, directories, and files, you can use the listRoots, listFiles, and list methods.

The last group presents some methods that you can use to work with files and directories. For instance, you can use the setReadOnly method to create a file or directory that only allows read operations, and you can use the delete method to delete a file or directory. Before you can delete a directory, though, the directory must be empty. Since all four of the methods in this group return a boolean value that indicates whether the operation was successful, you can write code that checks the return values whenever you need to know if the method ran successfully.

Methods that check a File object

Method	Description
`exists()`	Returns a true value if the pathname exists.
`canRead()`	Returns a true value if the pathname exists and can be read by the program.
`canWrite()`	Returns a true value if the pathname exists and a program can write to it.
`isDirectory()`	Returns a true value if the pathname exists and refers to a directory.
`isFile()`	Returns a true value if the pathname exists and refers to a file.

Methods that get information about a File object

Method	Description
`getName()`	Returns the name of the file or directory as a String object.
`getPath()`	Returns the pathname as represented in the constructor as a String object.
`getAbsolutePath()`	Returns the absolute pathname as a String object.
`getCanonicalFile()`	Returns a String object that represents the canonical pathname. This method throws an IOException.
`length()`	Returns the length of the file in bytes as a long type.
`lastModified()`	Returns a long value representing the time that the file was last modified as the number of milliseconds since January 1, 1970. If the file doesn't exist, this method returns 0L.
`listRoots()`	A static method that returns an array of File objects representing the drives available to the current system.
`listFiles()`	If the object is a directory, this method returns an array of File objects for the files and subdirectories of this directory. If the object is a file, this method returns a null value.
`list()`	If the object is a directory, this method returns an array of String objects for the files and subdirectories of this directory. If the object refers to a file, this method returns a null value.

Methods that work with File objects

Method	Description
`setReadOnly()`	Makes the pathname read-only. If successful, this method returns a true value.
`createNewFile()`	Creates a new file for the file represented by the File object if one doesn't already exist. Returns a true value if the file is created. This method throws an IOException.
`mkdir()`	Creates a new directory for the directory represented by this File object. Returns a true value if the directory is created.
`delete()`	Deletes the file or directory represented by the File object. If successful, this method returns a true value. A directory can only be deleted if it's empty.

Figure 16-5 Methods of the File class

Code examples that work with directories and files

Figure 16-6 presents four examples that show how to work with files and directories. These examples illustrate several important skills.

The first example shows how to get information about a file. Here, the first statement creates a File object that refers to a file. Then, an if statement checks whether the file exists. If so, five statements print information about the file to the console. Otherwise, a single statement prints a message that says that the file doesn't exist.

The screen below the first example shows the result of the five statements that are executed when the file exists. First, the getName method returns the name of the file specified in the constructor. Then, the getPath method returns the pathname specified in the constructor. The next two statements show the two ways a full pathname can be returned. Here, the getCanonicalPath returns the full pathname, while the getAbsolutePath method returns the full pathname plus the relative pathname. Finally, the canWrite method returns a true value to show that you can write data to the file.

The second example shows how to create a new file. To do this, the first statement creates a File object. Then, the second statement calls the createNewFile method to create the file. If the file doesn't already exist, this statement will create the file.

The third example shows how to list the names of files and subdirectories in a directory. Here, the first statement creates a File object that refers to a directory. Then, an if statement checks whether the directory exists and whether it is a directory. If both are true, the first statement in the if block prints the name of the directory to the console. Then, the second statement returns an array of strings that contains the names of the files and subdirectories of that directory. And finally, a loop prints each element of the array to the console. In this example, the directory only contains two files and one subdirectory.

The last example shows how to return all drives available to a system. Here, the first statement uses the static listRoots method of the File class to return an array of File objects. Then, a loop prints the pathname for each root drive to the console. In this example, the system contains four drives: A, C, D, and E.

Code that gets information about a file

```
File file = new File("..\\files\\books.txt");
if (file.exists()){
   System.out.println("File name:       " + file.getName());
   System.out.println("Path:            " + file.getPath());
   System.out.println("Canonical path: " + file.getCanonicalPath());
   System.out.println("Absolute path:  " + file.getAbsolutePath());
   System.out.println("Is writable:    " + file.canWrite());
}
else
   System.out.println("The " + file.getName() + " file doesn't exist.");
```

Output of the above code

```
File name:      books.txt
Path:           ..\files\books.txt
Canonical path: C:\java\ch16\files\books.txt
Absolute path:  C:\java\ch16\classes\..\files\books.txt
Is writable:    true
```

Code that creates a new file

```
File file = new File("newdata.txt");
file.createNewFile();
```

Code that lists the contents of a directory

```
File dir = new File("C:\\java\\ch16\\classes");
if ((dir.exists()) && (dir.isDirectory())){
   System.out.println("Directory: " + dir.getCanonicalPath());
   String[] files = dir.list();
   for (int i = 0; i < files.length; i++){
      System.out.println(files[i]);
   }
}
```

Output of the above code

```
Directory: C:\java\ch16\classes
FileTester.class
FileTester.java
files
```

Code that lists available roots

```
File[] myRoots = File.listRoots();
for (int i = 0; i < myRoots.length; i++){
   System.out.println(myRoots[i].getPath());
}
```

Output of the above code

Figure 16-6 Code examples that work with directories and files

Perspective

In this chapter, you learned the concepts and terms that you need to read and write files. In addition, you learned how to use the File class. Now, you can read chapter 17 to learn how to read and write text files, or you can skip to chapter 18 to learn how to read and write binary files.

Summary

- In Java, a *text file* contains text characters, while a *binary file* can contain seven primitive data types plus object data. As a result, binary files are used for most business applications.
- In Java, you use *character streams* to read and write text files and *binary streams* to read and write binary files. To get the functionality you need, you can *layer* two or more streams, thus creating a *filtered stream.*
- A *buffer* is a block of memory that is used to store the data in a stream before it is written to or after it is read from an I/O device. When an output buffer is full, its data is *flushed* to the I/O device.
- Buffering significantly improves the efficiency of disk operations because it reduces the number of operations that are done by a disk device. This means that less time is wasted while a disk rotates to the starting location for a read or write operation.
- When you work with I/O operations, you'll need to catch or throw three types of checked exceptions: IOException, FileNotFoundException, and EOFException.
- To identify a file when you create a File object, you can use an *absolute pathname* or a *relative pathname*. To identify a file on a remote computer, you can use the *Universal Naming Convention* (*UNC*).
- The File class provides many methods that you can use to check whether a file or directory exists, to get information about a File object, and to create or delete directories and files.

Terms

input file
output file
I/O operation
file I/O
text file
binary file
stream
output stream
input stream
character stream
binary stream
layer
filtered stream
buffer
buffered stream
flush
absolute pathname
relative pathname
Universal Naming Convention (UNC)

Objectives

- Name and describe the two types of files that Java provides for.
- Explain why and how a filtered stream is created.
- Explain how a buffer for an output stream works and how it improves the performance of an I/O operation.
- Name and describe the three common types of I/O exceptions.
- Write code that handles the three common types of I/O exceptions.
- Write code that uses the File class to get information about a file.

Exercise 16-1 Use the File class

This exercise guides you through the process of using the File class to get information about a file.

1. Open the FileTester class that's in the c:\java\ch16\classes directory.
2. Inside the main method, create a File object that refers to the grades.txt file that's in the c:\java\ch16\files directory. To do this, you'll need to import the java.io package and you may want to refer to figure 16-6.
3. Add an if statement that determines whether the file exists as in figure 16-3. If it does, the application should print "File exists." Otherwise, it should print "File does not exist." Then, compile and run the application to make sure it's working properly.
4. Code statements that display information about the file as shown in figure 16-6. To do this, you'll need to write code that catches the IOException that may be thrown. Then, compile and run the program to make sure it's working properly.
5. Edit the code so it gets the same information from the books.txt file located in c:\java\ch16\classes\files directory. Then, compile and run the program to make sure it's working properly.

17

How to work with text files

In the last chapter, you learned some concepts and skills that apply to all I/O operations. Now, you'll learn how to create programs that write and read text files. Although text files are used infrequently for business applications, they are appropriate for some applications. Since some of the examples in this chapter use arrays, you should read the array portion of chapter 9 before you read this chapter.

How to write text files

To write a text file, you need to layer two or more classes to create a character output stream. That's why this topic begins with a general discussion of the classes that you can use to write text files. Then, this topic describes the methods that you can use to write text files, and it shows several examples that use these methods.

Classes that write character output streams

Figure 17-1 shows five of the classes that can be used to write text files. Although more classes for writing text files exist, these are five of the most commonly used classes for working with text files, and they're the ones that you'll learn how to use in this chapter.

In the Java API, all classes that are used to write text files descend from the abstract Writer class. You can use the PrintWriter and FileWriter classes to convert the binary data in your program to a character output stream and to write that stream to a file. To increase the efficiency of your I/O operations, you can use the BufferedWriter class to create a buffer.

Although the OutputStreamWriter class isn't covered in this chapter, you can use it to convert a character output stream to a binary output stream. That of course is the type of output stream that you'll learn about in the next chapter.

A subset of the Writer hierarchy

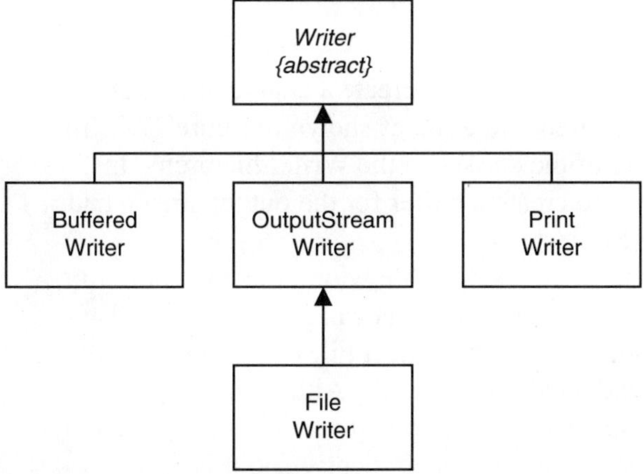

Classes that write character output streams

Class	Description
Writer	An abstract class that provides the foundation for all classes that write character output streams.
PrintWriter	A class that writes data to a character output steam.
BufferedWriter	A class that creates a buffer for a character output stream so the stream can be processed more efficiently.
FileWriter	A class that connects a character output stream to a file.
OutputStreamWriter	A class that creates a bridge from a character output stream to a binary stream.

Description

- The Writer hierarchy includes more classes than the ones in this figure. To learn more about them, you can check the documentation for the Java API. All classes in the java.io package that end with Writer are members of the Writer hierarchy.

Figure 17-1 Classes that write character output streams

How to connect a character output stream to a file

Before you can write to a text file, you need to create a character output stream and you need to connect that stream to a file as shown in figure 17-2. To do this, you must layer two or more of the classes in the Writer hierarchy. In addition, it's a good coding practice to create a buffer for the output stream and to use the File class to create a File object.

The first example shows how to write text to a file without using a buffer or a File object. First, you create a PrintWriter object that can print strings and other data types to an output stream. Then, you create a FileWriter object that uses a string to specify the name and location of the file. Although the output stream in this coding example uses fewer lines of code than the output stream in the second example, it doesn't process the data as efficiently and it isn't as flexible.

The second example shows how to include a buffer and a File object in the output stream. Since a buffer increases efficiency, you'll want to include one for any serious application. Similarly, since a File object lets you get information about the file that you're working with, you'll usually want to include one. That's why this example uses one variable to refer to the File object and another variable to refer to the output stream.

The constructors in this figure should help you understand how to layer output streams. Here, you can see that the PrintWriter constructor accepts any class derived from the Writer class. As a result, you can supply a BufferedWriter object as an argument of the PrintWriter constructor. Similarly, since the BufferedWriter constructor also accepts any Writer object, you can supply a FileWriter object as an argument of the BufferedWriter constructor. Then, to create a FileWriter object, you can supply either a File object or a String object that refers to a file.

Two of these constructors accept a second argument. If you set the second argument of the PrintWriter constructor to true, you turn on the *autoflush feature*. Then, the buffer is flushed whenever the println method is executed. If you set the second argument of the FileWriter constructor to true, you can append data to the file. To use this constructor, though, the file name must be a String object, not a File object. In this case, you can still create a File object to check the properties of the file, but you can't use it in the constructor.

Classes used to connect a character output stream to a file

PrintWriter	writes data to the stream
→ **BufferedWriter**	creates a buffer for the stream (optional)
→ **FileWriter**	connects the stream to a file
→ **File**	gives the name and location of the file (optional)

How to connect without a buffer or a File object (not recommended)

```
PrintWriter out = new PrintWriter(
                  new FileWriter("books.txt"));
```

How to connect with a buffer and a File object (preferred method)

```
File data = new File("books.txt");
PrintWriter out = new PrintWriter(
                  new BufferedWriter(
                  new FileWriter(data)));
```

Constructors of these classes

Constructor	Throws
`PrintWriter(Writer)`	None
`PrintWriter(Writer, booleanFlush)`	None
`BufferedWriter(Writer)`	None
`FileWriter(StringFilename)`	IOException
`FileWriter(File)`	IOException
`FileWriter(StringFilename, booleanAppend)`	IOException

Description

- By default, when you use a buffer, the data is flushed to the disk device when the buffer is full.
- If you set the second argument of the second PrintWriter constructor to true, the *autoflush feature* is turned on. Then, the buffer is flushed each time the println method is executed.
- If you set the second argument of the third FileWriter constructor to true, you can append data to an existing file. This means that you can write data starting at the end of the file.

Figure 17-2 How to connect a character output stream to a file

How to write a text file

Figure 17-3 shows how to write a text file. To start, it shows a simple application that writes data to a file. Then, it summarizes some of the methods of the PrintWriter class.

Within the main method of the TextWriterApp class, the first two statements create a File object and an object that refers to a buffered output stream. Then, the statements that follow use the print and println methods to write data to the buffer. Here, the first print statement writes a character representation of an int value, the second print statement writes a character, and the third print statement writes a character representation of a boolean value. Then, a println statement writes a string and follows it with an end of line character that's appropriate for the current platform.

After the println statement, a print statement writes another string to the file. Then, the last statement calls the close method. This flushes all of the characters from the buffer to the file, and it frees any resources used by the stream.

This figure also summarizes five methods of the PrintWriter class. Here, the first two methods write a character representation of the argument type to the stream. Since both of these methods can accept any of the argument types listed in this figure, they can convert any data type to a character representation. If you supply an object as an argument, these methods call the toString method of the object to return a string.

Note that the operation of the println method depends on whether the autoflush feature has been turned on by using the second PrintWriter constructor in the last figure. If this feature is on, all of the characters in the buffer are flushed to the file each time the println method is called. Otherwise, the buffer isn't flushed until it's full.

The last three methods in this figure also have an effect on the buffer. Since the print and println methods of the PrintWriter class don't throw exceptions, you don't need to throw or catch them. However, you can use the checkError method to flush the buffer and check whether any errors occurred when using these methods. Once an error occurs, though, all checkError calls return a boolean value of true.

In contrast, both the flush and close methods throw IOExceptions. Although you usually don't need to call the flush method, you can use it any time you want to flush all the data in the buffer to the file. On the other hand, you should always use the close method when you're done using a stream. Then, the buffer will flush its data to the file before the stream closes. If you don't call this method, you may lose data that hasn't been flushed to the file.

A class that writes data to a text file

```
import java.io.*;

public class TextWriterApp{
   public static void main(String args[]) throws IOException{
      File data = new File("example.txt");
      PrintWriter out = new PrintWriter(
                        new BufferedWriter(
                        new FileWriter(data)));
      out.print(5);
      out.print('c');
      out.print(true);
      out.println("Java");
      out.print("End of file");
      out.close();
   }
}
```

The file after it has been opened by a text editor

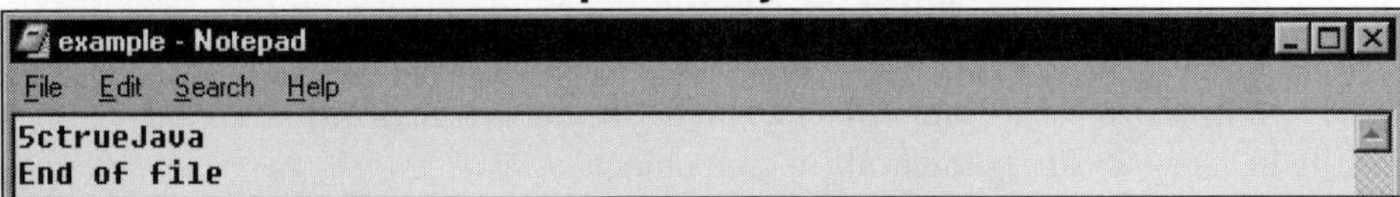

Common methods of the PrintWriter class

Method	Throws	Description
`print(argument)`	None	Writes the character representation of the argument type to the file.
`println(argument)`	None	Writes the character representation of the argument type to the file followed by the end of line character. If the autoflush feature is turned on, this also flushes the buffer.
`checkError()`	None	Flushes the stream and returns true if it finds an error.
`flush()`	IOException	Flushes the stream.
`close()`	IOException	Flushes the stream and closes it.

Argument types accepted by the print and println methods

`boolean`	`char`	`char[]`	`String`	`Object`
`int`	`long`	`double`	`float`	

Description

- To write a character representation of a data type to an output stream, you use the print and println methods of the PrintWriter class. If you supply an object as an argument, those methods will call the toString method of the object.
- To prevent data from being lost, you should always close the stream when you're done using it. Then, the program will flush all data to the file before it ends.

Figure 17-3 How to write a text file

Three examples that write text files

Figure 17-4 presents three examples that show how to write data to text files. This figure also shows what the text files will look like when opened by a text editor.

The first example shows how to use the println method to write character representations of three double values to a text file named doubles.txt. For the first double value, the println method converts the eight-byte double value that's used by Java to five one-byte character values. In this case, four of these character values represent the four digits and one character represents the decimal point. Since this example uses the println method for all three values, an end of line character follows each value.

The second example shows how to append a string and an object to a text file named log.txt. To start, the FileWriter constructor creates a FileWriter object that can append data to the file. If no file named log.txt exists in the current directory, this statement will create the file. Then, the print method prints a string, and the println method prints a Date object that represents the current date and time. Using a Date object as an argument of the println method automatically calls the toString method for that object.

The third example shows how to write records to a *delimited text file*. In this type of file, one type of *delimiter* is used to separate the *fields* (or *columns*) that are written to the file, and another type of delimiter is used to separate the *records* (or *rows*). In this example, the bar character (|) is used as the delimiter for the fields, and the end of line character is used as the delimiter for records. Note, however, that the tab character (\t) is commonly used as a field delimiter.

An example that writes doubles to a text file

```
File data = new File("doubles.txt");
PrintWriter out = new PrintWriter(
                  new BufferedWriter(
                  new FileWriter(data)));
out.println(59.75);
out.println(23.70);
out.println(92.22);
out.close();
```

The file opened in a text editor

```
59.75
23.7
92.22
```

An example that appends a string and an object to a text file

```
PrintWriter out = new PrintWriter(
                  new BufferedWriter(
                  new FileWriter("log.txt", true)));
out.print("This application was run on ");
Date today = new Date();
out.println(today);
out.close();
```

The file opened in a text editor

```
This application was run on Thu Dec 14 09:53:56 PST 2000
This application was run on Thu Dec 14 10:29:53 PST 2000
```

An example that writes a delimited text file

```
String[] names = {"Vicky Lewis", "Karen Doe", "Greg Smith"};
int[] grades = {94, 91, 86};
File data = new File("grades.txt");
PrintWriter out = new PrintWriter(new BufferedWriter(new
   FileWriter(data)));
for (int i = 0; i<names.length; i++){  //loops through each record
   out.print(names[i]);
   out.print('|'); //places a bar between each field
   out.println(grades[i]); //places a new line character after each record
}
out.close();
```

The file opened in a text editor

```
Vicky Lewis|94
Karen Doe|91
Greg Smith|86
```

Figure 17-4 Three examples that write text files

How to read text files

Now that you've learned how to write text files, you're ready to learn how to read those text files. To start, this topic discusses how to work with the classes that read text input streams. Then, this topic shows how to connect an input stream to a file, how to use the methods of an input stream to read a line of text, and how to read delimited text files.

Classes that read character input streams

Figure 17-5 shows six classes that can be used to read character input streams. Of these classes, two are abstract. Although these classes are only a subset of the entire Reader hierarchy, they include the classes that are most commonly used to read character input streams.

In the Java API, all classes that are used to read character input streams descend from the abstract Reader class. Of these classes, the BufferedReader and FileReader classes are the two most commonly used classes. In some coding situations, though, the PushbackReader and InputStreamReader classes are also useful.

A subset of the Reader hierarchy

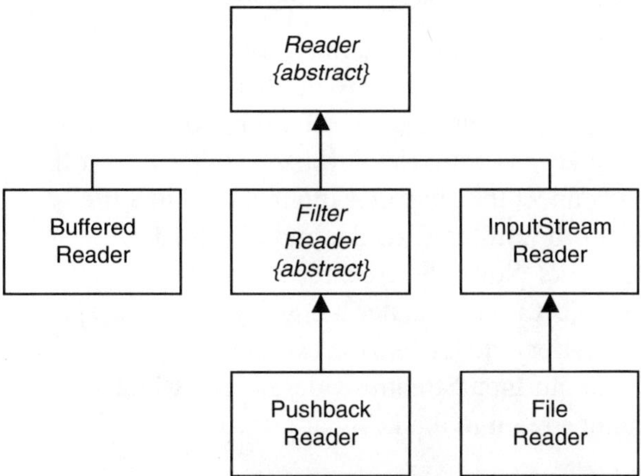

Classes that read character input streams

Class	Description
Reader	An abstract class that provides the foundation for all subclasses in the Reader hierarchy.
BufferedReader	A class that can be used to create a character input stream that uses a buffer. This class also contains useful methods for reading characters from a file.
InputSteamReader	A class that can be used as a bridge between binary streams and character input streams.
FileReader	A class for connecting any object in the Reader hierarchy to a file.
FilterReader	An abstract class for reading filtered character input streams.
PushbackReader	A class that can be used to read and unread characters in a character input stream.

Description

- The Reader hierarchy includes more classes than the ones in this figure. To learn more about them, you can check the documentation for the Java API. All classes in the java.io package that end with Reader are members of the Reader hierarchy.

Figure 17-5 Classes that read character input streams

How to connect a character input stream to a file

Before you can read characters from a text file, you must connect the character input stream to a file. Figure 17-6 shows how to do that with a buffer and a File object. Since the BufferedReader class creates a buffer and provides methods that read data, you'll almost always want to use this class. Then, you'll need to use the FileReader class to connect the character input stream to a file.

If you look at the constructors for the BufferedReader and FileReader classes, you can see why this code works. Since the constructor for the BufferedReader object accepts any object in the Reader hierarchy, it can accept a FileReader object that connects the stream to a file. However, the BufferedReader object can also accept an InputStreamReader object, which can be used to connect the character input stream to the keyboard or to a network connection rather than to a file.

Classes used to connect a character input stream to a file

BufferedReader reads data from the stream (optional)
→ **FileReader** connects the stream to a file
→ **File** gives the name and location of the file (optional)

How to connect with a buffer and a File object

```
File data = new File("books.txt");
BufferedReader in = new BufferedReader(
                    new FileReader(data));
```

Constructors of these classes

Constructor	Throws
`BufferedReader(Reader)`	None
`FileReader(StringFilename)`	FileNotFoundException
`FileReader(File)`	FileNotFoundException

Description

- Although you can read files with the FileReader class alone, the BufferedReader class improves efficiency and provides better methods for reading character input streams.

Figure 17-6 How to connect a character input stream to a file

How to read text files

Figure 17-7 shows how to read text files. To start, this figure shows a simple application that reads the text file that's created by the class in figure 17-3. Then, this figure summarizes the methods of the BufferedReader class.

Within the main method of the TextReaderApp class, the first statement creates a File object. Then, an if statement uses this File object to check if the file exists. If it does, the statements inside the if block read the file. Otherwise, the else block prints a message to the console indicating that the file wasn't found.

Within the if block, the first statement creates a character input stream and connects that stream to the file that's specified in the File object. Then, a while loop reads each line in the file and prints these lines to the console. When the readLine method attempts to read past the end of the file, it returns a null value, which causes the application to exit the loop and call the close method. This flushes the buffer and closes the input stream.

The rest of this figure summarizes some of the methods of the BufferedReader class. Here, the readLine method reads in one line of text as a string. Then, you can parse the numbers and other types of data from the string as shown in the next two figures.

Although you can also use the read method to read a text file, it's not commonly used. When this method reads a character, it returns an int value that represents the ASCII code for the character. Then, to get the character, you must cast the return type to a char value.

If you know the structure of the data in the input stream that you're working with, you may occasionally need to skip a specific number of characters. To do that, you can use the skip method. When you call this method, it tries to move the cursor forward the specified number of characters without reading new characters into the stream. However, if this method encounters the end of the file or can't continue for some other reason, it returns the actual number of characters that were skipped.

A class that reads text from a file

```
import java.io.*;

public class TextReaderApp{
   public static void main(String args[]) throws IOException{
      File data = new File("example.txt");
      if (data.exists()){
         BufferedReader in = new BufferedReader(
                                new FileReader(data));
         String line = in.readLine();
         while(line != null){
            System.out.println(line);
            line = in.readLine();
         }
         in.close();
      }
      else
         System.out.println("File not found - example.txt");
   }
}
```

The output to the console

Common methods of the BufferedReader class

Method	Throws	Description
`readLine()`	IOException	Reads a line of text and returns it as a string.
`read()`	IOException	Reads a single character and returns it as an int that represents the ASCII code for the character. When this method attempts to read past the end of the file, it returns an int value of -1.
`skip(longValue)`	IOException	Attempts to skip the specified number of characters, and returns an int value for the actual number of characters skipped.
`close()`	IOException	Closes the input stream and flushes the buffer.

Figure 17-7 How to read text files

An example that reads numbers from a text file

Figure 17-8 shows a coding example that reads numbers into a program from a text file. In particular, it shows how to read the three double values that were written to a text file by the code in the first example of figure 17-4. In this case, each double was written to a separate line in the text file. As a result, you can use the readLine method to return a String object that contains each value. Then, you can use the parseDouble method of the Double class to convert each String object to a double data type.

An example that reads numbers into a program from a text file

```
File data = new File("doubles.txt");
BufferedReader in = new BufferedReader(
                    new FileReader(data));
String line = in.readLine();
while(line != null){
   double number = Double.parseDouble(line);
   System.out.println("Double: " + number);
   line = in.readLine();
}
in.close();
```

The output to the console

```
Double: 59.75
Double: 23.7
Double: 92.22
Press any key to continue . . .
_
```

Description

- When a text file contains just one numeric field per line, you can convert each field to a primitive type as shown above.
- When a text file contains more than one field per line, you can use the StringTokenizer class to parse each line into fields as shown in the next figure. Then, you can convert the numeric fields into primitive types.

Figure 17-8 An example that reads numbers from a text file

How to read delimited text files

When you're working with delimited text files that contain more than one field in each line or record, you can use the StringTokenizer class to parse each record into substrings, or *tokens*. Then, you can treat each token as a field in a record. Figure 17-9 shows how this works.

When you create a StringTokenizer object, the first argument of the constructor supplies the string that you wish to break into tokens. By default, the StringTokenizer object uses spaces, tabs, new lines, and returns as the delimiters for finding the tokens. But if you want to specify your own delimiters, you can code a second argument that contains a string of one or more characters that you want to use as delimiters.

The first example in this figure shows how to use the StringTokenizer class to parse a string into tokens and print the contents of each token. Here, the constructor identifies the tab (\t) and return (\r) characters as the delimiters. As a result, the new object consists of three tokens. The first token is WARP, the next token is War and Peace, and the last token is 14.95. Although this last token looks like a number, remember that all of the tokens are actually strings. Then, to convert a numeric string to a double type, you can use the parseDouble method of the Double class.

The second example shows how to use the StringTokenizer class to work with the delimited file named grades.txt that was created by the third example in figure 17-4. Since the code in this figure is similar to the code in the previous figures, you should understand most of it. The main difference is that you can now use the StringTokenizer class to retrieve the individual fields of each record.

Inside the while loop, the first statement creates a StringTokenizer object for each line that is read with the bar character (|) used as the field delimiter. Then, the next two statements use this object to return one token for the name and one token for the grade. The last three statements in this loop convert each grade from a string to an int type, print a line that shows the name and the grade for each record, and read another line from the text file.

In the method summary in this figure, you can see that the methods for a StringTokenizer object let you work with the tokens. When you call the nextToken method for the first time, for example, it returns the first token in the string. Then, each subsequent call to the nextToken method returns the next token in the string. If no more tokens are available, though, the nextToken method throws an exception. To prevent this, you can call the countTokens or hasMoreTokens method to make sure you don't issue the nextToken method when there aren't any more tokens.

Although this figure uses the StringTokenizer class to work with delimited text files, you can also use it to work with other types of strings. Since it's part of the java.util package, though, you should import this package whenever you use this class.

The StringTokenizer class

```
java.util.StringTokenizer
```

Code that shows how the StringTokenizer class works

```
String record = "WARP\tWar and Peace\t14.95";
String tokenDelimiter = "\t\n";
StringTokenizer t = new StringTokenizer(record, tokenDelimiter);
int numberOfTokens = t.countTokens();
System.out.println("Number of tokens: " + numberOfTokens);
while (t.hasMoreTokens()){
   String token = t.nextToken();
   System.out.println(token);
}
```

Code that uses the StringTokenizer class to parse a text file

```
File data = new File("grades.txt");
BufferedReader in = new BufferedReader(
                    new FileReader(data));
String line = in.readLine();
while (line != null){
   StringTokenizer t = new StringTokenizer(line, "|");
   String name = t.nextToken();
   String gradeString = t.nextToken();
   int grade = Integer.parseInt(gradeString);
   System.out.println(name + " " + grade);
   line = in.readLine();
}
in.close();
```

Common constructors of the StringTokenizer class

Constructor	Description
`StringTokenizer(String)`	Creates a StringTokenizer object with default delimiters of spaces, tabs (\t), new lines (\n), and returns (\r).
`StringTokenizer(String, StringDelimiters)`	Creates a StringTokenizer object with the delimiters specified by the second argument.

Common methods of the StringTokenizer class

Method	Description
`nextToken()`	Returns the next token as a String.
`countTokens()`	Returns an int for the number of tokens.
`hasMoreTokens()`	Returns true if more tokens exist.
`hasMoreElements()`	Returns true if more tokens exist.
`nextElement()`	Returns the next token as an Object.

Description

- A *token* is a substring that has been extracted from a delimited string.

Figure 17-9 How to read delimited text files

Perspective

In this chapter, you've learned how to read and write text files. You've also learned how to parse a delimited text file into the fields and records that it is composed of. In the next chapter, you'll learn how to use many of the same skills as you read and write binary files.

Summary

- You can use the classes that end with Writer to create a character output stream that can write data to a text file.
- When you use the BufferedWriter class to add a buffer to a character output stream, the buffer is flushed when the buffer is full. However, if you turn the *autoflush feature* on, the buffer is flushed each time the println method is executed.
- In a *delimited text file*, *delimiters* are used to separate the *fields* and *records* of the file.
- You can use the classes that end with Reader to create a character input stream that can read data from a text file.
- You can use the StringTokenizer class to create an object that consists of the *tokens* that are extracted from a delimited text file or record.

Terms

autoflush feature
delimited text file
delimiter
field
column
record
row
token

Objectives

- Write code that writes data from a program to a text file.
- Write code that reads data from a text file into a program.
- Write code that writes and reads delimited text files.

Exercise 17-1 Write and view text files

This exercise guides you through the process of writing three text files. Then, it has you open these files in a text editor to see what you've written.

1. Open the TextWriterApp class that's in the c:\java\ch17 directory. Then, add the code for the TextWriterApp class that's in figure 17-3, and compile and run this application. When you're done, open the example.txt file that you just created with a text editor. It should contain the two lines of text shown in figure 17-3.
2. Open the LogWriterApp class that's stored in the c:\java\ch17 directory. Then, modify this class so it appends data to the file as in the second example of figure 17-4. Next, compile the code and run the application two or more times. When you're done, open the log.txt file with a text editor. It should contain two or more lines of text, one for the each time that you ran the application.
3. Open the GradesWriterApp class that's in the c:\java\ch17 directory. Then, edit the code so it prints the grades to a tab-delimited text file. To do that, you need to use the tab character (\t) instead of the bar character (|). When you're done, open the grades.txt file with a text editor. It should have three lines of text. Although you probably won't see the tab characters, your text editor uses these tabs to align the data.

Exercise 17-2 Read text files

This exercise guides you through the process of reading three text files.

1. Open the TextReaderApp class that's in the c:\java\ch17 directory. Then, edit the file so it reads both lines of text in the example.txt file as in figure 17-7. When you compile and run this application, it should print the two lines of text shown in this figure.
2. Open the DoublesReaderApp class that's in the c:\java\ch17 directory. Then, edit the code for this class so it reads the three doubles from the doubles.txt file as in figure 17-8. When you compile and run this application, it should print three lines of text, one for each double value.
3. Open the GradesReaderApp class that's stored in the c:\java\ch17 directory. Then, edit the code so it reads the grades from the tab-delimited text file. To do that, you need to supply a second argument for the StringTokenizer constructor as in figure 17-9. When you compile and run this application, it should print the names of three students and their grades to the console.

18

How to work with binary files

In chapter 16, you learned some general concepts and skills that apply to all input and output operations. In this chapter, you'll learn how to create programs that read and write binary files. This is the type of file that you're most likely to use for business applications. Since working with this type of file requires the use of arrays and vectors, you need to read chapter 9 before you read this chapter.

How to write binary files

To write a binary file, you need to use a combination of binary output streams. That's why this topic first presents an introduction to these streams. Then, this topic describes some of the methods that you can use to write data from your program to a binary file. And finally, it presents some examples that write data to a binary file.

Classes that write binary output streams

Figure 18-1 shows five classes and one interface that you can use to write binary output streams. You can use the DataOutputStream and FileOutputStream classes to send data to a binary output stream and to write that data to a binary file. Since the DataOutputStream class implements the DataOutput interface, you can call the standard methods of this interface to send data to the output stream. Later in this chapter, you'll learn more about these methods.

In the Java API, all classes that write data to binary output streams descend from the abstract OutputStream class. Most of these classes end with OutputStream and are stored in the java.io and java.util.zip packages. Most of the classes that are used to add functionality to an output stream class inherit the FilterOutputStream class. For instance, the BufferedOutputStream class adds functionality to a stream by adding a buffer that allows the stream to be processed more efficiently.

Note, however, that the Java API also contains many other OutputStream classes that inherit the FilterOutputStream class. To learn more about these classes, you can browse through the java.io and java.util.zip packages in the documentation for the Java API.

A subset of the OutputStream hierarchy

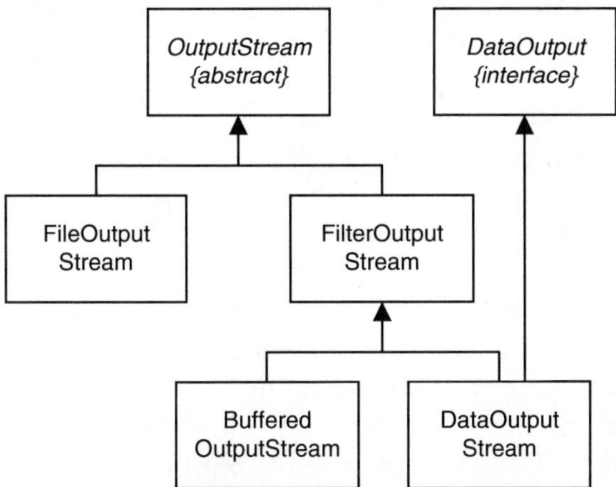

Summary of these classes

Class	Description
OutputStream	An abstract class that's inherited by all classes that write binary output streams.
FilterOutputStream	The superclass of all classes that filter binary output streams.
BufferedOutputStream	A class that creates a buffer for a binary output stream.
DataOutputStream	A class that writes data to a binary output stream.
FileOutputStream	A class that connects a binary output stream to a file.

Description

- The OutputStream hierarchy includes more classes than the ones in this figure. To learn more about them, you can check the documentation for the Java API. All classes in the java.io and java.util.zip packages that end with OutputStream are members of the OutputStream hierarchy.
- Classes that inherit the FilterOutputStream class typically add functionality to an existing output stream.
- The DataOutputStream class implements the DataOutput interface. As a result, you can use the methods of that interface to send data to the output stream.

Figure 18-1 Classes that write binary output streams

How to connect a binary output stream to a file

Before you can write data to a binary file, you need to create a binary output stream and you need to connect that stream to a file. To do this, you must layer two or more streams in the OutputStream hierarchy as shown in figure 18-2. It's also a good coding practice to create a buffer for the output stream and to create a File object for the file.

The first example shows how to connect your program to a file without using a buffer or File object. First, you create a DataOutputStream object that can write data to a binary output stream. Then, you supply an object of the FileOutputStream class as an argument of the DataOutputStream constructor.

The second example shows how to include a buffer and a File object in the output stream. Since a buffer increases efficiency, you'll want to include one for any serious application. Similarly, since a File object allows you to get information about the file that you're working with, you'll usually want to include one. That's why this example uses one variable to refer to the File object and another variable to refer to the output stream.

The constructors shown in this figure should help you understand how to layer output streams. Here, you can see that the DataOutputStream constructor accepts an object created from any class that's derived from the OutputStream class. As a result, you can supply a BufferedOutputStream object as an argument of the DataOutputStream constructor. Similarly, since the BufferedOutputStream constructor also accepts any OutputStream object, you can supply a FileOutputStream object as an argument of the BufferedOutputStream constructor. In contrast, to create a FileOutputStream object, you can supply either a File object or a String object that refers to a file.

If you use the first two constructors of the FileOutputStream class to create a file output stream, the output stream will delete all data in the existing file before it writes the new data to the file. However, you can use the third constructor of the FileOutputStream class to add data to the end of a file (append) by setting the second argument to true. When you use this constructor, though, the filename must be a String object, not a File object. If necessary, you can still create a File object to check the properties of the file, but you can't use it in the constructor of the FileOutputStream class.

Classes used to connect a binary output stream to a file

DataOutputStream	writes data to the stream
→ **BufferedOutputStream**	creates a buffer for the stream (optional)
→ **FileOutputStream**	connects the stream to a file
→ **File**	gives the name and location of the file (optional)

How to connect without a buffer or a File object (not recommended)

```
DataOutputStream out = new DataOutputStream(
                       new FileOutputStream("books.dat"));
```

How to connect with a buffer and File object (preferred method)

```
File data = new File("books.dat");
DataOutputStream out = new DataOutputStream(
                       new BufferedOutputStream(
                       new FileOutputStream(data)));
```

Constructors of these classes

Constructor	Throws
`DataOutputStream(OutputStream)`	None
`BufferedOutputStream(OutputStream)`	None
`FileOutputStream(File)`	FileNotFoundException
`FileOutputStream(StringFilename)`	FileNotFoundException
`FileOutputStream(StringFilename, booleanAppend)`	FileNotFoundException

Description

- Although a buffer isn't required, it makes output operations more efficient.
- By default, the FileOutputStream constructors overwrite the entire file. To append data to a file, use the last FileOutputStream constructor in this figure and set the second argument to true.

Figure 18-2 How to connect a binary output stream to a file

How to work with the DataOutput interface

Figure 18-3 shows the most commonly used methods of the DataOutput interface. Since most of the classes that write data to a binary output stream implement this interface, you can use these methods to write data to a binary file. Earlier in this chapter, you learned that the DataOutputStream class implements this interface. Later in this chapter, you'll learn how to work with another class that implements this interface.

You can use the first seven methods in this figure to write primitive data types to a binary output stream. For example, you can use the writeInt method to write an int value to a binary output stream. To read these data types, you sometimes need to know how many bytes each data type uses. That's why this figure includes the number of bytes that each of these methods uses.

You can use the last two methods in this figure to write strings to a binary output stream. When you use the writeChars method, it writes two bytes per character. When you use the writeUTF method, it starts by writing a two-byte number that indicates the length of the string. Then, it writes the *UTF* (*Universal Text Format*) representation of the string. Although this usually writes each ASCII character as one byte, it may write some Unicode characters as two or three bytes. In general, you can use the writeUTF method whenever it's okay to write strings with lengths that vary. But when you need to write strings that have equal lengths, you need to use the writeChars method. Later in this chapter, you'll learn why.

All of these methods throw an IOException that's checked by the compiler. As a result, you must either throw or catch this exception. Otherwise, you won't be able to compile your code.

Methods of the DataOutput interface

Method	Throws	Description
`writeBoolean(boolean)`	IOException	Writes a 1-byte boolean value to the output stream.
`writeShort(int)`	IOException	Writes a 2-byte short value to the output stream.
`writeInt(int)`	IOException	Writes a 4-byte int value to the output stream.
`writeLong(long)`	IOException	Writes an 8-byte long value to the output stream.
`writeFloat(float)`	IOException	Writes a 4-byte float value to the output stream.
`writeDouble(double)`	IOException	Writes an 8-byte double value to the output stream.
`writeChar(int)`	IOException	Writes a 2-byte char value to the output stream.
`writeChars(String)`	IOException	Writes a string using 2 bytes per character to the output stream.
`writeUTF(String)`	IOException	Writes a 2-byte value for the number of bytes in the string followed by the UTF representation of the string, which typically uses 1 byte per character.

Description

- Since the DataOutputStream class implements the DataOutput interface, you can call the methods shown above from a DataOutputStream object.
- The writeUTF method uses the *Universal Text Format (UTF)*. First, this method writes a two-byte number for the number of bytes in the string. Then, it writes the characters using the Universal Text Format. For most strings, UTF uses one byte per character.

Figure 18-3 How to work with the DataOutput interface

How to write a binary file

Figure 18-4 shows how to write data to a binary file. To start, it shows a class that uses the DataOutputStream class to write data to a binary file. Then, it shows three methods of the DataOutputStream class that go beyond the methods of the DataOutput interface.

The class in this figure contains a main method that throws an IOException. Within the main method, the first statement creates a File object that refers to a file named example.dat in the current directory. Then, the second statement creates a binary output stream by layering the DataOutputStream class, the BufferedOutputStream class, and the FileOutputStream class. After that, the next six statements write a variety of data types to a binary file: an int value, a char value, a boolean value, and several types of strings. The last statement closes the output stream, which flushes all data to the file and releases the resources that were used by the stream object.

The screen in this figure shows what a binary file looks like when it's opened in a text editor. Although it isn't as readable as a text file, it shows the number of bytes that were used for each data type. To start, the file uses four bytes for the int value, two bytes for the char value, and one byte for the boolean value. Then, the file uses six bytes to write the string that was written with the writeUTF method: two bytes for the length of the string, and one byte for each character in the string. Next, the file uses two bytes to store the new line character. And finally, the file uses two bytes per character to store the string that was written with the writeChars method.

Since the DataOutputStream class implements the DataOutput interface, you can use the methods summarized in the previous figure. In addition, you can use the three DataOutputStream methods shown in this figure. You can use these methods to retrieve the number of bytes currently written to the binary output stream, to flush the output stream, and to close the output stream.

A class that writes data to a binary file

```
import java.io.*;

public class BinaryWriterApp{
   public static void main(String[] args) throws IOException{
      File data = new File("example.dat");
      DataOutputStream out = new DataOutputStream(
                             new BufferedOutputStream(
                             new FileOutputStream(data)));
      out.writeInt(5);
      out.writeChar('c');
      out.writeBoolean(true);
      out.writeUTF("Java");
      out.writeChar('\n');
      out.writeChars("End of file");
      out.close();
   }
}
```

The file opened in a text editor

```
▮▮▮▮▮c▮▮▮Java▮
▮E▮n▮d▮ ▮o▮f▮ ▮f▮i▮l▮e
```

Methods of the DataOutputStream class

Method	Throws	Description
size()	None	Returns an int for the number of bytes written to this stream.
flush()	IOException	Flushes any data that's in the buffer to the file.
close()	IOException	Flushes any data that's in the buffer to the file and closes the stream.

Description

- When you use the DataOutputStream class, you can use the methods above as well as the methods of the DataOutput interface that this class implements.

Examples that write binary files

Figure 18-5 presents two more examples that show how to write data to a binary file. In addition, they show what the file will look like when opened in a text editor.

The first example shows how you can write three *records* of data to a binary file. In this example, each record contains two *fields*: one field for the student's name and one for the student's grade. To start, this example writes an int value for the number of records in the file. Later in this chapter, an example will use this number to read the records from the file. Then, a loop writes the three names and grades to a binary file. Within this loop, the first statement uses the writeUTF method to write the names of the students. Then, the second statement uses the writeInt method to write the grade for each student.

The second example shows how the writeUTF method differs from the writeChars method. To start, this example uses the writeUTF method to write a string that contains 35 characters (34 regular characters plus one end of line character). Then, it uses the size method to return the number of bytes that have been written to the stream. After that, this example uses the writeChars method to write the same string. Then, it uses the size method to return the number of bytes that this method writes. Last, this example prints the number of bytes used by each method to the console. To write these 35 characters, the writeUTF method used 37 bytes with two bytes for the length of the string and one byte for each of the 35 characters. In contrast, the writeChars method used two bytes per character, or 70 bytes.

An example that writes strings and int values to a binary file

```
String[] names = {"Vicky Lewis", "Karen Doe", "Greg Smith"};
int[] grades = {94, 91, 86};

File data = new File("grades.dat");
DataOutputStream out = new DataOutputStream(
                       new BufferedOutputStream(
                       new FileOutputStream(data)));

int numberOfRecords = names.length;
out.writeInt(numberOfRecords);

for (int i = 0; i < numberOfRecords; i++){
   out.writeUTF(names[i]);
   out.writeInt(grades[i]);
}
out.close();
```

The file opened in a text editor

```
1 ▮▮▮▮▮ Vicky Lewis▮▮▮^▮  Karen Doe▮▮▮[▮
2 Greg Smith▮▮▮V
```

An example that shows how to write strings two different ways

```
File data = new File("strings.dat");
DataOutputStream out = new DataOutputStream(
                       new BufferedOutputStream(
                       new FileOutputStream(data)));

out.writeUTF("How many bytes are in this string?\n");
int size1 = out.size();

out.writeChars("How many bytes are in this string?\n");
int size2 = out.size() - size1;

out.close();

System.out.println("The writeUTF method writes " + size1 + " bytes.");
System.out.println("The writeChars method writes " + size2 + " bytes.");
```

The file opened in a text editor

```
1 ▮#How many bytes are in this string?
2 ▮H▮o▮w▮ ▮m▮a▮n▮y▮ ▮b▮y▮t▮e▮s▮ ▮a▮r▮e▮ ▮i▮n▮ ▮t▮h▮i▮s▮ ▮s▮t▮r▮i▮n▮g▮?▮
3
```

The output to the console

```
The writeUTF method writes 37 bytes.
The writeChars method writes 70 bytes.
```

Figure 18-5 Examples that write binary files

How to read binary files

This topic shows how to read the binary files that you learned how to write in the last topic. Since reading binary files uses many of the same concepts as writing binary files, some of this material should feel like review.

Classes that read binary input streams

Figure 18-6 shows six classes and one interface that you can use to read binary input streams. These classes work much like the classes that are used to write binary output streams. In short, you can use the DataInputStream and FileInputStream classes to read data from a binary file. Since the DataInputStream class implements the DataInput interface, you can use all of the standard methods of this interface to retrieve data from the input stream.

In the Java API, all classes that read data from binary input streams descend from the abstract InputStream class. Most of these classes end with InputStream and are stored in the java.io and java.util.zip packages. Most of the classes that are used to add functionality to an input stream class inherit the FilterInputStream class. For instance, the BufferedInputStream class adds functionality to a stream by adding a buffer that allows the stream to be processed more efficiently.

Note, however, that the Java API also contains many other InputStream classes that inherit the FilterInputStream class. To learn more about these classes, you can browse through the java.io and java.util.zip packages in the documentation for the Java API.

A subset of the InputStream hierarchy

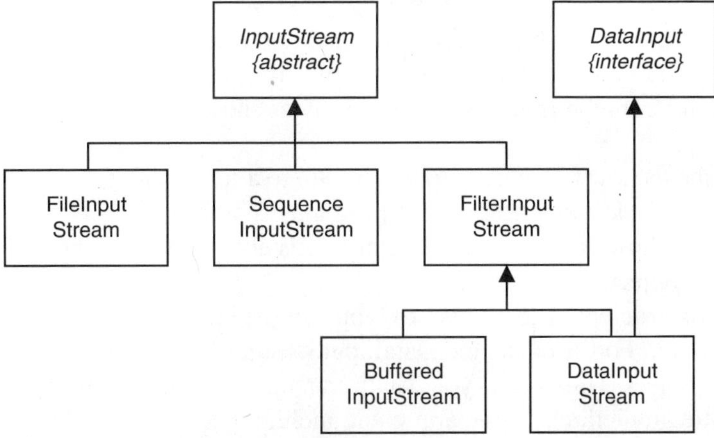

Summary of these classes

Class	Description
InputStream	An abstract class that provides the foundation for all classes that read binary input streams.
FilterInputStream	A superclass of classes that filter binary input streams.
BufferedInputStream	A class that creates a buffer for a binary input stream.
DataInputStream	A class that reads data from a binary input stream.
SequenceInputStream	A class that concatenates binary input streams.
FileInputStream	A class that connects a binary input stream to a file.

Description

- The InputStream hierarchy includes more classes than the ones in this figure. To learn more about them, you can check the documentation for the Java API. All classes in the java.io and java.util.zip packages that end with InputStream are members of the InputStream hierarchy.
- Classes that inherit the FilterInputStream class typically add functionality to an existing input stream.
- The DataInputStream class implements the DataInput interface. As a result, you can use the methods of that interface to retrieve data from the input stream.

Figure 18-6 Classes that read binary input streams

How to connect a binary input stream to a file

Before you can read data from a binary file, you need to create a binary input stream, and you need to connect that stream to a file. To do this, you must layer two or more streams from the InputStream hierarchy as shown in figure 18-7.

The first example shows how to connect your program to a file without using a buffer or File object. However, to improve program efficiency, you should include a buffer as shown in the second example. It's also a good coding practice to include a File object.

By looking at the constructors of these classes, you can see how they can be layered on top of each other. For instance, the DataInputStream constructor accepts an InputStream object. This means you can use an object created from any class in the InputStream hierarchy as an argument, including the BufferedInputStream or FileInputStream class. Similarly, the BufferedInputStream constructor accepts any object of the InputStream hierarchy.

For example, you can supply a BufferedInputStream object as an argument of the DataInputStream constructor. In contrast, when you create a FileInputStream object, you can supply either a File object or a String object that refers to a file.

Classes used to connect a binary input stream to a file

DataInputStream	reads data from the stream
→ **BufferedInputStream**	creates a buffer for the stream (optional)
→ **FileInputStream**	connects the stream to the file
→ **File**	gives the name and location of the file (optional)

How to connect without a buffer or a File object (not recommended)

```
DataInputStream out = new DataInputStream(
                      new FileInputStream("books.dat"));
```

How to connect with a buffer and a File object (preferred method)

```
File data = new File("books.dat");
DataInputStream out = new DataInputStream(
                      new BufferedInputStream(
                      new FileInputStream(data)));
```

Constructors of these classes

Constructor	Throws
`DataInputStream(InputStream)`	None
`BufferedInputStream(InputStream)`	None
`FileInputStream(File)`	FileNotFoundException
`FileInputStream(StringFilename)`	FileNotFoundException

Description

- Although a buffer isn't required, it makes input operations more efficient.

Figure 18-7 How to connect a binary input stream to a file

How to work with the DataInput interface

Figure 18-8 shows nine methods of the DataInput interface that you can use to read binary data. In general, these methods work like the methods of the DataOutput interface. Because the DataInputStream class implements the DataInput interface, you can call all of its methods from a DataInputStream object.

You can use the first seven methods in this figure to read primitive data types from a binary output stream. For example, you can use the readInt method to read an int value from a binary output stream. To read these data types, you sometimes need to know how many bytes each data type uses. That's why this figure includes the number of bytes that each of these methods uses.

You can use the readUTF method to read binary data that's stored in the Universal Text Format that was described earlier in this chapter. Usually, that means that you'll use the readUTF method to read the data that was written with the writeUTF method.

You can use the skipBytes method to skip a specified number of bytes in an input stream. If for some reason it can't skip that number of bytes, though, the method skips as many bytes as it can and returns an int value for the actual number that it skipped. This can happen, for example, if the method reaches the end of the file before it skips the specified number of bytes.

Although the read methods in this figure correspond with the write methods shown earlier, there is no corresponding read method for the writeChars method. As a result, to read strings written by the writeChars method, you need to create a loop that reads in each character using the readChar method. The next figure shows an example of how to do this.

Like the write methods shown earlier, all of these read methods throw an IOException that's checked by the compiler. As a result, you must either throw or catch this exception. Otherwise, you won't be able to compile your code.

Common methods of the DataInput interface

Method	Throws	Description
`readBoolean()`	EOFException	Reads 1 byte and returns a boolean value.
`readShort()`	EOFException	Reads 2 bytes and returns a short value.
`readInt()`	EOFException	Reads 4 bytes and returns an int value.
`readLong()`	EOFException	Reads 8 bytes and returns a long value.
`readFloat()`	EOFException	Reads 4 bytes and returns a float value.
`readDouble()`	EOFException	Reads 8 bytes and returns a double value.
`readChar()`	EOFException	Reads 2 bytes and returns a char value.
`readUTF()`	EOFException	Reads the string encoded with UTF.
`skipBytes(int)`	EOFException	Attempts to skip the specified number of bytes, and returns an int value for the actual number of bytes skipped.

Description

- Since the DataInputStream class implements the DataInput interface, you can call the methods shown above from an object of this class.
- The readUTF method reads characters that were written with the Universal Text Format.

Figure 18-8 How to work with the DataInput interface

How to read a binary file

Figure 18-9 shows how to read data from a binary file. To start, it shows a class that uses the DataInputStream class to read data from a binary file. Then, it summarizes two methods of the DataInputStream class that go beyond the methods of the DataOutput interface.

The class in this figure begins by importing the java.io package. Then, it declares a main method that throws an IOException. Within the main method, the first statement creates a File object that refers to the example.dat file that you learned how to write earlier in this chapter. Then, the example uses an if statement to check if this file exists. If it does, the first statement within the if clause creates a binary input stream by layering the DataInputStream class, the BufferedInputStream class, and the FileInputStream class. After that, the statements read the data, print that data to the console, and close the input stream.

These statements read an int value, a char value, a boolean value, and a string written in the Universal Text Format. Then, a statement reads the end of line character, but this character isn't stored in a variable or printed to the console. Last, a loop reads the characters stored at the end of this file and prints them to the console. To do that, this loop uses the available method to determine the number of bytes left in the file. Then, it divides this number by two since each char value uses two bytes. This prevents the loop from reading beyond the end of the file and throwing an EOFException.

Since the DataInputStream class implements the DataInput interface, you can use any methods in that interface on DataInputStream objects. In addition to those methods, you can use the available method to return the number of bytes left in the file and the close method to close the input stream and release any resources used by it.

A class that reads data from a binary file

```
import java.io.*;

public class BinaryReaderApp{
   public static void main(String[] args) throws IOException{
      File data = new File("example.dat");
      if (data.exists()){
         DataInputStream in = new DataInputStream(
                              new BufferedInputStream(
                              new FileInputStream(data)));

         int number = in.readInt();
         System.out.println(number);

         char letter = in.readChar();
         System.out.println(letter);

         boolean value = in.readBoolean();
         System.out.println(value);

         String string = in.readUTF();
         System.out.println(string);

         in.readChar();

         int numberOfChars = in.available()/2;
         String characters = "";
         for (int i = 0; i < numberOfChars; i++){
            char c = in.readChar();
            characters += c;
         }
         System.out.println(characters);

         in.close();

      }
   }
}
```

The output to the console

```
5
c
true
Java
End of file
```

Common methods of the DataInputStream class

Method	Throws	Description
`available()`	IOException	Returns the remaining number of bytes in the file.
`close()`	IOException	Closes the stream.

Description

- When you read data, you don't have to assign it to a variable. After the data is read, the cursor moves to the next byte in the file.

Figure 18-9 How to read a binary file

Examples that read binary files

Figure 18-10 presents two examples that show how to read data from a binary file. Both of these examples read from files that you learned how to write in figure 18-5. The first example shows how to read records, while the second example shows how to read strings that were written using the writeUTF and writeChars methods.

The first example reads a file that contains one record for each student. Each record contains one field for the student's name and another field for the student's grade. Since this file begins with an int value that indicates the number of records in the file, this example uses the readInt method to read that value. Then, this code uses that value to loop through each record in the file. This prevents the code from trying to read beyond the end of the file and throwing an EOFException. Within the loop, the first statement uses the readUTF method to return the name of the student as a string, and the second statement uses the readInt method to return the student's grade as an int value. The last statement in the loop prints this data to the console, separating the name and the grade with a tab character.

The second example reads two identical strings that were written by the writeUTF and writeChars methods. First, the readUTF method reads the string that was written by the writeUTF method. Then, this example uses the readChar method within a loop to read the string that was written by the writeChars method. But first, this code uses the available method to make sure that the readChar method in the loop doesn't attempt to read past the end of the file and throw an EOFException. Within the loop, the first statement returns the char value, and the second statement adds that value to the end of the string.

Although the binary file stores these two strings differently, the output for these methods shows that the same strings are returned to the program. For many applications, you can use the writeUTF and readUTF methods to write and read string data. But if you need to make sure that each string has the same length, you have to use the writeChars method and the readChar method. Later in this chapter, you'll see why.

An example that reads strings and int values from a binary file

```
File data = new File("grades.dat");
DataInputStream in = new DataInputStream(
                     new BufferedInputStream(
                     new FileInputStream(data)));

int numberOfRecords = in.readInt();

for (int i = 0; i < numberOfRecords; i++){
   String name = in.readUTF();
   int grade = in.readInt();
   System.out.println(name + "\t" + grade);
}

in.close();
```

The output to the console

```
Vicky Lewis     94
Karen Doe       91
Greg Smith      86
```

An example that reads strings two different ways from a binary file

```
File data = new File("strings.dat");
DataInputStream in = new DataInputStream(
                     new BufferedInputStream(
                     new FileInputStream(data)));

String string1 = in.readUTF();
System.out.print(string1);

String string2 = "";
int bytes = in.available();
int characters = bytes/2;
for (int i = 0; i < characters; i++){
   char c = in.readChar();
   string2 += c;
}
System.out.print(string2);

in.close();
```

The output to the console

```
How many bytes are in this string?
How many bytes are in this string?
```

Figure 18-10 Examples that read binary files

How to combine two files into a single input stream

Figure 18-11 shows how to use the SequenceInputStream class to combine the data from two files into a single input stream. Although you probably won't need to do that much, it shows how classes can add functionality to an input stream.

The diagram in this figure shows that the SequenceInputStream class doesn't create a new file. Instead, it lets you create one input stream from two files. Once you create the input stream, you can use the DataInputStream class to read the data as shown carlier in this topic.

An example that combines two files into a single input stream

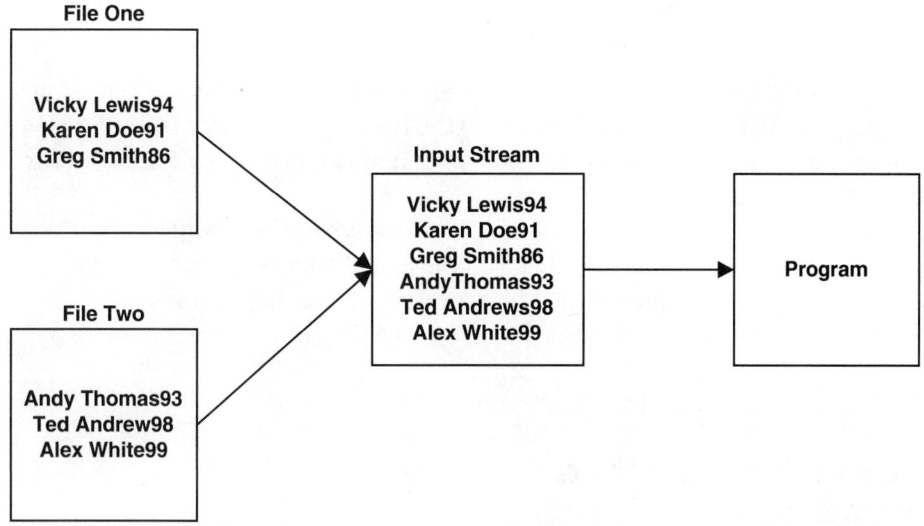

Classes used to concatenate streams

DataInputStream	reads data from the stream
→ **SequenceInputStream**	concatenates input streams
→ **FileInputStream**	connects the stream to a file
→ **File**	gives the name and location of the file (optional)

How to concatenate files

```
File data1 = new File("grades1.dat");
File data2 = new File("grades2.dat");
DataInputStream in = new DataInputStream(
                     new SequenceInputStream(
                        new FileInputStream(data1),
                        new FileInputStream(data2)));
```

Constructor of the SequenceInputStream class

```
SequenceInputStream(InputStream, InputStream);
```

Description

- The SequenceInputStream class combines two files into a single input stream without creating a new file.
- To combine more than two files into a single input stream, you can use a combined input stream as one of the arguments of the SequenceInputStream constructor.

Figure 18-11 How to combine two files into a single input stream

How to work with random-access files

So far, you've learned how to use streams to read and write files sequentially. That means that you read or write one record after another, from the first record in a file to the last. As a result, you have to read the first 49 records in a file before you can read the 50th record in a file. Files like that are known as *sequential-access files* (or just *sequential files*).

But now, you'll learn how to work with a special type of binary file known as a *random-access file*. This type of file lets you move a *pointer* (or *cursor*) to any location in the file. Then, you can read from or write to the file starting at that point, which means you can read the 50th record in a file without reading the first 49 records in the file. This type of access is far more efficient than sequential access for many types of business applications.

Constructors and methods of the RandomAccessFile class

Figure 18-12 shows the constructors and methods of the RandomAccessFile class. To start, it shows that this class implements both the DataOutput and DataInput interfaces. As a result, you can call the methods of those classes (see figures 18-3 and 18-8) when you work with random-access files.

When you use a constructor of the RandomAccessFile class, the first argument specifies the file that you want to use. As with sequential files, you can supply a File object or a String object for this argument. However, the second argument accepts a string that specifies the mode for the file. Here, you can specify "r" to open the file in read-only mode or "rw" to open the file in read-write mode.

Of the four methods summarized in this figure, it is the seek method that makes random access possible. This method lets you move the pointer to any location in the file without reading the records before that point. To use this method, you supply a long value that specifies the number of bytes from the beginning of the file that you want to move the pointer to. This lets you move the pointer forward or backward through the file. If you try to move the pointer beyond the end of the file, the pointer will be moved just beyond the last byte in the file so you can write a record at the end of the file.

The other three methods let you work with the length of a file and close a file. For instance, you can use the length method to return a long value that indicates the length of a file in bytes. You can also use the setLength method to change the length of a random-access file. If you use this method to make a random-access file shorter, it will truncate the file, thus deleting any data stored after the new length. When you're done working with a RandomAccessFile object, you can use the last method to close it and free the resources that are used by this object.

Note that you can't use buffered streams with random-access files. Because you normally read or write just one random-access record at a time and because you usually don't do those operations in sequence, this lack of buffering has only a minimal effect on efficiency.

The RandomAccessFile class

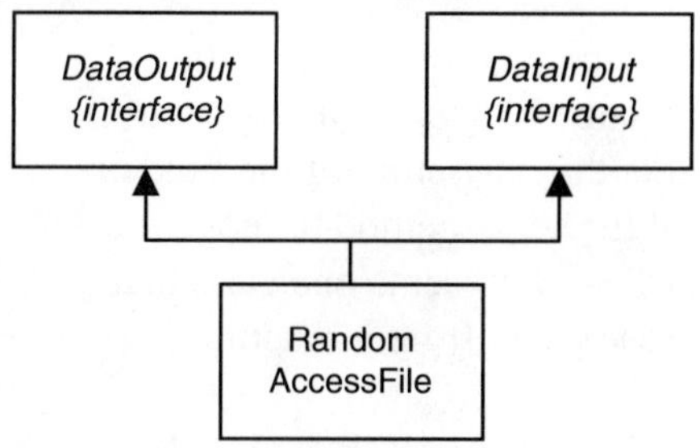

Constructors of the RandomAccessFile class

Constructor	Throws
RandomAccessFile(FileObject, StringMode)	FileNotFoundException
RandomAccessFile(StringFilename, StringMode)	FileNotFoundException

Methods of the RandomAccessFile class used for input and output

Method	Throws	Description
seek(long)	IOException	Sets the pointer the specified number of bytes from the beginning of the file. If the pointer is set beyond the end of the file, the pointer will be moved to the end of the file.
length()	IOException	Returns a long for the number of bytes in the file.
setLength(long)	IOException	Sets the length of the file to the specified number of bytes.
close()	IOException	Closes the stream.

Description

- You can use the classes in the OutputStream and InputStream hierarchies to read and write *sequential-access files*. When you work with these files, you read from the start of the file to the end of the file, and you can add data only at the end of the file.
- You can use the RandomAccessFile class to read and write *random-access files*. When you work with a random-access file, you can move a *pointer* to any point in the file. Then, you can read and write data starting at that point. This lets you modify part of a file without affecting the rest of the file.
- Since the RandomAccessFile class implements the DataOutput and DataInput interfaces, you can call the methods of those interfaces when working with a random-access file.
- In the constructor for the RandomAccessFile class, the second argument uses a string to specify a mode. For this argument, you can specify "r" for read-only mode or "rw" for read-write mode. When you specify read-write mode, you can read from and write to the same file.
- When you use a random-access file, you can't use buffered streams. That has only a minor effect on efficiency, though, because you normally read or write just one record at a time when you work with a random-access file.

Figure 18-12 Constructors and methods of the RandomAccessFile class

How to read and write random-access files

When you write data to a random-access file, each field should have the same length in bytes so each record will have the same length. That way, you can easily calculate the number of bytes that marks the beginning of the field or record that you want to access. Then, you can use the seek method to move the pointer to that field or record. To illustrate, figure 18-13 presents one class that writes data to a random-access file and one that reads data from a random-access file.

The first example shows a class that uses the RandomAccessFile class to write four records that contain two fields of equal length to a binary file. Within the main method, the third statement opens a random-access file in read-write mode. Then, a loop writes each record to the file using methods provided in the DataOutput interface. Within this loop, the first statement uses the writeChars method to write a string using two bytes per character.

The second example shows a class that reads the third record in the random-access file that was written by the first example. Within the main method for this class, the first statement opens a random-access file in read-only mode. Then, the second statement specifies the record to be read, which is the third record. After that, the third statement calculates the length of each record. To do that, it determines the number of bytes in the first field and adds the number of bytes used by the second field. In this case, the first field contains 8 bytes (four characters of 2 bytes each) and the second field contains 8 bytes (the number of bytes for a double value). Once the length of the record has been calculated, the fourth statement uses the seek method to move the pointer to the beginning of the third record. The rest of the statements read the data of the third record and print it to the console.

A class that writes to a random-access file

```
import java.io.*;

public class RandomAccessWriterApp{

    public static void main(String[] args) throws IOException{
        String[] codes = {"WARP", "MBDK", "CITR", "WUTH"};
        double[] prices = {14.95, 12.95, 9.95, 12.95};
        RandomAccessFile out = new RandomAccessFile("books.dat", "rw");
        for (int i = 0; i < codes.length; i++){
            out.writeChars(codes[i]);
            out.writeDouble(prices[i]);
        }
        out.close();
    }
}
```

A class that reads a random-access file

```
import java.io.*;

public class RandomAccessReaderApp{

    public static void main(String[] args) throws IOException{
        RandomAccessFile in = new RandomAccessFile("books.dat", "r");
        int recordNumber = 3;
        int recordLength = 4*2 + 8;
        in.seek((recordNumber-1) * (recordLength));
        String code = "";
        for (int i = 0; i < 4; i++){
            char c = in.readChar();
            code += c;
        }
        double price = in.readDouble();
        in.close();
        System.out.println(code);
        System.out.println(price);
    }
}
```

The output to the console

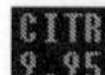

Description

- When writing random-access files, it's a common coding practice to write each record with the same number of bytes. This makes it possible to move the file pointer to the start of each record in the file.
- To read or write a record or field, you use the seek method to move the file pointer to the start of the record or field.

Figure 18-13 How to read and write random-access files

How to read and write fixed-length strings

When you write strings to a random-access file, you need to write each string with a fixed number of characters. In other words, you need to write *fixed-length strings*. If, for example, you want to create a field that stores last names, you might decide to use 20 characters for that field. Then, when you write a last name that has only 6 characters, you can add 14 Unicode zeros to the end of that last name. As a result, the field will contain 20 characters. When you read this field, you read the 6 characters and stop reading when you encounter the Unicode zeros.

To illustrate, figure 18-14 shows how to code a class named StringHelper that contains two static methods that you can use for writing and reading fixed-length strings. Then, the next figure shows some examples that use these methods.

Within the StringHelper class, the writeString method contains code that writes a fixed-length string. This method accepts three arguments and throws an IOException. The first argument is a DataOutput object, which is usually a RandomAccessFile object. The second argument is a String object that contains the string to be written. The third argument is an int value that specifies the length of the fixed-length string. Within the method, a loop writes each character of the string to the file. If the string is longer than the specified length, the method stops writing characters at that length. If the string is shorter than the specified length, the method writes Unicode zeros until it reaches the specified length.

Conversely, the readString method reads the fixed-length strings that were written by the writeString method, discarding any Unicode zeros. This method accepts two arguments and throws an IOException. The first argument is a DataInput object, which can be either a RandomAccessFile object or a DataInputStream object. The second argument is an int value that specifies the length of the fixed-length string. Within the method, the code reads each character in the string and builds a string that consists of all the characters up to the first Unicode zero. Then, it returns that string.

A class that writes and reads fixed-length strings

```
import java.io.*;

public class StringHelper{

   public static void writeString(DataOutput out, String s,
   int length) throws IOException{
      for (int i = 0; i < length; i++){
         if (i < s.length())
            out.writeChar(s.charAt(i));
         else
            out.writeChar(0);
      }
   }

   public static String readString(DataInput in, int length)
   throws IOException{
      String s = "";
      int i = 0;
      while (i < length){
         char c = in.readChar();
         if (c != 0)
            s += c;
         i++;
      }
      return s;
   }
}
```

Description

- When you write strings to a random-access file, you need to write *fixed-length strings*. That way, the length of the strings won't vary from one record to another, and all of the record lengths in the file will be the same.
- The two static methods in the StringHelper class shown above can be used to write and read fixed-length strings.
- The writeString method writes the characters of an input string to an output file followed by Unicode zeros for any unused positions in the fixed-length output string. The readString method reads a string written by the writeString method and builds a string that consists of all the characters up to the first Unicode zero.

Figure 18-14 How to read and write fixed-length strings

Examples that work with a random-access file

Figure 18-15 shows how to work with a random-access file. To start, it shows three statements that are used throughout the examples. Here, the first statement opens a random-access file in read-write mode. Then, the second statement defines a constant that specifies that the name field will contain 15 characters (30 bytes), and the third statement defines a constant for the length of the record. Since the grade field is an int type, it will use four bytes per field. As a result, each record will use 34 bytes.

The first example shows how to use the writeString method of the StringHelper class that's in the previous figure to write fixed-length strings to a random-access file. This example writes three records that contain two fields each to a file. Here, the first field contains a string for the student's name and the second field contains an int value for the student's grade. When this example calls the writeString method from the StringHelper class, it passes the random-access file as the first argument, the string as the second argument, and a constant that specifies the length of the name field as the third argument.

The second example shows how to use the readString method of the StringHelper class to read a fixed-length string into your program. In this example, the second statement uses the seek method to move the pointer to the beginning of the third record. Then, the third statement reads the fixed-length string. To do that, it calls the readString method of the StringHelper class and passes the random-access file as the first argument and a constant that specifies the length of the string as the second argument. Last, this example reads the int value for the grade and prints all of the data for the record to the console.

The third example shows how to add a record at the end of a file. Here, the first statement uses the seek method to move the pointer to the end of the file. To do that, it uses the length method to return the number of bytes in the file. Then, the next two statements write the student's name and grade.

The fourth example shows how to get the number of records in a file. To do that, you can divide the length of the file by the length of each record. For example, a file that is 100 bytes in length with 10 bytes per record contains 10 records.

The fifth example shows how to delete a record by using the setLength method to set the file length so it cuts off (truncates) the last record. To do that, you can subtract the length of one record from the current length of the file. Although this type of code only works when you want to delete the last record in a file, you'll learn how to delete any record in a file later in this chapter.

The sixth example shows how to update a record. Here, the first statement specifies that the third record should be updated. Then, the second statement uses the seek method to move the pointer to the beginning of the third record. To do that, you can subtract 1 from the record number and multiply the result by the number of bytes per record. Once the pointer is positioned, you can use the writeString method of the StringHelper class to overwrite the old name with the new name.

Code that's used by these examples

```
RandomAccessFile randomFile = new RandomAccessFile("grades.dat", "rw");
final int NAME_LENGTH = 15;
final int RECORD_LENGTH = NAME_LENGTH * 2 + 4;
```

Example 1: Writing fixed-length strings

```
String[] names = {"Vicky Lewis", "Karen Doe", "Greg Smith"};
int[] grades = {94, 91, 86};
for (int i = 0; i < names.length; i++){
   StringHelper.writeString(randomFile, names[i], NAME_LENGTH);
   randomFile.writeInt(grades[i]);
}
```

Example 2: Reading fixed-length strings

```
int recordNumber = 3;
randomFile.seek((recordNumber - 1) * RECORD_LENGTH);
String name = StringHelper.readString(randomFile, NAME_LENGTH);
int grade = randomFile.readInt();
System.out.println("Record " + recordNumber + "\n" +
                   "   Name:  " + name + "\n" +
                   "   Grade: " + grade);
```

The output to the console

```
Record 3
   Name:  Greg Smith
   Grade: 86
```

Example 3: Adding a record to the end of a file

```
randomFile.seek(randomFile.length());
StringHelper.writeString(randomFile, "Bob Chambers", NAME_LENGTH);
randomFile.writeInt(85);
```

Example 4: Getting the number of records in a file

```
int numberOfRecords = (int) randomFile.length() / RECORD_LENGTH;
```

Example 5: Deleting the last record in a file

```
randomFile.setLength(randomFile.length() - RECORD_LENGTH);
```

Example 6: Updating the first field in the third record

```
int recordNumber = 3;
randomFile.seek((recordNumber - 1) * RECORD_LENGTH);
StringHelper.writeString(randomFile, "Karen Tanner", NAME_LENGTH);
```

Figure 18-15 Examples that work with a random-access file

The I/O code for the Book Maintenance application

In chapter 12, you learned how to code the user interface for the Book Maintenance application. Now, you'll learn how to code the I/O operations for this application so it saves each book as a record in a random-access file. To do that, you'll learn how to code a class named BookIO that handles all I/O operations. Then, you'll learn how to code the Book class so you can create a Book object from the book data that's stored in a random-access file.

The user interface for this application

To refresh your memory about how this application works, figure 18-16 shows the user interface for the Book Maintenance application. To move from one record to another in the file, you click on the First, Prev, Next, and Last buttons. To change the data in the database, you click on the Add, Update (when it's enabled), and Delete buttons.

BookIO calls in the BookFrame and BookPanel classes

Figure 18-16 also shows the code in the BookFrame and BookPanel classes that calls the methods of the BookIO class. To review all the code for these classes, you can refer back to figure 12-20, but this gives you the highlights.

If you look first at the constructor for the BookPanel class, you can see that it uses the open method of the BookIO class to open the random-access file. Then, it uses the moveFirst method to return the current Book object, which is stored as an instance variable of the BookPanel object. If the file can't be found, a FileNotFoundException will be caught, a message will be displayed, and the application will end. If the file can't be opened or read properly, an IOException will be caught and a message will be displayed.

After the file is opened, the BookPanel class can use the other BookIO methods. These are called from the actionPerformed method in the BookPanel class. For instance, when the user clicks on the Exit button, the close method is called. And when the user clicks on the firstButton, the moveFirst method is called. Although the code for the other buttons isn't shown, this continues for all of the buttons. Since any of these methods can throw an IOException, the actionPerformed method is contained in a try/catch statement, and the third catch block catches this exception.

To end the program, the user can click on the Exit button, which leads to a call of the close method. But the user can also end the program by closing the window. That's why the windowClosing method in the BookFrame class must also call the close method. In the windowClosing method, though, the IOException isn't caught so it must be caught (not thrown) by the close method in the BookIO class.

The GUI for the Book Maintenance application

The code for the windowClosing method in the BookFrame class

```
public void windowClosing(WindowEvent e){
    BookIO.close();
    System.exit(0);
}
```

The code in the constructor for the BookPanel class

```
try{
    BookIO.open();
    currentBook = BookIO.moveFirst();
 }
 catch (FileNotFoundException e){
    JOptionPane.showMessageDialog(null, "FileNotFoundException");
    System.exit(1);
 }
 catch (IOException e){
    JOptionPane.showMessageDialog(null, "IOException");
 }
```

The code for the actionPerformed method of the BookPanel class

```
public void actionPerformed(ActionEvent e){
  try{
     Object source = e.getSource();
     if (source == exitButton){
        BookIO.close();
        System.exit(0);
     }
     else if (source == firstButton){
        currentBook = BookIO.moveFirst();
        performBookDisplay();
        enableButtons(true);
     }
     //the code for the other buttons
  }
  catch (FileNotFoundException fnfe){
     JOptionPane.showMessageDialog(this, "FileNotFoundException");
  }
  catch (NumberFormatException nfe){
     JOptionPane.showMessageDialog(this, "NumberFormatException");
  }
  catch (IOException ioe){
     JOptionPane.showMessageDialog(this, "IOException");
  }
}
```

Figure 18-16 BookIO calls in the BookFrame and BookPanel classes

The code for the BookIO class

Figure 18-17 presents the complete code for the BookIO class. This class contains 18 static methods. As you develop a class like this, you try to provide all the methods that other classes that use this file will need. That means you need to code the methods that are needed by business classes like Book and BookOrder, and also the methods that are needed by GUI classes like BookFrame, BookPanel, BookOrderFrame, and BookOrderPanel.

To start, this class imports two packages. The java.io package lets this class work with the I/O classes, and the java.util package lets this class use the Vector class. Then, this class declares three static variables and four static constants. This class uses the first static variable to refer to the current book, the second one to store an array of the book codes read in from the file, and the third one to refer to a random access file. Next, this class uses the constants to set the file name, the size of the fields in characters, and the size of the record in bytes.

The first static method is the open method. It opens the random-access file that's going to be used. Then, it calls the readCodes method on the next page of code to read all of the book codes into this array. Since this method throws exceptions, they have to be handled by the classes that call it.

The next static method is the close method. It just closes the random-access file when the user closes the window or clicks on the Exit button. Unlike the other methods in this class, though, this method catches the IOException instead of throwing it. That's why the windowClosing method of the BookFrame class doesn't have to catch an exception when it calls this method.

The getRecordCount method returns the number of records in the current file. To do that, this method divides the number of bytes in the file by the number of bytes in each record. This method is used by some of the other methods in this class.

The next method is the readString method, which helps the other methods in this class read fixed-length strings. The code for this method works the same as the code for the readString method that's in figure 18-14.

The overloaded readRecord method provides two ways to read a record. First, you can supply an int that specifies the record's number. Second, you can supply a string that specifies the record's book code. Either way, the readRecord method returns a Book object that's created from the data in the file.

The first readRecord method uses the seek method to position the pointer at the beginning of the specified record. Once this method positions the pointer, it reads each field in the record, using the readString method to read the strings. After that, this method creates a Book object from these fields and returns it.

The second readRecord method begins by passing the book code parameter to the getRecordNumber method that's shown on the next page. This method returns an int value for the record number that corresponds to the book code. Then, the second statement in this readRecord method passes that int value to the first readRecord method.

The BookIO class

```
import java.io.*;
import java.util.*;

public class BookIO{
   private static Book book = null;
   private static String[] codes = null;
   private static RandomAccessFile randomFile = null;

   private static final File BOOK_FILE = new File("books.dat");
   private static final int CODE_SIZE = 4;
   private static final int TITLE_SIZE = 20;
   private static final int RECORD_SIZE = CODE_SIZE*2 + TITLE_SIZE*2 + 8;

   public static void open() throws IOException{
      randomFile = new RandomAccessFile(BOOK_FILE, "rw");
      codes = readCodes();
   }
   public static void close(){
      try{
         randomFile.close();
      }
      catch(IOException e){
         System.out.println("IOException thrown when closing file.");
      }
   }
   public static int getRecordCount() throws IOException{
      long length = BOOK_FILE.length();
      int recordCount = (int) (length / RECORD_SIZE);
      return recordCount;
   }
   public static String readString(DataInput in, int length)
   throws IOException{
      String s = "";
      int i = 0;
      while (i < length){
         char c = in.readChar();
         if (c!=0)
            s += c;
         i++;
      }
      return s;
   }
   public static Book readRecord(int recordNumber) throws IOException{
      randomFile.seek((recordNumber-1) * RECORD_SIZE);
      String code = readString(randomFile, CODE_SIZE);
      String title = readString(randomFile, TITLE_SIZE);
      double price = randomFile.readDouble();
      book = new Book(code, title, price);
      return book;
   }
   public static Book readRecord(String bookCode) throws IOException{
      int recordNumber = getRecordNumber(bookCode);
      book = readRecord(recordNumber);
      return book;
   }
```

Figure 18-17 The code for the BookIO class (part 1 of 3)

The getRecordNumber method accepts a string that contains a book code and returns the record number for that book code. To do that, it compares each element in the codes array with the specified book code. When it finds a match, it returns the current position in the array plus one. If this method can't find the book code in the file, it returns a -1.

The readCodes method returns an array that contains every book code that's stored in the file. To start, this method declares an array of strings that has a length equal to the number of records in the file. Then, it uses a loop to read each code field from the file into the array. To do that, this method uses the getRecordCount method to return the number of records in the file as an int value, and it uses the readString method to read the string for the code field.

The readTitles method creates a string array of all of the book titles in the file. Here again, the getRecordCount method is used to specify the number of elements in the array. Although this method isn't used by the Book Maintenance application, it may be used by other applications, including the Book Order application in this book.

The writeString method helps other methods write fixed-length strings. The code for this method works the same as the code for the writeString method in figure 18-14.

The writeRecord method accepts a Book object argument and a record number argument. Then, it uses the record number argument to move the pointer to the beginning of that record, and it writes the data from the Book object to the file. To do that, this method uses the writeString method to write the strings for the book's code and title.

The BookIO class (continued)

```
public static int getRecordNumber(String bookCode) throws IOException{
   int match = -1;
   int i = 0;
   boolean flag = true;
   while ((i < getRecordCount()) && (flag==true)){
      if (bookCode.equals(codes[i])){
         match = i+1;
         flag = false;
      }
      i++;
   }
   return match;
}

public static String[] readCodes() throws IOException{
   codes = new String[getRecordCount()];
   for (int i = 0; i < getRecordCount(); i++){
      randomFile.seek(i * RECORD_SIZE);
      codes[i] = readString(randomFile, CODE_SIZE);
   }
   return codes;
}

public static String[] readTitles() throws IOException{
   String[] titles = new String[getRecordCount()];
   for (int i = 0; i < getRecordCount(); i++){
      randomFile.seek(i * RECORD_SIZE + 8);
      titles[i] = readString(randomFile, TITLE_SIZE);
   }
   return titles;
}

public static void writeString(DataOutput out, String s, int length)
throws IOException{
   for (int i = 0; i < length; i++){
      if (i < s.length())
         out.writeChar(s.charAt(i));
      else
         out.writeChar(0);
   }
}

public static void writeRecord(Book book, int recordNumber)
throws IOException{
   randomFile.seek((recordNumber-1) * RECORD_SIZE);
   writeString(randomFile, book.getCode(), CODE_SIZE);
   writeString(randomFile, book.getTitle(), TITLE_SIZE);
   randomFile.writeDouble(book.getPrice());
}
```

Figure 18-17 The code for the BookIO class (part 2 of 3)

You can use the next four methods in this class to scroll through the books in a file. For example, you can use the moveFirst method to return a Book object for the first record in the file, and you can use the moveNext method to return a Book object for the next record in the file. These four methods use the Book variable of the BookIO class to keep track of the current record, and they use the readRecord method that's in this class to create Book objects from the data that's stored in the file.

The movePrevious method moves back one record in the file. If, for example, the current record is the third record, this method sets the Book variable to the second record. However, if the current record is the first record in the file, this method doesn't change the Book variable.

The moveNext method moves forward one record in the file. If, for example, the current record is the third record, this method sets the Book variable to the fourth record. However, if the current record is the last record in the file, this method doesn't change the Book variable. To determine whether the current record is the last record, this method compares the number of the current record with the total number of records in the file.

The moveLast method moves the current record to the last record in the file. To do that, it determines the current number of records in the file and sets the Book variable to the last record.

You can use the last three methods in this class to add, update, and delete the records in a file. These methods are high-level methods that build upon the other methods in this class. As a result, these methods don't perform the actual I/O operations. Instead, they call other methods like the readRecord and writeRecord methods to perform the I/O operations.

The addRecord method adds a record to the end of a file. To do that, it accepts a Book object as an argument. Then, it writes the data for that Book object to the end of the file.

The updateRecord method updates, or modifies, the current record. To do that, it accepts a Book object as an argument. Then, the first statement determines the record number of the current Book object, and the second statement writes the data for specified Book object over the data for the current record.

The deleteRecord method deletes the current record from the file. To do that, a loop creates a Book object for every record in the file and stores those Book objects in a vector. Then, the remove method of the Vector object removes the book that's specified by the book code parameter from the vector, and the setLength method of the RandomAccessFile object truncates the file so it contains one less record. Once these statements remove the specified book from the vector and shorten the file, the second loop in this method writes each Book object stored in the vector to the file. After that, an if statement sets the current record equal to the next record in the file. However, if the deleted record was the last record in the file, the else clause sets the current record equal to the new last record in the file.

Please note that this delete method reads every record in the file, removes one record, and writes all the records back to the file, which is extremely inefficient (imagine a file with 5,000 records). This points out one serious

The BookIO class (continued)

```
    public static Book moveFirst() throws IOException{
        book = readRecord(1);
        return book;
    }

    public static Book movePrevious() throws IOException{
        int recordNumber = getRecordNumber(book.getCode());
        if (recordNumber != 1)
            book = readRecord(recordNumber - 1);
        return book;
    }

    public static Book moveNext() throws IOException{
        int recordNumber = getRecordNumber(book.getCode());
        if (recordNumber != getRecordCount())
            book = readRecord(recordNumber + 1);
        return book;
    }

    public static Book moveLast() throws IOException{
        int lastRecordNumber = getRecordCount();
        book = readRecord(lastRecordNumber);
        return book;
    }

    public static void addRecord(Book addBook) throws IOException{
        writeRecord(addBook, getRecordCount() + 1);
        close();
        open();
    }

    public static void updateRecord(Book book) throws IOException{
        int recordNumber = getRecordNumber(book.getCode());
        writeRecord(book, recordNumber);
    }

    public static void deleteRecord(String bookCode) throws IOException{
        int recordNumber = getRecordNumber(bookCode);
        Vector books = new Vector();
        for (int i = 0; i< getRecordCount(); i++){
            books.add(readRecord(i+1));
        }
        books.remove(recordNumber-1);
        randomFile.setLength(RECORD_SIZE *(getRecordCount() -1));
        for (int i = 0; i<books.size(); i++){
            writeRecord((Book)books.elementAt(i),i+1);
        }
        if (recordNumber < getRecordCount())
            book = readRecord(recordNumber);
        else
            book = readRecord(getRecordCount()-1);
        close();
        open();
    }
}
```

Figure 18-17 The code for the BookIO class (part 3 of 3)

limitation of random-access files. Although you can delete a record at the end of a file, there's no good way to delete a record in the middle of a file.

One traditional solution has been to mark the deleted records, instead of actually deleting them. For instance, this method could just change the book code for a deleted record to ZZZZ. Since that requires just one disk operation, that would be a major improvement in efficiency. But that would also require changes to several of the other methods and complicate the code overall.

The code for the Book class

Figure 18-18 presents the code for the Book class. Here, the first constructor has three parameters: book code, title, and price. It is used by the readRecord method of the BookIO class to create a Book object from the data retrieved from the file.

The second constructor has just one parameter, the book code. It can be used to create a Book object when only the book code is available to the calling class. To do that, this constructor creates a temporary Book object with the data from the book file. Then, it sets the title and price for the Book object that the constructor is creating equal to the temporary object's title and price. This constructor is written this way so it gets the data with just one read of the record.

The Book class

```
import java.io.*;

public class Book{
   private String code;
   private String title;
   private double price;

   public Book(String bookCode, String bookTitle, double bookPrice){
      code = bookCode;
      title = bookTitle;
      price = bookPrice;
   }

   public Book(String bookCode) throws IOException{
      code = bookCode;
      Book tempBook = BookIO.readRecord(bookCode);
      title = tempBook.getTitle();
      price = tempBook.getPrice();
   }

   public String getCode(){ return code; }
   public String getTitle(){ return title; }
   public double getPrice(){ return price; }
}
```

Figure 18-18 The code for the Book class

Perspective

In this chapter, you learned how to read and write binary files, including random-access versions of those files. If you've already read the chapters in section 3, this means that now at last you can see how all of the classes and methods in a business application work together. That includes GUI classes like Frame and Panel classes, business classes like Book and BookOrder classes, and data classes like the BookIO class.

To make sure you understand these relationships, it's worth taking the time to study all of the classes for a complete application like the Book Maintenance application. In particular, you should study how the GUI classes make use of the business classes and the BookIO class.

Keep in mind as you work with files, though, that they represent just one way to store the data for business objects. The other way is to store the data in a database. Since a database provides sophisticated features for organizing and managing data, this makes adding and deleting records much easier to do. That's one reason why databases are commonly used for business applications. In the next chapter, you can learn how to use them.

Summary

- You can use the classes that end with OutputStream to create a binary output stream that can write data to a binary file, and you can use the methods of the DataOutput interface to write data to the binary output stream.
- You can use the classes that end with InputStream to create a binary input stream that can read data from a binary file, and you can use the methods of the DataInput interface to read data from a binary input stream.
- You can use the RandomAccessFile class to create a *random-access file*, which is a special type of binary file that lets you move a *pointer* to any location in the file. Then, you can use the methods of this class to read and write data starting at that point.
- To work with random-access files, you use the writeChars and readChar methods to write and read *fixed-length strings*. That way, the files have the same number of bytes for each *field* within each *record*.
- Whenever you work with files, efficiency is an important consideration. In general, you goal should be to reduce the number of disk operations that an application requires because those operations are the most time-consuming.

Terms

Universal Text Format (UTF)
record
field
sequential-access file
sequential file
random-access file
pointer
cursor
fixed-length string

Objectives

- Write code that writes data from a program to a binary file.
- Write code that reads data from a binary file into a program.
- Write code that reads and writes random-access files.
- Explain the differences in the use of random-access and sequential-access files.

Exercise 18-1 Write and read binary files

This exercise guides you through the process of writing and reading a binary file, and it shows how to open these files in a text editor.

1. Open the BinaryWriterApp class that's in the c:\java\ch18 directory. Next, add the code for the BinaryWriterApp class that's in figure 18-4. Then, compile and run this application. To make sure it works, open the example.dat file with a text editor. You should see two lines of text.
2. Open the BinaryReaderApp class that's in the c:\java\ch18 directory. Then, edit the class so it reads both lines of text in the example.dat file as shown in figure 18-9. When you compile and run this application, it should print five lines to the console.

Exercise 18-2 Write and read binary files and random-access files

This exercise guides you through the process of writing and reading a binary file, and it shows how to convert this file to a random-access file.

1. Open the GradesWriterApp class that's in the c:\java\ch18 directory. Then, edit the code so it writes the grades to a binary file named grades.dat as in figure 18-5. Make sure to use the writeUTF method to write each student's name. After you compile and run this class, open the grades.dat file with a text editor to see that the writeUTF method has used one byte per character.
2. Open the GradesReaderApp class that's in the c:\java\ch18 directory. Then, edit the code so it reads the grades from the file as in figure 18-10. When you compile and run this application, it should print the names and grades of three students to the console.
3. Open the StringHelper class that's in the c:\java\ch18 directory. Then, compile this class.
4. Modify the GradesWriterApp class so it uses the StringHelper class to write each name with a fixed length of 15 characters as in figure 18-15. After you compile and run this class, open the grades.dat file with a text editor to see that the writeString method has used two bytes per character.

5. Modify the GradesReaderApp class so it uses the RandomAccessFile class and the StringHelper class to read the third record from the grades.dat file as in figure 18-15. When you compile and run this class, it should print the name and grade for the third student.
6. Code an application named ModifyRecord3App that modifies the third record in the file as in figure 18-15. When you compile and run this class, it should modify the name and grade for the third student. You can check to see the new record by running the GradesReaderApp, which should display the modified record.

Exercise 18-3 Fix some bugs in the BookIO class

This exercise gives you a version of the BookIO class that has some bugs in it. Then, it guides you through the process of fixing the bugs in this class.

1. Open the BookFrame class that's in c:\java\ch18\book. Then, compile and run it to see if it's working properly. If you click repeatedly on the Next and Prev buttons, you'll find that they aren't working properly. For instance, if you click on the Prev button when the first record is displayed or the Next button when the last record is displayed, an IOException will be thrown. In addition, if you attempt to update an existing record, the change isn't permanently written to the file.
2. Open the BookIO class that's in the c:\java\ch18\book directory. Fix the bug in the moveNext and movePrevious methods. Then, run the BookFrame class again to make sure that these buttons work properly.
3. In the BookIO class, fix the bug in the updateRecord method. Then, run the BookFrame class and check to make sure that this code works properly.
4. When you have the program working correctly, delete the readString and writeString methods from the BookIO class and modify the code in the BookIO class so it uses the readString and writeString methods from the StringHelper class.

Section 5

Advanced Java skills

This section presents two skills that aren't usually included in beginning Java books. As we see it, though, these skills are critical to your understanding of Java. That's why we included them in this book.

In chapter 19, you can learn how to use Java Database Connectivity (JDBC) to store the data for the business objects that you create in a database. In chapter 20, you can learn how to use threads with applications and applets so your application can do two or more tasks at the same time. Because these chapters are independent of each other, you can read either one first.

19

How to use JDBC to work with databases

If you've read section 4, you know how to work with data that's stored in files. Now, in this chapter, you'll learn how to use JDBC to work with data that's stored in a database. As you will see, databases are easier to work with than files. They also provide data management features that aren't offered with files. That's why you should use databases for all serious business applications.

How a relational database is organized

In 1970, Dr. E. F. Codd developed a model for a new type of *database* called a *relational database*. This type of database eliminated some of the problems that were associated with earlier types of databases like hierarchical databases. By using the relational model, you can reduce data redundancy, which saves disk storage and leads to more efficient data retrieval. You can also view and manipulate data in a way that is both intuitive and efficient. Today, relational databases are the de facto standard for database applications.

How a table is organized

A relational database stores data in *tables*. Each table contains *rows* and *columns* as shown in figure 19-1. In practice, rows and columns are often referred to by the traditional terms, *records* and *fields*. That's why this book uses these terms interchangeably.

In a relational database, a table has one column that's defined as the *primary key*. The primary key uniquely identifies each row in a table. That way, the rows in one table can easily be related to the rows in another table. In this table, the BookCode column is the primary key.

The software that manages a relational database is called the *database management system* (*DBMS*) or *relational database management system* (*RDBMS*). The DBMS provides features that let you design the database. After that, the DBMS manages all changes, additions, and deletions to the database. Four of the most popular database management systems today are Oracle, Microsoft SQL Server, IBM's DB2, and Microsoft Access.

The Books table in the MurachBooks database

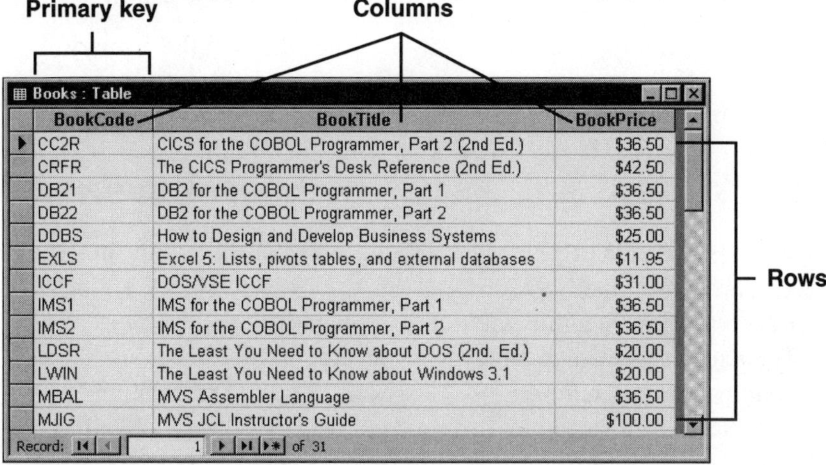

BookCode	BookTitle	BookPrice
CC2R	CICS for the COBOL Programmer, Part 2 (2nd Ed.)	$36.50
CRFR	The CICS Programmer's Desk Reference (2nd Ed.)	$42.50
DB21	DB2 for the COBOL Programmer, Part 1	$36.50
DB22	DB2 for the COBOL Programmer, Part 2	$36.50
DDBS	How to Design and Develop Business Systems	$25.00
EXLS	Excel 5: Lists, pivots tables, and external databases	$11.95
ICCF	DOS/VSE ICCF	$31.00
IMS1	IMS for the COBOL Programmer, Part 1	$36.50
IMS2	IMS for the COBOL Programmer, Part 2	$36.50
LDSR	The Least You Need to Know about DOS (2nd. Ed.)	$20.00
LWIN	The Least You Need to Know about Windows 3.1	$20.00
MBAL	MVS Assembler Language	$36.50
MJIG	MVS JCL Instructor's Guide	$100.00

Description

- A *relational database* uses *tables* to store and manipulate data. Each table contains one or more *records*, or *rows*, that contain the data for a single entry. Each row contains one or more *fields*, or *columns*, with each column representing a single item of data.
- Most tables contain a *primary key* that uniquely identifies each row in the table.
- The software that manages a relational database is called a *database management system* (*DBMS*). Four of the most popular database management systems today are Oracle, Microsoft SQL Server, IBM's DB2, and Microsoft Access.

Figure 19-1 How a table is organized

How the tables in a database are related

Figure 19-2 shows how a relational database uses the values in the primary key field to relate one table to another. Here, each BookCode field in the BookOrders table contains a value that identifies one row in the Books table. Since the BookCode field in the BookOrders table points to a primary key in another table, it's called a *foreign key*. Often, a table will have several foreign keys.

In this figure, each row in the Books table relates to one or more rows in the BookOrders table. As a result, the Books table has a *one-to-many relationship* with the BookOrders table. Although a one-to-many relationship is the most common type of relationship between tables, you can also have a *one-to-one relationship* or a *many-to-many relationship*. However, a one-to-one relationship between two tables is rare since the data can be stored in a single table. In contrast, a many-to-many relationship between two tables is typically implemented by using a third table that has a one-to-many relationship with both of the original tables.

Incidentally, the primary key in the BookOrders table is the BookOrderID field. It is automatically generated by the DBMS when a new record is added to the database. This type of primary key is often appropriate for tables like Invoice, Employee, and Customer tables.

The relationship between the Books and BookOrders tables

Books : Table

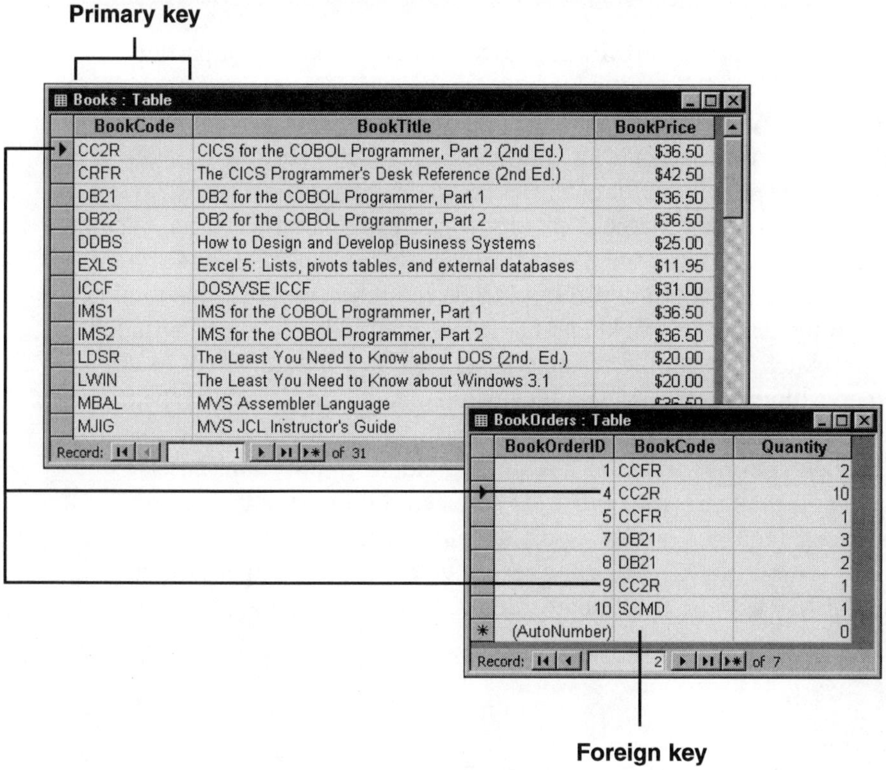

BookCode	BookTitle	BookPrice
CC2R	CICS for the COBOL Programmer, Part 2 (2nd Ed.)	$36.50
CRFR	The CICS Programmer's Desk Reference (2nd Ed.)	$42.50
DB21	DB2 for the COBOL Programmer, Part 1	$36.50
DB22	DB2 for the COBOL Programmer, Part 2	$36.50
DDBS	How to Design and Develop Business Systems	$25.00
EXLS	Excel 5: Lists, pivots tables, and external databases	$11.95
ICCF	DOS/VSE ICCF	$31.00
IMS1	IMS for the COBOL Programmer, Part 1	$36.50
IMS2	IMS for the COBOL Programmer, Part 2	$36.50
LDSR	The Least You Need to Know about DOS (2nd. Ed.)	$20.00
LWIN	The Least You Need to Know about Windows 3.1	$20.00
MBAL	MVS Assembler Language	
MJIG	MVS JCL Instructor's Guide	

Record: 1 of 31

BookOrders : Table

BookOrderID	BookCode	Quantity
1	CCFR	2
4	CC2R	10
5	CCFR	1
7	DB21	3
8	DB21	2
9	CC2R	1
10	SCMD	1
(AutoNumber)		0

Record: 2 of 7

Description

- The tables in a relational database are related to each other through their key fields. For example, the BookCode field is used to relate the Books and BookOrders tables. The BookCode field in the BookOrders table is called a *foreign key* because it identifies a related row in the Books table.
- Three types of relationships can exist between tables. The most common type is a *one-to-many relationship* as illustrated above. However, two tables can also have a *one-to-one relationship* or a *many-to-many relationship*.

Figure 19-2 How the tables in a database are related

How the fields in a database are defined

Figure 19-3 shows how a DBMS defines a field in a database. In particular, it shows how the DBMS defines a name and data type for each field. Although this figure shows an Access 2000 database, all relational databases require a name and a data type for each field. In addition, any modern relational database will let you set other properties for each field in the database such as a default value for new rows, whether the field is required, and so on.

This figure shows the names and data types for the fields in the Books table. Here, the key symbol to the left of the BookCode field indicates that it is the primary key for the table. This field and the BookTitle field are defined with the Text data type, which maps to the String type in Java. In contrast, the BookPrice field is defined with the Currency data type, which maps to the double type in Java.

When a DBMS defines a field as a required field, an application must provide a value for the field when it tries to add a record to the database. For some applications, though, you can supply a *default value* for the field. That way, if the application tries to add a new record without specifying a value for the field, the DBMS will use the default value.

The design of the Books table in Access 2000

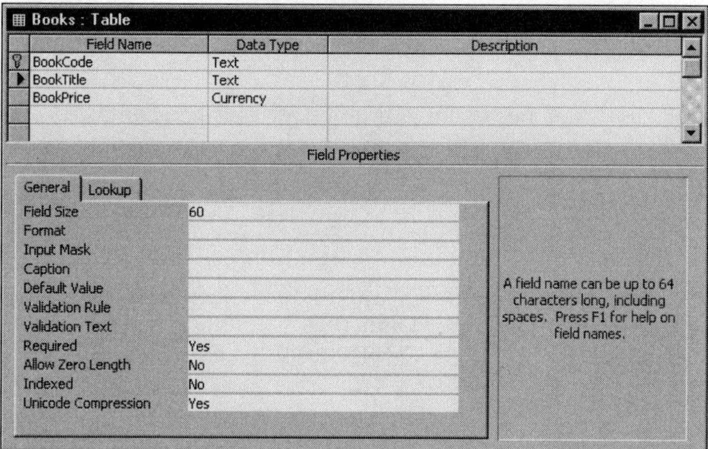

Description

- A database management system requires a name and data type for each field. Depending on the data type, you may be able to specify other attributes for the field such as field size, a value to be used as a label, whether the field is required by new rows or not, and so on.
- If you specify a *default value* for a field, that value is used for the field in a new record when no other value is supplied.

Figure 19-3 How the fields in a table are defined

How to use SQL to work with the data in a database

Structured Query Language (*SQL*) is a standard language that you can use to communicate with any modern DBMS. This language can be divided into two parts. The *Data Definition Language* (*DDL*) lets you define the tables in a database. The *Data Manipulation Language* (*DML*) lets you manipulate the data that's stored in those tables.

Since you'll normally use database software to define the tables in a database, this topic will focus on the four SQL statements that you can use to manipulate the data in a database: the SELECT, INSERT, UPDATE, and DELETE statements. These are the statements that you will use in your Java applications.

How to query a single table

Figure 19-4 shows how to use a SELECT statement to *query* a single table in a database. The SELECT statement is the most commonly used SQL statement. It returns a *result set* (or *result table*) that contains the rows and columns that are specified by the SELECT statement.

In the syntax summary for this statement, the capitalized words are SQL keywords and the lowercase words represent the items that you must supply. The brackets indicate an item that is optional; the bar (|) indicates a choice between the options on either side; and the ellipsis (...) indicates that you can code a series of like items. To separate the items in a statement, you can use one or more spaces, and you can use indentation whenever it helps improve the readability of a statement.

The first example in this figure shows how to retrieve three columns from the Books table. Here, the SELECT clause identifies the three columns and the FROM clause identifies the table. Then, the WHERE clause limits the number of rows that are retrieved by specifying that the statement should only retrieve rows where the value in the BookPrice field is greater than 35. Last, the ORDER BY clause indicates that the retrieved rows should be sorted in ascending order (from A to Z) by the BookCode field.

The result set is a logical table that's created temporarily within the database. Here, the *current row pointer*, or *cursor*, keeps track of the current row. If you make a change to the data in a result set, the change is also made to the table that the result set was created from.

As you might guess, queries can have a significant effect on the performance of a database application. The more columns and rows that a query returns, the more traffic the network has to bear. As a result, when you design queries, you should try to keep the number of columns and rows to a minimum.

SELECT syntax for selecting from one table

```
SELECT field-1 [, field-2] ...
FROM table-1
[WHERE selection-criteria]
[ORDER BY field-1 [ASC|DESC] [, field-2 [ASC|DESC] ...]]
```

A SELECT statement that gets selected columns and rows

```
SELECT BookCode, BookTitle, BookPrice
FROM Books
WHERE BookPrice > 35
ORDER BY BookCode ASC
```

The result set defined by the SELECT statement

Current row pointer →

	BookCode	BookTitle	BookPrice
▶	CC2R	CICS for the COBOL Programmer, Part 2 (2nd Ed.)	$36.55
	CRFR	The CICS Programmer's Desk Reference (2nd Ed.)	$42.50
	DB21	DB2 for the COBOL Programmer, Part 1	$36.50
	DB22	DB2 for the COBOL Programmer, Part 2	$36.50
	IMS1	IMS for the COBOL Programmer, Part 1	$36.50
	IMS2	IMS for the COBOL Programmer, Part 2	$36.50
	MBAL	MVS Assembler Language	$36.50
	MJIG	MVS JCL Instructor's Guide	$100.00
	MJLR	MVS JCL (2nd. Ed.)	$42.50
	SDIG	System Development Intructor's Guide	$100.00
	TSO1	MVS TSO, Part 1:Concepts and ISPF	$36.50
	TSO2	MVS TSO, Part 2:Commands,CLIST, and REXX	$36.50
	VBAL	DOS/VSE Assembler Language	$36.50

A SELECT statement that returns all columns and rows

```
SELECT * FROM Books
```

Description

- The SELECT statement is used to perform a *query* that retrieves rows and columns from a database.
- The *result set* (or *result table*) is the set of records that are retrieved by a query.
- The *current row pointer*, or *cursor*, identifies the current row in a result set. You can use this pointer to identify the row you want to update or delete from a result set. Any change to the result set is reflected in the table that the result set is based on.
- To select all of the columns in a table, you can code an asterisk (*) instead of coding field names.
- For efficiency, you should code your queries so the result set has as few rows and as few columns as possible.

Figure 19-4 How to query a single table

How to join data from two or more tables

Figure 19-5 shows how to use the SELECT statement to retrieve data from two tables. Since the data from the two tables is joined together into a single result set, this type of operation is known as a *join*. In this figure, for example, the SELECT statement joins data from the Books and BookOrders tables into a single result set.

An *inner join* is the most common type of join. When you use an inner join, which is sometimes called an *equi-join*, the records from the two tables in the join are included in the result set only if their related fields match. These matching fields are specified in the SELECT statement. In this figure, for example, records from the Books and BookOrders tables are included only if the value of the BookCode field of the Books table is equal to the BookCode field of the BookOrders table. In other words, if there isn't any data in the BookOrder table for a book, that Book won't be added to the result set.

Please note in this SELECT statement that the last field in the query, the Total field, is calculated by multiplying BookPrice and Quantity. In other words, a field by the name of Total doesn't actually exist in the database. This type of field is called a *calculated field*, and it exists only in the results of the query.

Another type of join is an *outer join*. With this type of join, all of the records in one of the tables are included in the result set whether or not there are matching records in the other table. In a *left outer join*, all of the records in the first table (the one on the left) are included in the result set. In a *right outer join*, all of the records in the second table are included. To illustrate, assume that the SELECT statement in this figure had used a left outer join. In that case, all of the records in the Book table whose price is greater than 35 would have been included in the result set…even if no matching record was found in the BookOrders table.

Although this figure only shows how to join data from two tables, you can extend this syntax to join data from additional tables. If, for example, you want to create a result set that includes data from three tables named Vendors, Invoices, and InvoiceLineItems, you could code the FROM clause of the SELECT statement like this:

```
FROM Vendors
    INNER JOIN Invoices
        ON Vendors.VendorID = Invoices.VendorID
    INNER JOIN InvoiceLineItems
        ON Invoices.InvoiceID = InvoiceLineItems.InvoiceID
```

Then, you could include any of the fields from the three tables in the field list of the SELECT statement.

This figure also shows an alternate SQL syntax that lets you join two tables by using the WHERE clause instead of the FROM clause. Using this syntax, the FROM clause lists all of the tables in the result set. Then, the WHERE clause identifies the join by using the AND keyword to connect all of the selection criteria that must be satisfied. This is an older syntax for joins that is still used by some older database management systems.

SELECT syntax for joining two tables

```
SELECT field-1 [, field-2] ...
FROM table-1
   {INNER | LEFT OUTER | RIGHT OUTER} JOIN table-2
   ON table-1.field-1 {=|<|>|<=|>=|<>} table-2.field-2
[WHERE selection-criteria]
[ORDER BY field-1 [ASC|DESC] [, field-2 [ASC|DESC] ...]]
```

A SELECT statement that retrieves and sorts selected fields and records from the Books table

```
SELECT BookCode, BookTitle, BookPrice, Quantity,
       BookPrice * Quantity AS Total
FROM Books
   INNER JOIN BookOrders
   ON Books.BookCode = BookOrders.BookCode
WHERE BookPrice > 35
ORDER BY BookCode ASC
```

Another way to write the SELECT statement shown above

```
SELECT BookCode, BookTitle, BookPrice, Quantity,
       BookPrice * Quantity AS Total
FROM Books, BookOrders
WHERE Books.BookCode = BookOrders.BookCode AND BookPrice > 35
ORDER BY BookCode ASC
```

The result set defined by the SELECT statement

BookCode	BookTitle	BookPrice	Quantity	Total
CC2R	CICS for the COBOL Programmer, Part 2 (2nd Ed.)	$36.50	1	$36.50
CC2R	CICS for the COBOL Programmer, Part 2 (2nd Ed.)	$36.50	10	$365.00
DB21	DB2 for the COBOL Programmer, Part 1	$36.50	2	$73.00
DB21	DB2 for the COBOL Programmer, Part 1	$36.50	3	$109.50

Description

- A *join* lets you combine data from two or more tables into a single result set.
- An *inner join*, or *equi-join*, returns records from both tables but only if their related fields match. An *outer join* returns records from one table in the join (the LEFT or RIGHT table) even if the records aren't matched by records in the other table.

Figure 19-5 How to join data from two or more tables

How to modify data in a result set

Figure 19-6 shows how to use the INSERT, UPDATE, and DELETE statements to add, update, or delete one or more records in a database. The queries done by these SQL statements are sometimes referred to as *action queries* because they actually change the data in a database.

The first syntax and example for the INSERT statement show how to use this statement to add one record to a database. To do that, the statement supplies the names of the fields that are going to receive values in the new record, followed by the values for those fields.

In contrast, the second syntax and example for the INSERT statement show how to add multiple records to a table. To do that, you include a SELECT statement within the INSERT INTO statement. Then, the SELECT statement selects the fields and records from one table, and the INSERT statement adds those records to another table. In this example, the SELECT statement selects all of the fields from the records in the Invoices table that have been paid in full (AmountDue = 0), and inserts them into the InvoiceArchive table. In this case, you don't have to specify the list of fields because both tables have the same fields.

Similarly, the syntax and examples for the UPDATE statement show how to update a single record and a group of records. In the first example, the UPDATE statement updates the BookTitle and BookPrice fields in the record where BookCode is equal to WARP. In the second example, the BookPrice field is updated to 36.95 in all of the records where BookPrice is equal to 36.50.

Last, the syntax and examples for the DELETE statement show how to delete a single record or a group of records. Here, the first example deletes the record from the Books table where the BookCode equals WARP. Since each record contains a unique value in the BookCode field, this only deletes a single record. However, in the second example, many records in the Invoices table may have an AmountDue field that equals 0. As a result, this statement deletes all invoices whose balance has been paid in full. That way, the Invoices table will only contain unpaid invoices.

When you issue an INSERT, UPDATE, or DELETE statement from a Java application, you usually work with one record at a time. You'll see this illustrated by the Book Maintenance application in this chapter. Action queries that affect more than one record are more often issued by database administrators and programmers by using query interfaces that are provided by the DBMS.

How to add records

INSERT INTO syntax for adding a single record

```
INSERT INTO table-name [(field-list)]
   VALUES (value-list)
```

A statement that adds a single record

```
INSERT INTO Books (BookCode, BookDescription, BookPrice)
   VALUES ('WARP', 'War and Peace', '14.95')
```

INSERT INTO syntax for adding multiple records

```
INSERT INTO table-name [(field-list)]
   SELECT-statement
```

A statement that adds multiple records

```
INSERT INTO InvoiceArchive
   SELECT * FROM Invoices WHERE AmountDue = 0
```

How to update records

UPDATE syntax

```
UPDATE table-name
   SET expression-1 [, expression-2] ...
   WHERE selection-criteria
```

A statement that updates a single record

```
UPDATE Books
   SET BookTitle = 'War and Peace',
       BookPrice = '14.95'
   WHERE BookCode = 'WARP'
```

A statement that updates multiple records

```
UPDATE Books
   SET BookPrice = '36.95'
   WHERE BookPrice = '36.50'
```

How to delete records

DELETE FROM syntax

```
DELETE FROM table-name
   WHERE selection-criteria
```

A statement that deletes a single record

```
DELETE FROM Books WHERE BookCode = 'WARP'
```

A statement that deletes multiple records

```
DELETE FROM Invoices WHERE AmountDue = 0
```

Figure 19-6 How to modify data in a result set

How to access a database with Java

Before an application can use *JDBC* (*Java Database Connectivity*) to manipulate the data in a database, you need to connect the application to the database. In this topic, you'll learn four ways that you can do that. Then, you'll learn how to configure two of these ways and how to write the code that creates the connection.

The four driver types

Figure 19-7 shows four ways a Java application can access a database. To start, the Java application uses the JDBC driver manager to load a *database driver*. Then, the Java application can use one or more of the driver types to connect to the database and manipulate the data.

You can use a type-1, *JDBC-ODBC bridge driver* to connect to a database through *ODBC* (*Open Database Connectivity*), which is a standard way to access databases that were developed by Microsoft. Since ODBC drivers exist for most modern databases, a type-1 driver provides a way to connect Java with almost any database type. And since a type-1 driver is included as a part of the Java 2 Platform, it's available to all Java programmers. However, in order for a type-1 driver to work, an ODBC data source must be registered on the client machine as shown in the next figure. In addition, the JDBC-ODBC bridge driver doesn't support some of the newer JDBC features introduced since Java 2.

You can use a type-2, *native protocol partly Java driver* to connect to a database without using ODBC. However, like ODBC, this driver requires that some binary code be installed on each client machine. As a result, you'll want to use a type-3 or type-4 driver if you plan to distribute the application on multiple client machines.

You can use a type-3, *net protocol all Java driver* to connect to a database by converting JDBC calls to an independent net protocol that's used by a specific vendor. Then, the vendor's middleware software, which runs on a server, will convert the net protocol into calls in the native protocol that's used by the DBMS. Since the middleware software can typically convert the net protocol into the native DBMS protocol for multiple databases, this solution is the most flexible.

You can also use a type-4, *native protocol all Java driver* to connect to a database. This type of driver, which runs on a server, converts JDBC calls directly to the native DBMS protocol. Since most DBMS protocols are proprietary, these types of drivers are typically available from the database vendors.

Although this chapter shows how to connect to a database using both a type-1 and type-3 driver, you'll want to use a type-3 or type-4 driver for any serious application. You can download type-3 and type-4 drivers for most databases from the Java web site (www.java.sun.com/products/jdbc/drivers). The documentation for these drivers typically shows how to install and configure the driver so it runs on a server.

Four ways to access a database

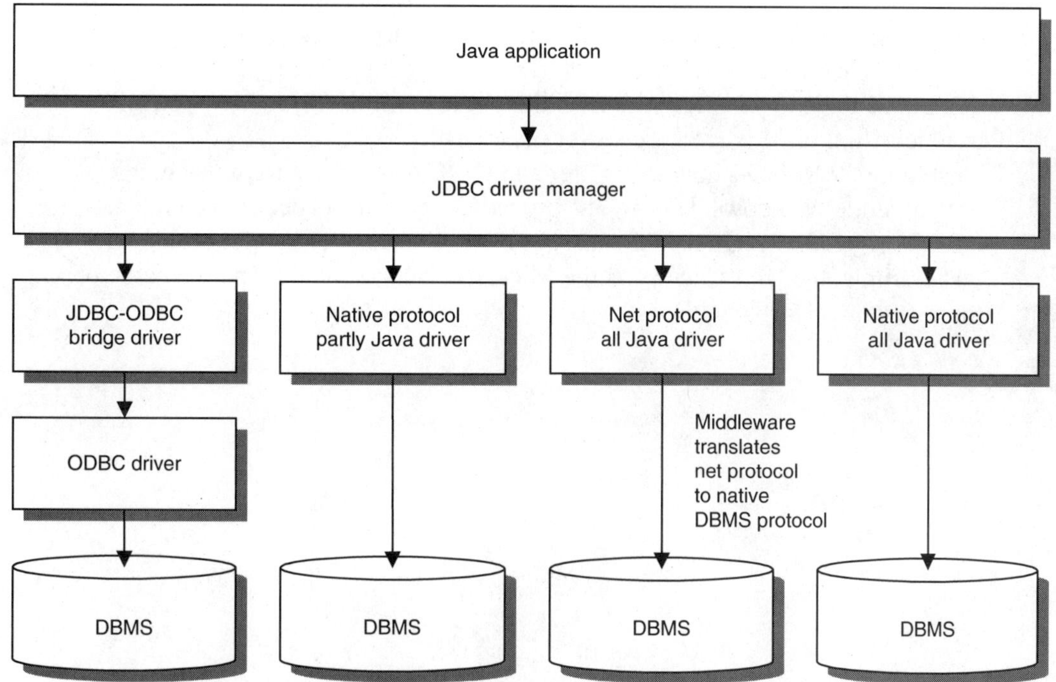

The four types of Java drivers

Type 1 A *JDBC-ODBC bridge driver* converts JDBC calls into ODBC calls that access the DBMS protocol. This data access method requires that the ODBC drivers be installed on the client machines.

Type 2 A *native protocol partly Java driver* converts JDBC calls into calls in the native DBMS protocol. Since this conversion takes place on the client, some binary code must be installed on the client machine.

Type 3 A *net protocol all Java driver* converts JDBC calls into a net protocol that's independent of any native DBMS protocol. Then, middleware software running on a server converts the net protocol to the native DBMS protocol. Since this conversion takes place on the server side, no installation is required on the client machine.

Type 4 A *native protocol all Java driver* converts JDBC calls into a native DBMS protocol. Since this conversion takes place on the server side, no installation is required on the client machine.

Notes

- To get information about the drivers that are currently available, check the Java web site at www.java.sun.com/products/jdbc and click on the List of Drivers Available link.
- Since type-1 and type-2 drivers require some client-side installation, they're not a good solution for Internet applications.

Figure 19-7 The four driver types

How to configure an ODBC data source

To use a JDBC-ODBC bridge driver, you need to configure the ODBC data source on each client machine. In contrast, to use a type-3 or type-4 driver, you don't need to do any configuration on the client machines. However, you still need to install the driver on the server machine.

Figure 19-8 shows how to register an ODBC data source for a machine running under Windows. During this procedure, you must specify the type of ODBC driver, the location of the database, and the name of the data source. In this example, the ODBC driver is the Microsoft Access Driver, and the name of the data source is MurachBooks.

How to register an ODBC data source

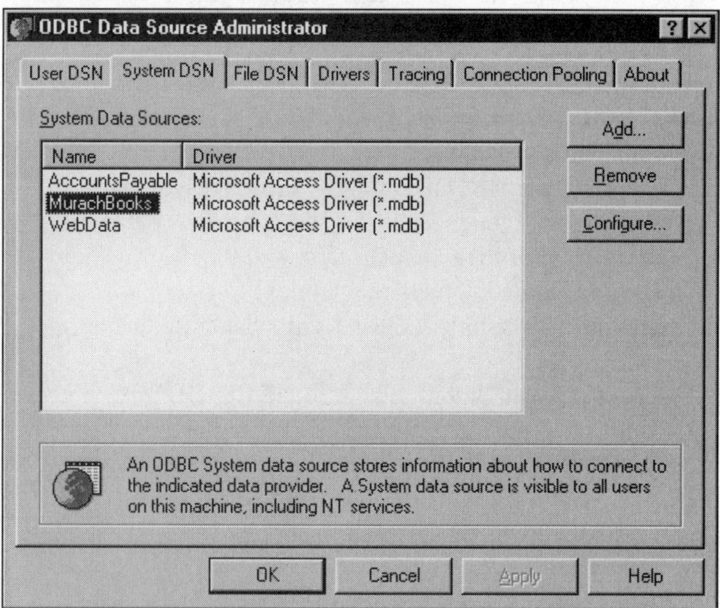

How to install the client driver for an ODBC data source

1. Go to the Control Panel and select the ODBC Data Sources (32 bit) icon.
2. From the ODBC Data Source Administrator dialog box, click on the System DSN tab, and then click on the Add button to add a data source.
3. From the Create New Data Source dialog box, select the type of database and click on the Finish button. Then, enter a name for the data source and select the database. When you're done, the ODBC Data Source Administrator should look similar to the dialog box shown above.

Note

- This procedure will vary slightly depending on the operating system and on the type of database. However, the general idea is the same. You must select a type of ODBC driver; you must provide a name for the data source; and you must locate the data source. That way, the client machine or server has all the data it needs to access the data source.

Figure 19-8 How to register an ODBC data source with Windows

How to connect to a database

Figure 19-9 shows the syntax and code needed to use JDBC to connect to a database. First, this figure shows the syntax that's used to specify the URL (Uniform Resource Locator) for the database. Then, this figure shows the code that illustrates two ways to connect to a database.

The first example shows how to use the JDBC-ODBC bridge driver that comes as a part of the Java 2 Platform to connect to the MurachBooks database. To start, you use the forName method of the Class class to load the driver. Then, you use the getConnection method of the DriverManager class to return a connection object. To do that, you must supply a URL for the database, a user name, and a password.

The URL for these drivers starts with "jdbc". Then, for JDBC-ODBC bridge drivers, the subprotocol is "odbc" and the database URL is the name that you used when you configured the ODBC data source. In this example, the default user name and password for an Access database are used. However, if the security for the database was enabled, you would need to supply a valid user name and password for the database.

The second example shows how to use a type-3 driver named JDataConnect to connect to the MurachBooks database. A trial version of this driver can be downloaded from NetDirect's website at www.j-netdirect.com. Although this example uses a driver named JDataConnect that's made by NetDirect, it just shows that the syntax for connecting to a database is similar no matter what type of driver you use. To load the driver, you specify the location of the driver class. But since this class isn't part of the Java API, you must download the class and set the Java classpath to the directory on the server that contains JData2_0\sql\$Driver.class.

All of the connection code in this second example is similar to the code in the first example except for the URL specification. Here, the subprotocol is the protocol that's used by JDataConnect, and the URL itself points to the server that the database is running on. This means you must configure the ODBC data source on that server. To point to a specific server, you can supply a URL, name, or IP address for that server. In this example, the database is running on a server named DBSERVER. However, you can test this driver by placing it on your local system and using localhost rather than the server's name.

Although this figure doesn't show any exception handling code, the forName method of the Class class throws a ClassNotFoundException, and the getConnection method of the DriverManager class throws an SQLException. As a result, you must either throw or catch these exceptions when you write the code that connects to your database, but it's good programming practice to eventually catch both of these exceptions. Then, if an error occurs, you can tell whether it's due to the driver connection (ClassNotFoundException) or the database connection (SQLException).

In practice, connecting to the database is often the most time-consuming and frustrating part of working with a database. So if some of your colleagues have already made a connection to the database you need to use, by all means get help from them. That can save you hours of frustration.

URL syntax

```
jdbc:subprotocolName:databaseURL
```

How to connect to the MurachBooks database with the JDBC-ODBC bridge driver

```
//load the JDBC-ODBC bridge driver
Class.forName("sun.jdbc.odbc.JdbcOdbcDriver");

//use the DriverManager to create a Connection object
String url = "jdbc:odbc:MurachBooks";
String user = "Admin";
String password = "";
Connection connection = DriverManager.getConnection(url, user, password);
```

How to connect to the MurachBooks database with a type-3 driver named JDataConnect

```
//load the type-3 driver
Class.forName("JData2_0.sql.$Driver"); //must set classpath to find driver

//use the DriverManager to create a Connection object
String url = "jdbc:JDataConnect://DBSERVER/MurachBooks";
String user = "Admin";
String password = "";
Connection connection = DriverManager.getConnection(url, user, password);
```

Description

- The forName method of the Class class throws a ClassNotFoundException.
- The getConnection method of the DriverManager class throws a SQLException.
- Since the Connection object will often be used by more than one method in a class, it's often declared as static instance variable.
- To learn more about the JDataConnect driver, check the NetDirect website (www.j-netdirect.com).

How to use Java to work with the data in a database

Once you connect to a database, you're ready to retrieve data from the database and to manipulate that data. So that's what you'll learn to do next.

How to return a result set

Figure 19-10 shows how to use Statement objects to return ResultSet objects. To start, this figure shows two examples of how to create a result set. Then, it shows five constants of the ResultSet interface that can be used to control the type of result set that's created.

The first example shows how to create a forward-only, read-only result set. Here, the createStatement method is called from a Connection object to return a Statement object. Then, the executeQuery method is called from the Statement object to execute an SQL SELECT statement that's coded as a string. Since this SELECT statement only identifies a single record (the book with the book code equal to WARP), this result set will be a table that contains only one row. This type of query lets a user search for a book by its book code.

The second example shows how to create a scrollable, updateable result set. To do this, the code supplies two arguments for the createStatement method of the Connection object. The first argument specifies the type of the result set. Here, the result set has been set to a scrollable result set that will display changes that have been made by other users to the data that's in the result set. Although this is the most flexible type of result set, it also requires the most system resources. In contrast, a scrollable result set that isn't sensitive to changes requires less resources.

The second argument in this second example specifies the concurrency of the result set. Here, the concurrency has been set to updateable. That means that you can update the values in the result set and those values will be stored in the database. Within this example, the SELECT statement returns three columns and all of the rows in the Books table. As a result, this statement uses more resources than the statement in the first example.

When you return a result set, you need to make sure that your driver supports the features of the result set. For example, some older drivers only support version 1.0 of the JDBC API. Since scrollable and updateable result sets were added in version 2.0 of the JDBC API, this means that those drivers don't support these types of result sets. In addition, not all drivers will support version 3.0 of the JDBC API. This version is included with SDK1.4 and includes newer features such as allowing multiple result sets to be open at the same time.

How to create a forward-only, read-only result set

```
Statement statement = connection.createStatement();
ResultSet books = statement.executeQuery("SELECT * FROM Books " +
                                         "WHERE BookCode = 'WARP'");
```

How to create a scrollable, updateable result set

```
Statement statement = connection.createStatement(
    ResultSet.TYPE_SCROLL_SENSITIVE,
    ResultSet.CONCUR_UPDATABLE);
String query = "SELECT BookCode, BookTitle, BookPrice "
             + "FROM Books ORDER BY BookCode ASC";
ResultSet books = statement.executeQuery(query);
```

Five ResultSet constants that set type and concurrency

Constant	Description
`TYPE_FORWARD_ONLY`	Creates a result set where the cursor can only move forward (default).
`TYPE_SCROLL_INSENSITIVE`	Creates a result set where the cursor can scroll through the result set but won't display changes made by others to the result set.
`TYPE_SCROLL_SENSITIVE`	Creates a result set where the cursor can scroll through the result set and will display changes made by others to the result set.
`CONCUR_READ_ONLY`	Creates a read-only result set (default).
`CONCUR_UPDATABLE`	Creates an updateable result.

Description

- The createStatement method of a Connection object creates a Statement object. Then, the executeQuery method of the Statement object executes a SELECT statement that returns a ResultSet object.
- By default, the createStatement method creates a forward-only, read-only result set. However, you can set the type and concurrency of a Statement object by coding the constants above for the two arguments of the createStatement method.
- Both the createStatement and executeQuery methods throw an exception of the SQLException type. As a result, any code that returns a result set will need to catch or throw this exception.

Figure 19-10 How to return a result set

How to move the cursor through a result set

Figure 19-11 shows how to move the cursor through a result set. To start, this figure shows 14 methods of the ResultSet object. Then, this figure shows examples that illustrate how to use some of these methods. Since the ResultSet object is created from the ResultSet interface, it's up to the driver software to fully implement these methods. As a result, older drivers may not support some of the methods that were added in versions 2.0 and 3.0 of the JDBC API. These methods include the methods for working with scrollable result sets such as the previous method.

If the result set is a forward-only result set, you'll only be able to use the next method to move through the result set. But if the result set is scrollable, you can use any of the methods. When you use the first, previous, next, last, absolute, and relative methods to move the cursor through the result set, they return a boolean value that indicates whether the cursor has been moved to a valid row. For example, the next method returns a true value until it reaches the end of the result set or until it hits a row that's invalid for other reasons. Since all of these methods throw an exception of the SQLException type, you either need to throw or catch this exception when you're working with these methods.

The examples in this figure show how to use the first, previous, next, last, absolute, and relative methods. Here, the first statement moves the cursor to the first row in the result set, and the second statement moves the cursor to the last row. Then, the first if statement moves the cursor to the previous row if the cursor isn't on the first row, and the second if statement moves the cursor to the next row if the cursor isn't on the last row. Finally, the fifth statement moves the cursor to the fourth record in the result set; the sixth statement moves the cursor back two rows; and the seventh statement moves the cursor forward three rows.

Methods of a ResultSet object that move through a result set

Method	Description
`beforeFirst()`	Moves the cursor before the first row in this result set.
`afterLast()`	Moves the cursor after the last row in this result set.
`first()`	Moves the cursor to the first row in this result set.
`previous()`	Moves the cursor up to the previous row in this result set.
`next()`	Moves the cursor down to the next row in this result set.
`last()`	Moves the cursor to the last row in this result set.
`absolute(intRow)`	Moves the cursor to the row specified by the int value where 1 is the first row, 2 is the second row, and so on.
`relative(intRow)`	Moves the cursor a relative number of rows where 2 moves down two rows and –3 moves up three rows.
`isBeforeFirst()`	Returns a true value if the cursor is positioned before the first row.
`isAfterLast()`	Returns a true value if the cursor is positioned after the last row.
`isFirst()`	Returns a true value if the cursor is positioned on the first row.
`isLast()`	Returns a true value if the cursor is positioned on the last row.
`close()`	Releases the result set's JDBC and database resources.
`getRow()`	Returns an int value that identifies the current row of the result set.

Code examples

```
books.first();
books.last();
if (books.isFirst() == false)
    books.previous();
if (books.isLast() == false)
    books.next();
books.absolute(4);
books.relative(-2);
books.relative(3);
```

Description

- When you create a result set, the cursor is positioned before the first record. As a result, the first time you call the next method, it will move to the first record in the result set.
- The first, previous, next, last, absolute, and relative methods all return a true value if the new row exists and a false value if the new row doesn't exist or the result isn't valid.
- All of the methods in this figure throw an exception of the SQLException type.

Figure 19-11 How to move the cursor through a result set

How to return data from a result set

Figure 19-12 shows how to return data from the current record in a result set. In particular, it shows how to use the getString and getDouble methods of the ResultSet object to return String values and double values. However, the same principles can be used for any of the getXXX methods.

The two methods in this figure show the two types of arguments accepted by the getXXX methods. The first method accepts an int value that specifies the number of the column in the result set, where 1 is the first column, 2 is the second column, and so on. The second getXXX method accepts a string that specifies the name of the column in the result set. Although the getXXX methods that specify the column index run slightly faster and require less typing, using the getXXX methods that specify the column name can be more flexible. As a result, you can decide which method to use based on the needs of your application.

The first example shows how to use column indexes to return data from a result set named books. Here, the first two statements use the getString method to return the code and title for the current book while the third statement uses the getDouble method to return the price of the book. Since these methods use the column index, the first column in the result set must contain the book code, the second column must contain the book title, and so on.

The second example shows how to use column names to return data from the books result set. Since this code uses the column name, the order of the columns in the result set doesn't matter. However, the column names must exist in the result set or an SQLException object will be thrown that indicates that a column wasn't found.

The third example shows how you can use the getXXX methods to create a Book object. Here, the constructor for the Book object uses three values that are returned by the getXXX methods to create a new book. Since objects are often created from data that's stored in a database, code like this is commonly used.

If you look up the ResultSet interface in the documentation for the API, you'll see that getXXX methods exist for all of the primitive types and for other types of data too. For example, getXXX methods exist for the Date, Time, and Timestamp classes that are a part of the java.sql package. In addition, they exist for *BLOB objects* (*Binary Large Objects*) and *CLOB objects* (*Character Large Objects*). These types of objects are used for storing large objects such as multimedia files in databases.

Methods of a ResultSet object that return data from a result set

Method	Description
`getXXX(intColumnIndex)`	Returns data from the specified column number.
`getXXX(StringColumnName)`	Returns data from the specified column name.

Code that uses column indexes to return fields from the books result set

```
String code = books.getString(1);
String title = books.getString(2);
double price = books.getDouble(3);
```

Code that uses column names to return the same fields

```
String code = books.getString("BookCode");
String title = books.getString("BookTitle");
double price = books.getDouble("BookPrice");
```

Code that creates a Book object from the books result set

```
Book firstBook = new Book(books.getString(1),
                          books.getString(2),
                          books.getDouble(3));
```

Description

- The getXXX methods can be used to return all eight primitive types. For example, the getInt method returns the int type and the getLong method returns the long type.
- The getXXX methods can also be used to return strings, dates, and times. For example, the getString method returns any object of the String class while the getDate, getTime, and getTimestamp methods return objects of the Date, Time, and Timestamp classes of the java.sql package.
- Although they aren't widely used, the getBlob and getClob methods can be used to return *BLOB objects* (*Binary Large Objects*) and *CLOB objects* (*Character Large Objects*).

Figure 19-12 How to return data from a result set

How to modify data in a result set

Figure 19-13 shows how to use Java to modify the data in a database. First, it shows how to use the executeUpdate method of a Statement object to execute SQL statements that add, update, and delete data. Then, this figure shows how to use newer methods from the JDBC 2.0 API to add, update, and delete data. Since the executeUpdate method has been a part of Java since version 1.0 of JDBC, this method should work for all JDBC drivers. In contrast, the newer methods of JDBC 2.0 and 3.0 may not work with older JDBC drivers. In particular, these methods don't work with the JDBC-ODBC bridge driver included with the SDK1.3.1. However, later SDK versions may eventually contain an updated bridge driver that can use these methods.

When you work with the executeUpdate method, you just pass an SQL statement to the database. In these examples, the code adds, updates, and deletes a book in the Book table. To do that, the code combines data from a Book object with the appropriate SQL statement. For the UPDATE and DELETE statements, the SQL statement uses the book's code in the WHERE clause to select a single book.

When you work with the newer methods of the JDBC, you don't have to use any SQL statements. Instead, you just call methods from the ResultSet object to add, update, and delete records from the current result set. In these examples, you can assume that the ResultSet object named books contains three columns and many rows.

To add a record, you call the moveToInsertRow method to move the cursor to a special buffer area that's used to construct a new row. Then, you call the updateXXX method for each column in the row. Here, the first argument specifies the name of the column and the second argument specifies the value of the column. When you're done providing values for all of the columns in the row, you call the insertRow method to commit the changes to the database. Then, you can call the moveToCurrentRow method to move back to the row that you were on before you called the moveToInsertRow method.

To update or delete a row, you start by moving to that row using the methods that were described earlier in this chapter. Then, you can update a record by calling the updateXXX method for any of the columns that you wish to update and by calling the updateRow method after that. Or, you can delete a record by calling the deleteRow method.

Depending on the driver that you're using, the modifications that you make to a result set may cause some problems. For example, when you add a row, you may not be able to move to that row. Worse, when you delete a row, an invalid row may remain in the result set where the deleted row used to be. Then, if you try to move to that row, your application will throw an SQLException. The best way to solve these problems is to get a better driver or change the way your program retrieves data. However, you can also solve these problems by closing the result set and opening it again. Although that isn't efficient, it will refresh all rows in the result set.

How to use the executeUpdate method to modify data

How to add a record

```
String query =
   "INSERT INTO Books (BookCode, BookTitle, BookPrice) " +
   "VALUES ('" + book.getCode() + "', " +
           "'" + book.getTitle() + "', " +
           "'" + book.getPrice() + "')";
Statement statement = connection.createStatement();
statement.executeUpdate(query);
```

How to update a record

```
String query = "UPDATE Books SET " +
   "BookCode = '" + book.getCode() + "', " +
   "BookTitle = '" + book.getTitle() + "', " +
   "BookPrice = '" + book.getPrice() + "' " +
   "WHERE BookCode = '" + book.getCode() + "'";
Statement statement = connection.createStatement();
statement.executeUpdate(query);
```

How to delete a record

```
String query = "DELETE FROM Books " +
               "WHERE BookCode = '" + bookCode + "'";
Statement statement = connection.createStatement();
statement.executeUpdate(query);
```

How to use methods from JDBC 2.0 and later to modify data

How to add a record

```
books.moveToInsertRow();
books.updateString("BookCode", book.getCode());
books.updateString("BookTitle", book.getTitle());
books.updateDouble("BookPrice", book.getPrice());
books.insertRow();
books.moveToCurrentRow();
```

How to update a record

```
books.updateString("BookCode", book.getCode());
books.updateString("BookTitle", book.getTitle());
books.updateDouble("BookPrice", book.getPrice());
books.updateRow();
```

How to delete a record

```
books.deleteRow();
```

Description

- The executeUpdate method is an older method that works with most JDBC drivers. The newer methods may not work properly with older JDBC drivers.
- The executeUpdate method returns an int value that identifies the number of records that were affected by the update.
- When you delete a record, the result set may contain an invalid row where the deleted row used to be. To solve this problem, you can close the result set and reopen it.

Figure 19-13 How to modify data in a result set

How to work with prepared statements

Figure 19-14 shows how to use a prepared SQL statement to return a result set or to modify data. Since *prepared statements* let Java compile the SQL statement with parameters that can be supplied later, they execute faster than regular statements. As a result, you should use prepared statements whenever you're coding a statement that will be executed more than once.

The first example shows how to use a prepared statement to create a result set that contains a single book. Here, the first statement uses a question mark (?) to identify the parameter for the SELECT statement, which is the book code for the book. The second statement uses the prepareStatement method of the Connection object to return a PreparedStatement object. The third statement uses a setXXX method (the setString method) of the PreparedStatement object to set a value for the first parameter in the SELECT statement. And the fourth statement uses the executeQuery method of the PreparedStatement object to return a ResultSet object.

The second example shows how to use a prepared statement to execute an UPDATE query that requires four parameters. Here, the first statement uses four question marks (?) to identify the four parameters of the UPDATE statement, and the second statement creates the PreparedStatement object. Then, the next four statements use the setXXX methods to set the four parameters in the order that they appear in the UPDATE statement. The last statement uses the executeUpdate method of the PreparedStatement object to execute the UPDATE statement.

The third and fourth examples show how to insert and delete records with prepared statements. Here, you can see that the type of SQL statement that you're using determines whether you use the executeQuery method or the executeUpdate method. If you're using a SELECT statement to return a result set, you use the executeQuery method. But if you're using an INSERT INTO, UPDATE, or DELETE statement, you use the executeUpdate method. This holds true whether you're using a Statement object or a PreparedStatement object.

By default, the prepareStatement method of the Connection object creates a forward-only, read-only result set. However, you can set the type and concurrency of a PreparedStatement object just as you can for Statement objects as shown in figure 19-10. That way, you can create a scrollable, updateable result set.

How to use a prepared statement

To return a read-only result set

```
String preparedSQL = "SELECT BookCode, BookTitle, BookPrice " +
                     "FROM Books WHERE BookCode = ?";
PreparedStatement ps = connection.prepareStatement(preparedSQL);
ps.setString(1, bookCode);
ResultSet book = ps.executeQuery();
```

To modify data

```
String preparedSQL = "UPDATE Books SET " +
                     "BookCode = ?, BookTitle = ?, BookPrice = ?" +
                     "WHERE BookCode = ?";
PreparedStatement ps = connection.prepareStatement(preparedSQL);
ps.setString(1, book.getCode());
ps.setString(2, book.getTitle());
ps.setDouble(3, book.getPrice());
ps.setString(4, book.getCode());
ps.executeUpdate();
```

To insert a record

```
String preparedQuery = "INSERT INTO Books (BookCode, BookTitle, "
                     + "BookPrice) VALUES (?, ?, ?)";
PreparedStatement ps = connection.prepareStatement(preparedQuery);
ps.setString(1, book.getCode());
ps.setString(2, book.getTitle());
ps.setDouble(3, book.getPrice());
ps.executeUpdate();
```

To delete a record

```
String preparedQuery = "DELETE FROM Books "
                     + "WHERE BookCode = ?";
PreparedStatement ps = connection.prepareStatement(preparedQuery);
ps.setString(1, bookCode);
ps.executeUpdate();
```

Description

- To specify a parameter, type a question mark (?) in the SQL statement.
- To supply values for the parameters in a prepared statement, use the setXXX methods of the PreparedStatement interface. For a complete list of setXXX methods, look up the PreparedStatement interface of the java.sql package in the documentation for the Java API.
- To execute a SELECT statement, use the executeQuery method. To execute an INSERT INTO, UPDATE, or DELETE statement, use the executeUpdate method.

Figure 19-14 How to work with prepared statements

The Book Maintenance application

In chapter 12, you learned how to code the user interface for the Book Maintenance application. If you've read chapter 18, you've also learned how to code the BookIO class that provides the methods that the user interface needs for maintaining the book data in a random-access file.

Now, in this chapter, you'll learn how to code a BookDB class that provides the methods that the user interface needs for maintaining the book data in a database. This will illustrate how using a database is superior to using a random-access file. It will also show how separating the GUI, business, and data access code makes it easy to change the way an application is implemented.

The user interface for this application

To refresh your memory about how this application works, figure 19-15 shows the user interface for the Book Maintenance application. In chapters 12 and 18, you've seen this interface used with other data. Now, this version shows this interface with different data because the application connects to the MurachBooks database. Otherwise, the interface looks and works the same.

BookDB calls in the BookFrame and BookPanel classes

Figure 19-15 also shows the code in the BookFrame and BookPanel classes that calls the methods of the BookDB class. To review all the code for these classes, you can refer back to figure 12-20, but this gives you the highlights. The primary difference between the code in this figure and the code in figure 12-20 is the use of the connect method and the change of the class name from BookIO to BookDB.

If you look first at the constructor for the BookPanel class, you can see that it uses the connect method of the BookDB class to connect to a database, and it uses the open method to open a record set. Then, it uses the moveFirst method to return the current Book object, which is stored as an instance variable of the BookPanel object. If the driver can't be loaded or the database connection can't be made, this class catches any ClassNotFoundException or SQLException and displays the related error message.

After the database is opened, the BookPanel class can use the other BookDB methods. These are all issued from the actionPerformed method in the BookPanel class. For instance, when the user clicks on the Exit button, this method calls the close method. When the user clicks on the First button, this method calls the moveFirst method. Although the code for the other buttons isn't shown, this continues for all of the buttons. Since any of these methods can throw an SQLException, the actionPerformed method is contained in a try/catch statement, and the second catch block catches the SQLException.

The GUI for the Book Maintenance application

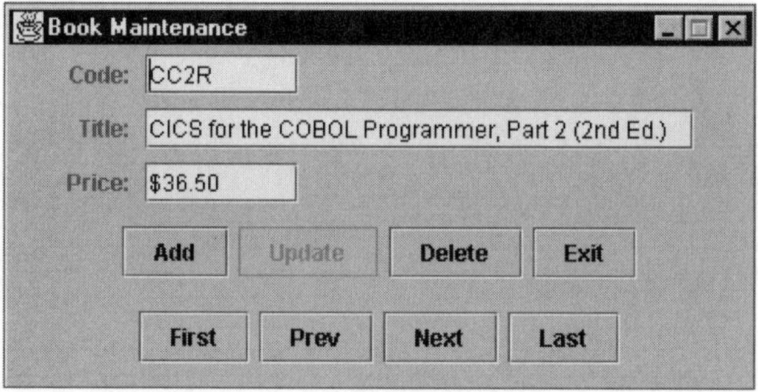

The code for the windowClosing method in the BookFrame class

```
public void windowClosing(WindowEvent e){
   BookDB.close();
   System.exit(0);
}
```

The code in the constructor for the BookPanel class

```
try{
   BookDB.connect();
   BookDB.open();
   currentBook = BookDB.moveFirst();
}
catch(ClassNotFoundException e){
   JOptionPane.showMessageDialog(null, e.getMessage());
   System.exit(1);
}
catch(SQLException e){
   JOptionPane.showMessageDialog(null, e.getMessage());
}
```

The code for the actionPerformed method

```
public void actionPerformed(ActionEvent e){
   try{
      Object source = e.getSource();
      if (source == exitButton){
         BookDB.close();
         System.exit(0);
      }
      else if (source == firstButton){
         currentBook = BookDB.moveFirst();
         performBookDisplay();
         enableButtons(true);
      }
      //else if blocks for the other buttons
   }
   catch(NumberFormatException nfe){
      JOptionPane.showMessageDialog(this, nfe.getMessage());
   }
   catch(SQLException sqle){
      JOptionPane.showMessageDialog(this, sqle.getMessage());
   }
}
```

Figure 19-15 BookDB calls in the BookFrame and BookPanel classes

To end the program, the user can click on the Exit button, which as you've already seen leads to a call of the close method from the actionPerformed method. But the user can also end the program by closing the window. That's why the windowClosing method in the BookFrame class must also call the BookDB.close method. This time, though, the SQLException isn't caught so it must be caught (not thrown) by the close method in the BookDB class.

The code for the BookDB class

Figure 19-16 shows the code for the BookDB class. This class provides the static variables and methods that are used to connect to a database, open a result set, scroll through the result set, modify the data in the result set, and close the result set. Although this class mixes some JDBC 1.0 methods with JDBC 2.0 methods, the JDBC-ODBC bridge driver supports all of these methods.

To start, the BookDB class declares static variables for the Connection, Statement, and ResultSet objects. Then, it uses the connect method to provide all the code needed to connect to the MurachBooks database with the JDBC-ODBC bridge driver that comes with the SDK. For this code to work, the ODBC driver must be configured for a data source named MurachBooks. In addition, the user name and password that are supplied must be valid for the database.

The open method opens a scrollable and updateable result set that contains the BookCode, BookTitle, and BookPrice columns for all of the books in the Books table of the MurachBooks database. In addition, this method sorts the result set in ascending order by the BookCode column. If an error occurs in the createStatement or executeQuery methods, an SQLException may be thrown that will be caught in the BookPanel class.

The close method closes the ResultSet object. Then, it closes the Statement object. In this case, you must close the ResultSet before you close the Statement object. Otherwise, calling the close method of the ResultSet object will throw an SQLException. Please note that unlike the other methods in this class, this method catches the SQLException instead of throwing it. That's why the call of the close method in the windowClosing method of the BookPanel class doesn't need to catch this exception.

The next four methods use the JDBC 2.0 methods to move the cursor through the result set that's created by the open method. All of these methods return a Book object that corresponds to the row that the cursor is on in the table. In addition, all of these methods throw an SQLException. That's why the code in the BookPanel class must catch these exceptions.

If you study the code for these methods, you shouldn't have any trouble understanding them. They just use the methods of the ResultSet object to move the cursor. The moveFirst method returns a Book object that corresponds to the first row in the result set. The movePrevious method usually returns a Book object that corresponds to the previous row in the result set. However, if the cursor is positioned on the first row of the result set, the movePrevious method returns a Book object that corresponds to the first row in the result set.

The code for the BookDB class

```
import java.sql.*;
import javax.swing.*;

public class BookDB{
   private static Connection connection;
   private static Statement scrollStatement;
   private static ResultSet books;

   public static void connect() throws ClassNotFoundException, SQLException{
      Class.forName("sun.jdbc.odbc.JdbcOdbcDriver");
      String url = "jdbc:odbc:MurachBooks";
      String user = "Admin";
      String password = "";
      connection = DriverManager.getConnection(url, user, password)
   }

   public static void open() throws SQLException{
      scrollStatement = connection.createStatement(
            ResultSet.TYPE_SCROLL_SENSITIVE, ResultSet.CONCUR_UPDATABLE);
      String query = "SELECT BookCode, BookTitle, BookPrice "
                  + "FROM Books ORDER BY BookCode ASC";
      books = scrollStatement.executeQuery(query);
   }

   public static void close(){
      try{
         books.close();
         scrollStatement.close();
      }
      catch(SQLException sqle){
         JOptionPane.showMessageDialog(null, sql.getMessage());
      }
   }

   public static Book moveFirst() throws SQLException{
      books.first();
      Book firstBook = new Book(books.getString("BookCode"),
                                books.getString("BookTitle"),
                                books.getDouble("BookPrice"));
      return firstBook;
   }

   public static Book movePrevious() throws SQLException{
      if (books.isFirst() == false)
         books.previous();
      else
         books.first();
      Book previousBook = new Book(books.getString(1),
                                   books.getString(2),
                                   books.getDouble(3));
      return previousBook;
   }
```

Figure 19-16 The code for the BookDB class (part 1 of 2)

Another way to write the code for the movePrevious method is to use the previous method to move the cursor and return a false value if the move doesn't work:

```
if (books.previous() == false)
   books.first();
```

Although this code is shorter than the code used in this figure, it's more difficult to understand. Yet another way to write this code is to use the not operator (!) to reverse the boolean value like this:

```
if (!books.previous())
   books.first();
```

Although this code is even shorter, it's even more difficult to understand. Because your applications will be easier to maintain when they're easier to read, it's a good coding practice to write code like this in the way that's easiest to read.

After the moveNext and moveLast methods, which work like the movePrevious and moveFirst methods, the BookDB class continues with the addRecord, updateRecord, and deleteRecord methods. These methods use JDBC 1.0 methods to modify the data that's stored in the database. The first two methods accept a Book object as a parameter while the last one accepts a String that represents a book code.

The addRecord method adds a new row to the Books table. To do that, the first statement creates a string that contains an INSERT statement that includes the data from the Book object that was passed to the method. Then, the second statement creates a forward-only, read-only Statement object. The third statement uses the executeUpdate method to execute the query. The fourth statement closes the Statement object. And the last two statements call the close and open methods of the BookDB class to refresh the result set. This ensures that the newly added row will be displayed properly. With the right driver, though, these last two statements shouldn't be necessary.

The updateRecord method works like the addRecord method. However, the updateRecord method uses an UPDATE statement instead of an INSERT statement. And since no records have been added or removed from the result set, this method doesn't need to close and open the result set to refresh it.

The deleteRecord method also works like the addRecord method. However, the deleteRecord method uses the DELETE statement instead of the INSERT statement. In addition, the deleteRecord method only accepts a book code as a parameter. That's because this method only needs to identify the book that should be deleted. Here again, the method ends by closing and opening the result set to refresh it, but this shouldn't be necessary with the right driver.

If you compare the methods in this class with those that work with the random-access file in figure 18-17, you'll see that the code for working with databases is much easier to read and understand. It should also run more efficiently. That's why databases are commonly used for serious business applications.

The code for the BookDB class (continued)

```
    public static Book moveNext() throws SQLException{
        if (books.isLast() == false)
            books.next();
        else
            books.last();
        Book nextBook = new Book(books.getString(1),
                                 books.getString(2),
                                 books.getDouble(3));
        return nextBook;
    }

    public static Book moveLast() throws SQLException{
        books.last();
        Book lastBook = new Book(books.getString(1),
                                 books.getString(2),
                                 books.getDouble(3));
        return lastBook;
    }

    public static void addRecord(Book book) throws SQLException{
        String query = "INSERT INTO Books (BookCode, BookTitle, BookPrice) " +
            "VALUES ('" + book.getCode() + "', " +
            "'" + book.getTitle() + "', " +
            "'" + book.getPrice() + "')";
        Statement statement = connection.createStatement();
        statement.executeUpdate(query);
        statement.close();
        close();
        open();
    }

    public static void updateRecord(Book book) throws SQLException{
        String query = "UPDATE Books SET " +
            "BookCode = '" + book.getCode() + "', " +
            "BookTitle = '" + book.getTitle() + "', " +
            "BookPrice = '" + book.getPrice() + "' " +
            "WHERE BookCode = '" + book.getCode() + "'";
        Statement statement = connection.createStatement();
        statement.executeUpdate(query);
        statement.close();
    }

    public static void deleteRecord(String bookCode) throws SQLException{
        String query = "DELETE FROM Books " +
            "WHERE BookCode = '" + bookCode + "'";
        Statement statement = connection.createStatement();
        statement.executeUpdate(query);
        statement.close();
        close();
        open();
    }
}
```

Figure 19-16 The code for the BookDB class (part 2 of 2)

An introduction to working with meta data

When you work with a result set, you can get data about the definition of the result set. This type of information is known as *meta data*. For example, the meta data of a result set includes the number of columns, names of the columns, and the data type that's stored in each column. Although working with meta data is an advanced skill that you don't need for normal business applications, this topic gives you a taste of what you can do with it.

How to work with meta data

Figure 19-17 shows the basic skills for working with meta data. First, this figure shows how to return a ResultSetMetaData object from a ResultSet object. Then, it shows five methods that are commonly used to work with meta data, plus two typical programmer-defined methods that work with meta data.

When you use the last four methods in this figure, you use an integer value to specify the column, where 1 is the first column. The difference between the second and third methods is that the second method returns the *name* that the DBMS uses to identify the column while the third method returns the *label* that's used as a heading for GUIs and reports. If a label hasn't been defined for a column, the DBMS often uses the column name as a default. The difference between the fourth and fifth methods is that the fourth method returns an int type that represents an SQL data type while the fifth method returns the name of the SQL data type.

The first example shows a static method that returns the column names for a result set. This method accepts a ResultSet object as a parameter and returns a Vector object that contains all of the column names. To do that, the first statement defines a blank vector. Then, the second statement gets the ResultSetMetaData object from the result set that has been passed to the method, and the third statement uses the getColumnCount method to get the column count. After that, a for loop cycles through all of the columns in the result set and uses the getColumnName method to add each column name to the vector. The last statement in this method returns the vector.

The second example shows a static method that returns the data for each row in a result set. This method also accepts a ResultSet object as a parameter and returns a Vector object. However, the vector that's returned in this example is a two-dimensional vector. That way, the outer vector can store one inner vector for each row in the result set. To do that, this method uses a while loop to cycle through all of the records in the result set. Inside the while loop, the for loop cycles through each column in the result set using the getColumnType method to check the data type for the column. Depending on the data type, the appropriate getXXX method is used to add the data to the inner vector. In this example, the code uses the constants of the Types class to check for the VARCHAR and INTEGER types. In addition, this code checks for the SQL data type with an int value of 2 (which corresponds with the CURRENCY type that's used by Microsoft Access).

How to use the getMetaData method to create a ResultSetMetaData object

```
ResultSetMetaData metaData = resultSet.getMetaData();
```

Methods for working with meta data

Method	Description
`getColumnCount()`	Returns the number of columns in this RecordSet object as an int type.
`getColumnName(intColumn)`	Returns the name of this column as a String object.
`getColumnLabel(intColumn)`	Returns the label of this column as a String object.
`getColumnType(intColumn)`	Returns an int type that represents the SQL data type that's used to store the data in this column.
`getColumnTypeName(intColumn)`	Returns a String object that identifies the SQL data type that's used to store the data in this column.

A method that returns the column names of a result set

```
public static Vector getColumnNames(ResultSet results) throws SQLException{
   Vector columnNames = new Vector();
   ResultSetMetaData metaData = results.getMetaData();
   int columnCount = metaData.getColumnCount();
   for (int i = 1; i <= columnCount; i++)
      columnNames.add(metaData.getColumnName(i));
   return columnNames;
}
```

A method that returns the rows of a result set

```
public static Vector getRows(ResultSet results) throws SQLException{
   Vector rows = new Vector();
   ResultSetMetaData metaData = results.getMetaData();
   int columnCount = metaData.getColumnCount();
   while (results.next()){
      Vector row = new Vector();
      for (int i = 1; i <= columnCount; i++){
         if (metaData.getColumnType(i) == Types.VARCHAR)
            row.add(results.getString(i));
         else if (metaData.getColumnType(i) == Types.INTEGER)
            row.add(new Integer(results.getInt(i)));
         else if (metaData.getColumnType(i) == 2)
            row.add(new Double(results.getDouble(i)));
      }
      rows.add(row);
   }
   return rows;
}
```

Description

- When you specify an index value for one of the methods shown in this figure, use 1 for the first column, 2 for the second column, and so on.
- You can use the constants of the Types class of the java.sql package to specify an int value for a SQL data type.

Figure 19-17 How to work with meta data

How SQL data types map to Java data types

Figure 19-18 shows how some of the most common SQL data types map to the Java data types. Some of these conversions are intuitive. For example, the SQL INTEGER type corresponds to the Java int type. However, some of these conversions aren't as intuitive. For example, the SQL REAL type maps to the Java float type.

When you write code that converts SQL types to Java types, you can use the constants in the Types class of the java.sql package to refer to the SQL types as shown in the previous figure. And if a constant doesn't exist for the data type, you can use an int value to refer to the data type. To get the int value for a data type in your record set, you can use the getColumnType method described in the previous figure. Or, to get the string that describes the data type, you can use the getColumnTypeName. For example, the Access field that defines the BookPrice column uses a non-standard Currency data type. In an SQL result set, the int value for this data type is 2 and the name for this data type is CURRENCY.

How SQL data types map to Java data types

SQL data type	Java data type
VARCHAR, LONGVARCHAR	String
BIT	boolean
TINYBIT	byte
SMALLINT	short
INTEGER	int
BIGINT	long
REAL	float
DOUBLE	double
VARBINARY, LONGVARBINARY	byte[]
NUMERIC	java.math.BigDecimal
DATE	java.sql.Date
TIME	java.sql.Time
TIMESTAMP	java.sql.Timestamp

Description

- To get the SQL data type that's used in the column of a result set, you can use the getColumnType and getColumnTypeName methods of the ResultSetMetaData object.

Figure 19-18 How SQL data types map to Java data types

Perspective

Now that you've finished this chapter, you should understand how to use JDBC to store data in a database and to retrieve data from a database. Although there's much more to learn about working with databases, those are the essential skills. To enhance your database skills, you can learn more about SQL, you can learn more about database management systems like Oracle or SQL Server, and you can learn more about the other JDBC features that are provided by Java.

Summary

- A *relational database* uses tables to store and manipulate data. Each table contains one or more *rows*, or *records*, while each row contains one or more *columns*, or *fields*.
- A *primary key* is used to identify each row in a table. A *foreign key* is a key in one table that is used to relate rows to another table.
- Each database is managed by a *database management system* (*DBMS*) that supports the use of the *Standard Query Language* (*SQL*). To manipulate the data in a database, you use the SQL SELECT, INSERT, UPDATE, and DELETE statements.
- The SELECT statement is used to return data from one or more tables in a *result set*. To return data from two or more tables, you *join* the data based on the data in related fields.
- An *inner join* returns a result set that includes data only if the related fields match. An *outer join* returns a result set that includes data from all of the rows in one table plus the data from the rows in the other table that match the related fields.
- Before you use JDBC to access data in a database, you have to connect the application to a database through a *database driver*.
- A Java program can use one of four driver types to access a database. *Type-1* and *type-2 drivers* run on the client's machine, while *type-3* and *type-4 drivers* can run on a server machine.
- When working with databases, you often need to handle the SQLException and the ClassNotFoundExeption.
- You can use JDBC to execute SQL statements that select, add, update, or delete one or more records in a database. You can also control the location of the *cursor* in the result set.
- You can use *prepared statements* to compile SQL statements with parameters that can be supplied later.
- You can return a list of the column names and types in a result set by using *meta data*.

Terms

database
relational database
table
row
column
record
field
primary key
database management system (DBMS)
relational database management system (RDBMS)
foreign key
one-to-many relationship
one-to-one relationship
many-to-many relationship
default value
Structured Query Language (SQL)
Data Definition Language (DDL)
Data Manipulation Language (DML)
query
result set
result table
current row pointer
cursor
join
inner join
equi-join
calculated field
outer join
left outer join
right outer join
action query
Java Database Connectivity (JDBC)
database driver
JDBC-ODBC bridge driver
Open Database Connectivity(ODBC)
native protocol partly Java driver
net protocol all Java driver
native protocol all Java driver
BLOB object
Binary Large Object
CLOB object
Character Large Object
prepared statement
meta data

Objectives

- Write simple SELECT statements that select, add, update, or delete records in a database.
- Given a database, configure an ODBC data source for it.
- Write code that loads the JDBC-ODBC bridge driver.
- Write code that connects an application to a database.
- Write code that returns a result set from a database.
- Write code that adds, updates, and deletes records in a database.
- Write code that uses prepared statements to add, update, and delete records in a database.
- Use meta data to return the name and data type of each column.
- Identify these terms: database, row, column, DBMS, and SQL.
- Distinguish between a primary key and a foreign key.
- Distinguish between an inner join and an outer join.

Exercise 19-1 Create the Book Maintenance application

This exercise guides you through the process of creating a version of the Book Maintenance application that uses the MurachBooks database. This database has been supplied in the Microsoft Access 2000 and 97 formats.

1. Install an ODBC data source named MurachBooks for the MurachBooks database that's in the c:\java\ch19\database directory as shown in figure 19-8. If the ODBC driver for Access on your system doesn't support the Access 2000 format, use the database named MurachBooks97 instead, but still use MurachBooks as the name for the data source.
2. Open and compile the BookDB class in the c:\java\ch19\scroll directory. Then, test this class by coding a main method that prints the first record in the database to the console. To do that, you can use the connect, open, and moveFirst methods. When you compile and run the BookDB class, it should print the first record in the database to the console.
3. Modify the code for the BookFrame class that's in the c:\java\ch19\scroll directory so it uses the BookDB class as in figure 19-15. Then, test this class to make sure it works properly. To do that, experiment with the First, Prev, Next, and Last buttons. In addition, try to add a record and then delete it, and try to modify a record. Due to errors and incomplete code in the BookDB class, the Next and Prev buttons won't work properly. In addition, the Update and Delete buttons won't work properly when updating and deleting records.
4. Go to the BookDB class, and fix the moveNext and movePrevious methods. Then, run the BookFrame class again to make sure that these buttons work properly.
5. In the BookDB class, fill in the code for the updateRecord method. Then, run the BookFrame class and check to make sure that this code works properly.
6. In the BookDB class, fill in the code for the deleteRecord method. Then, run the BookFrame class to make sure that this code works properly.
7. Modify the addRecord, updateRecord, and deleteRecord methods so they use prepared statements. Then, run the BookFrame class to make sure that the application works properly.

Exercise 19-2 Modify the Book Maintenance application

This exercise guides you through the process of modifying the Book Maintenance application so it doesn't return the entire Books table as a result set.

1. Open the code for the BookFrame class that's stored in the c:\java\ch19\find directory and run it. It should display a dialog box like this one:

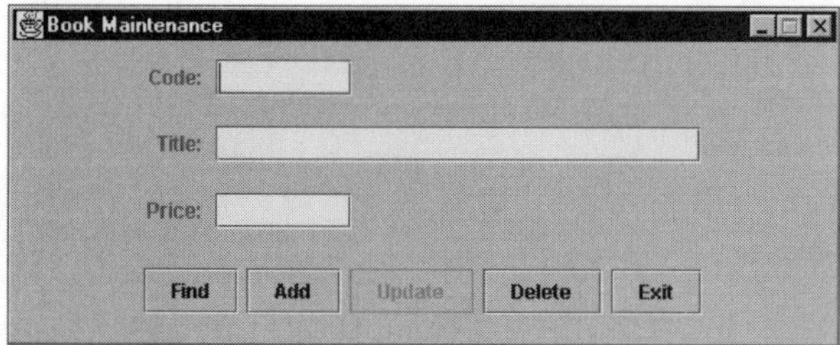

2. Open the BookDB class that's stored in the c:\java\ch19\find directory. Then, add a method named findOnCode that accepts a book code as a parameter and returns the matching Book object.
3. Modify the code for the actionPerformed method in the BookFrame class so this user interface works properly. When you click on the Find button, you can use the JOptionPane class to display a dialog box like this one:

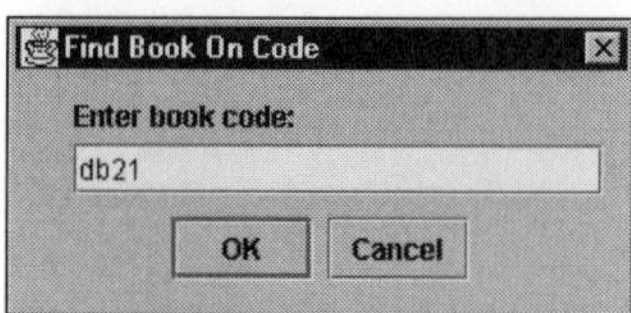

4. If you enter a valid book code, the user interface should display the record. Then, you should be able to update or delete that record. If you don't enter a valid book code, the user interface should display a dialog box like this one:

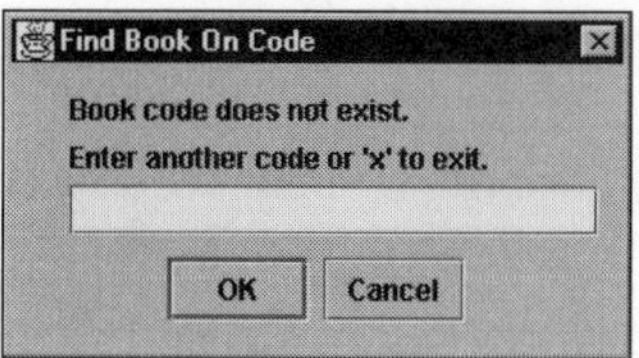

5. Test the application by displaying the records for these book codes:

   CC2R
   DB21
   SCMD

   Next, modify the prices for these records, and add a couple test records of your own to the database. Then, use the Find button to find them and use the Delete button to delete them.

20

How to work with threads

When you run a program in Java, the program runs in one or more threads. In previous chapters, you learned how to run each program within a single thread. In this chapter, you'll learn how to use multiple threads to allow a program to alternate between tasks. For example, you can use one thread to display animation while another thread makes a calculation.

An introduction to threads

This topic begins by presenting a brief overview of how threads work. Then, it summarizes two classes and an interface as well as some of the constructors and methods that are commonly used to work with threads.

How threads work

Figure 20-1 shows how *threads*, or *threads of execution,* work. To start, it shows a diagram that compares a program that contains a single thread with a program that contains two threads. Then, it shows a diagram that describes the life cycle of a thread.

The first diagram shows how the *central processing unit*, or *CPU*, of your computer runs a program. If the program contains only a single thread, the CPU executes each action sequentially. When the program contains multiple threads, though, the CPU can switch between the threads. This is known as *multithreading*, and it can allow your program to be more responsive to the user. Although the CPU can't run each thread at the same time, it can quickly switch between the two threads. This gives the appearance that both threads are executing at the same time.

When would you want to use threads? Threads are often used to allow a time-consuming task to occur in the background. To illustrate, let's say a program needs to display an image that's very large. Without multiple threads, the user would have to wait until the program displayed the image before the user could continue with any other parts of the program. To solve this problem, you can run the code that displays the image in its own thread. Then, the CPU can continue to work on displaying the image while the user can continue using other parts of the program.

The second diagram shows the life cycle of a thread. To start, the programmer writes code that defines and starts the thread. Once the thread is started, it's registered with the *thread scheduler*. Since the thread scheduler isn't completely platform independent, it may schedule threads differently depending on the operating system. Once the thread is scheduled, the scheduler places the thread in the ready state. Then, the scheduler runs the thread whenever it can.

When you write code that works with threads, you can move a thread into the waiting state. Usually, this causes the thread to wait for a specified period of time or until it receives a message. This lets you use threads to run a task at specified intervals, and it lets you synchronize multiple tasks. Once the thread is done waiting, the scheduler moves it back to the ready state where it can compete with other threads for CPU time. Once a thread finishes running, the thread is dead.

How using threads can improve performance

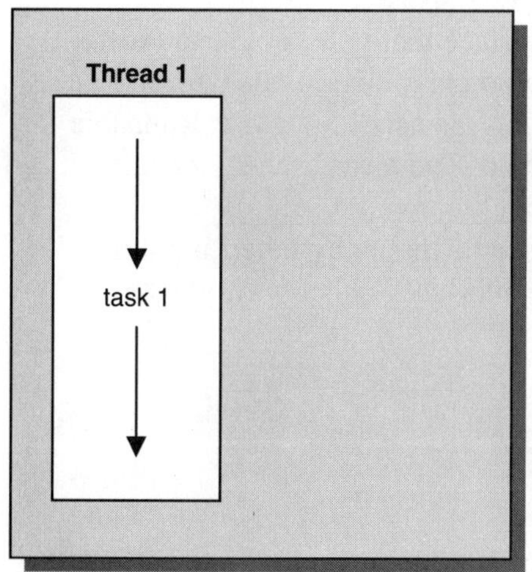

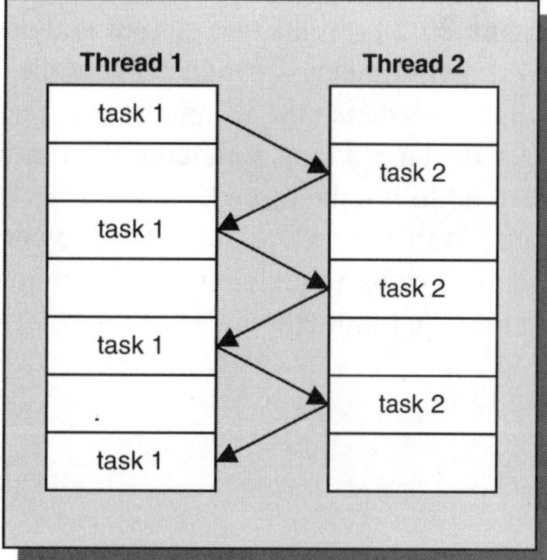

The life cycle of a thread

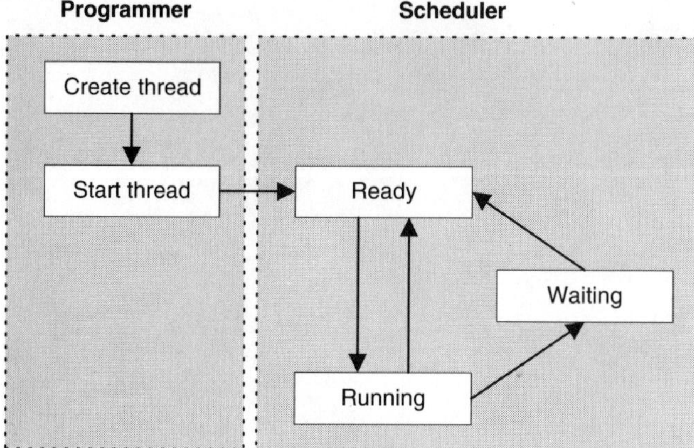

Description

- A *thread*, or *thread of execution*, is a single sequential flow of control within a program. A thread often completes a specific task.
- A typical computer only has one *central processing unit*, or *CPU*. As a result, two tasks can't physically run at the same time. However, a program that uses *multithreading* allows two or more tasks to share a computer's processor. This gives the appearance that all of the tasks are running at the same time, and this can make an application work more efficiently.
- Since a processor can only execute one thread at a time, the *thread scheduler* determines which thread runs at a given time.

Figure 20-1 How threads work

Classes and interfaces for working with threads

Figure 20-2 presents two classes and an interface that you can use to create and work with threads. This shows that the Thread class inherits the Object class and implements the Runnable interface. This also shows that the Runnable interface declares a single method, the run method. The thread scheduler calls this method to run the thread.

Later in this chapter, you'll learn how to create a thread by inheriting the Thread class or by implementing the Runnable interface. Either way, you need to override the run method.

Classes and interfaces used to create threads

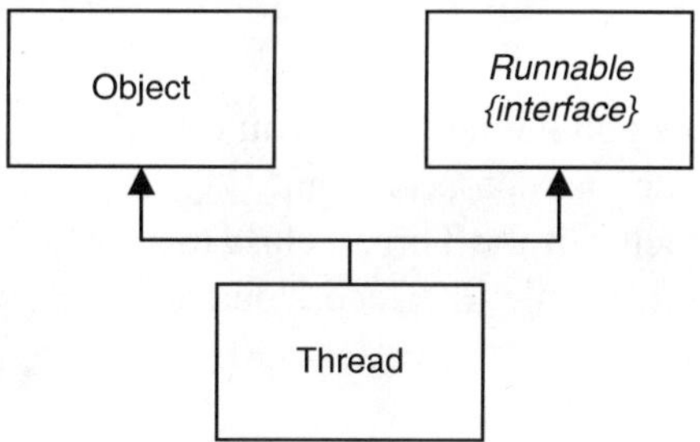

Summary of these classes and interfaces

Class/Interface	Description
Thread	A class that defines a thread.
Runnable	An interface that must be implemented by any class whose objects are going to be executed by a thread. The only method in this interface is the run method.

The Runnable interface

Method	Description
`void run()`	The thread scheduler calls this method to run the thread.

Figure 20-2 Classes and interfaces for working with threads

Constructors and methods for working with threads

Figure 20-3 summarizes some of the constructors and methods that you can use to work with threads. To start, it summarizes one constructor and ten methods of the Thread class. You can use the constructor of the Thread class to create a thread from any object that implements the Runnable interface. You can use the methods of the Thread class to get information about a thread and to control when a thread runs, when it waits, and when it ends.

Although most of these methods are self-explanatory, two require further explanation. First, you can use the setDaemon method to create a subordinate thread known as a *daemon thread*. When you create a daemon thread, that thread will end when the thread that started it ends. If you don't use this method to explicitly create a daemon thread, the thread is considered a *user thread*. User threads continue running even if the thread that created them ends.

Second, you use the setPriority thread to set the priority of a thread. This method accepts an integer from 1 to 10 where 1 is the lowest priority and 10 is the highest priority, and you can use the three fields summarized in this figure to set the priority of the thread.

The rest of this figure shows three methods of the Object class. You can use these methods when you need to synchronize the actions of several threads. If, for example, two threads use the same resource, you can use the wait method to tell one thread to wait until another thread is done using a resource. Then, when one thread is done using the resource, you can use the notify or notifyAll method to let the other threads know.

A common constructor of the Thread class

Constructor	Description
`Thread(Runnable)`	Creates a Thread object from any object that implements the Runnable interface.

Methods of the Thread class

Method	Description
`run()`	This method should be overridden in all subclasses.
`start()`	Registers this thread with the thread scheduler.
`getName()`	Returns the name of the thread. By default, threads are named numerically.
`currentThread()`	A static method that returns a reference to the currently executing thread.
`setDaemon(boolean)`	If the boolean value is true, then this thread is a *daemon thread*. This means it's a subordinate thread that ends when the thread that created it ends.
`yield()`	A static method that causes the current thread to pause so other threads can run.
`sleep(longMS)`	Makes the current thread wait for at least the specified number of milliseconds, which gives the CPU time to run other threads.
`interrupt()`	Interrupts this thread.
`isInterrupted()`	Returns a true value if this thread has been interrupted.
`setPriority(int)`	Changes this thread's priority to an int value from 1 to 10.

Fields of the Thread class used to set thread priorities

Field	Description
`MAX_PRIORITY`	The maximum priority of any thread (an int value of 10).
`MIN_PRIORITY`	The minimum priority of any thread (an int value of 1).
`NORM_PRIORITY`	The default priority of any thread (an int value of 5).

Methods of the Object class

Method	Description
`wait()`	Relinquishes the lock on the object. Causes the current thread to wait until another thread calls either the notify or notifyAll method on this object.
`notify()`	Wakes up one arbitrary thread waiting for this object's monitor.
`notifyAll()`	Wakes up all threads waiting for the object to compete for the CPU.

Description

- The sleep and wait methods throw a checked exception of the InterruptedException type. As a result, you must throw or catch this exception when you use these methods.

Figure 20-3 Constructors and methods for working with threads

How to create and start threads

This topic shows two ways to create a thread. First, you'll learn how to create a thread by inheriting the Thread class. Then, you'll learn how to create a thread by implementing the Runnable interface. In addition, you'll learn how to create an applet that runs in its own thread.

How to extend the Thread class

Figure 20-4 shows how to create two threads by inheriting the Thread class. Although these threads don't illustrate a practical use of multithreading, they do illustrate some of the concepts for defining and working with threads.

The first code example defines a class that creates a thread that counts down from 6 using only even numbers. To start, the CountDownEven class inherits the Thread class. Then, this class overrides the run method of the Thread class. This method contains a loop that prints three numbers to the console: 6, 4, and 2. Within this loop, the first statement uses the getName method to display the name of the thread followed by an even number. Then, the second statement calls the static yield method of the Thread class. This allows the thread scheduler to run any other threads that are ready to be run.

The second code example shows a class that defines a thread that counts down from 5 using only odd numbers. It works like the previous class except that it prints three odd numbers to the console: 5, 3, and 1.

The third code example shows a class that contains a main method that creates and starts the threads defined by the first two examples. Within the main method, the first two statements create the two threads. Then, the last two statements start the threads. In other words, the second two statements register the threads with the thread scheduler. Then, the thread scheduler calls the run methods of these threads.

The screen at the bottom of the figure shows the output that's generated by the three classes shown in this figure. Each line begins by printing the name of the thread. Here, the name that's assigned to the CountDownEven thread is thread-0 while the name that's assigned to the CountDownOdd class is thread-1. Then, each line prints the number that's generated by the for loop. Since both of these classes use the yield method, the scheduler switches between these two classes. However, in this example, the order that the scheduler uses varies due to factors that are beyond your control. Later in this chapter, you'll learn more techniques for controlling the order of execution among threads.

In this example, the main method runs in its own thread, the *main thread*. As a result, this program actually uses three threads: one for the main thread, one for the CountDownEven class, and one for the CountDownOdd class.

How to create a thread by extending the Thread class

- Create a class that inherits the Thread class.
- Override the run method to perform the desired task.
- Create the thread by creating an object from the class.

A class that defines a thread that counts down even values

```
public class CountDownEven extends Thread{
   public void run(){
      for (int i = 6; i > 0; i-=2){
         System.out.println(this.getName() + " Count " + i);
         Thread.yield();
      }
   }
}
```

A class that defines a thread that counts down odd values

```
public class CountDownOdd extends Thread{
   public void run(){
      for (int i = 5; i > 0; i -= 2){
         System.out.println(this.getName() + " Count " + i);
         Thread.yield();
      }
   }
}
```

A class that starts two threads

```
public class CountDownApp{
   public static void main(String[] args){
      Thread count1 = new CountDownEven();
      Thread count2 = new CountDownOdd();
      count1.start();
      count2.start();
   }
}
```

Output of the code shown above

Figure 20-4 How to extend the Thread class

How to implement the Runnable interface

Figure 20-5 shows how to create threads by implementing the Runnable interface. Although this method of creating threads requires a little more code than the previous figure, it's also more flexible. As a result, it's used more often than the technique in the previous figure.

The first two examples in this figure define the CountDownEven and CountDownOdd classes that you were introduced to in the last figure. However, these classes implement the Runnable interface instead of inheriting the Thread class. To create a reference to the current thread, they use the static currentThread method of the Thread class.

The third example also works much like its counterpart in the previous figure. However, the first two statements of the main method use a constructor of the Thread class to create a Thread object. Since this constructor accepts any object that implements the Runnable interface, you can supply objects created from the CountDownEven and CountDownOdd classes to create these two threads.

How to create a thread by implementing the Runnable interface

- Create a class that implements the Runnable interface.
- Code the run method to perform the desired task.
- Create the thread by supplying a Runnable object to the Thread constructor.

A class that defines a thread that counts down even values

```
public class CountDownEven implements Runnable{
   public void run(){
      Thread currentThread = Thread.currentThread();
      for (int i = 6; i > 0; i-=2){
         System.out.println(currentThread.getName() + " Count " + i);
         Thread.yield();
      }
   }
}
```

A class that defines a thread that counts down odd values

```
public class CountDownOdd implements Runnable{
   public void run(){
      Thread currentThread = Thread.currentThread();
      for (int i = 5; i > 0; i -= 2){
         System.out.println(currentThread.getName() + " Count " + i);
         Thread.yield();
      }
   }
}
```

A class that starts two threads

```
public class CountDownApp{
   public static void main(String[] args){
      Thread count1 = new Thread(new CountDownEven());
      Thread count2 = new Thread(new CountDownOdd());
      count1.start();
      count2.start();
   }
}
```

Output of the code shown above

Figure 20-5 How to implement the Runnable interface

How to run an applet in its own thread

Figure 20-6 provides a framework that you can use to code applets that run in their own threads. This framework runs the applet when the user moves to the web page and stops running the applet when the user moves away from the web page. This allows resource-intensive applets to share the processor with other applets on the same web page. For example, it's a common practice to run an applet that displays graphics in its own thread.

The example in this figure begins by declaring that the class that defines the applet implements the Runnable interface. Then, this applet declares an instance variable that refers to the thread for the applet and initializes the instance variable to a null value. After that, the start method checks if the instance variable equals a null value. If so, it creates the thread for the applet and calls the start method for the applet, which calls the run method. Within the run method, the first statement returns the current thread. Then, a loop checks if the current thread is equal to the thread for the applet. If so, this method executes the code for the applet, which may call other methods. Finally, the stop method sets the thread for the applet equal to null, which will cause the while loop in the run method to exit.

This figure also summarizes two methods of the Applet class that are typically used to work with threads. Since the start method is called every time the user displays the web page for the applet, this method is used to create and start the thread for the applet. Since the stop method is called every time the user moves from the web page, this method is used to stop the thread for the applet.

How to run an applet in a thread

- Declare that the class implements the Runnable interface.
- Declare a thread as an instance variable and initialize it to null.
- Override the applet's start method. If the thread is equal to null, this method should create and start the thread.
- Code a run method for the thread.
- Override the applet's stop method. This method should set the thread equal to null.

The code for an applet that runs in a thread

```
public class MyApplet extends Applet implements Runnable{
   private Thread myThread = null;

   public void start() {
      if (myThread == null) {
         myThread = new Thread(this);
         myThread.start();
      }
   }

   public void run() {
      Thread currentThread = Thread.currentThread();
      while (myThread == currentThread) {
         //code for the applet goes here
      }
   }

   public void stop() {
      myThread = null;
   }
}
```

Two methods of the Applet class that are used to work with threads

Method	Description
`public void start()`	This method is called when an applet should start execution. It is called when the web page is first displayed and every time the user visits the web page.
`public void stop()`	This method is called when an applet should stop executing. It is called when a user moves to another web page and when the user closes the browser.

Figure 20-6 How to run an applet in its own thread

How to schedule threads

In the last topic, you learned how to create and start threads. In addition, you were introduced to the yield method that allows multiple threads to share the processor. Now, you'll learn some other ways to control threads. In particular, you'll learn how to run a thread at a specified time interval, how to interrupt a thread, how to prioritize threads, and how to synchronize threads.

How to put a thread to sleep

Figure 20-7 shows how to use the sleep method of a thread to execute a task at specific time intervals. In particular, it shows how to use the sleep method to create a banner that moves across an applet. Although simple, this concept is the basis for creating more complex animations.

The first screen in this figure shows the text that's initially displayed by the applet when it runs within the Applet Viewer. Then, the second screen shows how this text moves from left to right.

The code in this figure defines an applet that runs in its own thread. As a result, the start, stop, and run methods work like they did in the last figure. However, within the run method's loop, this applet uses the sleep method to repaint the applet every 100 milliseconds (10 times per second). Since the sleep method throws an InterruptException, you must code a try/catch statement around the sleep method, but you don't need to do anything if this exception is thrown.

This applet adjusts the x value for the position of the text to make the text move from left to right. To start, this applet declares an instance variable for the x value. Next, the init method sets the initial x value to 10. Then, the paint method resets the x value every 100 milliseconds, moving the text 5 pixels to the right. To make sure the banner is displayed within the area defined by the applet, the second statement in the paint method uses the getSize method of the Applet class to return a Dimension object that defines the applet's area. Then, the next statement uses the width field of that object.

An applet with a moving banner

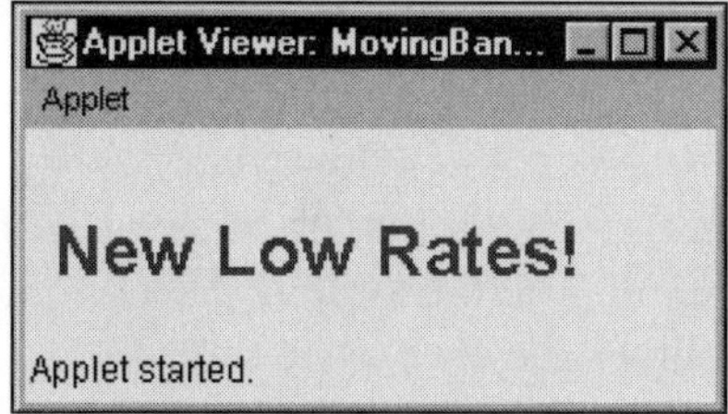

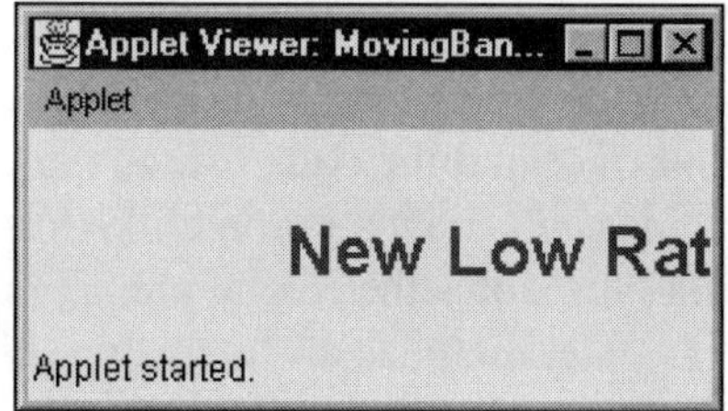

The code for this applet

```
import java.awt.*;
import java.applet.*;

public class MovingBannerApplet extends Applet implements Runnable {
   private Thread bannerThread = null;
   private int x;

   public void init(){
      setBackground(Color.white);
      x = 10;
   }

   public void start() {
      if (bannerThread == null) {
         bannerThread = new Thread(this);
         bannerThread.start();
      }
   }

   public void run() {
      Thread myThread = Thread.currentThread();
      while (bannerThread == myThread) {
         try{
            Thread.sleep(100);
         }
         catch (InterruptedException e){}
         repaint();
      }
   }

   public void paint(Graphics g) {
      x += 5;
      Dimension d = getSize();
      if (x > (d.width - 10))
         x = 10;
      g.setFont(new Font("SansSerif", Font.BOLD, 24));
      g.setColor(Color.red);
      g.drawString("New Low Rates!", x, 50);
   }

   public void stop() {
      bannerThread = null;
   }

}
```

Figure 20-7 How to put a thread to sleep

How to interrupt a thread

Figure 20-8 shows how to interrupt a thread. In particular, this figure shows the user interface and the code for an applet that draws a graphic. However, most systems can't draw a graphic like this one quickly. In addition, drawing a graphic like this slows the rest of the applications running on the system. As a result, this applet includes an Interrupt button that allows the user to stop the image from being drawn.

In many ways, the code in this figure works like the code for the Moving Banner applet in the previous figure. It defines an applet that runs in a thread that displays a graphic. However, it also provides an Interrupt button that lets the user stop the image from being drawn. When the user clicks on this button, the event handler for the button calls the interrupt method from the thread for the applet. Note, however, that calling this method doesn't immediately end the thread. Instead, it marks the thread as interrupted. Then, within the run method of the thread, the if statement uses the isInterrupted method to exit the loops that draw the image.

The two loops in the run method draw an image that's 255 pixels tall by 255 pixels wide, and they change the color for every pixel. That's why it takes so long to draw the image on most systems.

An applet that interrupts a time-consuming task

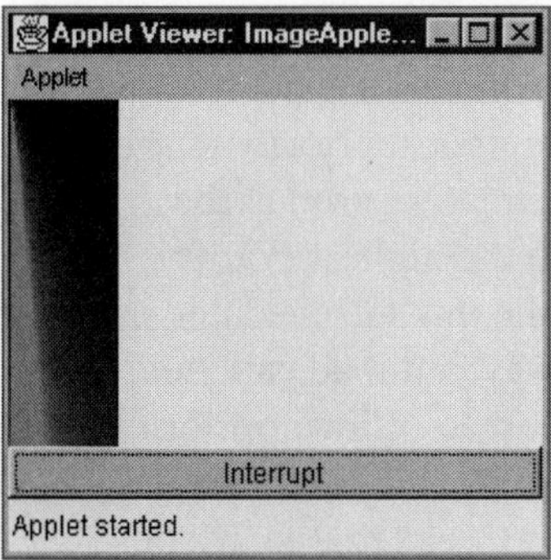

The code for this applet

```
import java.awt.*;
import java.awt.event.*;
import java.applet.*;

public class DrawImageApplet extends Applet
                             implements ActionListener, Runnable {
   private Thread drawImageThread = null;
   private Button interruptButton;

   public void init(){
      setLayout(new BorderLayout());
      interruptButton = new Button("Interrupt");
      interruptButton.addActionListener(this);
      add(interruptButton, BorderLayout.SOUTH);
   }

   public void actionPerformed(ActionEvent e){
      drawImageThread.interrupt();
   }

   public void run() {
      Thread currentThread = Thread.currentThread();
      while(currentThread == drawImageThread){
         for (int i = 0; i < 255; i++){
            for (int j = 0; j < 255; j++){
               if (drawImageThread.isInterrupted() == false){
                  Graphics g = getGraphics();
                  g.setColor(new Color(i, j, (i+j)/2));
                  g.drawLine(i, j, 1, 1);
                  Thread.yield();
               }
            }
         }
      }
   }
}
```

Note

- The start and stop methods work as they did for the previous two figures.

Figure 20-8 How to interrupt a thread

How to prioritize threads

Figure 20-9 shows how to prioritize threads. When a thread is created, it is given a priority value between 1 and 10, where 10 is the highest priority and 1 is the lowest priority. Then, when multiple threads become ready to run at the same time, the thread scheduler executes the thread with the highest priority first. If multiple threads have the same priority setting, the thread scheduler will run these threads until they're finished running. Either way, a thread can yield to a thread of equal or higher priority, but can't yield to a thread of lower priority.

This lets you create low-priority threads that will run when none of the other threads are running. For example, you could give a thread that loads an image a low priority so the image will load when all other threads have finished running. When you create a thread like this, though, it's still a good idea to include a yield method so the thread will yield to threads that have higher priorities if those threads become ready to run.

The first two examples shows how to set priorities for the threads for the CountDownEven and CountDownOdd classes. Here, the first example uses the setPriority method to set the priority for the CountDownEven thread to minimum. Conversely, the second example uses the setPriority method to set the priority for the CountDownOdd thread to maximum. The output of this code shows that the CountDownOdd thread finishes running before it yields to the CountDownEven thread.

The third example shows how to set priorities for the thread for the DrawImageApplet class. Since this thread takes a long time to run, and since it's not critical to any other applets on the page, this thread is set to a minimum priority. To do that, the first statement creates the thread, and the second statement sets the priority of the thread.

How to set the even count down thread to low priority

```
Thread currentThread = Thread.currentThread();
currentThread.setPriority(Thread.MIN_PRIORITY);
```

How to set the odd count down thread to high priority

```
Thread currentThread = Thread.currentThread();
currentThread.setPriority(Thread.MAX_PRIORITY);
```

Output of the code shown above

How to set the draw image thread to low priority

```
drawImageThread = new Thread(this);
drawImageThread.setPriority(Thread.MIN_PRIORITY);
drawImageThread.start();
```

Description

- If two or more ready-to-run threads have different priority settings, the scheduler executes the threads with the highest priority setting first.
- If two or more ready-to-run threads have the same priority, the scheduler executes the threads in a round-robin order.
- A thread can't yield to a thread of lower priority.
- By default, every thread is given the priority of the thread that created it.
- Since thread scheduling relies on the underlying system, the final result may vary depending on the platform.

Figure 20-9 How to prioritize threads

How to synchronize threads

So far, you've been working with threads that execute independently of each other. These types of threads are known as *asynchronous threads*. Now, you'll learn how to work with threads that share resources and must be synchronized. These types of threads are known as *synchronous threads*.

The diagram in figure 20-10 shows how two threads can share a resource. In this diagram, a thread on the server machine retrieves an order and processes it. Since this thread uses the data, it's known as the *consumer thread*. Meanwhile, threads on client machines can send data. Since these threads produce the data, they're known as *producer threads*.

With asynchronous threads, two problems can occur. First, the consumer thread can run faster than the producer thread. This can cause the consumer thread to attempt to retrieve an order when no order exists, or it can cause the consumer thread to retrieve the same order twice. On the other hand, the producer thread can run faster than the consumer thread. Then, the producer can send two orders while the consumer only retrieves one. To prevent these conditions, you can use a *monitor class*.

The monitor class in this figure uses the synchronized keyword to prevent the sendOrder method and the retrieveOrder method from being executed at the same time. In other words, this code locks the monitor class so that only one of the synchronized methods can be executed at a time. Although this example synchronizes methods, you can also use the synchronized keyword to work with blocks of code.

The monitor class in this figure also uses the methods of the Object class to prevent the retrieveOrder method from being executed before the sendOrder method. To start, it declares a boolean instance variable and sets that instance variable to false. This variable is used to alternate between sending and retrieving orders, and it starts by sending an order. Inside the retrieveOrder method, the boolean instance variable is checked to determine if an order has been sent. If not, this code calls the wait method from the current OrderMonitor object. This unlocks the OrderMonitor object and allows other threads to call synchronized methods. In this example, the retrieveOrder method waits until the sendOrder method calls the notifyAll method. This notifies all threads waiting on the monitor that an order has been sent.

If you use the notify method instead of the notifyAll method, Java will notify one arbitrary thread. Since that's not what you usually want, it's more common to use the notifyAll method. Then, all threads waiting for the monitor object can compete to execute.

An example that requires synchronized threads

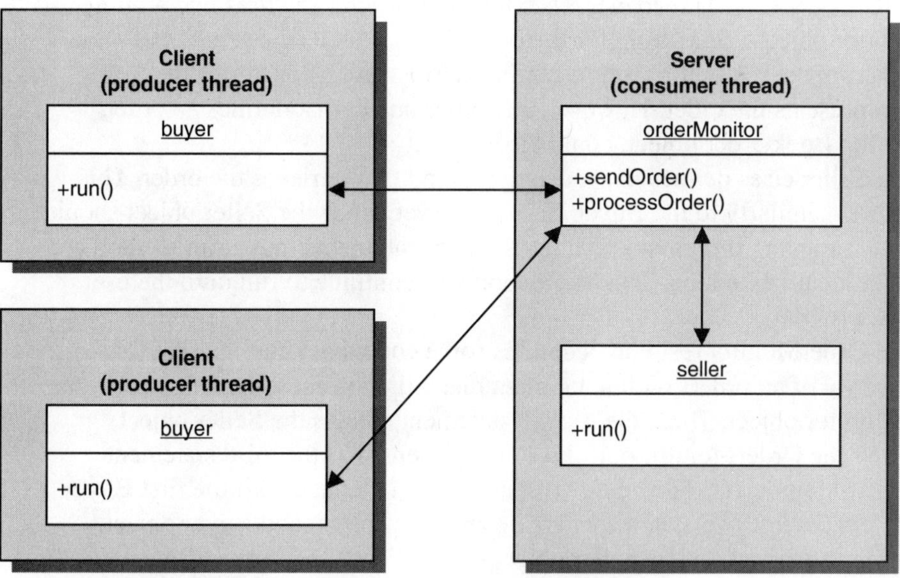

The monitor class

```
public class OrderMonitor{
   private boolean request = false;
   private String orderString;

   public synchronized String retrieveOrder(){
      while (request == false){
         try{
            wait();
         }
         catch(InterruptedException e){}
      }
      request = false;
      notifyAll();
      return orderString;
   }

   public synchronized void sendOrder(String s){
      while(request == true){
         try{
            wait();
         }
         catch(InterruptedException e){}
      }
      request = true;
      notifyAll();
      orderString = s;
   }

}
```

Figure 20-10 How to synchronize threads (part 1 of 2)

The Buyer class defines the producer thread that sends an order. To start, this class extends the Thread class. Next, its constructor requires two arguments, the monitor object and a string for the order. Then, it calls the sendOrder method from the monitor object to send the string. In this example, the String object represents the order. However, any other object that defines an order, such as the BookOrder object, could also be sent.

The Seller class defines the consumer thread that retrieves the order. This class works similarly to the Buyer class. However, since the Seller object should continue retrieving orders indefinitely, the two statements in the run method are coded within a while loop. This while loop will continue to run until the user exits the program.

The OrderMonitorTest class contains some code that simulates the sending and retrieval of an order. Within the main method, the first statement creates the OrderMonitor object. Then, the second statement creates the Seller object, supplying the OrderMonitor object as an argument, and the third statement starts the Seller object. The next two statements create and start the first Buyer object, and the last two statements create and start the second Buyer object.

When the thread for the Seller object starts, it calls the retrieveOrder method. Since no order has been sent, this thread calls the wait method and waits for an order. When the first Buyer thread starts, it calls the sendOrder method. This method sends an order and calls the notifyAll method to let the Seller thread know it's finished. Then, the Seller thread can retrieve the order. The output for this code shows that the monitor class causes one order to be retrieved for every order that's sent.

Since the Seller class uses an indefinite while loop, it will continue to run until the program ends. In this example, you'll need to press Ctrl+C at the console to end the program. Otherwise, the Seller object will continue to wait for more orders to be sent in by a Buyer object. However, in a real-world application, the program would include a more elegant way to end the Seller class.

A thread that sends orders

```
public class Buyer extends Thread{
   private OrderMonitor monitor;
   private String orderString;

   public Buyer(OrderMonitor m, String s){
      monitor = m;
      orderString = s;
   }

   public void run(){
      monitor.sendOrder(orderString);
      System.out.println("Buyer sent: " + orderString);
   }

}
```

A thread that retrieves orders

```
public class Seller extends Thread{
   private OrderMonitor monitor;

   public Seller(OrderMonitor m){
      monitor = m;
   }

   public void run(){
      while (true){
         String orderString = monitor.retrieveOrder();
         System.out.println("Seller retrieved: " + orderString);
         //code that processes the order
      }
   }
}
```

Code that simulates how synchronized methods work

```
public class OrderMonitorTest{
   public static void main(String[] args){
      OrderMonitor monitor = new OrderMonitor();
      Seller s = new Seller(monitor);
      s.start();
      Buyer b1 = new Buyer(monitor, "Order one");
      b1.start();
      Buyer b2 = new Buyer(monitor, "Order two");
      b2.start();
   }
}
```

Output of the above code

Figure 20-10 How to synchronize threads (part 2 of 2)

How to work with timers

In the last topic, you learned how to use threads to execute a task at a specified number of milliseconds. Since it can be difficult to use threads to schedule and repeatedly execute tasks, version 1.3 of Java added some timer classes to the API that make it easier do that. In particular, version 1.3 added a Timer class to both the java.util and javax.swing packages.

In this topic, you'll learn how to use the utility timer to work with applications that don't have graphical user interfaces. Then, you'll learn how to use the Swing timer to work with applications that use Swing components.

How to use the utility timer

Figure 20-11 shows how to use the Timer class and TimerTask classes that are stored in the java.util package. To start, you define a class that inherits the TimerTask class and you override the run method for that class so it performs the task. Then, you can create Timer objects in another class that run the specified task at the specified times. Part 1 of this figure shows an example of this, and part 2 summarizes the constructors and methods of these classes.

In the example in part 1, the AlarmTask class inherits the TimerTask class and overrides its run method. In this case, the run method displays a dialog box that tells the user that it's time for a meeting. However, this method could perform any type of task. In addition, the AlarmTask class could include a constructor that accepts one or more parameters.

The Alarm class in this example begins by declaring an instance of the Timer class that's stored in the java.util directory. Since all classes in the java.util and javax.swing packages are available to the application, the code uses the full name of the Timer class. Otherwise, the Java compiler won't know which Timer class to use and will display a compile-time error when you try to compile the code.

Within the constructor, the first two statements define a Date object that specifies the date and time that the AlarmTask object will be run. Then, the third statement defines a Timer class using the full name of the Timer class. Finally, the fourth statement uses the schedule method of the Timer class to set the task and the date and time that the task will be run. As a result, the dialog box will be displayed at 2 PM on May 21, 2001.

How to use the java.util.Timer class

- Create a class that inherits the TimerTask class and override its run method.
- Create an object from the java.util.Timer class. Then, use the schedule method to call the specified TimerTask object at the specified time.

An example that uses a timer to schedule an alarm

```
import javax.swing.*;
import java.util.*;
import java.text.*;

public class Alarm{
   private java.util.Timer timer;

   public Alarm(){
      GregorianCalendar alarmGregDateTime =
         new GregorianCalendar(2001, Calendar.MAY, 21, 14, 00);
      Date alarmDateTime = alarmGregDateTime.getTime();
      timer = new java.util.Timer();
      timer.schedule(new AlarmTask(), alarmDateTime);
   }

   public static void main(String[] args){
      Alarm alarm = new Alarm();
   }
}

class AlarmTask extends TimerTask{
   public void run(){
      JOptionPane.showMessageDialog(null, "Time for your meeting!");
      System.exit(0);
   }
}
```

Figure 20-11 How to use the java.util.Timer class (part 1 of 2)

Part 2 of figure 20-11 summarizes the constructors and methods that you can use when working with the TimerTask and Timer classes of the java.util package. To start, this figure reviews the constructor and method of the TimerTask class that were shown in part 1 of the figure. Then, this figure shows two constructors and five methods of the Timer class. These constructors and methods allow you to specify a timer that executes a task at fixed intervals, and they allow you to control when a timer starts and when it ends.

To create a Timer object, you can use either of the constructors in this figure. Then, you use one of the methods to specify a TimerTask object and to set the initial delay time for the task and the time interval for subsequent tasks. When you use the schedule method, you can run the task once. The second argument in this method allows you to schedule the initial delay for the task by specifying a Date object as shown in part 1 of this figure or by specifying the delay in milliseconds. When you use the scheduleAtFixedRate method, you can run the task at a specified time interval. The first two arguments for this method work the same as the schedule method. However, the third argument allows you to repeatedly execute a task by specifying a time interval in milliseconds.

There are three ways to end a Timer object. First, you can invoke the exit method of the System class to terminate all threads. Second, you can use the second constructor shown in this figure to create a Timer object that runs in a daemon thread. Then, the Timer object will automatically end when the object that created it ends. And finally, you can call the cancel method directly from the Timer object.

Constructor and methods of the TimerTask class

Constructor	Description
`TimerTask()`	Creates a new timer task.

Method	Description
`run()`	Must be overridden to handle the specific action to occur by this timer task.

Constructors and methods of the java.util.Timer class

Constructor	Description
`Timer()`	Creates a new Timer object that runs in a user thread.
`Timer(booleanDaemon)`	If a true value is specified, this method creates a new Timer object that runs in a daemon thread.

Method	Description
`schedule(TimerTask, Date)`	Schedules the specified TimerTask to execute at the specified date/time.
`schedule(TimerTask, longDelay)`	Schedules the specified TimerTask to execute after the specified delay in milliseconds.
`scheduleAtFixedRate(TimerTask, Date, longSubsequentDelay)`	Schedules the specified TimerTask to execute starting at the specified date/time and repeated after each specified subsequent delay in milliseconds.
`scheduleAtFixedRate(TimerTask, longFirstDelay, longSubsequentDelay)`	Schedules the specified TimerTask to execute starting at the specified first delay and repeated after each specified subsequent delay in milliseconds.
`cancel()`	Terminates this timer and cancels any scheduled tasks.

Description

- The Timer and TimerTask classes were included as part of the API with version 1.3 of Java in the java.util package. These classes make it easy to perform tasks that could only be accomplished with threads in early versions of Java.
- The TimerTask class implements the Runnable interface and can be used to define a task that's started by the java.util.Timer class.
- Since a Timer class also exists in the javax.swing package, it's common to refer to these timers by using their full path names: java.util.Timer and javax.swing.Timer.

Figure 20-11 How to use the java.util.Timer class (part 2 of 2)

How to use the Swing timer

When you work with Swing components, you shouldn't normally use threads. Instead, you should use the Timer class in the javax.swing package to schedule tasks as shown in figure 20-12. That's because most Swing components aren't *thread safe*. As a result, for most Swing components, the thread that created the component is the only thread that can modify the component once the component is painted or about to be painted.

The example in this two-part figure shows how to use the Timer class to display the current time on the Loan Calculator application. Here, the import statements for the application only import the Date class from the java.util package. That way, you can use the shorthand notation to refer to the Timer class and the compiler will only have access to the Timer class in the javax.swing package, not the Timer class in the java.util package. Within the class for the frame, one instance variable refers to the Timer object while another instance variable refers to the JLabel object that displays the time.

Within the constructor, the code that sets up the frame and adds the other panels to the frame runs as it did in chapter 11. Then, the eight statements in this figure add a label that displays the current time to the frame. To do that, the first five statements create a panel for the label and add the label to the frame. Then, the sixth statement creates a Timer object that notifies its action listeners every second (1000 milliseconds), and the seventh statement sets the initial delay to zero. As a result, the timer will send the first action performed event immediately. Finally, the eighth statement starts the timer.

Within the actionPerformed method, an if statement is used to check whether the Timer is the source of the ActionEvent object. If so, this example executes four statements. The first statement returns the current date and time, the second statement returns a medium time format, and the third statement returns a string that contains the time. Then, the fourth statement uses that string to set the text for the label that's used to display the current time.

How to use the javax.swing.Timer class

- In the constructor or init method, create and start the timer.
- Code the actionPerformed method in the listener's class to handle the timer's task.

The Loan Calculator user interface with a clock

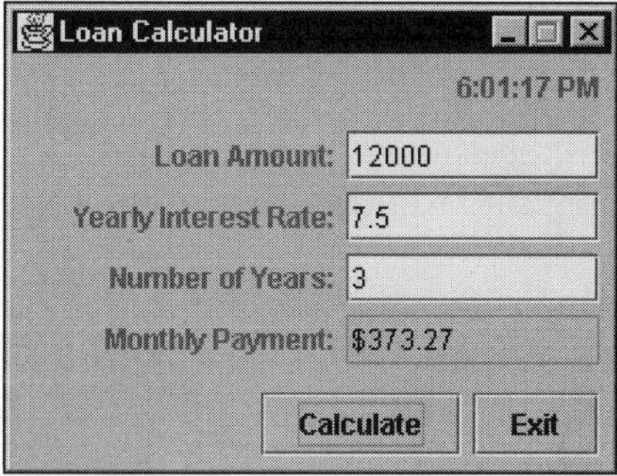

Code that adds a clock to the Loan Calculator application

```
import java.awt.*;
import java.awt.event.*;
import javax.swing.*;
import java.text.*;
import java.util.Date;

public class LoanCalculatorFrame extends JFrame implements ActionListener{

   // code for other instance variables
   private Timer timer;
   private JLabel clockLabel;

   public LoanCalculatorFrame() {
      //code that sets up the frame and its other panels
      JPanel clockPanel = new JPanel();
      clockPanel.setLayout(new FlowLayout(FlowLayout.RIGHT));
      clockLabel = new JLabel("Starting...");
      clockPanel.add(clockLabel);
      loanCalculatorPanel.add(clockPanel, BorderLayout.NORTH);

      timer = new Timer(1000, this);
      timer.setInitialDelay(0);
      timer.start();
   }

   public void actionPerformed(ActionEvent e){
      Object source = e.getSource();
      if (source == timer){
         Date t = new Date();
         DateFormat df = DateFormat.getTimeInstance(DateFormat.MEDIUM);
         String time = df.format(t);
         clockLabel.setText(time);
      }
      //code that handles the other events for the frame
   }

}
```

Figure 20-12 How to use the javax.swing.Timer class (part 1 of 2)

Part 2 of figure 20-12 summarizes some constructors and methods that you can use to work with the Swing timer. To start, you can create a Timer object by using the constructor to specify a delay interval in milliseconds and to specify an action listener. Once the Timer is created, you can start it with the start method, and you can stop it with the stop method. In addition, you can use the setDelay and setInitialDelay methods to control when the timer notifies its action listeners. Last, if you don't want the action to repeat, you can supply a false value to the setRepeats method. Then, the timer will only notify its action listener once.

Constructor of the javax.swing.Timer class

Constructor	Description
Timer(intDelay, ActionListener)	Creates a Timer object that notifies its listeners after the specified delay in milliseconds.

Methods of the javax.swing.Timer class

Method	Description
start()	Starts the Timer object.
stop()	Stops the Timer object.
setInitialDelay(intDelay)	Sets the initial delay in milliseconds before the first action event.
setDelay(intDelay)	Sets the delay in milliseconds between action events.
setRepeats(boolean)	If the boolean value is set to false, the Timer will only execute one time. By default, this value is set to true.

Description

- Most Swing components are not *thread safe*. As a result, you shouldn't use threads to modify them. Instead, you should use the Timer class of the javax.swing package to modify them.

Figure 20-12 How to use the javax.swing.Timer class (part 2 of 2)

Perspective

In this chapter, you learned the essential skills for working with threads. In addition, you learned how to work with two types of timers that can accomplish many of the tasks that were previously accomplished with threads. You can use these skills with both applications and applets.

Summary

- You can use multiple *threads* to allow a computer's *central processing unit* (*CPU*) to quickly switch between two or more tasks. When an application or applet does operations like I/O operations that are time-consuming but don't require much processing, *multithreading* can often improve performance.
- Since a processor can only run one task at a time, the *thread scheduler* determines which task to run. Once a thread has been started, it can be in three states: running, waiting, or ready. In the ready state, it competes with other threads for the processor.
- You can use the Thread class or the Runnable interface to create a thread. You can use the methods of the Thread class to start and end a thread and to control when a thread runs.
- You can run an applet in a thread by implementing the Runnable interface for the class that defines the applet by using the start and stop methods of the Applet class to start and stop the thread.
- By default, the constructor of the Thread class creates a *user thread* that ends when it has finished executing. However, you can also create a *daemon thread* that ends when the thread that started it ends.
- All programs contain a *main thread* that the program runs in.
- When multiple threads run independently of each other, they're known as *asynchronous threads*. When threads need to communicate with each other, they're known as *synchronous threads*.
- When a thread produces data that needs to be processed by another thread it's known as a *producer thread*. When a thread consumes data that's produced by a producer thread, it's known as a *consumer thread*. To synchronize producer and consumer threads, you can code a *monitor class*.
- Version 1.3 of Java added two Timer classes that you can use to perform tasks that were accomplished with threads in previous versions of Java.
- You can use the Timer and TimerTask classes of the java.util package to work with applications that don't use Swing components.
- You can use the Timer class of the javax.swing package to work with Swing components. Since most Swing components are not *thread safe*, you shouldn't use threads to work with them.

Terms

thread
thread of execution
central processing unit (CPU)
multithreading
thread scheduler
daemon thread
user thread
asynchronous threads
synchronous threads
consumer thread
producer thread
monitor class
thread safe

Objectives

- Describe when and how threads can improve the performance of a program.
- Use the Thread class or the Runnable interface to create a thread.
- Run an applet in its own thread.
- Use the methods of the Thread class to control when the processor executes a thread.
- Use the methods of the Object class to control when the processor executes a thread.
- Describe when to use the timer classes there were included with version 1.3 of Java.
- Use the Timer and TimerTask classes of the java.util class to schedule tasks.
- Use the Timer class of the javax.swing package to schedule tasks.

Exercise 20-1 Create the Count Down application

1. Open the CountDownEven, CountDownOdd, and CountDownApp classes in the c:\java\ch20\count directory. Then, read through the code for these classes to make sure you understand them. When you're done, compile and run the application. Since these classes don't contain a yield method, the even thread won't let the odd thread run until it's done executing. However, some operating systems automatically yield threads. This means that the processor may switch between the two threads even though you haven't coded the yield method.
2. Code the yield method for the CountDownEven and CountDownOdd classes as shown in figure 20-4. Then, run the application several times. When you do, the processor should randomly switch between the two threads.
3. Convert the three classes so they use the Runnable interface as shown in figure 20-5. Then, compile these classes and run the application to make sure it works the same as it did in the previous step.
4. Use the setPriority method to assign a low priority to the even numbers and a high priority to odd numbers as shown in figure 20-9. Then, compile these classes and run the application. It should print the odd numbers first and then even numbers. Then, remove the code that uses the setPriority method.
5. Create a CountDownMonitor class that insures that the count down will always go from the highest number to the lowest number. To do this, you can code two synchronized methods named printOdd and printEven. Then, you'll need to add a constructor to both the CountDownEven and CountDownOdd classes that accept a CountDownMonitor object. After that, you can call the printEven and printOdd methods within the run methods. To test this application, you can code a main method similar to the one in figure 20-10.

Exercise 20-2 Create the Moving Banner applet

1. Open the MovingBannerApplet class that's stored in the c:\java\ch20\banner directory. Add code to this applet so it works as shown in figure 20-7. When you're done, compile the code and use the Applet Viewer to view this applet.
2. Use a web browser to view the LoanCalculator HTML page that's stored in the c:\java\ch20\banner directory. This web page displays both the Moving Banner applet and the Loan Calculator applet. Since the Moving Banner applet runs in its own thread, you should be able to use the Loan Calculator application to make a calculation while the Moving Banner applet is running.
3. Add a Stop button to the Moving Banner applet that allows you to stop the banner from moving. To stop this banner, set the thread for the applet equal to null.

Exercise 20-3 Create the Alarm application

1. Open the Alarm class that's in the c:\java\ch20\alarm directory. Then, run this class. Since the code sets the date and time of the meeting to a time that has already passed, this application should immediately display a dialog box that says, "It's time for your meeting."
2. Modify the statement that sets the alarm date and time of the meeting so that the dialog box will be displayed two minutes from the current time that's displayed by your computer. Then, compile and run the application. When the application displays a blank console, switch to another application and work on something else for a couple minutes. In two minutes, the application should display the dialog box.
3. Comment out the first two statements that create the Date object. Next, use the second schedule method shown in part 2 of figure 20-11 to use a long value to specify a delay of 2 minutes (120000 ms). Then, compile and run the application. In two minutes, the application should display the dialog box.

Exercise 20-4 Enhance the Loan Calculator application

1. Open the LoanCalculatorFrame class that's stored in the c:\java\ch20\clock directory. Then, run this class. It should display label that says, "Starting…", but the label won't display the current time.
2. Add code to the LoanCalculatorFrame so the label displays the current time every second as shown in figure 20-12. When you compile and run this class, it should display the current time once every second.
3. Modify the code for the LoanCalculatorFrame so the time that's displayed by the label doesn't include seconds. To do that, you can use the SHORT field of the DateFormat class. In addition, modify the code so it creates a Timer object that only causes the time to be updated once every 10 seconds. That way, the time that's displayed by the label will never be more than 10 seconds off from your computer's clock. Then, compile and run this class to make sure the application is working correctly.

Index

A

B

C

D

E

F

G

H

I

J

K

L

M

N

O

P

Q

R

S

T

U

V

W

Y

What the CD contains

- Java™ 2 Software Development Kit (SDK), Standard Edition, version 1.3.1 for Windows
- A trial version of TextPad, a program for Windows systems that makes it easier for you to enter, edit, compile, and test Java code
- The Java source code and data for all of the book examples and exercises
- The Java API documentation for SDK 1.3.1
- Forte for Java, release 2.0, Community Edition for All Platforms

Read chapter 1 first

- Chapter 1 describes the products that are on the CD and gets you started using them. Although the procedures that follow are for Windows systems, chapter 1 explains how you can install these products on other systems.

How to install the Java SDK 1.3.1 for Windows

- Navigate to the directory on the CD named WindowsSDK. Then, double-click on the file named j2sdk1_3_1-win.exe, and respond to the dialog boxes that follow. For more information, see figure 1-4 on page 11.

How to install TextPad for Windows

- Navigate to the directory on the CD named TextPadSetup. Then, double-click on the file named TextPadSetup.exe, and respond to the dialog boxes that follow. For more information, go to figure 1-11 on page 24.

How to install the Murach source code and data

- From the root directory of the CD, double-click on the file named Install.exe and respond to the dialog boxes that follow. This will install the source code and test files into a directory structure that starts with c:\Murach\Java2.
- Navigate to c:\Murach\Java2\ExerciseStarts\Java. Then, copy (not move) the Java directory and all of its subdirectories to the root directory of the C drive. From that point on, you can find the source and data files that you need in subdirectories like c:\java\ch01 (for chapter 1), c:\java\ch02 (for chapter 2); and so on.

How to install the Java API documentation

- Use the procedure in figure 3-11 on page 101.

How to install Forte for Java

- Navigate to the directory (folder) on the CD named Forte. Then, double-click on the file named forte_ce_1_0_2.exe, and respond to the dialog boxes that follow.